CATHOLIC

AND

PROTESTANT NATIONS COMPARED

IN THEIR THREEFOLD RELATIONS TO

WEALTH, KNOWLEDGE, AND MORALITY.

BY REV. NAPOLEON ROUSSEL,

OF PARIS,

AUTHOR OF MON VOYAGE EN ALGERIE, SCENES PATRIARCHALES, LE CULTE DOMESTIQUE, LES ELANS DE L'AME, ETC., ETC.

WITH AN INTRODUCTION,

BY THE

HON. AND REV. BAPTISTE NOEL,

OF LONDON.

BOSTON:

PUBLISHED BY JOHN P. JEWETT AND COMPANY.

CLEVELAND, OHIO:

JEWETT, PROCTOR AND WORTHINGTON.

NEW YORK: SHELDON, LAMPORT AND COMPANY.

1855.

DEDICATED TO

WILLIAM R. LAWRENCE, M.D.,

OF BOSTON,

AS A TRIBUTE OF GRATITUDE

FOR HIS DEVOTION TO THE CAUSE OF CHRISTIAN EDUCATION

AMONG THE YOUTH OF FRANCE,

BY HIS FRIEND,

THE AUTHOR.

TABLE OF CONTENTS.

VOLUME FIRST.

VOLUME SECOND.

PREFACE.

Without any reference to effects, the claims of the Church of Rome may be proved to be without foundation. It is destitute of the moral marks which characterize the Church of Christ, Unity, Holiness, and Apostolicity; while its Catholicity, being the result of force, is its disgrace. On the other hand, any reader, by an attentive examination of the word of God, may arrive at the following conclusion: —

The Church of Rome, instead of being the Church of Christ, is the rival and enemy of that Church.

The Apostle Peter was neither the Bishop of Rome, nor the Prince of the Apostles.

The Pope instead of being the successor to the Apostle Peter, has contradicted his doctrine, and concealed his writings from the people.

Instead of being the Vicar of Christ, the Pope, by a flagrant usurpation of his rights, holds an office which is essentially antichristian.

The hierarchy of the Church of Rome, instead of having from Christ an exclusive authority, has been constituted in opposition to his directions, and is destitute of all sanction from him.

The Latin worship of the Church of Rome, among nations not speaking Latin, is contrary to the will of God.

Some of its doctrines are subversive of the Gospel.

Its sacraments contradict Scripture, materialize religion, and injure society in order to exalt the priests.

Its sacrifice of the mass is a corrupt invention, which contradicts Scripture, and is derogatory to the sacrifice made by the Redeemer on the cross.

Its Latin worship is against Scripture and contrary to the the will of God.

Its worship of the mass is the worhip of a wafer as God.

Its worship of Mary is idolatry.

Its doctrine of purgatory, according to which the Redeemer sentences his regenerated and justified disciples to be tormented in fire, is contrary to Scripture and blasphemous.

Its practice of the confessional, with the accompaniment of priestly absolution, is contrary to Scripture, degrading to those who practise it, and mischievous in its effects upon society.

Its prohibition of the free use of the word of God by its adherents, is a cruel tyranny, dishonorable to Christ, and fatal to Catholics.

Thus the Church of Rome is condemned by Scripture distinctly, unequivocally, and completely; nor need we suspend our judgment of its character till we have examined its effects upon society.

But at the same time, the examination of its effects is exceedingly instructive;— God has given his Gospel to bless and to save mankind, so that whatever is in harmony with the Gospel must be beneficial, and whatever is injurious must be opposed to the Gospel; we may therefore further determine the character of the Church of Rome by an examination of its effects. Since it has now been established for a long period, and in many lands, those effects are no longer uncertain, and if they are mischievous, then it is a corruption of Christianity and ought to be abandoned.

In the following work, Mr. Roussell has examined those effects, and having compared the condition of Catholic and Protestant States with respect to their knowledge, their morals, and their prosperity, he has established unanswerably that in these respects the Protestant nations are superior. He has compared contiguous nations and nations placed in similar circumstances; North America, which is Protestant, is compared with South America which is Catholic; Prussia is compared with Austria; Holland with Belgium; and the Protestant cantons of Switzerland with its Catholic cantons. He has compared different parts of the same empire when placed under the same laws and in similar circumstances; as Protestant Scotland and Catholic Ireland. He has compared the different States of a nation, which has continued exclusively Catholic, as Spain in the 10th century, with the same country in the 19th. He has examined the effect of the Roman Catholic system in a country where the Church of Rome is entirely dominant, as in Italy; and its effects in a country where that Church is depressed, as in Ireland. He has compared the effects of Protestantism under persecution with those of Romanism under persecution; e. g. the history of Protestantism in France with that of Romanism in Ireland; and finally, he has compared the effects of Catholic and Protestant missions.

All these inquiries guide us to two conclusions: —

1st. That Protestantism has given to Protestant nations knowledge, morality, and prosperity, while Catholicism has left Catholic nations ignorant, immoral, and poor; 2d, That Protestantism must be more consonant to the Word of God than Catholicism is.

If it be objected that as Protestants hold very opposite opinions, their opinions cannot all be true. I answer that Protestants hold certain truths in common, which truths, and not the errors into which individual Protestants have fallen, have given to Protestant nations the superiority which they possess; Protestants in general have renounced the errors and the abuses of the Church of Rome, through which act alone they have thrown off much that is detrimental to the interests of nations; they agree in believing that the word of God is the standard of truth and duty, and that it is the duty of all men to read it; they have retained free from Catholic appendages many of the great truths of revelation; and these Protestant principles have done much to launch the nations which have received them in a career of self-improvement.

But it must never be forgotten that the Protestantism which has prevailed in Europe has been chiefly evangelical and not sceptical. The Reformed Churches in Germany, Switzerland, Holland, and Great Britain, had all of them, at the time of the Reformation, evangelical creeds; and it is to the Gospel, as freed from Roman Catholic corruptions, not to a scepticism which has recently in some places been substituted for the Gospel, that the knowledge, morals, and prosperity of Protestant nations are due. I must add, that wherever Protestantism has been the most evangelical, its good effects have been the most conspicuous. The two nations, which in knowledge, morality, and prosperity, are now at the head of the nations, are by the acknowledgment of Catholic as well as Protestant writers, Great Britain and United States; but these are also the nations in which Protestantism is the most evangelical.

Thus we arrive at the conclusion that Evangelical Protestantism, which bears the most abundant good fruit, is also the nearest to the word of God; and has the least error mingling with the truths which it upholds.

Mr. Roussell anticipates, therefore, with much reason, the future benefits of Protestantism. Nations, once emancipated from the tyranny of the Church of Rome, will never submit to it again. North America may draw the Catholic South to its light, but glorious as it is in knowledge, morality, and propriety, will never beg from the Catholic South its ignorance, vice, and pauperism; Prussia will never wish to become Austrian; Berne will not adopt the creed which has ruined Freibourg. The Canton de Vaud will not embrace the opinions of the Valias or of Tessin; and Scotland will not renounce the principles which have made it one of the foremost of the nations, in favor of those which have made Ireland almost the last and the lowest among them. Almost all Europe shrinks from a Catholicism, which, when enthroned, exclusive and all powerful, has chained, brutalized, and ruined Spain, once so glorious, and the magnificent regions of Catholic South America; and especially the Papal States, the seat and centre of Catholicism, are longing to expel from them as the representative of spiritual and of secular tyranny, the Pontiff to whom they once bowed down as the Vicar of God.

I heartily hope that this useful book will be read extensively. It is short and conclusive. The facts which are collected rest generally upon Catholic authorities, and the conclusions which it establishes are most important. Here the English reader may see what educated Frenchmen and Germans think of the influence of the Church of Rome, and he can scarcely rise from the perusal without thankfulness that he is an Englishman, without fresh confidence in his Protestant principles, and without fresh hope that the dominion of Roman Catholic superstition is hastening to its close.

BAPTISTE NOEL.

London, January, 1855.

CATHOLIC NATIONS

AND

PROTESTANT NATIONS

COMPARED IN THEIR THREEFOLD RELATION TO

WEALTH, KNOWLEDGE, AND MORALITY.

PLAN OF THE WORK.

Good deeds are the result of truth; evil is the result of falsehood; two modes of expressing the same idea. The true and the good are intimately connected, or, to speak more correctly, they are but one.

All understand what is meant by "true," but what do we mean by "good?" It will be useful here to explain.

Morality, knowledge, wealth, are, in our estimation, three things good in themselves, and for all mankind.

If the reader dispute this assertion, it will be well to pause here; for upon this all our argument rests, as upon an axiom.

We have said that good deeds are the result of truth, and evil of falsehood. The Gospel has proclaimed the same truth in more striking terms. Christ has said, "you shall know them by their fruits." "A good tree cannot bring forth evil fruit, neither can a corrupt tree bring forth good fruit." "Do men gather grapes of thorns, or figs of thistles?"

If this be so, then, wherever wealth, knowledge, and morality shall be found, it may be said, here the truth exists; and where misery, ignorance, and vice shall be found, there error reigns.

Without doubt, if all the good should be found in one hemisphere, and all the evil in the other, the demonstration would amount to proof. But if, without arriving at this complete separation of good and evil, we should yet find, dispersed over all the quarters of the globe, nations moral, enlightened, and prosperous to a certain degree, may we not still say, here truth reigns? If at the same time, in close contact with these nations, we should meet with others comparatively miserable, ignorant, and immoral, shall we not have a right to add, there error reigns? Lastly, if this twofold experience should recur in several parts of the world, will not these simple probabilities become certainties? Such at least is our opinion, and it is in reliance on this principle that we proceed to handle our subject.

During the three last centuries a great question has been agitated in Christendom. Catholicism and Reform, opposed in their principles, say, each with equal confidence, "I am the truth." Certain it is that one of the two is mistaken; but which? It is for the consequences of these two doctrines to furnish the answer. Where morality, knowledge, and wealth exist, there truth will be found. Where misery, ignorance, and vice exist, there error will be found. Let us then study successively the protestant nations, placing by the side of each her catholic neighbour; and the result of the comparison will be, to make us know where error is, and where the truth. Here an objection may present itself. We may be told that neither all the good, nor all the evil, is the product of any particular religious faith; that climate, race, and a thousand other accidental causes, may contribute to develope or to destroy the wealth, the intellect, and the morals of a nation. This is true, but their influence is less than it is generally supposed to be. In the first place, most of the accidental causes of the civilisation of a people, such as legislation, are themselves the products of a religious principle; in the second place, climate and races lose their importance as soon as we compare men placed in the same latitude, and sprung from the same stock. Further, after allowing their due weight to all these accessory circumstances, there will always remain to be taken into account the most important circumstance of all, the religious conviction; that conviction, even though it be completely erroneous. Unless man is pronounced to be only a machine, the mere sport of exterior influences, it must be granted that we regulate our conduct by good or bad motives, vacillation or firmness. People may give to these motives what name they please; but we call them here religious principles, and we maintain that they have a great influence on individual conduct.

Lastly, to lessen the chances of error arising from the differences of geographical position, political institutions, origin, etc., we shall take the elements of each of our comparisons in two nations placed as nearly as possible in the same circumstances of latitude, government, and nationality. When, in spite of all our efforts, differences still remain, we shall take these matters into account in our final appreciation.

We shall now proceed to place in parallel lines North America and South America; Ireland and Scotland; the Swiss protestant cantons, and the Swiss catholic cantons; Austria and Prussia, etc.

If these several comparisons should all give us the same result, it may be safely concludedthat the problem often worked, and always yielding a similar solution, has at last led us to the discovery of the truth. But we shall not rest satisfied even then; we shall resume the question under another form. Going back three centuries, and selecting two nations, one essentially protestant, and the other essentially catholic, we shall study the case of each separately, and consider its starting point, its progress, and the height that it has reached, in order to ascertain which of the two has ascended, and which has descended, in the scale of civilisation, under the influence of its religious faith. England and Spain will furnish the element of this additional demonstration. To learn the intrinsic value of the two religions, we shall then inquire what their followers have become under favour or persecution. This will lead us to study the catholics in Italy, and the protestants in France. We shall afterwards compare the results obtained by the two churches in the fields of their respective missions.

Whatever may be the conclusion at which we shall ultimately arrive, we can imagine beforehand that there are persons who have arrived at a contrary one. We ought here, then, to weigh their arguments. We do not conceal from ourselves that our undertaking exposes us to a danger, that of partiality. We feel that we are liable to an unconscious partiality, resulting from the religious faith of the writer. In order to escape from it, the author will shelter himself as much as possible behind authorities. He will present facts; even the statement of these will not be his own. The authorities will be taken, neither from among his friends, nor from among his co-religionists; but, for the most part, from writers animated by a different faith from his own, or, at least, from writers who have no religious pre-occupations.

Staticians, geographers, naturalists, will come forward to furnish, unintentionally, their testimony in this controversy.

We are not aware of more than a single point in respect to which our work can be attacked; and that is, as to the choice of documents. We may be told that the same writers, if cited in other pages of their works, would perhaps have established contrary results. With regard to this, we can only affirm that such is not our opinion. We are thoroughly convinced that it would be impossible to pick out from the same writers passages to contradict the results which they have given us. We have laboured, in reference to this, with an uprightness of intention, which is to us a guarantee for the truth of our conclusions. Let any one attempt to read the whole of our authors, and to extract from them passages giving a sense opposed to that contained in those which we have borrowed, and we feel confident that the most skilful hand will be unable to compile from them a work which shall counterbalance our statements.

Lastly, to be strictly accurate, we ought to allow that it would undoubtedly be possible to glean, in the field of protestant and catholic nations which we have passed over, a few tares in the midst of the wheat, and some ears of corn on a barren soil. All the good is not in one camp; nor all the evil in the other; in other words, it is necessary here to apply the popular adage: "There is no rule without an exception." But we affirm, that the general state of these nations is such as we have described it; and if any doubt should still remain in the mind of the reader, the work itself, we hope, will have the effect of removing it.

The present is not a literary performance: the author scarcely takes a part in it, but for the choice and classification of documents. His work consists in a great measure of the labours of others. It is precisely this which gives the greater solidity to his conclusions. The more numerous and various our authorities are, the more unassailable becomes the cause which they unitedly defend.

The question relates, not to us who have edited the book, but to the truth itself. It matters little that we remain in the shade, provided the truth be brought to light; and, for that purpose, the united torches of a hundred different writers are worth far more than our simple affirmations.

Next to the variety and the multiplicity of the authors cited, what we ought to cause to be specially remarked, and have already pointed out, is, that these authors bring their contingent of proofs without knowing or intending it. It is neither our thesis, nor their own, which they defend; they have spoken, without thinking of the use to which we should put their words. Are not such witnesses worthy of confidence? We have, therefore, uniformly sought for our authorities, by preference, in the camp opposed to the one to which they should naturally have belonged.

This work might have been composed either of stastistical data, or of moral descriptions. The first method has more of precision; the second, more of interest. The best method of all, however, as it appears to us, is to combine the two; to require of staticians their figures, and of travellers their impressions. We shall check the former by the latter, and on the agreement of the two, we shall rest our convictions. At the same time, we ought to promise that we shall assign the smaller space to statistics; first, because that science has said everything when it has given certain numerals; secondly, because, being in their nature dry, statistics fail to leave on the mind any very permanent impressions. Our descriptive citations will occupy much more space, and the diversity of hands that will have traced them will secure to them that confidence which no single authority could have acquired for them. The simple traveller, the studious geographer, the learned naturalist, the statesman, will come, each in his turn, to add a stroke of his brush to the canvas; and, if the result should be an harmonious picture, we must conclude that this *ensemble* of impressions equals in precision statistical science itself.

Before we proceed to the study of details, let us take a general view of the whole; before we speak of any particular nation, let us say a few words of the Catholic world and of the Protestant world.

GENERAL VIEW.

It is from statistics that we shall seek our first general ideas. But, before entering on the subject, let us class in two categories, according to their religions, the nations that are to engage our attention :

CATHOLIC NATIONS.	PROTESTANT NATIONS.
South America.	North America.
Ireland.	Scotland.
Switzerland, catholic.	Switzerland, protestant.
Austria.	Prussia.
Belgium.	Holland.
Spain.	England.
Italy.	
France.	

These two families may be studied in three different points of view : Wealth, Knowledge, and Morality.

WEALTH. — Under this title we shall include all that can contribute to the material prosperity of a nation :

Agriculture, Industry, Commerce. Let us say a word on each of these subdivisions.

Here is what we read in a work written by M. Moreau de Jonnès, a learned statician :

Extent of cultivation.

Great Britain	one-third.
Italy	"
Prussia	"
The Low-Countries	"
Austria, properly so called	"

This equality is only apparent. " The British territory, " says M. Jonnès, " is almost entirely stripped of forests, and is smitten with sterility in a fourth part of its surface [1]. " Besides, the natural fertility of England is nothing compared to that of Italy. In the next place, the south of Germany, Austria, is also much more highly favoured in this respect than is the north, Prussia. The extent of cultivation being the same in proportion to the extent of the countries, the superiority in civilisation is on the side the least favoured by nature. In other words, agriculture is more advanced, better understood, in England and in Prussia, than in

1. Vol. I, pp. 41 and 44.

Italy and Austria; that is to say, the advantage is on the protestant side.

The industry of a country cannot be measured with accuracy by its exports, for these include merchandise that has been only warehoused. However, with reference to our subject, this confusion is unimportant; for, what we might withdraw from industry, we should add to commerce.

We shall then take the exports for the proximate measure of industry; and afterwards, adding them to the imports, we shall take the sum total to measure the extent of commerce.

The following table is extracted from the same work of M. Jonnès; we have, however, omitted countries such as Russia, which are alien to our subject, and have divided the list into two parts, in order not to have to compare nations that hold the first rank with those that are the last in the scale of industry :

Exports.

FIRST CLASS.

Holland..........	(in 1835)..............	75 fr.	»»	per head.
British Isles.......	(1835)..............	60	»»	—
United States......	(1834)..............	32	»»	—
Wurtemberg.......	(1822)..............	27	»»	—
France............	(1835)..............	25	»»	—
Portugal..........	(1830)..............	20	»»	—

SECOND CLASS.

Danish States......	(in 1831)..............	16 fr.	»»	—
Sweden and Norway	(1831)..............	15	»»	—
Kingdom of Naples.	(1828)..............	7	50	—
Roman States......	(1830)..............	7	»»	—
Spain.............	(1829)..............	4	50	—
Austria............	(1829)..............	3	50	—

In the first class, four protestant states commence the list, and two catholic states conclude it. In the second, two protestant states take the lead, and four catholics are in the last ranks. If we unite the two lists,

In the 1st, 4 protestant states have the advantage over 2 catholic states.
In the 2nd, 2 protestant states have the advantage over 4 catholic states.

ON THE WHOLE, 6 protestant states have the advantage over 6 catholic states.

Consequently, the six protestant nations show themselves to be more industrious than the six catholic nations. Will the equilibrium be re-established by adding the imports to the exports, to get at the sum total of general commerce?

Let us ask another author.

We copy from M. Schnitzler the following table :

Absolute importance of the chief commercial Powers [1].

British Empire............	1,443,638,241 +	2,002,051,641 =	3,445,689,882
France....................	871,600,000 +	902,600,000 =	1,774,200,000
United States.............	749,478,710 +	608,467,885 =	1,357,946,595
Austrian Monarchy.........	325,449,326 +	319,827,168 =	645,276,494
Belgium...................	212,401,858 +	162,178,520 =	374,580,378
Spain.....................	114,490,000 +	65,547,000 =	180,037,000

In this list, taking into account the population, two of the countries should be differently placed : 1st, the United States, the population of which is but half that of France; 2nd, Belgium, the population of which is but the fifteenth part of that of Austria. By effecting these changes, we alter the order of absolute importance into that of relative importance, the only one necessary for our subject, and then we have the following order :

British Empire.
United States.
France.
Belgium.
Austrian Monarchy.
Spain.

This result confirms that which M. Moreau de Jonnès has given us. The two first nations in the order of relative commercial importance are protestant nations; the two last are Catholic nations. Might we venture to add, that the two intermediate nations, although catholic, are less exclusively so? However this may be, it results from all that precedes, that, to judge by the state of agriculture, by the progress of industry, and by the extent of commerce, the advantage is always on the same side. Now, these elements constitute Wealth; there is more Wealth, then, among the protestant nations than among the catholic nations. Still, let us not decide from such general data; let us defer forming an opinion until we have studied each of these nations separately; and, for the present, let us proceed to our second point of comparison, namely, Knowledge.

Knowledge.—The number of pupils in the primary schools may be given as the measure of the diffusion of knowledge among the popular masses; but it does not prejudge the question as to the knowledge of the upper classes. It may suit the policy of a govern-

1. Schnitzler, vol. IV, p. 269.

ment to grant to its people elementary knowledge, while it puts impediments in the way of propagating the sciences. Nevertheless, we must rest content with the means that statistical science furnishes : she can count pupils; she cannot measure intellects.

Let us first present a document the most simple and brief; we will afterwards check it by another more complete.

We read in M. Schnitzler :

Primary Instruction.

In Saxony, one pupil for........................	6	inhabitants.
In the Low Countries, one for..................	6	—
In Prussia, one for..............................	6 1/6	—
In Great Britain (England and Wales), one for....	8	—
In Belgium, one for..............................	9	—
In Austria, one for..............................	10 1/2	—
In France, one for..............................	11 [1]	—

The four first nations are protestant; the three last are catholic. If we take the two averages, we have :

1 pupil for 6 1/2 protestants,
1 pupil for 10 catholics.

In other words, the protestants who know how to read an write are to the catholics in the proportion of 13 to 20.

Will M. Jonnès come to confirm, or to contradict M. Schnitzler? We read in M. Jonnès :

British Isles.................	1	pupil for	6	inhabitants in	1833.
Switzerland, canton de Vaud...	1	—	6	—	1828.
Baden........................	1	—	7	—	1825.
Bavaria......................	1	—	7	—	1825.
Wurtemberg...................	1	—	8	—	1827.
Low Countries...............	1	—	10	—	1826.
Prussia......................	1	—	10	—	1825.
Holland......................	1	—	8	—	1835.
Austrian Empire..............	1	—	16	—	1822.
France.......................	1	—	17	—	1834.
Denmark......................	1	—	30	—	1825.
Kingdom of Naples...........	1	—	45	—	1818.
— of Poland...........	1	—	100	—	1823.
Portugal.....................	1	—	109	—	1819.
Hungary......................	1	—	350	—	1835.
Spain........................	1	—	350	—	1803. [2]

In this table, copied from Jonnès, we have omitted those countries that would cause a double reckoning, as Scotland and Ireland, which are included in the British Isles.

One glance thrown upon this list of sixteen states makes us aware

1. Vol. II, p. 343. — 2. Vol. II, pp. 333, 334.

that, with almost a single exception on each side, the first half is protestant, and the second catholic. We can even account for the anomaly in regard to Bavaria, by observing that a catholic nation, situated in the midst of protestant nations, has been compelled to receive the light which came to it from all sides, and to follow the general impulse. But let us seek a measure more exact; let us place Bavaria among the catholic nations, and Denmark among the protestant; let us no longer count nations, but individuals, and we shall have as the average:

1 pupil for 124 catholics.
and 1 pupil for 10 protestants.

In order to be still more exact, let us reduce the catholic return to 1 in 100, on account of the earlier dates affixed to some of the countries that help to compose it, and we have even then this astonishing result, that there are ten times more pupils in the aggregate of protestant countries, than in the aggregate of catholic countries.

This report given by Jonnès is infinitely more favourable to protestants than the report of 13 to 20 found in Schnitzler, because it extends to more nations, and above all to catholic nations more remote from the radiation of protestant light, such as Spain, Portugal, and Italy. The same cannot be said of these countries, that can be said of Bavaria, borrowing the words of M. G. de Beaumont and of M. A. de Tocqueville; "In the case of a nation surrounded by enlightened neighbours, instruction is a political necessity." (*Système pénitentiaire, part I, ch. III.*) An evidence corresponding with that of the number of pupils in schools is to be found in the number of the readers of journals. The following is the order in which Jonnès places them in the different nations of Europe:

Journals.

Denmark	80	journals,	1	copy for	24,000	inhabitants.
Low Countries	150	—	1	—	40,000	—
Switzerland	54	—	1	—	40,000	—
Germany	305	—	1	—	40,000	—
Prussia	300	—	1	—	44,000	—
Sweden and Norway	82	—	1	—	44,000	—
Scotland	41	—	1	—	50,000	—
France	490	—	1	—	66,000	—
England	179		1	—	71,000	—
British Isles	274	—	1	—	88,000	—
Ireland	54	—	1	—	135,000	—
Portugal	17	—	1	—	200,000	—
Poland (1830)	13	—	1	—	300,000	—
Greece	3	—	1	—	300,000	—

Austria	80 journals,	1 copy for		400,000	inhabitants.
Italy.....................	29	— 1	—	750,000	—
Spain (before 1833).......	16	— 1	—	900,000	—
Russia....................	31	— 1	—	1,500,000	—

This table is an exact reproduction of that of Jonnès. With a view to our subject, we ought to modify it as follows: 1st, let us not take account of the number of journals, but only of the number of copies, because one journal may print a far greater number of copies than another: 2ndly, let us omit Greece and Russia, countries which are neither catholic nor protestant; and also Germany, because its mixed population might give occasion to dispute in which class it ought to be placed; lastly, the British Isles, the three divisions of which are already in the list. Being thus rid of these elements foreign to our subject, this table shows that, with regard to the extent of the publicity of journals, the six first states are protestant, and the six last, are catholic. Now, to obtain an exact average, let us take into our calculation France and England, placed between the two extremes, and we shall have:

1 copy for 315 protestants,
1 copy for 2,715 catholics.

which shows that nine copies are circulated among protestants for one copy among catholics. This result confirms and verifies that which we found as to the pupils, which was 10 to 1.

This approximation also proves that the knowledge acquired is in general turned to account, for we see that ten pupils furnish eventually nine readers.

Let us again check Jonnès by Schnitzler. We read in this last author:

"On the 1st of January, 1844, there appeared in all 541 journals, of which 119 were published in London, 237 in the country, 11 in Wales, 93 in Scotland (the capital of which, Edinburgh, ranks immediately after London), and 71 in Ireland, of which 30 in Dublin.

"In Germany also (a country the greater part of which is protestant), the number of journals is greater than in most other countries. There appear in it, it is said, more than 850 periodical publications of every kind; while in Austria, a country essentially catholic, there appeared in the year 1841 only 31 political journals, disposing of 5, 350 copies, and 52 journals not political, disposing of 4000. If we add to these all the subscriptions to foreign journals, there are not distributed, in all that vast monarchy (Hungary excepted), more than 25,500 copies a day (official).

"In Spain there appeared on the 1st of January, 1837, 135 journals, of which 108 were official bulletins; not taking these into account, there were 27 journals in Madrid, and 60 in the provinces.

"Denmark and Sweden possess, in proportion to their population, a very great number of journals.

"In the United States, the total, in 1843, was 1,641 journals, of which 148 appeared every day; 1,141 every week; 125 twice or thrice a week; and 227 at more distant periods [1]."

On the whole, as respects the number of copies circulated, Schnitzler gives to England, Germany, Denmark, and Sweden, protestant countries, the advantage over Austria, Ireland, and Spain, catholic countries. This general result of Schnitzler, then, confirms the more exac one of Jonnès. We have often seen that our studies with reference to nations, viewed collectively, have ended in verifying those we have pursued with regard to individuals. In thus studying nations, we have more than a simple probability of accuracy, we have a complete demonstration; an evident proof that the result is not owing to any accidental circumstance, but rather to a law. If, for example, in taking the averages, we included as an element a return very favourable to protestantism, but borrowed from a single nation, a return which, often appealed to, would tend to influence exceedingly the final average, it might be said with reason, that this final result was owing to a particular nation. But we have not done this: it is not by seeking only the averages that we have been led to give the superiority to protestantism, but also by taking special account of each member of the series. We have seen that, in the lists of 12 or 15 nations, all the protestant nations rank first, all the catholic nations rank last. When an arithmetical calculation is verified by proofs worked out in ten different ways, does any one think of disputing its correctness?

Still, we shall proceed as if this arithmetical calculation, proved ten times over, might after all be false, and we shall suspend our judgment in regard to Knowledge, as we have suspended it in regard to Wealth, until we have seen it confirmed or contradicted by our further researches with reference to each particular nation.

Let us then, for the present, proceed to the last point:

Morality. — While we have judged of Wealth and Knowledge by their presence, is it not strange that it is only by negative evidence that we are able to solve the question of Morality? It is a sad necessity of our nature to have to ascertain which of us has the

1. Vol. 2. pp. 369, 370.

least of moral miseries, in order to know which has the most of virtue!

Be this as it may, these moral miseries manifest themselves under two principal aspects; acts of violence, and acts of profligacy; assassinations and corrupt manners. A word on each of these two points.

As many causes contribute to make the appreciation of judges differ, we shall take account not only of crimes that have been consummated, but also of crimes the perpetration whereof has only been begun. Taken alone, the first only indicate the severity of human law; joined with the second, they measure more correctly the perversity of man. Here, then, is what we read in Jonnès:

Justice.

ASSASSINATIONS AND ATTEMPTS TO ASSASSINATE IN EUROPE.

Scotland	1835...........	1 for 270,000
England...........................		1 for 178,000
Low Countries	1824...........	1 for 163,000
Prussia	1824...........	1 for 100,000
Austria	1809...........	1 for 57,000
Spain	1826...........	1 for 4,113
Naples...........................		1 for 2,750
Roman States......................		1 for 750[1] "

In this decreasing table of morality, extracted from Jonnès, the first four states are protestant; the four last are catholic. To obtain a more exact measure, let us take the average, and we shall have one assassination, or one attempt to assassinate, for 180,222 inhabitants in the aggregate of the four protestant nations; and one assassination, or one attempt to assassinate, for 16,153 inhabitants in the four catholic nations; in other words, eleven times more crime among the Roman catholic nations.

Let us proceed to the second point, to Morals properly so called, which we shall uniformly appreciate by their deficiencies.

We acknowledge that illegitimate births are not a very certain sign by which to estimate the immorality of a nation. *Here* legal marriage is surrounded by so many obstacles, that many unions dispense with it. *There*, the cicisbeos, that is to say, the lovers by the side of the husband, are so completely sanctioned by public opinion, that immorality, thus legalized, has only the effect of changing impurity into adultery. Besides, there is prostitution, which destroys the traces of illegitimate unions. In all these cases the remedy is worse than the disease. But as we do not pretend to

1. Jonnès, vol. II, p. 257.

give exact data on such subjects, we will content ourselves with citing such indications as statistics afford us; we shall afterwards have an opportunity of verifying their results by other means.

Here, then, is the table of illegitimate births among the nations which are to occupy our attention.

In this table we no longer place the nations in the order of the figures, but we make two sections: one catholic, the other protestant. Nor do we limit our inquiry to those nations which we shall have to compare further on; but we bring together all the data that we have been able to discover in different authors. The employment of such means is indispensable in a subject so complicated, and, by resorting to more numerous elements, we have more chances of getting near the truth:

Natural children.

Their proportion to legitimate children.

CATHOLIC NATIONS.		PROTESTANT NATIONS.	
France	13,98	British Isles (in 1830), according to Jonnès	19
Lombardy	23	Prussia (from 1820 to 1834)	13,12
Gallicia	12	Sweden... 15 or.... 17,50 } aver	16,25
Bohemia	6		
Austria, properly so called	3		
	57,98		48,37
Divided by 5 the average. is	11,59	Divided by 3 the average. is	16,12

Leaving the fractions, the proportion of natural children among these catholic and protestant nations is then as 16 to 11. If we had not taken Lombardy into the account, where, very evidently, the number of natural children is not a just standard of morals (for the reason pointed out above), we should have had, as the final result, twice as many illegitimate children among the catholic nations as among the protestant. To avail ourselves of the remark made by the authors from whom we have extracted this information: "These data confer no great honour on the morals of Austria (catholic)[1]."

Having thus taken a summary view of the statistical data of wealth, knowledge, and morality, we should like to find some further kind of evidence that would illustrate these three subjects, and corroborate the statistical data. It has struck us that the Savings-Banks furnish this *desideratum*. They indicate, in fact, the wealth of the people, their spirit of order, as well as a wise economy of their

1. Schnitzler, vol. I, pp. 284, 285.

resources. Without attaching too much importance to them, let us cite, on this subject, from the same author :

SAVINGS-BANKS.

" It was in England that Savings-Banks were first elevated to the rank of an institution. In 1841, there were 563. The amount of deposits exceeded 400 millions of francs, belonging to 841,204 depositors. In 1839, there had been only 748,396 depositors, of whom 734,089 were individuals, and 14,308 (!!) were charitable societies, or of mutual aid. The average deposit of individuals was 725 francs; that of charitable associations, 1,525.

" After England, the country most distinguished in this respect is Switzerland (the greater part of which is protestant).

" In the Austrian monarchy, the official reports have registered, for 1841, 11 savings-banks, each with many branches. The year (1841) has commenced with a deposit of nearly 100 millions [1]. "

Thus, the first place belongs to a protestant country; the second, to a country with a mixed population; the third, to a catholic country.

It is not the first time that we have arrived at this threefo result.

But it is time to leave these generalities. Let us not attach too much importance to them; let us wait before we confide in them, or distrust them until we have studied each nation separately; not so much by the data of statistics, the elements of which the reader might fear our prejudiced mind had ill chosen; but, above all, by giving the opinions, clearly expressed, of travellers and learned men.

We have cast a glance over the whole of the globe; let us now fix our attention, for the present, on a single hemisphere, the two Americas; hereafter, we shall direct it to regions more circumscribed.

1. Schnitzler, vol. 2, p. 268.

THE

TWO AMERICAS COMPARED.

In the plan of our work the two Americas naturally call for a comparison; but we must exclude from this comparison the elements which, by their nature, do not belong to our subject; such as, in the North, the Russian colonies and others of small importance; and in the south, the nations that are strangers to all forms of christian worship, in order to have only before us, on the one hand, the United States, essentially protestant, and on the other, Brazil, Peru, Chili, etc., all catholic states, and of Spanish origin.

But, before we describe the nations, let us say a few words of these regions.

A difference in the climate does not necessarily produce a corresponding difference in the inhabitants.

"The same nations," says M. de Tocqueville, "have shown themselves, at different epochs of their history, chaste or dissolute : consequently the regularity, or the disorder of their conduct, was produced by some variable cause, and not by the nature of the country, which was unchanged [1]."

If the influence of climate is considerable elsewhere, facts show that it is not so in America.

"Physical causes have not so great an influence as is supposed on the destiny of nations," says the same writer. "I have met with men in New England ready to leave their native land, where they

1. De Tocqueville, vol. IV, pp. 84, 87.

might have lived in the back-woods, and close to them I have seen the French population of Canada crowd themselves into a space much too narrow for them, with the same back-woods close at hand; and whilst the emigrant from the United States acquired, for the price of a few days' labour, a large domain, the Canadian paid for his land as dearly as if he were in France. Thus nature, in giving up the New World to Europeans, offers them riches, of which they do not always know how to make use. Other nations in America possess (excepting their laws and morals,) the same elements and prosperities as the Anglo-Americans, and these nations are miserable : therefore the laws and morals of the Anglo-Americans are the foundation of their greatness, and form the cause of predominance that I seek [1]. "

If climate must be taken into account, the advantage is on the side of South America, blessed with a clear sky, a fertile soil, and majestic rivers, the longest in the world. " In Brazil," says Rougemont, " the maritime districts are extremely fertile; the table-land is much less productive, but it is rich in diamonds and metals [2]. " " The soil, " adds d'Orbigny, " could be easily cultivated, and made very productive like that of Buenos-Ayres, where, when they choose to sow, wheat yields fifty-fold, but the time is not come for agriculture [3]. " " In the provinces of Rio-Janeiro, " according to Malte-Brun, " all the fruits and grains of Europe invariably succeed, but their cultivation is neglected; the grapes yield very good wine, but water in the neighbourhood of the rich gold mines is preferred. The horned cattle, obliged to seek their own food, often perish with hunger [4]. " " Peru and Mexico, " according to Balbi, " although situated between the tropics, owe to their elevation a perpetual spring [5]. "

On the other side, on the contrary, a cloudy sky, a much less fertile soil, and obstacles of all kinds, oppose the establishment of colonists. It is acknowledged that the natural advantages of a country give a right to expect from the inhabitants a more rapid and higher civilization. The greater the fertility of a soil, the more guilty are the people who neglect it; as the original sterility of a land afterwards covered with abundant harvests bears witness to the skill of the people who cultivated it. If then, with a fine climate, and in the most advantageous circumstances, we find a people ignorant, lazy, miserable, and immoral, our conclusions against the actuating principle of their conduct would be singularly

1. De Tocqueville, vol. II, p. 250. — 2. Rougemont, p. 679. — 3. D'Orbigny, vol. I, p. 472. — 4. Malte-Brun, vol. IX, p. 681. — 5. Balbi, p. 944.

strengthened. — But let us enter upon our subject: the comparison of the United States of North America, with the several Republics of the South.

We have said that the United States are protestant, the South, catholic: before we describe their present condition, let us relate their origin, and begin with the Anglo-Americans.

"The emigrants who came to settle on the shores of New England all belonged to the middle classes in the mother-country. Their assemblage on American ground presented, from the beginning, the singular phenomenon of a society where there were neither great lords nor common people, neither rich nor poor. There was proportionately a greater mass of misery amongst them than in the midst of any European nation in these days [1]."

"The emigrants, or as they called themselves so well, the pilgrims, belonged to that sect in England, which, on account of the austerity of its principles, was called Puritan.

"When scarcely disembarked upon this inhospitable shore, which Nathaniel Morton has described, the first occupation of the emigrants was to organise themselves into a society. They passed immediately an act which read thus: "We, the undersigned, who, for the glory of God, the advancement of the christian faith, and honour of our king and country, have undertaken to plant the first colony in these distant regions; we do, by these presents, solemnly and mutually, in the presence of God and of each other, covenant and combine ourselves together into a civil body politic, for the better ordering and preservation and furtherance of our designs: by virtue hereof to enact, constitute, and frame such just and equal laws, ordinances, acts, constitutions, and offices from time to time as shall be thought most meet and convenient for the general good of the colony; unto which we promise all due submission and obedience [2]."

"The legislators in this body of penal laws are above all anxious to maintain good morals and virtuous conduct; for which reason they penetrate continually into the domain of conscience, and there is scarcely a sin which they do not succeed in placing under the control of the magistrate [3]."

"What distinguished these emigrants from all others," says Malte-Brun, "was the object of their enterprise. It was not poverty that forced them to abandon their country; they left behind them a respectable place in society, and sure means of existence.

1 De Tocqueville, vol. I, pp. 23, 24. — 2. Vol. I, pp. 28 et 29. — 3. Vol. I, p. 34.

Neither did they pass into the New World to better their condition, or to augment their fortune; they tore themselves from all the delights of their native land to satisfy a purely intellectual desire, and exposed themselves to the miseries of exile in order to obtain the triumph of an idea[1]. "

Now let us consult Michel Chevalier :

" The Anglo-Americans, who quitted Europe the last, that is to say, after the Spaniards had established their domination in Southern and Central America, did not leave the Old World until it had been completely ploughed up by the intellectual revolution of which Luther was the Mirabeau, and Henry the Eighth in England the Robespierre and the Napoleon. This great event had already deposited in the human mind a germ, which succeeding ages were destined to see flourish. England was already pregnant with these habits of labour, method, and legality, which were to make her the first commercial and political nation in the Old World; they the refore started with the principles which were to insure their political and commercial supremacy in the New[2]. "

Such is the origin of the United States of North America. We shall not follow the different phases of the history of this people; it does not enter into our subject : all we have to do, after having described their starting point, is to show the end attained. And here again we shall allow eye-witnesses to speak :

" The United States is the greatest nation of the New World. Their mercantile navy is only surpassed by that of England; their public works, their canals, their scientific and literary establishments rival those of Europe. The population, already considerable in itself, is still more so when we compare it with that of the other States of America, over which it exercises a twofold influence by its mass and by the enterprising activity of its government. In short, the United States are at the head of that civilization which is advancing so rapidly from one end to the other of this part of the World.

" It is difficult to form a just idea of the extraordinary progress of the population of the Union, the prodigious developement of agriculture, manufactures, and commerce, the foundation of fresh towns, the opening of new canals, and formation of new roads. Villages, and even simple hamlets, become in a few months great and opulent cities by the construction of a railroad, by the opening of a canal, or by the working of a new mine[3]. "

1. De Tocqueville, vol. xi, p. 222. — 2. Vol. i, pp. 374, 375. — 3. Balbi, introd., pp. 63 et 64.

"No where, in America, can the philosopher contemplate a more imposing spectacle than that which is offered him by the Anglo-American Confederation; it is truly a phenomenon, hitherto without example in the history of nations. Great and flourishing from her very infancy, this powerful Confederation is a demonstration of what may be effected by liberty sustained by wise institutions, the spirit of concord, the love of one's country, respect for the laws and religion, activity and persevering labour. With a political existence of scarcely half a century, her immense shores are studded with rich and populous cities, her primeval forests are exchanged for a well cultivated country, ornamented by the richest gifts of nature, and enriched by numerous manufactories. Sumptuous edifices, magnificent churches, elegant houses, superb squares, canals and railroads of extraordinary length, immense stores, numerous dock-yards, workshops of every description, take the place of the miserable huts of the former inhabitants; and thousands of vessels, laden with the manufactures of the most industrious nations, with the productions of every climate, plough the waters of her rivers, which in olden time only drifted the shapeless canoe of the savage. It is impossible sufficiently to admire the rapid progress which every year marks the existence of this new Europe, rich in all the knowledge and activity of the Old World, which she even appears ready to outvie. Without distant colonies, it has developed to an immense extent its commercial shipping: inferior only to that of England, and already superior to that of all the other nations of the globe. Never have similar wonders been wrought in so short a time, even by the most powerful monarchies, and after many glorious reigns. Civilization now flourishes where formerly all was barbarous; the authority of wise laws has been substituted for the violence of brutal force; numerous philanthropical institutions, and the consolations of a religion of peace, relieve and comfort mankind, on the same spots where so much was suffered from the barbarity and superstition of the ancient inhabitants [1]."

"Here is a real moving picture, a scene of perpetual action, without a moment of rest: towns and whole Republics rise up more rapidly than an edifice in Europe. New England is the centre of commercial and maritime enterprise, and the seat of the most generally diffused civilization: the people, well informed and laborious, know how to appreciate and defend their political rights. Gloomy presbyterianism shows its influence solely in the austerity

1. Balbi, pp. 975, 976.

of morals and in the respect for public worship, which are characteristic marks of the inhabitants of New England [1]. "

Lastly, we will quote a modern author :

" At this time, the Republic of the United States, whose origin is so recent, has not its equal in power in the New World, or in the Old. Amid the old powers of Europe she already occupies a foremost place. Prodigious progress! which may be justly considered as the wonder of modern ages. Other nations perhaps have started from a lower state of existence, and arrived at the summit of power, the Romans for example; but it must be remarked that their elevation was the slow and gradual work of ages, whilst the American Republic has increased her population fivefold, tripled her territory, and increased at least tenfold her power of production in half a century; and this without an army, without war, without conquest; thanks alone to the gradual and pacific developement of her natural resources, fructified by labour. Raynal wrote in 1781 : *If ten millions of men ever find an assured subsistence in these provinces, it will be a great deal.* In less than forty years the *ever* of Raynal had arrived; and now, that is to say, sixty-five years after, the ten millions that he stated as the extreme limit of what was possible are more than doubled. What is more, this progression perserves its astonishing rapidity, and promises not only tens, but hundreds of millions. The result has thus baffled all foresight, and surpassed all expectation [2]. "

To this sketch of Protestant America in the North, what has Catholic America in the South to oppose? This is the statement of Roman Catholic authors :

" In the Republics of South America, which preserve the blood and the indolent pride of the Spaniards, constitutions are destroyed hourly by the will of some dictator; and the people, after a transient appearance in the career of civilization, fall back into the darkness of barbarism, and are not even conscious that they have been free for a day. Society, in short, stumbles at the first step it attempts to take forward, and falls helpless at the entrance of that path in which modern civilization springs forward, radiant and proud, to the goal. All that is a grievous assemblage of ignorance, disorder, and misery [3]. "

" In the countries occupied by the descendants of the European colonists, public education is very defective, and private education, in general, neglected. Agriculture, except in some few localities, is

1. Malte-Brun, vol. XI, pp. 210, 211. — 2 *Revue Britannique*, 1848, July and August. — 3. January and February, p. 244.

in a deplorable state; as to manufactures, they are in their infancy. The natural feelings are on a level with such an education. Scarcely is an individual attacked with leprosy, than he is torn from his family, and thrown into a special hospital; and there, deprived of all external communication, and abandoned to the brutality of an impatient mercenary, the unhappy being sees himself lost without resource, and gives himself up to despair; the disease increases, and he falls a victim to the ignorance and prejudices of his countrymen.

" In the Cundinamarca exists the barbarous custom of travelling on the back of a man, as elsewhere on the back of a mule. The unhappy Cargueros, lightly clothed, and armed with a long stick, travel during several successive days across a stony and rugged country, carrying a load on their shoulders which weighs abont two hundred pounds. Two straps round the shoulders support a chair on which the traveller is seated, and when he finds that his steed does not go fast enough, that his foot is not sure, or his trot gentle enough, he does not hesitate to strike him with his riding whip, or to run his spurs into his sides [1]. "

Leaving the country, let us turn to a large city, and cast a glance at Rio de Janeiro, the capital of Brazil:

" Here the use of cemeteries is not yet prevalent. There happens what used to take place in the charnel houses of our great cities. Fresh funerals are continually throwing up bones, which are not always treated with the respect due to the dead. Sometimes, " as M. Walsh says, " the soil has been so often turned up, that it is impossible to find a fresh spot of earth deep enough to contain the dead body, which necessarily remains above the level of the soil, and the gravedigger is obliged to use an instrument like that employed by our paviers to make it enter into its grave. The spectators look on with the most perfect indifference [2]. "

" In order to give a complete idea of the strange system which had been adopted by the mother-country with regard to the Portuguese colonies, we may mention the fact that, about the year 1800, a cotton spinning manufactory having been established near Bahia, it was destroyed by order of the governor, and the proprietor was sent to Europe to be judged according to the laws which forbad the introduction of manufactures [3]. "

If any one wishes to know what the Argentines were doing while the Anglo-Americans were laying down railroads, they have only to

1. *Union pittoresque*, Colombie, p. 21. — 2. *Idem*, p. 139. — 3. From Warden, *Chronologie Historique de l'Amérique*, vol. XIII, p. 109.

read : " In the Argentine Republic, " says d'Orbigny, " instead of making new roads, and opening fresh communications in the midst of the wilds, the Europeans neglect those that have been in their possession for ages, and, to the shame of civilization be it spoken, they are driven back to the gates of their cities [1]. "

" In town and country, all persons who are not of a certain rank in society go barefoot. Shoes have only lately been introduced, and it is not at all uncommon to see a woman shoeless, who is otherwise well dressed. The use of stockings is still less common, because they cost more [2]. "

" The children go completely naked in the house until they are six or eight years old ; and when they go out, scarcely a simple cotton shift is thrown about them, so that they always remain strangers to modesty. "

" At Lesquina commences a change of manners. I found no longer the frank hospitality of the North ; but that insolence and hatred of strangers which is met with in the province of Entre-Rios, which I was going to enter [3]. "

" Caballa-Matia is a group of a few poor huts, where live suspicious and uncommunicative men, with faces as ferocious as those of the jaguars, their neighbours [4]. "

" The inhabitants of Bajada dislike agriculture, and none of their houses are ornamented with gardens ; they never plant a tree : on the contrary, they cut down all they can find, so that the country appears as if it had been ravaged by a general conflagration [5]. "

" When I traversed the forest of the Conception, my enterprise appeared very bold ; but my guide confessed that he was in communication with the brigands who were concealed there, and that with the help of some presents, with which he was always provided, he had no fear of being ill treated [6]. "

" A great number of the inhabitants (Pampas), instead of accepting any improvement in their condition, persist in their filthiness and rudeness, regarding it as a point of personal pride not to renounce habits which they consider as indispensable, and withdrawing from circulation enormous sums, which they hoard to the great prejudice of the country ; boasting of their occupation as the most useful in the world, of their violent exercises as the most noble, and despising supremely all kinds of science, education, and politeness [7]."

" The bad state of the roads has long been the chief obstacle to the extension of commerce, and this state of things is maintained by

1. D'Orbigny, vol. I, p. 313. — 2. *Idem*, p. 384. — 3. *Idem*, p. 413. — 4. *Idem*, p. 421. — 5. *Idem*, p. 427. — 6. *Idem*, p. 431 — 7. *Idem*, p. 627.

the civil and religious authorities, in order to preserve the exclusive monopoly of the exchanges. Miry roads are covered with trunks of trees, across which the poor mule makes its way, at the risk of breaking a leg, or sinking up to the breast[1]. "

" The commerce of the province (Corrientes) is insignificant; and it is forbidden to let any money go out of it. To exercise any kind of trade is a dishonour to a man of condition, so that there are neither artisans, nor manufacturers, except among the Indians, the mulattoes, or the women. The whites must not do any thing[2]."

" It is singular to see men, who would blush to employ themselves in any manual labour, think it quite natural that their wives should do so : it would be easy to establish manufactories, as labour is cheap. When will civilization, and the spirit of industry, be sufficiently advanced among the Correntinos to turn to account the riches which only require to be made use of ? [3] "

" The upper classes are proud and conceited; their siesta is very long, and they only devote to business the time that is not given to smoking; talking of politics sometimes, but more usually of horses and cattle, and still oftener of scandalous adventures and women. In fact their occupation consists in doing nothing[4]. "

" Felling trees, their transport, the loading of boats, etc., would be labours incompatible with the indolence of the proud Entre-Rianos, who, although these occupations are very lucrative, regard them as beneath them; the little labour which the occupation of shepherd exacts suits them much better than any kind of industry[5]. "

" Little is done at Santa-Cruz : the chief employment consists in visits and festivals. Literature is scarcely known : the men read little, and the women not at all. Men and women go barefooted[6]. "

The Pampas willingly lend to each other their wives, who indeed abandon themselves to all their relations. At the approach of death they meet together, and shut the eyes, mouth, and nostrils of the dying person, in order, they say, that death may not pass from his body into that of the other inhabitants of the house. It thus often happens that these savages, taking a fainting fit for death, hasten by suffocation the last moments of their relations[7]. "

Is the contrast that we have placed before the eyes of our readers the fruit of our imagination? Does it result from a choice of quotations, which other quotations would contradict? Are we the only

1 D'Orbigny, vol. I, pp. 390, 391. — 2. *Idem*, p. 351. — 3. *Idem*, p. 352. — 4. *Idem*, p. 369. — 5. *Idem*, p. 438. — 6. *Idem*, vol. II, p. 571. — 7. *Idem*, vol. III, p. 98.

persons struck by this contrast? No, our author remarks it himself: " When one sees North America traversed in every direction by numerous steamboats and railroads, one is astonished that the nations who have colonised South America should have remained so far behind, without ever taking the first steps towards progress [1]. "

Michel Chevalier pronounces a similar judgment: " The Anglo-American people will lay the foundation of a race, although it is possible that the type that now predominates may be eclipsed by another; whilst the Hispano-Americans will leave no posterity, unless, by one of those inundations called conquests, a flood of more generous blood from the North or East comes to fill their impoverished veins [2]. "

To render the parallel exact and conclusive between the two hemispheres, it is not necessary to oppose to the mechanic and farmer of the United States their counterpart in the nations of German origin, idiom, and religion; it is only necessary to open one's eyes to recognise that the mass of the population of the French, Spaniards, and Italians, are far from having attained each in his own way the degree of perfection to which the masses in North America have advanced in their own peculiar direction [3]. "

" If the United States were to snatch the Mexican provinces from the Spanish race, they would be responsible to mankind and to God for the consequences of a theft; but if the countries of which they had taken possession prospered in their hands, posterity would pardon their having seized them. On the contrary, it would pronounce a severe judgment on the Mexicans, who, with such neighbours near at hand, should remain as they are at present in a state of base inactivity and stupid security; and on the European powers, if they had neglected to warn and help them to shake off their lethargy [4]. "

Lastly, M. de Tocqueville expresses himself in the same terms: " Democratical institutions, " says he, " only prosper in the United States. The American Union has no enemies to struggle against: she is alone in the midst of the Ocean. Nature had isolated in a like manner the Spaniards of South America, but this did not prevent their keeping up an army: and when they had no strangers to fight against, they turned their arms against each other. The Anglo-American democracy is the only one that has been able to remain at peace. The territory of the Union presents a boundless field for human activity, and inexhaustible materials for labour and

1. D'Orbigny, vol. III, p. 113. — 2. Michel Chevalier, p. 378. — 3. *Idem*, pp. 385, 386. — 4. *Idem*, pp. 387, 388.

industry. Then, the love of wealth takes the place of ambition, and a life of comfort subdues the fierceness of party spirit. But in what part of the world are there more fertile wastes, more magnificent rivers, more inexhaustible riches to be met with, than in South America? And yet South America cannot bear a democracy. Were it sufficient for the happiness of a people to be placed in a corner of the universe where they could spread themselves as they pleased over uninhabited lands, the Spaniards of South America would have no reason to complain of their lot.

And even if they could not enjoy the same happiness as the inhabitants of the United States, they might, at least, excite the envy of European nations. Yet there are no nations upon the face of the earth so miserable as those of South America [1]. "

The scale of morals is not more elevated than that of civilization : " The Spaniards let loose their dogs upon the Indians as if they were wild beasts; they pillaged the New World like a town taken by storm, without discernment and without pity, but all could not be destroyed, fury must needs wear itself out : and the rest of the Indian population, which had escaped the massacre, ended by mixing with the conquerors, and by adopting their language and customs.

" On the contrary, the conduct of the Americans of the United States towards the natives breathes the purest love of forms and legality. Provided that the Indians remain in their savage state, the Americans do not interfere in their affairs in any way, but treat them as independent nations; and they will not occupy their lands without having duly acquired them by contract.

" The Spaniards, in spite of unexampled barbarities, which have covered them with lasting shame, have not succeeded in exterminating the Indian race, nor even in hindering their sharing their rights. The Americans of the United States have attained this double result with a wonderful facility; quietly, legally, philanthropically, without bloodshed, without violating any of the great principles of morality in the eyes of the world [2]. "

To convince you that the difference of these two nations consists in men, and not in things, suppose that they have the same institutions, the same contract will still exist. Facts have realised this supposition. " Mexico, " says M. de Tocqueville, " which is as happily situated as the Anglo-American Union, has chosen the same laws, and yet cannot get accustomed to a democratical government.

1. De Tocqueville, vol. II, pp. 250, 253, — 2. *Idem*, p. 311.

There must then be, independent of physical causes and laws, something which enables democracy to govern the United States [1]. "

We have already hinted that the civilization of the United States was a fruit of the Protestant faith. Without any fresh demonstration, we might now conclude that the Catholic faith is the source from which flows the state of things we have been considering in South America. But, in the room of this simple deduction, we prefer placing the eloquent testimony of a writer, who explains, as we do, the difference of these two civilizations by the difference of the two religious principles which has inspired them. Let us listen then to M. Edgard Quinet:

" In order to appreciate the struggle between modern Catholicism and Protestantism, we must leave Europe. Here they are both embarrassed in their movements by too many old establishments and customs. Providence has placed them in a vast arena, where each being surrounded solely by its own deeds will be judged by them alone. The Church of the Middle Ages and the Reformation have, each in America, a world in which to try their strength at ease. A duel which has Heaven and Earth for witnesses! A few men land, one by one, on the shores of North America, poor, humble, and unknown; they bring with them but one book, the Bible; they open it on the strand, and begin immediately to build up the new city on the plan of the book recovered by Luther [2]. "

" See the calmness and boldness of these men! We discover, in the constitution of this rising empire, the fire of Luther united to the coolness of Calvin. What intrepidity, to rush into this visible infinity, to push back the barriers, to tame the hydra of the forests! Herculean labour, performed by a christian mind! sacred work of man to bend a whole hemisphere to his will! An empire bows to labour a new universe for its field; its instruments are rivers; Christ again becomes the carpenter.

" Hearken to the sound of his axe; he fells the primeval oak in the virgin forests; the sweat inundates his brow. To all appearance his thoughts are concentrated in his rule and compass. He builds, with toil and trouble, an unknown hut near a running stream. The traveller scarce deigns to turn his head towards this humble dwelling, where the noise of the axe and hammer mingles with the chant of a psalm. But if, a few years later, he pass again by the same spot, he sees, by a sort of social miracle, in the

1. De Tocqueville, vol. II, pp. 250, 255. — 2. Quinet, p. 291.

place of the hut, a mighty empire rising from the earth. The Carpenter has become the teacher of the world [1]. "

" In this immense arena the lists are opened between two religions; the Catholicism of the Council of Trent has received, for the display of her strength, South America. There the founders are not isolated individuals; on the contrary, according to Catholic principles, an association already formed, a powerful empire, with all its resources, comes to take possession of the soil. Spain established herself in America with her Church, her authority, and her armies; and enhancing the value of her portion, on one side the nation that takes its place on this scene is the right arm of Catholicism, and, on the other, the country that is assigned to it is the most visibly favoured by the Creator. Rich valleys and fertile plains seem to demand the living energy which would give birth to new empires. In order that the trial may be more decisive, Catholicism alone is allowed to approach these shores; the civilization of the natives, which might have embarrassed her actions, disappears. Nothing remains but mighty nature, who, in her solitude, invites man to crown her with vast ideas, projects, innovations, *societies*, kingdoms, gigantic as herself. But man remains motionless, bound by an invisible force.

" His mind neither rises nor expands in this mould newly opened to receive it. Three ages pass away; all withers around him. In the midst of primeval forests, not one new thought buds out in the form of institution, an enterprise, or even a book. The morning breeze of the universe fans the brow, but cannot give new life to decrepitude. What are these infant empires, Mexico, Rio-Janeiro, Buenos-Ayres, Lima, that have in the first days of their existence the wrinkles of Byzantium? Chili alone seems yet to preserve the spirit of the ancient Araucans in the poem of Ercilla.

" What means this wondrous sterility in a New World, except that the idea brought thither had given elsewhere all its fruit; that Catholicism, essentially conservative during three ages, has lost the power of impulse, the creative spirit; that she is incapable henceforth of giving to the wide expanse the word alone pregnant of a new social world; that her soul, imprisoned in the cathedrals of the medioeval ages, has no longer the strength of divine tempests to purify chaos and baptise continents [2]. "

" Let these nations of the South do what they will, they end inevitably by realising in their government the ideal which they have

1. Quinet, p. 293.— 2. *Idem*, p. 295.

inscribed in their state religion, that is, absolute power. All they can do is to change dictators : and thus we see republic succeed in nothing but in tightening the bands of their thraldom. Progressive punishment! South America lies as it were at the foot of a vast upas tree, ever distilling its torpor, while the trunk, rooted in another Continent, remains invisible[1]. "

Until now we have only considered the two states of society from afar, and in a general way; let us now draw nearer, and study them in detail; and first let us examine the religious principles which inspire them :

Religion. — " It is religion, " says M. de Tocqueville, " that has given rise to the Anglo-American communities. In the United States, religion is blended with the national customs, and with all those feelings that one's native land inspires; this gives it a special influence. In this country, religion, it may be said, has fixed her own limits; religious order here remains entirely distinct from political order; so much so, that it has been easy to change the old laws, without unsettling the old systems of faith. Christianity has retained a great ascendancy over the mind.

In the United States, Christian sects are infinitely varied, and undergo continual modifications; but Christianity itself is an established and undeniable fact.

The revolutionists of America are obliged to profess a certain respect for Christian morality and equity, which does not permit them easily to violate the laws, even when these are opposed to the carrying out of their designs; and, if they could surmount their own scruples, they would still feel themselves checked by those of their partisans. Hitherto, no one in the United States has dared to advance the maxim, that everything is allowable for the interest of society : an impious maxim, which appears to have been invented in an age of freedom, in order to justify all future tyrants! Thus, while the law permits the American people to do every thing, religion hinders them from conceiving everything, and prohibits them from daring everything. Religion, which, among the Americans, never directly interferes with the government of society, should be regarded as the first of their political institutions, which singularly promotes the exercise of liberty. It is also in this point of view that the people of the United States themselves regard religious convictions.

" When a political man attacks a sect there, it is not a reason

1. Quinet, p. 298.

for the members of that sect to refuse to support him; but, if he attacks all the sects together, all men desert him, and he remains alone."

But what spirit animates this religion, so generally diffused in the United States? A spirit of light and liberty: "The Americans," as the same author tells us, "blend so completely in their minds the idea of Christianity with that of liberty, that it is nearly impossible to bring them to conceive the existence of the one apart from the other; and this is not, among them, one of those barren convictions that the past bequeaths to the present, and which appears less to live than to vegetate in the bottom of the soul [1]."

"There are European populations whose infidelity is only equalled by their depravity and ignorance; whilst in America we see one of the most free and enlightened nations in the world cheerfully fulfilling all the outward duties of religion. On my arrival in the United States, it was the religious aspect of the country which first attracted my attention. By degrees, as I prolonged my stay, I perceived the great political results of these facts, so new to me. Among ourselves I had seen the spirit of liberty almost always move in opposite directions. Here I found them closely connected [2]."

According to the authors quoted, religion is the source of all the civilization of the United States. But what religion? Protestantism; M. Quinet tells us so: "The protestant principle is realized there with a manifest result; and it is surprising that many writers amongst us, who have treated of American democracy, have only seen in these institutions the vague influence of religion in general. These institutions bear the exclusive stamp of the Reformation; for each one of their founders turned aside from the resort of men into the depths of the forests; he was there, so to speak, king of the world; there was no appeal in the physical and moral universe but to himself. Nature and the Bible encompassed him. In this immensity, he was himself a church; uniting in himself the offices of priest, king, and artizan, he baptised his children, he celebrated their marriage. By slow degrees, other sovereigns like himself found themselves almost unconsciously touching his boundaries; intervals were filled up; the cabin became a village, the village a town. A community was formed without the individual ceding any of his power; and this spectacle

1. Tocqueville, p. 226. — 2. *Idem*, vol. II, p. 229.

is unique. The Gospel, open everywhere, was the primitive contract which made these solitary men the citizens of a republic of equals [1]. "

Such are the religious principles of the United States : what are those of South America? Let us examine.

M. d'Orbigny, whom we have already quoted, is a man of learning, sent by the French government on a scientific expedition to South America; he passed several years in travelling over these countries, he is therefore well acquainted with them. In describing the climate, plants, mines, etc., he often expresses his opinion of the inhabitants. As the naturalist, when writing, could have had no idea of the use that we should make of his reports, his testimony is so much the more valuable to us. He thus expresses himself on the religion of the Brazilians : " What a singular contrast! What outward religion, and what corruption in grain! The conscience of the inhabitants of Corrientes must be unscrupulous indeed, or they must have a religion for themselves altogether different from the true one; a religion teaching the Spanish belief, that confession effaces all sins [2]. " " Notwithstanding the dissipated lives led by both sexes at Corrientes, they never neglect going to mass on Sundays and festivals [3] ; they offer numberless prayers, and are continually asking for blessings; these are remains of the system of education established by the Jesuits in their missions. But, if we consider their religious belief in its true point of view, we shall see that for the inhabitants of these provinces religion is rather a matter of habit than of conviction; for it does not hinder them from indulging, when they are young, in all kinds of excesses, without much fear of future punishment, notwithstanding the bloody spectacles of the Holy Week, and the awful penances to which the aged men and women submit themselves [4]. "

" The most bloody representations of the Passion are exhibited in the churches during Passion week : all there breathes horror. It is then that faults are expiated; if indeed the superstitious acts of an exaggerated worship have ever borne the characteristic marks of real repentance [5]. "

" Women sometimes die from the effects of their penances. Some may feel justly astonished at seeing so much austerity allied to such laxity of morals, but I have always met the one accompanying the other. The ministers of religion would undoubtedly

1. Quinet, p. 291. — 2. D'Orbigny, vol. I, pp. 377, 378, 379. — 3. *Idem*, p. 387. — 4. *Idem*, p. 388. — 5. *Idem*, 395.

obtain more advantageous results by preaching sound morality, and supporting it by the example of a pure and spotless life[1]."

"The Spaniards, in general, exaggerate everything relating to the externals of religion. Thus it is difficult to recognize a likeness to anything human under the wounds and blood with which the statues are covered. Perhaps I was ill-disposed, but this frightful spectacle filled me with horror, and I could share but slightly in the enthusiasm with which the priest extolled each of these groups to me, repeating, in every possible form, that true religion existed nowhere but in Moxos. After vespers, a troop of Italians, dressed in a burlesque manner in red and other glaring colours, and performing the characters of Jews, went slowly over the mission searching for Jesus Christ. The melancholy sounds of the drums, half unstrung, and the plaintive notes of the flutes, produced upon me an effect that I cannot describe; my whole nervous system seemed shaken. The priest told me that the drums represented the noise of the populace enraged against Jesus Christ; the flutes counterfeited cries; and the calabashes imitated the earthquake[2]."

At Christmas, I was spectator at Chuquisaca of a singular custom. All the ladies decorate altars, where are exposed images of the child Jesus surrounded by playthings. In order to see these altars, every one visits the ladies, who rival each other in luxury. On these occasions, it is the custom to play practical jokes. You are invited, for example, to take some whipped cream; instead of which you find cotton: this excites the hilarity of the bystanders[3]."

More than ten different bands grotesquely dressed danced before the Holy Sacrament at Tiaguanaco, as well as at La Paz; and, in the evening, they did as much around the square. Going from chapel to chapel, the music, executed without any attempt at harmony, produced a most extraordinary cacophony. Afterwards I called down vengeance upon the authors of these dances; for two nights running they never ceased to go about the streets, executing their wild concert[4]."

"At Corrientes, during Passion Week, I had the opportunity of observing the remains of the fanatical rites which seem to have presided in this country since the first dawning of civilization. But, as I had been warned that this excess of outward devotion generally concealed a great amount of depravity, I silently quitted the wretched scene of this religious parody, pained at seeing the profanation of the mysteries of a religion, which is always respected when

1. D'Orbigny, vol. I, p. 396. — 2. *Idem*, vol. III, pp. 134, 135. — 3. *Idem*, p. 282. — 4. *Idem*, p. 348.

its ministers know how to render it respectable, by respecting themselves [1]. " I saw practised there the *velario*, a custom which seems to unite the fanaticism of the first ages of Christianity with the barbarism of the savage state. Strangers and relations for two leagues round assemble in the house where a child has died, dance the *ciéléto*, drink brandy, smoke, and indulge in foolish merriment. They afterwards go to bury the body, accompanied by a fiddle, at least. In order to multiply these festivals (a monstrous mixture of superstition and debauchery, which violates the rights of humanity, and effaces or perverts the sentiments of nature !) they even go so far as to borrow the body of a child, which often passes from house to house until it is putrefied [2]. "

To complete this picture of the state of religion in South America, let us give some traits of the clergy, who, in catholicism, are so completely identified with religion itself.

M. Auguste de Saint-Hilaire cannot refrain from noticing a number of abuses which may be observed in the clergy of the country of Minas (Brazil). " The stipend of the priests being insufficient since the suppression of tithes, an arrangement known by the name of the Constitution of Bahia grants to the priests forty reis (twopence-halfpenny), for each proprietor and his wife; and twenty reis (a pennyfarthing), for each slave. This contribution had been voluntary; but the clergy soon advanced other claims, and on pretence of being indemnified for the Easter confession, which European catholics will happily have some difficulty in believing, the priests succeeded in introducing the custom of being paid three hundred reis (one shilling and sevenpence halfpenny) by each communicant. Priests have been seen (one hardly dares to say so), who, at the moment of giving the communion at Easter, have interrupted the solemn act to demand of the poor the accustomed gratuity. It is, without doubt, in this way that certain benefices produce as much as nine thousand cruzados." The author points out, with a moderation which gives additional authority to his words, the monstrous abuses which, as he proves, are opposed to the prosperity of the country.

" Confession, " he continues, " is, of all the sacerdotal functions, that which takes up most of the priest's time, and I have seen five negroes despatched in a quarter of an hour. If the ecclesiastics read their breviary, it must be very secretly; for I never but once chanced to meet one in the performance of this study. To be a

1. D'Orbigny, vol. I, p. 123. — 2. *Idem*, pp. 146, 147.

priest is a kind of trade, and the ecclesiastics themselves find it quite natural thus to consider the priesthood.

" There have not been wanting instances of ecclesiastics devoting themselves to trade (literally), and even selling in a shop; at the same time, it is some satisfaction to know that they do not add hypocrisy to their other faults. They show themselves for what they are, and do not seek to deceive any one by grave discourses or an austere deportment..... We may add to this strange picture, that we ourselves have seen, in the neighbourhood of San-Salvador, a priest making his parishioners dance to the sound of a guitar, and without any person being scandalised thereby [1]. "

" In order to convert the natives the more easily to the catholic religion, " says M. d'Orbigny, " the Jesuits and other enlightened ecclesiastics had introduced into the christian festivals the religious dances of the Incas, a highly politic concession; but, subsequently, these festivals were multiplied to such a degree by the importunities of the priests interested in maintaining them, that they now constitute one of the heaviest imposts by which these poor creatures are oppressed [2]. "

The manner in which these ecclesiastics enter on their office is worthy of their ministry. " At Santa-Cruz, they celebrate a solemn festival on the day on which a young ecclesiastic says his first mass. A drum summons to the door of his relatives the persons invited; there are assembled the religious, civil, and military authorities. They go in procession to the church, preceded by music. On returning home, the young priest stands at his door, and offers his hand to kiss to those who present themselves. A table is spread with sweetmeats, wine, and liquors of every kind; and they invite each other to drink [3]. "

" However painful it is to speak of it, I cannot pass over in silence the conduct of the *curé* of San-Juan. A deputation of native judges came to Santa-Ana, to declare that his connexions with the women of the place rendered it impossible for him to confess any one, as in America custom forbids an ecclesiastic to confess any of the relations of the women with whom the *curé* has been too intimate. All the native authorities unanimously deposed that the priest had not respected their wives any more than their daughters. Of the nineteen Indian females, who had been the last victims of this monster, the eldest was not more than twelve years old. The examination brought horrors to light : the miserable

1. Brésil, *Univers pittoresque*, pp. 352, 353. — 2. D'Orbigny, vol. II, p. 421. — 3. *Idem*, p. 531.

wretch had made use of religion, and the fear of hell, in order to satisfy his passion with the most revolting cynicalness and shameless libertinism. The culprit did not deny any of his acts, deeming them quite natural.....

" The manner of living of the *curés* and the administrators explains these abuses, which often occur in a lonely district of 30 or 40 leagues, exempt from all control.

" These two men (the *curé* and the administrator) share between them unlimited power, and can satisfy all their caprices and fancies.

" Penances and excommunications on the one hand, and the fear of corporal punishments on the other, compel the natives to suffer in silence. The bad dispositions of the *curés* and the administrators (men for the most part ill-educated) are increased by idleness and impunity.

" The priest at Ascension, a worthy man of no capacity, was more busied about his temporal affairs, than with the salvation of the Indians [1]. "

" Among the Guarayos I met the *curé*, who had been informed, I know not how, of what had taken place (certain pagan and indecent festivals had been celebrated by the neophytes in my presence). I expected that I should, at the very least, receive some censures from him; but it was otherwise [2]. The priests, having no professional education, and being ignorant of the language of the country, changed nothing in the order of things at Chiquitos. Only, as they were far from the control of government, they worked the missions for their own profit. Things remained in this state until 1789, when Don Lazaro Bibera revealed to the audience of Charcas the abuses introduced by the priests, who had not only allowed arts and industry to languish in the province, but had carried on a traffic with Brazil in sacred vessels and in cattle [3]. "

" The governors of Moxos having no right to interfere with the administration of the priests, there followed the greatest disturbances. The priests being only busied with their temporal affairs, the missions became mere shadows of what they had been. The greatest part of their wealth was pillaged, the Indians lost the fruits of their good education; vice flourished under the cover of idleness, and all the industrial arts were forgotten [4]. "

" At Caupolican, as on the Bolivian Table-land, the abuses introduced by the clergy, on the occasion of catholic festivals, have,

1. D'Orbigny, vol. III, p. 12. — 2. *Idem*, p. 13. — 3. *Idem*, vol. III, p. 48. — 4. *Idem*, p. 233.

without doubt, been the principal cause of the disorder and ruin of the country [1]."

"The natives of Carmen de Moxos are extremely gentle. They have borne for many years the infamous conduct of their administrator and of their priest, who, having divided the mission between them as a common harem, caused all the young Indian girls to be brought to them successively, as soon as they reached eight or ten years of age, and that under pain of fifty lashes. The number of the victims of these monsters, and the horrible details which I learnt from the interpreters themselves, make one shudder [2]." "Since Don Marcelino de la Pena has been governor, the workwomen at Chiquitos are no longer chastised; but at Moxos, the rapacity of the administrators and priests perpetuates and even multiplies the chastisements..... In this country the Indians have not a single day to themselves, except Sunday and festivals, which are completely devoted to religious practices. All the rest of the year they are worked by their administrators and priests, who do not leave them a moment's respite. The women are even less spared than the men..... I had never seen, under a free government, more slavery and despotism [3]."

Such are the resources, the men and things, the clergy and the religion, that have been employed, on both sides, to civilize the two Americas. Now let us see what results have been obtained on either hand. Let us first study the two systems of legislation, and seek in them the traces of the two religious creeds which have inspired them.

Administration. —"It is impossible to deny," says M. de Tocqueville, "that the legislation of the Americans, taken as a whole, is well adapted to the genius of the people that it governs, and to the nature of the country. The American laws are therefore good, and it is to them must be attributed a great part of the success which the democratic form of government ob ains in America [4]."

"The general principles upon which modern constitutions rest, those principles which were scarcely comprehended by most Europeans of the XVIIth century, and which then partially triumphed in Great Britain alone, are all recognised and fixed by the laws of New-England: the intervention of the people in public affairs, the voluntary grant of taxes, the responsibility of the government agents, individual liberty, and trial by jury, were established there without discussion, and are in full activity [1]."

1. D'Orbigny, vol. III, p. 385. — 2. *Idem*, p. 88. — 3. *Idem*, p. 93. — 4. Tocqueville, vol. II, p. 255.

Such are the laws; now for the administration: "A strict economy in the management of the public funds renders a budget of twenty-five millions of dollars sufficient to meet all the expenses of the Union, and to pay off the public debt, which will soon cease to exist. It is with these resources, which appear so trifling in comparison with the population, that the Union has been able, since 1816, to supply her navy with roadsteads, safe and well defended ports, dockyards for repairing and building, and to construct a line of fortifications which defend all the vulnerable points of her vast territory [2]."

"The government of the United States has adopted the principle of allowing none but productive expenses: therefore the standing army consists of only seven thousand men, and the navy has only forty ships afloat [3]."

There is no country where justice is administered more leniently than in the United States: "North America," says M. de Tocqueville, "is, I think, the only country upon earth where, for the last fifty years, not a single individual has been put to death for political offences [4]."

It appears to us that one of the best criteria by which to judge of the excellence of a people, is the obedience of that people to the laws. It is not from the legislation, mild or severe, that we can judge of the morals of a nation; but a respect for the laws is a strong proof of its morality. Let us apply this rule to the United States of America.

"It must be acknowledged," says M. Michel Chevalier, "to the honour of the English race, that it is more imbued than all others with the sentiment of respect for the laws. Even down to the present time, the Anglo-Americans in this respect, as in many others, have shown themselves to be English re-invigorated. There are nations that only comprehend the power of the law under a living form; that is to say, personified in a man. They know how to obey a chief; but they cannot bring themselves to respect a dead letter. To them, the glory and prosperity of a state depend very little upon the excellence of the laws, but very much upon the men who are appointed to interpret them. In their opinion, an empire flourishes or decays by turns, according as the sovereign, whatever may be his title, is a superior or an ordinary man. This appears to be, in general, the character of the Asiatic nations. The Englishman is formed in a different mould. It costs him but little to bow before a

1 Tocqueville, vol. I. p. 36. — 2. Malte-Brun, vol. XI, pp. 335, 336. — 3. *Idem*, p. 339. — 4. Tocqueville, vol. IV, p. 8 and 9.

text; but he bows with an ill grace before a man. There is no necessity for his fellow-man to enjoin him to observe the laws; he obeys them without effort, and by instinct. In a word, the Englishman possesses in himself the principle of *self-government*. This explains the success which this political system has obtained in the United States, where the English race has freely developed itself according to its nature [1]. "

" In their political existence, the mass of the American people have arrived at a state of initiation superior to that of the European mass, for they do not so much need to be governed. Every man here supports in himself, in a high degree, the principle of self-government, and is more fit to take part in public affairs [2]. "

In the face of this legislation and administration of the protestant United States, what do we find in the catholic States of the South? Allow M. d'Orbigny to speak : " The volumes of laws and decrees that have been published in a spirit of emulation by each of these governments, which succeed each other with so much rapidity, have neither improved the administration of justice, nor better guaranteed public prosperity and individual security. One might say that the laws are no sooner promulgated than they are forgotten, even by the magistrates who had proposed or discussed them, and that the greater part of the citizens pay no attention even to those that are registered in the code. It is impossible to enforce the observance of the most simple police regulation : the insolence of the inhabitants renders them hostile to every kind of control, and presents an amount of passive resistance, which could be vanquished only by the energy of the government [3]. "

" The new regulations at Moxos prohibited all commerce, under the severest penalties. The Indians were more complete slaves than ever; instead of one absolute master (the priest), they had two (the priest and the administrators), whose continual quarrels and bad conduct caused the ruin of the missions..... The measure adopted by the court of Charcas was the origin of all kinds of disorder, in consequence of the rivalry between the religious and secular authorities, and of the ignorance of the delegates of all classes. Covetous agents overburdened the Indians with labour for their own private advantage, the revenues decreased, and the province did but vegetate [4]. "

" The greatest merit of the Spanish agents was to augment the revenues of the State; every measure that had this result was highly

1. Michel Chevalier, pp. 314, 315. — 2. *Idem*, p. 379. — 3. D'Orbigny, vol. I, p. 513. — 4. *Idem*, vol. III, p. 234.

recompensed. When the inhabitants of the missionary stations had been subjected to the burdens imposed on them by Don José Santa Cruz, other tribes, who were on the point of submitting, retreated into the depths of the forests in order to escape the annual tribute, and more especially the innumerable vexations and violence too often exercised by the agents employed in collecting it [1]. "

" If commerce had continued in the province of Caupolican, the inhabitants would certainly have progressed in civilization, against which their rulers are ever struggling, under the vain pretext that strangers would corrupt their morals [2]. But they are wanting in men who, laying aside personal interest, would devote themselves to the development of their intellectual faculties and to their moral education [3]. "

" At Bojada, there is no police at all, any more than there is justice. The old Spanish laws, still nominally in force in the country, have but little authority..... In the evening, I kept upon my guard, lest I should be attacked and robbed on the quay by the ragged *gauchos* with their long knives and stern looks, as such attacks were often witnessed [4].

" The discipline of the soldiers (Pampas) is as bad as their appearance: the recruits bring with them all the dominant vices of the country — the love of gaming and strong liquors, laziness, dirty habits, and quarrelsome dispositions, which probably costs the nation as many men as the wars. The punishments are corporeal, and very cruel; but they are not a sufficient check to these disorders. The bad choice of the officers is another obstacle to a better state of things: they are generally young men, who are fit for nothing else, and whose irregular conduct makes them a burden to their families [5]. "

" As soon as war breaks out in the country, they collect together all the criminals and vagabonds. They hastily give them a little drilling, equip and arm them, and the corps is formed. The prisons serve as a nursery for the soldiers of the Republic: brigands, guilty of numerous crimes, escape with a hundred lashes; after which their irons are taken off, and they become soldiers [6]. " This is their first education: " The regulation in Chalejo is, to chain together the soldiers on a march, like our galley slaves; after which they put them on a waitscoat made out of a bullock's skin, quite fresh, which, in drying, squeezes the upper part of the arms so tightly that all motion is impossible. This barbarous measure

1. D'Orbigny, vol. III, p. 367. — 2. *Idem*, p. 373. — 3. *Idem*, p. 374. — 4. *Idem*, vol. I, pp. 436, 437. — 5. *Idem*, p. 556. — 6. D'Orbigny, vol. I, p. 557.

causes them to arrive half-dead with fatigue, and I have been assured that sometimes the flies lay their eggs under these leathern waistcoats, and the unhappy recruits, after a march of a hundred and twenty-five leagues, are covered with wounds, and eaten alive by worms [1]. "

" The Indian Chiquitos, when they are attacked by epidemical diseases, have no one to attend or watch over them. Attacked by a burning fever in the epidemy of 1825, they found certain death by bathing in the coldest waters of the running streams. Some measures of precaution, taken by those whose position gives them the most unlimited power, would have prevented this deplorable result [2]. "

The trader is no better treated than the soldier: " At Conception, the cotton is magnificent, the indigo of the best quality, and the neighbouring forests yield plenty of wax and vanilla : but the severity of the present administrator has disgusted the Indians, who, to avoid his exactions, fly into the woods, and return to their savage state. Having no wants, these Indians find themselves happier than at the mission; where, besides doing the government-work, they have to labour for the administrator and the priest, who do not spare them [3]. "

The simple husbandman is no better governed than the trader. " During a drought of seven years' continuance, many of the inhabitants of San-José died of hunger, through want of foresight on the part of the administrator... Nothing is now to be seen around the habitations but stunted trees, and an impoverished vegetation, which is constantly diminishing [4]. "

" Some Indian families of Chiquitos, carried off from Santa-Ana, are treated, at Casalbasco, like transported criminals. They are shut up every night, escorted by soldiers when they go into the fields; and when surprised in the open country, or suspected of wishing to escape, are chastised with rigour. Except in the towns of la Paz-Chuquisoca and Patos, there are nowhere medical men to take care of the sick poor, who are generally allowed to die for want of attention [5]. "

But, if the administrators neglect those confided to them, they take care of themselves. Read this : " The governors of Chiquitos, in the absence of all control, worked the province for their own profit: their pride grew in proportion to the extent of their own power. They even arrogated to themselves all the pomp of ceremo-

1. D'Orbigny, vol. II, p. 505. — 2. *Idem*, p. 592. — 3. *Idem*, p. 597. — 4. *Idem*, p. 625. — 5. *Idem*, p. 445, 446.

nies, which, until then, had been reserved for the great solemnities of the Church. Nothing could exceed their arrogance and absolutism : reigning by terror, they satisfied their slightest caprices, even at the expense of morality. The Indians, men and women, were slaves, who, under pain of fifty lashes, could refuse nothing to the governor, who indulged himself in the most scandalous libertinism. The whole province, being considered as the farm of this functionary, was ground down and oppressed in every possible way [1]. "

" The administrators, in their turn, beyond the control of their governor, and occupied with every thing except the good of the country, imitated their chief in his exactions. The inevitable result of this was a dilapidation of the revenues of the state, a general system of bribery, continual disputes for authority between the priest and the administrator, and recriminations which lowered both of them in the opinion of the natives; the more so, that these unhappy beings, while forced to give all their time to the State, had still to satisfy the numberless demands of men who only thought of harrassing them, in order the sooner to enrich themselves with the fruit of their labour. The Indians, shocked at first, by degrees lost their innocence, and habituated themselves to corruption by imitating their chief. Their religion became merely external, being unaccompanied by any moral sentiment. The government had considerably augmented their burdens, while it had taken from them many of their rights. The amount of labour exacted from them increased according to the caprice or the particular wants of the administrators and priests. The revenues of the State diminishing every year, all was employed in paying the agents [2]. "

" Don Gil Poledo, sent as governor to Chiquitos, endeavoured to establish there the old faith of the Incas, by ordering the adoration of the sun. Every morning, followed by his soldiers, he assembled the Indians, and compelled them, at the sound of music, to kneel down before the rising orb. In the evening, when finishing its career, he caused it to be saluted with the like ceremony...

" Before the emancipation, the Spanish governors participated in the worship paid to the Divinity in the churches, regarding themselves as absolute kings in civil matters, and, in moral concerns, as equal to God. What astonishes me most, is the culpable

1. D'Orbigny, vol. III, p. 50. — 2. *Idem*, p. 51.

weakness with which the clergy complied with demands of such a nature[1]. "

We have seen how these governors treat their countrymen; let us see how they treat the natives: "The public revenues being no longer sufficient to pay the salaries of the agents, they endeavoured to make up the deficiency by speculations. Misery was at its height. The Indians, not knowing the value of things, and it being the interest of their rulers to keep them in ignorance on this point, saw themselves made use of by the relatives of the administrators and priests, without any bettering of their own condition[2].

"The Indians owe to the State the Monday, Wednesday, and Friday of every week. Legally, Tuesday and Saturday belong to them; but, extra service being required of them, they rarely profit by the days which the law allows them. Compelled to snatch time on these days to cultivate the ground, in order to feed their families, they live in the greatest misery, in want of every thing; and this misery entails the greatest dissoluteness in their morals. They have always the liberty of trading with certain privileged persons, such as the relations of the priests and administrators; but they are shamefully cheated, and they part with the produce of their labour in exchange for useless trifles[3]. "

When we reflect on the immense advantages that the commerce of Chiquitos would derive from good means of communication, which would enable the inhabitants to profit by the varied productions of the most fertile soil in the world, we are astonished that the government does not establish, in the interest of all, a network of interior navigation, of which the advantages would be so certain[4]. "As the administrators and priests of Moxos are entirely engrossed by their private interests, they abandon all their rights to the *caciques*, who, for the most part, do not scruple to abuse them. They are continually drinking chica of maize, until they are intoxicated, and then administer justice according to their caprice. They abuse to such a degree the plenty they enjoy, that they become immensely corpulent, and destroy their health[5]. "

Such are respectively the laws and modes of governing of the two Americas. The facts speak so plainly, that it would be superfluous to comment upon them: let us then proceed to another point of comparison. We have seen, on either hand, what light the two religious torches have shed, or what darkness they have left, among the leaders of the two nations; let us endeavour now

1. D'Orbigny, vol. II, p. 645. — 2. *Idem*, vol. III, p. 53. — 3. *Idem*, p. 58. — 4. *Idem*, p. 78. — 5. *Idem*, p. 95.

to ascertain what amount of instruction they have communicated, or what amount of ignorance they have left, among the people themselves.

It will be understood beforehand that if one of these two religious systems challenges investigation in order to make itself accepted, by so doing it invites to the study of all other subjects. The branches of knowledge acquired with a view to religion will be applicable to every thing else. If, for example, it is a principle that the dogmas to be believed, and morals to be practised, are contained in certain sacred books, it is very necessary that the believer should know how to read. If it is the rule that each individual should examine these books before he admits them as authority, it is very necessary that he should study, more or less, what relates to them : history, geography, antiquities. Without doubt, all will not do this; but it is not the less true that such a religion invites all its adherents to do it, and that, by so doing, it leads the people to study, and to the acquisition of knowledge.

But if the contrary should be the case; if, for instance, it should be a principle in a religious system that the simple believer should defer in every thing to the authority of his priest; or, at least, that he should only examine on condition of arriving at a pre-determined result, it is very evident that such a religious system would suppress intellect, and extinguish learning. The faculty of thought, no longer exercised in religion, would cease to be so in what is connected with it; that is, in everything. Or, if there should be intellects bold enough to venture into the field of human knowledge, this would only be after having broken loose from the religious authority that sought to fetter them. There might then, perhaps, be learning without piety; but, most probably, there would be neither the one nor the other.

Having laid down these principles, let us compare the degrees of knowledge which the two religious systems have introduced into the Americas that are respectively subject to them.

Knowledge. "Elementary instruction is more generally diffused in the United States than in any other part of the world; this is owing to the enlightened foresight of the first colonists; for each time that a town or even a village was founded, a school was erected, a schoolmaster appointed, and their maintenance insured; and, ever since, all the legislatures have rivalled each other in their zeal to improve public instruction. Therefore the number of scholars, as compared with the population, is much greater in the United States than in any other country in the world. This number is 1 to

4 inhabitants; whilst in France, it is 1 to 18. It may be said that the American Union reaps the fruits of a system so wisely planned, that it was impossible it should remain unproductive. It is in the schools that the character of the mass of the people is formed; it is there that each one acquires from his infancy an enlightened sense of his rights and of his duties [1]. "

" In 1834, the elementary schools of the state of New York were frequented by 541,401 public scholars : now the number of children between five and sixteen years of age, in the districts of which we have the returns, and which comprehend nearly the whole state, is only 543,085. The total of the expenses was 7,000,000 francs, of which 4,000,000 had been employed in paying the schoolmasters. In France, four years ago, the whole sum granted for elementary instruction by the state, the departments, and the parishes together, was only 4,000,000 francs. Now, thanks to the efforts of M. Guizot, this sum has been raised to nearly twelve millions. But it is still only three times as much as that which is consecrated to the same purpose in the state of New-York, which is sixteen times less populous than France. The number of children who frequent the schools in France is 2,450,000, that is to say, a thirteenth of the population, or three times less, in proportion, than in the state of New-York [2]. "

" What will enable us to appreciate the degree of civilization to which the Anglo-American Confederation has arrived, is the development of the periodical press. No European state, not even Great Britain, can enter into competition with her in this point of view. In 1828, for a population of 12 millions, there existed not less than 802 newspapers, without including the other periodical publications. In 1833, the number of the political newspapers amounted to 840, and that of the periodical publications to nearly 400, among which sixty treated exclusively of religious subjects. The city of New York alone published 65 daily or monthly journals; and in the entire state there were not less than 263, a considerable number for a population of 1 million of inhabitants [3]. "

" At this time the number of newspapers and periodical writings published in the

United States amounts to	2,800
The circulation to	5,000,000
The number of copies printed each year to	422,000,000 [4] "

1. Malte-Brun, vol. XI, pp. 335, 336. — 2. Michel Chevalier pp. 292, 293. — 3. Malte-Brun, vol. XI. — 4. United States' Census for 1851.

"The conquests of the human mind, of which the Reformation was the signal and the starting point, the great discoveries in sciences and industry, which in Europe are still hidden from the view of the greater part of the people by a veil of ignorance and clouds of theories, are in North America exhibited to the eyes of all, and placed within the reach of all capacities; here the common people know how to handle and make use of them. Examine our rustic population, study the minds of our peasants, and you will see that the mainspring of all their actions is a confused jumble of the biblical parables and the old legends of a gross superstition. Repeat the experiment on the American farmer, and you will find that the great traditions of the Bible are allied in his mind, harmoniously enough, with the precepts of modern science, as taught by Bacon and Descartes; with the principles of moral and religious independence, promulgated by Luther; and with the most modern ideas of political independence: he is initiated. With us, the great industrial and scientific machines, such as the steam-engine, the balloon, the voltaic pile, the lightning-conductor, inspire the greater part of the population with a religious terror. In France, among a hundred peasants from the heart of our provinces, you would not find one, who, after witnessing their effects, would venture to touch them; they would fear to be struck dead, like the sacrilegious man who touched the Ark of the Lord. On the contrary, for the American, they are familiar objects; he knows them all, at least by name; he feels that he has a right of possession over them. To the French peasant they would be beings as mysterious and terrible as the fetiche for the negro, or the manitou for the Indian. The cultivator of the far West regards them in the same light as a member of the French Institute — as a tool, an instrument of labour, or of experiments: I repeat it, he is initiated. In the United States, there is no *profanum vulgus,* at least among the whites [1]."

"He who desires to form a judgment on the state of knowledge among the Anglo-Americans is, therefore, liable to see the same object under two different aspects. If he only fixes his attention on the learned, he will be astonished at the smallness of their number; and if he counts the ignorant, the Americans will appear to him the most enlightened people on the face of the earth. The whole population is placed between these two extremes; I have already said so elsewhere. In New England, every citizen

1. Michel Chevalier, p. 379.

receives the elementary notions of human knowledge, and learns, besides, what are the doctrines and the proofs of his religion; he is taught the history of his country, and the principal features of the Constitution which governs him. In Connecticut, it is very rare to find a man who has but an imperfect knowledge of all these things; and he who is entirely ignorant of them is in some sort a phenomenon!... In the states on the shores of the Gulf of Mexico may be found, as amongst ourselves, a certain number of individuals who are strangers to the elements of human knowledge; but, in the United States, it would be vain to seek a single district still remaining buried in ignorance [1]. "

" Americans never employ the word peasant; they cannot use the word, because they have no idea of what it means. The ignorance of the early ages, the simplicity of the fields, the rusticity of the village, have not been preserved among them; and they form no conception of the virtues or the vices, of the vulgar habits or the simple graces, of a dawning civilization. At the farthest extremity of the Confederate States, on the confines of society and the desert, there exists a population of hardy adventurers, who, to avoid the poverty which would have been their lot under the paternal roof, have not feared to penetrate into the solitudes of America, in search of a new country. As soon as he is arrived on the chosen spot, the pioneer hastily fells some trees, and builds a cabin under the remaining foliage. Nothing can be more miserable than the aspect of these isolated dwellings. The traveller who approaches them in the evening sees from afar the flame in the chimney shining through the walls; and at night, if the flame mounts high, he hears the leafy roof crackle among the trees of the forest. Who would not imagine that this poor hut was the asylum of coarseness and ignorance? But there is no comparison to be made between the pioneer and his asylum. Every thing is primitive and wild around him; but he is, so to speak, the result of eighteen centuries of labour and experience. He wears the garb of cities, he speaks their language; he is acquainted with the past, curious as to the future, and reasons upon the present. He is a man highly civilized, who, for a time, submits to living in the woods, and penetrates into the wildernesses of the New World, with his Bible, a hatchet, and some newspapers. It is difficult to imagine with what rapidity thought circulates in these wilds: I do not believe that in the most enlightened and populous districts in France, there is so great an intel-

1. De Tocqueville, p. 242.

lectual movement. There can be no doubt that in the United States the instruction diffused among the people conduces powerfully to the maintenance of the democratic republic. It will be the same, I think, wherever the instruction that enlightens the understanding is not separated from the education that regulates the morals [1]. "

Such is the North, illumined by the protestant torch. Let us now proceed to the South, and seek for catholic enlightenment.

"Every where, in South America, the whites have introduced anarchy and immorality. Every where monarchical despotism, or the ambition of certain intriguers, destitute of talent, has caused the most deplorable disorder, and obstructed the normal development of nations the most highly favoured in point of intelligence. From the northern provinces of Brazil to Buenos-Ayres; from Bolivia and Peru even to the southern frontiers of Chili, nothing is found but bloody struggles, continual divisions, and forced halts in the old ruts of barbarism and ignorance. It is not, then, astonishing, that the people of the South (the natives) have not yet been tempted to take their share in the miserable advantages of such a civilization [2]. "

"The natives, who, in Mexico, form the greater number of the citizens, have been oppressed to such a degree, that their moral faculties are more degraded than those of the Indianos bravos. All their religion consists in going to mass and in repeating a few prayers. Only a short time ago there were several schools in which neither reading nor writing were taught, but only certain forms of prayers. In the country, and even near large towns, scarcely one person in two hundred could be found able to read. They are superstitious, bigoted, slaves to the clergy, ignorant, and poor. The universities and colleges inculcated the principles of servile obedience, political and religious; and the people were left entirely without elementary schools. Those who wish to found schools meet with great obstacles in the intolerance of the clergy, sanctioned by the Congress and the states [3]. "

"The ignorance and superstition of the people (in Mexico), and perhaps also the absence of all public spirit, will long render this country the seat of political storms, which hitherto have continually agitated it [4]. "

"After the last war, the Spaniards abandoned to the people of New Mexico one or two leagues of land round their villages, the

1 De Tocqueville, pp. 242 to 246. — 2. Patagonie. *Univers pittoresque.* — 3. Rougemont, pp. 735, 736. — 4. Malte-Brun, vol. XI, p. 369.

conquerors receiving for themselves the rest of the territory. These Indians are the best husbandmen in the country; the finest fruits in the market come from their fields; the finest horses from their stables. They are, moreover, distinguished in the midst of the foreign race that has enslaved them by the probity of their character, by their principles of morality, and by their habits of sobriety...

" At the time of the conquest, a large number of pueblos manufactured different stuffs; the loss of their liberty seems to have destroyed their industry; besides they live in a state of complete ignorance. Although they observe regularly enough the forms of Christianity, they have not entirely relinquished their old superstitions. Not a school is to be found among them, not a book, and only some of the children learn to speak Spanish [1]. "

" The South-Americans could not acquire any instruction under the Spanish government, whose wretched policy consisted in brutalizing its subjects, rather than in developing their minds [2]. "

" About thirty houses are dispersed over the missionary station of Duro; its native population does not exceed two hundred and fifty individuals. A great number of the men wear nothing but a piece of calico round the loins; the girls go entirely naked until the age of ten years, and the boys until twelve or fourteen..... The ordinary food of the population is entirely vegetable. It consists of the products of wild trees, chiefly of various kinds of palm-tree nuts. The mission is superintended at present by a priest from *la Nativité*. The Aldea has no school; the two only persons in the community who can read are the two captains [3]. "

" Evidently, that part of New Mexico which borders on the Rio del Morte would produce abundant crops, but the inhabitants do not know how to cultivate their lands. Their natural indolence prevents their making any kind of progress; and it is probable, " says M. Gregg, " that there is not a region in any part of the world, bordering upon the empire of civilization, where the arts and sciences are so backward as here. Whoever has learnt to read and write, is considered a very learned personage; and elementary education does not rise so high as even the first rules of arithmetic. This ignorant and indolent population increases but very slowly. Literature and the fine arts are scarcely known in New Mexico Elementary instruction there, as we have already said, is confined within the narrowest limits; so confined, that a woman who can

1. *Revue Britannique*, July and August, 1848, pp. 113, 115. — 2. *Idem*, May, 1853, p. 116. — 3. *Idem*, July and August, 1847, pp. 49 à 61.

write a few lines to her husband, is considered as a kind of phenomenon. Some years ago, an American caravan brought a printing press to Santa-Fé; the inhabitants of the town had never before seen any thing of the kind. A clever Mexican guessed the use he could make of it, and employed it during three weeks in printing a newspaper,, by means of which he got himself elected Member of the Congress. This great undertaking accomplished, he discontinued his newspaper and abandoned the press, which is now only used for printing forms of prayer and catechisms [1]. "

" Civilization and literature can experience no development while under the influence of the deplorable circumstances that continue to keep down the beautiful and unfortunate country of Columbia [2], where the arts and sciences languish [3]. "

Nothing is more calculated to prove how little civilization is to be found among the South Americans, than the curious incidents related in the travels of M. d'Orbigny : " I obtained at last, " says the learned traveller, " the *indispensable* permission to leave Montevideo. The Brazilian officer on guard at the gate — these officers frequently cannot read — appeared to see me do so with regret, to judge by the ill-humour and impertinence with which he met the exhibition of my passport [4]. "

" During a barometrical observation on the sea-shore, an officer of the same nation asked me if I had leave to draw the plan of Montevideo. I thought I had sufficiently answered his question by showing him the nature of my instrument; but I was mistaken, so great is the ignorance of the Brazilians! Another time, accompanied by twenty soldiers, he repeated his question : I gave him the same answer. They conducted me to the fortress of San-José as a state criminal; and, after two interrogatories, dragged me to the guard-house without allowing me to write to the general, and I was thrown into a damp dungeon, where I found twenty other persons, of whom fifteen, at least, were in chains [5]. "

" At Corrientes, you recognize immediately the persons who have been educated out of the province; comparatively speaking, their manners and conversation are quite different from those of the inhabitants who have never left the country, and who can scarcely write legibly in their native tongue [6].

" The superstition of the inhabitants of Buenos-Ayres was so great, that the women were persuaded that the English had tails

1. *Revue Britonnique*, July, August, 1848, p. 111. — 2. Colombie, *Univers pittoresque*, p. 23. — 3. Malte-Brun, vol. XI, p. 545. — 4. D'Orbigny, vol. I, p. 35. — 5. *Idem*, vol. II, pp. 50, 51. — 6. *Idem*, vol. I, p. 357.

like the devil : a conviction which lasted a long time, and only disappeared at the first alliance between the English and the Argentines [1]. "

" Mine host at Del Monte, who talked politics, and read the newspapers and a little history, passed for an enlightened man in the midst of this rude population [2]. "

" In the opinion of the Spaniards of Yungos, my profession of naturalist necessarily included that of medicine; not that they the less frequently importuned me to mend their watches. [3] "

" A governor, in the opinion of the poor people of Santa-Ana, is a supernatural being, invested with all imaginable rights [4]. The inhabitants of Santo-Corazon did not know whether a governor, whose powers had been so highly extolled to them, was a man or a god. They inquired whether his head was shaved, as the priest was the first person after God [5]. "

After such recitals, it requires a strong effort of memory to call to mind that the title of this chapter is ***Knowledge;*** but, on this subject, we shall present no more reflections than we have on the preceding ones. It is better to let the reader form his own conclusions.

Having spoken of the light which intellect diffuses, we are naturally led to speak of the discoveries of industry, of commercial enterprises, and of the wealth that flows from them; we shall unite all these subjects under the general title of prosperity.

Prosperity. — Let us hear an eye-witness very competent on this subject : " North America, " says M. Michel Chevalier, " is a country of blessings for the working man and the peasant. What a contrast between our Europe and this America! After I had disembarked at New York, I thought every day was Sunday, for the population that fills Broadway seemed to be always in their holiday clothes. I did not see any of those countenances faded by privations or the noxious vapours of Paris : nothing that resembled our miserable scavengers, our rag-gatherers, or our barrow-women. Every man was comfortably wrapped up in his great coat, and every woman had a cloak and a bonnet made in the last Paris fashion : rags, dirt, and misery, degrade women still more than men [6]."

"The admirable prosperity of the United States is much more the fruit of labour than the reform of taxation [7]. "

" . . . . . Here every one enjoys, or at least spends. The means

1. D'Orbigny, vol. I, p. 485. — 2. *Idem*, p. 631. — 3. *Idem*, vol. II, p. 446. — 4. *idem*, p. 604. — 5. *idem*, p. 644. — 6. Michel Chevalier, p. 210. — 7. *Idem*, p. 218.

of living are ample; they wear plenty of clothing. Every one produces largely, because the country consumes largely, and every one consumes largely, because he gains largely [1]."

"The newspaper *Le Pays*, in a recent article, publishes some reflections on the message which the President of the United States has just addressed to Congress. It acknowledges, with that statement before it, that it is a grand and wonderful spectacle, this unheard of prosperity, this gigantic development, that has already absorbed one half of the New World! We really must admit that this society, democratic in the highest sense of the term, presents at this moment a great example to the universe. Where is there a happier, a quieter, a more powerful, or a more prosperous country to be found than this North America, which has not yet existed a hundred years? When we consider all that has been achieved by this energetic Anglo-Saxon race, we wonder as to what degree of prosperity and grandeur these transatlantic republicans will shortly attain: these Americans, that a witty man lately named the English of the future [2]."

From the testimony of Balbi, no country in the world has ever undertaken, in so short a space of time, such immense labours in canals and railroads as the United States. These works surpass in extent all similar constructions that have been executed elsewhere, and the short time in which they have been completed is without a precedent in the annals of nations [3].

"Since the last war with England, industry and commerce have made immense progress in the United States. The number of spinning machines, at this time, is estimated at little short of a million. The book-trade has made an astonishing progress, and the productions of the periodical press have increased to a degree that has never been attained by the most polished nations of the earth. The merchants of the United States have extended their operations to every part of the globe. They are the factors of nearly the whole world, and their commerce becomes every day more flourishing [4]."

"It is in North America that industry has arrived at the highest pitch [5]."

"The United States are not only one of the principal maritime nations of the globe, but the second commercial power in the world. Their navy sustained in a signal manner her honour and her independence against the Queen of the Ocean. Her flag waves

1. Michel Chevalier, pp. 219, 220. — 2. *Siècle*, December 23, 1853. — 3. Balbi, p. 984. — 4. *Idem*, pp. 991, 992. — 5. *Idem*, p. 969.

in every port, and her commerce is so extensive that her merchants have become, we may say, the factors of the Old and New World [1]."

"Brought into existence but yesterday, and agitated from her cradle by the efforts of a dawning civilization, North America has found in herself a profusion of life, courage, intelligence, which has made her equal to the most terrible exigences. Without respected and strong traditions, such as those which sustain monarchies; without that display of bayonets which youthful governments seek to make up for the want of that moral *prestige* which they have been unable to acquire; in a word, without support in the past, or even in the present, the Union has been able to resist violent storms, and to survive the prophecies that have so often threatened her with infallible ruin [2]."

"It is not a question, then, of the past for this country, but of the future! When we see the progress accomplished in so short a time; plenty everywhere, and misery nowhere; churches, schools, towns, rising on every side, as if by enchantment, in the midst of forests, which, a short time ago, were scarcely inhabited or known; this hardy population, active, persevering, still rude, but eager for knowledge, and always advancing, we feel a lively impression of joy; and the mind, soothed with pleasing ideas, yields at last without resistance to the most ambitious hopes [3]."

"Although the aspect of New England," says M. Goodrich, "is rugged and unpleasing, labour and taste have endowed her with pleasant and prosperous towns and villages. The heights and the valleys are enriched by cultivation; and the traveller would with difficulty find in any other country a people living in such a state of comfort. If, in this country, there are few persons immensely rich, there are also very few who are poor.

"The inhabitants of this region are moral and religious in a high degree. The churches and other places for public worship are numerous, and the day of rest is strictly observed. There is also a number of charitable societies; and colleges, where public lectures are delivered, have been instituted in nearly all the towns, and in a great many villages [4]."

We will not multiply quotations which would fatigue the reader, nor can we enter into details worthy of the industry and commerce of a nation, whose outward march nearly equals in rapidity that of its steam engines; but we cannot refrain from showing, by a few

1 Balbi, p. 970. — 2. *Revue Britannique*, 1848, January, February, p. 279. — 3. *Idem*, p. 183 to 249. — 4. Goodrich, p. 69.

figures, the results contained in the work recently published (1850) by M. Goodrich, Consul of the United States:

Marine products	14	millions.
Products of woods and forests	34	—
Agricultural products	53	—
Vegetable products	79	—
Manufactured products	26	—
Miscellaneous	113	—

Total, including the different fractions omitted above, 700 millions of francs!

" There are now (1853) more than 4,000 leagues of railroads completed, and 2,000 leagues of canals. The electric telegraph, established on more than 3,000 leagues, is come into common use. A message of 20 words is sent a distance of 2,000 leagues for 5 francs, and an answer is returned in an hour. In these last years, the average number of emigrants who have annually arrived in the United States has been 400,000[1]. "

" The increase of the population is in proportion to that of trade. According to the census of 1851, the total number of inhabitants in the United States on the 1st of June, 1850, amouted to 23,263,488. The positive increase since the 1st June, 1840, has been 6,194,035, and the relative increase is thirty-six per cent.

" The decennial increase in the most favoured regions of Europe is less than one-and-a-half per cent; whilst, in the United States, it reaches three-and-a-half per cent. If the increase in this country and that of the European nations continue in the same proportions, in forty years the population of the United States will exceed the population of the following States united: England, France, Spain, Portugal, Sweden, and Switzerland. "

Let us now take a survey of South America with M. d'Orbigny; and let us see in these lands, so richly endowed by Providence, what elements of prosperity we can put on a parallel with the civilization of the United States:

" There is not a single manufactory in Buenos-Ayres," says M. d'Orbigny, " that takes advantage of the products of the soil: thus the country necessarily grows poorer and poorer. It is the same in all the Republics of South America [2]. It is greatly to be wished, for the Correntinos, that the progress of industry would reveal to them the new modes of employing the raw materials, so as to perfect the manipulation among themselves. This would free them from the tribute they pay to strangers; for, possessing all the

1. Goodrich, pp. 27, 28, 357 and following pages. — 2. D'Orbigny, vol. I, p. 523.

elements of prosperity, they only want to know how to turn them to account. The cultivation of cotton, notwithstanding its good quality, produces next to nothing [1]. "

" The environs of some of the towns in San-Nicolas remind one sometimes of France; but, on looking a little farther, we find ourselves in America. No cultivated fields, no bright country houses: the plain, the naked plain, as far as the eye can see, without the ornament of a single tree. At distant intervals, a wretched cabin is with difficulty discovered.

" If, profiting by the mercantile tastes of the inhabitants of Cochachamba, and by their enterprising disposition, a firm government would encourage the establishment of woollen, linen, cotton, and silk manufactures, of which the raw materials abound in the country, it would be easy to naturalize them in this town. It would be the more easy to create a manufacturing city here, that the inhabitants live in idleness, and consequently in misery, and have a natural taste among them for manufactures [2]. "

" Industry, strictly speaking, is very backward at Santa-Cruz; no establishment for weaving is to be found there, nor indeed have they a manufactory of any sort [3]. "

" Formerly, all kinds of furniture were made at Chiquitos; but now, I only see rosaries mentioned in the returns [4]. The natural productions make it easy to conceive what agricultural and commercial improvements might be introduced there, and that incalculable advantages might be derived from them [5]. "

" Potosi, so rich in former times, declines daily, and is threatened with total ruin. What is wanted in this city is an industrious population, capable of making use of all the advantages that are to be found there [6]. "

" On approaching Oruro, I was struck with the miserable aspect of the town, and with the great number of ruined habitations that I saw in every direction: there are so few inhabitants, that it appears abandoned [7]. "

" At San-Pedro, the country around the inhabited districts is changed since the arrival of the Europeans: a great part of the land is covered with thistles.

" In the province of Argentine the growth of weeds is so rapid that there is reason to fear that the province of Buenos-Ayres will end by being entirely overrun with them [8]. "

1. D'Orbigny, vol. I, pp. 347, 348. — 2. *Idem*, vol. II, p. 480. — 3. *Idem*, p. 572. — 4. *Idem*, vol. III, p. 63. — 5. *idem*, pp. 70, 74. — 6. *idem*, p. 299. — 7. *idem*, p. 313. — 8. *idem*, vol. I, pp. 472, 473.

"At Chicasica the abundance of flat hemp and wool would amply supply materials for industry in a province where the number of running streams and the downward course of the rivers would furnish every facility for establishing manufactories. Working the mines, however, is deemed sufficient, and agriculture is restrained to supplying the miners with the necessaries of life [1]."

"Is it credible that for the last sixty years the unhappy natives of Caupolican have been forced to carry on their backs, for a distance of fifty or sixty leagues, the productions of several villages?... Is it credible that with such a magnificent river as the Beni at their command they should hitherto have used but simple rafts [2]?"

"Cadelaria has been destroyed for some years, with all the other small towns and villages in its neighbourhood. The university of Cordova, formerly considerable, has long ago fallen into decay, as well as the public library, which had remained almost without readers for many years [3]." Chucuito has fallen very low: nothing remains but the ruins of the monuments formerly situated in the environs of Cuzco. Huanuco is but the shadow of what she was under the dominion of the Incas. Junin is nothing but a wretched village [4]."

"At Cochabamba agriculture is confined to the mere necessaries of life. The oleaginous plants, and those used in dyeing, as well as numbers of others useful to industry and the arts, are not even known [5]."

"The original industry of Valle-Grande has been lost; agriculture was gradually neglected, and reduced at length to the cultivation of a little Indian corn, which provides in some degree for the sustenance of the inhabitants; of a little barley, for the beasts of burden; and of aji, or red pimento, as the only article for exportation [6]."

"I traversed the town of Del Monte, which has a most wretched appearance. All the houses are roofed with straw, and are in a state of dilapidation, showing extreme poverty. The ancient fort is totally abandoned. The building once used for barracks is falling into ruins: rubbish and weeds alone forbid an entrance [7]. The pasture lands of Bojada, so rich in horned cattle a short time ago, are now reduced to the most miserable state [8]. If we except the principal villages, in the rest of the country nothing exists but wretched huts, the only furniture of which consists of a pallet

1. D'Orbigny, vol. II, p. 461. — 2. *idem*, vol. III, p. 395. — 3. Balbi, pp. 1071, 1072. — 4. *idem*, p. 1059. — 5. D'Orbigny, vol. II, p. 481. — 6. *idem*, p. 503. — 7. *idem*, vol. I, p. 628. — 8. *idem*, p. 432.

of sticks covered with cow hide, a rude table, and a few broken chairs or stools, which are often exchanged for blocks of wood, or cows' heads. The kitchen utensils consist of an iron kettle, a coffee pot, a tin mug, for which is often substituted a cow's horn, a pewter dish, and two or three iron or horn spoons. The use of plates is far from general; they commonly eat out of the dish [1]. The disorder and filth which reigns in the houses of Navaro are the distinguishing characteristics of the inhabitants of the provinces [2]."

"In the less opulent houses, plates and forks are very rare: all eat with their fingers. The animals used for food are cut up on the ground upon their skin, so that the flesh is always covered with blood, soiled by the mud and dung, and rarely washed before it is roasted. The dairy is no better managed, so that the cheese is detestable, and the butter, badly washed, and being put like grease into bladders, has almost always a bad taste [3]."

"In these days," says M. Lesson, a traveller as learned as he is impartial, "nothing reminds us of those times of opulence, in which the traders of Lima were rich enough to pave the principal street with massive silver. Trade was recovering, when civil war put a stop to every thing, and plunged Peru back into misery [4]."

"This city, the richest in the New World, is also the most corrupt. The extraordinary luxury of the few elbows the utter wretchedness of the many. The result of this is an extraordinary degree of corruption, daily increasing. Securely disguised by their dress, the women can act intrigues, even with their own husbands if it so please them. The extreme licentiousness and general misery of the country lead them to misconduct themselves to feed their luxury. In the evening they fill the streets and theatres, where they attack strangers [5]."

"In Mexico, the completion of the great canal has been interrupted not only by revolutions, but by the want of keeping it in repair; the old works are in the most deplorable state, and threaten the city with the greatest disasters. It has been proposed several times to abandon this country. The suburbs of the town are encumbered with ruined houses, rubbish, and filth; you often find extreme wretchedness and dirt in the interior of elegant buildings. These suburbs are the ordinary resort of twenty thousand beggars, who display all the marks of the most hideous misery [6]."

What a distance between these two degrees of civilization! But, as it is not rare to find prosperity the result of knavery, and poverty

1. D'Orbigny, vol. I, p. 547. — 2. *idem*, p. 620. — 3. *idem*, p. 545. — 4. Balbi, p. 1036. — 5. D'Orbigny, vol. III, p. 403. — 6. Balbi, pp. 1020, 1023.

that of rustic simplicity, let us see whether such is the case in the two Americas, or whether good morals are there the companions of prosperity, and vice the associate of misery.

Morality. — Our readers doubtless have noticed that, in the wish to avoid even the appearance of partiality, we have, as much as possible, refrained from expressing an opinion. We have done more, we have abstained from stating the facts ourselves. Our readers will be pleased at our resolution to persevere in this reserve, and even to keep absolute silence, when we might say so much! Let them listen to the recitals of men, who cannot be suspected of partiality, since they neither belong to the nation, nor to the creed, of which they unwittingly show us the admirable fruits :

" I sought, " says M. de Tocqueville, " for the causes to which is to be attributed the maintenance of the political institutions of the Americans, and religion appeared to me one of the principal. Now, that I am studying individuals, I find it again; and I perceive that it is no less useful to the citizen than to the entire people. It directs the morals; and by regulating the household it succeeds in regulating the State. I do not doubt for an instant that the great strictness of morals to be noticed in the United States originates in their creed. Religion, there, is often too weak to restrain man amidst the numberless temptations which fortune presents to him : she may not be able to moderate in him the thirst for gain which all around excites; but she reigns supreme over the mind of woman; woman gives the tone to morals. America is certainly in the whole world the country where the marriage tie is the most respected, and where the highest and most just idea of conjugal happiness has been formed. In Europe, nearly all the disorders of society take their rise around the family hearth, and not far from the nuptial couch. It is there that men imbibe a contempt for the ties of nature and for lawful pleasures, and acquire a taste for disorder, excitement, and change. Agitated by the tumultuous passions which have often troubled his own dwelling, the European only submits with difficulty to the authority of the legislators of the State. When the American retires from the agitations of the political world, and returns to his family, he breathes an atmosphere of peace and order. There all his pleasures are simple and natural, his enjoyments innocent and tranquil, and as he arrives at happiness by the regularity of his life, he accustoms himself without difficulty to regulate his opinions as well as his tastes. Whilst the European endeavours to escape from his domestic cares by disturbing society, the American seeks in his home the love of order, which he carries with him into the affairs of the State. In the United States, religion not only forms the morals, but extends her empire over the mind [1]."

Let us hear also M. Michel Chevalier on the same subject: "The American masses are more completely initiated than the European masses in all that concerns family, and above all married life. The union of man and wife is more sacred amongst the labouring classes in America, than amongst the independent classes of all the countries in Europe.

"Although, in America, the celebration of marriage is surrounded with much fewer formalities and less show than with us, and although the marriage tie is not indissoluble, as in our country, the cases of adultery are very rare. The unfaithful wife there would be a woman lost to society; and any man guilty of seduction, or known to have an illegitimate attachment, would be excommunicated by the public. In the United States, even amongst the labouring classes, man is more completely initiated into the duties of the stronger towards the weaker sex than he is in a portion of the middle classes in France. Not only the American mechanic or farmer spares his wife, as much as possible, all fatiguing work or laborious occupation, but he has, besides, for her and for all women in general, attentions which are unknown amongst us, even by people who pride themselves upon a certain elevation of mind, and even on a literary education. In the United States, in public places and in travelling, every man is equal; but a woman, whatever may be the rank or fortune of her husband, is secure of commanding respect and attention from every one.

"All books in America, without excepting novels, suppose the women to be chaste, and no one relates scandalous adventures.

"Literature in our country (France) has a perfectly different character. When a European undertakes to describe in fiction some of those great catastrophes which are seen amongst us in married life, he takes care to excite the pity of the reader by showing two uncongenial beings, united by constraint. Although a long tolerance has relaxed our morals, he would succeed with difficulty in exciting our interest for his characters, if he did not begin by excusing their faults. This artifice generally succeeds; we are prepared to be indulgent, by the events that are continually passing before our eyes.

"The Americans could not make such excuses plausible in the eyes of their readers; their customs and their laws are opposed to

1. Tocqueville, vol. II, p. 222.

such reasoning; and, despairing; to render immorality acceptable, they do not describe it. This is partly the cause of the small number of novels published in the United States [1]. "

"One would suppose that, with regard to morals, we have granted a singular immunity to man; there appears to be one standard of morality for him, and another for his wife: and, according to public opinion, the same act is considered in one case as a crime, in the other, as a simple fault.

"The Americans do not acknowledge this singular allotment of duties and rights; amongst them, the seducer is as much dishonoured as his victim.

"It is true that the Americans rarely pay to woman those assiduous attentions which she receives in Europe; but they always testify, by their conduct, that they believe her to be modest and virtuous; and they respect so completely her moral liberty, that, in her presence, every one is careful that not a word should be uttered in conversation which might wound her delicacy. It is common for a young, girl to undertake, without fear, a long journey alone [2]."

"I have no hesitation in saying, that, although in the United States woman rarely goes beyond her domestic circle where, however, she is in many respects very independent), nowhere, in my opinion, does she occupy a higher sphere [3]."

"North America," says an Anglo-American writer, quoted by Malte-Brun, "is the paradise of women; they neither labour in the fields, or perform the hard work of the house. A husband, whose wife were to be seen fulfilling these toilsome duties, would be considered an unfeeling man, or not sufficiently industrious to maintain her. He would blush at it. All that the women have to do is confined to working at their needle for themselves and their negresses, overlooking them, setting them their tasks, and keeping up good conduct and cleanliness in the family. For this reason, even in the lowest stations, we find a degree of education and good manners which honour mankind."

To complete the description of these domestic habits, we shall transcribe what a late publication relates of the order and morality that reign in the great manufactories of the United States : that is to say, under circumstances in which, as every one knows, there is the greatest difficulty in preserving purity of morals.

" Lowell, the town of all others in which the genius of the

1. Tocqueville, vol. IV, pp. 84, 85, 86, 87. — 2. *idem*, pp. 102, 103. — 3. *idem*, p. 104.

Anglo-Americans displays its greatest originality, presents a singular aspect. From whatever side you approach, nothing is perceived but large buildings, surrounded by detached houses prettily decorated. Every where are to be seen pyramids of balls of cotton; manufactories three and four stories high; forges, workshops, manufactured articles of all kinds, and the perpetual movement of an ant-hill. Raw materials arrive from all quarters, and manufactured articles are imported with the same alacrity.

"Each industrial company has as many boarding-houses as are necessary for lodging all the persons attached to its manufactories. These boarding-houses are neat buildings, with green shutters, constructed so as to lodge from twenty to twenty-five persons. They contain invariably, besides the private rooms, a dining-room and a saloon : all plainly but comfortably furnished. They are let to middle-aged women, in general widows of good reputation, who are answerable for the conduct of their boarders. Besides, any complaint made of them to the director of the company, whether by the boarders or any other person, is carefully examined, and followed up by a strict investigation.

"Since 1836, the year of its foundation, the authorities of Lowell have laboured incessantly to embellish their town, to promote its salubrity, and to increase the comforts of the population. They have paved the streets, made footways, facilitated the drainage, adopted a fine system of lighting, and erected public buildings for religious instruction, popular education, and benevolent societies. Their solicitude has induced the establishment of a preparatory school, in which the elements of general knowledge are taught to pupils who intend to follow the lectures of the superior schools : 8 intermediary, and 36 elementary schools, are frequented by 3,500 scholars. Wants of another kind have not been neglected; there are two banks, with a joint capital exceeding four millions of francs, and a fire-insurance company. Nor have the future prospects of the town been neglected. Comfortable and even elegant lodgings have been prepared, not only for the inhabitants who may stand in want of them, but also for visitors who might wish to stay there awhile. In short, every means that the most sagacious foresight could adopt has been employed, in the interest of the population, to lay the foundation of great and lasting prosperity upon the widest bases.

"In order to be thoroughly acquainted with the present state of this great manufacturing centre, we must examine the comfort and morality of the working classes, and the means that have been employed to insure the ulterior improvement of their intellectual and moral faculties. First, there is an inspector-general, who keeps active and vigorous watch over the whole corporation. In the manufactories, which are also submitted to strict regulations, there is, in every chamber, a trustworthy overseer, who is answerable for the order and good conduct of those under his care; and, lastly, there is a guardian, whose special duty is to inspect the manufactories several times during the night, in such a way as to render any infraction of the regulations an impossibility. Any person found to be notoriously dissolute, lazy, dishonest, intemperate, or having contracted the habit of absenting himself from divine service, or otherwise violating the Sabbath, is dismissed from the company's service. No kinds of spirituous liquors are allowed, unless ordered by a medical man, and all games of chance, or cards, are forbidden throughout the territory.

"The health of the working people employed in the manufactories is also considered, and with just reason, as an object of the most serious importance; and, in consequence, every measure has been taken to insure the comfort of all, and to diminish the causes of disease. For this purpose, the chambers and working-rooms are kept well aired, and heated at a uniform temperature, whilst the greatest precautions are taken to prevent accidents. The different companies have established jointly a large hospital in a healthy spot, where the sick are admirably tended under the care of an eminent physician. The workwomen are well dressed, without luxury, but with a certain degree of elegance, and, above all, with the strictest attention to cleanliness. They all appear very satisfied with their situation; and not a trace of depression or suffering is to be met with on their faces. I declare solemnly that, amongst the crowds I had the opportunity of examining in the different manufactories, I did not notice a single countenance which left a painful impression on my mind, nor see one young girl obliged to work for her livelihood, whom I could have wished to rescue from these works.

"The moral police established there is excellent, and insures the good conduct of individuals, and the purity of the public morals. Whoever is guilty of the slightest immorality, or even of a blamable action, is either not employed, or, on discovery, ceases to be so immediately. To keep company with a person of doubtful reputation is sufficient not only to hinder admission into the manufactories, but to procure a dismissal, if already employed. The names of all the persons dismissed for ill behaviour are inscribed in a book, which is open to all the establishments in the town, and thus prevents these persons from ever being employed there again. This strict watchfulness produces the best results. Thus the statistical reports of the manufactories of Lowell prove, without contradiction, that there exists amongst the working classes of this town a high degree of morality, fit to serve in every respect as an example to all other manufacturing districts. But we must also admit that nothing has been neglected to attain so lofty an aim. Measures have been taken in order that the population may easily enjoy the recreation of reading during the intervals of labour, in the evenings, and on Sundays and holidays. Books may be obtained from the libraries and reading-rooms, and the workmen even receive, direct from their offices, newspapers and reviews. It is extremely easy to procure books, but always good books. The town has a public library, containing five thousand volumes, and the working men's association another, of three thousand three hundred volumes, without mentioning numerous religious congregations, who all have collections more or less extensive.

"A great number of the young workwomen frequent evening-schools during the winter; and sometimes join together in classes to take lessons in foreign languages, at a trifling expense. There are also clubs, named in general circles of emulation, of which the members meet every fortnight, in order to submit their literary compositions to the critical examination of the assembly. Thus everything contributes to raise the moral tone of the population: material and moral inspection, churches, schools, libraries, literary circles, exterior comfort, savings-banks, and benevolent institutions. Besides, it is easy to imagine that persons, brought up at home with all the rigidity of manners of New-England, bring with them to the manufactories a high tone of morality, and easily become, with the help of the good administration of Lowell, an incomparable working population[1]."

"The American mechanic knows better how to work, and is more fond of it, than the European. The American artisan is acquainted with labour, not only in its sorrows, but in its rewards; his clothes are as good as those of a Senator in Congress, and he likes to see his wife as well dressed as the wives and daughters of the rich merchants in New York, and following, like

1. *Revue Britannique*, 1847, July, August, pp. 69 to 85.

them, the Parisian fashions. His house is solidly built, very warm, and very clean; and his table is almost as abundantly covered as that of his more opulent countrymen. In that country the mere necessaries of life, for the whites, includes several things which, amongst us, are considered as luxuries, not only by the working population, but, in certain ranks, amongst the middle classes[1]."

"The American masses appreciate much more fully than the European all that relates to the dignity of man, or at least to his own dignity. The American workman is full of self-respect, and shows it, not only by an extreme susceptibility, but by exactions which to us, citizens of Europe, would appear inconceivable, by his repugnance to make use of the European word ***master***, which he exchanges for that of ***employer***, and also by much greater honesty, punctuality, and scrupulousness in his transactions. The American workman is exempt from the slavish vices of lying and stealing, so frequent amongst our labouring classes, particularly in our towns and manufactories.

"The French workman is much more submissive outwardly; but, pressed by want, and surrounded by temptations, he rarely lets slip an opportunity of cheating his ***bourgeois*** when he thinks he can do so with impunity. The workman of Lyons takes the ***peignage d'onces;*** at Reims he pilfers the wool. It is certain that frauds are committed in America; there is more than one clerk whose conscience is burdened with innumerable peccadilloes, but these petty thefts are exceptions. The character of the American artisan, considered as a workman, is highly respected, and excites the envy of the European, who draws a comparison between what he sees there, and what he has left in his own country.

"What I have said of the artisan may be applied with still greater force to the peasant. The American farmer, not being obliged daily to battle with his master for the price of his work, surrounded by husbandmen like himself, and ignorant of the temptations to which the inhabitants of large towns are exposed, possesses all the qualities of the artisan, and fewer defects: he is less unjust, and less jealous of the rich and cultivated classes.

"If, then, we examine the existence in general of the mass of the American people, we shall find it superior to that of Europeans.

"Perfection for the masses, in every country, consists, above

1. Michel Chevalier, p. 382.

all things, in knowing and observing punctually their duties towards God, their country, their families, and themselves; in working assiduously and conscientiously, in being honest citizens, attentive husbands, and good fathers, and in watching over the comfort and good conduct of those related to them. In order to compare with equity, and without fear of gross error, the most numerous class of American and European society, we must compare them under these differents points of view; for they belong to every scale of civilization, and every variety of the human race, and it is upon their degree of development and permanence amongst the greater number that depends the degree of stability of empires[1]."

"Strong, vigorous, intelligent, active, full of daring and energy, but, at the same time, prudent and determined, the American," says the ***Revue Britannique***, "makes an incomparable labourer. No difficulty discourages him, no obstacle stops him. It is particularly to him that may be applied the fine idea of M. Guizot: 'Nothing is an obstacle without being at the same time a means. Clear-headed and practical, he always tries to accomplish his designs by the simplest means and the shortest way: he is ready to admit all kinds of methods, but only as helps, and in order to have the pleasure of perfecting them; his enterprising disposition leaves no means untried, no experiment unverified, no process unemployed; possessing in rare proportion daring and skill, he undertakes the most difficult enterprises without anxiety or hesitation, and succeeds in them while he playfully gets rid of a thousand obstacles that others, from the first, would have deemed insurmountable. Patient and resolute, nothing discourages and nothing stops him; above all he is a man of action, and as such is always on the breach: and, with more reason than Beaumarchais, he might adopt for his motto: My life is a struggle.'

"The American scarcely takes any relaxation. If he quits his private business for a few moments, it is only to be busied with public affairs. From morning till night, from his rising up to his lying down, he is constantly occupied; even his meals takes him but a few minutes.

"Frequently, in the solitudes of the West, Frenchmen and Americans may be seen living close to each other: nothing could afford a more striking contrast. The Frenchman rises much earlier, but he bustles about and makes a great noise, gives orders,

1. Michel Chevalier, p. 378.

and ends by setting off to gossip with a fellow-countryman, who lives at a distance of several leagues. On his return, he breakfasts and begins to work, if, indeed, some hunting or fishing party has not been made up during his morning's visit..... He lives from day to day, amuses himself, drinks, and vegetates; having no fixed purpose in view, he squanders his life with the carelessness of a child.

"By his side, the American rises every day exactly at the same hour, not before dawn, but just in time to begin work, which he does not quit for the whole day, except for the few minutes which are strictly necessary for his meals. He labours in silence with zeal and assiduity, and adapts with wonderful facility every method capable of improving the quality or quantity of his productions. By his enlightened foresight no detail is neglected, nothing is left to chance, and, in some degree, he forces Nature to stand his friend.

"His aptness for all kinds of works is the greater, because he is ignorant of the very meaning of the word *routine*. He is anxious to acquaint himself with all kinds of methods, but it is in order to choose the best. It is easy to imagine the influence which such qualities must have upon the prosperity of a nation. The most laborious, and above all the one who works with the greatest power, sagacity, and energy, must advance much more rapidly than others in the track to wealth [1]."

Such are the morals and habits of the Protestant United States. To complete our parallel, we must sketch the moral physiognomy of the Roman Catholic States in the South; let us leave the pencil to one who paints from Nature :

"The habits of immorality in the province of Corrientes are disgusting. After supper, every one retires to rest : it is the time for intrigues. The lover wraps himself in his *poucho*, and, to avoid being recognised, changes his hat for one that he does not wear in the day. On all sides favoured mortals may be seen entering at doors gently opened, at an appointed signal, by a young girl making every effort not to be heard by her mother, who sleeps in the adjoining room, and who often, on her side, receives in secret a favoured lover; though the daughter is as perfectly aware of her mother's conduct, as the mother is of hers..... The husband, on his side, pays court to his mistresses, caring very little about what goes on at home, provided he finds his mate,

1. *Revue Britannique*, 1848, July, August; J. Magne, pp. 122 to 132.

cigars ready, and something to eat. It is not even a rare thing, in families of a small fortune, to see the men the first to provoke intrigues in their own families, with the hope of deriving some benefit from them..... A woman is not in the least degraded in the eyes of her countrywomen for having one or two lovers, or for having had children by different fathers. The reader who would dare to accompany me into the houses of the poorer classes would shudder at the spectacle presented to his view. He would see all the children on the ground together, in the same room: the young slave keeping by the side of his young mistress, often naked, or half-dressed. In the kitchen the servants of both sexes are huddled together, just as they please; friends, enemies, men, women, girls, boys, married people, talking of every thing, naming every thing, and learning to do and say every thing. Thus, in this class corruption is carried to an extent, the very thought of which makes one shudder. Incest between brother and sister is not uncommon, especially in the country [1]."

"The women at Corrientes complain of the inconstancy of the other sex... They themselves are more faithful to their lovers than to their husbands..... There is neither sincerity nor confidence in the inhabitants. On the contrary, they are distrustful to a ridiculous degree, especially towards strangers [2]."

"A buffoon, by jests more obscene than witty, and accompanied by gestures still more indecent, excited general hilarity in the town by scenes which made me blush for the spectators, and which would have been unjustifiable even in the rudest and most barbarous ages [3]."

"The corruption of morals has produced many diseases in this country: syphilis, which, amongst the creoles, is accompanied with alarming symptoms, occasions agonizing pains that are rarely relieved, and is transmitted from father to child to such a degree, that it is not unusual to see unhappy babes disfigured by hideous buboes [4]."

Libertinism naturally leads to theft: "The peasants have little scruple in stealing their neighbour's cattle. In Buenos-Ayres these thefts are committed in open day, in the very sight of their owner [5]." In time, it also produces cruelty.

"Soon after my arrival in this country, the French, Italians, and other strangers warned me not to go from the port to the town without arms during the siesta, or in the evening; other-

1. D'Orbigny, vol. I, pp. 377, 378, 379. — 2. *Idem*, p. 382. — 3. *Idem*, p. 135. — 4. *Idem*, p. 388. — 5. *Idem*, p. 163.

wise I should run the risk of being assassinated: and all strengthened their advice by the recital of tragical adventures. They whispered, while pointing to several men on horseback, each with a long knife in his girdle: this one has already killed five persons, that other six; and if I were to believe them, the most innocent had been guilty of the death of, at least, one of his fellow-creatures. I asked if there was no justice in the country? and I acquired the certainty that in this town, as well as in the whole Argentine Republic, the laws have no power against crime. When an assassin is incarcerated, it is only for a short time. The war of partisans and the bloodthirsty dispositions of the shepherds (gauchos), has rendered them as indifferent to the death of a man as to that of the beasts they are in the habit of killing. No trouble is taken to secure a criminal, so that the country is infected with banditti, who are considered as honest citizens[1]."

"At Buenos-Ayres, when the men have quitted the coffee-houses, where they have passed the evening in gaming, and all is silent, woe to him who strays beyond the centre of the city, or returns too late, unless armed with good pistols! for he may be robbed even in the streets, near the square, by men who, putting a knife to his throat, will politely force him to strip[2]."

"Even the children in this country are early accustomed to cruelty, and amuse themselves in cutting with their knives the ham-strings of dogs, as they see their fathers do with oxen. In their childish sport, they show what will be the ferocity of their future disposition; for provided already with arms proportioned to their age, they are continually threatening to mutilate or kill each other when they quarrel. But let us turn from this disgusting picture of rustic manners[3]."

"The pulperias, which serve as resting-places for travellers, are the resort of all the idle vagabonds around, so that they are continually the scene of quarrels generally ending in bloodshed[4]."

"A knife is indispensable to all who travel in the interior of the country, and the natives laugh at those who have forgotten to provide themselves with one[5]."

"Highway robbery is but too frequent in a country where the enforcement of the laws is unknown from being generally eluded, and it is very common to see armed men behave as if they were upon an enemy's territory[6]. The Gauchos of White Bay are vagabonds, passionately fond of gaming, brandy, and women; essen-

1 D'Orbigny, vol. 1, pp. 425, 426. — 2. *Idem*, p. 508. — 3. *Idem*, p. 512. — 4. *Idem*, pp 528, 529. — 5. *Idem*, p. 530. — 6. *Idem*, p. 622.

tially lazy, of ferocious habits, and completely destitute of feeling. A man of the militia, in a quarrel, will rise without saying a word, draw his knife, and plunge it up to the haft in the side of his antagonist, who falls bathed in blood. If asked with indignation what is the motive of so horrid a crime, he replies with the utmost coolness that he had received a box on the ear, but, at least, he has had the pleasure of ripping up his enemy. Stabbing is an every-day occurrence amongst the inhabitants of the country around Buenos-Ayres: all the quarrels between the shepherds are decided by their knives... In general, they endeavour to strike their adversary in the face, and to leave a deep scar; this is what they call *marking their enemy*, in allusion to marking the cattle with a hot iron[1]."

"I know not how much punch I was forced to drink at the festival given in honour of my arrival at Santa-Cruz; I had need of all my strength to support it. The licentiousness of the dances bordered on madness; the men exciting the women more and more by the liquors, which were profusely served in uninterrupted streams. The frenzy was heightened by the doors being closed, to prevent any one from leaving, and a penalty enforced of ten glasses of punch for the men, and six for the women, who should be detected in endeavouring to quit the ball[2]."

"In this town the greater part of the year is passed in visits, amusements, and dances. At the parties given by married and single women, every one is forced to drink wine or liquors, very often until the senses attain the most extravagant degree of excitement[3]."

"The Tobas are far from cleanly in their habits[4]. The women of the country, out of vanity, resort in their youth to the abominable practice of abortion; and for that purpose, during their pregnancy, they lay down on their backs, and get some one to strike their body. It is only when they become of a certain age that they bear the only child they choose to rear. In consequence, the vast plains of Chaco are nearly depopulated. The children go naked until the age of puberty, do just as they please, and never obey their mother, who is a slave to their slightest caprices[5]."

"The woman who leads a profligate life is at length sent into exile, if she persists in disorderly conduct, which is not considered any crime in the men. But it must be allowed that this measure does not remedy the evil. The first woman placed in this situa-

1. D'Orbigny, vol. I, p. 664. — 2. *Idem*, vol. II, p. 528 — 3. *Idem*, p. 550. — 4. *Idem*, vol. I, p. 307. — 5. *Idem*, pp. 308, 309.

tion, and who was to be sent to Bueno-Vista, answered arrogantly that she was ready to obey, but that she would like to be accompanied by the concubines of all the Government agents, beginning with those of the Governor and his brother[1]."

"The present governors of Brazil set the example of misconduct; the Indians do not srcuple to follow it, so that universal corruption reigns in the province[2]." If it were only the civil and political chiefs! but listen: "At San-Iago they have a dance during which the women complain, in their songs, that they are bitten by ants, and whilst they scratch and hunt for these troublesome insects, they uncover the greater part of their bodies: the cries and shrill whistling which accompany this dance carried me back, by their wildness, to the original state of the nation... In another dance, the women raise their hands in the air, and seizing one of the bystanders shake him soundly, in order to make him dance the better. They seized hold of us all by turns, without even excepting the priest. While the women were dancing at the Governor's, the men were singing wild and discordant airs in the square[3]."

"The corruption of the inhabitants is carried to the highest pitch. The young girls, who go entirely naked until the age of puberty, are lost to all feelings of modesty. When older, they make no scruple of misconduct. Unrestrained by any sound religious principle, they return to the original customs of their country, and abandon themselves indifferently to all their relations[4]."

"All the vices are allied; impurity leads to gaming. The inhabitants of San-Roque are proud, and above all great gamblers," says M. d'Orbigny. "The love of gaming, which is general throughout South America, is there beyond bounds. They gamble not only during the day, but all night long. All the skill of the gambler consists in cheating cleverly. Often a poor mother remains without food for her children, whilst her husband gambles all away, even to his horse[5]."

"The usual occupations of the richer inhabitants of Itaty are those of the rich of the other parts of the country: sleeping, smoking, drinking *maté*, and gaming. Every time I called on the priest I found him, as well as the governor, playing at *moute*, instead of endeavouring to eradicate the love of gaming so ardent and ungovernable in nearly all the Americans[6]." And then, gaming bears its own fruits: "A number of individuals have made immense

1. D'Orbigny, vol. I, pp. 355, 356. — 2. *Idem*, vol. II, p. 606. — 3. *Idem*, p. 638. — 4. *Idem*, vol. III, p. 95. — 5. *Idem*, vol. I, pp. 146, 147. — 6. *Idem*, p. 203.

fortunes by the odious trade of gambling at the pulperias, where are often enacted scenes which end tragically for the proprietor, for scarcely any are free from bloodshed, and the master often falls a victim to the fury of the gamesters and drunkards [1]."

Such morals must be betrayed by the language; it is said by Him who knew the heart of man: "Out of the abundance of the heart, the mouth speaketh." This is verified here:

"At Yotaïty-Guaçu," says M. d'Orbigny, "at dinner parties, and, indeed, in all numerous assemblies, my delicacy was continually wounded by the vulgarity, the coarse jests, and the obscenity of the conversation indulged in by both men and women before young people, who, however, did not testify the least surprise at it. What a cynical language! what rude manners! Will it be believed that at the dessert disgusting tricks formed part of the entertainment, that the guests threw dirty things at one another's heads, and that some pratical jesters defiled even the dishes of preserves, in order to prevent any one else from touching them?... And let it be understood that far from heightening the colours of this picture, I have softened them down. How often have I painfully endured what I heard and saw with disgust [2]."

Such was the state of Brazil some years ago, when M. d'Orbigny travelled through it. Has it changed since then? We shall see by the more recent works of M. Kidder, who, like the former, resided some time in the country:

"The favourable position and the vast extent of the Brazilian Empire must always secure for it a prominent place in the eyes of the world.

"The internal resources of the empire are such as might be expected from its favoured position and extent of territory. Nature, who enriched Brazil with the most precious minerals, has been still more prodigal of her gifts in the vegetable kingdom.

"Brazil combines all that is beautiful, rich, and magnificent in Nature, with the blessing of an agreeable and healthy climate. But at present it suffers severely from two causes: firstly, the embarrassed state of the finances; and, secondly, the want of a free and intelligent population.

"These evils have in some respects a common origin. The revenues of the empire are derived almost exclusively from heavy duties levied upon trade. Unfortunately, the nation has no manufactures that require a tariff to protect their interest; and, without

1. D'Orbigny, vol. I, p. 584. — 2. *Idem*, p. 251.

the assistance of some skilful mind, years, if not ages, must elapse before the resources of that immense empire will be fully developed.

"It is true that the ancient system of absolutism no longer exists, which scarcely allowed a stranger to set foot on the Brazilian territory; but very little progress has been made since, or whence the necessity of hiring Europeans to settle in one of the most enchanting countries of the New World? And why is the number of immigrants, who land yearly in all the ports of Brazil, less than the average of the monthly arrivals in the port of New York alone? It is easy to answer: there are, in these matters, radical defects in the policy of the country.

"It is painful, yet true, to observe that the present regulations of the Brazilian Government tend rather to prevent, than to encourage, immigration. These regulations are jealous, illiberal, and degrading.

"One would naturally suppose that the Irish Catholics would rather immigrate to a Catholic country than to one colonised by Protestants. Facts prove, on the contrary, that Catholic immigrants find more toleration amongst Protestants than even in a country professing their own faith. Various plans, both public and private, have been formed to encourage immigration to Brazil, but they will all prove abortive, until the principles of perfect toleration prevail in the country. I am aware that the Constitution tolerates all religions, and that very liberal sentiments are professed by enlightened and educated Brazilians generally; but the lower classes, particularly the Portuguese and their immediate descendants, have a mass of national prejudice and bigotry of their own to overcome, before the position of foreign colonists can be at all pleasant amongst them.

"Besides, it appears they prefer the system of settling foreigners in distinct communities, to that of encouraging them to intermingle with the inhabitants. These colonies have seen little or no prosperity. But what is especially wanting in all parts of Brazil is, a sufficient number of practical industrious mechanics, from no matter what nation; these would be of great use to the country.

"The day ought ardently to be desired when Brazil shall be able to dispense with special exemptions, and, what is worse, lotteries, as a means of promoting her manufactures.

"It is generally known that notwithstanding all the laws, regulations, conventions, and treaties, for the prevention of the slave trade, it is still carried on between the coasts of Africa and Brazil.

"The subject of education in this empire is one of great and increasing interest; but the people being constrained to bear the burden in the shape of an involuntary tax, have none of their sympathies enlisted in favour of the schools, and too often neglect to take advantage of them when established.

"Complaints are made in all the provinces of the want of competent teachers; a want that will doubtless continue to be felt until more liberal salaries are paid for their services.

"Another serious obstacle to the progress of education is the almost universal want of suitable school-books. In certain parts of the interior, children are taught to read from manuscripts. Anything printed is very rare and very wretched. A newspaper or a book which finds its way to the school becomes, in a manner, public property, and is passed from hand to hand as an acquisition from which all, by the common laws of humanity, are entitled to derive some sort of benefit.

"Moreover, it is to be feared that the most serious obstacles are to be found in the mind and manners of the great mass of the people. Their tastes are those of other times: their highest ambition of intellectual enjoyment is associated with the dull excitement of the *festas*. What degrades them still more is the spiritual subjection in which they are held by men who are jealous of improvements, and who resist every effort in its behalf as a scandalous innovation.

"In corroboration of these remarks may be quoted the words of a distinguished Brazilian statesman, uttered before the Legislative Assembly: 'As to the civilization of the Brazilian people, almost nothing, unfortunately, has been done. A narrow strip of land along the coast alone enjoys the blessing of civilization, while, in the interior, our people are still plunged in the grossest barbarism.' Further he adds: 'We have been unable to remedy the evil, nor can anything be done without the aid of a moral and enlightened clergy.'

"There are few subjects on which Brazilian writers express themselves with greater unanimity of opinion than on the state of religion in the country. Laymen and ecclesiastics, officers of the state, men of business, and politicians, all agree in representing the condition and prospects of religion as low as they are unpromising.

"Monachism is on the decline, the number of secular priests is diminishing, the churches are falling to ruins, and the spirit and principles of infidelity are already disseminated far and wide, and this in a country peopled by the descendants of Inquisitors, and in which, from the period of its discovery, the Roman Catholic religion has held absolute sway."

The following statements are borrowed from the Report of the Minister of Justice and Ecclesiastical Affairs to the Legislative Assembly of 1843 :

"The retrograde movement of our clergy is well known; the necessity of adopting measures to remedy such an evil is also evident. On the 9th of September, 1842, the Government addressed inquiries on this subject to the bishops and capitular vicars. Although complete answers have not yet been received from all of them, the following particulars are certified :

"The want of priests who would devote themselves to the cure of souls, or even come forward as candidates, is surprising. In the province of Para, there are parishes which, for twelve years and upwards, have been without a pastor. The district of the river Negro, containing about fourteen settlements, has but one priest; that of the river Solimoens is similarly circumstanced. In the three *camarcas* of Belem, and the Upper and Lower Amazon, there are thirty-six vacant parishes. At Maranham, twenty-five churches have several times been designated as wanting curates, and not a single candidate has applied for either of the vacant places.

"The Bishop of San-Paulo gives a similar account of vacant churches in his diocese; and the diocese of Guyabà is no exception to the rule; not a single church is provided with a curate having a fixed residence; and those priests who officiate as vicars treat the efforts of the bishop to instruct and improve them with great indifference.

"In the bishopric of Rio-Janeiro most of the churches are supplied with pastors, but a great number of them only temporarily. This diocese embraces four provinces, but during the last nine years not more than five or six priests have been ordained annually, and, even of these, few devote themselves to their pastoral duties. Either they turn their attention to secular pursuits as a means of procuring themselves more comfort, emolument, and respect, or they look out for chaplaincies and other situations which offer equal or superior inducements, without subjecting them to the *literary examination*, the trouble, and the expense necessary to secure an ecclesiastical benefice. In short, there are in Brazil elements of disorder which grow up and strengthen under the shelter of firm bulwarks built for them by ignorance, superstition, intolerance, and vice."

But here we leave the two Americas. The documents and the evidence brought forward on the trial are too explicit to need any commentary. The defender of a good cause may be silent after the statement of facts: we rely on the force of truth. Let us now leave the New World to study the Old; and let us begin by comparing Scotland with Ireland[1].

[1] We have said nothing of slavery, because our task is not to judge, but to compare. If any one could think of making it in this place a subject of reproach to the United States, we should have a right to ask whether it was the English Protestants or the Catholic Spaniards who introduced slavery into America? — The Roman Catholics! To which of the markets of America do the slave-ships carry their cargo of human flesh? — To Catholic Cuba, to Catholic Brazil! And where is the entrance of this cargo so positively forbidden that it is not even attempted? — In the Protestant United States, which were the first, in 1808, to decree this interdiction. Where, at the present day, is slavery completely and seriously abolished? — In half the States of the Protestant Union, where the negroes are free, and where the whites are striving to obtain the emancipation of their brethren in the rest of the States! Where are the slaves best treated? M. de Tocqueville will reply: "What proves that the singular mildness of the Americans is principally owing to their social condition, is the way in which they treat their slaves. There is probably no colony in the New World where, upon the whole, the physical condition of the negro is less hard than in the United States" (Tocqueville, vol. IV, pp. 8 and 9.)

ROMAN CATHOLIC IRELAND

AND

PROTESTANT SCOTLAND

COMPARED.

We have seen how, in the two Americas, religious faith is one of the most powerful causes in the development of the morality, intelligence, and well-being of a nation. What is true in the New World is also true in the Old, and especially respecting Ireland and Scotland.

The reader may here, however, raise an objection which we shall anticipate. May not the distance which separates moral, educated, and prosperous Scotland from debased, ignorant, and miserable Ireland, be explained by the respective histories of the two nations? Although united to the same capital, placed under the same firmament and subject to the same laws, have not the two countries been connected with England under very different auspices? Is not Scotland simply an annexed kingdom; while Ireland is a conquered country, which was for a long time oppressed by the conqueror?

There is some truth in this remark. We shall take this difference into consideration with a view to relieve Ireland from a part of her responsibility. The difference in the origin of the two sisters, and in the treatment they have received from the mother country, is not, however, a sufficient explanation of the moral distance which separates them. We shall go further: the difference in the conduct of England, in regard to the two nations, has not always been in favour of Scotland. If, indeed, it ever was the case, it is not at present. For more than half a century the conduct of Great Britain towards Ireland has been greatly changed. England makes enormous sacrifices for Ireland, and none for Scotland; and Ireland, which we are about to compare with Scotland, is not that of former times, but the nation of the present day.

However, it may be insisted, if the objection does not acquit Roman Catholic Ireland, it does not the less blame Protestant England, which persecuted her. We do not think it does; and an obvious reflection will convince the reader of it.

England has only been Protestant about three hundred years, while more than seven centuries have elapsed since the conquest of Ireland : the reproaches which are directed against England for her long persecutions are, therefore, applicable to the Roman Catholic England of a former age.

Great Britain, we know, persevered even after her adhesion to her new faith in oppressing Ireland: but is it to be expected that the policy of a nation shall change suddenly, and her new principles penetrate into her actions from the very instant they are proclaimed? In the moral conversions of individuals, do we not see for a long time the traces of their old characters? What may reasonably be expected of a people as of an individual is, not that he shall change his morals in a certain time, but that he shall change them gradually in such a way as that, after a period which it does not belong to us to fix, especially in regard to a people, the change shall be complete and satisfactory : now, has not this change for the better in the conduct of England taken place? Have not the bad laws, after falling into desuetude, been repealed? Have not the ecclesiastical taxes which were condemned by the whole nation been abolished by the State? Have not the episcopal sees of the Anglican Church been reduced in number? Has not Catholic emancipation been voted by Parliament? Finally, has not England endowed a Roman Catholic college in Ireland, national schools, and given assistance of different kinds to the priest? Yes: the answer in the affirmative makes it, then, only equitable to judge of Protestant England, not by the actions of her infancy, but by the conduct of her mature age.

Moreover, another answer can be given to the objection : If persecution prevents the development of the natural good fruits of Catholicism in Ireland, why did it not smother those of Protestantism in France? Was not Louis XIV. as severe as Cromwell? Were not the *dragonnades* as oppressive as the taxes? And yet the French Protestants have struggled victoriously with these difficulties, and prospered at home and abroad. "From the commencement of the seventeenth century," says the *Revue Britannique*, "there is no misfortune or persecution which the Protestants have not had to support. Amidst many dangers and sufferings, while excluded from all public employments, deprived of their civil rights, trodden down into the lowest grades, they have taken a great and glorious part in the progress of their country, in industry, in science, in intelligence, and in civilization. In 1787, when the paternal justice of Louis XVI., and in 1789 the decrees of the Constituent Assembly, restored to them their rights as men and citizens, they returned to their natural positions in the highest ranks of French society. Their political emancipation found them prepared to fulfil all the duties which a free country imposes upon its children, and to merit the honours which it accords to them.[1]"

Is there not in this difference in the destinies of Catholics and Protestants, equally persecuted, an indication that, in the first case, the persecution was employed against error, which was in the end vanquished; and, in the second, against the truth, which is always victorious?

Let us, at any rate, suppose that Scotland, in the protection of her religion, has enjoyed a concession refused to Ireland; Ireland has over Scotland advantages of various kinds: a climate more agreeable, a soil more fertile, a geographical position and an insular form more favourable to commerce. In the comparison of their degrees of prosperity, these circumstances are compensations for disadvantages.

Moreover, to render our parallel more irreproachable, after comparing Ireland with Scotland, we shall compare Ireland with Ireland: the Protestant North with the Catholic South of Ireland. We shall have here the same conditions of prosperity; with the lands, the administration, and the country, the same. The difference of climate and of fertility will be in favour of the South, where Nature has cut out harbours much superior to those of the North, and far more convenient for the wants of commerce.

After all, even admitting that in some respects the lot of Scotland has been better than that of Ireland, will the difference suffice to explain the superiority of the first of these two countries over the second, without taking their respective religions into the account?

1. *Revue Britannique*, July, August, 1848, p. 413.

We do not think it, and we hope that the following pages will suffice to convince the reader of it.

This preliminary question settled, we shall enter upon the matter in hand, and compare Ireland with Scotland in various respects.

The Irishman is first of all an Irishman, a patriot. The Romish clergy have worked on this element of his character until it has become, at present, impossible to say whether religious principles or national pride has most influence over his actions.

The dexterous combination of patriotism and religion reveals already the immense power which the Irish clergy must exercise over the people; and it must be added that this power is doubled by the very nature of Catholicism. The priest, in fact, holds a great place in the Romish Church; he is the dispenser of pardon by the confessional; the operator of salvation by mass; and the infallible interpreter of the Sacred Code: he identifies religion with himself until he ends by becoming himself religion and salvation incarnate! From the double circumstance then of the confusion of politics and religion, and that his creed makes him the representative of the Deity, the Irish priest, in his domination over the faithful, becomes omnipotent. It is then into his domicile that we ought to go to search for the mould into which he is pleased to cast the Irishman. By studying the master, we shall prepare ourselves to understand the pupil; and let us look then, before anything else, at the Roman Catholic clergy:

"The Catholic religion," says M. de Beaumont, "has a public existence in Ireland; her temples are erected, her clergy organized, her ceremonies performed in open day: she has four archbishops, two thousand five hundred churches, and two thousand and seventy-four priests or vicars[1]."

If you add to these the college at Maynooth, and the national schools, you have a considerable body. Let us now see to what purposes it is applied. The Irish priest is, above all, a politician. He is both a tribune and a preacher; as a tribune he is described by M. de Beaumont: "No election can take place in Ireland without the clergy giving their advice if not their commands to the people. The clergy take a share in all the affairs of the country; they attend the meetings, and make many speeches. The priest is changed into the demagogue, and the very tongue which insisted upon the duty of giving to Cæsar the things which are Cæsar's, pro-

1. De Beaumont, vol. I, p. 48.

claims aloud that every good Catholic ought to vote against the Protestants. Nobody now denies, in Ireland, that the success of the elections is entirely dependent upon the influence of the priests, who hold in their hands the souls of the people."

M. Pichat makes us acquainted with the priest as a preacher. He says: "To obtain an idea of the authority exercised by the Irish priest, we must enter his humble chapel upon a day on which he has announced his intention of talking to them about a private affair interesting to them all. The congregation is crowded, for the Irish know that the priest is sure to make them weep or laugh, and perhaps both. The Irish like the drama at the church as well as on the platform, and to succeed the orator must be pathetic and comic in turns, and sometimes a buffoon. The church is therefore thronged; Father Kavanagh, in passing through the crowd, gives a few slight taps to two or three roguish urchins who try to hold him by his surplice; then he ascends the pulpit, makes the sign of the cross, and gives out his text: 'Blessed is he who gives his money to the needy.'"

"'These words, my brethren, are taken from St. Paul, who, we may say between ourselves, knew that a friend in need was a friend indeed. The text, at any rate, is very clear. The Apostle meant to say that we ought to give our money, when we have any, be it well understood, for the text is not made for him who has none, and who with an empty purse may whistle at thieves. I wish that none of you, my dear parishioners, may ever hum that tune upon the day when your priest has need of a pair of new boots (general laughter), because I know you are too good Christians to allow him to go about with holes in his boots, when the fat parson his neighbour, with three chins and jolly red cheeks, makes his high heels ring upon the pavement like an officer of dragoons (renewed burst of laughter)

"'I suppose a man has no money; I may be right, or I may be wrong; but, to make myself sure of it, I shall choose a logical example — Peter Donovan!'

"'I'm here, yer reverence!' replies the parishioner who has been called by his name.

"'Look here, Peter, I suppose now you have no money; am I right or wrong?'

"'Oh! I'd be sorry to put yer reverence in the wrong, but I must.'

"'How much, then, have you in your pocket, Peter?'

"'Without looking, I may tell yer reverence, since you press me so closely, that I would have had ten shillings if I hadn't to take out of it the price of an ounce of tobacco which I bought in coming to the church.'

" 'Very well, Peter, hand them to me just to serve as an illustration.'

"Peter Donovan made a grimace, and prior to putting his hands into his pockets said cunningly, 'Will yer reverence give me leave to quote also a proverb: A fool and his money are soon parted. I see well enough you're going to play me a trick.'

" 'Give him the money, Peter,' cried a hundred voices, 'give him the money, you niggard! What are you afraid of?'

" 'Here it is, here it is,' cried Peter at last, 'I would not for all I have offend yer reverence.'

" 'Thank you, Peter, or rather, it is a stingy fellow like you who ought to thank me. Must I employ all the arts of eloquence to draw out of you a few pieces of vile metal? Are ye not ashamed of clinging to your money in that way? Thank me then for the good action I intend to do in your name with your nine shillings. Alas! it will perhaps be your first, you cold Christian that you are; but I hope that when you have tasted the happiness of being charitable, you will not stop short there, which would not be logical.'

"The roars of laughter now become universal, and the merry priest laughs like the rest at the success of his trick."

"Is this an imaginary sermon that I have transcribed? No: I have only abridged and Frenchified a little in style a scene of real life, the truth of which can be verified by the author from whom I have taken it[1]."

We do not think this a fair specimen of the preaching of all the Roman Catholic priests in Ireland. We are willing to suppose the picture is too highly coloured, but it is given to us as a specimen. After passing a sponge over it, and removing the exaggerations, enough will remain to give us a poor idea of the Irish Roman Catholic pulpit.

Let us follow the priest in the discharge of his ministerial functions, always according to the accounts of Roman Catholic writers. Let us go to a marriage. "The priest," says M. Prevost, "celebrates the ceremony of marriage in the village church; and, it appears, in most of the counties requests the husband, after the mass, to give his wife the kiss of peace. The new married couple kiss, *sans façon*, at the very foot of the altar, and the joking lookers-on do not scruple to criticize at the very moment how they do it.

1. Pichat, pp. 317 to 324.

Nothing pleases them better than to make the bride blush by their jokes. Some priests however, now-a-days, oppose the old national custom, and I have heard of one who gave a vigorous cuff to a husband who was about to kiss his wife in the church..... After the national dances of jigs and reels, come country-dances, in which there are the most numerous performers. The priest is always present: he speaks to every body, and sometimes handles the fiddlestick or blows the bag-pipe, to the great satisfaction of his flock [1].

From a marriage let us pass to a funeral. "When the defunct," says the same writer, "has left a large sum for his interment, the chamber set apart for the wake is abundantly supplied with provisions, tobacco, and whiskey; and then, in the intervals of the chants and ceremonies, the men and women, smoking and talking, dine plentifully and drink to the memory of him who, alas! alone, of all the company, cannot partake of the feast..... The wakes may last three or four days, or as long as there is anything to eat or drink..... Dirges and lamentations are kept up incessantly upon the road to the grave-yard; and I assure you a traveller feels considerably astonished when he meets suddenly, in a lonely valley, a procession in which everybody, man, woman, and child, send doleful cries up to Heaven.

"If unfortunately two funerals take place at the same time, and the two processions take the same road to the same cemetery, scandalous scenes sometimes occur. At first, each procession quickens its pace in order to enter before the other; but if they chance to meet at the gate, they form into two hostiles parties, who begin by abusing each other, and always end by coming to blows. Vanity is not the only cause of these deplorable collisions; for, according to an old tradition, it is solemnly declared that he who enters last into a grave-yard is forced to be the servant of the rest of the dead, and he must fetch their drink and obey their commands until a new arrival relieves him from his humiliating functions [2]."

In this place we shall mention the part which the Irish priest takes in a multitude of superstitions; and show him, for instance, at the Purgatory of Saint Patrick, where the pilgrims, on paying for it, obtain the privilege of submitting to severe penances, particularly that of passing twenty-four hours in a cellar without food, drink, or sleep, for fear the devil should come as he had done before, and carry off the cellar and every thing in it; but as the

1. Prevost, p. 93. — 2. *Idem*, pp. 193 to 195.

subject is inexhaustible, we shall limit ourselves to two short quotations:

"In the ancient abbey of Burrishoob we had pointed out to us a large hole, full of the bones of the monks of the abbey. I observed with astonishment that most of the skulls which appeared upon the surface were black with smoke. One of our guides gave me the following explanation of it: 'The peasants of the neighbourhood have,' he said, 'great confidence in these relics of the monks, and when any one falls ill they hurry off for a skull to Burrishoob. The drink or soup prescribed by the doctor is boiled in it, and it rarely happens that the patient is not preserved by it. After the cure, the skull is faithfully carried back, and restored to its place [1].'

" Whilst I was surveying the humble grave-stones, 'tumuli,' or 'cairns' upon the road from Cong, I saw a poor woman at prayer, and laying prostrate for some minutes, after which she took up a flint, and threw it into a cavity which I had not previously remarked. I examined the tumulus or 'cairn' more attentively, and I observed that every one of them had a similar hole; my guide told me that the hole was called the window or bowl of purgatory. Every time that any one comes to kneel before a pyramid or heap of stones, it is usual to deposit a flint in the bowl of the dead for whom they pray, and when the bowl is full it is a sign of the deliverance of the soul from the torments of purgatory [2]."

It is astonishing that any clergy, no matter of what creed, should have so little regard for the dignity of her ministry. But a French writer, who is a sincere friend of Catholicism, informs us how this happens to the Roman Catholic clergy of Ireland: " The Irish priests," says Baron d'Haussez, ex-minister of Charles X, " are recruited from the lowest classes of society; too poor to have been able to acquire the education necessary for their office, they make up for the deficiency by a blind fanaticism, which they most dangerously communicate to those classes whose religious sentiments, being incapable of enlightenment, they can only inflame [3]."

By the side of this clergy, which represents the Romish religion in Ireland, let us place the Protestant religion in Scotland. M. Custine, a Roman Catholic, is the person who speaks as follows: "It may be said almost literally that the whole population of the Scottish towns assemble morning and evening to hear with profound attention moral and reasonable discourses upon the Gospel,

1. Prevost, p. 389. — 2. *Idem*, p. 420. — 3. *Idem*, p. 197.

and listen to the sounds of pious psalms, which dispose the soul to contemplation. These men are wearisome when amusing themselves, but they are affecting in prayer.

"I am too good a Catholic by habit and conviction to be suspected of partiality in the praises which I give to the Presbyterian worship; but I have also too much good faith not to avow the respect which every Christian communion inspires, when its precepts are observed by the whole community.

"The first prejudice which any one receives against a doctrine comes generally from the lukewarmness of those who profess it. In this point of view the Presbyterian and even the Anglican religion recommend themselves to the esteem of foreigners. They ask with astonishment what is the authority which understands so well how to make itself obeyed? It is not here, as amongst certain continental nations, a few women more sensitive, or weaker, or stronger than the rest of the world, who keep alive the traditions of true piety; it is a whole people, without exception, who are eager to avow publicly their submission to the public faith.

"The sentiment of religion does not appear to be less sincere in being protected by the civil power. When I see a Scottish pulpit, I cannot prevent myself from being moved, and I bow with veneration before it, as the source whence have flowed the virtues I have admired in a nation essentially consequent and conscientious. The Scottish Reformers avoided scrupulously calling to their aid the help of imagination and sentiment; nothing, in their austere doctrines, speaks to the senses, nothing seduces the heart; every thing is there to subdue the mind by mind alone; every thing is inward worship; conviction is all in all; and the severe language spoken is that of reason [1]."

Such are, according to Roman Catholic authorities, the sources whence, in Scotland and in Ireland, the people derive their morals. Let us see what are the streams which flow from them; and especially let us listen, in regard to the latter country, to what is said by a zealous defender of the Irish Catholics.

M. de Beaumont says: "It would be to contradict well-known facts to deny the vices of the Irish. The Irishman is lazy, false, intemperate, and violent. He has notoriously a sort of invincible aversion for the truth. Even when he is disinterested, between truth and falsehood it may be calculated that he will prefer falsehood. Every thing he says he supports with an oath, and he swears

1. Custine, pp. 405 to 407.

always upon his honour: *Upon my honour, upon my word;* familiar phrases in the mouths of persons who do not speak the truth. His repugnance for work is not less singular. What he does he does without taste, care, or zeal; and he is more frequently idle. Many Irishmen who are miserable add to their misery by their indolence; to alleviate their misfortunes nothing more is necessary than a little industry and activity; but nothing can drag them out of their apathy and indifference; they seem to like their misery, and they lie down in it and remain in it, in spite of the distress and wants which they have ceased to feel.

"These are deplorable vices; but there are others which are terrible. Violent and vindictive, the Irishman displays, in his deeds of vengeance, the most ferocious cruelty. We have seen how the farmer, who has been expelled from his farm, or who has had his goods seized for tithes, proceeds to reprisals characterised by the most ferocious barbarism. No one can remember without horror the tortures which he invents in his savage fury. Sometimes incendiarism and assassination do not suffice, and he must inflict longevous agonies upon his victim. He is often as unjust as cruel in his fury, and he wreaks his vengeance upon persons entirely innocent of the injury he has sustained. It is not only upon the squire and the parson that he takes satisfaction for the severities for which they alone are responsible. His violence makes him rush upon the agent of the proprietor, upon the new-come farmer, or upon the clergyman's lawyer; sometimes he goes still farther away from the author of his wrongs, and violently abducts the wives and daughters of these individuals, and dishonours them to punish fathers and husbands who are in no way culpable [1]."

"What happens when a factory is set up in Ireland? The workmen, who have at first consented to work for small wages, are no sooner installed in their new position than they forthwith club together for a rise of wages, and applying to industry the practices of Whiteboyism, arbitrarily fix the price of a day's work, threaten with terrible penalties the master who pays a smaller salary, and the workman who consents to receive it; the threats of this barbarous code not being empty menaces, the punishment usually following the offence very closely [2].

"It is difficult to form an idea of the number of cattle which are killed or mutilated maliciously every year; the woods and buildings which are burnt, the grass dug up and turned over, and the trees

1. De Beaumont, vol. I, p. 350, etc. — 2. *Idem*, p. 116.

which are cut, from sheer spite or vengeance. In 1833, I find that in the province of Munster more offences were committed with a design to injure the landlords than with a view to benefit the wrong-doers. Thus, of the whole number of crimes, while there were 59 thefts, I noticed that 178 offences were dictated by the instincts of brutal and vindictive violence[1]."

It might be imagined that such barbarism is exercised only against the English and the rich, whom the poor Irishman has been taught to regard as his enemies; but it is not so, and this barbarism is found in their whole conduct and manners, against their countrymen as much as against foreigners, in their pleasures as well as in their affairs.

"On returning to the house of Mr. W...," M. Raumer tells us, "I saw a distant crowd, and I expected to find, as in Scotland, an itinerant preacher; but they told me it was an Irish game. Two men, naked to their waists, were fighting, not like the noble Greeks of the Olympia, nor like the noble and trained boxers of England, but with great whips. After they were both bruised, covered with blood, and almost skinned alive, one of them fell senseless in the gutter. To take him up by the arms and legs, carry him to dry ground, open his mouth to pour into it half a bottle of brandy, and throw a bucket of water over him; all these things were accomplished in a minute. After that, the furious combatants were excited to renew the fight like mad dogs. Meanwhile, the judges of the field were displaying an activity incredible; they made room by distributing right and left amongst the crowd lashes of their whips, the least of which would have made me keep my bed for several weeks, but which have not here more effect than if any one amongst us was to say : 'Will you be good enough to stand back a little out of the way[2].' ".

Prince Muskau has published a piquant description of Donnybrook Fair. He says :

"Nothing could be more national. The misery, filth, and noise everywhere equalled the joy and turbulence with which they gave themselves up to the meanest pleasures. I saw them consuming viands and drinks which forced me to turn away my head to conceal the disgust I felt. The heat and dust, the crowd and the stench, were really intolerable : but the Irish did not appear to be aware of them. Several hundreds of tents chokefull of people, were erected, surmounted with rags of different colours instead

1. De Beaumont, vol. I, p. 169. — 2. Raumer, pp. 307, 308.

of flags. There were some which had no other sign than a cross and a walnut Kernac. The sign over the door of one of them was a dead and half rotten cat. In the midst of all this, the meanest mountebanks, covered with old tinsels, displayed their tricks in the wind, and wearied themselves in singing and grimacing with most frightful zeal. A third of the public was staggering about, or lay upon the ground dead drunk, while the rest eat, screamed, or fought[1]."

And as if on purpose to prove that these manners derive their origin from religious truth: "The Irish people," M. d'Haussez assures us, "is one of the nations most attached to their practices of religion, and one of those the least enlightened in regard to its veritable spirit; one of the most brave, and yet the most inclined to base and cruel acts of revenge; the most accustomed to privations, and the least sober; the most persisting in its resolutions, and the most frivolous in its designs; the most willing to work, and yet the laziest. It may be said of the Irishman that he has always a vice to spoil a virtue. In his character may be found both the Gascon and Beotian.

"Their passions are quick and unsubmissive to contradiction, are easily excited, and soon degenerate into rage. Hence extreme resolutions, the execution of which is never suspended by reflection; anger is the adviser they consult, and violence the means to which they resort most willingly; thus they are guilty of many faults, the first effect of which is to aggravate their own miseries.

"By the oddities and contradictions of which it is composed, the Irish character may be considered at once as the cause and the effect of the state of things which has been described[2]."

"The number of troops," says M. Dill, "stationed in Ireland now for many years is surprising : the annual average of the last eight years has been upwards of 25,000 men! Thus, to control 7,000,000 of professing Christians, it requires near one-fourth of that magnificent army which is found sufficient (our native Indian troops excepted) to control the greatest empire on which the sun ever shone, containing 156,000,000 of subjects and tributaries; of whom 120,000,000 are heathens and Mohammedans! And if to this military force we add 13,000 constabulary and metropolitan police, we have in this small island a constant army of occupation of 38,000 men!

"You exclaim : *Can* such a force be required? at least must it

1. Saint-Germain Leduc, p. 258. — 2. D'Haussez, pp. 225 to 227.

not supersede the necessity of jails and gibbets? Alas! it is a country of prisons as well as garrisons. There are in Ireland 155 jails and bridewells; near 700 law courts, from assizes to petty sessions; and 10,000 persons ministering justice, from the judge to the bailiff. And *can* this array of tribunals be required? Enter any southern court whatever; mark the crowds who throng the building and hang round the door; see the piles of indictments, processes and summonses; observe the prodigious mass of business transacted during one single term; and then you may form some conception of the gross amount of *law* going on continually over the land, with all its disorganising influences. Yes, and though weeks are frequently spent at the assizes of one single county, yet the business is often left unfinished, and special commissions are required to relieve the crowded prisons. In fact, our chief public buildings, in addition to *poorhouses*, are jails and court-houses, and our most flourishing business is that of lawyers and solicitors.

" Again, in Great Britain, with thrice the population of Ireland, and this consisting largely of the depraved manufacturing classes, there were in 1850, only 31,281 committals, while there were in Ireland in the same year, 33,326, or upwards of 3 to 1! Yet this gives no accurate idea of the proportion of *actual* crime in these two countries; for conspiracy against the laws is in many parts of Ireland so perfect, that even assassinations take place in open day, within view of the people, and not only do they not inform, but so screen the assassin that he often eludes the utmost vigilance of the police. Nor is a less mournful fact brought out by the relative proportion of *convictions*. The same conspiracy against law and justice appears in our very courts; scenes of perjury the most revolting are common on the witness table; and in party cases, the frequent expression even of jurors, before entering their box at all, is that they will " eat their boots " with hunger before they find against the prisoner! Hence the striking fact, that while in Britain, of the above 31,281 committals, there were 23,900 convictions, or nearly three-fourths, of the 33,326 prisoners committed in Ireland, there were only 17,108 convicted, or not much over one half[1]. "

"As in general the Irishman does not like work, he has not consequently the zeal and the attention to details of the laborious and persevering man. He is lazy, deceitful, intemperate, and inclined to violence, and is particularly pleased when out of work. His in-

1. Dill, pp. 74 to 76.

dolence increases his misery, and prevents his being industrious of his own accord. With a little more application to work, he might improve his condition most essentially, instead of which he abandons himself to his lot, and gives way to apathy, in spite of the privations which his negligence imposes upon him. The most simple ideas of right and wrong, of just and unjust, are confused and often entirely erroneous in the minds of the lowest classes. The Irishman does not always love the truth; he flatters his superiors, and is rude and insolent to his inferiors. Secret associations, such as those of the Ribbonmen, preach pillage, incendiarism, and murder in different parts of the country. United by oaths, the violation of which is punished with death, these secret societies give themselves up to the most cruel excesses, and escape punishment by the vengeance which they threaten against the witnesses who may inform against them. Their bands are spread over the whole island, and form the centres of all the commotions which disturb the peace of the provinces[1]."

It is especially in agrarian crimes that the daring of the Irishman is shown: "The characteristic trait of these crimes is that the mass of the population seem to sympathize with the criminal. This sympathy is an indirect complicity which encourages and protects the homicide, the incendiary, and the destroyer of private property. One of the witnesses heard upon an inquest said: 'There exists a lively sympathy amongst the small farmers with criminals, and they endeavour to protect them, calling it opposition to the landlord.' The report adds: We are assured that in consequence of that sympathy it is very difficult, as difficult as it can be, to get any one to give evidence against an agrarian criminal, and every criminal of this kind is sure of a good reception wherever he goes. Intimidation is universal in Ireland; for the fear of offending somebody, of becoming unpopular, or of being shot, induces people to endure things in Ireland which no one would submit to in England for any consideration whatever. It is necessary to notice here an observation of Lord Rosse, who, to show that the law has not the force in Ireland which it has in England, proves the indirect complicity of the juries with the accused. On every ten trials for murder in England and Scotland, there are, he says, nine condemnations, while there is only one in Ireland[2]."

Let us oppose to these Irish morals, formed by Catholicism, those which the Reformation has created in Scotland: Let us first hear

1. Solitaire, pp. 555 to 557. — 2. *Revue Britannique*, 1850, February, p. 382.

M. Jonnès, a French statistician: "Scotland is a country by itself... In its morals are found that puritan rigidness, that Scandinavian honesty, of which Norway (a Protestant country) offers still in Europe the example and model.

"The small number of crimes committed in Scotland bears the most favourable evidence as to the morality of the inhabitants of the country. It is not a gift of civilization, for figures which carry us back sixty-eight years, an epoch at which the population was still very little advanced, shows that crimes were at that time very rare. Howard states that in fourteen years, from 1768 to 1782, there were in Scotland only 76 persons condemned to death, of whom 54 were executed. As the population amounted to 1,360,000 inhabitants, an average of 5 capital crimes yearly gives the result of 1 in 252,000. The proportion is now 1 in 350,000. Thus, Scotland of the present day has not degenerated. There were in former times 4 executions yearly, or 1 in 340,000 inhabitants; at the present day there is 1 in 600,000; consequently justice has become almost one-half less rigid, and yet the number of crimes has diminished [1]."

"I shall mention a trait of the character of the Scotchman, which is the key to his history. There is in the Scotchman something interior, grave, reflective, which seems sometimes to resemble reserve or pride, but which is rather the firmness of independence and liberty. The lofty air and the severe looks show only that there is, in their souls, hidden and powerful principles, noble and profound passions, which if they were to unchain them would rise up and combat as the lion when he is attacked. Christianity has penetrated into these men more than any other nation. The Christian sap is grafted in them, not as on the feeble descendants of the Romans, but as on a young, wild, and vigorous stock which grows up finely [2]."

"The Scotch are grave but courteous, and they possess to a great degree a look of kindness, a demonstration of hospitality, an expression of goodness which is always confirmed by a trial of their dispositions [3]."

"Theft, plunder and housebreaking are things unheard of in Scotland, and public security is so great that bolts and locks are considered unnecessary precautions. They do not think of shutting their doors even during the night. Capital punishments are so rare that there is only one or two executions yearly in the whole

1. Jonnès, vol. II, p. 275. — 2. Aubigné, p. 55. — 3. D'Haussez, p. 149 to 151.

kingdom. Every family attends divine service with its servants; and, in every house, morning and evening devotions are performed, while charity to the poor is never forgotten... Coincident with the French Revolution, which found much sympathy in the middle class, there was a relaxation of morals. Wise and energetic measures, however, preserved the public spirit of order and morality, and each family assumed a certain watch over the conduct of its children. Thus morals were re-established with the tranquillity which had been momentarily troubled. To-day, the mass of the Scotch population occupy, in regard to morality, a distinguished place amongst the most respected nations. The occurrence of riots is rare; the masses of country people seem, in cases of unforseen misfortunes, full of resignation, which appears to be the result of a feeling of public morality and religion. It was thus that, in 1837, entire families became victims of famine rather than commit the smallest theft, although they had no reason to fear the consequences."

Any one might distrust the impressions of travellers or party men. But how can they question the facts which we have just read, when they are verified by impartial statistics? Let us then consult M. de Jonnès when comparing the criminality in Ireland and Scotland:

Accusations of crimes and offences.

(Average from 1831 to 1835.)

Scotland........................ 1 in 880 inhabitants.
Ireland......................... 1 in 460 inhabitants.

Thus already commitments are, in proportion to the populations, nearly twice as numerous in Ireland as in Scotland. Let us pass on to the crimes proved and punished :

Thefts.

Scotland, from 1834 to 1836, 186 thefts: 1 in 13,000 inhabitants.
Ireland, from 1834 to 1836, 3,026 thefts: 1 in 2,700 inhabitants.

Thefts, then, are five times more numerous in Ireland than in Scotland!

Crimes committed against persons.

(Average from 1830 to 1835.)

SCOTLAND.

Assassinations, 1 in 400,000 inhabitants; homicides, 1 in 266,000; thefts, 1 in 19,460.

IRELAND.

Assassinations, 1 in 107,000 inhabitants; homicides, 1 in 46,000; thefts, 1 in 63,340.

"Ireland, compared with Scotland, presents the following differences : homicide is six times, assassination four times, and thefts, from three to four times, more common in Ireland than in Scotland.

"Offences against public order are so multiplied in Ireland that it is necessary to treat them separately :

Homicides and attempts (in 1832)	224
Shots fired at persons	211
Incendiaries	571
Destruction of houses	87
Attacks on houses	2,122
Demands of arms	673
Illegal oaths	317
Illegal notices	2,149
TOTAL	6,374

"These numbers are augmented by smuggling offences, attended with violence, against the Excise and Customs :

Condemnations to death (1804 *to* 1811).

Scotland, 1 in 257,000 inhabitants.
Ireland, 1 in 52,900 inhabitants.

"The condemnations to death in Ireland are ten times more numerous than in Scotland, and executions three times; there is consequently :

In Scotland, 1 individual condemned to death in 235 convicted of crime.
In Ireland, 1 individual condemned to death in 49 convicted of crime.

Executions.

(Average from 1831 to 1835.)

Scotland	1 in 610,000 inhabitants.
Ireland	1 in 221,000 inhabitants[1]."

According to Quetelet and other statisticians, the affinity between the numbers of the accused and the condemned measures the severity of the judges. Following this principle, the law is enforced with more rigour in Scotland than in Ireland; for, in the first country, more than half of those condemned to death are executed, whereas in the second, there is only one in six.

To sum up, the numbers of accused, condemned, and executed, are always much greater in Ireland than in Scotland, and the average ratio is three to one! If morality could be counted, it ought to be said that there is three times more morality in Scotland than in Ireland.

If religious faith and morals are intimately united, it is not

1. Jonnès, vol. II, pp. 275, etc.

always so with morals and intelligence. In treating the first question, then, we have necessarily not prejudiced the second. Therefore let us compare the two nations in regard to knowledge.

We have wished to know the names of the illustrious men that Ireland has produced. Malte-Brun has furnished us with the following list :

"Boyle enlarged the sphere of physical knowledge; — Steele associated his pen with that of Addison; — Congreve enriched the theatrical catalogue with many lively comedies, of which some are still played; — Swift received from Voltaire the name of the Rabelais of good society; — Sloane, a skilful doctor, studied botany with success; — Bishop Berkely gave himself to the study of the exact sciences, and threw new light on metaphysics;— Sterne, by the originality which distinguished his novels, acquired an European reputation; — Nell made himself known by his light and easy poetry; — Goldsmith, as a scholar, historian, and naturalist; and lastly Burke, Sheridan, Flood, and many others, who shone as orators at the national tribune [1]."

But, asking ourselves afterwards if all these men were Roman Catholics, we looked nearer, and we have found that they were all Protestants!

Undoubtedly we shall not conclude from this that Catholic Ireland does not produce distinguished men. The remembrance of Thomas Moore and O'Connell would be there to protest against it. But then it must be owned that the circumstance that a French writer, when making a list of Irish celebrities, mentions only Protestant names, is a very remarkable one.

Nevertheless, the same author explains himself clearly on this subject:

"Ireland, he says, is certainly less enlightened than England, and especially Scotland. She has fewer scholars than these two kingdoms, but about the same number as France. The thing which distinguishes it principally from other nations is the kind of instruction which is obtained. The great majority of the people, being guided by a poor Catholic clergy, who are ill educated and full of prejudices, are kept in a state of appalling superstition, the only principle of the ignorance with which they are reproached.

"The elementary instruction of the populous class ought not to consist merely in the knowledge of reading and writing. Morality ought to teach the Irishman the extent of his duties; religion

1. Malte-Brun, pp. 228, 229.

ought to encourage him to fulfil them. Whence can he derive the mental knowledge indispensable to his situation, if it is not from the books destined to enlighten the Christian? The Irish Catholic clergy do not permit the people to read the Bible; and it is by ridiculous works, destined to perpetuate superstition and ignorance, that they mould them into that sort of dependence, which makes them nothing but blind instruments of enmity towards England, and hypocritical Christians always ready for revolt[1].

" The island has only one establishment for ecclesiastical education; it is the Royal College of Saint Patrick, at Maynooth, which is conducted by Jesuits, and destined to educate Catholic priests; none come out of it but those brought up in prejudices and pretensions unfavourable to England[2]. "

M. de Jonnès enters more into details : " In 1734 there was in Ireland 1 scholar in 770 inhabitants; and at the same time in Scotland 1 in 250. "

At present this disproportion does not exist, but it must be remarked that the amelioration of Ireland, in this respect, is due to the Protestants; not only because they have created schools for their own children, but also because they have opened them for Catholics. This can be inferred from the following table, which we borrow from M. de Jonnès, showing the state of education in Ireland in 1824 :

	Schools		Scholars	
" Association for the suppression of vice	226	schools	12,769	scholars.
Institution of Erasmus Smith	113	—	9,011	—
Kildare-Street Association	919	—	58,205	—
London Irish Society	618	—	37,507	—
Baptist Society	88	—	4,566	—
Charter Schools	32	—	2,255	—
Other Protestant schools	123	—	1,550	—
	2,119		125,863	
Catholic schools, supported by nuns	46	schools	7,136	scholars.
— — by friars	24	—	5,454	—
Other Catholic schools	352	—	33,825	—
	452		46,415[3]. "	

If we class the schools, not after the scholars which present themselves, but after the societies which support them, we shall have :

For the Protestants,	2,119 schools,	125,863 scholars.
For the Catholics,	422 —	46,415 —

1. Malte-Brun, book LXI, pp. 199 and 200. — 2. *Idem*, p. 101. — 3. De Jonnès, vol. II, p. 326, etc.

And this at an epoch when the Catholics were three times more numerous than the Protestants.

Since then two circumstances have happened which have modified the state of things in a manner honourable to England. Government has established numerous schools for the Catholics, and a powerful Protestant propagation has organised itself to cover the country with benevolent institutions of all kinds. It thus happens that everywhere in Ireland instruction is spread to the profit of one church, and at the expense of another. But, without dwelling upon the Protestant source whence the instruction for the Catholics flows, let us look at the extent of it:

"Of the *fourth part* who *can* read and write, while very many are most highly educated, the attainments of the majority are, we fear, but slender. In 6 counties and 74 towns, with populations ranging from 2,500 to 12,400 each, there was not in 1849 a single book-shop; and in the entire island there was, in proportion to the population, only one for every nine which then existed in Scotland! While, as to private libraries, it is said that in the greater part of Connaught there do not exist as many books as would stock a book-shop in a small English town [1]."

We might quote documents which show that instruction is at the lowest ebb amongst the Irish Catholics; that there are towns of 40,000 inhabitants without a book-shop or a reading-room; that there is a million of children destitute of all education; but, weary of the contemplation of such ignorance, we prefer to turn our eyes towards a country upon which they may rest more agreeably.

"May we be permitted," says a Review, "to state our conclusions in favour of the Scottish race, whom neither difficulties nor insufficient assistance has induced to lag behind on the march of progress. The sacred fire of intellectual ambition has always been kept up by that nation, which has always counted so many men illustrious in science, literature, and industry; poets like Burns and Hogg; inventors like Ferguson and Watts; financiers like Paterson and Horner; superior men of all kinds for whom elementary education of the parish school proved sufficient. What chiefly distinguishes Scotland is the laudable intellectual activity of the whole nation, which M. Chambers affirms to be superior to the parish schools, and where four-fifths of the population receive their elementary education. The Scottish workmen can scientifically perfect their professional education, and acquire all sorts of

1. Dill, p. 72.

accessory knowledge, in the 'Mechanic's Institutes;' a sort of club in which they have the use of a library, literary conversations, and lectures. Since 1825, these institutions have multiplied greatly. The lyceums of working classes are another sort of club-schools, supported by small subscriptions, and they give the names of 'Unions' to a certain number of societies of working men, who are associated amongst themselves for mutual aid and assistance [1]."

"What a country!" cries a French traveller, speaking of Scotland; "a country interesting and curious, instructive and orderly, rich and well cultivated, rural and picturesque, with its castles, its parks, its fields, its rocks, its grand and beautiful lakes. Why it would take many volumes to describe it! Every thing there breathes of the opulence of a happy existence [2]."

"The Scotchman loves study. He is a thoughtful and great reader. Food for his mind is to him a necessity of his intellectual existence. The tendency of the nation towards instruction appears to have been the result of a general civilization, which extends through all classes of society. The capital is in this point of view the centre of education and culture. The numerous political and literary journals which are published there appears to be scarcely sufficient, notwithstanding their high price, to the daily wants of the reading population [3]!"

"It would be difficult to give a just idea of the zeal with which the poor are animated in Scotland to give their children the advantages of a good elementary education. This is in the eyes of all a duty so essential that the most obscure and even vicious men would reproach themselves for neglecting it. If we except some remote corner of the highlands, it would be difficult to find in this country any one who does not know how to read and sign his name. In the middle class, classical education is rarely omitted, and the poor are often known to impose sacrifices upon themselves, and even the privation of necessaries, to secure the education of their sons. The parish schoolmasters of Scotland form a class of men who are respected, and deserve to be so [4]."

"The extraordinary number of illustrious men which Scotland produced towards the end of the last century," says M. Moreau de Jonnès, "gave the country the knowledge of itself. The Presbyterian clergy used their powerful influence to spread instruction

1. *Revue Britannique*, 1849, July, pp. 90, 91. — 2. Solitaire, vol. II, p. 566. — 3. *Idem* vol. II, p. 605. — 4. Saint-Germain Leduc, vol. II, p. 316.

amongst the people, and succeeded marvellously. In 1820, the day-schools established in Scotland gave instruction to

	110,770 free pupils.
	65,533 paying pupils.
TOTAL	176,303 pupils.

" It is a tenth of the population, and since then no infant remains without instruction. This happy state of things has been maintained and perpetuated.

" The family affections and the love of country have facilitated in Scotland the establishment of public schools. Children who cannot be supported by their parents are supported by their friends, their benefactors, or by patriotic associations; and an entire generation has passed away without any diminution being observable in the honourable sentiment which imposes this voluntary tribute. It appears that in the Scottish schools, they do not confine themselves, as nearly everywhere else, to giving an automatic instruction, but busy themselves in developing the real fruits of education. The superiority observable in the Scotchman, in divers circumstances, is attributed to these educational influences.

" As a sign of the worth of Scotchmen, the following anecdote is worth mentioning: In 1807, a body of English troops, a part of the expedition of General Fraser, fell into the hands of the Turks, who sold their prisoners, and they were dispersed in Upper Egypt. When they were re-purchased, it was remarked that the highest ransoms were demanded for the Scotchmen, on account, no doubt, of their intelligence, their good conduct, and their education. It was necessary to redeem them at the price of a hundred sequins, while they obtained the redemption of the others at the rate of from twenty to thirty sequins [1]."

" Reading, and the instruction it produces, " says M. de Jonnès, " are promoted in the British islands by religious duties, and the interest of the country. There is not a family in which the Bible is not read; also, there is not one, however poor it may be, which does not procure newspapers, and occupy itself more or less with public affairs. These national habits furnish every body with the means and the occasions for reading daily. Thus it becomes for every one a duty, a pleasure, a necessity, a want [2]."

" There is in Scotland more than one copy of a newspaper for every individual, and, in Ireland, one for four inhabitants. "

1. De Jonnès, vol. II, p. 326. — 2. *Idem*, p. 330.

This account would be singularly modified in favour of Protestantism, if we remark that the immense majority of newspapers published in Ireland are published and read by the Protestant minority.

Thus Scotland is not less distinguished by its intelligence than by its morals, when it is compared with Ireland. We can foresee then, already, that it will be the same thing in regard to its material prosperity. But here the distance is so great between these two neighbouring countries, that it will undoubtedly surpass all the anticipations of the reader.

Let us commence our parallel by showing the physical condition of the Irish Catholics. Baron d'Haussez, ancient Minister of Charles X., shall open the investigation by a deposition which ought not to be suspected by Catholics, and which is all the more imposing that it points out what has always appeared to us to be the real cause of the miseries of Ireland:

"The effect upon the Irish," says M. d'Haussez, "of the bad direction which the priest gives to their minds, is a prostration of their moral force, which annihilates all their intellectual faculties, and blunts even the consciousness of misfortune and the desire to put an end to it. The Irish peasant is stimulated only by the sense of hunger; insensible to all others, he does not concern himself either with the nakedness of his family or the dirtiness of his house, which he shares with the animals, who are few, and of little value, and whose produce place in his hand now and then a few pieces of money, which are quickly exchanged for whiskey, his favourite liquor [1].

"Ireland is peopled with poor, and comfort is an exceptional state, limited to a very small number of families, in comparison with those who live in complete destitution; the only relief which distress meets with, when carried further than in any other country, is that it has become common, the condition enforced upon the whole nation, and that at least those who suffer find no occasion for making comparisons, which would aggravate their lot [2].

"England every year sees thousands of Irish who come in flocks to crowd amongst the workmen already to onumerous by whom she is encumbered; they bring strong arms, which are often turned aside from useful employment by heads excited by the immoderate use of gin; and they mix in all quarrels of the workshops. They are seen everywhere where there is work or disorder,

1. D'Haussez, vol. II, pp. 206, 207. — 2. *Idem*, p. 211.

equally disposed for the one or the other, noisy, intermeddling, and troublesome everywhere. These dispositions make it more difficult for them to find employment for their strength, and adds to the causes of their extreme misery [1]. "

" The Irish beggars might be called the lazzaroni of Great Britain. At every step, in the streets of London, you meet an Irishman who asks charity; by their manners and their pronunciation, even a stranger cannot help knowing them [2]. "

" At the time I visited George Yard, Wentworth-street, Saint Giles of London," says M. Pichot, " it was Irish colonies chieflywhich had there established their misery and filth. I read also in an old report of parliamentary inquiries, which reduced every thing to figures, that of 15,000 beggars in London at that time, there were 5,000 Irish. At the same time, it was calculated that a fourth of the prostitutes of London came from the same nation [3]. "

" The commerce and industry of Ireland, like the other sources from which her prosperity ought to flow, are in an absolute state of depression. The extreme poverty of the country prevents an active consumption of commodities, which is everywhere the most certain base of the rapidity and importance of commercial transactions [4]. "

" Ireland contains one of the most miserable populations of the earth; and the one of all others, which, whilst trying to do it, adopts the means the least adapted to enable them to escape from their miseries; one of the most enslaved, and which justifies the most this enslavement by its tendency to free itself from an authority which has always shown itself to be moderate [5]. "

In a report addressed by Patrick M'Rye to the Lord Lieutenant of Ireland, we read the following details of the parish of West-Tullegobegly, county of Donegal : " The inhabitants are in the most needy condition; the most famished, the most destitute that I have ever known. Although I have gone over nine Irish counties, a part of Scotland and England, many colonies of North America, and walked on foot 2,253 miles, across seven of the Union States, nowhere have I seen the tenth part of such misery, want, and destitution.

" I shall now draw up the tabular statement of it with all the exactitude of truth, but without the least exaggeration. This parish contains 4,000 inhabitants, all Catholics, who possess between them only : one cart, one plough, sixteen harrows, eight

1. D'Haussez, vol. II, p. 216. — 2. Saint-Germain, vol. IV, pp. 258 to 260. — 3. Pichot, vol. I, p. 271. — 4. D'Haussez, vol. II, p. 219. — 5. *Idem*, p. 225.

men's saddles, two women's saddles, eleven bridles, twenty shovels, thirty-two rakes, seven table-forks, minety-three chairs, two hundred and forty-three stools, ten iron forks, twenty-seven geese, three turkeys, two mattresses, eight straw-mattresses, two stables for horses, six stables for cows, eight brass candlesticks, three watches, one national school, one priest, no cart with four wheels, no other carriage of any sort, no hats, no clocks, no looking-glass above the value of threepence, no boots, no fruit-trees, no turnips, no carrots, no parsnips, no clover, nor any other horticultural products, except potatoes and cabbages; about ten feet square of glass for all the houses, except the chapel, the school, the presbytery, the house of M. Dombrain, and the guard-house of the constables.

"No woman, married or unmarried, can be said to have more than one shift; the majority have none, and at least one-half of the men and women have no shoes on their feet; also there are not many families who have two beds, but in many the boys and girls of a mature age sleep pell-mell with their parents. Their beds are of straw, green or dry rushes and heath, with coarse sheets or none at all, and blankets in tatters [1]."

"If," says M. Nichols, in a report addressed to Lord John Russell, "you reason with the Irish peasants, and show them how easy it would be to ameliorate their lot, they fall back on their poverty. You see a man at his door warming himself lazily in the sun, or seated beside his peat-fire, whilst his cabin is surrounded with stinking mire across which it is impossible for you to pass. You tell him that with the water of the stream he could, in a few hours, clean all this filth. Oh! he answers, we are so poor! And yet he smokes his pipe, and probably does not deny himself a drop of whiskey [2]."

"As for the other necessities of life, the Irish have scarcely enough to clothe themselves by day and cover themselves by night. In the winter, notwithstanding the temperance of the climate, they die of cold as of hunger; in many cabins there is but one coat for two individuals. They put it on by turns to go to mass on the Sunday; the rest of the day they are covered in tatters [3]. In all countries there are more or less poor; but a nation of beggars is what only Ireland can offer. Ireland seems destined to show how far human misfortunes can go [4]."

"The country people have rarely shoes or stockings; they envelope their bodies in an immense great coat; the men and women

1. *Revue Britannique*, 1847, March; April, pp. 98 to 100. — 2. *Idem*, p. 98. — 3. Nougarède, vol. III, p. 642. — 4. *Idem*, p. 645.

are bareheaded, and nearly always barefooted. As for the children, they are almost stark-naked. A rag of a shift or trowsers, or sometimes an old shawl or ragged petticoat, with which they cover themselves the best way they can, is their ordinary costume. On the roads, at the entrance of every village, swarms of poor children, half naked, appear all of a sudden, and seem to come out of the earth. They besiege all the carriages, follow them with cries of distress, and do not stop until they have received charity [1].

" Potatoes cooked in a little milk from the cow which shares the house, and rendered a little insipid by a little salt, when they have enough of money to buy it, forms the nourishment of seven-eighths of the inhabitants of Ireland. The little which the woman gains from spinning flax, and the man from digging, goes to buy whiskey. As for clothes, they wear little or none, and shoes and stockings are things completely unknown. The more comfortable farmers, however, wear a little straw in their coarse shoes or *brogues;* but this is a rare luxury. A labourer rich enough, as they say, to put hay in his boots, is a Cresus in comparison with the ordinary Irishman. Some have a horse to themselves, whilst others unite with two or three neighbours to keep one. Under the same yoke they harness their horse and a stout labourer, who serves as a second horse, and who is not safer from the whip of the driver than his four-footed companion at the plough."

" The peasants lounge about upon the road-sides, with the indifferent air of travellers; those men who have the palest complexions, and the most broken hats, sport the cast-off but repatched coats of gentlemen, taking care to make the patches more remarkable, persuading themselves that it is better to look like a broken down "gent." than to appear to be a poor peasant. The urchins even wear cast-off clothes, and play amongst the household pigs with what were in former times an old riding frock, a small coat, and a little hat. Nothing appears to be more rare in Ireland than old shoes. Paddy walks at his ease barefooted in spite of the formal cut of his rags [2]. "

Mr. Edward Wakefield could say without contradiction in 1812: " An estimable writer of this country acknowledged frankly that the Irish peasant is not much above the savage, either in regard to just notions of liberty, or in respect for the laws and civil institutions of men [3]. " In such a state of manners, the most barbarous practices are not rare. At Gweedore, for instance, besides

1. Prévost, p. 142. — 2. Pichot, vol. I, pp. 224 to 229. — 3. *Idem*, vol. II, p. 258.

the shearing to which the sheep are subjected once a year, every one has recourse to the wool whenever it is wanted. A woman who is knitting a pair of stockings for the next fair, if she need some more wool, catches a sheep or a lamb, and shears or tears off from the back as much as she chooses. The poor beast, thus shorn, presents a strange and ridiculous spectacle.

"Under the influence of the wandering habits of these populations, it may be readily understood that the home is ill cared for, as it is only in fixed habitations that men try to obtain domestic comforts. The huts of these Bedouins consist of four walls, built of stones, sometimes of nothing but turf put together, without mortar; no chimney, two doors, one in front, and the other behind, to take advantage of the wind; and an opening, by courtesy called a window, in which the glass has been replaced by sheepskin in the state of parchment.

"In the inside may be seen two or three wooden stools, an iron pot, an old wooden bed full of heather or potatoes, without curtains and without blankets, a churn, two or three plates, a shovel, a spade, and a pipe. The cow, if there is one, has no other stable than the kitchen, or even the room itself, under the pretext that it is more convenient to have the animal at hand when her milk is wanted [1]."

"At Dungarvan," says M. Pichot, "our carriage was suddenly surrounded by about thirty real Irish mendicants. If I were to believe my imagination, I should say there were a hundred instead of thirty. I still have before my eyes that horrible spectacle, I hear those lamentables cries, I smell those stinking exhalations. Sometimes they seem to surround me like the head of the hydra, more terrible than any of the monsters of any mythology or of the Virgilian or Dantean pandemonium, such was the agglomeration of grimacing faces around us. Sometimes, on the contrary, all these livid heads, all these dislocated bodies, seemed to multiply themselves by the effects of the eagerness with which they separated and crossed to go round the carriage and hold out their hands wherever they heard the clink of a bit of money."

"At Dungarvan, as elsewhere, no trade or labour is so profitable for a family as the lucky accident of an infirmity, or a deformity which permits them to go and hold out their hands, and sing their complaints in the streets. Poor homes are envied for their lame, their cripple, their rickety child or blind old men, as these are

1. Pichot, vol. II, pp. 463 to 465.

the most useful members of the family. The new-born which was drowned in the Eurotas at Sparta, is at Dungarvan reared with particular care[1]."

"At Kilkenny, the carriage was completely surrounded by mendicants, and nothing could be heard anywhere except the varied cries distinguishable by the difference of their voices, and their ages and sexes. Their clothes, that is to say the tatters of the women, which hung down to their ancles, allowed to be seen what is concealed everywhere else, although here they are not deemed shameful. I saw a mother picking up the skins of gooseberries, which one of my companions had spit out, and push them into the mouth of her infant. Since I left Fondi, in the kingdom of Naples, I have never seen anything like it[2]."

"If industry had made more progress, and a good use were made of the resources of the country, Ireland could nourish three times her present number of inhabitants. During the whole winter there is no work to be had; and the peasants subsist upon the produce of the potatoe field which adjoins their cabins. When spring returns, the Irishman shuts up his cabin, and his wife and ragged children drag themselves along the roads, and beg at the doors of the farmers to support existence until the arrival of the potato harvest. Other peasants, who are without families, quit for ever the scene of their miseries, in order to find a living more or less certain in the English factories[3]."

"The poor of the suburbs cross in hundreds the most beautiful quarters of Dublin to receive in one of the principal houses of refuge, situated upon the quay in the centre of the town, their daily allowance of food, distributed in three meals: breakfast, dinner, and supper. These mobs of beggars are to be seen in the streets going and coming, producing the most powerful and painful impression which can possibly accompany the traveller in his way, and which does not leave him when he quits the capital of Ireland[4]."

"In the cabins of the fishermen may be seen little half-naked fair-haired children upon the floors of holes hollowed out of the earth, and covered with turf and mud which are called cabins, living, playing, and wallowing amongst the little pigs which reside with them. The interior of these habitations presents everywhere the same aspect of extreme poverty, which at every step oppresses the heart, and renders an excursion into the interior

1. Pichot, vol. I, pp. 224, 229. — 2. Raumer, pp. 309, 310. — 3. Solitaire, vol. II, p. 532. — 4. *Idem*. p. 547.

of the country ineffably painful. Every where misfortune provokes compassion, every where it seems to claim alms, which your heart cannot refuse at the sight of entire populations plunged in distress whom you meet at every step in a fertile land full of uncultivated estates. This distress of the Irish people reaches the extremest limits of poverty. Their costume presents nothing to the view except rags similar to the rubbish of the shop of a *chiffonnier*, or rag-merchant. The cottages of the peasants, without comparing them to the subterraneous huts of which we have spoken, would scarcely be considered in England or Scotland fit for barns for cattle [1]."

But let us take courage, and descend into the lowest and last retreat of misery, into the Irish cottage which is found everywhere, and which becomes finally the true type of the habitations of the country. "An Irish cottage," says M. Prévost, "is a sort of shed, about twelve feet long and ten broad. The walls are made of mud and flints, or of old and almost rotten planks; the roof is composed of a layer of clods of heather, spread over the laths. To prevent the wind from sweeping away this frail covering, the peasant has thrown over it some large stones, which often help not a little to ruin the feeble edifice. Generally, no windows are to be seen; light enters only by means of the door, or the hole which has been made in the roof, a hole which as may be supposed serves as a chimney, and which is surmounted outside by the remains of an old wicker basket instead of a chimney-pot. At first sight, the traveller thinks it impossible to penetrate into these sombre retreats, for the entrance is almost always obstructed by a dunghill, in which manure and filth swim about between gutters of foul and muddy water. This fetid receptacle is crossed by means of stepping stones, and he must deem himself lucky who crosses without splashing. I asked a farmer one day why he did not throw dung-heap behind his cabin, instead of leaving it at the entry. 'It is,' he replied, 'because we have no other place.' You have scarcely succeeded in entering one of these houses when you are almost suffocated by a thick smoke, which descends into your throat, and prevents you for some minutes from distinguishing any thing else except a peat-fire opposite the door. When your eyes are somewhat accustomed to the obscurity, and you can see around you, you are seized with pity by a spectacle of misery surpassing everything you have imagined. In this same damp room live

1. Solitaire, vol. II, p. 552.

pell-mell two, three, and sometimes four generations of human beings. The sow seems a member of the family as she lies crouched in her corner, surrounded by the children. The hens are roosted in the holes under the thatch, or upon the top of some old trunk. In the closest and best-sheltered corner is seen an old shake-down, which is the bed of the grandfather. As for the other members of the family, they all lie down together upon straw, or some handfuls of heather. The catalogue of the furniture is soon made; it consists first of all of an iron pot for boiling the potatoes, a wicker basket to hold them in, two stone seats or banks of earth set in the wall, a three-legged stool upon which they seat the guest they receive; an old dresser to which are hooked some broken plates; add to these some garden tools scattered here and there, or set up in corners, a crucifix crowned with a glory of laurels which has been blessed by the priest, some strangely illuminated saints, and you will have a complete Irish home: yet the inhabitants of these huts so naked and shattered, less wholesome and comfortable than the wigwam of the Indian, are not at all regarded as belonging to the most miserable class. There are thousands of human beings with still more to complain of, who have neither a bit of land to grub up, nor a den in which to shelter themselves, and who are reduced to wander as mendicants or to go into the workhouse, exchanging their liberty for two rations of potatoes per day [1]."

"The grandfather's chair, in the house into which I entered, consisted of three small planks of wood arranged as a triangle, and leaving a void in the middle; the seat was supported by three girders, two of which served as legs, and the third rose up two or three feet, and answered the purpose of a back. The wooden goblet called *mether*, in which I was offered some whiskey, was square and not round, as all the glasses and cups are which are known and used in other parts of the world. I confess that the first time I raised it to my lips I spilt at least half the liquid which it contained; it was necessary that I should study awhile prior to succeeding in adjusting my mouth conveniently to one of the large angular sides of that ancient oaken vase, which might have been in use at the feasts of the Druids. The means of transport employed by the peasants of Connaught are just as comfortable as the memorable *mether* of which I have given you a description. The first vehicle that I met on leaving

1. Prévost, pp. 375, etc.

the cabin consisted simply of a plank of wood fixed between two massive wheels without spokes, like the card-board wheels which children cut for their little carts, which they make to be drawn along by flies and beetles. Two gigantic pigs drew with difficulty this heavy rolling machine, upon which sat at their ease three robust lads [1]. "

" You are not surprised to see coming out of the Irish cottages men, women, and children, all equally ragged. The mud huts have generally no opening except the door, as if the misery they conceal were afraid of the light. An idea of their internal arrangement can be obtained from those left empty by emigration, and through a hole in the roof or a gap in the walls, by which the passer-by may gaze freely. Those which are still inhabited or habitable have adjoined to them a sty for the sow; but there are some in which this animal shares familiarly the common apartment, which is luckier than its master, for if the leavings of human food are insufficient for her, as generally happens, she has other resources, and can seek her fortune upon the sides of the road [2]. "

" Here there are no words which can describe what strikes the eye upon all sides; it is necessary to have seen those houses. What have I said, houses? no, those cabins..... Have I said cabins? no, those holes, mostly without windows or light of any kind, the same outlet serving for men and pigs; lying together in the same small space, the pigs fresh and well fed, and the men clothed in rags. The comfortable inhabitants of the town excepted, I have not seen a single Irishman, in a thousand, who had a coat, shirt, and trowsers without holes [3]. "

Such are the doleful habitations of the Irish in the country. Let us glance at the towns, in favour of which the last writer has made his reservations; and, to see the best, let us survey the capital. Undoubtedly the following picture does not include the whole of Dublin, but it is the picture of the part most essentially Catholic, and it is precisely what is most suitable to our subject. " All the picturesque aspects, " says the same writer, " of the beautiful capital of Ireland are spoiled or I may say sullied by those swarms of mendicants who seem to issue out of the earth. As for me, thought I, when walking the other day with a respectable gentleman, who was obliging enough to act as my *cicerone*, it is impossible to admire at my ease your edifices and your works of art, while I meet at each step my fellow-creatures who are dying of fa

1. Prévost, pp. 381, 383. — 2. Pichot, vol. I, p. 224. — 3. Raumer, vol. II, p. 315.

mine; now a ghostly woman with a dying infant hanging at her breast; and then a tottering and infirm old man showing in the sun his hideous sores and fleshless limbs.

"It is difficult to form an idea of the horrible misery which reigns here. Day and night, upon the steps of the most beautiful hotels, or under the porticoes of the churches or public buildings, you knock your feet in passing against wretches who have scarcely strength to implore your charity in a doleful voice. Parliament votes a new poor law in vain, and the local authorities in vain issue severe regulations for the prevention and suppression of mendicity; the constables themselves, in spite of the orders they have received, cannot and dare not prevent wretches dying of famine from holding out their hands and begging from the passers-by. But it is especially in the ancient quarter, known under the name of the Liberties, that Irish pauperism may be seen in all its nakedness. Courage is needed to enter alone and on foot into this dark labyrinth, this abyss of misery and corruption. In the evening, unfortunate women in rags, sometimes quite young girls, infants of twelve years old, accost the stranger and offer him their bodies at a low price, and if he refuses they try to move his pity, and merely ask alms.

"Those mansions in which dwelt the rich and noble and most of the English race, but lately so brilliant and so splendid, are, now that the nobility have emigrated to the other side of the Liffey, black and dilapidated; the poor having thrown themselves into these abandoned palaces, and multiplied in them in frightful numbers. Some of these houses have no roofs, others neither doors nor windows; also, it is chiefly in the cellars that the wretched population of the Liberties searches for shelter from the cold and wet. Sometimes upon the steps of these retreats you may see squatted down two or three generations of these wretched creatures; half naked children tumbling and playing carelessly about: these are least to be pitied; they do not understand as yet as the sadness of their lot; the father and mother are grave and gloomy; they know what they have suffered, and they despair of the future; with them is the grandmother, the head of the unhappy tribe; she is generally quite brutified by a long life of sufferings and privations; with a steady look and a motionless body, she smokes tranquilly her old black pipe, and appears to have become equally insensible to pleasure and pain. The pencil and palette of a Murillo or a Ribeira are necessary to sketch all these desolate heads, all these sinister faces, to paint all these rags so strangely torn, slashed, and patched. When a puff of wind throws open up to the neck the cloak which hides the misery of most of the Irish, it is seen that the wearer has only on some fragments of shirts and pantaloons, and it is a thought to make one shiver to reflect that in a few weeks winter will come and undoubtedly decimate that unfortunate *caste*. When famine makes itself cruelly felt and become intolerable, they are seen leaving their holes in bands and spreading over the town, the squares, and the public walks. They march together in silence, asking nothing, contenting themselves with showing to the rich their ragged vestments as their only reproach; a few sobs or a wailing cry is sometimes however torn by anxiety and want from the bosom of some poor mother carrying her infant upon her back, in the folds of her coarse cloak. This ragged procession, this ill-looking *cortége*, inspires at least terror into those who have not been touched by compassion. Every one hurries to give alms to these poor creatures, who then return to their brethren, who have been waiting for them impatiently in their doleful abodes[1]. "

" Dublin alone possesses more mendicants than Scotland altogether has had in twenty years. "

But this last word reminds us of the second part of our comparison; let us then cross the channel, and after having seen the miseries of Catholic Ireland, witness the prosperity of Protestant Scotland.

We read the following in the *Revue des Deux-Mondes*, of the year and month in which we write, January, 1854 : " Scotland is one of the greatest examples which exists in the world of the power of man over nature. I know nothing to rival to it except Holland; even Switzerland does not offer greater obstacles to human industry. What adds to the marvellousness of this development of prosperity upon an ungrateful soil is that it is quite recent. A century ago, Scotland was still one of the poorest and most barbarous countries in Europe. It may now be asserted that there is not under the sun a happier or better-regulated country. Her total production has increased tenfold in the course of this century. Agricultural produce has alone increased in enormous proportions. Food is yearly produced there in an abundance which permits an immense annual exportation. The English themselves confess that Scottish agriculture is now superior to English agriculture, at least in several respects; it is into Scotland

1, Prévost, pp. 5 to 8.

that the cultivators send their sons as apprentices upon the model farms; the best books on agriculture which have appeared of late have been published in Scotland, and when English landlords wish for a good factor or *bailiff,* they go into Scotland in search of him. The average consumption there is two hundred pounds a-head as in England, while in France it is only one hundred and forty. How has Scotland reached this fair result in spite of a soil and climate naturally unfertile? The Scotch make up for the inferiority of their capital in comparison with the English by a greater spirit of economy, and more rude and assiduous personal toil. The farmers more generally work themselves, and, besides, their capital increases quickly.

" Nowhere has the nature of leases been the subject of such a profound study. They may be said to have arrived in this respect at perfection. We must go into Scotland to find models when we undertake to introduce leases into a country in which they do not exist, and to transform poor and ignorant cultivators, *des métayers* (persons who work for half the produce), *des bordiers,* the servants at wages, into comfortable and intelligent farmers. Rents are on an average nearly as high in the best parts of Scotland as they are in England; there are even places where they are higher, and the interior of the farms, formerly so poor, present a striking air of comfort.

" In aid of the excellent system of leases has come the best organization of credit in the world. Coolness, exactitude, sobriety, the genius of calculation, are in Scotland such profoundly national qualities, that a large system of credit has been established without inconvenience, and borne the most magnificent fruits. All the countrymen of Adam Smith are more or less impregnated with his sagacious and mater-of-fact spirit. The admirable mechanism of the banks affords incredible facilities in the transaction of business; and agriculture is as perfect as industry. It may be said that there never is any want of any reasonable amount of money even for agricultural speculations. Every one makes it a point of honour not to abuse it, and thus it is maintained universally.

" The means for the diffusion of the knowledge of good methods or improvements are at least as much employed in Scotland as in England. The Agricultural Society distributes yearly many prizes divided into different classes; agricultural methods, special cultures, woods and plantations, clearing waste lands, agricultural machines, cattle of all kinds, dairy produce, rural buildings. These competitions, at which the humblest farmer sits side by side with the highest of the aristocracy, are at least as renowned as those of the same kind in England. The society possesses a museum in Edinburgh, where models are to be found of all the instruments used in Europe, specimens of all the grains cultivated, and correct pictures of all the prize cattle since the commencement of the competitions.

"All these encouragements, however powerful they may be, do not suffice to explain the prodigious progress of Scotch agriculture; the true causes are the same as in England; — I mean industrial wealth and free institutions. If the history of English industry is admirable, what is to be said of that of Scotland! The vale of Clyde, formerly a desert, now rivals the rich county of Lancashire for its coal-pits, factories of all kinds, and its immense navigation. The germ of this wealth did not exist in 1750; it is English capital which, aided by the frugal and laborious genius of Scotland, has transformed to such a degree in so few years that inert land. This industrial impulse has been followed, as it always is, by a corresponding agricultural progress."

"When brought suddenly into contact with English manners and laws, the Scottish people shewed themselves to be one of the fittest to understand the benefits of individual independence and voluntary order. She has from the very first surpassed England herself, for it may be said in a political point of view that Scotland is England improved. Nowhere in Europe there is less of governmental and administrative machinery, and we must go to America to find equal simplicity. The much-vaunted system of administrative centralization which fleeces three-fourths of France, to the profit of the remaining fourth, and which everywhere suffocates individual or local enterprize (*et qui étouffe partout l'initiative personnelle ou locale*) is there absolutely unknown; the places are few, and mostly unpaid.

"The spirit of order and economy which every one carries into his private affairs, passes into the management of public affairs, and they effect these more with little money than is accomplished elsewhere with much. What the taxes cannot do, the spirit of association and enterprize achieves quicker and cheaper. The lessons of economical science have found in Scotland their most direct and complete application.

"A Scotchman never thinks of any other support than himself. He does not pass his time in agitation and useless errands; he has nothing to ask or beg. Giving himself entirely to his own affairs, he conducts them well, because nothing leads him away or astray.

There are none of those rivalries to which ambition gives rise; every one lives as he likes in his own home, and when they can be of use to each other, as is often the case, arrangements are easily made for objects of common utility. Scotland is a family.

"On descending the Lammermoor Hills, the undulating plains are seen, which surround Edinburgh for more than a million acres (500,000 hectares), which are called the Lothians. The cultivation is here really unrivalled. Rents of 100, or 200, or 300 francs, or four, eight, or twelve pounds the *hectare* (more than two acres) are quite common. The soil was formerly deemed incapable of growing rye, and they grew nothing but barley and oats. Notwithstanding their enormous rents, the Lothian farmers get on very well. They have all handsome houses, and whatever may be said of their national frugality, they live as well as many of our proprietors, even those who are best off. All the arable land in Scotland is now under cultivation, and even the waste lands are reclaimed intelligently and profitably. This country lives thus sheltered from the sufferings and anxieties which arise from over-population. It never can have anything to fear for its subsistence, since it voluntarily exports much of its agricultural produce; while the small number and the sobriety of its consumers permits it to change into capital a great part of its receipts.

"In the Highlands, the most barren part of Scotland, which formerly contained a race so troublesome to their neighbours, marauding habits have given place to regular and laborious pursuits; there has not been, as M. Sismondi has said, an economy of labour and of happiness, but a notable increase of both. The profound security enjoyed in this country makes residence in these mountains exceedingly attractive, notwithstanding the dulness of the climate. The overthrown huts of the clans have been succeeded by comfortable residences. Not only have the ancient chiefs built mansions upon the ruins of cottages, but rich Englishmen have purchased estates, and gone to live upon them. If the outside of the house is rough and solitary, the inside always presents all the appliances of luxury. Excellent roads and steam-boats upon the lakes make accessible with ease even the most solitary corners[1]."

Does the agricultural prosperity of Scotland date from Catholic times? The *Dictionnaire de la Conversation* answers:

"Until the commencement of the fifteenth century, Scotland had made little progress in civilization. War was the only busi-

1. *Revue Britannique*, 1854, 1st of January. — Lavergne, pp. 149 to 182.

ness of the chieftains, and they found their only pastime in the chase and drunkenness. The direct consequences of despotism, servility, laziness, and misery shewed themselves in Scotland in their most hideous forms. The people followed the example set them by their leaders; they lived upon the charity of the great, and were ignorant of every kind of industry; nearly every article of consumption came from Flanders. At that time agriculture produced nothing in Scotland beyond what was strictly necessary. Bread was looked upon as a delicacy. Civil wars disturbed continually the reign of the laws."

Such was the Scotland of the fifteenth century. What was it that changed it even according to the testimony of our author? Read: "Protestant beliefs were early spread in Scotland, and, from the fifteenth century, there were amongst the mountains of the Highlands a great number of secret partisans of the doctrine of Wycliff, who read in the bosom of their solitudes the English translation of the Bible. The ignorance of the churchmen and laymen of Scotland opposed for a long time the propagation of the new faith. While the churches struggled agamst the propagation of protestantism by the most violent means, the new religion acquired powerful partisans amongst the nobility. The bishops had long been the object of the envy and jealousy of the nobles, while the churchmen of inferior rank were generally despised for their ignorance, and hated for the oppressions they practised against the lower classes of the people. The inclination of the Scotch to meditation greatly facilitated the propagation of the new doctrines. The decree of the Parliament of 1543, which permitted the people to read the Bible in their own tongue, was one of the most active means of this propagation."

If the admirable agriculture of Scotland does not date from Catholic times, may we not suppose that at that epoch at least the seeds of it had been sown? No, on the contrary the Reformation had to work a long time in the country, prior to bringing out the love of labour, and the intelligence of which we now see the results.

Saint-Germain Leduc says in effect: "For a long time Scotland had nothing but wretched oaten and barley cakes, which was found upon every table. The farms, the villages, and even the small towns, were ignorant of wheaten bread.

In the year 1727 a field of wheat, in the neighbourhood of Edinburgh, was regarded as a prodigious attempt, and many honest Scotchmen came down from their mountains to see it with their own eyes. Scotland now produces ten times more wheat than in 1780, and it is now the bread in the towns, the villages, and even most of the farms[1]."

When the prosperity of a people springs from their virtues and from accidental circumstances, we may be sure that it will show itself under different forms: thus Scotland is flourishing not only in agriculture, but also in industry and commerce; nearly all the workshops and factories have been brought in this country into as high a degree of perfection as in England. Since 1750, they have especially worked in flax and hemp. Nevertheless, the fabrication of fine linen has diminished considerably, in consequence of the competition of the Northern or Protestant parts of Ireland.

"Scotland possesses also an immense number of factories of soap, candles, starch, immense tanneries, important distilleries, etc. Fishing occupies many hands. Scotland has an infinite number of saw-mills. Most of the machines now used in manufactures are of Scottish origin. Their construction, that particularly of steam-engines, forms an important branch of trade. In the Scottish ports may be seen a multitude of carpenters' yards for building and repairing many ships of all sizes."

"Scotland did not in former times take more than a small share in foreign commerce. Her commerce with the North and West of Europe dates from the time of Cromwell. In the middle of the following century, immense cargoes of goods were sent to Holland, Sweden, and the ports of the Baltic. Scottish trade sent its products chiefly to Archangel, Spain, Portugal, the Mediterranean, and Canada. The Clyde is the *rendez-vous* of most of the ships sent to North and South America. A very active commerce also takes place with London. The merchant marine of Scotland has 2,500 ships[2]."

Let us complete the parallel by adding a picture of a Scottish town, as we have given one of an Irish town. We have seen Catholic Dublin; let us see Protestant Edinburgh:

"The city of Edinburgh is remarkable for its University, the activity of its printing presses, and the importance of its publishing trade, which has earned it the name of the Modern Athens, for its libraries, for its collection of natural history, for its numerous institutions for the spread of instruction and virtue amongst the working classes, for its industry, and for its commerce[3]."

"Everything grateful in hospitality, and everything varied in learning, presents itself in turns to the foreigner who is admitted

1. Saint-Germain Leduc, vol. III, p. 162. — 2. *Dictionnaire de la Conversation*, at the word ÉCOSSE. — 3. Balbi, p. 515.

into the *salons* of Edinburgh. Nowhere will he find more kindness, more obligingness, or more desire to please. The Scotch have well-founded pretensions in science and in arts, and every one tries to master some branch or other. There results from this more general information than is found elsewhere [1]."

"The University has long been celebrated for the talents of its professors, and especially for its School of Medicine. The number of professors is 27, that of students more than 2,000. They have the use of a library of more than 50,000 volumes, a beautiful museum of natural history, a botanical garden with hothouses; a basin for aquatic plants, and a hall for the lectures. The High School is frequented by more than 800 scholars. There are, besides, four English schools, under the protection of a Town Council, a drawing academy, a royal riding school, and several other establishments. The city possesses besides 25 scientific and literary societies, amongst which may be mentioned the Royal Society, established in 1782, the Wernerian Society, the Royal Society of Antiquaries, the Astronomical Institution, which possesses an observatory supplied with all the necessary instruments; they have there, moreover, several other useful associations, such as that of the Advocates', the Physicians' and Surgeons', and the Highland Society, formed by the nobility and gentry, and intended to grant rewards for reclamation of waste lands, for the advancement of agriculture, and the improvement of cattle and sheep. Commerce supports there twelve private banks, possessed of the privilege of circulating a certain number of bank-notes. Philanthropic views are dominant over the management of the prisons, of 11 hospitals, of 60 houses of charity, and a crowd of other benevolent institutions. Finally, the Scottish capital possesses seven public libraries, and publishes eleven literary, learned, or political journals. It has been remarked that this combination of learned men has diffused through the different classes of society the gentle frankness, the polished manners, and the toleration of opinions which distinguishes ordinarily the great capitals [2]."

"The new town of Edinburgh shines chiefly by its regularity, cleanliness, aristocratic decorations, and all the social and domestic advantages. The large streets, squares, gardens, belong to all the styles, Greek or Gothic; colonnades, ogives, statues, compose the exterior of the city. The social advantages which make Edinburgh, without a single exception in Great Britain, a place at least

1. D'Haussez, vol. II, p. 149. — 2. Malte-Brun, book the 60th, pp. 164 and 165.

in the first rank, draw to it justly persons who love the fine arts, sciences, and letters, and who take pleasure in moral and instructive conversations. How is possible not to love Scotland with such advantages and attractions?

"I avow that I have never experienced a more agreeable or durable impression than that derived from my sojourn in that royal metropolis of the East of Scotland. To what kind of superiority can a modern town aspire, if it is not to that of shining at once by graceful and imposing buildings, by the ineffable charm of a society of men and women who add almost always to the piquant traits of wit solidity of judgment, and austere and religious chastity of morals! Edinburgh is a beacon light, to which intelligent men ought to turn who fear the rocks. Edinburgh is like a star of civilization which shines upon the Old and the New World, and it would be wise to take it as our guide in the obscurity in which we walk often without circumspection [1]."

But does not Edinburgh, as the capital, much surpass what is to be seen in the provinces? To know it, let us follow our traveller: "I do not know a coach-service comparable to that which took us to Aberdeen, in dignity, cleanliness, and rapidity. Coachman, guard, coach, and horses, are irreproachably got up, and it is rather the carriage of a king in red livery which carries you along than that of a public service. An active and intelligent population of merchants, agriculturists, and workmen has succeeded in raising out of ruins a town like Aberdeen. Look at the great markets, the post-office, the great cemetery with its Ionian colonnade, Marshal College, its statues, its churches, its hospitals, its multiplied benevolent institutions, its well-regulated factories, and you will be convinced that labour and religious generosity alone found such rich and useful creations.

"No doubt women are not entirely sheltered from the inconveniences of industrial labour in the factories of the town; but on the other hand how many evils may be prevented by assiduous occupation with one task? What a grand spectacle is this feminine world assembled upon a few square yards, and successively transforming the raw material into thread of all dimensions, from the thickest to the imperceptible, for the use of all the nations of the globe! It is not astonishing that Scotland should be the country of Adam Smith and James Watt!

"The library, and there is no want of books in the public esta-

1. Trabaud, pp. 292, 299.

blishments of Great Britain, was naturally supplied with works on christian morals, and industrial and commercial economy; and when I reflected that the cotton manufacture was in its infancy only a century ago, the spectacle at Banner-Mill appeared to me still more grand [1].

"Industrial activity has been added to the commercial opulence of Glasgow, and from this sum of wealth, achieved by intelligence, labour, and some natural advantages, has sprung this little world of three hundred thousand souls, living in the midst of one of the most magnificent cities of the globe. This population has increased in a manner almost fabulous; in 1651, the most ancient census known, it was only 14,000 souls; in 1789, it was 50,000; in 1830, 200,000; and in 1840, 250,000 souls. If by first town or capital we meant what has always been the official capital, a monumental city inhabited by a peaceful society of intelligent and literary men the palm of precedence must be assigned to Edinburgh; Glasgow, on the contrary, will obtain the precedence, if to an illustrious past they add a prodigious quantity of modern documents, majestic quarters sometimes superior to those of Paris and London, and a commercial movement never before heard of, sustained by a numerous population[2]."

We have compared Ireland and Scotland, and we have seen where the superiority is found. We shall not insist upon it to make it more felt, but before finishing we shall reply to an objection which we have ourselves raised: does not this difference arise from other causes than differences of religious belief? From the difference of geographical position, legislation, etc.? Our reply shall be very simple; leave Scotland aside, and compare Ireland with Ireland, that is to say the Catholic South with the Protestant North. If the same conclusion is returned, it will be all the stronger, because the South of Ireland enjoys a soil, a climate, and natural ports much superior to those of the North. Here, as elsewhere, we shall above all allow Roman Catholic authors to speak:

"The Irish of the North," says M. Prévost, "have from times immemorial devoted themselves to the linen manufacture, yet they were still much behind and much below the people of the continent. When the revocation of the Edict of Nantes drove from France so many industrious Protestants, the English government shewed much zeal in attracting these exiles into Ireland. The Parliament voted a sum which was set apart to their establishment, and in

1. Trabaud, pp. 322 to 327. — 2. *Idem*, p. 332.

exchange confided to them the mission of instructing and training the native workmen. The first great linen and cambric factories of Belfast were founded by French immigrants, and in looking over the *Commercial Almanack* of that city, you may still discover French names. The population increased; Belfast felt suffocated in its girdle of walls; the fortifications were destroyed, the ditches were filled up, and the ruins of the citadel served to erect new factories...

"Few towns possess so many establishments destined to succour the unfortunate as Belfast; houses of refuge are to be seen there for almost all sorts of misfortune. There are special hospitals for the blind, the deaf and dumb, the fever-patients, lunatics, the feeble; with asylums for penitent girls, liberated convicts, domestics out of place, and women out of work. There are at Belfast thirteen Presbyterian chapels, three chapels set apart to the Anglican worship, and two Catholic churches. It may thus be seen that the puritan sect is alone more powerful than the two others. Belfast is not only the capital of commerce in Ireland; it is also the metropolis of puritanism.[1]"

Belfast is a remarkable example of the prosperity of the Irish and Protestant towns of the North: "In 1786, Belfast was an unimportant place, with a wretched harbour; and the revenue of its port was but 1,500*l.* In 1838, it contained 50 factory steam-engines; in 1841, its mills for spinning linen-yarn alone amounted to 25, one of the principal employing 800 hands; in 1846, the Tidal Harbour commissioners pronounced it 'the first town in Ireland for enterprise and commercial prosperity,' and in 1850, its port revenues had increased to 29,000*l.* [2]."

"Londonderry, in the North, appears to be in a very flourishing state; a great activity reigns there, and the inhabitants are almost all Presbyterians and merchants. The houses are well built, the quays large and convenient. The sojourn which I had previously made at Belfast rendered it unnecessary for me to stop at Londonderry, where I should not have anything to observe but the laborious habits, the regular and uniform morals, of a population which is not really Irish, but Anglo-Scottish in its origin and character.

"The city is surrounded with ravishing scenery. During the first half of the day I traversed fertile fields and well-kept and beautiful domains. I was still in one of the favoured districts of the North of Ireland, which owe their prosperity to rich and industrious English and Scottish colonists[3]."

1. Prevost, pp. 335, 337. — 2. Dill, p. 29. — 3. Prevost, p. 362.

"The village *Morevian*, established at Grace-Hill, always in the Protestant North, at about two miles from Ballymeno, contains about four hundred persons of the two sexes; it consists of four streets and is built with much taste; the church, which is a pretty edifice, is placed in the centre. Every house has a garden behind it. The profusion of flowers which they place before their houses, as well as those of their gardens and the palissades which surround all, produce an extremely agreeable effect, and give the whole an air of happiness. The establishment seemed perfectly regulated. The most minutious order seemed to have presided over the details [1]."

Has this contrast between the North and the South struck none but the eyes of Protestants? No, hear the voice of a Catholic who is about to point it out: "I left the industrious colonies of the North," says M. Prévost, "and suddenly the scene changed, and I found again the deserts, heather, bogs, tottering hovels, in which are huddled together successions of famished generations. Still sadder pictures revealed to me that I had penetrated into the heart of Donegal, one of the poorest and most backward counties of Ireland. As I advanced, the scenery became more sombre and savage... The city of Donegal, the county-town, is large and populous; it is quite an Irish town, with crooked streets and ruinous houses scattered here and there in disorder. The whole population seemed to live upon the public road. The squares are continually encumbered with men, women, and children, almost naked. The spectacle affected me painfully; I recollected that at Belfast, and on the previous evening at Londonderry, I had seen a whole people busy at work. Capital is deficient at Donegal, as in many other Irish towns, which are equally gorged with able and robust inhabitants doomed to vegetate rather than live, and spend their days without being able to find work [2]."

"Kilkenny was an important town when Belfast was only a village; it has had several factories, eleven water-mills, and such a carpet factory that its English rival, to avoid the competition, demanded the repeal of the Union! In 1834, Mr. Inglis saw only one man in the principal factory which formerly employed two hundred workmen. He says, of the eleven water mills only one goes, and that not to move machinery, but only to prevent them rotting [3]."

The prosperity of the North of Ireland has something in it which rejoices the heart of a Frenchman when he knows the origin of it,

1. Saint-Germain Leduc, p. 209. — 2. Prevost, pp. 362 to 365. — 3. Dill, p. 30.

and we sympathize with the writer who expressed himself as follows only a few days ago in the *Siècle* : —

" Allow me to say in passing, for the honour of the French name, that in Ireland, not less than in Germany, in the two Hessies, in Prussia, at Berlin, the French refugees expelled from their country by the intolerance of the *grand roi*, have always and everywhere distinguished themselves by their rare intelligence, by their inventive spirit, and their ability and activity in industry. In 1693, three French congregations were founded in Dublin. A regiment of French Protestants fought under William III. at the battle of the Boyne, and became resident in Ireland after the peace. Even to this day traces of these French refugees are found at Waterford, at Lisburn, and especially at Portarlington, where they founded good schools. They conducted themselves well in these different localities, and made themselves remarkable by the fabrication of silk, by the culture of flowers, and even by their success in literature and arts : and they conciliated general esteem by the purity of their morals [1]."

But we shall not confine ourselves to the impression of travellers; let us consult an Irishman upon Ireland, and as he is a Protestant, let us not accept any of his documents except those which, by being taken from statistics, cannot be suspected of partiality :

" By the census of 1841, the proportions of the population in *each* province who could neither read nor write were : Protestant Ulster, 33 per cent.; Roman Connaught, 64. Thus, it appears that, of persons totally ignorant, there were then in Ulster one-half less than in Connaught. Not *less* difference is found in the *general* intelligence of those who can read and write; and *much more* in their *religious* knowledge ; the northern child evincing an acquaintance with revealed truth not often found in the southern grandfather. Indeed, the great educational superiority of Ulster is clearly proved by the fact, that, while Connaught almost exclusively depends on national schools for education, Ulster has many others besides, yet, with twice the population, the latter province contains thrice as many national schools as the former. And, though a large number of the youth of Ulster are educated at the Scotch universities, yet, during the session of 1849, the students attending the Belfast Queen's College amounted to 192 ; while in that of Cork, there were 115 ; in that of Galway, 68 ; and of this latter number, some of the most eminent were natives of Ulster. While, as to industrial

1. *Le Siècle*, 4th August, 1853.

knowledge, we shall only add, that the south has been sending individuals to the north to learn the cultivation and manufacture of flax; and the National Board is obliged to employ northern females to teach their southern schools the sewed muslin manufacture.

"The difference in moral character is still more remarkable. Of the 25,000 troops usually stationed in Ireland, scarce 3,000 are found in Ulster, and, except in its southern counties, even these are wholly unnecessary. Not a soldier is stationed betwen Belfast and Derry, a distance of 70 miles, embracing two most populous counties and various large towns. Of our 13,000 police, the number stationed in Ulster, in 1851, was 1,901, little more than a seventh of the force for a third of the population. And our prison statistics prove that even these are comparatively unnecessary. Of our 33,326 committals in 1850, the number in Ulster was 5,260, not one-sixth part. Yet, considering how many crimes escape detection in the south from the prevailing conspiracy against the laws, and how few, in the north, from the opposite cause, even this is too large a figure to represent the proportion of actual crime.

"The *character* of crime shows a still more remarkable difference. At almost every northern assizes, the first sentence of the judge's opening address to the grand jury is one of congratulation on the peace of their county, and the lightness of their calendar. Comparatively few are transported from Ulster; and capital crimes occur there so rarely, that of 23 executions which took place in Ireland, in the year 1849 and 1850, only two occurred in Ulster.

"In short, the vast moral superiority of that province is seen on every hand. In many districts, the doors of the dwellings are seldom locked; in numbers of shops a child can safely deal; while the atrocities which are the rule elsewhere are the exception in Ulster. There landlords are scarce ever shot, murderers sheltered, or wretches known to swear away innocent life; while in most counties assizes last a day or two, jails are half empty, and gibbets scarce ever required. During the assassinations of 1848, one threatening letter was sent to the county Derry to a landlord of high respectability; and it came from *Connaught!* The excitement it created was intense (abundant proof of the novelty of the occurrence); and the people formed themselves into a guard, and kept sentry for weeks round the gentleman's demesne; yet some journals would persuade us that, for the last few years, Ulster has become a scene of agrarian disturbance!

"Now, of course, it is impossible fully to estimate the influence exerted on Ulster's prosperity by its superior light and virtue, in the security of property, the influx of capital, the encouragement of enterprise, and, above all, that general elevation and success which are the sure fruits of education and morality. But some idea of its magnitude may be formed from the fact that with one-third of the population, Ulster's share of the police, jail, and poor-law expenses of Ireland, is, in round numbers, but one-eighth [1]."

"From the census of 1834, in Ulster the Protestants then were to the Roman Catholics in round numbers as 11 to 19; in Leinster as 2 to 11; in Munster as 1 to 20; and in Connaught as 1 to 23. But any one who consults the same authorities from which we have taken those of the other three provinces will find that *in all four*, as with Protestantism, so are the knowledge, virtue, and prosperity. To give one mere sample, in the year ending 1848, there were, in round numbers, 3 persons receiving relief out of every 100 in Ulster; 7 in Leinster; 14 in Munster; and 19 in Connaught! Here is a graduated scale singularly correspondent to the Protestantism of each province, and, excepting Connaught, the very reverse of what we were entitled to expect. For, besides other advantages, Leinster has long been the seat of government, and enjoyed the benefits of the "English pale;" not only is Munster the garden of Ireland, but its population are the oldest inhabitants of the island; while Ulster is a mere colony little more than 200 years old, and composed for the most part of a few Scotch adventurers, who were doomed to struggle for years against a host of difficulties.

"If from the *provinces* we descend to the *counties*, we find the same proportions prevailing with singular exactness. To make this perfectly clear, we shall contrast a few of the most Protestant with a few of the most Roman Catholic counties. In Antrim, the Protestants are to the Roman Catholics nearly as 3 to 1; in Down, more than 2 to 1; in Derry, about 1 to 1; and in Donegal, 1 to 3, while in Cork they are 1 to 16; Limerick, 1 to 22; Kerry and Waterford, 1 to 23; Mayo and Galway, 1 to 24. Now, mark how the light of each county is as to its Protestantism, with only an exception which establishes the rule; Donegal being mountainous, without a single large town; while Cork and Limerick are full of populous towns, with all their educational facilities. In 1841, the proportions who could neither read nor write, were: Antrim, 23 per cent.; Down, 27; Derry, 29; Limerick, 55; Donegal, 62; Cork, 68; Kerry, 72; Waterford, 73; Galway, 78; and Mayo, 80. Thus, in the most Roman Catholic counties, we have four-fifths of

1 Dill, pp. 80 to 82.

the people in total ignorance; in the most Protestant only one-fifth; and in all, with the above exception, the ignorance increasing as the Protestantism diminishes! We might further prove, that in all these counties those who can neither read nor write are almost *all* Roman Catholics. Instance Donegal, the only county out of its place in the above scale; and, according to a report of the Rev. E. M. Clarke, chaplain and local inspector, of 138 Protestants confined in Lifford jail in 1849, 91, or near three-fourths, could read; while of 922 Roman Catholic prisoners, only 213, or not one-fourth, could read. Indeed, all those districts which are remarkable for their religious and general ignorance, such as the West-coast region above noticed, are those in which the Church of Rome has for ages held unbroken sway.

"Nor is the contrast less remarkable in the crime than in the ignorance of these counties. In the four Protestant counties of Antrim, Down, Derry, and Donegal, the gross number of committals in 1848 was not in proportion to the population *one-fourth* that of the four Roman Catholic counties of Kerry, Limerick, Galway, and Mayo; yet, of the latter, none but Limerick belong to the 'disturbed districts.' Again, while from the prevailing conspiracy against justice in the latter, their convictions are not much over a *third* of their committals, in the former they are nearly *four-fifths*. And there is really no comparison as to the *character* of offences; for example, of 69 criminals hanged in Ireland in the years ending 1850, 13 were executed in Limerick alone, only 4 were hanged in Ulster, and only 1 in any of the above Protestant counties viz., in Donegal, the *least* Protestant. Finally, as a mere sample of their *temporal condition*, we find that, in the 4 Roman Catholic unions of Kanturk, Listowel, Castlebar, and Ballinrobe, there were, in 1848, *twelve times* as many paupers relieved, in proportion to their population, as in the 4 Protestant unions of Larne, Kilkeel, Coleraine, and Newton Limavady. And the awful state of these unions may be conceived from the fact, that half the population of Listowel, and one-third that of Castlebar and Ballinrobe, were at that period obliged to support the remainder!

"Lest any remnant of doubt should hang on the reader's mind as to the extent of the coincidence we are tracing; lest he should cherish the least suspicion that Ulster owes its superiority to some other cause which we are unable to discover, or unwilling to disclose, let us turn for a moment to its own counties. While in Antrim, its most Protestant county, the percentage who cannot read or write is 23, in Cavan, its most Roman Catholic, it is 51. With a population a little over that of Derry, that county has annually twice as many committals, and not one-third the proportional number of convictions. The number of police stationed in Derry in 1850 was 106, at the expense of 5,299*l.*; while in Cavan there were 396, at the cost of 16,985*l.*, — over thrice the expense, and near four times the force. In short, Cavan is notoriously the most turbulent county in Ulster, and constantly occupied by a large body of military; while the only troops in the entire county of Derry are a depot stationed in Londonderry city, whose services are scarcely ever required. From counties we might even descend to *parishes*. One of the richest in Antrim is the parish of Killagan, and one of the poorest, that of Cushenden; yet in the former the Protestants are to the Roman Catholics as 6 to 1, and in the latter as 1 to 9. Do you say the northern Roman Catholic was driven back to the mountains by the Ulster settlers? Then we ask, what has so generally driven the southern Roman Catholics to the mountains, too? By what other foes has he been pursued thither than those evils habits which compel men to retire before the advance of light and virtue? But not to dwell on this: go to some of our finest *plains*, where no stranger has disturbed the southern. In the diocese of Cashel, Roman Catholics are to Protestants in the enormous disproportion of 28 to 1; and that naturally luxuriant region has long been known as the place where the demon of murder holds his court, and those assassination clubs have existed where each deed of blood is deliberately planned. Do you impute these crimes to landlord oppression? We ask not why such oppression, often as intolerable in Ulster, occasions there so few dreadful crimes, and why these few are almost exclusively committed by ***Roman Catholics***; but we take you at once to the ***towns***, where no landlord can rack, but men rise or sink by their own conduct. Instance Belfast and Cork, in the former of which Roman Catholics are to Protestants as 1 to 2 1/2, and in the latter as 5 to 1; and in the 10 years ending 1851, the population of Belfast had increased 24,400, or near 33 per cent, and its trade and manufactures proportionally; while the population of Cork had in the same period increased 5,700, or not 5 per cent; and even this consists for the most part of paupers, whom during the last five years want has driven from the surrounding country! Nay, pass if you please through the ***streets*** of each town, and you will find that in ***both***, and with the very same opportunities, the Protestants are the highest and the Roman Catholics the lowest of the people.

"We really must not weary the reader; but, as the last resistless proof of the fact we are establishing, examine the ***individuals*** of each persuasion, and you will find the Roman Catholics as a ***class*** everywhere the lowest in knowledge, virtue, and wealth, the uneducated, the criminals, the servants of their own land. It is notorious that during the late famine, even in Ireland's most Protestant parts, the immense proportion of the ***relieving*** were Protestants, and of the ***relieved***, Roman Catholics. And our poor-house, jail, and hospital statistics usually show from twice to four times as many Romanist as Protestant inmates, in proportion to the denominations of each district. On the 8th of May, 1850, there were in Derry 41 Protestant and 118 Roman Catholic prisoners, being three times as many of the latter, in proportion to the population of the county; and on the 14th of May, in the same year, there were in Tralee jail 572 Roman Catholic and only 4 Protestant prisoners. In short, turn where you will, and the result is the same; you can generally tell the prevailing denomination from the appearance of every parish, every village, and almost every house in the land[1].

"If you next turn to the period of the famine, those scenes of horror which were so common in the south were scarcely known in the north of Ireland; and many of those who did perish there were natives of Connaught and Leinster, who poured into Ulster in quest of food. Of 10,000,000 *l.* of relief sent to Ireland at that period by public and private charity, scarce 1,000,000 *l.* is supposed to have reached Ulster; while that province actually contributed large sums for the relief of the south and west, and has ever since paid the rate-in-aid tax for the same end. Finally, if you look to its condition since 1847, you find that those calamities which have prostrated Munster and Connaught have fallen upon it with but mitigated severity. While Ireland has lost one-fifth of its inhabitants, Munster almost one-fourth, and Connaught nearly one-third, Ulster has not lost one-sixth. Its pauperism is not half so great as that of the other provinces, its proportion of the entire poor-rates of the country being also about an eighth. In a word, you find that Ulster, though exposed to every ordinary influence felt by Munster and Connaught, has scarce known the miseries which have given them such fearful notoriety. So soon as you enter that province, the entire aspect of the country changes. All around assume that air of social health which is so easily perceived, yet so

1. Dill, pp. 86 to 92.

difficult fully to describe. You have left behind the region of filthy cabins and swarming beggars, ruined villages and deserted farms, and you enter a territory of comparatively rich cultivation, studded with comfortable dwellings and thrifty towns. And you cannot but feel that, from whatever cause, Ulster is at least fifty years ahead of its sister provinces in all the true elements of national progress; and in its general aspect so much more resembles Britain than Ireland, that one could almost fancy some physical convulsion to have severed it from the one island and attached it to the other.[1] "

The objection could be made to this comparison between the North and the South, that the Protestants have been transplanted, are not of the same race as the Catholics of the South, and that therefore the signal distance between their degree of civilization is not to be explained solely by the opposition of their faith.

So be it; let us search elsewhere for men of the same origin and of the same race as the Irish Catholics. We find them in the Highlanders of Scotland. If it is race which makes civilization, these will not be civilized. If, on the contrary, the civilization is due to the religious faith, those Celts become Protestants ought to differ from the Celts who have remained Catholics in Ireland. The following is the answer which has been made to this objection in the Edinburgh *Witness* : " It is asserted that the same vices and the same miseries are found amongst the Highlanders of Scotland, under the wing of Presbyterianism, which are attributed to Popery in Ireland, and it is inferred that if these mountaineers are not only as poor but as vicious as the Irish people, it is an error to suppose that their religion has any thing to do with their perversity.

" We grant that the Highland Presbyterians are almost as poor as the Irish Papists; but we have never told that Popery was the sole cause of poverty. There are others, and there has been no want of them either in Ireland or amongst the Highlanders; what we wish to prove is that Romanism is the most influential cause of ruin and demoralization. When comparing the poverty of the two countries, to be just we ought to search what have been the relative advantages on each side. On the one side we find a soil full of riches, and on the other a poor and barren soil. In the one we find a climate, the natural warmth of which is enough to ripen grain equal to those of the most beautiful corn-fields of Europe; in the other we see a country a prey to flies and bogs, full of wild valleys and lakes, covered by a sky which does not permit the sun to show itself except at

1. Dill, pp. 29 to 32.

rare intervals; a country in which the ice and frost only go away to give place to deluges of rain. In the one, the earth conceals mineral riches, the materials for the arts and commerce, while there are not in the other any of these treasures. In the one, we find natural bays and harbours; in the other, the waves break in bays which afford no kind of shelter. In the one, we find great and numerous towns which promote industry by providing *depots* for its products; in the other, you have to go several hundred miles, and sometimes to cross an arm of the sea, to discover a market. In the one, they have exhausted all the resources and treasures of legislation, and spent millions in alms; in the other, nothing has been done by the nation; every thing which has been done has come from the spontaneous generosity and benevolence of individuals. Thus, in regard to everything necessary for the comfort of life and prosperity, these two countries are two extremes, whence seem to flow necessarily the poverty of the Scottish Highlanders and the wealth of the Irish. There certainly is a difference between the man who has not succeeded in turning a desert into a garden, and the man who has allowed a garden to change into a desert. In the first case, we see the labour and skill of men, unskilfully helped and insufficiently encouraged by the nation, unable to surmount the immense difficulties they have encountered; and in the latter, we see all the gifts of nature and all the benefits of legislation made useless, and the combined influences of these two resources rendered incapable of stopping the constant march of the people towards the abyss of physical evils and social ruin. We are obliged to confess before these features both sad that the most painful is still that which represents Ireland. In fact, misery has there attained a degree of intensity to which nothing comparable is to be found amongst the Highlanders.

"Where do we see in Scotland what is seen in Ireland? Men dying of famine in hundreds and thousands, the roads and ditches full of the sick and dead, villages the whole population of which have been abandoned by the owners to the wind and rain, and church-yards presenting the revolting spectacle of dogs fighting for the ill-entered corpses? But it is not only a difference of degree that we wish to establish in this affair to ascertain which is the poorer of the two countries. We admit the fact of the excessive misery of the Highlanders, but we maintain that the causes above-mentioned, added to the feudal system which has always flourished in full force in the Highlands, explains the miserable condition of the Highlanders. It is not to any of these causes that the complicated evils of Ireland can be ascribed. Of all the evils stated, the only one found in Ireland is the feudal system; and moreover its influence has been modified by a great variety of circumstances.

"But the decisive point of our argument is here. The Papists of Ireland and the Protestants of the Highlands have this much in common, they are poor, very poor even; but the difference is that crime, which is a prevailing vice with the first, is scarcely known amongst the second. The one are poor and criminal, the other is content to be poor; now we ask how does it happen that both being equally in a bad physical condition, and weighed down by the same sufferings, the Irish Catholics are flagrant violators of the law, while the Protestant Highlanders are exemplary for their virtuous and peaceable conduct! The political misgovernment of Ireland, however bad it may be, is nothing compared with the terrible social and moral disorganization which reigns there, and certainly it is this last evil which leaves the least ground of hope in the history of that people. Nowhere, on the contrary, does the moral element present itself in the form of social disorganization. Now, to what is it to be ascribed, if not to Protestantism, that this people, in the midst of great privations, have maintained their moral and social character intact, while the Irish, deprived of this preserving salt, and having instead of it a principle of disorder and debasement, have broken down into complete corruption under the weight of evils comparatively light. Can we have any more striking proof of innate vigour and purity of true Protestantism on the one hand, and on the other of the innate depravity and ruinous tendency of Popery?

"But it is said: 'The same vices which amongst the Irish are ascribed to Popery exist in all their ugliness amongst a people who are the most fanatical Protestants of Scotland: I mean the Highlanders. It is this assertion, given as a fact, which has raised the objection. But this fact is denied by every body, and it is exactly the reverse of the fact. We do not say that the Highlanders are faultless; what people upon the surface of the earth in circumstances similar to theirs would not have yielded to the temptation to become indolent, or have ceased to show an activity which has every where been rejected. But to say that the vices which have rendered Ireland so unhappily famous in all the countries of the world are to be found in all their force amongst the Scotch Highlanders, would be to exhibit absolute madness. Where do they find amongst the Highlanders the accounts of homicides and murders committed in broad day, of midnight robberies, of crimes which have changed

Ireland into a sea of blood? Is there to be found in the history of the Highlanders a landlord murdered by his own tenants upon his threshold, or of a pastor who, on returning from worship on the sabbath, was killed upon the public road? Where will they find the perjured witnesses, and the juries who refuse to give a verdict, paralyzing the law and arresting the course of justice? Where are the soldiers planted to keep the Highlanders in awe? When the Queen goes into the north to live amongst these fanatical Highlanders without law and without faith, how many regiments are deemed necessary to protect her person? Not a single soldier was posted in the neighbourhood of her castle [1]!"

We cannot conceive but one more objection possible derived from the different positions of the Celts in Ireland and Scotland; the Irish Celts, it will be said, are Catholics; they are a majority in Ireland separated from the Protestants by national hatreds, while the Scotch Celts are Protestants; they are a minority, and united by their patriotism with the rest of the Scotch. It may be understood from this that the stain of Celtic origin has disappeared in Scotland, and persisted in Ireland.

Again, so be it. Let us see then if the Celtic race in Ireland, amongst the most unmixt Catholics in majority, and animated by political prejudices, has always withstood the civilizing influences of Protestant principles.

We have ourselves travelled through Ireland at three different epochs. In 1853, the last time, on purpose to study the Catholic populations which have recently adopted the Protestant faith, and the following is what we have witnessed: in several localities, such as the colony of Achill, that of Dingle and of Ventry, the little town of Clifden, and others composed of persons formerly Catholics, we have seen the same men, who were recently miserable, ignorant, and fanatic, become Protestants, initiating themselves in active life by the knowledge derived from reading and by morality of conduct. The transformation has been complete, and the means of accomplishing it unique: the preaching of the Protestant faith.

We have seen in the island of Achill a prosperous colony firmly fixed upon a soil which was recently wild; order, cleanliness, abundance, establishing themselves upon a spot where but yesterday reigned misery, idleness, and ignorance. The new buildings contrast there with the remains of the old. Where recently were huddled together a few huts of fishermen, there are now erected

1. *Witness*, 20th of January, 1850.

an agricultural institution, a printing-office, schools, an asylum for orphans, a hostel, a church, a manse, and farmers who, if not rich, gain their subsistence without difficulty.

At Ventry, the same spectacle — school, church, manse, and white and clean farm-houses, contrasting with the only Catholic house which remains as a *souvenir* of the past!

At Clifden, there was an equally admirable transformation: a whole country torn from barbarism, its natural resources used profitably, commerce created, workshops opened, and the soil every where made green by the waters of the Reformed Faith.

At different localities there are industrial schools where they give the foremost place to the study of the Gospel and to apprenticeship to a trade in such a way as to spread at the same time over the country morals and prosperity: such are the things we have ourselves seen, and which will show to any one, who wishes to enjoy the spectacle, that it is neither intelligence nor heart which is deficient in the Irish race, but a cordial acceptance of religious truth.

Moreover, to place ourselves at the point of view of the sceptic himself, we can say that the absence of all faith would be better for Ireland than the mass of superstitions and of hatreds which the Roman clergy nourish in the heart of their flocks. Sceptical France is not moral, but she is intelligent, active, and to some degree prosperous; while grossly superstitious Ireland is neither moral, nor educated, nor active, nor prosperous. One half of the Catholics there die of famine, and the other half go to seek their bread in America, a Protestant country!

In passing from the parallel of the Two Americas to that of Ireland and of Scotland, we have brought together the terms of the comparison to make them more striking; here, in fact, the two countries were neighbours, and under the same mother-country. Let us now take another step in this direction; let us bring the elements of contrast still nearer to each other; let us take them in the same little Republic, Switzerland, and compare canton by canton.

CATHOLIC

AND

PROTESTANT SWITZERLAND

COMPARED.

Viewed in relation to our subject, the Swiss Cantons may be divided into three classes: Catholic, Protestant, and mixed. As it would be difficult and even impossible to assign to each of the two faiths its share of influence in the mixed Cantons, we shall abstain from speaking of them, and compare only the Catholic with the Protestant Cantons.

But here we ought to anticipate a difficulty : admitting that certain Cantons are superior to others in civilisation, may it not be presumed that they were so prior to the introduction of Protestantism, and that the superiority comes from other causes than their religious faith ? Our reply shall be a picture of Switzerland taken at a time when it was entirely Roman Catholic, and which, when placed in presence of Modern Switzerland, will give us the measure of the intervening changes. Muller, the historian *par excellence* of the Helvetian Confederation, brings these two pictures before our eyes :

" Everything bad has been said respecting the misery of the people and the corruption of the clergy at the time of the Reformation. No matter whether you inquire of Catholics or Protestants, there is no one who will not shew you the land ill-cultivated, a population of monks fattened upon the sweat of the peasants, the holy monasteries changed into brothels, and the temples into markets of indulgences. No more science, no more consolation, the Church blessed no more : commerce was stopped in its impulse, industry in its progress, and the middle classes in the development of their liberties. Lausanne had formally and loudly complained of its Chapter, representing the life of the canons as one long orgy. No place of prostitution was comparable to their residences; they were seen full of wine descending from the city of an evening, sometimes disguised as men of arms, striking the citizens with drawn swords, and penetrating furtively into the houses, where they were guilty of violation and adultery : no fear, no shame restrained them; oftener than once the holy places themselves witnessed their disorders; they have been seen in the temples in the midst of divine service quarrelling, and giving each other great blows [1]."

"Meanwhile, the morals of the Reformation developed with its faith; a fact worthy of attention. The Swiss towns twenty years before were what the indulgences and mercenary worship of the Church had made them, towns of riot and pleasure : but from the time when the cities glorified themselves with the name of regenerated, they all struggled against their ancient manners. The courts of law and the pulpits were of one accord against disorder. The prostitutes were driven from the streets which they occupied. In all the parishes, consistories composed of laymen and ecclesiastics watched over the administration of the disciplinary laws, particularly the sanctity of marriage and the peace of families. The pulpit taught the duty of purity of life, and led the way to those lofty sources whence man derives the chastity and force of the soul. By degrees they were led back from their ancient manners to domestic life, to labour, to order, to simple tastes, and severe piety [2]."

"A great zeal was shewn for the study and especially a great love was manifested for Sacred Literature. The Reformers had appealed to the Bible as to the Charter of the Christian people. It was with the Bible in their hands that they had stood up before God and before kings. The sacred book was reprinted in numerous editions, which succeeded each other rapidly. After having opened the Bible to the poor people, the Reformation founded schools for them because they could not read. It created teachers. When the pastor did not find any, his devotion supplied the want, and he himself taught the children their letters. Nothing seemed too low to these sons of the Gospel. Haller, Bullinger, no more neglected visiting the schools

1. Muller, pp. 33 to 35. — 2. *Idem*, pp. 186 to 188.

than the churches. They inquired not only what was taught, but also how it was taught. It was asserted of Bullinger that he knew all the scholars in the schools of Zurich. These men preached every day, and often several times a day. They assiduously visited the poor, the afflicted, the sick; and employed their days in labour and their nights in study. Their lamp was seldom extinguished before midnight, and at five o'clock they were up and again at work. Their correspondence was vast and active. The more their letters are familiar, the more do they prove their virtues. Few confidential epistles will stand this test; but these men had God for their friend, and their hearts were one.

"Most of these laborious men were poor. Léon Jude, when he died, left 80 florins. For months he had shared his hardly-earned bread with the exiles; his lute was his only relaxation; and his wife procured by spinning day and night the food which she shared with the poor.

"The sacred writings were studied by preachers who might at any hour find themselves called upon to answer their opponents; by the magistrates, some of whom obeyed the dictates of their hearts, and others a necessity of the age; and by the people, of whom war was no longer the sole thought. Conferences were opened upon market-days for the instruction of the country people[1]."

"The revival penetrated (after the Reformation) into all branches of knowledge. The printers had made it a rule never to allow any work to leave their presses of which they had not corrected the last proofs. The law, out of respect for the time they devoted to such noble labours, released them from the duty of mounting the city guard. The instant they issued from the press, the works of antiquity were expounded; at Zurich by Bibliander, Pellican, the two Collins; at Basle, by Bar, Plater, Borhans, Sebastian Munster, Phigio, Myconius. It was a worship; the hand of God had impressed upon their brows I know not what seal of grandeur and devotion. The Reformation had not less raised the condition of material than of moral things. The time lost in taverns, the strength consumed in mercenary worship, was employed after the religious revolution in fertilising the soil or in the service of industry. The earth was cultivated with a more intelligent and successful hand. The peasant who possessed a patrimony seated himself with pride beside a hearth which he could call his own. What he formerly lavished on the purchase of indulgences or the embellishment of a cathedral,

1. Muller, pp. 186 to 195.

he learned to apply to the improvement of his dwelling. Until then he had been under the thatch, as if he were only encamped upon the soil. Beggars overran the country; after the Reformation, it became a proverb (at least at Berne) that indigence was only to be found by the side of indolence. Labour and the law concurred in effacing the last traces of serfdom. A very few years sufficed to enable the Evangelical Cantons to distinguish themselves by their activity and riches from those which had preserved the old faith. After the Reformation, the sword hung rusting against the wall. The attention of every one was turned towards religion, agriculture, literature — the works of peace. The Catholic Cantons presented a very different aspect [1]."

"Every year (in the Catholic Cantons) when the recruiting sergeants made the king's gold clink, a phantom of military glory passed over the Alps, the taverns were full, and the echoes repeated nothing but the impatient cries and songs of the soldiers; in the villages of the Evangelical Cantons it was psalms which were sung; the contrast was great; and it was remarked even in the features and in the costume. The traveller who passes in the present day from the canton de Vaud into that of Fribourg, is struck with the contrast of the physiognomies and the clothes. Here order with rich simplicity; there carelessness with foolish and gay colours. It is the Reformation which has produced this difference between populations formerly the same [2]."

"The refugees for the sake of religion divided their time between prayers, study, and action. They have all the more merited well of our country; they reconciled the people to the Reformation. If any taste for study, if any love for the best things, if any zeal for what makes the purest glory of man, is displayed in Roman Helvetia, it is to these exiles she owes it. The knowledge of the Gospel spread from parish to parish, and a more enlightened faith begot purer morals [3]."

"Lavish of indulgences, Lucerne had sunk at the end of the sixteenth century down to the level of the general manners. The worship deceived the conscience by the performance of ceremonies; and thence they rushed to the taverns, to the joys of the carnival, or to the dances upon the mussegg.

"The priests passed their nights in the *cabarets* or wine shops, and could not tear themselves from their beds to perform divine service. During the processions, they were seen with the cup hanging at

1. Muller, pp. 207, 208, 211. — 2. *Idem*, t. XI, p. 231. — 3. *Idem*, p. 349.

their sides, stopping at every wayside inn to quench their thirst. The credulous and ignorant people were sent to sleep with fables. The angel of death was represented to them as a wild hunter followed by three red three-legged dogs running continually over the forests and fields[1]."

"The Gospel had effaced the last traces of the law of mortmain in the Reformed Cantons, as it had in the first centuries in the Roman Empire broken the chains of slavery. During the half century which succeeded the Reformation, the population of these Cantons increased one-fourth; at Zurich one-third; and nevertheless it had scarcely attained one-half the numbers to which liberty, agriculture, and industry have borne it in our day. Agriculture had made less progress in the Catholic Cantons, and in more than one place had even receded before pastoral life[2]."

"The progress of the epoch of course gave umbrage to the Church. Spain, which most faithfully represented her spirit, embraced the side of the bishop against the inhabitants during the struggles which took place in Valais. It tried to withdraw the Canton from the influence of the Reformation. The task was difficult. The indifference and the bad lives of the Valaisian priests had deprived them of the respect of the people; most of them could scarcely read; and the churches were without splendour. When a clergyman had been driven out of his neighbourhood for misconduct or incapacity, he was sure to be consecrated in the Valais; if one in ten was found with some learning or some piety, it was among the sectaries[3]."

Everybody will admit without difficulty that the present state of Switzerland differs from that of the sixteenth century; but is the difference due, as Muller affirms, to the influence of Protestantism? If it is not, the improvements will be found spread equally over all the Cantons, or spread in accordance with a geography different from the religious geography: but if, on the contrary, Protestantism is the source of this modern civilisation, it ought to be most especially remarkable in the Reformed Cantons. This conducts us directly to our subject: the comparison of the Cantons of the two communions. First of all, we give the complete list of the two Cantons, with their populations as divided between the two religions. We prefer to take this table from Malte-Brun, because it relates to an average date in comparison with the dates of the documents we shall have to quote.

1. Muller, t. XII, p. 171. — 2. *Idem*, pp. 341 to 343. — 3. *Idem*, t. XII, p. 371.

Religious Statistics for 1822.

CATHOLIC CANTONS.	NUMBER OF PROTESTANTS.	NUMBER OF CATHOLICS.	PROTESTANT CANTONS.	NUMBER OF PROTESTANTS.	NUMBER OF CATHOLICS.
Ticino	0	93,800	Zurich	191,700	1,350
Fribourg. . . .	5,100	67,400	Vaud.	155,000	3,200
Lucerne	0	103,900	Berne.	300,500	41,700
Schwitz	0	34,900	Appenzell . . .	41,200	13,800
Underwald . . .	0	24,800	Glaris.	23,845	3,285
Soleure	4,200	49,500	Neuchatel . . .	50,000	2,200
Uri	0	12,000	Basle.	0	5,900
Zug	0	15,000	Schaffhausen . .	26,900	200
Valais.	0	67,400	Geneva	27,080	14,400

Mixed Cantons [1].

	Number of Protestants.	Number of Catholics.
Saint-Gall. . .	81,829	61,371
Grisons. . . .	49,000	34,500
Argovie . . .	76,500	68,800
Thurgovie. . .	63,900	19,000

After deducting from our table the four mixed Cantons, there remain eighteen Cantons which can fortunately be separated into two categories of equal numbers. We shall therefore group them two and two, and oblige ourselves to place in each parallel the two Cantons most provocative of comparison by their geographical proximity, and by the equal importance of their populations. Paying as much attention as possible to this double rule, we succeed in forming the following nine groups :

I.	TICINO Catholic	and	ZURICH Protestant.
II.	FRIBOURG Catholic	and	VAUD Protestant.
III.	LUCERNE Catholic	and	BERNE Protestant.
IV.	SCHWITZ Catholic	and	APPENZELL Protestant.
V.	UNDERWALD Catholic	and	GLARIS Protestant.
VI.	SOLEURE Catholic	and	NEUCHATEL Protestant.
VII.	URI Catholic	and	BASLE Protestant.
VIII.	ZUG Catholic	and	SCHAFFHAUSEN Protestant.
IX.	VALAIS Catholic	and	GENEVA Protestant.

1. Although Geneva may *now* be placed, strictly speaking, among the mixed, owe have placed it among the Protestant Cantons ; partly because Geneva was much less Catholic at the time of which we treat, and also because the Catholic population, consisting chiefly of the working classes, has never had any share in the direction of public affairs.

Appenzeli might also be classed among the mixed cantons; but it will only be the Protestant part that we shall compare with Schwitz; further on, we shall compare together the two parts of the canton.

I. TESSEN Catholic, and ZURICH Protestant. — Let us listen to Count Walsh, the champion of Catholicism, upon the Tessenese:

"This race of men is handsome, and evidently belongs to the privileged races of the South, for whom nature has done so much, and who do so little for themselves. The country moreover is poor, if we except some districts, such as Bellinzona, Lugano, and Locarno. The inhabitants emigrate in crowds every year to seek among strangers the means of existence, and in most of the villages during the summer season nobody remains except the old women, the old men, and the children. It is remarked that the Tessenese, who have made their fortunes elsewhere, do not return like the other Swiss to enjoy it in their country[1]." So much for the people, now for their guides: "Fines are exacted for the profit of the magistrates called *Baillis*, or bailiffs of the cantons, who inflict them; they have been known to present occasions to their *administrés* to commit certain high-taxed offences, and to give premiums to *provocateurs* from Milan, who had been brought by themselves on purpose. Justice was not administered, but sold. Bunstetten says, some judges took money from both parties, and others more scrupulous sold their decisions in good faith. It is but just to say that in the midst of these infamies and exactions, the two cantons of Berne and Zurich (both Protestant) always made themselves remarkable by the virtue and probity of their magistrates. The lower classes of Tessen are too ignorant and too demoralised to know how to be free[2]."

"Tessen presents a singular phenomenon in Europe: that of a population which has notably diminished since the end of the last century. Prior to the Revolution, it had 160,000 inhabitants, and now there are not more than 90,000. The decrease amounted to about 3,000 souls from 1817 to 1827. Has emigration increased? or is it because agricultural labour, which is left to the women, makes them old before their time? The Tessenese do not trouble themselves either with the culture or the multiplication of their trees... they are noted for their want of cleanliness... M. Bunstetten says jocularly that a Swiss German pig would refuse to enter the house of a Tessenese peasant. Indeed, from the first night I slept there, I saw in fact that the inns were not kept with the same care and cleanliness as elsewhere.

"Shall I own that this promised land is robbed of its enchantment to my eyes by the men who inhabit it? In fact, it is difficult to see anything more repulsive than the aspect of the peasant of

1. Walsh, t. I, pp. 459, 460. — 2. *Idem*, pp. 459, 460.

this Canton. I was much struck by it. His countenance, always ignoble and false, would it is obvious become on provocation ferocious. His tattered garments, which shew more negligence and dirtiness than misery, augment the repugnance inspired by his appearance. Perhaps I wrong these poor people of Tessen, but in truth it seems to me that a band of brigands could nowhere be raised more easily than here; indeed, in this respect it is said the inhabitants of the valley of Verzasca are not in any way inferior to those of the most sadly celebrated passes of Calabria and the Apennines.

"Tessen is a prey to rapacious and ignorant *baillis* or tax-gatherers. The country is devastated by epidemic maladies, and by bands of brigands. The population is Italian, and is inferior to all the other Swiss populations in morality, knowledge, activity, and comfort; agriculture is neglected; there is little industry, and more new laws than improvements in morals[1]."

To the testimony of the journalist of Charles X, let us add that of his minister: "Whatever may be the future of Magadino (Canton of Tessen), the population which begs upon the only road which leads to it does not incline us to form a favourable opinion of the inhabitants which it will have. This population is weak, feeble, dirty, and ragged. It follows with inveterate importunities the persons from whom it hopes to extract an alms. It shews itself to be what a population might be expected to be which almost exclusively furnishes Europe with showmen of bears, monkeys, and camels, and persons who trade in this sort of exhibitions in the fairs. Instead of doing as they do in China, where they throw into the stream which flows past their cabin the unfortunate creature which would add to the embarrassments of its parents, here they bring it up well or ill, and as soon as its limbs can support it to the nearest town they place it upon the road which leads to it. A few chesnuts and a bit of black bread pay its pretensions to the paternal, and a kiss perhaps a tear to the maternal, heritage[2]."

The description which we have read is sufficiently significative to render more than probable the traits which M. Picot adds to this picture, which is already somewhat sombre. The following passage relates to an evil to which the misery and the recklessness of the inhabitants are not such strangers as might be supposed at a first glance:

"The industry and national spirit of Tessen are not as yet what they ought to be. The inhabitants do not extract all the benefits they

1. Walsh, t. I, p. 330. — 2. D'Haussez, t. I, pp. 311 to 314.

ought from their soil and geographical position. Nowhere are more deformed men to be met in consequence of the negligence with which they nurse their infants. Cretinism or *goître* exists in their valleys, and cases of it are even still more numerous in Valais and in Savoy. Men of a very advanced age are rarely seen among them. Bad food and the immoderate use of wine and brandy cause premature death. They have natural wit and an imagination full of fire, but also prejudice and ignorance; few of them are addicted to study, and they spend as little money as possible on books; and thence, although endowed with the most felicitous dispositions, they want the love of work, industry, and resources to such a degree that they are inferior to the other populations of Switzerland in morality and comfort, in spite of all that nature has done for them. Crimes are unhappily common in the Canton. A great number of the population do not care for their native soil, which makes them without fear of expatriation, and disinclined to observe the laws as they are observed by the citizens of countries in which patriotism has great sway. Several causes contribute to the bad cultivation of the soil in Tessen; such as a defective knowledge of rural economy, and the want of hands, produced by emigration. The inhabitants of Tessen are destitute of industry, which is a consequence of their ignorance. Manufactories are not found among them, except at Lugano and Mendrisio. The trade even in the products of their country is not altogether in their hands; it may be remarked also that they are generally poor; they want good agricultural utensils; their carts with wheels, which are made of a single piece of wood, have all the clumsy simplicity of the remotest ages. The use of fire-engines is unknown to them; they do not know how to erect breakwaters against the fury of torrents; and in other respects they are behind the present state of knowledge. The emigrations, as we have seen, injure considerably the cultivation of the land; and the women, in the absence of their husbands, suffer more than the most miserable beasts of burden. All the emigrants are replaced by foreign workmen, who take away from the Canton a share of the advantage which it might reap from the products of its soil." This circumstance will appear all the more regrettable to the reader, that he has seen above all the natural advantages assigned to the country by Catholic writers; wherever misery is found which the resources of the soil ought to prevent, the misery must be traced to the principles of the inhabitants themselves; and it is this which our author seems to insinuate when he adds almost immediately : "The Catholic religion has been up to the end of the eighteenth century accompanied in Tessen with superstitions, and even the most revolting abuses. Assassins found asylums and protection in the churches and convents. Justice was not better administered in other respects; and honest men trembled in the midst of a smiling and fertile country which nature seems to have wished to make a paradise. The educational condition of the Canton is not brilliant. Many communes are without primary schools, and it is remarked that the *curés* do not give themselves much trouble about the education of the children of their parishes. Hence comes the ignorance which reigns over the mass of the nation. Many first magistrates of *Communes* do not know how to read and write. There is not in the Canton any council for the particular inspection of public instruction, any literary society, any society of educated men, and scarcely any library. The inhabitants of Tessen are behind their age in regard to the useful arts [1]. "

Without entering into the same details, other writers allow the same thoughts to be seen. According to Sommerlatt [2], the brutalising labours and the unwholesome nurture of the women bring about the degeneracy of the human species; land naturally fertile produces almost nothing in unskilful hands; and public instruction is in such a backward state that it will not bear a comparison with that of the other Cantons. According to Buchon [3], this country is infinitely beneath Germany in useful knowledge. Malte-Brun [4] describes the country, in regard to knowledge and civilisation, as most miserable and most backward. And finally Cambry [5], at the sight of so much misery united to so much superstition, cries : " What filth, what yellow, black, and livid complexions [6] ! The coast of Canabio is embellished with houses painted like the insides of chapels. Jesus Christ, the Virgin, and Saint Christopher and the Holy Spirit may there be seen mingled with *cordeliers, capucins*, and hermits; the usual means adopted by Catholicism to attract towards earthly saints the respect and the adoration which is due only to the God of Heaven. The rapacity, the rudeness, the misery, the very great filthiness and the infectious odours shocked us upon intering into the town [7]. "

Not far from this Canton of Tessen, formed by Catholicism, what will Zurich be found to be, which was educated by the Reformation? Let us hear the same travellers, who in the same day may have passed perhaps from the one Canton to the other, and who

1. Picot, pp. 445 to 465. — 2. Sommerlatt, p. 486, 492, 496. — 3. Buchon, p. 200. — 4. Malte-Brun, t. VII, p. 186. — 5. Cambry, pp. 313, 322, 323. — 6. *Idem*, p. 313. — 7. *Idem*, pp. 322, 323.

have therefore applied the same judgment and the same measure to the two countries:

"Ever since the middle ages," says Malte-Brun, "Zurich has been celebrated by the talents of Zuinglius, the Reformer, and the distinguished men to which it has given birth. It suffices to name S. Gessner, Lavater, and Pestallozzi, to justify its titles to celebrity. Its schools are numerous, its university is in good repute; its learned societies would do honour to more important cities. It contains only 11,000 or 12,000 inhabitants[1]."

"The present generation offers at Zurich to the eyes of the Catholic Walsh an assemblage of learned men, writers, and artists, whose reputation is not confined within the narrow limits of their country[2]."

"There, more than in any other great town in Switzerland, may be remarked the independence and the zeal for liberty which distinguished the founders of that brave nation. The magistrates, less submissive than elsewhere to the influence of foreign powers, and above corruption, consult in general the real advantage of their Canton, and the Helvetian Confederation. Zurich has preserved up to the present day a very great preponderance in the general Diet, which she owes more to the idea which the other states have of her republican opinions, than to her real power. They regard her as the most independent and just of all the Cantons[3].

"In consequence of the unceasing attention which the government has given to the education of youth since the Reformation, several learned men have appeared at Zurich in the different branches of literature, and there is not a town in all Switzerland where letters are more encouraged, nor where they are cultivated with more success[4]."

"The principal object of the Natural History and Physical Science Society at Zurich is to encourage and perfect practical agriculture. For this purpose, the members correspond with the landlords in the different parts of the Canton, make tours in the different districts in turns, invite to Zurich the most intelligent farmers, inform themselves respecting the rural economy of each of them, give them instructions, offer prizes for improvements in cultivation, furnish the poor peasants with pecuniary supplies, and communicate to the public the result of their researches and observations[5]."

"Zurich has been called the Athens of Switzerland, and has produced a great number of learned men, of authors, poets, and

1. Malte-Brun, t. VII, p. 130. — 2. Walsh, p. 88. — 3. Coxe, t. I, p. 85, 86. — 4. *Idem*, p. 91. — 5. *Idem*, p. 101, 102.

celebrated artists. A commercial, industrial, and learned city, Zurich has purchased rather than conquered the districts which form its Canton. Its inhabitants are distinguished for their wisdom, their ability, their prudence, their benevolence, and their good humour. The Canton owes its fertility not to the nature of the soil, but to the activity of man. Its industry is very considerable, most of the workmen being both labourers and vine-keepers. The inhabitants of the Canton are generally laborious, friends of order, economical, fond of the arts and mechanical inventions, and benevolent. Zurich was one of the centres of the Reformation[1]."

"Do not fancy that the luxury of mind is in this city the lot of only a few opulent families; a wholesome education is here generally spread among all classes of society; there is not perhaps a people in Europe who read so much as the inhabitants of Zurich; I have seen in that city devoted to industry and commerce a book upon every counter, and almost in every hand; and I would not be surprised if the humblest artisan of Zurich had not as much literature as some of our *beaux esprits* of Paris. After that, as they do not write in this country for the sake of writing, *le bel esprit* not merely does not constitute a particular profession at Zurich, but does not distinguish any one, and the title of man of letters, « homme de lettres, » which is taken among us by those who have no other, is not given to anybody, because there every one pursues some honest trade. A man who knew only how to make pamphlets and operas would not find a place there even among the tribe of weavers; he would be good for nothing, not even to amuse the leisure of the populace, as there are not at Zurich neither comedians, nor mountebanks, nor newsmen[2]."

"The continually increasing progress of commerce and of industry, the acquisition of a rich and fertile territory, an excellent public spirit, the fruit of moderation and labour, morals pure and even severe, joined to an advanced culture of the mind, were the arguments by which the partisans of the ancient government of Zurich vindicated their attachment to the institutions of their forefathers, when the Directory sent an army there to proclaim the rights of man[3]."

"In this country the manners serve as correctives and supplements to the laws. The balance of power does not depend there upon an equation, nor the fate of the state upon an arithmetical combination, and it may be said that the twenty-six votes of Zurich are still

1. Rougemont, p. 310. — 2. Raoul Rochette, t. II, p. 310. — 3. *idem*, p. 315.

at the present time the oracle of the nation as they were when the whole nation resided at Zurich [1]. "

"The members of the demagogy are still in a minority in the councils of Zurich; salutary concessions, just regard for all reasonable pretensions, a moderation full of force and dignity on the part of those who administer the State, reduce their adversaries to play the ungrateful part of a legitimate opposition. The clergy of Zurich are imbued with excellent political principles, as they are gifted with all the virtues of their profession, and their actual chief, Hesse, maintains by the authority of his irreproachable life, as well as by his ministry, the ancient doctrines of a Church distinguished in all times for the purity of its morals and the severity of its maxims [2]."

"Zurich is still a very moral town in comparison with those which surround it, and there does not exist perhaps in Europe a city, great or small, which might not be profited by acquiring what remains. Opinion, the last check upon bad morals, which restrains them when the fear of God is weakened in the heart, has lost almost nothing of its ancient severity. The chiefs of the State submit to it in their conduct like the humblest citizens [3]."

" I should never have done about Zurich if I were to tell you all I have seen agreeable, instructive, and above all honourable for this city; but everything must have an end, even the most legitimate eulogiums, and this letter is already so long that I fear it will appear too long even at Zurich [4]. "

"The simplicity of antique manners characterises the Zurichese. If nothing is more respectable than the civil condition of this Canton, nothing is also more interesting than its moral condition, nor more touching than the spectacle of the interior of the families. Conjugal affection is there both a sentiment and a custom. Filial piety has there something of the respect which was the virtue of the children of the patriarchal times [5]."

" The inhabitants of the town as of the Canton of Zurich are generally industrious and active; they all like work. The child occupies himself with it as well as the old man. Those who do not devote themselves to letters, apply themselves with great activity to commerce [6]."

"Zurich has always governed with equal equity and wisdom the subject *communes* of the Republic, knows how to maintain them in a respectful submission, and to make the Canton flourish by an

1. Raoul Rochette, t. II, p. 317. — 2. *idem*, p. 322. — 3. *idem*, p. 329. — 4. *idem*, p. 335. — 5. *idem*, p. 188. — 6. *idem*, p. 148.

enlightened administration. The subjects have rarely had to reproach their magistrates with acts of severity or injustice. They acknowledge the integrity of their administrators [1]."

"What smiling scenes," cries the tourist Cambry, "environs the *Lemat* which leaves the lake and encircles the town of Zurich! It is adorned with a beautiful amphitheatre, covered with gardens. Fortune seems to reside there as a wise and happy mediocrity. In the west, the riches of nature are unimaginable. What dales! what culture! what abundance and industry! It is a country of enchantment. Zurich and its beautiful environs appear to me to be the asylum of wisdom, moderation, comfort, and happiness [2]."

"Let us leave the town, and traverse the country; we can scarcely go a hundred paces, without seeing some pretty cottage, or meeting peasants who salute as they pass. Every part of the ground is cultivated to the highest degree of perfection [3]."

"We learned with pleasure that every village had a schoolmaster paid entirely or partly by the government, and a child is scarcely to be seen in the whole Canton who has not learned to read and write.

"A little further on we entered into a cottage, the mistress of which presented us with milk and cherries, and placed upon the table nine or ten large silver spoons [4]."

"The town of Winterthur is small, and its inhabitants, about 2,000, are extremely industrious. The schools of this little state are well endowed and regulated. The public library contains a small collection of books, and a great number of Roman coins and medals [5]."

"In the Canton of Zurich the population, which is half agricultural and half manufacturing, enjoys as great an abundance of food as it is possible to wish; and the interior of the houses proves the comfortable condition of their inhabitants [6]."

Let us recall to mind the miserable state of agriculture in fertile Tessen, and we shall all the better appreciate what the Zurichese have made of a naturally sterile soil, in the words of Sommerlatt: "Zurich is one of the most important Cantons of the Swiss Confederation, not merely as the directing Canton, and in regard to political influence, but in regard to extent, population, education, and industry [7]."

"Zurich is in general more indebted for its productiveness to the industrious activity of man than to nature; but it is not only the indefatigable toil of the Zurichese which has shed such blessings

1. Zschokke, t. II, p. 291. — 2. Cambry, t. II, pp. 322, 323. — 3. Coxe, t. I, p. 113. — 4. *idem*, p. 117. — 5. *idem*, p. 129. — 6. Sommerlatt, p. 123. — 7. *idem*, p. 126.

upon their country, it is above all an enlightened rural economy and the zeal of scientific societies, which of late years have occupied themselves with the progress of agriculture. The spirit of industry and activity at Zurich is remarkable. Its manufactures and commerce have attained a high rank [1]."

"The Zurichese are upright, hospitable, and benevolent. If their intelligence has distinguished itself in the mechanical and industrial sphere, the spirit of this people has shone still more in the sphere of the arts and sciences. Zurichese names have acquired a merited celebrity in all branches [2]. In an ecclesiastical point of view, the predominant system is the Presbyterian, professing with very few exceptions the Reformed religion [3]. Zurich is placed in direct communication with the neighbouring communes by means of a multitude of new and tasteful erections [4]."

We have seen Catholic Tessen and Protestant Zurich, as estimated by the same authors; let the reader judge them in his turn, while we for our parts pass on towards our second comparison:

II. Catholic Fribourg and Protestant Vaud.—We have some good to say of Catholic Fribourg, at least for the past; we can therefore give our attention to a Protestant author : "The downfall of liberty in the Canton involved that of the national industry. Prior to the establishment of the Secret Chamber, Fribourg had numerous linen manufactures, which spread comfort in the country. It annually sent more than 26,000 pieces of linen to Venise. One single quarter of the town, it was estimated, contained more than 2,000 workmen employed in tanning leather. All that industry fell.

"The inhabitants of the rural districts near the town, and known under the name of the old territory, deplore also the loss of liberty, and lament to see themselves reduced to the condition of subjects under a despotic *régime*. Deaf to all complaints, the government has constantly punished as acts of sedition the statements of grievances which simple citizens or even entire *communes* permitted themselves to address to it [5]."

After these lines of Zschokke, we need not be surprised to hear from the lips of the Baron d'Haussez the following avowals: "Everywhere in the environs of Fribourg the view is arrested by fields and meadows which are very ill-cultivated, and by crops which excite a presentiment of indigence. Beggary re-appears, and the dress of the wretched creatures who exercise it show that

1. Sommerlatt, p. 127. — 2. *idem*, p. 129. — 3. *idem*, p. 130. — 4. *idem*, p. 151. — 5. Zschokke, t. II, pp. 250 and 251.

it is more the result of speculation than of real want. The town of Fribourg is destitute of the prospect of improvement, because there is nothing to attract a population different from that already fixed there by habit. Very ugly houses, distributed across a country the inequalities of which injure the circulation more than they contribute to the beauty of the views, form altogether a monotonous and unattractive scenery. The agricultural population of the Canton of Fribourg cannot be enjoying any great degree of comfort. The cultivation allows to be seen the signs of a negligence which is found wherever you may carry your observations. The public administration does not escape any more than private habits from the reproach of inertness. The roads, made without intelligence and kept without care, contrast disadvantageously with those of the Protestant Cantons upon their frontiers. The churches and public edificies are in a bad condition. Everything bears the mark of disorder, improvidence, and discomfort [1]. "

After the words of the minister of Charles X, let us quote those of M. Raoul Rochette, not less worthy of confidence in the eyes of a Roman Catholic: " Fribourg is a town very little attractive in itself. The want of population, and consequently of activity and movement, does not help to weaken the painful impression which the traveller experiences there. This void is felt, as it were, by all the senses at once, from the profound silence which reigns everywhere, and from the grass which grows in the streets and public places, and it penetrated and saddens the soul; on the whole, when we have contemplated the exterior and the situation of Fribourg, the best thing to be done is to get out of it.

" The Canton is wholly Catholic, and it might be by its extent one of the most important in Switzerland, if it were better cultivated; but I have remarked upon a great part of the road I gone over lands from which they might have derived greater advantages, and I have been able to convince myself, when crossing the Cantons of Neufchatel and Fribourg, that the reproach which is made here to the Catholics of being less industrious than the Protestants is not altogether without foundation; I shall return to this point when speaking of the government of the country. The Fribourgese are extremely devout. My first impression at the sight of all the coarse imitations of the most respectable objects (images, crucifixes), was a movement of surprise only moderately pious, and still further from being agreeable [2]. "

1. D'Haussez, t. I, p. 206. — 2. Raoul Rochette, t. I, pp. 45 to 48.

"If any reproach can be addressed to the government of Fribourg, it is that of a want of vigour, activity, and industry. I have already observed that many of the estates were badly cultivated; and I have since been assured that a great number are still uncultivated. Industry and commerce are scarcely more advanced; everything languishes; everything drags in the capital; the roads are ill-kept, and the country is in want of the outlets which might be easily procured. Finally, the government has with inconceivable indifference tolerated and even promoted the emigration of a great number of Fribourgese families, which have left the country in mourning and deprived it of many of its most useful hands. Fribourg alone has contributed nearly one-half to the formation of the colony derived from different Swiss Cantons which is established in Brazil[1]."

"Agriculture, confining itself to the flat country of the Canton, is far from being sufficient for the consumption of the inhabitants, who are obliged to procure supplies from without[2]. Their commerce and manufactures are of small importance[3]."

"There is very little industry in the country; the roads have been ill kept up until of late years. The inhabitants are ignorant and superstitious. The chief city counts one ecclesiastic for every 18 inhabitants; this Canton has produced very few celebrated men[4]."

"Superstition is still in all its force at Fribourg, pious farces being performed still in its church as they were all over Europe in the thirteenth century. At Pentecost or Whitsuntide, for example, the Holy Spirit, a radient wooden pigeon, descends from the sky upon the Canons who hold the wax candle in their hand, the material emblem of the gift of the tongues and of lights which in the form of tongues of fire established themselves in the minds of the apostles[5]."

A circumstance which is astonishing, although it has been several times reproduced in the course of our observations, is the appearance of a bright point upon this sombre picture — the reformed district of Morat. An eulogium interrupts the unanimous concert of accusations and of sadness, and this praise is bestowed precisely upon the only portion of the country which professes the evangelical worship: "The prefecture of Morat, the population of which is Protestant, is one of the best cultivated of the Canton, the inhabitants distinguishing themselves from their neighbours by superior agriculture and more industry[6]."

It would be difficult for a people to be very advanced in civilisation when their religious condition is such as is described in the

1. Raoul Rochette, vol. I, pp. 57, 58. — 2. *idem*, p. 313. — 3. *idem*, p. 320. — 4. Rougemont, p. 317. — 5. Cambry, p. 153. — 6. Picot, p. 315.

following lines by the Catholic Zurlauben: "Every year, upon the Day of Kings, *jour des Rois*, an exhibition is made upon a platform of King Herod consulting with the doctors of the law concerning the appearance of the Star of the East. The three magi or the three kings, one of whom has his face blackened, arrive upon horseback. Herod orders the prophecies to be read respecting the appearance of the Messiah, and disputes with the Pharisees relative to their interpretation. The Virgin Mary, seated upon an ass, and holding the infant Jesus, parades the town meanwhile, followed by Saint Joseph, whilst a brilliant star attached to a cord stretched from one end of the street to the other escorted them in the air [1]."

But it is time to cross the frontier; let us enter into the neighbouring Canton; the change is so rapid and so complete, that in truth it seems as if they had brought us a torch in the midst of darkness.

"We perceived in the distance the slopes of the Vaud country, the best cultivated in all Switzerland [2]. The fields displayed everywhere order, activity, and comfort. What agreeable ideas of repose and retirement are given to the agitated traveller by those rustic residences so well placed near those clumps of elms, those orchards, and those fertile meadows! What milk ought to be furnished by the numerous flocks half concealed in the thick grass! Luxury and opulence dot not reign in the towns which you traverse, but neither do rags and misery give pain there to the friends of the poor and of equality. Fresh and calm complexions, and a simple and slow walk, shows the absence of the boiling passions which elsewhere form the torments of life [3]."

"Nature had not given anything to the Vaudois on the Vevay side, except rocks and sunshine; but they have cultivated these mountains and supplied them with earth which they have had to carry from a distance; now they have fields, vines, and meadows of the greatest fertility; a multitude of artificial terraces rising in pyramids from the foot of the lake support the lands, and present to the eye a most delightful amphitheatre; you ascend upon the left of the road to the rustic village which is almost concealed by the walnut, chestnut, and apple trees which surround it [4]."

"How all these places are adorned by the aspect of a population established in the midst of the richest and most varied cultivation, whose costume displays comfort, whose air reveals happiness, whose proud and quick step betrays the spirit of independence and energy! There are no beggars, and scarcely any objects for the exercise of

1. Zurlauben, t. II, p. 224. — 2. Cambry. p. 25. — 3. *idem*, p. 78. — 4. *idem*, pp. 85, 86.

benevolence; the resources which, however fertile it may be, the soil refuses to a part of its inhabitants, industry procures them; the cultivation of the land and the anxieties of commerce have not absorbed the activity of the Vaudois so as to make them negligent of the lofty wants of intelligence, and in that happy land mental occupations go hand in hand with the manual labours which fertilise it. Everybody knows here how to read and write well, and almost every one, no matter of what station, procures for himself the pleasure of habitual reading. Up to the present time it must be admitted this instruction has not led to any deviation from the customs to which the country owes the wellbeing it enjoys. It has not made them ashamed of their habitual labours, nor led them to abandon them for apparently more elevated careers; they remain cultivators, workmen, merchants, and they are not withdrawn by disgust or disdain from the toils which these professions impose; they preserve even the dresses of them and do not blush for them [1]."

"The Canton of Vaud is particularly renowned for its cultivation and for its vineyards, which produce an excellent wine. Nature is there at once agreeable and severe; it is there that more than anywhere else she spreads out her green verdure and green shades in the midst of which clear and limpid streams roll everywhere their silver waters. This part of Switzerland is one of those where the purity of manners is best preserved; everything there breathes of the peace of the early ages. Almost everywhere an air of comfort and contentment reigns; nobody is poor there, and nowhere do you meet with beggars. The inhabitants are laborious and sober, proud and spiritual; their habits gentle and regular; everything tends to keep up among them the love of the domestic hearth; it is sacred for them, and it is very rarely that corruption comes to trouble their happy homes. There is in the single parish of Montreux more zeal for the general good than in many cities. A library is to be found there, established by the inhabitants themselves; a reading-room, where they have the newspapers; and several schools, one of them for music."

"There is not a height, if you have the courage to climb it, which does not offer you a striking picture of animation, freshness, and life. Families are to be seen everywhere laboriously and zealously occupied, and at some steps from them stands the hospitable cottage where the stranger is received with that frankness which charms at once, and commands confidence. This hospitality is never paid

1. D'Haussez, vol. I, pp. 107, 109.

for in money at Montreux : beware of offering it; they will regard it as an insult; it is there only, under these humble roofs, that is found the pure and simple life which recalls the manners of the patriarchs[1]. "

" The road from Lausanne to Vevay stretches along the sides of the mountains, in the midst of numerous vineyards. The industry of the Swiss is nowhere to be seen more advantageously than in that neighbourhood; the mountains, which were formerly sterile and inaccessible rocks, are now entirely covered with vines. They have carried earth from a great distance to the place to create a soil, and they have heaped up stones which, arranged symmetrically, serve as walls[2]. "

"In the plain," says M. de Rougemont, "a transport traffic takes place; the inhabitants there have simplicity and frankness[3]. "

" The good society, the urbanity, and the comfort of the inhabitants render Vevay dear to strangers. There is a very good college, and boarding schools for young persons of both sexes[4]."

" I ought to say that I have seen in the Vaud country nothing but the unequivocal signs of an always increasing prosperity, and I add that I was all the more struck with it that I had carried to Lausanne unfavourable prejudices[5]. "

" The advantages of an enlightened and active administration always penetrating more and more into all classes of society fortifies patriotism in proportion to the wellbeing they diffuse. It is surprising how in so few years, and with such limited means, the government has been able to form the establishments of public utility, elementary schools in every commune, hospitals for the sick and the insane, prisons for civil and criminal offences, superb bridges and roads, and which already rival the most beautiful works of this sort by the Bernese Republic; and above all the agricultural institutions, which are daily improving the cultivation and developing the private industry of the Canton. The cultivation of this country has in unencumbered hands made rapid progress; the vitality of the social body shews itself here by regular movements, by sustained activity equally remote from lassitude and turbulence; and the words liberty and country, which might pass elsewhere for cruel irony, or for an ambitious device, are here not only imprinted upon the money and upon the seal of the State, but they are engraved upon the hearts and expressed in all the actions of the citizens[6]. "

1. Madame Aragon, pp. 18, 22. — 2. Coxe, vol. II, pp. 78, 79. — 3. Rougemont, p. 331. — 4. Sommerlatt, p. 525. — 5. Raoul Rochette, vol. II, p. 27. — 6. Raoul Rochette, pp. 30, 31.

" It is astonishing how the taste for reading has gained ground, of late years, in the Vaud country and the country of Neufchatel, not only among the middle classes, but also among the peasants. The peasants of these countries have facilities for acquiring books of all sorts. The printing presses of Geneva, of Lausanne, Yverdun, and of Neufchatel, publish nearly all the foreign books which express the tastes and the opinions of the Swiss [1]. "

" Nothing can be more agreeable than the part of the Vaud country which borders the Lake of Geneva. We admire its rich and charming banks, and are astonished at the quantity of towns in the neighbourhood, and the numerous populations which inhabit them. An enrapturing picture is formed by the adorned and smiling dales on all sides; and this country, which is everywhere cultivated and everywhere fruitful, offers to the labourers, the shepherds, and vinedressers, the certain fruits of their soils, which are not devoured by the greedy tax-gatherers. Chablais (which is Catholic, as everybody knows) upon the opposite coast, is a country not less favoured by nature, but which does not present to view anything but a spectacle of misery. We can discern distinctly the different effects of the two governments upon the wealth, the number of men, and the lot they enjoy. It is thus that the earth opens its fertile bosom and lavishes its treasures upon the happy nations which cultivate it for themselves. She seems to smile and become animated at the sweet spectacle of liberty [2]. "

" The peasant of the Vaud country frequents very assiduously his parish church upon Sundays, and is careful to avoid the public-houses; those of the Canton of Fribourg do not observe the same regularity; their conduct presents a remarkable contrast; upon Sundays and fête-days they go into the territory of Berne to dance and drink in the public-houses [3]. "

Let us finish this Canton with a short summary, made not by a passing traveller but by a learned geographer, who examines and meditates to write at leasure :

" One of the Cantons the most important for its territorial riches is that of Vaud. It is one of those in which civilisation is most advanced, and education most diffused. Crimes are there few, or unknown [4]. "

III. Catholic LUCERNE, and Protestant BERNE. — Our quotations will be so explicit here that we shall deem it our duty to abstain from adding any reflection whatever. If our extracts are shorter

1. *Tableau de la Suisse*, par Zurlauben, vol. II, p. 3. — 2. *Idem*, p. 149. — 3. *Idem*, p. 220. — 4. Malte-Brun, vol. VII, p. 166.

upon Lucerne than upon Berne, it is because all the writers are infinitely more copious upon this last Canton; a sign of its relative importance, which we have thought it right to preserve :

"The town of Lucerne is not peopled in proportion to its extent; it will be, without doubt, if commerce becomes more flourishing, and the inhabitants profit by their advantageous situation. Lucerne was formerly much more populous, and even very commercial [1]. "

"Lucerne, being the first in rank and in power among the Catholic Cantons, is the place of residence of the Nuncio of the Pope; all the affairs which have to do with religion are transacted in the annual Diet which meets in that town, and at which the deputies of these Cantons are present. The city contains scarcely 3,000 inhabitants. It has not any manufactures of importance, and its commerce is very weak. As to education, it nowhere receives less encouragement than here, and consequently it is nowhere less cultivated. What a contrast between it and Zurich [2]!"

"The Canton of Lucerne, almost in the centre of Switzerland, is one of the most fertile of them; it produces more corn than it consumes; most of the inhabitants are engaged in agriculture, and manufacturing industry is very little developed [3]. "

"The soil of the Canton is very favourable to agriculture... Industry and commerce have not in general any great importance, although the neighbourhood of the lake and the road from Saint-Gothard are favourable to land and water carriage [4]. "

"No one can imagine how many difficulties are opposed in the Canton of Lucerne to the completion of the great roads; the peasants, imbued with ancient and ridiculous prejudices, believe that by enlarging the roads we open the country to the enemy [5]. "

To Lucerne, the first Catholic town of Switzerland, we oppose Berne, the first Protestant town. The one receives the Nuncio of the Pope, the other receives consuls; a difference which is already an omen. Let us hear our authors :

"In entering Berne, I was extremely struck with its beauty and cleanliness; except Bath, I do not remember to have ever seen a town which has given me so much pleasure. The principal streets are broad and long; they form gentle curves; and the houses, which are nearly uniform, are of grey stones, and built in arcades. In the midst of the streets flows in stone channels a limpid stream, which, along with agreeably ornamented fountains, supplies the

1. Zurlauben, vol. II, p. 290. — 2. Coxe, vol. I, p. 264. — 3. Malte-Brun, vol. VII, p. 146. — 4. Sommerlatt, p. 220. — 5. Zurlauben, vol. I, towards the end.

wants of the inhabitants [1]. Easy circumstances and even wealth distinguish in a particular manner the peasants of the Canton of Berne; and a particular attachment to the government is observable in the German district [2]. The charitable institutions of Berne are numerous, and administered with much wisdom. The hospitals are vast, clean, and well-aired [3]."

"The environs of Berne are pretty, not merely from the variety and the hills and vales of the scenery, but from the charming habitations in which the Bernese live during the summer. We are received in them with a simple and frank hospitality, a grand and noble ease, but without pomp or luxury; things which they consider (and this shews their good sense) as essentially destructive of the real wellbeing of families, and as conducing to a relaxation of morals mortally dangerous to society [4]."

"When observing the fertility of the Berne country, its excellent cultivation so striking when compared to that of other Cantons; when admiring the cleanliness, order, and comfort of its inhabitants, the industry and the wealth of Berne, we are strongly tempted to believe that the government of this Canton is one of the wisest and most paternal of all those which it has been given to the poor human species to create in a lucid interval of reason [5]."

"M. Coxe justly makes a great eulogium upon the politeness of the Bernese towards strangers; he celebrates the singular frankness and cordiality, which he has so often admired in the Swiss. The Bernese are infinitely honest; the mobility of thought gives a distinguished superiority to their character [6]."

"In the plain of the Canton of Berne lives a people well known for their beauty, their easy circumstances, and their wealth, which is superior to that of all their neighbours [7]."

"Berne holds one of the first ranks among the most beautiful cities of Europe, and perhaps there is no town which can present like it a street of nearly half a league in length, bordered on both sides by magnificent and contiguous hotels, ornamented at certain distances with columns, with painted or gilded statues, and washed by a current of flowing water, which maintains cleanliness and freshness. Criminal justice is administered with the rarest equity and humanity, but there is generally nothing to do. Happy country which nourishes few criminals! a proof both of the goodness of the government and of the morals [8]."

1 Coxe, vol. II, p. 222. — 2. *Idem*, pp. 226, 227. — 3. *Idem*, p. 227. — 4. Aragon, p. 225. — 5. *Idem*, p. 232. — 6. Zurlauben, p. 164. — 7. Rougemont, p. 313. — 8. Lautier, vol. III pp. 220, 221.

" The Canton is fertile, populous, smiling, and embellished with a number of wealthy cities, burghs, and villages. The gentle and easy manners of the Bernese render their society very agreeable. They are opulent without pomp, great without pride; trained to business from their youth, they are engaged in it almost all their lives. At Berne the fathers are the first teachers of their children, and the first lessons inculcated are the love of country and the advantages of moderation, equity, and sobriety. The city, although of moderate extent, is one ot the most beautiful in Switzerland. It has an Academy of Sciences, made illustrious by several learned men, a redoubtable arsenal, and many rich and well-administered hospitals [1]. "

" We admired the cultivation and the air of comfort and cleanliness in the neighbourhood of Berne. This city is, beyond contradiction, the most beautiful and best kept in Switzerland. Everything seen around Berne announces order and peace, well-regulated wealth, which is enjoyed without ostentation; nothing degraded or neglected is presented to the eye of the traveller. Fertility and happiness appear to reign in the country [2]. "

" Nothing has been spared for the elevation of the lower classes. Different learned societies and libraries attest the taste for intellectual culture and the sciences [3]."

"The finances are in a flourishing condition. The State of Berne has always made many sacrifices to make and maintain roads, and this zeal increases every day [4]. "

" There does not perhaps exist in the world a country which, by a combination of a fertile soil, an excellent cultivation, and an enlightened administration, can in the same degree satisfy at once the eye and the heart. A multitude of rustic habitations, disseminated alone the road from Berne to Thun, shine with a cleanliness so *recherchée* in their uniform structure that there reigns even outside such a grand air of plenty and such a perfect image of order, that the exterior alone of these houses attests the opulence of those who inhabit them. The citizen who sits in the counsel of the Republic, and the peasant who cultivates the soil, occupy similar residences; a visible and touching sign of the republican equality which is found here in the general welfare.

" If the sight of their homes impresses the traveller thus favourably, it is but justice to ascribe the wealth and industry of the people of Berne to their institutions. A country so well cul-

1. Lautier, vol. III, p. 308. — 2. Cambry, vol. II, p. 370. — 3. Sommerlatt, p. 161. — 4. *Idem*, p. 170.

tivated, such general prosperity, the air of content and dignity which is here the universal expression, are proofs of good government, which might render any further examination unnecessary, and we need not hesitate to pronounce the government of Berne one of the best in Europe, judging of it merely from the external evidence which we have adduced[1]. "

IV. SCHWITZ Catholic, and APPENZELL, Protestant. — We might have spared ourselves this comparison by contrasting the two distinct parties of the Canton of Appenzell; but, as we shall have to retrace our steps in a subsequent chapter, we shall pursue our previous method. With reference to Schwitz, we can only speak of its religion and its agriculture, the only subjects that occupy the people.

" Agriculture is very much neglected; here and there are valleys where the plough and the flail are unknown; the inhabitants consume but little corn, and live chiefly on the various products of their flocks. Some have imagined that the fogs and mists that hang about the hills prevent the ripening of the corn, but the real cause of scarcity is neglect of cultivation [2]." " If their prejudices could be overcome, there is no doubt that agriculture would be more advantageous than the usual occupations of the people [3]. " He who neglects his field, is little likely to adorn his house : " The furniture consists generally of a few wretched articles made of wood, and of the most indispensable kind[4]. " Is it study that takes the place of manual labour? " A library founded for the use of schoolmasters was never resorted to [5]. "

" What a contrast offered itself when we entered the Canton Zurich after having traversed an angle of Schwitz! The latter covered with misery and squalor; as everywhere in Switzerland Romanism announces itself by rags, sores, and beggary, and Protestantism by opulence and fertility [6]. "

" A hundred thousand ignorant pilgrims visit yearly the abbey of Einsidlen, and deposit their offerings with covetous Benedictins. Superstition and darkness accompany them; they kneel, beat their breasts, chant mournful hymns, wash their hands and their eyes in miraculous springs, see hell and its flames, boiling caldrons, horrible toads and serpents; while hungry bears haunt and stupify their feeble minds[7]. " " From early dawn till nightfall, men, women, and children throng around the feet of the saint in a locality about 20 feet long by 10 or 12 broad. Moved by our liberality, a strong Benedictin conducted us to the altar, and found

1. Raoul, vol. I, p. 116. — 2. Picot, p. 247. — 3. Sommerlatt, p. 265. — 4. *Idem*, p. 264. — 5. *Idem*, p. 274. — 6. Cambry, p. 330. — 7. *Idem*, p. 338.

a passage by distributing cuffs and kicks among the free and hardy Swiss who blocked up the way, and who fled at his approach. We visited the Goddess; the monk raised her petticoat, her veil, her trimmings, her gauzes, and even her scapularies; in fact, he treated her very lightly [1]. "

"During the celebration of mass, I saw a stalwart Benedictin play the policeman somewhat fiercely; the goods brought for sale had been exposed too early; he enteréd every stall, took from one a dozen of handkerchiefs, from another a couple of hats, here a piece of cloth, a cheese, or some lace, with which he loaded a stout follower, for the good of the convent and the glory of God! No one complained; every sufferer conducted the thief with the utmost respect to the door, hat in hand, making lowliest obeisance, and promising to be more discreet and less covetous in future [2]. "

" The natives of Einsidlen, although accustomed to the arrival of so many pilgrims to their abbey which is in Schwitz, have neglected labour, and betaken themselves to beggary and idleness; thus we find them a prey to misery, ignorance, and superstition. They are in general bigoted and fanatical, much addicted to pilgrimages and processions, regard the externals of worship as the whole of religion, and can neither read nor write. The clergy whose duty it is to instruct them are responsible for this state of brutal ignorance [3]. "

We might be tempted to infer from this extract that M. Cambry was not a very zealous Catholic, and that he might even be suspected of exaggeration. Count Walsh will guarantee the fidelity of the picture:

" There is one old woman who has performed the pilgrimage some twenty or thirty times for the benefit of others. The time spent thus is a total loss to the family; work and duty are suspended, and they are living on the product of their wretched economy. Moreover, it is difficult to persuade oneself that the same fervour would not have obtained the same favour if they had staid at home, instead of coming to ask it fifty leagues away. The opportunities of dissipation and amusement must offer to many the compensation of this increased devotion [4]. "

" The cross of saint Magnus exhibited in the church of Schwitz is held in great veneration, and is regarded as of peculiar virtue in averting calamities. Not long since it was employed vith success, we are told, in driving away the beetles and caterpillars that in-

1. Cambry, vol. 2, p. 338. — 2. *Idem*, p. 345. — 3. *Idem*, p. 347. — 4. Walsh, p. 132.

fested the country. It was carried in procession by the clergy, followed by immense crowds of people, who probably helped on the miracle by crushing heaps of the insects as they went. These good people are passionately fond of sights, and the Jesuits who have the charge of the College here are ready to indulge them. They have had theatricals, in which they and their pupils were the actors. The clergy in general countenanced the performances, and even lent the sacred vestments to enhance the show [1]. "

" Public instruction is very backward in Canton Schwitz, and agriculture is not in advance of it. The little corn that is consumed is brought from Germany. You scarcely ever see a cultivated field, and thirty or forty years ago the use of the plough and the flail was unknown. Wheat was at that period cultivated in gardens as an object of curiosity, and bread is still regarded as a luxury in most places.

" When at the season of the great famine that followed the Revolution the benevolent committees distributed lentiles, the people of Schwitz refused to eat this vegetable, doubtless because they were previously unacquainted with it. The soil would bear wheat cultivation here, as well as in other parts of Switzerland; but the fear of unproductive harvests, the force of habit, and the fetters of idleness, have hitherto rejected every proposal for improvement [2]."

Let us refresh ourselves with the other side of the picture. Let us step over to Appenzell, and that we may be sure of an impartial statement let us follow M. Raoul Rochette, a zealous Catholic, in our review of this Protestant Canton : " I reached Gais, a village of Protestant Appenzell, just as the people were leaving the church, and returning to their solitary dwellings in the plain. If the uniformity of costume bear witness to the equality of political rights, the exceeding cleanliness of their persons and attire are evidence of their wealth, while the dignity of their bearing attests the elevation of their character and position. You cannot conceive a more interesting spectacle than that offered by this people of Appenzell, so calm in a state of the most absolute freedom. It is scarcely possible to describe their condition without exposing oneself to the reproach of exaggeration. The exterior of the houses at Gais, where I was living, is so carefully preserved, that I would defy any artist to exaggerate the details of this rustic architecture. Nowhere have I seen the expression of such an exquisite sentiment of cleanliness as in Appenzell, from the threshold which is

1. Walsh, p. 158. — 2. *Idem*, p. 137.

cleaned every day, to the polished lightning conductor that surmounts every roof in the village. It is impossible to unite a more exquisite taste with a more perfect simplicity; and if the embellishment of home be criterion of the love for home, the inhabitant of Appenzell is undoubtedly the happiest man on earth, as he is perhaps also the most free."

But is it indeed the Protestant district of Appenzell that is here referred to? we shall see: "The town of Appenzell is infinitely less attractive than the smallest village of the reformed districts. The religious festivals, which are very numerous, fall in with the natural character; the pomp displayed on these occasions is just a dissipation and a spectacle; but, besides this, any act of religion, a marriage, a baptism for instance, is constantly followed by dancing, and a ball is here, so to speak, a part of the sacrament[1]."

"Trogen, one of the principal towns of Protestant Appenzell, is a pattern of wealth and industry. The houses of the wealthier citizens are ornamented within with the finest marbles; and even in France there are few persons whose dwellings are decorated in a purer taste than that of the venerable landamman Zellweger. Thus, what were formerly the huts of the shepherd serfs of the abbot of Saint-Gall, are become the palaces of a free people; and a country that derives all its wealth from its pastures, imports the arts and the luxury of Italy. It is but justice to observe, that never was liberty more gratefully cherished by those whom she has so largely blessed[2]."

"Throughout Protestant Appenzell, I never saw one dilapidated house or one ruined cottage. The whole district seems in holiday costume; the houses are spacious and well placed, and have the lower story built of stone, the upper part of wood; they are scattered about on hills, in vallies on the mountain-sides, so that wherever you turn your eyes, you see, as in the centre of an English park, a large and commodious dwelling-house, white and well kept; with French windows opening on to a richly cultivated garden. Before reading what follows, let us remember that it is in the Protestant part of the Canton that the manufactures are carried on. The flourishing condition of the cotton manufactories in the Protestant district has placed many persons in easy circumstances, and has rendered some rich. This is evident in the villages of Irogen and Undevil, from the regularity of the buildings, and their extreme cleanliness[3]."

"In our journey across the outer portion of the Canton of Appen-

1. Raoul Rochette, vol. II, pp. 216 to 221. — 2. Bachon, p. 172. — 3. Coxe, vol. I, p. 33.

zell, which is Protestant, we entered several houses, and everywhere found a remarkable degree of order and cleanliness, such as to make it plain that these are become necessary to the people. The result is a series of the most agreeable landscapes, along a chain of cultivated mountains, richly wooded and covered with hamlets, which seem to have been placed there by the hand of taste to produce a picturesque effect. One might think they were independent tribes united only by the love of society; but they are so still more by the maintenance or enactment of laws and government, and for the preservation of the common liberties [1]. "

V. Unterwalden Catholic, and Glaris Protestant. — Although these Cantons have no positive importance, they have a bearing on our general conclusions, always the same. If we were to suppress them, it might be thought that the result of our comparisons was for the first time different.

"The Canton of Unterwalden is generally poor," says Depping. "There are few large fortunes, and there is much indigence. A Swiss author attributes both facts to the excessive devotion of the people. The numerous services and festivals consume much precious time, and poverty leads to beggary. Buried in profound and brutal ignorance, the peasants have opposed all improvements. Dark and gloomy, they upheld the practices of bribery and corruption, and set themselves against the introduction of knowledge as an innovation [2]. "

"The people do not take advantage, as they might, of the natural productions of their country, but purchase at a high price the manufactured articles which they might make for themselves, as they have the materials at hand. We may indeed apply to Unterwalden what is the general remark of all travellers and writers on Switzerland, of the superior industry that characterises the Protestant Cantons, the result of want of education among the Catholics, and of the time wasted in festivals and superstitious exercises. The cantonal schools are neglected, which may be traced back to divers causes, and especially to the poverty of the State, and of individuals [3]. "

"The existence of the people of Schwitz, Uri, and Unterwalden, is a miserable one, and they make few efforts to render it otherwise. They might certainly keep their houses cleaner; they might adopt a mode of clothing themselves more in keeping with the exigences of the climate; they might improve their diet and their beds. But

1. Coxe, pp. 34 and 35. — 2. Depping, vol. III, p. 145. — 3. Picot, p. 270.

no! the thought never occurs to them! they live in cabins that are black with the smoke of their fathers' fires, and shiver through the snows of winter in garments that oppressed them in summer. Rye bread, softened in whey, is their chief article of food. March-beans, potatoes, cabbages eaten with salt, pies prepared and cooked in grease, and in the case of the rich, the addition of a little lard; such is their bill of fare [1]. Neither trade nor manufactures prosper in this Canton [2]."

Let us turn the medal to the Protestant side, and see what the same author says of Glaris: "Trade and manufactures flourish."

"The people of Glaris are remarkably industrious. In the seventeenth century they had begun to establish manufactories among them; they then worked for the merchants of Zurich, but they soon learned to do without them, and to work for themselves, and their manufactures of cottons and of muslins have long made them opulent and independent [3]."

"The number of Protestants has increased considerably within the last century, and their ability in every branch of trade greatly exceeds that of the Catholics, which is a clear proof that the dogmas of Rome are less favourable to liberty and to the progress of the useful arts [4]."

This last extract may lead the reader to suppose that Glaris is not exclusively Protestant. "About one-eighth is Catholic," says M. Oscar M'Carthy, "and a glance is sufficient to show the difference between them and the rest of the population, who are addicted to commerce and manufactures, whence they have attained riches and competence [5]."

VI. Soleure Catholic, and Neufchatel Protestant. — It is possible that to those who know nothing more of Switzerland than the relative importance of the Cantons, our comparisons may appear to have been purposely made between districts differing widely in size. But we would observe that we have not been left to choose; after having disposed of the four mixed Cantons, there remained nine Catholic and nine Protestant Cantons. If the latter be the more important, that is not our fault. This is often the result of the truth that we are asserting. If for instance we hear far more of Neufchatel than of Soleure, it is not that the population or the extent of the former Canton is greater; on the contrary, but that the industry and instruction of Neufchatel have made it known far and wide, while Soleure remains in obscurity. We may also

1. D'Haussez, vol. I, p. 149. — 2. Sommerlatt. p. 282. — 3. Picot, p. 286. — 4. Coxe, vol. I, p. 49. — 5. *Dictionnaire de la Conversation*, Glaris.

remark that the civilisation of Neufchatel is in nowise the result of superior natural advantages; for perhaps there is no part of Switzerland where the people have had more obstacles to contend with. "Soleure, then," says Depping, "where the Catholic religion is in the ascendant, is greatly behind the other Cantons; the people are ignorant and superstitious, and the schools are bad. A talented Swiss writer, M. Glutz-Blozheim, attributes this to the Jesuits; for although the superintendence of education is no longer in their hands, the spirit of their method prevails, and the government is so little alive to the necessity of any improvement that it has proposed the recall of the Jesuits. Aristocratic influence has been prejudicial to the state, as the influence of the clergy has been to the progress of knowledge[1]." "Soleure is more interesting from its trade, than from the state of education there. The schools of the town are even worse than those of the country[2]." Are we to infer from this that the commerce of Soleure is flourishing? Coxe shall answer: "The commerce of Soleure is very inconsiderable, although from the situation of the place it might be extensive[3]." To this M. Sommerlatt in a more recent publication adds: "The manufactures are almost entirely confined to the products of the soil[4]." And as if to indicate the source of this apathy he says elsewhere: "The inhabitants are apt to be influenced by superstition[5]." While it is difficult to collect any characteristic details with regard to Soleure, it is scarcely possible to bring those referring to Neufchatel within the limits of a brief comparison.

In surveying the general aspect of the country, M. Cambry exclaims: "What a marvellous state of cultivation! Twenty-four villages are within sight! Pasture lands, corn-fields, pine-woods, scattered groups of firs, announce to the traveller the opulence and the happiness of the peasantry[6]; agriculture is here in great perfection[7]." Nor does education lag behind: "The rudiments of knowledge are generally accessible to all classes, and are well taught[8]." Neufchatel has good schools for the youth of both sexes; libraries, printing-houses, and museums[9]." To which Coxe adds: "The people are well-informed, and for the most part devote all their leisure to reading. Their tastes are divided between labour and study, and I was surprised to find, even in the villages, excellent and well-chosen libraries[10]."

And now let us glance at Malte-Brun's more detailed account:

1. Depping, vol. II, pp. 7 to 10. — 2. Malte-Brun, vol. VII, p. 138. — 3. Coxe, t. I, p. 124. 4. *Idem*, p. 325. — 5. Sommerlatt, p. 323. — 6. Cambry, p. 235. — 7. Sommerlatt, p. 551. — 8. Picot, p. 536. — 9. *Idem*, p. 561. — 10. Coxe, vol. II, p. 122.

"We might have expected that a district which from its elevation is exposed to all the rigours of a northern climate, would have paralysed the energies of its inhabitants. Far from it, and indeed it would be difficult to find a country more interesting from the industry, the information, and opulence of its people. The arts of painting and engraving, and especially of watchmaking, are cultivated in those mountains with great success. At Locle, a town situated at a great elevation, the population is almost entirely employed in working on gold, silver, and steel, for the cutler and the watchmaker.

"At Chaux-de-fonds, formerly a village, now a town of some magnitude, and situated at a greater elevation than Locle, there is a large manufactory of watches and other minute objects of art, as well as of lace. This town was the birthplace of the Droz, skilful mechanics, celebrated for their automatons. At Couvert, Travers, and other places we find the same industry and activity. We can scarcely conceive the limits of man's inventive powers when these are free to develope themselves; and here we see this realised. Peasants, moved solely by the desire of improving their condition, have brought from the bowels of the earth a force which multiplies their natural strength, so as to increase its productive pover. We shall not then find it matter of surprise that in the industrious Canton of Neufchatel there should be 5,000 lace-makers, 3,300 watchmakers, a large body of engravers, and 700 artists occupied solely in designing patterns for the manufactures of muslins and cottons. The annual production of the last is estimated at 60,000 pieces, and the number of watches exported to Germany, Italy, Spain, Turkey, and even America, at 130,000. In a country enclosed by mountains like Neufchatel, the condition is not to be estimated by the number of cities: 3 of these, 3 municipal towns, 67 villages, and 45 hamlets, including a population of 1,350 to the square league, afford the most striking evidence of prosperity. And to what is this prosperity to be attributed? Shall we ascribe it to that tendency to reflect, to examine, to discuss all sorts of questions, which led them in 1530 to adopt, by a plurality of votes, the Reformation as preached to them by Farel? for there are only two Romish parishes in Neufchatel: Landeron and Crellier. Is it rather to be attributed to the perfect freedom both civil and religious that the people enjoy? to the exemption from taxes and burdens? to a state of peace unbroken for centuries? Doubtless all these things have had a share in exciting that spirit of emulation which tends to preserve purity of morals and the love of labour; that passionate craving for liberty which is as a spur to the acquisition of knowledge, and that spirit of fellowship among those engaged in the same works, which annihilates the petty strivings of rivalry so often observed in manufacturers[1]."

And what has Nature done for the development of this prosperity? Niggard of her gifts, hers has been a forced co-operation. "The stratification of the Jura being loose and hollow, the rains and snows penetrate the crevices, and form subterraneous channels; these the peasants have made use of to turn water-mills, which, after an infinity of labour bestowed on their construction, serve to facilitate the cultivation of the soil. Engineers have found means of setting wheels, where this seemed impossible; they have devised a new species of scaffolding, and a multitude of other expedients, and that not for the sake of amassing fortunes to gratify a covetous ambition, but to secure the quiet enjoyment of a competence legitimately acquired.

"Their houses, which are small, well-built, and very convenient, are all plastered and whitewashed on the outside; they are clean and even elegant, which here in this mountainous region might appear astonishing[2]." "A beggar is scarcely to be met with, for labour keeps off poverty[3]." We rejoice when, along with all this prosperity, we find a state of morals which proves that it is not abused: "The morals of the inhabitants of this happy country," says Coxe, "are so excellent, and theircharacter is so mild, that flagitious crimes are scarcely known among them; indeed, it is rare to meet with the smallest instance of the infraction of the law[4]."

"It must be remarked that in the municipality of Sainte-Côte, in the Canton of Neufchatel, the moral and physical qualities of the people are admirably balanced; and if they are exhausted by the cultivation of the soil, they are refreshed by the enjoyment of freedom. The cleanliness is very striking. In the four villages that compose the district the houses are well and regularly built, the public places and fountains are carefully kept, and the streets are better paved than in many larger towns. And, with all this, one is pleased to find that abundance and benevolence go hand-in-hand, and that everywhere the spirit of kindness manifests itself, either in the charity that alleviates or in the hospitality that prevents[5]."

Now what we have to ask is, whether all this is to be traced to a period so remote as to afford evidence of its being the fruit of a

1. Malte-Brun, vol. VII, p. 161. — 2. Coxe, vol. II, pp. 121, 122. — 3. *Idem*, pp. 122, 123. — 4. *Idem*, p. 134. — 5. Zurlauben, vol. II, p. 543.

Catholic-tree; or whether it be of so recent a date as to prove itself the result of the great Reformation of the sixteenth century? "It is scarcely half a century," says Durand, "since the forests and deserts of this fertile country have been converted into rich pasture-lands and populous villages, that obliterate all trace of the sterility of the soil. Since this, industry and energy have done wonders. On all sides the traveller sees miracles of industry[1]."

And now let us verify these testimonies from the pages of M. Raoul Rochette, whom we are pleased to cite with reference to a Protestant Canton, from the fact of being of the Romish religion:

"Cultivation of mind is so common in this happy Canton of Neufchatel, that it is matter of surprise to none but strangers. It is the result of that widely-diffused competence which flows from the development of all the resources of the soil, and of the human energies, to an extent unknown perhaps elsewhere[2]."

"The government of Neufchatel is one of the mildest and most paternal in Switzerland. I never heard any complaint whatever of the magistracy from any one of the people whom I have questioned. I found nothing but contentment with their lot[3]."

"I cannot quit Neufchatel without bearing testimony to the excellent character of its inhabitants. The people are indeed citizens and brothers; I found no poor among them; the government is so mild that it leaves to the cultivator all the fruits of his toil. Public charity is neither showy nor interested, as with us, and is always ready to come to the aid of honourable indigence. The peasantry bear in their faces the stamp of happiness and the marks of health; they never meet without a friendly greeting, even where they have no previous acquaintance, and this appears to me one of the strongest proofs of the kindly feeling by which all are alike animated. They are generally a talented people[4]."

Now, to what cause does M. Raoul Rochette himself ascribe this prosperity, this diffusion of knowledge, this exemplary morality? The following words, which we copy from his pages, may serve as an answer: "The faith is as fresh as on the day when the Gospel was first brought by the preacher to these vallies[5]."

VII. Uri Catholic, and Basle Protestant. — The Canton Uri is too small to be spoken of much at length; still we will give the impressions of those who have written about it: "Many of the inhabitants of Canton Uri, left by the clergy, as the purveyors of

1. Durand, vol. IV, pp. 79 to 81. — 2. Raoul Rochette, vol. I, p. 3. — 3. *Idem*, p. 29. — 4. *Idem*, pp. 38, 39. — 5. *Idem*, vol. III, p. 24.

education, in a state of shameful ignorance, subsist by begging on the high roads, while the better part of the population devote themselves to commerce. The influence of the clergy is slightly diminished; there are fewer pilgrimages and processions, and the people work more. Nevertheless, this Canton, which is entirely Catholic, has much progress to make. A certain French traveller has said that Uri does not enjoy the liberty of the press. I go further; I believe that there is no press, and the state of public education is such that few citizens would be found capable of administering the affairs of the State, if they were not prepared for the office by commerce and by military service[1]."

"Uri is, of the three primary Cantons, the largest, the least populous, and the most uncivilised[2]."

"These Cantons have never produced any poets or authors of distinction[3]," "and there is not a single manufactory in either of the three Cantons of Uri, Schwitz, and Unterwalden[4]."

"About two o'clock we reached Fluetten; this home of Catholicism announced itself by four men with goître, divers with other complaints, and half-a-dozen wretches in rags who looked as if they had come out of the tombs. Never did poverty, disease, and misery show themselves under a sadder aspect than in these narrow vallies and gorges that we traversed after leaving Altdorf. — Never did I behold human nature more degraded in form and organisation. I could have supposed myself transported to the Valais, or to Tartary; I could have believed I was looking on those Huns who, by the terror they inspired, were regarded as monsters in Thrace, in Gaul, and in Italy[5]."

"The communes are, for the most part, too poor to support schools; and where they do exist, they are in many cases only open in winter. Parents who can afford it send their children away for education. Throughout the Canton there is neither library, nor literary society deserving of any attention[6]."

And now let us do for Basle what we have done for Uri; let us consult the pages of the tourist and the geographer:

"Basle, like Zurich and Geneva, is remarkable for the industry and cultivation of its inhabitants, and for the extent of its commerce. It was here that the first printing press was erected in Switzerland; and in point of fertility of soil and of agriculture, Basle is not a whit behind the other Cantons[7]."

1. Depping, vol. III, pp. 117 to 123. — 2. Rougemont, p. 305. — 3. *Idem*, p. 306. — 4. Zurlauben, p. 153. — 5. Cambry, vol. I, pp. 295, 296. — 6. *Idem*, p. 238. — 7. Sommerlatt; p. 344.

"The agriculturist and the manufacturer are alike distinguished for their activity and their industry [1]."

"There is no village without good primary schools [2]."

"The natives of Basle-Campagne are remarkable for their natural vivacity and wit [3]."

"In all ages the city of Basle has regarded public instruction as the only base of civilisation, and science as the noblest ornament of their town and of its inhabitants, so that Troxler could say: "Basle has set Switzerland the example of noble sentiments and heroic efforts [4]."

"Basle has thirteen literary and scientific societies [5]."

"The children of citizens receive in general an excellent education. They are always taught Latin, sometimes Greek, and it is by no means unusual to find petty shopkeepers reading Horace, Virgil, or Plutarch at their leisure moments [6]."

"The arts and sciences have been cultivated at Basle with great success. The Canton is well farmed, and the factories are numerous. Basle is the first city in Switzerland with regard to commerce [7]." It is also the richest; there are 40 houses having a business of more than a million of francs [8]." "The trade is daily increasing, and has increased wonderfully within the last four-and-twenty years [9]."

VIII. Zug Catholic, and Schaffhausen Protestant. — Before we say anything of the inhabitants, let us say a word about the soil of Canton Zug. — "The soil is generally productive, and the climate healthy and mild," writes M. Sommerlatt [10]. — And what is the result of these advantages? "There is little trade, and little industry," replies the same author.

"The peasants of Zug and Uri have the reputation of being the least civilised and the most intractable of the whole league. The former are distinguished for a turbulent spirit, of which their public assemblies have given sanguinary proof [11]."

The portrait is not flattering, but we would acknowledge that this, the smallest of the Catholic Cantons, has appeared to us the best. Now let us compare Schaffhausen: "The inhabitants of this Canton have more points of resemblance with their Suabian neighbours than with their Swiss countrymen. The artisans of the towns are industrious, and live well; the peasants are sober, active, and laborious, and exhibit none of the marks of poverty. Their language is less corrupt than that of the German Swiss in general.

1. Sommerlatt, p. 346. — 2. *Idem*, p. 348. — 3. *Idem*, p. 346. — 4. *Idem*, p. 348. — 5. *Idem*, p. 358. — 6. Coxe, vol. I, p. 179. — 7. *Idem*, p. 319. — 8. Sommerlatt, p. 344. — 9. Coxe, vol. I, p. 144. — 10. Sommerlatt, p. 306. — 11. Zurlauben, vol. II, p. 175.

There are primary schools in all the communes of the Canton, and the masters, though ill-paid, discharge their duties with zeal[1]."

"The finances are well administered, and there is a balance in favour of the State[2]".

"There are several literary and benevolent institutions[3]."

We are approaching the end of our task; our last comparison will not perhaps be the least conclusive.

IX. The VALAIS Catholic, and GENEVA Protestant. — "The inhabitants of the Valais are behind the other Cantons, even in regard to agricultural operations, and the management of cattle. They are also inferior in education, knowledge, and science. The people of the Lower Valais are specially idle, negligent, and dirty[4]."

"This region, surrounded by high mountains, has an isolated population exercising little influence on its neighbours; uncivilised, slothful, poor, and ignorant[5]."

"The population inhabiting the miserable villages of the Valais is in perfect keeping with the smoky hovels they reside in. Rags, dirt, and goître, that hideous deformity of which the Valais is the classic ground, cause one to avert the eyes in disgust. The costume of the women is like that of the people of the towns, except in its filthiness, which is nowhere equalled.

"The property of the communes is managed with a degree of recklessness beyond what is elsewhere to be met with. There is no restraint of law; every one uses or abuses it according to his necessities or his caprice. The pastures are overstocked; the forest-trees are cut down at pleasure, without any reference to the authorities. As the Valaisans made no efforts to free themselves from their present condition of obscurity, ignorance, and wretchedness, it might be supposed that all, even the upper classes, are well pleased with it. There is little industry among them, and their improvement would seem hopeless when we consider how little change has been effected by the opening of the great road which brings the travellers and the merchandise of France and Italyto their doors[6]."

"Picture to yourself immense tracts of valuable land lying waste; acres of undrained marshes; woods browsed by cattle, and devastated by man; and alongside of all the roads, here and there, a woman employed in keeping either a few goats, a cow, or a pig, and a crétin holding out his hand for the alms wrung from the disgust, rather than the compassion, of the traveller; picture to yourself, I say, all this, and you have some idea of the state of things

1. Picot, pp. 347, 350. — 2. Sommerlatt, p. 369. — 3. *Idem*, p. 372. — 4. Rougemont pp. 333, 334. — 5. *Idem*, p. 294. — 6. D'Haussez, vol. I, pp. 229 to 235.

that saddens the heart as you journey through the Valais, which under a better administration might be rendered so productive and so picturesque[1]."

"The inhabitants have refused to employ themselves as manufacturers. Mining, iron-foundries, and the making of glass are operations carried on exclusively by foreigners, and Valaisans, sunk in the most abject poverty, will yet refuse to take work in them.

"Their wretchedness is not only the result of an inadequate provision, it is also the consequence of bad habits received from their ancestors, and which will be in turn transmitted to their children. The people have all the vices that are born of idleness — intemperance, disorder, and the most revolting filthiness. The small profit realised by the sale of any superfluous produce is spent without thought, and adds no comforts to their store. The most indispensable articles of furniture are wanting in their houses, and such as they have soon become shabby, like their garments, from the want of care. Education is either bad or neglected. Some of the children indeed are taught to read and write after a fashion, but no pains are taken with their moral training, and nothing is done to withdraw them from the career which has brought their fathers to poverty. Here all are poor, all are suffering, all are ignorant. Better manners and a measure of pride keep some aloof from the populace; and the families marry only among themselves; but in reality the only difference is between discomfort and destitution[2]."

Apropos of the Valais, we would suggest an inquiry as to whether the causes of its crétinism are not moral as well as physical. We will hear what M. Raoul Rochette has to say on the subject of this scourge, on finding it in another Catholic country, the Val d'Aosta: "I shall never forget the sensations I experienced on beholding at every door of every village of the Val d'Aosta this frightful multitude of crétins, sickly, wretched, languishing, with an enormous head, lost in an enormous goître, their faces swollen and livid, the eyes sunk under the thick and heavy lids; the flabby cheeks, the half-opened lips with the tongue hanging out, and a filthy saliva round it; incapable of motion except by means of a sort of machine in which they are enclosed, and which is impelled by the weight of their bodies. Some lay warming their limbs, which were scarcely covered by rags, in the sun; others, seated on the laps of half-crétinised old women, resigned to them the inspection of their dirty heads and hideous beards; all were motionless, dejected, sitting in

1. D'Haussez, vol. *I*, p. 264. — 2. *Idem*, pp. 273 to 277.

profound silence, or, sometimes stirred by sudden passion at the sight of a stranger, would seize a stone which they were impotent to fling, or form a curse which died away upon their voiceless lips. At the sight of these abject creatures, these unformed sketches of the human race one shudders to see how small is the interval that separates man from the brute. Surely the warlike Solassi, the indigenous race of these vallies, before whom the genius of ancient Rome retired defeated, could not have been crétins. Neither were those Pretorians inhabitants of Aosta, whose duty it was to defend this important barrier of the Empire. And where are now the descendants of the conquerors of Appius? as well as those of the Pretorians of Augustus? Who could recognise them in the locality, which nevertheless has neither changed its aspect nor its nature; but where the spectre of the kings of Sardinia has given place to the legislation of ancient Rome.

"It was remarked that under the French administration, which lasted from 1798 to 1814, the number of crétins, born such, had sensibly diminished, and it has recently been stated in documents, which have not been contradicted, that since the restoration of the Sardinian rule the number of these unfortunate beings has increased annually to a frightful extent. It was natural to conclude that the administrations had been conducted on different principles, and so it was[1]."

M. Lautier follows in the same track: "The neglect of education is one of the causes of this imbecility (crétinism). The lower classes in the Valais neglect their children, who exist like the beast. They wallow in the mire, seizing and devouring all they find there; in the winter they pass whole days stretched in a room warmed by a stove[2]." "The Valaisans are poor, indifferent to pleasure, even to comfort; they are paralysed by idleness. Their filthiness is disgusting. Drunkenness is the prevailing vice. They are very superstitious, and quite insensible to their own interests; moreover, intractable and obstinate[3]."

"The houses of the Valais, from which the light of day seems carefully excluded, and where the commonest necessaries are not to be found, appear to belong to another age of the world. And, with regard to science and education, the Valais is indeed behind the rest of Switzerland[4]."

And of all these evils what is the primary cause? "There are," says one of our travellers, "obstacles more terrible perhaps than

1. Raoul Rochette, vol. III, p. 392. — 2. Lautier, vol. II, p. 204. — 3. — *Idem*, p. 231. — 4. Picot, pp. 510 to 512.

those of nature in convulsion, which always oppose the progress of cultivation and industry: I mean those of natural indolence, of superstition, and of prejudices that time has not yet destroyed, which lead them to repulse all that would tend to draw them out of their wretched ignorance in which they prefer to grovel[1]."

But we will come down Lake Leman; and, with the Valais still fresh in our memory, contemplate Geneva.

We must observe, in the first place, that the line of deviation and of development is the epoch of the Reformation: "Since the Reformation, Geneva is become one of the most luminous points of a centre of light, literature, and science[2]." Its superiority over the other capital cities of Switzerland is in some respects purely intellectual; nothing has been spared to perfect the educational institutions. The library has some 50 or 60,000 volumes, and a large collection of manuscripts; its Academy, founded by Calvin, has chairs of theology, law, medicine, and other literary and scientific branches; its observatory is fitted up with good instruments; its botanic garden is rich in fine plants; many societies of arts and literature keep alive the taste for solid pleasures, and perhaps conspire with a rigid form of Church discipline to produce that purity of morals, which is more common here than elsewhere. One of the characteristic traits of the Genevese is their love of reading; more than 2,000 volumes of the public library are constantly in circulation among the workmen, and it is not known that a single volume has ever been lost[3]."

"Geneva is justly regarded as the Swiss Athens of France. It is the most populous and the most industrious city of the Cantons, and that in which the greatest number of newspapers are published; some of these rank with the best in Europe. This scientific, manufacturing, and mercantile city has indeed few places of public amusement; it is only of late years that it possesses a theatre; it owes its attractiveness, which draws such an immense concourse of foreigners, to the admirable social order which prevails[4]."

"Geneva is now one of the most beautiful of European cities; not only by its quays, its bridges, its hotels, its public places, but by its industry, its manufactures, its commerce, its civilisation, and its riches. The Genevese are, in general, distinguished for their information and their love of order. The love of their native country is very strong, a sort of link and fraternity unite them whenever they may happen to meet, and anything that recalls the

1. Aragon, p. 74. — 2. Malte-Brun, vol. VII, p. 189. — 3. *Idem*, p. 191. — 4. Balbi, pp. 217, 218, 219.

fatherland operates upon them as an instantaneous and powerful charm [1]."

"Geneva is perhaps the place where the full resources of the human mind are most entirely developed. We cannot, without astonishment, look through the catalogue of ***savants*** and of celebrated artists of all kinds that this city has produced within the last two centuries [2]. "

"The land in the vicinity is so well cultivated, and the number of elegant country-houses is so great, that the whole resembles a garden, or a public promenade. The soil of Geneva is not naturally fertile; but they are skilfully managed, and all the resources afforded by a great population are brought to bear on their improvement.

"The Protestant clergy have enjoyed a great reputation for learning, talent, wisdom, and zeal ever since the Reformation; their principal aim is to do good by setting an example of the virtues they recommend. "

"If Geneva, in spite of its smallness, has gained a European reputation, she owes it essentially to her educational etablishments and to the distinguished men found in them. The education of women is conducted with as much care as that of the other sex. Divers institutions aid the Government in this matter. The education of country children has not been overlooked, and in every parish there are one or more primary schools [3]."

"If the Genevese, shut up in a corner and as to domain reduced almost to the use of their arms, and with scarcely any soil but their industry to cultivate if we may so speak, if they have been enabled not only to be self-sufficing but to put Europe under contribution by their arts and their machinery, we do indeed recognise in all this the power of the genius of man [4]. "

Educational advantages here are by no means the exclusive prerogatives of the rich : "We are astonished," says Coxe, "to find at Geneva men perfectly well-informed among the very lowest of the people, and there is no town in Europe where knowledge is so universally diffused. I have enjoyed many a conversational treat on politics and literature with mechanics, and was surprised with the amount of their information [5]. "

The testimony of Baron d'Haussez is no less valuable than that of M. Raoul Rochette. Let us listen to it : "The freedom that is enjoyed at Geneva, the watchfulness of an enlightened

1. Aragon, p. 7. — 2. Durand, vol. IV, p. 72. — 3. Picot, p. 546. — 4. Raoul Rochette, vol. II, p. 361. — 5. *idem*, vol. III, pp. 271 to 274. — 6. Coxe, vol. II, p. 337.

Government, and the mild and orderly manners of all classes of the people, render life here as pleasant to strangers as it is to the inhabitants. Nowhere is society so select, nor is it easy to find elsewhere such an union of all that can make life tranquil and agreeable.

"In the first class of peculiarities which place Geneva very high in the circle of important cities; we must rank the taste and skill of the people for the higher branches of knowledge, and for the useful arts. Public and gratuitous courses of lectures are given by some of the most distinguished citizens, who with the most perfect disinterestedness consecrate to the edification of the people the information and talents they possess, thus employing for the good of their country an activity of mind which elsewhere is but too frequently devoted to the excitement of political commotions. Hence a more widely-diffused information, and an education so admirably adapted to the special wants of each particular class, that each takes only what he requires for his special, individual career; and thus ambition is circumscribed in those circles which, without dividing, part the population. We must seek in this permanent disposition the secret of the tranquillity that distinguishes Geneva from the generality of Republics. Previous to the Reformation, the pretensions of the house of Savoy gave rise during several centuries to a succession of struggles. Since that great movement, Geneva has only twice been disturbed by any of those convulsions that are so apt to be intermittent in countries where the same form of government prevails. Every one finds a measure of relative consideration, and such a portion of comfort as suffices for happiness; for on looking round on the admirable state of order that prevails, each rejoices in it as though it were his own work; and since no single name shines so as to eclipse the rest, and absorb the merit of the whole, every one is at liberty to believe that his personal influence has a bearing on the whole; and, indeed, such is the fact. Moreover, the authority is wielded in a spirit of gentleness and benevolence.

"The tranquillity of mind and the leisure which are realised at Geneva are consecrated to science and to public affairs. Here, without effort and without fatigue, without jostling his neighbour, the citizen has time for everything; he contributes to the public advantage, and he receives his reward in the esteem of his fellow-citizens, which is rather felt than expressed. If there be any overplus of time or talent, he employs it still to the advantage of his country by filling the professor's chair, by taking office in some branch of the administration, by consecrating his leisure to the creation or the superintendence of such things as may contribute to the general welfare.

"The arts go hand in hand with the sciences at Geneva, and if we come down to these branches of industry which without becoming trades are on the verge of ceasing to be arts, we shall find that here also Geneva is in the ascendant. Nowhere else do we find such vast workshops, and such an amount of first-rate production in watchmaking and jewellery, and in all that appertains to them.

"There are but few enterprises of real utility in which Genevan capital has not a share; and such is the confidence generally felt in their prudence and management, that the association of Genevese partners is always found to attract others.

"The result of all this is a general ease of fortune, position, and even of mind; for all have more money, more relative consideration, more mind than they are called on to dispense, and thus we find nowhere else a population which presents the appearance of so great a degree of comfort and prosperity.

"I have claimed for Geneva a superiority of mind as well as of fortune; and, to justify my opinion, let any one make his way into the social meetings of the élite of the city, here more numerous and more distinguished than in most places, making allowance for the difference of population. The conversational talent which has been supposed to exist exclusively in Paris, is here found in all its piquancy, its wit, and its gracefulness. What diversity, what elegance, what talent in those conversations, arising from the apropos of the moment, and enlivened by the information and the wit of women devoid of pedantry and spite; where mental culture is equal in the sexes, and where the result is an interchange of thought upon all subjects, and in every variety of style.

"It becomes a duty for the stranger to proclaim the noble and generous kindness with which he has been received; the solicitude which bore the impress and sometimes the character of affection. For my own part, I could have fancied myself in the centre of a circle of my early friends; and all my efforts to penetrate beneath the surface have confirmed me in the belief that this kindness is no mere form, but the true expression of the feelings of the heart. Under the name of Sunday-Societies, the daughters of families connected by the ties of blood or of class meet at each others' houses, and are brought up in habits of friendship and intimacy, which are to be permanent. The results of this system are deeply interesting. The tone of cordiality which presides in the habits of daily life, the sympathy that is at all times manifested as it is called forth by circumstances, tell of one heart and of one mind, as though all formed but one family. Is any sick or afflicted? It is a rivalry of care and consolation!

"To a vast amount of useful knowledge, calculated to prepare them for the duties of domestic life, the Genevese ladies add many accomplishments. In drawing and music, which are generally cultivated, some of them excel, and these arts are frequently turned to benevolent purposes.

"Occupying so exalted a position on the ladder of civilisation, Geneva should also take the lead in her charitable institutions; and she does so. There is help at hand for all who need it, and the importunity of rags and beggary is unknown [1]."

"It will be seen, from what I have said, that Geneva is in my eyes one of those exceptional countries, where, in politics as well as in morals, all that can be good is good; all that admits of improvement has a tendency towards it [2]."

"Geneva, once free, attained in consequence of her independence to a height of prosperity without any other domain than the narrow tract of territory that borders her walls! She soon secured an honourable position among the cities of Switzerland by her industry and her talent [3]."

Reader! How far removed is all this from the state of the Valais! What centuries of distance between the adjoining Cantons! What contrasts between Catholic and Protestant! Is your opinion still on the balance? other writers shall turn it for you. Hitherto *we* have made the comparisons, although in the words of others. They shall now draw them for themselves. We shall be brief: the length to which we have already gone demands it, and we shall not follow our authors through the whole length of their parallels; we shall content ourselves with such short extracts as suffice to indicate the judgment they have formed. Let us enter Switzerland from the side of France. M. Cambry introduces us: "In a moment you pass from the poverty, the disorder, and the neglect of the pays de Gex (Catholic France), to the Canton de Vaud, where all is order, industry, and propriety."

From the centre of this Protestant Canton, let us cast a glimpse north or south over two Catholic Cantons. On the one side Coxe tells us: "A comparison of the pays-de-Vaud with the sterile hills of Catholic Chablais, which present only a few towns situate

1. D'Haussez, vol. I, pp. 56 to 82. — 2. *Idem*, p. 101. — 3. Schokke, vol. II, p. 22.

at the water's edge, you will see the happy consequences of freedom under a mild and equitable government [1]. "

A second traveller adds : " On leaving the Canton of Friburg Catholic, we enter the smiling, prosperous vale of the Canton of Vaud. The pleasure of the contrast kept us there some hours [2]. "

We will cross this Canton of Friburg in order to visit Protestant Berne, and we will put ourselves under the guidance of the learned M. Raoul Rochette : " Without an inspection of the heraldic-insignia, the eye of the traveller will at once detect the line of demarcation between the States of Friburg and Berne; the admirable cultivation of the fields, the size and neatness of the rustic dwellings of Berne, offer such a contrast to the aspect of Friburg, that it could not escape notice; we cannot go fifty yards upon the high road without being sensible of the difference from the beauty of the route, which is not excelled by anything of the kind in France, and never perhaps, within so short a distance and in the same country, do we meet with signs so striking of the different effects of Governments. Berne is the region that in former days was styled Terra-inculta; and now, under the administration of its Senate, it is become one of the richest in Europe. If then I had retained any doubts as to the carelessness and incapacity of the government of Friburg, they must have vanished the moment I quitted its boundary; and if on the other I had brought with me any lingering prejudices against the Bernese aristocracy, I must have renounced them as soon as I had set foot within their territory [3]. "

Let us enter Saint-Gall, a mixed Canton, of which we have not hitherto spoken : " The populous class, " says Malte-Brun, " is sunk in wretchedness, especially in the Catholic part [4]. "

" At Saint-Gall (the Protestant-town) all was animation, " says Coxe, " all were busy; and the aspect contrasted strongly with that of Constance, which we had just quitted [5]. "

" In this town, which is exclusively of the Reformed Faith, the streets are wide and handsome, and the houses are well-kept. Cleanliness everywhere presides. Many of the private houses have their own fountain. All is bustle and activity; and the flourishing condition of the place is the result of the almost inconceivable industry of its citizens, who have manufactures of linen, muslin, and embroidery [6]. "

" In a town so devoted to commerce I was surprised to find the

1. Coxe, vol. II, pp. 85, 86. — 2. Aragon, p. 108. — 3. Raoul Rochette, vol. I, pp. 62, 63. — 4. Malte-Brun, vol. VII, p. 127. — 5. Coxe, vol. I, p. 28. — 6. Zurlauben, vol. II, p. 475.

arts and sciences cultivated, and literature in high repute. In the library there are thirteen folio volumes of M.S. letters of the Great Swiss and German Reformers[1]. "

We turn to mixed Appenzell, as a Canton peculiarly adapted to our purpose, as the members of the two communions live at distinct points. We have ten guides, who all lead us to the same conclusion. And first, we will take a Protestant author, were it but to compare his production with that of our subsequent authorities: "The Canton consists of two separate Republics: Rhodes interior, or Catholic; and Rhodes exterior, or Protestant. The second ranks with the most industrious and commercial countries of Europe; it reminds one of a vast English garden, where the most varied rural prospects alternate with the finest mountain scenery[2]. "

Coxe is rather more explicit: "Rhodes exterior is larger, and more populous in proportion than Rhodes interior, and the Protestants are in general better calculated for commercial pursuits, and more industrious than the Catholics[3]. "

Sommerlatt adds a new trait: "In Inner Rhodes the public education is sadly neglected, which is not the case in the other district, where in 1827 there were already 73 schools[4]. "

We will now hear a traveller whom we are especially pleased to cite, on account of his being himself a Catholic: "Civilisation is further advanced," says Count Walsh; "information and competence are more widely diffused in Protestant than in Catholic Appenzell. The population is also greater by two-thirds. Generous citizens, enriched by commerce, have made a noble use of their fortunes by founding establishments of benevolence and public utility, such as orphan-houses and schools for destitute children[5]. "

"Inner Rhodes is inhabited by a population of lax morality, uncivilised and fierce, idle, and therefore poor. Outer Rhodes is one of the most populous districts of Europe, as well as the most industrious and commercial. The people are distinguished for their skill in the mechanical arts. The number of manufactories is considerable[6]. "

"We find but few instances of poverty in Appenzell. Competence is general, particularly among the Protestants, who are more industrious than the Catholics[7]. "

"The same facts are reproduced in Canton Argovia. There are several manufactories in an advanced state of progress, especially in

1. Coxe, vol. I, p. 29. — 2. Picot, pp. 353, 359. — 3. Coxe, vol. I, p. 31. — 4. Sommerlatt, p. 381. — 5. Walsh, vol. I, p. 420. — 6. Rougemont, pp. 321, 322. — 7. Zurlauben, vol. II, p. 150.

the Protestant part. Trade flourishes, favoured by the admirable order of the roads [1]."

We finish our tour with the Valais and Geneva, thus returning to our starting-point: "Although the Lower Valais is greatly in advance of the part of Savoy which we had just left, it is nevertheless very miserable, especially when compared with the luxuriant Canton of Vaud. Covered with vines, and tall maize planted between them, and growing together without injury to either, such is the fertility of the soil [2]."

"At length, at the little village of Chêne, we entered the territory of Geneva. After having sighed over the poverty of the Savoyards, our hearts were gladdened by the sight of the cleanliness and prosperity of Geneva, the abundant population, the fertility of the soil, and the number of country-houses scattered on the banks of the Lake [3]."

We will now turn from the comparison of cantonal details to more generalising statements, and we shall see how on all points the superiority is awarded to the Protestant Cantons.

Superiority of Numbers. — "In general," says Baron Zurlauben, "the Protestant Cantons are more populous than the Catholic."

Superiority of Commerce. — "The Protestant populations carry on a greater trade than the Catholic; the consequence of which is a larger measure of prosperity [4]."

Superiority in Agriculture and Industry. — "The Catholics, who are obliged to keep many holidays besides Sundays, are thus greatly hindered in their labour. All field-work is then suspended, by order of the Church. In order to make up for this interruption, it becomes necessary to employ other hands; and if from poverty this is impossible, the crops suffer. We remarked that the Protestant peasant has generally prepared his land or his vineyard earlier than his Catholic neighbour [5]."

"Agriculture is as much neglected in Unterwalden as in Schwitz. The valley of Enghelbert is the most industrious; but it is here in general, more than in any other part, that we realise what has been observed by sundry travellers, that the Catholic Cantons are less industrious than the Protestant, the consequence of a deficient education, and of time lost in fêtes. The faults of the people, ignorance, superstition, dislike of improvements, all spring from the same source. The Catholic religion is professed here.

"The Cantons of the North and East are the most industrious;

1. Sommerlatt, pp. 445, 446. — 2. Aragon, p. 74. — 3. Coxe, vol. II, pp. 66, 67. — 4. Zurlauben, vol. I, p. 451. — 5. *idem*, pp. 451 to 454.

that is to say, the Protestant Cantons. It is very common in Switzerland to find excellent artists and manufacturers among the agriculturists; and doubtless it is owing to this circumstance that the country is able to compete advantageously with the manufactures of Alsace for cotton stuffs, and with those of Lyons for silks. The Cantons of Zurich, Basle, Geneva, Glaris, Neufchatel, and outer Appenzell are distinguished above the rest for their industry[1]."

Superiority of Information. — Coxe tells us that: "The people are not generally so well educated in the Catholic as in the Protestant Cantons[2]."

A tabular view will prove this:

Number of presses in Switzerland.

PROTESTANT.		CATHOLIC.	
Zurich	17	Lucerne	6
Berne	9	Uri	1
Glaris	1	Schwitz	3
Basle	16	Unterwalden	0
Schaffausen	3	Zug	2
Vaud	12	Friburg	2
Neufchatel	3	Soleure	4
Appenzell	1	Tessin	2
Geneva	18	Valais	2
	80		22 [3]

Journals.

PROTESTANT.	CATHOLIC.
Messager de la Suisse.	Gazette de Zug.
Correspondant général de la Suisse.	Courrier Suisse.
Gazette du Vendredi.	Gazette du Tessin.
Nouvelle Gazette.	
Narrateur hebdomadaire.	
L'ami des Suisses.	
Gazette de Lausanne.	
Nouvelliste Vaudois.	
Journal de Genève.	
Bibliothèque Universelle.	

Great men of Switzerland.

(As cited by Zurlauben, vol. II, p. 23, etc.)

Divines	128	Protestants.	50	Catholics.
Lawyers	24	—	1	—
Mathematicians	51	—	5	—
Physicians, chymists, botanists	75	—	12	—
Poets and musicians	18	—	16	—
Antiquaries, etc	69	—	7	—
Historians	104	—	35	—
	469	Protestants.	126	Catholics.

1. Balbi, p. 212. — 2. Coxe, vol. I, p. 408. — 3. Malte-Brun, vol. VII, p. 197.

Thus, in a population where the Protestants are to the Catholics as 3 to 2, their distinction is as 4 to 1, according to a Catholic authority.

"In the Catholic Cantons," adds Madame Aragon, "information is less rapidly diffused; and, education being much less liberal, improvements are not so readily adopted [1]."

"Switzerland, and especially Protestant Switzerland, is one of the countries in which information is the most widely diffused. The Cantons in which education is the most carefully attended to are Zurich, Berne, Basle, Schaffhausen, Argovia, Vaud, Neufchatel, and Geneva. Those in which the industrial arts flourish most are Zurich, Thurgovia, Argovia, Basle, Glaris, Geneva, Outer Appenzell, and Neufchatel [2]."

That is to say, in the Protestant Cantons. "We will trace the literary career of Catholic Switzerland, which is by no means so brilliant as that of ProtestantSwitzerland [3]."

"In the Catholic Cantons ignorance and misery sometimes go hand-in-hand, and distress the eyes of the traveller. The taste for processions, pilgrimages, and other acts of useless devotion introduced by the monks, has encouraged a spirit of idleness which is the bane of trade and agriculture, and which augments the numbers of the poor. Hence we see in some parts the most grievous neglect of the resources of the soil, while elsewhere we find a state of cultivation which might serve as a model to the neighbouring countries. In the Cantons where the peasants bow the neck to the yoke of the clergy, men had lost all energy, all elevation of mind; servile and taciturn as slaves, they had forgotten their rights, and knew nothing beyond the performance of a mechanical and unreasoning obedience [4]."

Superiority in Beneficence. — Proved by the silence of a Swiss, Catholic author in the following passage:

"Switzerland offers admirable examples of all that is necessary for the maintenance of health, and the general well-being of society. This is shown in the institutions and the mode of providing for the preservation of health. Zurich, Vaud, Basle, Geneva, and Berne" (all Protestant Cantons), "possess establishments of this kind, which may compete with the most vaunted of all other countries. The other Cantons suffer so severely from the want of similar institutions, that it is difficult to comprehend the reason [5]."

Superiority in Financial Position. — "There are three Catholic

1, Aragon, p. 99. — 2. Rougemont, p. 302. — 3. Zurlauben. — 4. Depping, vol. 1, pp. 35 to 49. — 5. Franscini, p. 171.

Cantons, Lucerne, Friburg, and Soleure, each of which enjoys a pretty considerable revenue; but it is said that after the expenses of the government are paid, what goes into the public treasury does not amount to much; moreover, in these and the other Catholic Cantons the larger revenue is that enjoyed by the clergy and the monks. It must be observed that the revenues of the Protestant Cantons are greater in proportion than those of the Catholic Cantons; in the latter the income always exceeds the expenditure. Basle and Schaffhausen, though of small extent, are yet through their trade proportionably richer than the three Cantons of Lucerne, Friburg, and Soleure; but the wealthiest of the Cantons are Berne and Zurich; the latter especially, by means of its trade and in proportion to its territory; although, in fact, the revenue of Berne is double that of Zurich, if we take into the account its great extent of territory [1]. "

Superiority in Freedom from Crime. — Proved by the praise awarded exclusively to the Protestant Cantons by Franscini: " As to capital punishments, we might be convinced that, in spite of the severity of the law, Switzerland is one of the countries where it is least frequently called into operation; it is well known that at Geneva, Basle, and Neufchatel, long periods pass over without a single execution taking place. In the Protestant Canton-de-Vaud, for instance, with a population of 200,000, there had been an interval of 25 years between the executions [2]. "

Whence this general superiority? Malte-Brun replies: " Christianity, while it banished the ancient deities of Helvetia, brought in a new growth of popular superstitions. In the Catholic Cantons, religion consists only in a round of external practices. In the others, it is a benignant influence. Perhaps it is to the ascendancy of Protestantism in Switzerland that we must attribute the universal diffusion of the spirit of concord and toleration [3]. "

In order to be strictly just, we will subjoin the reason given for this Protestant superiority by a zealous Catholic: " Generally, in Glaris as in Appenzell, the Catholics have continued to be shepherds, while the Protestants have turned their attention to trade or manufactures; the mediocrity of the one contrasts with the competence of the other, and it would seem at first sight that in this world it is better to live with the latter than with the Catholics; BUT THERE IS ANOTHER WORLD, IN WHICH THIS INFERIORITY IS PROBABLY COMPENSATED [4]. "

1. Zurlauben, vol. I, p. 308. — 2. Franscini, p. 101. — 3. Malte-Brun, vol. II, p. 120. — 4. Rochette, vol. II, p. 154.

To such an argument we have no answer!

The conclusion of every comparison brings the same embarrassment. We fear lest we seem to exult in an easy victory, and we leave the matter in the hands of the reader, although our moderation almost assumes the appearance of treachery to the cause of truth. So be it. Strong in the purity of our motives, we shall persevere in this course; and we shall say to both Catholic and Protestant — you have seen Geneva and the Valais, the Canton-de-Vaud and Friburg : decide for yourself.

But we are on the borders of Germany, where Protestant Prussia and Catholic Austria, towering above the petty states by which they are surrounded, naturally provoke comparison. What will be its result?

ROMAN CATHOLIC AUSTRIA

AND

PROTESTANT PRUSSIA

COMPARED.

Although our title is confined to these two monarchies, our subject will overflow and extend to the whole of Germany, which we shall view as divided into two parts: Germany of the South, Catholic; Germany of the North, Protestant. Here, Austria and Prussia will appear as the heads of these two bodies; in fact, it is they who direct, inspire, influence, and impel all the Germanic members.

Our parallel will here be on a different plan to the one we have hitherto followed. Instead of comparing successively the two nations in each of their component details, we shall study both of them uninterruptedly, as a whole, so as to bring into juxta-position two complete pictures.

We shall commence by the Empire of Austria. Here again is a difference between the method which we followed with regard to other nations, and the one that we intend to adapt for these. Instead of confining ourselves to the enumeration of the different classes of society, and their different aspects, we propose at once to present the primary idea of the whole Austrian system of Government, and then to bring to the support of our declaration the documents which we have collected.

1. Austria. — In Austria, two powers, the government and the clergy, have united in working the nation to their mutual advantage. The Catholic clergy, at first, strove to govern both the people and the nobles; but the nobles resisted, and took the place coveted by the clergy. The civil power is therefore master, only it reigns in the nation by the means and tutoring of the Church. A compromise exists; the Church is the instrument, the government is the hand; but the instrument acts according to its own aptitude, so that a harmonious concurrence exists between the two powers. Here, more than anywhere else, Catholicism may be studied in statesmen. Rome has fashioned Austria, although Rome obeys Austria. This fact is important to us, who are seeking above all the influence of religion. But what spring have these two forces brought into play to enthrall the nation? In one word: they have deprived it, as much as possible, of liberty and instruction. We say *as much as possible*, for we shall see that, more than once, they are obliged to give way, under the pressure of external circumstances, to the general movement of Germany, and to let in a few rays of that light which cannot be totally extinguished; but we shall see also that the curtain is drawn aside with such precaution, that it may be guessed that the hand which withdraws it wishes to admit, not the free light of day, but a deceitful twilight.

Were this theory on the Popish government of Austria supported only by one authority, we might suspect it to be untrue. But no: a multitude of writers unanimously bear witness to its reality; and, since we wish to be believed only after having produced our proofs, we shall allow our authors to speak for themselves.

We said that the clergy had, at first, striven to enthrall the people upon its own account; that afterwards, itself had been made serviceable to the state, and, at length, that both unitedly had laboured to work the nation to their mutual advantage. Here are our proofs: —

"Morally, the clergy exercise more authority than the nobility, and to this day they have over the ignorant masses numerous means of action; but the danger of ecclesiastical influence has been long ago provided against, by rigorously subordinating it to that of the State; and, far from the clerical power being willing to act against the calculating and directing power, it can use no better instrument of administration and police[1]."

"The Austrian aristocracy take advantage of the indifference of

1. Desprez, vol. I, p. 188.

the people, and of their attachment to their prejudices, in the one aim of keeping up among them their old habits of servile obedience and superstition. They regard ignorance as the sacred pledge of their hereditary supremacy. There is no college or court councillor so insignificant but he draws himself up in the presence of a man of low birth, and treats him as a paria.

" Nor are the priests backward to keep up the spirit of uncertainty, and the degradation proper to men, whose happiness appears to consist in not thinking. Concealed behind the curtain of religious belief, they propagate widely the principle of obliged ignorance, or the more fatal one still, of demi-civilisation, in order to give a permanent seat to their sacerdotal authority.

" Had the people the privilege of looking a little into public affairs, were the press to inform them daily of what was passing without, they might perhaps conceive the wish to know the origin and price of their happiness. But they are satisfied to live penned up like cattle, and their fatherland is to them nothing more than a manger, where the master, depositing oats and forage in quantities proportioned to his caprice or to the exigencies of his lords, allows him just enough to prevent his dying of hunger [1]. "

Such weakening of the faculties supposes a very long and very powerful pressure. The spirit is evidently broken, and so completely so that when a liberal prince attempted to raise the people, the people repelled the hand outstretched towards them : " The premature attempts of the Emperor Joseph," says the ***Revue Britannique***, " to force upon an ignorant people reforms which this people was incapable of appreciating, were followed by a reaction. For the instruction of those who fancy that a good government is compatible with popular ignorance, the tragical history of this illustrious martyr of zealous, but autocratic, philanthropy should be written. The violent prejudice resulting from it against every thing like an amelioration, threw the power into the hands of the most inveterate enemies of progress [2]. "

It is clear that the evil had passed into a chronic state; the palliative disappeared with the royal physician, and the gangrene reached, one after another, as far as the nations protected by the gasping patient : " To maintain the German supremacy, a persevering machiavelism corrupted, in the countries swayed by the Austrian sceptre or patronage, all the civil and military institutions, education, and even religion. To corrupt in order to

1. Tardif, p. 48. — 2. *Revue Britannique*, 1847, Nov., Dec., p. 258.

reign, has always been the maxim of the Viennese Cabinet [1]. "

But let us enter into details, and see whether it be true, as we have affirmed, that the first Austrian means of Government is repression of all liberty.

First, no liberty of thought : " As to affairs of censorship, " says M. Bernard, " there are twelve offices for the revision of books, and as many censors, at Vienna, Prague, and Milan. Works are prohibited by one of these two formulas : ***Damnatur,*** and ***erga Schedam.*** The learned alone obtain condemned books of the first class; as to those of the second, any learned or rich man may obtain them by signing a paper, in which he declares that the prohibited books he wants are exclusively intended for his private use. The books upon which the Council of Censors places ***admittitur*** may be sold, and meet with no difficulties in the market; but works which have only been admitted with the formula ***transeat***, cannot be advertised in the journals [2]. "

No liberty of commerce : " The advance of industry, " says the same author, " is stopped by an exaggerated, prohibitive system. Commerce pays for the blunders of the fatal policy of the timid Cabinet of Vienna, which dares not resist the invasions of a rival power. Austria is trying in vain to open fresh outlets to her threatened commerce, and to give a new impulse to her merchant service, which visibly tends, rather to grow weaker, than to increase [3]. "

" The foreign trade of Austria in nowise answers to the extent of the monarchy, and the internal trade is far from having attained the degree of development it might enjoy. The bad policy of the government sacrifices the interests of the country to a ridiculous fear of any progress. Agricultural progress, increased during these latter years, does not yet answer to the fruitfulness of the soil [4]. "

Not even individual liberty : " Until the year 1846, the lord was the only land-proprietor in Austria; the subject is a simple tenant; he cannot be more. By the side of this principle so withering to labour, was another which aggravated its consequences : the lords judged between his subjects; he did more in Gallicia and elsewhere, he judged in his own cause. And then, although in Hungary, the peasant might emigrate, buy, sell, make a will, marry without authorisation, and as he liked, he could not do so in the other provinces. There, he was not free to move,

1. *Revue Britannique*, Nov., Dec., p. 149. — 2. Bernard, pp. 16 to 18. — 3. *idem*, p. 228. — 4. *idem*, p. 23.

or to contract any agreement. He was a minor kept by the legislature under perpetual guardianship; often blind, always haughty, and naturally selfish[1]. In Gallicia, for a whole farm, a peasant owed no less than three days' labour in the week, with six oxen and two men; that is, 156 days per year. In Hungary, he was only bound to give 108 days of one man's labour, but the loans in kind were rather more considerable; for, besides the small taxes varying from one province to another, and the tithes on the produce levied by the whole body of the clergy, the Hungarian lords took in addition a ninth portion of the corn. Happy would they still have been had they been freed from all other obligation, after having settled with the nobility and the church; but the State claimed its part also, and demanded the more, as it had less to take from the privileged classes. In Gallica, in Bohemia, in all the provinces which are not constitutional, the nobles were subject to taxation; but the heaviest part, as may be well understood, fell upon the people. In Hungary and in Transylvania, where the nobles were not taxed, the people paid for all. The public burdens fell amost exclusively upon the laborious classes of the Empire.

" Such was, until 1846, the law on property in Austria. The feudal system not only hampered social progress, but created very serious evils, and very great political perplexities in all the provinces of the Empire; but none received more terrible blows than Gallicia. It is a dismal example set forth for the consideration of all Eastern Europe. Nowhere, save in the lands of slavery and thraldom, has the law been more ungrateful to the laborious classes, nor armed the nobles whith a more unjust and extensive power. It would be harsh to say that the lower classes had been premeditatingly pushed on to their ruin, but when on the brink they have not been kept back. A country, possessing all the elements of wealth, has thus remained barren, and a frightful indigence bore sway there even before fresh woes called for mourning and famine.

" What accumulated miseries in these wretched and repulsive-looking villages! Narrow dark huts formed of the branches of trees, rudely kept together with osier bands, and covered with straw and clay, unsymmetrically surround a ruined church; such is the outside. Under the humble roof, men and cattle sleep promiscuously in winter upon the same straw bed. Rarely is there

1. Desprez, vol. v, p. 164.

found within a camp bedstead, wooden seats, or cooking utensils.

"Nothing can be more painful than the sight of the family at home, except it be the crowd of ragged labourers, whom the officers of the domain drive before them like a herd of vile cattle, at dawn of day, to their forced drudgery. While their tattered garments attest their indigence, their careworn and depressed countenances shew clearer still their want of courage. It is easy to see here that their moral sufferings are not the lightest they endure.

"Yet these poor creatures, until 1846, had always borne with patience the excessive rigours of their destiny, and of the laws; and more than one interesting proof of their resignation might be given. Here is an example taken out of a thousand others: the poor inhabitants of a village had for lord an Austrian Count, who, for thirty years, had been in the habit of exacting and obtaining from them an increase of drudgery entirely illegal. One day, to conquer their refusal, he called in the aid of the commissary of circle, who presented himself escorted by a squadron of dragoons. The elders of the village, spokesmen of the community, said that they had for several years, and in vain, complained of an abuse of power, and that, on this occasion, they humbly petitioned to be authorised to quit their farms with their families, and to seek another lord. The commissary's only answer was, to have them stretched out, one after the other, in the position of criminals going to be beaten. The youngest was past seventy. They submitted, and received six blows. This treatment was to continue, and increase by twenty additional blows to each victim; such was the gradation in this sort of torture, often mortal; but the old men could not endure this fresh trial; they gave way, acknowledged themselves to blame, and returned sorrowfully to their task [1]."

It must not be supposed that this kind of degrading punishment is peculiar to these provinces: far from it; it is the national correction of Austria: "The salutary and venerable institution of the *schlague* (punishment of beating) exists in Austria in all its primeval vigour. It is a pleasant addition to the other pleasures of the soldier's profession. No commentary is necessary to prove the immeasurable distance this alone creates between our institutions and those which rule Austria. Honour and beating are two things so opposite to each other, that they cannot associate. The degrading and afflictive penalty of the *schlague* shews, of itself, to what a

1. Desprez, vol. I, pp. 166 to 171.

degree of debasement and brutality are still reduced the populations swayed by the sceptre of Ferdinand I. When the emperors of Austria engaged in fatal and ruinous warfare, it was through a feeling of pride, in which the nation had no part. Because it was commanded to march, it marched; it is too debased and enthralled to reason upon its victories or defeats [1]."

"There exists no system of government so absolute, no Cabinet so wily, so devoid of delicacy, so contemptible, and consequently none more versatile, than that of Vienna [2]."

"And what other means were there for repressing liberty? Let us hear: "The timorous Cabinet of Vienna, as its sole means of preventing a revolt, places cannon on all the thoroughfares, and sentinels at every street-corner. The army seems to exist for no other purpose. The primary condition of a really national army is entirely wanting; no trace is perceived in it of any energetic feeling of nationality or morality. The penalties of the rod and the bastinado, existing in the military legislation, and the law which incorporates vagabonds into the army, are not likely to raise the sentiment of dignity in the soldier, who, in fact, embraces his profession with repugnance, since he views himself as in a treadmill. The Austrian soldier, debased to the level of a machine, never examines whether the order given him is just or unjust; he obeys like a musket, and is, himself, like one in the hands of his superior.

"The same mechanical discipline which characterises the military organisation, also distinguishes the civil administration. It is a state machine of unexampled complexity, having no other tendency than to preserve what exists; a tendency which arrests every independent development of public life, and embarrasses the smallest acts by a multitude of formalities and chicaneries. This machine has absorbed every movement of the State, and the most trifling step of the citizens is as much as possible watched over, controlled, and brought into the sphere of supreme inspection. The race of Austrian bureaucracy is a veritable plague. Without any high political tendency, knowing no interest but their own, crouching with mercenary humility at the feet of the superior classes, and full of insolent pride in presence of their inferiors, before whom they love to strut as masters, these officials devour the substance of general wealth and private industry.

"The fact must be tested with one's own eyes before an idea can

1. Tardif, pp. 43 to 45. — 2. *idem*, p. 48.

be formed of the incredible number of these agents. In the civil service alone they outnumber 150,000.

"Beside the armed force, everywhere visible, besides the universally-meddling officials, there glides in the shade the occult influence of the police, which, marching in the same rank as the censorship, has everywhere and always its ear turned to all that is said, and its eye open upon all that is printed [1]."

To conceive a just idea of this police, read the following lines:

"The different professions were enrolled to serve the police; I omit the most scandalous to mention only twelve hundred hackney-coachmen; about thirty thousand servants, called up now and then to open their hearts respecting their masters, and the appearance of their households; eight thousand door-keepers of the city (Vienna) and its outskirts; tradesmen and their clerks might also render some service. Sum total: one-half of the people were spies upon the other half. Mysteries of vexations, treasures of annoyance and weariness, were accumulated in the people's heart [2]."

Thus, no liberty of thought, no liberty of commerce, no individual liberty; drudgery for the peasants, the *schlague* for the soldier, humiliation for officials, and secret police exercised even by the citizens themselves : such is the justification of our statement. The first means of government for Austria is the thwarting of all freedom. We shall see that the second is to oppose the free progress of education :

"The way of the Austrian government," says the *Dictionnaire de la Conversation*, "has ever been to ensure the strengthening and development of the *statu quo*. Thanks to the zeal and severity of the President of the Aulic Police, foreigners, for the most part Swiss, who occupied places of professors or preceptors, were obliged to quit the Empire in 1821; and in 1824, the soil of Austria was interdicted to certain persons on account of their writings or political opinions. And lastly, the order which prescribes that all works of Austrian subjects, intended for the foreign press, shall be previously submitted to the censure of the government, was extended in 1824 to engravings, lithographies, or any other kind of prints [3]."

"Since 1821, no private person has obtained the authorisation to give to his own children a foreign tutor; one is tempted to believe that the government wish the education and instruction of youth to be confided to the Jesuits. Since 1829, dissenters from Roman-

1. Rey, p. 63. — 2. Bernard. — 3. *Dictionnaire de la Conversation*, p. 460.

ism are forbidden to teach anything to young Catholics, except music, dancing, and fencing. Studies in any foreign land count for nothing, and must be gone over again in the country. The prohibition from selling or distributing Bibles published by Bible Societies, and notably those in the Bohemian tongue, printed at Berlin, was renewed in November, 1822 [1]".

So true it is that the Austrian Government derives its inspirations on this subject from Romanism, that the Popes have tried to apply the same principles to all Catholic Germany. " The Popes," says the same authority, " under the pretext of reconstituting the Church, shaken in consequence of the Reformation, treated Catholic Germany with the greatest despotism. In order to attain their end with greater ease, they made use of the Jesuits, who, in concert with the mendicant friars, filled the universities, while at court, as confessors and councillors of princes, they mixed themselves up in everything, and secured in their own hands the entire education of youth. Thus was systematically compressed the glorious burst of reason and scientific culture, which had promised so much, especially in the depths of Germany during the latter years of the XV th; and the first years of the XVI th century. From that time, every means of enlightenment through the light of Protestantism was taken from the population; while they were given over to new superstitions, and to a multitude of institutions established in the sole aim of propagating error, and blinding and stupifying the mind, until it should bend itself patiently and without effort to all the designs of the hierarchy. Besides an ignoble bigotry and gross ignorance, the greatest vices and most monstrous immorality appeared to have become the portion of the Catholic Church. The sincere friends of truth and learned philanthropists were the only beings towards whom she shewed herself inexorable. All the forms of Catholic worship, however fantastical, were regarded as so many privileges, and consecrated with so much the more tenacity, that they were the objects of satire and contempt. To avoid the danger of proselytism, the church was not ashamed to throw the human mind into darkness, and to keep it methodically there; and then, to shew herself more Catholic than the Gallican Church, she allowed herself to be totally subjugated by the Court of Rome [2]."

Mirabeau makes a similar remark: " The want of knowledge and industry of Catholic Germany must be attributed to the bigotry,

1. *Dictionnaire de la Conversation*, p. 463. — 2. *idem*, pp. 369, 370.

which, in those superb countries, sways both government and people. Festivals, processions, pilgrimages, mummery, render the latter idle, stupid, and careless; the sway of the priests renders the former ignorant, oppressive, despotic, cruel, and, above all, implacably inimical to everything that might enlighten the human mind. These two causes are eternally destructive of all knowledge, and the ruin of knowledge brings on that of commerce and industry [1]."

"The Catholic universities in Germany are in the worst possible state, and have never contributed to the progress of knowledge. The Elector of Mayence has, however, just formed one which projects some light around; but to do this he has called in learned Protestants, and those are the only professors deserving of any reputation [2]."

But, to confine ourselves to Austria, let us hear, on her distrust of all light, an author as commendable by his knowledge as by his moderation: "Every professor (in Austria), is compelled either to write out a manual of the branch he professes to teach, or to adopt one of the existing manuals, in order, it is said, to spare the students the fatigue of making long extracts from books, and also, doubtless, that the text of the lessons should be submitted to the authorities, approved of by them, and the professor prevented from going beyond his bounds [3]. In oral extemporaneous teaching, the professor would have too much opportunity to be free and say what he chose.

"The University of Vienna has no fame; it has no professor of renown; no celebrated work has proceeded from it. What is the reason of this, when it has so much encouragement, and so many pupils? Is it the fault of the country, or that of the government? The influence of the Jesuits, and their method of teaching, is felt in the frequent examinations of the faculty, and in the division of the classes in the colleges [4]."

"The only fault I shall find with the articles of discipline in the Theresian Academy is, that they attempt to rule in too much detail the conduct of the young men, and become impracticable from their minuteness. I find more serious fault with the following: "As the pupils should have an equally kindly feeling towards each other, it is necessary that they should have no private connexion or

1. Mirabeau, vol. I, p. 34. — 2. *Idem*, p. 223. — 3. The intention is to spare the students the trouble of writing from the dictation of the professor, and committing to paper the course of lectures. The professors must therefore have a book which forms the basis and text of their lessons. This book is examined and approved by the authorities; it is even frequently enjoined on professors to take such and such authors for text. (Girardin, p. 205.) — 4. *Idem*, pp. 182, 183.

friendship. It is necessary for other motives also. These friendships are injurious to mutual esteem, and also to the universal harmony of the house. The pupils are therefore to have neither exclusive preference nor repugnance for each other." This is surely carrying out too far the love of directing and inspecting. I cannot blame too severely such a spirit of police and inquisition. To prevent the disorder sometimes accruing from the friendships of young people, is the duty of masters; but to proscribe friendship, to forbid confidence, is a crime against human nature, for it is destroying a great good to prevent an evil rarely met with. Doubtless it is convenient for the prefects (Jesuit chiefs) to take young men one by one; they are more dependent and submissive, having no idea of supporting one another; but it is with this college police, carried to such a degree of annoyance and umbrage, as it is with public police when carried too far, it prevents a few bad actions, but dries up the spring of all good ones, and thus injures more than it benefits[1]."

"'There must be instilled into the children (says the Manual), 'those ideas only, which are suitable to men of their state and 'condition; above all, the will must be acted upon; they must be 'accustomed to respect authority, and this respect must be the 'motive of their obedience. Examples will be in this respect the 'best lesson; school books must present such examples as are fitted 'to make an impression upon their minds; the priests especially 'have this care in charge, because it devolves upon them to form 'the morals of the people.' As it is seen, the Austrian government is fond of directing the will and mind of the people; such is its constant aim. Austria has formed its schools upon the plan of its government, seeking to fashion from infancy the people into what it chooses them to be and to remain. In this country, good and evil, all is agreed[2]."

If we were to characterise in a single word the governmental and clerical system of Austria, we should say that it is essentially stationary. "The death of Francis I," says M. Bernard, "and the advent to the throne of his successor, Ferdinand I, brought about no change of system from the Austrian Government, ever devoted to immobility. A horror of change preserves it from all militant ardour. In its idolatrous respect for facts, it suffers facts to take place in a direction totally opposed to its sympathies, wishes, and secret efforts. It tries to let nothing move; but, when it cannot prevent a change, it submits to it, and does all it can that at least

1. Girardin, pp. 207, 208. — 2. *Idem*, pp. 224, 225.

it may be the last change. In politics, it worships nothing but repose. A lasting usurpation, in its eyes, is but a commencing legitimacy. The system followed out hitherto by the Austrian government is that temporising, palliating system, wholly passive, in which a vague and purile fear of all movement, all action, and all progress, takes the place of political ideas; and which may be summed up in the famous words: 'After me, the Deluge!'

"Prince Metternich, in the Austrian oligarchy, which for two centuries has been working the government solely on its own account, has no friends, no rivals; this shews little ambition, little activity of mind. The great Austrian lords live in their families, or among each other; play, walk, go to the theatre, are assiduously intent upon the plays, the actors, their horses, their sport, their lands, and leave without debate the management of the State to M. de Metternich.

"Who does not know it? For a long, a very long, time Austria has been what we see it to-day. Since the XVIth century, not to go further back, no internal change in its government or social state has forced it to alter its policy. It is the classic ground of traditions and habits, observed to-day, because they were observed yesterday. There the past is all powerful over the present, and the present is scarcely more than the continuation and reproduction of the past. The thing endowed in Austria with strength and power is neither the nation, nor public opinion, nor the nobility, nor the officials, noryet the Emperor, who possesses the least of any; it is habit, custom, life by the day, routine.

"For three centuries the cause of Austria has been that of stationary rule, of absolute stability; under this rule she lives; all her affairs, all her interests, are measured by it. Should she try to become a little liberal, what would she do with the throes of Italy, the recollections of Bohemia, the weak heavings of Hungary, the cries of Gallicia? These populations ask nothing from her to-day, because they expect nothing; but, if the faintest opportunity were opened for them, what a deluge of complaints, recriminations, desires, attempts, would overflow [1]."

Such are the administrative means set to work by the government, aided by the clergy. Now, of these very Catholic means, what has been the result? Such is the question which remains for us to study.

Here is, first, a general answer:

1. Bernard, p. 213.

" The people have remained backward in the career of progress, and, with the exception of Bohemia, Moldavia, and Lombardy, where the progress that may be found must be attributed to particular, and, so to speak, local causes, the Austrian empire is to this day at the same degree of material prosperity as it was in the first years after the war.

" What, above all else, must be looked upon as the cause of this backward state of Austria, is that inconceivable political system, which consists in conjuring away every question, in putting aside, without destroying, every cause of change.

" What have been the results of this policy? Within, the government has alienated from itself the sympathies of the people; the State is burdened with a mass of ever-increasing debts; material prosperity has made and still makes none but infinitely slow and almost derisory progress; intellectual interests are entirely set aside. Without, Austria has lost power, respect, and influence; she owes the place she occupies among the great powers of Europe merely to a certain veneration for her ancient power; as to her real influence, she has lost it long since, and although she has the presidency in the German Diet, and notwithstanding the fascination of days of old which her name awakens, she has seen all her influence in Germany carried away and engrossed by Prussia. The Austrian influence is completely annihilated in the East, and in Italy it is restricted to a few Papal Legations, and to the *great powers* of Parma, Modena, Lucca, and San Marino! Such are the splendid results and valuable fruits that a peace of five-and-twenty years has brought forth and matured for Austria and her government! Devoid of all solid bases, and of every life-giving principle; fallen, as to its outward relations, in the public opinion of Europe; given up to foreign and hostile influences upon all its frontiers, the Austrian Empire cannot even secure to its own subjects the temporary and exclusive comfort of an assured and flourishing existence. An inanimate mechanism can produce nothing that has life. The Austrian Empire is being carefully embalmed; it is being wound round minutely to make it last, thus, powerless and immovable, as long as possible; but swathe it as they may, it will inevitably fall into dissolution, somewhat like the bodies overwhelmed at Pompeii, which dissolve into dust as soon as a ray of sun or the slightest breath lights upon them [1]. "

1. Bernard, p. 213 to 232.

After this general view of the results obtained by the Austrian Government, let us enter into particulars.

The first result of this coalition of Church and State to work the nation has necessarily been fatal to the two conspirators. A religion preached without conviction creates unbelievers; administrative agents formed to grind the people profit by the lesson, and grind their masters, and thus the snare formed for others entraps those who laid it. This is taught by the history of all nations, especially that of Austria. And first for the Church : " To say that the government is bigoted would be erroneous; a pompous religion, admitted without reflection, much music, and few words, that is what was given to the people; they came to the churches to have their ears and eyes charmed, and might unite the greatest vices with an apathetic admiration for holy things; this Catholicism, far more material than that of France, may be expressed as the worship of two of the five senses [1]. "

" Notwithstanding the universal respect paid to all religious observances in Austria, it is clear, for all who have the opportunity of noticing the manners of the country, and of interrogating the popular feeling, that little by little, and in silence, superstitious practices are falling into disuse among the enlightened classes; now they exclusively form the appanage of poverty and ignorance, just as the black bread and knitted jacket do [2]. "

The just punishment fallen upon the Church has also fallen upon the State. It had formed its agents for bribery, and its corrupt agents have deceived it: " Each province is governed one way or another; each state agent follows out his private end, often diametrically opposite to that of the other agents. The financial administration has differences with the political authorities, and the military administration with both. The one has lawsuits against the other, lasting for years, and glories in its victory when it is able to wrench anything from its adversary; while it never comes to any one's mind, that, after all, they serve one and the same country."

The fatal caste of the aristocracy has caused corruption to overflow widely around. It is to the nobility that Austria owes her vitiation to the very core. It must be left to skulking statistics, concealed as much as may be by the government, to form into figures the ruin of families, and the great anti-social effects of universal corruption.

1. Rey, p. 59. — 2. Trollope, vol. I, p. 235.

"There were too many agents in Austria, and too many useless ones, to be well paid; the majority did not gain half their livelihood, and they were left to procure the remainder from the pockets of the public; from thence arises that universal venality so odious to foreigners. With a wretched bank-note, a man might obtain anything, even simple justice! and without it the agents would subject him to interminable annoyances." These things will lead us to understand the state of finances : "Austria, during twenty-five years of thorough peace, has not yet been able to establish an equilibrium between her receipts and her expenditure, nor to get rid of the deficit, which, by returning at regular periods, exacts fresh loans, and unceasingly augments the public debt [1]."

Go through, now, the different classes of the people, and penetrate to the very sources of public welfare, and everywhere you will find a state of things in harmony with the corruption of the governing powers, and the ruin of the finances. Let this be judged of by the state of agriculture. And, first, let us go back by a few years : "The mountainous parts of the country are only suited for the cultivation of corn, on condition of being tilled with the irresistible sedulousness of the Swiss, upon which it would be folly to depend in Austria. Agriculture demands cattle, instruments, ready money; how could the poor vine-dresser obtain it all? It is computed that the peasant pays in taxes double what the nobles pay; that is to say, what with direct and indirect taxation, he gives away more than half his income, as in the fifteenth century. Now, agriculture being a fatiguing and complicated work, so long as the largest *portion* of the Austrian nation will not come to the resolution of giving up its laziness, or rather, so long as a greater degree of liberty will not stimulate it thereto, the best views of the government will be of no effect [2]."

In sixty years has much progress been made on this point? A writer of our own day replies: "The state of agriculture being generally backward, commerce does not find corn a considerable source of exportation; the importations, for certain grains, are even larger than the exportations. The vine is not cultivated with the care it demands. Agriculture is insignificant in its developments; it is wanting in capital and credit. On account of the imperfection of internal communication, it has no market for its produce, and when it finds one, it is hampered by a thousand vexatious and injurious fiscal measures. It groans under a land-

1. Rey, p. 53 to 55, and following. — 2. Mirabeau, vol. VII, pp. 486 and 520.

tax beyond all reasonable proportion, and, besides, in the greater number of the provinces, it is weighed down under the feudal system, with its loans in kind and others, together with the most deplorable consequences, without mentioning an entangled system of mortgage with endless delays [1]."

"In Austria, in that fertile country placed in the centre of Europe, in the midst of the most civilised nations, from two-thirds to two pounds of sugar only are consumed annually by each person; that is to say, that sugar is totally unknown to the inhabitants of the country, the greatest portion of the population. We find in this circumstance that Austria is at the bottom of the European scale, side by side with Russia and Turkey; one would think that sugar had chosen to conform itself, with regard to her, to the rank she occupies in so many other respects among the nations of Europe. In truth, it would be in vain to find a country in which the masses are so ignorant, so easily led, and oppressed, in which the land is so completely wanting in all the advantages with which modern civilisation has endowed us, and in which money is so rare among the people. I am well aware that sugar is not like meat, corn, linen, and wool, an absolutely indispensable article; but it is one of those things which necessity alone deprives one of, and by whose presence or absence we judge whether a family is well or ill-off. See Ireland, compared with England; there we find 4 lbs of sugar against 20 lbs; Bavaria with Prussia; there it is 2 1/2 lbs against 5; Italy with Holland, there it is 2 lbs against 14 [2]."

To this state of agriculture corresponds an analogous state of industry. Half a century ago, Mirabeau said: "The people are in a state of thraldom too hard and too general, in almost all the provinces under the Austrian sway, for industry to be universal. More liberty and more light would be necessary for that. In truth, the shackles which impede the progress of industry in the Austrian states come principally from the want of light; for ignorance, the lover of routine, fancies that wisdom consists in letting things alone. These are real calamities, to which the imperial authority should apply a remedy [3]."

In the present day, William Rey says further: "In passing under review the more advanced fabrics — the tissues, for instance, — a singular fact made its appearance; I observed more carefully, saw many workshops, and always with the same result; this was

1. Bernard, p. 20. — 2. Jacquemin. — 3. Mirabeau, vol. VII, p. 358.

the fact : At Vienna, nothing is made except on designs and models of novelties from Paris. Poverty of invention is absolute, and perhaps exceeds what we know of China. It is no more possible to believe in a return to originality in industry where it has so completely perished, and given way to servile imitations.

These censures fall even upon those things of which they boast. "We cannot understand the praises which are lavished upon the Austrian Government for undertaking the execution of the principal lines of railway, since this resolution was not adopted until after it had allowed commerce to fall into a most deplorable condition. The merchants are in fact much discouraged for want of credit; and they see nothing before their eyes but abortive enterprises such as the unfinished road from Gmunden to Budweis, the service upon which is made by horses. The enthusiasm manifested upon that occasion will not deceive those persons who know the spirit of the Austrian Government, and they will only see in it a profound ignorance of the facts[1]."

Education is as little advanced as industry. Austria, it must be admitted, invites professors from abroad, and opens schools, academies, and museums, but with obvious unwillingness, and under the pressure of the Protestant atmosphere by which she is enveloped. In Austria, they accept the torch of science, but it is behind a veil, and only because they cannot hide it under a bushel.

"Notwithstanding the splendid and expensive establishments for the cultivation of literature and sciences," says Catteau, "the public libraries, the botanical gardens, and the university, the taste for knowledge is not diffused in Vienna. A censorship, notoriously severe, has inflicted upon the press and the book trade disadvantages which have produced the most striking effects[2]."

"If the importance of a people is to be estimated by its literature, and the celebrated men it has produced, the Austrians do not occupy apparently a very distinguished rank. In fact, their literature is next to nothing at all. The small number of writers which this country has produced have been imitators, or more or less judicious critics. This people, who are very little susceptible of enthusiasm for the fine arts, have found it more convenient to imitate than to produce. They have tried with labour and taste to know and appreciate books already in existence. They have thus done without a talent which they might have needed, and which they do not

1. Rey, pp. 114 and 115. — 2. Catteau, vol. I, p. 216.

seem to have received from nature; the talent which forms models and founds a national literature. As able critics and laborious scholars, the Germans occupy a distinguished rank; it is the same with the Austrians, with this difference, that they have not attained the same degree of perfection; and they have remained far below perfection in the higher walks of literature. The Germans have advanced to the conception of the great beauties of literature, although in the midst of their most beautiful productions we are always sensible of the inequality of their talent; but the Austrians have not advanced so far, and nothing in their literature displays even the first essays of genius[1]."

"If some writers in the North of Germany have been able to escape from the influence of despotic institutions, they owe it to the society in the midst of which they have found themselves placed. In fact, several princes of the North of Germany have endeavoured to make their little capitals imitations of Ancient Athens; by giving freedom to thought, and exercising their power moderately, they have prepared and perhaps given birth to that literature which is a part of the glory of the nation. Monuments perish, conquests are obliterated, but a beautiful book survives everything, and becomes an imperishable title of glory for ever."

"If we apply these general remarks to Austria, we shall understand more easily how it is possible that she should be still without literature, and why the cultivation of the fine arts there has never shed much brilliancy.

"There is a certain flight which literature cannot take without encouragement, or at least men must be borne towards the cultivation of letters by motives more or less powerful. Far from dreaming of encouraging them, the sovereigns of Austria have always tried to keep down every literary impulse of the nation; not of itself, by the way, over much inclined to such pursuits; and, in consequence of determining to restrain everything, they have finished by extinguishing all. The whole nation is content with the repose and comfort which it owes to the fertility of the soil, and to institutions tolerably wise. It knows no better, and is contented with the passive wellbeing of the enjoyment of which it feels assured. None of those who form a part of the nation has ever thought that noble motives are needful to create the sacred faith, and thrill men with the sacred love of country. Hence it has happened that when any sovereign has wished to shake them out of their lethargy,

1. Marcel de Serres, vol. IV, pp. 30 to 32.

these populations have not in the least understood him, and have opposed his innovations with the calmness of apathy, and the icy silence of indifference. How, I ask, with such elements and such a nation, can Austria have a national literature? If the patriotic sentiment of a people is composed of the memories which great men have bequeathed to it, or of the admiration inspired by the master-pieces of the national genius, how can it exist among the Austrians? Who are the great men of Austria? where are the master-pieces produced by them? The former are few in number, and the latter have no existence[1]. "

" The want of emulation has hitherto suffocated in Austria the love of the fine arts, and if imagination exalts itself enough among us to create the hope of living by the arts in the future, something more positive is necessary nevertheless to the nations which love nothing but the realities of life. The government of Austria seems to wish to push equity further than is natural by treating talent and mediocrity equally. All minds thus remain in profound repose, and the calm of the senses contributes to prolong still further that of the soul. At what epoch will such a people awake, and when will they appear with glory in the literary world[2]? "

Such as the spiritual world is; such will be the physical world. " Most of the countries, " says Mirabeau, " under the House of Austria, stagnate in superstition and ignorance; nevertheless, the natural products are manufactured in all the provinces. There is nothing but the government which obstructs the factories by impeding industry; by obliging, for example, such a country to cast its metals into such a form, and sell them at such a place; and by subjecting industry to a thousand absurd impediments. What a system is that of a country in which there are not only tolls and customs between the country and foreigners, but also between one province and another; where exportation and importation are equally impeded; where there is a general prohibition against all goods of foreign manufacture; where they burn everything that they seize; where the people have nowhere neither liberty nor property; where they prescribe to the makers the works which they ought to make, and where they ought to sell them[3]. "

" The causes which have prevented, up to the present time, the improvement of industry in the Austrian States, are the education, and the prejudices to which the people of all classes still cling, and certain political institutions, such as serfdom, severe *corvées*,

1. Marcel de Serres, vol. IV, pp. 70 to 75. — 2. *Idem*, p. 85. — 3. Mirabeau, vol. VII, p. 378.

impediments to commerce, and taxes upon the exportation of merchandise, and the productions of the country. 'I speak,' says M. Hermann, 'as a patriot who suffers when he sees all around his country the arts and sciences flourishing, and already arrived almost at perfection, in many lands destitute of the natural advantages of Austria; and that in a great part of the monarchy ignorance and prejudices oppose a thousand obstacles to the wisest measures, and that industry should be almost extinct in the remote districts and provinces [1].'"

The preceding applies to the Austrian Empire as a whole; but this vast state, composed of parts related to each other, must be studied in each of them. They are all Catholic, and this is enough for our purpose; it is useful to see how Catholicism bears fruits of the same savour, even when grafted upon different nations.

Let us start from the capital as from a centre: "Little familiar with good society, the young men of Vienna appear out of place in it, or without amiability. Without employment, and very often ill-educated, their way of life is even still more futile than those of the lightest of the women; gaming and hunting are their only resources; and insipid conversations are the only means left them to render supportable to other people the weight of their uselessness. These creatures, as weary as wearisome, are more common at Vienna than anywhere else. Literature is so little honoured in that capital, and consequently so little cultivated, that it never becomes a serious occupation except to a small number of men. Men of science and letters form there a class apart, with little communication with the fashionable world. The results are that the former are deficient in grace and ease, and the latter boast of their ignorance, or, which is almost the same thing, of their stupidity [2]."

Let us enter a neighbouring province:

"In Lower Carinthia the peasant must work three or four days a-week for his lord, who takes, besides, a half of the harvest. However accustomed we may be to see man endure every thing, it is still difficult to conceive how he can endure such sufferings, without crushing a thousand times such oppressive tyrants [3]."

"M. Campe, a writer worthy of credit, assures us that he has never seen numbers of beggars approaching those which he met in crossing the Brisgau, in the environs of the four frontier towns. You cannot, he says, form an idea of it. When the Emperor crosses

1. Mirabeau, vol. VII, p. 414. — 2. Marcel de Serres, vol. V, p. 151. — 3. Mirabeau, vol. VII, p. 259.

these countries, great pains are taken to send them away, that at least there may be presented to the eyes of the monarch an appearance of prosperity[1]. "

" The people of Illyria are, in general, governed absolutely by their clergy. They are of the Greek rite, although not united; they are kept in the densest ignorance, says the author of a memoir, who was a long time physician to a Greek bishop in Croatia, to facilitate Catholic proselytism, as if it were not necessary to make men *men*, prior to making them orthodox. It is by educating the clergy that it is necessary to commence the civilisation of these populations. The government has often been urged to consent to the establishment of schools for the clergy; but, convinced that their ignorance is favourable to the introduction of Catholicism into the country, the government has constantly refused. We might here agitate the question, if the maintenance of superstition and barbarism is not a feature of the profound policy of the House of Austria, since it is more than probable that these populations, by civilising and instructing themselves, would become less fit for the kind of war which they wage in such a superior manner; but we shall regard this question as too atrocious to be discussed. To brutify a part of the human species to make them more perfect beasts of prey, would be one of the most frightful crimes of *lèse-humanité*, or treason against humanity[2]. "

" The soil of Hungary is cultivated without intelligence and without care. Nothing is wanting to enable this country to take the first rank among the most favoured countries of Europe, except a more enlightened direction of its rural economy. It would seem that Hungary, which had been so favourably treated by nature, ought to be the richest and the most beautiful country in the world. But it is nothing in the world, and many causes combine to prevent its becoming anything in it.

" The indolence, the ignorance, and the carelessness of the inhabitants drive away the happiness which offers itself. The earth is badly cultivated; the stagnant waters exhale, during summer, malignant miasms, which engender destructive maladies among men and animals. Education might elevate the lower classes towards better habits, but this education is almost absolutely wanting; dreaded perhaps by the classes who could spread it, the want is not felt by those to whom it would be most useful[3]. "

" Assuredly the kingdom of Hungary is admirably endowed by

1. Mirabeau, vol. VII, p. 269. — 2. *Idem*, pp. 298 to 300. — 3. D'Haussez, vol. II, pp. 191 to 195.

nature, the territory is nearly everywhere of a rare fertility, but, unfortunately, agriculture and industry are there in their infancy. Man has not undertaken anything as yet to draw forth the riches of the soil, which await the hand of the skilful and laborious workman, and enterprising capitalists who shall undertake to extract them, and turn them to profit[1]."

Such is the general state of the country; but an exception is mentioned; and we shall see that it is to the profit of another principle than that of Catholicism. The fact which we have shown in Ireland is produced in Germany, that is to say, that in the same circumstances of climate and administration, the Protestant populations have, over the Catholic populations with which they are mingled, an incontestable superiority.

"In Hungary are found Germans called Saxons by the Magyars; they have been drawn from the North of Germany by the ancient kings to teach agriculture, work the mines, and build castles; they enjoy certain privileges, and are Lutherans[2]."

The effects of this Protestant colonisation have been such as are seen generally; but they are all the more remarkable here, that they shew themselves beside the Catholic populations, who still remain inferior to these industrious foreigners.

"Civilisation, in Hungary, owes its most marked progress to Germans. They make more than half the population in the towns worthy of the name, and where the arts and skilled trades are carried on. Agriculture has also profited from the residence of the Germans: in cultivating the same land as the Magyars and the Wallachians, they always derive from it superior maize, or tobacco, or fuller corn, less soiled with earth and tares, and for which a higher price will be given. This is so true, that in the Banat they speak of German corn and Hungarian corn as if they were two different kinds of grain. The German has always had a feeling of his superiority over the disorderly and debt-ridden Hungarian nobility[3]."

But let us return to the Catholic populations and their ignorance: "In the elevated Cantons of the Tyrol, the peasants believe in good and evil sprites. The village maidens scarcely dare to go out in the twilight, or after the time of vespers, for fear of falling into some trap laid for them by infernal spirits. There is nothing, not even the murmur produced by the fresh evening breeze, which their exalted imaginations does not believe to be an announcement of

1. Desprez, vol. I, p. 251. — 2. Rougemont, p. 373. — 3. Rey, pp. 103, 104.

the presence of ghosts. The clouds which collect together before a storm, appear equally to them to be malignant divinities coming into collision. Thus, their superstitious dreams animate all nature. To protect themselves from these pretended sprites, many Tyrolese, and even some of the women, carve in their own flesh, by pricking with needles, and rubbing gunpowder into the holes, figures of Christ or of saints, and thus think themselves preserved for ever [1]."

Does this religious faith purify the morals? we may judge: "The very young girls of Voralberg (Tyrol) wear red sleeves, until about their fifteenth year, when they change them for black. A custom which is rigorously kept forbids the young men from making any attempts against the virtue of the girls with red sleeves; another custom, which they say does not admit of any more exceptions, authorises the most entire liberty in regard to those with the black sleeves. The unfortunate girl who has committed a fault is forced by her companions to substitute, for the ribbon knots and long gold or silver pin which keeps up her hair, a very little white cap, which she is obliged to wear. I have met, in my journies, a considerable number of white caps, and have been assured that I might have counted a much greater number, if, from the time that they perceive a change of head-dress inevitable, the families did not take means to prevent the shame, which nevertheless has no influence on the future estimation of the woman who has submitted to it.

"The first time that I entered into an inn to obtain the means of satisfying my hunger, which a long and painful road had made very exacting, they told me I might partake of the family meal. I was about to decline this honour, when my guide warned me that by doing so I should be guilty of a great incivility; and that, besides, the man who offered me this kind of politeness was an important personage, the chief magistrate of the place. I then resigned myself. I asked myself how they could take what was served to eat while the table was without plates. The host did not leave me long in uncertainty; he took one of the spoons, which were thrown in a heap upon the table, plunged it into the soup tureen, carried it to his mouth, and, leaning on the left elbow, while his right hand was in action, continued this exercise; every body imitated him, and myself like the rest, in spite of my repugnance. I remarked that those of the guests who piqued themselves on their good manners

1. Marcel de Serres, vol. VI, p. 88.

advanced the left hand, at the same time as the right, to catch what fell from the spoon before it reached the table-cloth [1]."

"Notwithstanding the innumerable resources which the fertility of the soil, the working of the mines and the woods, and the different manufactures created since the last century, present to the inhabitants of Bohemia, the country is not very flourishing. The villagers are reduced to the condition of serfs; and discouragement and apathy, the necessary fruits of slavery, always keep up in Bohemia a multitude of beggars and vagabonds. Such is the state of degradation of these poor creatures: the man is clothed in rags, and covered with a bad hairy cap; a stick helps to keep him up in a reckless attitude; he walks with bare feet, and he remains steeped in sloth, until an imperious necessity compels him to work [2]."

"In Dalmatia, there are not seven in twenty of the children who go to school; in Illyria not one-half; and in Gallicia not eighteen in twenty. The country people in Hungary remain buried in the deepest ignorance [3]."

"Industry is not proportionate to the richness of the soil, and the abundance of raw materials. Agriculture and the rearing of cattle are not well understood, except in the districts inhabited by the Germans (the author thus designates the Protestant district) [4]."

"In Gallicia, the industrial class is still in its infancy, the nobility uneducated, and the serfs ignorant and lazy [5]."

"The Zingarians, those even who have abandoned vagabondage and become Austrian peasants, most frequently do not possess even the cabin and the rags of the subject. They live under the earth, in holes covered with straw or faggots and clay, and shut by doors made of willows. Sometimes, near a great road, while you are looking for some new horizon, suddenly a few paces off, and at the side of a rock, human heads appear like spectres coming out of dilapidated tombs. These are Zingarian peasants attracted by the noise of your steps, and who come to ask charity. In these infected holes, children of both sexes are brought up almost to the age of puberty entirely naked, and with more than primitive liberty. To be just, I cannot throw upon the legislation and the proprietors all the responsibility of such destitution; but, because generous spirits have lost their labour in misdirected attempts at reformation, it does not follow that the Transylvanian nobles have ac-

1. D'Haussez, vol. I, pp. 355 to 358. — 2. Marcel de Serres, vol. V, p. 69. — 3. Rougemont, p. 348. — 4. *Idem*, p. 349. — 5. *Idem*, p. 367.

quired the right, in regard to these unhappy populations, to erect contempt and cruelty into a system.

"The peasants merit still less to be treated with this culpable indifference, as they are the noblest people in the principality. Those of Transylvania are not laborious, because up to the present time they have not been free. Their love of repose has no other cause. When refusing them the means of quitting their social apathy, the proprietors have been influenced no doubt by the prospect of the dangers by which they might be menaced by the development of nationality.

"In the two kingdoms of Hungary and Croatia, misery does not present the hideous aspect, the frightful nakedness, which it displays in Transylvania. However, it is necessary that the material condition of the country should be made what it might be under milder laws and government. Hungary is a generous land. The soil yields everything demanded of it; unfortunately, the means of carriage and transport are either impossible, or extremely dear. Very often the bridges are in ruins, and it is dangerous to cross by them in the night. In the villages, and sometimes in certain inland towns, the streets are not better kept. It sometimes happens that we are obliged to take a horse to get along them [1]."

"The part of Croatia situated beyond St. Georges is that where the absence of civilisation is most shockingly remarkable. From the ferocious air of the inhabitants, from their dress, which is composed of square bits of cotton or coarse stuff, and a mantle of sheepskin, from the nakedness of different parts of their bodies, from the sourness of their manners, from the form of their houses, we might believe ourselves amidst the savannas of Canada, or on the banks of some river of New Holland [2]."

"The Wallachians, who have established their residences in the mountains of Siebenbourg, may be considered as the European nation among whom civilisation is least advanced. Deprived of activity and industry, they lead a reckless life, and know no other occupation than that of keeping their flocks. There are few of them who will take the trouble of cultivating the earth, and these only when forced by extreme necessity. The Wallachians are distrustful and vindictive, and cordially hate all other nations. Drunkenness and the basest inclinations proceed from their bad education and the examples of the r forefathers. They allow their beards and hair to grow, which present a most disgusting appear-

1. Desprez, vol. I, pp. 178 to 182. — 2. D'Haussez, vol. II, p. 174.

ance; and they do not take the trouble to tie them, much less to comb them. Their whole dress consists of a coarse shirt, fastened round the waist by a leather belt, garnished with several buttons, on which are suspended their knives, their forks, and their short sabres[1]. "

If it is observed to us that it is not the Austrian government which has fashioned all these populations, we shall answer, no more is it the government which we accuse, but the primary cause which has formed these different nations, and even the government itself—we mean Roman Catholicism. Moreover, there is a creation which belongs entirely to this government; let it be judged. " Has Austrian society profited by the creation of the military colonies? is the population happy which lives in subjection to the *régime* of that establishment? Can we hope for it any progress or civilisation, or any amelioration of its lot? A negative answer it would appear ought to be made to each of these questions, when we consider the time which has passed since the formation of these establishments, the state of the population of which they are composed, and the country in which they exist.

" Eighty years have passed over the work of the genius of Maria Theresa. There is always the same brutality, the same immorality, the same ignorance of the most essential things, the same disdain for the comforts of life, and the same incapacity for procuring them. From so many efforts, and so much perseverance, all the results are some thousands more of coarse creatures, some cabins to shelter them, and some cultivated fields to nourish them. As for any real amelioration in the physical and moral state of the population, anything superior or even mediocre cannot be cited. I do not think that there exists in all Europe a population more backward in civilisation or intelligence than those of this country. The most simple circumstance embarrasses and stops individuals whose position and supposed education ought to make us believe them to be more intelligent; their only means is the brutal and uncontrolled exercise of an authority which extends to everything. It cannot be otherwise in a state of things which transmits its principle of stagnation to the society which it rules. A similar organisation cannot reproduce anything, but that which has created itself. Soldiers and not citizens; creatures condemned not to move except to the sound of the drum, to offer their backs to the lash of the

1. Marcel de Serres, vol. III, p. 32.

corporal, and, when war has spared them, to die upon the spot where they have lived, the lives of brutes, and almost those of vegetables. No progress can therefore be expected from society thus organised; these institutions have no other results than to extract from lands, previously sterile, the subsistence of a certain number of individuals, whose whole aptitudes, and only destiny, are confined to killing and being killed, and to create other individuals to succeed them, stupid, miserable, and enslaved, like themselves, and accepting life upon the same conditions. It was not worth while to do so much to go so far, and not go any farther[1]."

What we have said of Austria may be said of the other Catholic countries of Germany, and especially of Bavaria. A few short quotations will suffice to estimate the resemblance of the two nations.

First of all, let us hear Mirabeau. If the condition he describes is not exactly that of our times, it is at least contemporary with the condition of Prussia, of which the same author will inform us farther on, and this is enough for our comparison. More recent documents will follow elsewhere the testimony of Mirabeau: "Whence comes the condition of the commerce of Bavaria?" asks the illustrious orator. "The primary cause is found in the ignorance into which all classes of the people are plunged. We are assured that one-third of the people of Bavaria do not know how to read. A peasant who knows how to read is there a rare being. There is often only one school for a whole bailiwick, and moreover the schoolmasters are ignorant and ill-paid. The priests govern the whole nation, and they wish this state of things to last, as it is advantageous to them: they increase superstition all they can, and this superstition is destructive of every kind of industry. The infinite numbers of fêtes, pilgrimages, and processions keep up idleness and misery. The number of government stipendiaries are enormous, and also the number of overseers in the country, who, being as ignorant as they are rapacious, torment the peasants in the most cruel fashion. To form an idea of the oppressions which the unhappy cultivator has to support, it will suffice to know that when he takes possession of a property of the value of about 4,000 *l.*, he pays in fees to the overseers of the government 1,216 *l.*, without counting the expenses of the commission and of the inventory. How can he preserve the idea of escaping from his miserable condition? thus he cares for nothing but to consume the fruits which a fertile soil

1. D'Haussez, t. II, pp. 178 to 181.

renders him, without thinking of securing the permanent improvement of his condition. Another very sad consequence of this state of things is, that there is no country in all Germany where crimes are so frequent, and the wheel and the gibbet so active as in Bavaria. It is said that the great roads form in this respect an atrocious spectacle for sensitive travellers, as they are bordered on both sides by gibbets, as other roads are by useful trees. This is atrocious, no doubt, but it does not the less show the excess of evil which has been the cause of it. We feel that in such a situation it need not be asked if there is any commerce in Bavaria. How can a country, although endowed with a fertile soil, be worth a crown in money, while oppressed by ecclesiastical and secular power, without manufacturing industry, without commerce, and obliged to derive the satisfaction of nearly all its wants from the works of foreigners?

"It is not that Bavaria might not be infinitely more prosperous. Let them deliver it from a clergy who possess nearly one-third of the revenue of the country, and still more from the ignorance in which this clergy holds it; let them relieve it from the immense pressure of the holydays, which cause the working classes to lose such an infinitude of time; let them allow intelligence to penetrate into it, which would be followed by an improved agriculture; let them destroy the immense crowd of stipendiaries, and especially the overseers of the government, who oppress the cultivator at will; and soon the population will increase, and the country attain all the wealth that nature has destined it to[1]."

"The mendicant friars are one of the small plagues of Catholic countries. We remember to have read in a little German work, entitled, *Voyages dans le cercle de Bavière*, 1784, that they overran Bavaria like a sort of holy constabulary; laying peasants, shopkeepers, and artisans under contribution because gentlemen will not suffer them to enter into their mansions, and keep them aloof as if they were a sort of stinking and rapacious vermin[2]."

"The horrible persecutions suffered by the members of the society to maintain and diffuse information in Bavaria still draw tears from the eyes of all enlightened and sensible men in Germany, and will be the eternal shame of the present government in Bavaria."

"The superstitious party triumphs there completely at present, and of course there is no occasion to say that the education of the people and even of persons of rank is in the most miserable condition. The University of Ingoldstadt is entirely in the hands of ex-

1. Mirabeau, vol. VIII, pp. 336 to 338. — 2. *Idem*, p. 367.

Jesuits, and of all those men whose unique object is to increase ignorance and barbarism. In Bavaria, the colleges are workshops, in which they mutilate minds by teaching them nothing except barbarous Latin and brutilising theology. The schools of the people are, if possible, in a still more deplorable state. They are too few in number, and in consequence of the ignorance of the clergy and the schoolmasters the few there are do more harm than good. It is owing, apparently, to the ignorance of the people that an enormous quantity of crimes are committed in Bavaria.

"The monks themselves are guilty of strange atrocities, and if justice examines the facts and discovers them, the ecclesiastical power, by superior orders, withdraws the criminals from secular punishment.

"M. Nicolaï assures us that in 1781, eighteen executions took place in Munich, and that in 1775 it was a common thing to have two or three a-week. From whatever cause it may be, the ignorance of the clergy, and hence for the best of all reasons that of all classes of the people whom the clergy ought to instruct, is incredible[1]."

This description, written in the end of the last century, compared with one of our own day, will have the advantage of proving what indeed Catholicism boasts of, that under her rule people do not change: "The Bavarians," says M. Marcel de Serres, "seem much attached to the faith of their forefathers; the people, naturally less informed, appear to be more religious than educated persons, if we regard in religion only its observances. They owe to their great love for religious observances the taint of superstition from which they are not yet free. Their superstition is confined generally to the belief in good and evil spirits, and that these last trouble good order. The peasants even think that these spirits appear upon the earth in certain cases either to increase the ailments of their bodies, or to destroy the fruits of their labour. Almost all, and especially the inhabitants of the mountains, equally believe that the dead reappear after a certain time, and thus there is not a village nor a hamlet in which they do not narrate adventures with ghosts each more marvellous than the other. Here, it is a husband who has come back to devour his widow while she was giving herself up to amorous pleasures. There, it is a *curé* who has been seen reproaching young people for their indecent conduct; and farther on it is a miser who has seen a frightful spectre when about to count his gold. There is nothing which their imaginations does not

1. Mirabeau, vol. VIII, pp. 375 to 377.

animate, even the clouds; whilst others see the lines of happiness or misfortune in the manner in which the meteors and shooting stars glide in the skies. The graveyards are places which the people dread passing after dark, such is their fear of meeting malignant ghosts or spirits[1]."

"The greatest fault of the Bavarians is to be slow and lazy. Naturally far from active, they are not industrious except when driven to it by poverty or by indispensable work. The love of strong liquors often deranges their feeble brains. This passion is all the more dangerous for them, as it goes on increasing continually. The girls, like the women, share in this taste of the men, and their hearts often go astray when their heads can no longer resist the effects of these perfidious liquors[2]."

"Bavaria offers an example of the trist results produced by a bad administration. It is one of the most fertile countries in Germany. Upon entering into Bavaria I expected to see agriculture in a more prosperous state, but two-thirds of the country showed me I had deluded myself, so true it is that the paralysis of industry and commerce throws perturbation into all branches of agriculture. Bavaria, which is not or rather has almost entirely ceased to be industrial and commercial, has nothing more than a disorganised agriculture. There is not, perhaps in all Germany, a country in which agriculture has less capital, in which there is less money in circulation, where the country people are less provided with cash, or are more in debt. The debt of the kingdom, which amounts to more than 800 millions, presses with all its weight upon the soil. Nowhere have the products of the earth fallen to so low a price. Agricultural legislation is there most backward, and they not only do not in the least protect agriculture, and agricultural instruction is not merely neglected, but it is even repelled from the country as an object of repugnance. An agricultural institution, which might effect much good in the country, has waited for many long years for the sanction of the Crown to the assignment of funds to it which were voted in the budget, and it is probable that they will still have to wait a long time, as the king Louis has a horror of agriculture.

"In this state of things the products of agriculture are of scarcely any value, and are disposed of with difficulty. Hence the great quantity of uncultivated land, or which merely serves for pasturage. More than 300,000 arpents of land need only a little labour to become very productive, but where are the means to be found of covering

1. Marcel de Serres, vol. VI, pp. 53 to 56. — 2. *Idem*, vol. VI, p. 61.

the first expenses? It is the same with the grass lands, nine-tenths of which demand in vain the most simple modern improvements. Such is the general condition of agriculture in Bavaria. Almost the whole nation devotes itself to agricultural labours, but they are far from productive; as the Bavarian government, I repeat, does not encourage them in any way. No government in Germany pursues a more retrograde or more anti-national course[1]. "

In running over the different works which we have quoted upon Catholic Germany, and in particular on Austria, we have asked ourselves if our authors, as foreigners and travellers, had not become angry against a government which does not agree with their personal opinions, or at least have deceived themselves about a country in which they had not lived a long time. We have therefore been glad to find a writer, himself an Austrian, who can describe his country for us. We shall quote him with all the more confidence that everything in his book bespeaks a man who is calm, impartial, and well-informed on the subject upon which he treats. The confidence with which he inspires us will not fail to gain our readers. This last quotation upon Austria, if longer than its predecessors, is also more interesting:

"There exists no Autrian nationality, except in the narrow circle which surrounds Vienna. Without sympathies, without glorious memories, there is a dearth of facts in their history. The patriotism which broods in the heart of a Austrian embraces only his village, or at best only his province. The Frenchmen, when he speaks of his France, of *sa grande nation*, seems to grow bigger, however middling or little he may otherwise be, in his person. The Englishman, proud of his isolation amidst the waves, thinks himself a king when he compares himself with other nations. How small, on the contrary, ought the Austrian to appear to himself when he finds none of these sentiments in his soul, and no other pride than what may be inspired by the hope of becoming chamberlain or aulic councillor[2]. "

"Is it necessary that a state, which like Austria contains so many elements of strength and development, should be condemned to drag on its existence for ever under an overwhelming sense of insignificance. Austria has had her epoch of complete political apathy, and perhaps it still exists; she has also given a sad example of indifference to everything which does not concern her material wants. Governments who find it convenient to rule over nations buried in

1. Jacquemin, pp. 27 to 29. — 2. *De l'Autriche et de son avenir*, vol. I, pp. 8 to 10.

sleep, praise to their subjects the Austrian populations as examples and models: hence the pretty tales told to put these great infants to sleep about the perfect happiness and idyllic contentment of these populations. But these times are gone. In Austria, as elsewhere, the wants of the age, wants of an elevated order, and such as are felt by an intelligence which has begun to understand itself, have claimed their rights. An apathetic indifference to public affairs, a complete carelessness of the progress of time and of humanity, cannot subsist in this country any more than in any other in Europe. Nothing has as yet been seen having the remotest resemblance to the birth of an Austrian national sentiment, of a public spirit which embraces the State as a whole. This could not be otherwise, as the government has itself neglected to give to these sentiments an impulse and a rallying point. It would not call to life the forces which it believed to be buried in annihilation, and they have therefore turned away from it. At the point at which we have arrived, there may still be, although it may be doubted, the means of arresting this decomposition; but if the times in which we live are not skillfully turned to profit, the moment is not far distant in which four great and armed nationalities will be seen assuming hostile attitudes to each other, and having nothing in common except aversion and hatred against the government, if the latter does not give any heed to the demands always increasing, and always more pressing, which are addressed to it. The fatal crisis of this discontent cannot be far off, and its results are not doubtful.

"Already a total absence of affection and interest for the Government is observed everywhere in Austria; nowhere is the feeling of union found which in other countries makes the citizens like so many brothers; and the painful impression produced by this observation becomes all the stronger when we compare this apathetic disregard for the government with the lively, active, and always vigilant interest which without intermission attaches itself to the material and intellectual wants of the province or of the race. Another and a still graver symptom is the want of confidence in the future which distresses the inhabitant of the Austrian Empire, without his being able to explain it to himself; everybody in this country seems to be a prey to the sinister presentiment that the present state of things cannot last; that great changes are about to take place; that the policy of the government is only palliative, and that it only tends to prolong the actual situation, and save the present moment without caring for what is to come after it[1]."

1. *De l'Autriche et de son avenir*, vol. I, pp. 19 to 24.

" Meanwhile, the spirit has left the old governmental machine of Austria. A pernicious centralisation, a deplorable bureaucracy, has annihilated these venerable institutions, the Estates are without force, and, what is worse, without consideration. Mere shadows of national representation, they are every year exposed to the eyes of the multitude to amuse them at the expense of deputies, all of whose rights resolve themselves into one, that of *wearing a certain uniform!* and any attempt on their part to do anything more would be a crime!

" At the commencement of this century, shortly after the great struggle of nations, and during a dearth which killed by famine and misery thousands of men, the Estates of a province dared to lay before the throne a respectful remonstrance, and solicit from the Emperor a temporary diminution of taxes. The result of this proceeding was the most complete disgrace for the province and the Estates; and this disgrace lasted until after the death of the Emperor Francis. They had permitted themselves to usurp a sort of constitutional right of petition, and it was this which excited the wrath of the master [1]. "

" The principal and almost the only functions of the Estates are to cause the taxes to be collected and thrown into the government treasury. That in such a situation they should be destitute of all moral credit, and every kind of importance in the eyes of the people, is quite right, and a matter of course.

" Every extraordinary movement which happens unforeseen, be it good or bad, is foreign to Austria. Everything is there regulated and measured beforehand by the iron hand of habit. Everything moves within limits which it cannot quit neither by the most daring ambition, nor the most powerful influence. They might write upon the cradle of every Austrian who is born the history of his future destinies. Austria is the classic land of routine — of the customs which are observed to-day, because they were observed yesterday.

" The Austrian gentleman, deprived of all political importance, and imprisoned in a formalism which excluded all free development of the mind, and still more all profitable, practical activity, cannot preserve any other ambition than that of dragging on his life in a monotonous garrison, or of rolling out of one office into another without object, without tendency and without inner life, and curbing his mind beneath the miserable trifles which compose administrative routine. When old, he will become governor or

1. *De l'Autriche et de son avenir*, vol. I, pp. 38 to 39.

president, and will descend to the tomb conscious that he has not, during his long life of a polype, done a single useful, influential, or beneficent action which he can call his own, and leave with legitimate pride as an inheritance to his children. The thing which alone possesses force and power in Austria, is habit, custom, the daily course of routine. There is no reasonable indemnity for such a shabby existence, for this absence of all spiritual action; this life-long winter sleep, which does not receive from all the great vital questions which agitate our age anything but a far-off echo, like a confused dream, or a doubtful vibration. An intellectual suicide so blameable could not appear supportable except to one whose mind had been early confined within narrow limits, and who has not learned any other object than that of securing his daily bread. All the intelligent classes in Austria suffer from this painful and false position, and the nobility feel it most profoundly and most severely. When all other classes develope their activity, theirs is without object; being shut out from commerce by what may be a prejudice, but which is not on that account the less powerful. The absence of social and public life, and of publicity, takes from them all independent and personal activity, and they are reduced to the poor and ungrateful pursuits which the favour of the most mechanical of all governments permits to its friends.

"Every official at his commencement must pass, in all, sixteen years in his noviciate : they do not take the least notice of the differences of talents, or the different doses of the sciences, with which they may be provided. The poor infant is thus scarcely born before he ought to put himself on the wheel of the great machine which will henceforth carry him along to his last moment in the continued movement which it describes. Not a moment is allowed to this human being, during his whole life, to enjoy his liberty or take his breath; not a moment in which he might collect himself in the midst of the stupifying rotation and ask himself, why he is placed in that machine? if it is worth such a great sacrifice? and if *it* exists for his sake, or *he* for its sake?

"Sixteen years! and sixteen years of infancy and of youth! what a treasure of time and of faculties given to the State! what things might be learned in these sixteen years, the most important and the most decisive of the human life! How many fruitful seeds might have been thrown over this virgin soil! But, alas! the educational establishments of Austria do not comprehend the importance of their mission, and the possibility of fulfilling them. An unhappy pedantry, a shameful negligence of what is most important to the man and the citizen, dwarfs the young minds, impressing on them a restricted and unintelligent direction, turning aside their flight from every superior object, guiding them towards the vulgar road, and making them desire only their pitiful daily bread. There is no liberty of discussion or of thought. They have an educational book prescribed for each science, generally the true work of a pedant, and they are never allowed to go from it even by verbal commentaries. There is no social intercourse, or tie of the affections or of the soul between the professors and the scholars; there is nothing between them except the fear which the pupil has of an unfavourable report. They strengthen the memories of the pupils at the expense of their minds, by filling their heads with such a mass of useless and inapplicable things that there is no room left for thought. Their character and their moral development are entirely set aside, or limited to giving them some undigested religious instruction. Out of school, the life of the pupils is rendered painful by a contemptible and pedantic oversight, the lofty object of which manifests itself in a ridiculous war against smoking, sticks, and moustaches.

"Hence, very few auditors are seen in the educational establishments of Austria who are attracted there by the love of science. Nearly all regard their studies as a necessary evil; the only means of obtaining an office, or rather a salary — that only and grand object of the pupils, in their most golden dreams. To reach this object, they drag themselves painfully through the prescribed years, they support patiently the meagre lessons of the professor, and they reach with pleasure the end of a pleasureless career, and enter into another which is not less punctiliously regulated, nor less destitute of enjoyments.

"From his most tender youth, the Austrian has his spirit confined as in a fold; he has been brought up with one idea, and for one sole object, namely, to procure his daily bread. A stranger to every real interest, and to every elevated view, he has not from his earliest years seen anything but one winding, dull, and obscure path, which he has not chosen for the object to which it leads, nor for its noble destination; but only for the bread which he finds on it.

"It may be that there are other countries in which scientific education is not superior to that of Austria; but in these countries life outside the school has more liberty, and fewer impediments. Juvenile action, the development of ideas, is not so confined; there is none of that unreasonable and calculated pedantry which tends to suffocate liberty and spiritual life. The time of study passed, the young man enjoys an interval of full and absolute leisure. He can then disembarrass himself of the chain which a life of routine has riveted around him. He can, in the consciousness of his liberty, consider the course he would like best. He will not give way to a necessity which is often imaginary, and will not submit passively to the immediate consequences of the present. This short and only moment of liberty is forbidden to the future Austrian functionary. Hence it would be difficult to find a class so full of lost and broken existences, of souls so tormented by discontent, as that of the Austrian functionaries. In fact, most of them have adopted their trade without a taste or inward vocation for it, and even many of them with marked repugnance.

"If the past presents itself to them deprived of enjoyment, the perspective of the future is not less unprovided with every excitement to activity. For them, the weak thread of life unrols itself with an excessive slowness. The day of advancement arrives, without anything being able to accelerate or retard it a single hour. No mark of distinction, no gratitude, no public encouragement comes to recompense extraordinary efforts, or a capacity a little superior to mediocrity.

"The Austrian administration leaves to the *communes* so little liberty of action, that they cannot nominate any of their functionaries, not even their clerks, attornies, etc.; the nomination and dismissal of these subaltern *employés* is entirely at the mercy of the government, which is not in the least obliged to make known the motive of its acts. The administration of the expenses and receipts of the *commune*, like that of the common funds, is placed under the special inspection of the government of the State. No meeting for any object can take place without the permission of the authorities, nor without their presence, and these restrictions apply not only to rural *communes*, but also to towns, whatever may be their extent or their importance.

"When a few centuries hence our descendants shall study the institutions of their ancestors, when they shall see how the management of affairs the most important to individuals, and which affect them the most, were forbidden to the only persons who were directly interested in them, when they shall know that their management was confided to indifferent strangers, they will doubt the existence of such a state of things, and will be astonished at the stupidity of the governments and the good-nature of the governed.

"It is easy to understand what must be the influence of judicial functionaries whose power is neither limited by the institution of the jury, nor by the publicity of their proceedings, and who decide upon the property as upon the lives of the citizens. An influence not less great, and perhaps not less odious, is that of the officers of the Exchequer and the Excise, who are in constant contact with the people, and who have the right to control their daily income, and its consumption. The people ought to see in the functionaries auxiliaries to their efforts towards progress and improvement; the guides, in fact, of their knowledge and intelligence; they ought to recognise in them the will to do good, a sympathy for it, and, in a word, the opposite of what they now see in them. The antipathy of the Austrian people for the officials is thus all the stronger, that they know they have they right to make complaints against them, and that instead of hastening to do justice, they have a want of all interest in it, and an indifference without limits in regard to the men out of whose ranks they have nevertheless themselves risen [1]. "

" The deficit always returns in a regular manner in the Austrian administration. Where does such a state of the finances lead? The debt of the State, which augments every year, absorbs in a continually increasing proportion the public revenue, and the whole administration is annually becoming more costly and more complicated. The number of officials, which is augmenting incessantly, presents a frightful perspective. In such a situation, the only remedy for the disorder of the finances is a complete change of the present system [2]."

" The severity of the fiscal measures has now become vexatious beyond imagination. The tax-gatherers and excise men pursue their victims into the minutest details of their domestic affairs when they believe that they see an actual or an intended fraud against the Exchequer; and these agents not only have the right, and the duty, but, what is more important, it is their personal interest, to proceed to the most rigorous search upon any suspicion whatever. The natural consequences of this state of things is that a number of small producers and small traders have given up their businesses, because they did not find it worth while to subject themselves to such vexations, or because they were not able to meet the expenses which, *per fas* or *per nefas*, were always joined to such official acts. The result is the profound hatred which the people have against the tax-gatherers, a hatred which becomes more deeply rooted every day, and which is even already shown too frequently by bloody struggles, and sometimes murders [3]."

1. *De l'Autriche et de son avenir*, vol. I, pp. 38 to 64. — 2. *Idem*, p. 95. — 3. *Idem*, p. 104.

"Agriculture and rural economy are very far from having reached in Austria the degree of improvement which they have attained in other countries, especially in England and some parts of Germany. This state of things ought to be attributed to the land tax (*l'impôt foncier*), which has been raised most unreasonably. In the hereditary countries of Austria these taxes bring in about triple what they yield in England; a country in which the average price of rural produce is double what it is in Austria [1].

"Austria has not as yet attained its agricultural development; and the system of mortages, so perplexed, so full of delays, so little fixed, does not appear to be well adapted to facilitate her progress. Agriculture needs capital, credit, and encouraging examples to excite emulation. In consequence of defective interior arrangements, there are no markets for their produce, and even if they could be found they would be impeded by a thousand noxious and vexatious fiscal regulations. Agriculture groans under taxes which it is almost impossible to pay, and in most of the provinces under the feudal system with its offerings in kind and otherwise, and all its most disastrous consequences. The result of this shameful situation is that Austria, a country almost exclusively agricultural, does not produce enough of corn for its own consumption, and that the importations of certain cereals is much greater than its exportations.[2] The commercial policy of Austria is still very far from being what it ought to be, and it cannot be otherwise under the system which prevails; for, in a country where the wants and wishes of the people have no organ, and where they are submitted to the routine of a careless bureaucracy, they generally do not reach till it is too late, and sometimes only by chance, the knowledge of the government; and in such a country they do not know how to apply a large and energetic policy, which goes in advance of the wants of the age. Every province continues to be administered well or ill, as it was in past times, and every official pursues his own object, although often diametrically opposed to that of others. The financial administration quarrels with the political authority, and the military administration with them both. The one sustains against the other a lawsuit which endures for years, and boasts of its victory when it succeeds in extracting anything from the other; and it never enters into the mind of anybody that they are not only the servants of the same prince, but of the same country. This want of unity in the authorities is doubly pernicious in Austria, because all the government is concentrated

1. *De l'Autriche et de son avenir*, vol. I, pp. 108, 109. — 2. *Idem*, p. 110.

in authority into which all the political life drawn from the other members of the state has been crowded, and with which therefore the whole body is paralysed. Like every other Austrian institution, the Council of State founded by the Emperor Francis was attainted from the first year of its existence by the dissolving force of the bureaucracy; a force which takes away the soul of everything which ought to live. This council was also changed into a simple chamber, where everything was done by writing in separate sections, where all the nominations, and moreover all the tendencies, are bureaucratic. Since then, the ancient disorder and chaos have continued to reign with more strength than ever.

"Consequently, we witness the commercial and consular relations of Austria with other States suffer from privileged vices; we see also the good openings for commerce and good markets neglected; and, finally, we see the merchant marine degenerating instead of improving.

"If it be true, and we do not think it necessary to prove it in our day, that every advancement in general prosperity, every intellectual and material improvement of nations, depends on the free development of their common life, it flows naturally from thence that a government which opposes so many obstacles to it cannot be otherwise than prejudicial to the national progress. Experience has established the truth only too incontestably of this principle in Austria [1]."

"The Austrian functionaries form a body which, obstructing, dividing, and perplexing everything, place themselves between the prince and the people, intercept the benevolent intentions of the one, as the wishes and petitions of the other, and produce as the result a work unrecognisable and absurd. The government lets it alone. The system which has prevailed, and which still prevails, is the system of temporising, palliating, remaining passive, letting alone, and avoiding every energetic measure and every radical reform.

"What have been the results of the Austrian policy? At home, the government has alienated the sympathies of the people, the State is involved in a continually increasing mass of debts, the material prosperity has made and makes an infinitely slow progress, intellectual interests are neglected, and finally the empire seems to be on the eve of splitting up, in consequence of the constantly diverging tendencies of its different parts. Abroad, Austria has lost her strength, consideration, and influence. She owes the place which

1. *De l'Autriche et de son avenir*, vol. I, pp. 195 to 111.

she occupies among the great nations of Europe only to a certain veneration for her ancient power. As to her veritable influence, that which is founded upon the intrinsic value of nations, and derived from a tendency which is pursued without deviation, it has long been lost by Austria [1]."

" Whilst all the governments are profiting from the long peace to march in advance, Austria, like the unfaithful servant, is hiding the talents which the Lord has confided to her. She believes that she remains stationary, and does not perceive that, in the midst of the universal progress, those who do not advance go backward. Although she possesses the presidency of the Diet, she has seen, in spite of the ancient recollections which her name awakes, Prussia obtain an influence which, instead of lessening, is continually on the increase.

" Austria is despised, neglected, and hated in Germany, because she is regarded as the support of superannuated and retrograde principles, while Prussia has, wisely calculating her interests, placed herself at the head of liberal progress. When the great European powers have sustained by their efforts the decisive movements which were made towards liberty and civilisation, there was one among them which withdrew alone; and when the whole of Christendom palpitated at the spectacle of the heroic struggle of our brethren against the barbarians, remained aloof with a sulky air, a motionless spectator of the conflict; she did not dare to oppose the general movement of Europe, and take openly the side of the barbarian oppressors, but her sympathies, her wishes, and her secret efforts, were in their favour. This power was Austria; and nevertheless her dearest interests required her to contract a close alliance with Oriental Christendom. This inconceivable policy has borne its fruits: Austrian influence is entirely lost in the East; it has passed to other nations, who gain there every day more and more preponderance; and Austrian commerce, which is almost all in these latitudes, suffers considerably from it [2]."

" We have conscientiously applied the scalpel to the dissection of Austria, and we have found her to be destitute of a solid basis, and that she does not rest upon any principle likely to endure; we have seen how she has decayed in her foreign relations, in the public opinion of Europe, and in her influence, and we have seen her abandoned to foreign and hostile influences upon all her frontiers. We have found her to be at home a medley of nationalities which

1. *De l'Autriche et de son avenir*, vol. I, pp. 143, 144. — 2. *Idem*, pp. 148, 149.

are enemies of each other; and in one word we have found a governmental machine without animation, without intelligence, and consequently without vigour[1]."

"The first part of the work entitled ***De l'Autriche et de son Avenir***, was written with the intention of indicating the deep wounds by which all the vitality of our country threatens to escape; to shew that the system of the government leads to disorganisation, ruins the soil under our feet, and drags the State to total wreck, while the governors weaken at their pleasure their natural supports, and even overturn them, although they have been endowed with them by certain and historic laws and this is done to lean upon institutions which have neither guarantees of duration, nor strength, nor authority. It remains to draw the induction from so many evils; we have drawn it without fear and without compromise, and we have said that to save a monarchy ready to fall to pieces, a complete change ought to take place in the system of government[2]."

"Let them tell us who in Austria, from the throne to the cottage, has not a sincere conviction of the imperious necessity of an absolute reform, and who is happy enough to rock himself asleep in the agreeable delusion that the vaunted stability of Austria can last twenty years! or even ten years! This question will receive the same answer in the palaces of the great, in the imperial residences, in the chancelleries, and in the streets and places of our towns and of our villages; the moral revolution is accomplished[3]."

"Ever since 1809, Austria has gone back, to the profound affliction of all true patriots. Every sacred and fruitful idea, whether it comes from the Crown, the Estates, or the people, is quickly suppressed by the functionaries. Thanks to them, all progress, all development, every national impulse becomes impossible; it is to them we must ascribe the deplorable stagnation of our material and intellectual life, as well as the continually increasing disorganisation of our fine monarchy. The provinces isolate themselves, popular agitations are incessantly renewed in obscurity: yes, the redemption is near[4]."

"The liberty of the press does not exist in the Austrian States; it is impossible for them, although they have the feeling of their right and the desire, to appeal by it to the opinions and intelligence of the most instructed part of the nation; their most important prerogatives are destroyed or mutilated, and in favour of a bureaucratic despotism, which absorbs the power of the monarch and the liberty

1. *De l'Autriche et de son avenir*, vol. I, p. 154. — 2. *Idem*, vol. II, pp. 1 to 10. — 3. *Idem*, p. 10. — 4. *Idem*, p. 22.

of the people for its own advantage, without calculating the damage which results to the nation. This despotism suppresses at home the free tendencies of the people and their intellectual progress; whilst abroad they wish to appear the champions of civilisation and the defenders of the lower classes, whose degradation they contrive meanwhile to make eternal[1]."

"A system of mutism, unprecedented in history, has arrested the development and aspirations of mind in Austria. Power continues to resist firmly against all the efforts of the nation, and finds every means good for suppressing thought and intelligence; and this it does not only in directing education, but also in permitting the representation at the theatre of none but insignificant plays, which elevate neither the heart nor the mind. It would be admirable, if the adjective admirable could be applied to anything so melancholy, to observe with what constancy and cunning the power marches towards its object. When other governments try to improve the education and the morals of the people, with us they exert themselves to corrupt them or to let them stagnate in ignorance; and the press is surrounded with obstructions.

"When comparing the number of schools which were founded after the war of independence with those of the present time; when comparing the number of learned men with those of that day, although the number was still insufficient, with those of our day, we will be convinced that we have done nothing but go backwards during the last thirty years. When the nineteenth century came, with its liberty of the press and its political and moral progress, all these precious impulses had an influence upon Austria as upon the rest of Europe; they did not try then, as formerly, to draw the curtain of ignorance over our languishing country; and there was between Austria and its rulers a dumb war, which has never relaxed during thirty years, and, painful avowal! the advantage has been on the side of power, and this in great part by the fault of the nation. It is useless to deceive ourselves; the Austrians are despised by every body, and are the *parias* of intelligence and progress; their countrymen, the Germans of other States, will not fraternise with them, and reproach them for their culpable indolence. Indeed, if they had renounced their affected gentleness, and laid their hands upon property, they would have acted less cruelly, for the most holy and the most precious possessions of man are virtue and intelligence, and those who try to deprive him of these blessings attack the

1. *De l'Autriche et de son avenir*, vol. II, p. 42.

dignity of man, and the immutable laws of his development. Can it be reasonable that a State containing 38 millions of inhabitants, and surrounded on all sides by countries in which unlimited publicity reigns, should not have the shadow even of the liberty of the press? Tell us: is it becoming that Austria should be obliged to read foreign journals to learn what is passing in Austria? The most absurd abuses remain unremedied, simply because it is not possible to make them known, and the ignorance of the public comes in aid of the interests and the laziness of the subaltern officials. Who is the Austrian, or who is the foreigner even, who, after having gone over Europe, will not confirm what we have advanced? The fact has become so intolerable that the bitterest enemies of the liberty of the press admit it themselves, and do not apply the remedy from the strength of that inertia which is the original sin of the nation. If Austria had, as Prussia has already long had, a publicity capable of fixing opinion, the clamour raised by the friends and enemies of power would not take place; but as long as only one party can talk, and the other is forced to be silent, those who speak will never be able to persuade. It is thus that the government, by its own fault, finds itself impotent before opinion; and that the world, and particularly its own subjects, throw dirt in its face. It is wounded with its own arms; and the falsehood with which it wishes to kill the truth kills itself.

"Why not then boldly recognise the imperious want of the age, felt both by the rulers and the ruled, of a reasonable publicity; and, instead of having recourse to all those indirect means, as dishonourable as useless, proclaim at once the liberty of the press? Certainly, it would not be a rash act. Prussia, in which the monarchical principle is not less solid than among us, already possesses this benefit of the age, and the government increases even at the present moment the number of its organs, in order to be able to struggle more effectually with its adversaries. Such is the conduct of a strong government, conscious of its own rights, and the purity of its intentions. But to entrench always behind the brutal power of the censorship, is on the one hand to confess weakness, and on the other to leave the field open to suspicion and reproaches.

"If this demi-liberty had existed, the government would have had less powerful arguments against it, and in return would have had stronger ones in its own defence. At present, it may be truly said that it has purposely pushed into the opposition party the first minds of the nation, for no man of honour and conviction dare take its part. This is so true, that the writings published in such abundance in its favour are either not read, or, if read, it is with the resolution taken in advance not to believe a word they say [1]. "

" Never has the censorship been, at any epoch, more rigorous than it is at present, chiefly in regard to literature; and we may say that during a century we have marched backwards. The government has taken a hostile and ridiculous position against intelligence, science, and literature, without deriving any thing from it except disadvantage. Every year, and every month, for thirty years, the censorship has become more severe and more abstruse, and at present it has reached a point at which it is absurd. There are certain anecdotes of the Austrian censorship which would make the fortune of a comic almanack [2]."

" With the exception of that of the lower class, education in Austria is, it must be said, in a most pitiable condition, and in organising it they seem to have abstracted the principle that the student ought to have for his constant object *science, the knowledge of truth.* All they have wished is, that our colleges and universities should form bureaucracies, adapted to perpetuate the existing order of things. Physicians, advocates, ecclesiastics, receive these inspirations. Properly speaking, our lyceums are nothing but schools for civil cadets, where science and literature are completely neglected, and all particular lectures, no matter upon what subject, are forbidden, or permitted only in extraordinary circumstances [3]."

" Thanks to the pusillanimity of the chiefs and their partisans, Austria has fallen very low in opinion; the distrust and discontent which the government excites, without thinking of the future, germinates like fertile seeds, and will one day bear bitter fruits, of which it ought to taste itself the bitter savour; for, without any doubt, the reaction will come, and the effect of this exaggerated despotism is to predispose to radicalism; as long as the government shall continue in its old routine, opinion will be always against it, even when it acts for the public good [4]."

In commencing our study of Austria, we said that the government and the clergy were united together to rule the nation by depriving it of liberty and light. We may say that Prussia has followed a directly opposite course, and is endeavouring to guide

1. *De l'Autriche et de son avenir*, vol. II, pp. 61 to 71. — 2. *Idem*, p. 78. — 3. *Idem*, pp. 80 to 83. — 4. *Idem*, pp. 152, 153.

the people by gradually bestowing on them this intellectual light and liberty. We shall not stay to develope this assertion; the authorities we shall quote will suffice to convince the reader. All that we have to do is to exhibit the Prussian government, animated with a Protestant spirit, diffusing instruction and liberty with the same eagerness which Austria displays in restraining the former, and enchaining the latter. When we have thus proved that these two germs of Protestant life really exist in the Prussian soil, we shall see what fruits they produce there.

After having examined Prussia, we shall pass to neighbouring states, which profess the same religious faith, to prove that the same principles elsewhere produce the same results. We might here leave the reader to compare for himself Southern Germany, which we have considered, with Northern Germany, which we are about to consider; but, for the sake of further evidence, we shall again refer to our various authors. Finally, we shall conclude by asking these same writers what is the cause of the contrast we have noticed, and thus our plan will be complete. Our first question then is the following: Whilst Austria extinguishes the light of knowledge, and forbids liberty of thought, is it true that Prussia, on the contrary, governs by means of that light and that liberty? First, take the testimony of Mirabeau, who, having been already quoted with respect to Austria, must also be referred to as regards Prussia: "The constitution of Prussia well deserves the attention of every thinking man. It is a vast and beautiful machine, in the construction of which superior artists have laboured for centuries. It possesses many excellent qualities; the spirit of order and regularity may be said to be inehrent; liberty of thought and religious toleration are governing principles. This example affords a salutary and irresistible demonstration of the fact that, far from being incompatible with a monarchical government, these two treasures of mankind are most favourable to it.

"Civil liberty extends almost as far as is possible in a country under the absolute government of a single individual. There exists a military system, which requires but little change to rendre it perfect. The Prussian monarchy, in short, presents to Europe the example of a legislation to which no other nation approaches. Surely these points deserve attention[1]."

Listen now to more modern authorities: "Prussia," says M. de Rougemont, "is one of those states in which instruction is very

1. Mirabeau, vol. VI, p. 360, 361.

generally diffused, and watched over with the greatest care. The number of schools increases annually. There is no country where science and learning are more encouraged, or cultivated with greater success. The inhabitants have reached a high degree of moral and intellectual attainment [1]. "

" The Prussian government pays the greatest attention to public education, and the advancement of the arts and sciences; and the people are probably more generally instructed in this than in any other kingdom. Freedom is granted to all religious denominations in the Prussian monarchy [2]. "

" Prussia pursues her laudable efforts to extend instruction amongst all classes. In execution of the law of May 16, 1853, all the proprietors of workshops and manufactories, having among their artisans young persons under 16 years of age, have just been summoned to prove that they oblige them to attend school at least three hours every day [3]. "

" In Prussia, instruction is adorned with all that can render it attractive and honourable. The university professorship leads to the highest positions in the land. Professional education is most carefully attended to; individual capacities are called forth and brought into exercise. Young men destined for public positions are obliged to follow a course of instruction in constitutional law and political economy. After a rigorous examination, every student, without exception, is required to pass through a certain course of study, and thus, by constant practice, the theoretical part of education is completed. It can easily be believed that such a system sceures a greater amount of morality and knowledge in those to whom the direction of public affairs is confided than that which prevails with us [4]. "

" The greatest title which Prussia possesses to the admiration of Modern Europe is in the organisation of education. Instruction is there regarded in the light of a debt owed by the State to the people. Offered gratuitously to the poor, and at a trifling cost to others, it is imposed by the law on all. Such a system, based on the principle that religion, knowledge, and good morals, are necessary for the welfare of the people, evidently flows from the sincere desire of inspiring the rising generation with the love of God, of their country, and their family; and of establishing Prussian society on the firm groundwork of a morality which at all times dignifies its possessor.

1. Rougemont, p. 486. — 2. Omalius, pp. 208 to 210. — 3. Edm. Texier, *Siècle* du 28 th December, 1853. — 4. De Jonnès, Introduction, pp. 1 to 12.

"The census of 1843 shows that, in Prussia, out of a population of 2,992,124 children, including all from six to fourteen years of age, 2,328,146 attend elementary schools; that is, seventy-nine per cent. throughout Prussia. In the province of Saxony, the proportion is raised to ninety-four per cent. In no other country in Europe is instruction so widely diffused[1].

"We must in justice acknowledge that the philosophic school of Germany is worthy of the renown it has acquired, for no other since the days of Plato has been able to boast of so many celebrated masters. The opinions of Descartes, imbibed by Leibnitz, have been transplanted to a fruitful soil. If in other countries the problem of human destiny has been solved with greater clearness, it has nowhere been adorned with more dignity, nor enlivened by such bright expectations. By means of professional instruction, and the universal diffusion of education, philosophy has found its way in Prussia into general society, and into the government itself. The knowledge of right and duty, ideas of beauty, truth, and justice, the moral application of history, are not there mere theories of the learned; they stamp intelligence, reflection, and moral dignity everywhere, even among the women and children. In France, philosophy is only a barren abstraction to the great mass of the people; but in Germany it is a popular and practical science. Human perfectibility has there become a matter of belief, and intellectual progress an object of worship. This philosophic faith of the Germans makes them vigorous and hopeful; we are astonished elsewhere to find a lower standard of morality, and to discover that selfishness and love of gain can overcome integrity, wither the heart, and depress the genius; the evil which destroys us, is scepticism.

"Notwithstanding the great variety of sects and doctrines in Prussia, there exists there an excessive attachment to certain dogmas. The people cannot remain in a state of indifference; and the desire for unity which fills their minds disposes them to seek means for making these various sects agree among themselves, and they even endeavour to amalgamate religious belief and philosophil cal reasoning. It is difficult to comprehend all the intellectuaefforts which open-hearted Germany has made to bring about this general uniformity of opinion[2]."

"In the 17th century, freedom of opinion was protected and favoured in Prussia; it was there that its power first became mani-

1. De Jonnès, p. 179. — 2. *Idem*, pp. 189, 190.

fest. People began to philosophise upon different sciences; upon the history of jurisprudence for example; and this mode of study was soon found to exercise an important influence upon the cultivation of history, and other kindred sciences; as well as upon the civil and individual rights of the people. The Academy of Science at Berlin, established under the auspices of Leibnitz, greatly increased the progress made in mathematics and the physical sciences. Literary societies and clubs were formed in various places. The book trade became an important branch of commerce, and journals devoted to criticism were put forth, which gave their influence in favour of arts and science [1]."

"With what spirit and intelligence did the king himself encourage the progress of education among the people! How many collections have been made, institutions founded, and voyages of discovery undertaken at the expense of government since 1816! No country of the same extent and resources devotes so much money to education and to religious purposes. There are 107 gymnasia in Prussia, and an examining jury in every province. The religious education of the people is an object of anxious attention to the government. It is based upon pure Protestantism. The king himself sets an example of earnestness in religious duties [2]."

"This prince considers no sacrifice too great, if made for the encouragement of arts, science, and education; and such strict economy is observed, that the public treasury has continued in a thriving state, notwithstanding the large sums expended for these purposes [3]."

But if any one may be considered as an authority on such points, it would be assuredly that learned individual who was sent by a neighbouring nation to examine into the state of education in Prussia. We quote, then, in the next place the testimony of M. Cousin:

"No one can undertake any public situation in Prussia before undergoing a strict examination. As those who fill such situations are for the most part taken from all classes of society, and have all received a literary education, they bring the general spirit of the country into their professional employments, while at the same time they acquire the habit of legislation [4]." "The smallest parish is obliged to have an elementary school, where the whole course of instruction prescribed by law, or, at least, its most indispensable parts, must be taught. Such schools, there-

1. *Dictionnaire de la Conversation*, article *Allemagne*, pp. 384, 385. — 2. *Idem*, article *Prusse*, p. 390. — 3. *Idem*, p. 396. — 4. Cousin, p. 156.

fore, are to be found in every part of Prussia; but it is not sufficient to establish them; they must be also maintained. Provision to this effect is made by clause V of the law of 1819. This law begins by fixing such a complete maintenance for every school as may enable it to answer its proper end.

"1. A suitable income for the schoolmasters and mistresses; and a pension secured to them when no longer able to continue their services.

"2. A building for exercise and instruction, properly arranged and comfortably warmed.

"3. Furniture, books, pictures, instruments, and every other requisite for study and exercise.

"4. Pecuniary assistance for needy scholars.

"If any village is so situated that it can neither connect itself with schools in other villages, nor maintain one for itself, from want of necessary funds, assistance may be obtained from the department.

"In towns, the education of youth and the means for its support must never be considered secondary to any effort for the public good, but must be regarded as an object of primary importance, and provided for accordingly[1]."

"The main end of every school," says the law of 1819, "is, so to train up the rising generation that they may not only be well acquainted with the relation in which man stands to God, but may also be imbued with an earnest desire to regulate their lives according to the spirit and principles of Christianity. In the school, children will be early trained to habits of piety, and thus home instructions will be seconded and completed.

"The work of the day should be begun and ended by a short prayer, and a few religious remarks, which the master should offer in such a manner that these exercises may never sink into a mere form.

"The masters should also take care that the children attend divine worship punctually on the Sundays and festival. Sacred songs and hymns should be included among the religious lessons. Particular attention should be paid to inculcate on the young obedience to the laws, and faithful attachment to the Prince and the State, that they may thus be early inspired with devoted love of their country. Paternal feeling, affection, and kindness on the part of masters towards their pupils will prove the most effectual

1. Cousin, pp. 177 to 180.

security against surrounding evil influence, and the best means of guiding them in the right way.

"No punishment should at any time be inflicted, the nature of which might weaken the sense of honour, and in cases where corporal discipline may be necessary, undue severity should be carefully avoided, so that modesty may never be wounded, nor the health injured [1].

"In every commune of the kingdom, without exception, ministers of all denominations should seize every opportunity, whether in the church, during their visit to the school, or in their opening addresses, to remind the heads of schools of the importance of their task, and the people of their duties towards the school. The civil and ecclesiastical authorities and the masters should everywhere combine to draw more closely together those links of respect and attachment which should bind the people to the school, so that they may be more and more accustomed to regard it as an essential part of the common welfare, and be daily more interested in its progress [2]."

"This law of 1819 only served to systematise the existing order of things. It is not therefore an Utopian scheme, metaphysical, arbitrary, and artificial, like the majority of our laws on elementary education, but is founded on reality and experience. It has therefore been put into execution, and has rapidly produced the happiest results. The determination of the authorities to bring it into force has been so firm, the scrutiny of the government inspector so strict, and the authorities of the communes, departments, and provinces set over the schools have displayed such persevering and well-directed zeal, that at the present moment the requirements of the law are almost everywhere more than carried out: I mean, in every point in which zeal only is demanded. For instance, a large normal elementary school is established by law in every department; but, besides this, small branch normal schools are often to be met with [3]. Such schools in Prussia are not often conspicuous. They are more frequently concealed, and this is both honourable and meritorious. They differ from the larger schools, not only because the pupils are much fewer in number, but chiefly because most of them are intended to train village schoolmasters for the poorest parishes. That is strictly their original design, for which they are well and usefully adapted. There are many poor districts, where one

1. Cousin, pp. 192, 193. — 2. *Idem*, p. 199. — 3. *Idem*, pp. 242, 243.

would hesitate to send a talented schoolmaster, yet it is just in such places that instruction is most needed. These small normal schools are calculated to supply the deficiencies of the larger. They are organised expressly for the poor and ignorant parts of the country, for whose benefit they carry on their labours, their studies, their discipline. The large normal schools of Prussia doubtless deserve our highest esteem; but we can never sufficiently respect these smaller seminaries, which, as before remarked, are more desirous of concealment than of show. While the former seek to be enriched, the latter are willing to be poor because they labour for the poor; they cost very little, and do a great deal of good. They are established with the greatest ease, on one single condition: that directors and pupils be devoted to their work, without seeking the praise of men. Religion alone can engender and maintain such true devotedness of spirit. When we are willing to serve our fellow creatures without being known or esteemed, our eye must be directed towards the providence of God; and we must seek his approbation, rather than that of men. The originators and directors of these small schools are therefore generally either clergymen, animated with Christian love, or laymen of piety, filled with an earnest desire for the instruction of the people. The spirit of Christianity, combined with love for their fellow creatures, especially for the poor, pervades these humble institutions[1]. "

"I abstain from any remark on the regulation of these normal schools, which seem to have been derived from Saint Vincent de Paule. Most of the small normal schools of Prussia are founded and conducted in this spirit. They are all based on the sacred groundwork of Christianity, and, notwithstanding their humble appearance, every suspicion of vulgarity is removed by the earnest desire for solid instruction, and the taste for music and for works of nature which are there found. It would be well if some worlhy ecclesiastic in France would acquaint himself with the regulations of these schools, and undertake a similar mission[2]. "

"I have seen the actual working of the normal school at Potsdam; the arrangement of that institution in all its various details and the system of instruction are excellent. I was present at several lessons, when (from politeness to myself) the pupils were questioned on French history. These young persons answered very well, and were quite conversant with the dates and principal facts. M. Striez, the director, is a minister and preacher of the

1. Cousin, p. 296. — 2. *Idem*, p. 306.

Gospel; a serious intelligent man, who reminded me of M. Schweitzer, of the normal school at Weimar. I ought also to mention that all the pupils in this school appeared happy, and that they were very well-behaved. If they had brought any vulgarity with them to school, they had entirely lost it. I left the institution much gratified, filled with esteem for their director, and with respect for a country where popular education had attained so high a point [1]."

We have seen how limited is the course of study in Austria. We shall now see that in Protestant Prussia it is more extended than in any other country: "The examinations for the University take place in every *gymnasium*, in the case of those who have there completed their studies, and are called "*examen de départ.*" In the case of such young men as have not studied in the *gymnasia*, these examinations are held before a scientific commission. This examination comprehends, in a very remarkable degree, mathematics and science, as well as ancient languages and literature; the French language even forms a part. The grand trial at this examination consists in the written compositions; the oral examination is also very difficult. I have seen the compositions of such an examination in one of the best schools at Berlin, which appeared to me to exhibit a solid acquaintance with the different branches of learning in which instruction was given. In my opinion, this examination, as it regards rhetoric, is not only stricter than our examination for the degree of Bachelor of Arts, but it is even stricter than our examination for a licentiate [2]."

"We may consider that system of public instruction to be well organised where the four following points are secured:

"1. That the whole population, all, I mean, without exception, boys and girls, in town and in country, should attend elementary schools, with or without payment;

"2. That all the middle class, in towns, should attend superior elementary schools;

"3. That a sufficient number of youths, from the middle and upper classes, should attend the lower division of the colleges;

"4. That a selection of pupils should be made from this number, not on account of superiority of birth or fortune, but on account of talent and diligence in their studies, who, after suitable trial, should pass into the higher division of the college; from thence to the University, and from thence again into the higher ranks of society.

1. Cousin, p. 381. — 2. *Idem, Instruction secondaire*, pp. 69, 70.

" This idea is almost realised in Prussia. We have elsewhere proved that in 1831 out of a population of 12,726,823, 2,403,030 children, that is to say, all who were old enough to go to school, were in actual attendance; and that, of this number, 56,889 boys, and 46,598 girls, in all 103,487 children, attended superior elementary schools[1]. "

" There are five gymnasia in Berlin, without reckoning the royal gymnasium, which, on account of certain modifications in the rules, is gradually becoming an ordinary gymnasium. Of these 6 gymnasia, three belong to the state, and three to the town, and yet Berlin contains a population of no more than 200,000. In the same proportion, a town of 800,000 inhabitants, such as Paris, ought to have four times as many; that is to say, nearly 20 colleges; instead of which, Paris contains only 7, five of which belong to the State, and two to the town. In Prussia, there are a considerable number of cities, containing from 30,000 to 40,000 inhabitants, possessing several gymnasia, which, far from being ill attended, are very well filled, especially in the lower and middle classes. A college must always be judged of by the character of the studies, and the excellence of the discipline; in this respect, the gymnasia of Prussia may be regarded as models. Besides the gymnasium of Scholpfort, in the province of Saxony, I have carefully examined the six gymnasia in Berlin, and can bear my testimony that a solid and first-rate education (I speak of literary education, of which alone I am capable of judging), is imparted in every one of them[2]."

" The hope of the country lies in the students who have passed three or four years at the University; from their ranks proceed the theologians, lawyers, medical men, professors of schools and Universities, and all who hold public situations of the first and second class; for these situations are only given in Prussia to those who have passed through a literary examination. It is for this very purpose the gymnasia have been instituted, and in this point of view they must be regarded not only as literary establishments, but also, in conjunction with the Universities to which they are preparatory, as the centres of the moral strength and vigour of the nation, and of its existing political institution[3]. "

" The high importance assigned to religious instruction, is no less striking a feature in the Prussian gymnasia. In each of the six classes of which the gymnasium is composed, a course of religious

1. Cousin, *Instruction secondaire*, pp. 118, 119. — 2. *Idem*, pp. 123, 124. — 3. *Idem*, p. 127.

instruction is given as regularly as that of Latin, Greek, or mathematics. The performance of divine worship alone is not sufficient for young persons of reflecting minds; thorough religious instruction is indispensable, and nothing is so well calculated to afford that instruction, at once full, systematic, and varied in its character, as Christianity itself. One might have supposed that such instruction would have been established at the time of the Restoration in France, when religion was incessantly spoken of. Such was far from being the case, and all the zeal then displayed was expended on the multiplication of outward services. I know no government which has more injured the cause of religion. The Restoration reduced the chaplain to the grade of a curate, or even of a catechist for the lower classes. Christianity without instruction, reduced to an unmeaning spectacle, instead of elevating and delighting the mind, serves only to weary and degrade it[1]."

But we have said enough on education; let us pass now to its effects. We may say that the Prussian government has been able from that time to grant these wise, progressive, practical rights and privileges, without danger to itself, and much to the advantage of every kind of progress.

"Prussia," says Moreau de Jonnès, "in remoulding her society, has successively cast into the crucible of reform, property, civil rights, religion, administration, the army, public education, industry, commerce, political power, and territorial division. Forty years ago, Prussia was monarchical in government, and feudal in civil constitution; now, she is a free state, almost representative, and occupies an important position as an industrial and commercial country. Such a transformation in an intelligent, powerful, and well-governed nation of 16,000,000, cannot be a matter of indifference to any one. The Protestant and sensitive Germany of the North (widely different from the Catholic and lethargic Germany of the South), is convulsed by the shocks of empires, and trembles at the slightest excitement among the nations. Her people have been either the heroes or the auxiliaries of the most memorable events of the modern world. In the course of the two centuries which comprise her short existence, we have witnessed the growth and the education of a great nation; we have seen that nation, in spite of every obstacle, attaining strength and stability, proclaiming liberty of conscience, and becoming the first to open the way of emancipation to the world. Philosophy seated on the throne,

1. Cousin, *Instruction secondaire*, pp. 143, 144.

exercises toleration for half a century; at a later period slavery is abolished; civil privileges, and equality of rights are granted, and all those glorious principles are established which have been gained elsewhere by means of insurrection. Prussia continues to rise by industry in peace, after having already risen by courage in war. She is the land of discipline and of perseverance. The Zollverein constitutes for her a commercial empire, of which she herself holds the sceptre. The railways which extend from the capital in all directions entwine the Germanic body with a network of living fibres, of which Berlin is the centre. Prussia draws Germany to herself by a concentration of feeling and interests, and rules her by a much more irresistible and lasting ascendancy than that which is acquired by conquest. This universal development, accomplished at first for the advantage of one intelligent and progressing dynasty, has become, after 30 years, the united work of a whole nation raised to the highest rank by the sole power of its own genius and institutions. Amongst the most conspicuous promoters of modern civilisation, should we not mention the aristocracy of England, the people in France, and the monarchy in Prussia? The facilities afforded for intellectual development, the attention bestowed in Prussia upon education, the increase of pecuniary resources, by means of labour, the wonderful improvements in agriculture; all testify to the energy of the efforts made by Prussia to extend the necessaries of life to all, instead of allowing luxury to be the privilege of a few, while poverty is the lot of a far larger number[1]."

"In extending his plans of intellectual improvement, Frederick William, with the wisdom he always displays in civil administration, has not overlooked those secular matters which tend to encourage labour, to stimulate ingenuity, and to promote individual convenience as well as the prosperity of the State. Public works have been carried on to a great extent; new roads, ports, canals, river navigation, improvements in tillage and farming, have raised agriculture to a degree of perfection which is surpassed only in Holland and England. Nothing has proved more satisfactorily the intelligence of the Prussian government, and the sincere desire for improvement which animates it, than the rapid formation of railways. Although this work is entrusted to companies, the State has frequently assisted in its progress, either by taking a certain number of shares, or by granting a minimum of interest of three per cent. to the shareholders. A well arranged junction of the lines

1. De Jonnès, Introduction, pp. 1 to 12.

of the Rhenish Province with those of Belgium, and of the Prussian northern lines with those of Saxony and Austria, has in the course of a few years, and as if by magic, covered the centre of the continent from Holland to Switzerland, from Hambourg to Venice, and from Cologne to Varsovie, with a net-work of immense lines, skilfully intertwined; thus approximating the inhabitants of distant nations, and uniting, as it were, seas and countries in one common centre[1]. Nothing is wanting to complete the glory of Prussia; neither the palm of the great Captain, nor the civic crown of the legislator. If we examine attentively the system of legislation pursued by Frederick William III during the peaceful period of his reign, we shall perceive that one grand idea, a most generous and philosophical one, occupied his mind, and that in uniting the various parts of that system, he constructed a noble monument of social organisation. We may follow out this idea, and conceive the edifice of moral and physical power in Prussia to rest upon four stately columns; religion, military force, education, and industry. To raise the moral and intellectual standard of the nation, to increase public wealth and individual prosperity by promoting industry and commerce; such is the grand object of the admirable institutions we have enumerated, and which Frederick William has carried into operation with a zeal for the well-being of society and for intellectual progress which will transmit his name with honour to posterity[2]."

M. de Rougemont sums up in a few words the rights and privileges enjoyed by Prussia: "Since the commencement of this century, the peasantry have been freed from those taxes which formerly pressed so heavily upon them, and upon their land. The cities have received municipal institutions[3]." "Prussia is the powerful kingdom upon which, more than upon any other, depend the liberty and the greatness of Germany[4]." And now, we may inquire, what fruits have been produced in Prussia and in the other Protestant states of Germany from these two principles of science and liberty which we have seen springing up under the influence of religious reform? The question will be answered by the following quotation:

"The result of Luther's reformation in Germany was what may be called liberty of thought and opinion. Opinion became a matter of right. The Church had never given free permission to discussion, and, as if to protest against such a liberty, she had been wont, from time to time, to hand over some unhappy scholar to the flames! But, from Luther's time, things were different. No distinction was

1. De Jonnès, pp. 179 to 181. — 2. *Idem*, p. 193. — 3. Rougemont, pp. 486 to 490. — 4. *Idem*, p. 491.

now made between theological truth and philosophical truth, and public disputations were held in the German language without opposition. The princes who received the reformed religion allowed this liberty of thought, and the introduction of the German system of philosophy was one of the most important results that followed. No where, not even in Greece, has the human mind been permitted so to express itself and to expand so freely as it has in Germany, from the middle of the last century to the period of the French Revolution[1]. Liberty of thought and Protestantism are united by strong ties in Germany; these two things are as closely connected as mother and daughter. Although the Protestant Church has been reproached with narrow-mindedness, it must be remembered, to her immortal glory, that in permitting free examination in the Christian Church, she has released the human mind from the yoke of authority; and that this liberty of examination, in Germany especially, has led to the unrestrained development of science. German philosophy, though she may consider herself in the present day to be as high in position as the Protestant Church, or even higher, is nevertheless only the daughter of that Church[2]."

"The mental activity which remained unchecked even during the long occupation of the French, is the strongest evidence that can be adduced of the advanced civilisation of the people of Prussia, and of the wisdom of the government. Though less favourably circumstanced than the South, Northern Germany is more active and inventive. Prussia is powerful from her history, which abounds in glorious deeds; from the rank which she holds as the first Protestant nation of the continent; and from the national spirit of her intelligent and enterprising population. Germany owes her deliverance to Prussia; it is to be hoped that she will become indebted to her for internal prosperity also.

"Notwithstanding the tendency to autocracy, political freedom since the reign of Frederick II has made its way into the government of Prussia with greater ease than into the more independent States; the cause of this is, the re-establishment of individual liberty, and the suppression of servitude. Merit is sufficient to lead to employment, even of the highest kind; and as long as such wise principles continue in vigorous operation, Prussia may boast of a government too strong to fear disturbance.

"Prompt justice, conscientiously discharged without respect of persons, has long been the characteristic of the Prussian tribunal.

1. Heine, vol. I, pp. 54 to 56. — 2. *Idem*, p. 285.

Any Prussian may write to the King, and make complaints even of the chief minister of the State. He is sure that he will receive a reply, and that justice will be done him. How different is this mode of proceeding from what we have witnessed in Austria, where the poor old men, who dare to complain of their lord, are answered only by the bastinado[1]."

"We find in Prussia a people belonging to the same stock as the Austrians, but far more vigorous, active, and enterprising. Prussia's political existence is of scarcely three centuries' duration: by what mysterious process can she have been raised, in so short a time, to rank among the five great European powers? What was Prussia in the 16th century? Her name was hardly deemed worthy of a place in the catalogue of the geographer! and yet this little nation has risen up suddenly from the midst of Meclenbourg and Brandenbourg, where she has established herself in spite of every obstacle. Whatever may be the opinion of their neighbours, certain it is that the Prussians are more advanced in civilisation than any other nation in Germany[2]."

"Prussia is making rapid progress, both physically and intellectually. Agriculture is improving, trade flourishes, the army is large and well-disciplined; the learned men, the writers, the artists, excite the admiration, and the jealousy too, of other nations, the rivals of Prussia in power and fame; amongst those nations she occupies the position which of right belongs to her[3]. Prussia will be a model for all the other countries of Germany to endeavour to imitate, and the firm basis on which may be reared the great edifice of general unity[4]."

In speaking of the dwellings of the Prussian farmers on the shores of the Baltic, M. Salter tells us that they "are well built, healthy, tiled, and that they contain three large and airy apartments. The principal dwelling-house is surrounded by exterior buildings, which are sometimes superior to those of Norfolk. The condition of the labourers is equally comfortable. An excellent school is frequently established on the premises for the education of the children, and supported by the proprietor himself. The moral and physical state of the people is in every way satisfactory[5]."

"The revolution which the state of property has undergone in Prussia has been almost as important as that which has taken place in France; it has given relief, maintenance, and property to a

1. *Dictionnaire de la Conversation*, article *Prusse*, pp. 390 to 396. — 2. Tardif, pp. 49 to 51. — 3. *Revue Britannique*, March, April, p. 6. — 4. *Idem*, p. 9. — 5. *Idem*, pp. 300, 302.

nation of serfs; it has raised their physical and moral condition. But the prosperous state of Prussia is the best proof we can give of the well-timed measures adopted, and of the efficient manner in which they have been carried into operation. Did we need any further proof, we might mention the ardour with which all the other German States (Austria excepted) have followed the example of Prussia[1]."

"Prussia affords us a singular instance of the formation of a State. So rapid, indeed, has been the progress of this kingdom, which now claims to be the head of a new empire, that persons yet living may remember the time when the Sovereigns of Prussia could not obtain the recognition of their title from the Republic of Poland! As to the name of Prussia, it was then confined to an uncultivated little spot in the north-eastern corner of the present kingdom, given up to the knights of the Teutonic order. Half of the other States of Germany have assisted, in spite of themselves, to increase the power of the chief of a small duchy, which the ability and valour of the princes and people raised, in a century and a half, to the highest rank among the nations of the world. In the time of Charles V no State in the Germanic body was able to dispute the supremacy of the House of Austria. It was the rivalry of the German and Spanish branches of that house, which formed the basis of the regulation system of the European policy, until Prussia's sudden appearance removed apprehensions, and caused new alliances to be made[2]."

"By a united system of custom-house tariff, Prussia has acquired an influence over Germany which can never be destroyed. She heads the intellectual movement of this country, and the Germans are now, in pride and confidence, expecting from her the realisation of their hopes of unity and greatness. The noble successor of the great Frederick has invited his people to take part in public affairs, and the citizens have shown themselves worthy of the confidence of their prince. The sympathy of all Europe, and the goodwill of the Germanic race, are directed towards Prussia. Every day tends to consolidate Germanic nationality, at the head of which stands Prussia and her political institutions. In a short time, this union will be completed; and then those lingerers, who were once invited on account of their origin and early history to join in the general movement, will be finally excluded[3]."

We will nove give the more explicit testimony of a wise politi-

1. *Revue Britannique*, 1847, September, October, pp. 331. — 2. *Idem*, 1848, July, August, pp. 253 to 256. — 3. *De l'Autriche et de son avenir*, vol. I, pp. 146, 147.

cian : " Certain industrial localities," says M. de Jonnès," such as the valley of the Oder, in Silesia, upon the Rhine, Crefeld, and the valley of Bormen and of Elberfeld, have been transformed into streets many leagues in length, formed by lines of manufactories and workshops. The marshes, which once seemed likely to baffle the efforts of the Grand Elector, are now converted into verdant meadows, or lakes shaded by trees, on which is situated the royal city of Potsdam, surrounded by villas which vie in elegance and magnificence with those of Italy. Surely, when we consider the point and the epoch from whence the Prussian people started, we must acknowledge that few contemporary nations have made such rapid progress in so short a time; no country, excepting Holland perhaps, has had more to struggle with in regard to national disadvantages, the state of the people, and internal weakness. None ever rose from such insignificance to so high a position as that which Prussia now occupies; and if genius is to be estimated by the amount of difficulties and dangers overcome, she has indeed an undisputable right to head the nations in the march of civilisation[1]. "

" The people who conquered Napoleon knew their own power; the people among whom appeard Kant, Niebuhr, Herder, Lessing, Schlegel, and many other distinguished men, must have been conscious of the genius they possessed. Prussia is resolved to march on fearlessly, yet with caution, in the new course upon which she has entered. Prussia, the first of the Germanic nations in the struggle for independence, in the victory gained for religious liberty, in the establishment of civil emancipation; Prussia, the first in every movement, from her youthful ardour and intelligence, now asserts her just right and privilege of forming that grand compact which preserves the dignity and the interests of the people[2]. "

" Notwithstanding our desire to avoid any appearance of exaggeration, we cannot forbear mentioning the effects of the amelioration alluded to in the condition of the people. Let us reflect what an amelioration it must be for a humble establishment of 1,200 fr. to be raised to 2,000, and if the benefit be extended to other classes in the same proportion, how important will be the result! It is a change from anxiety, privation, misery, to sufficiency, and even comfort. And how has this change been effected? More powerful energy has been infused into every class of society by means of industry, by the suppression of the previous arbitrary and unpopular

1 De Jonnès, p. 199. — 2. *Idem*, p. 203.

form of government, by the grant of individual liberty, and the freedom allowed to intellectual development.

" A long continuance of peace has afforded time for the fruits of industry to appear, to ripen, and to multiply. Wise legislation has broken down the barriers which stood in the way of freedom and personal liberty. The national intelligence has made good use of these favourable circumstances for accelerating its progress, and promoting its well-being; and a vigilant administration has, at the same time, secured for each individual the assistance and protection which good conduct and industry have a right to claim [1]."

" The lesson of the illustrious Thaer have not proved fruitless in Prussia. Most of his precepts and instructions are followed by intelligent disciples, and are becoming more extensively diffused.

" Agriculture has received a new impulse. The King and the public functionaries bestow much attention upon this subject; rewards are offered; agricultural schools are founded, and general meetings are held in all the provinces to discuss the best modes of labour, and to try their effects by experiment. The small landed proprietors attend these meetings, and are enabled practically to study agriculture at the model farms established for their benefit [2]."

" In fifteen years, Prussia has expended a capital of 270,000,000 francs in roads and railways; yet, notwithstanding this outlay, and the additional capital employed in forming new industrial establishments, the ordinary expenditure necessary for the well-being of the nation has been increased rather than diminished; and it has been possible so to economise this vast amount of wealth and productive labour, as to convert it into a fixed capital producing interest. In stating these facts, we have, we think, proved to demonstration the industrial progress of Prussia. If industry proceeds steadily, without being forced by artificial excitement (and this is the way in which it does proceed in Prussia, through the wise legislation of the government), if manufacturers are becoming convinced that the best labour is that which is the best remunerated, then the rational development of industry, and the numerous opportunities of making money which it affords, are valuable boons offered to the poor [3]. "

Hitherto we have been listening to the political economist; let us now follow the traveller: " I came into Germany by Rhenish Prussia, which is undoubtedly the finest entrance. In my route from the frontier to Aix-la-Chapelle, I was struck with the beauty of the villages, which I saw scattered here and there in the midst of

1. De Jonnès, p. 376. — 2. *Idem*, p. 419. — 3. *Idem*, pp. 428 to 430.

verdure and cultivation. The houses are well-built, and almost concealed by their thick covering of vine leaves. Each has its little garden tastefully laid out, and the people are seen passing to and fro, all looking healthy, and well-clad. There is here an ardent desire for improvement, and a greater degree of liberality of feeling and opinion than in other parts of Germany. The inhabitants of these localities are ready to give up their old prejudices, and to adopt modern ideas and civilisation. Nowhere in Germany does agricultural improvement proceed so rapidly, or with more complete success [1]. "

" I wish you could see these interesting villagers of Rhenish Prussia. Their bright, happy countenances, and their courteous manners, as well as their costume, which on both banks of the Rhine is particularly elegant and picturesque, all bespeak the contentment and comfort which reign among them. Every Prussian is obliged to serve in the army, and this circumstance contributes not a little to give to the country people that love of order and neatness which so characterises them. Happy the nation that is both agricultural and military! Happy the subject who, after paying his debt of service to his country, can retire to the little plot of ground which his own hands have cultivated, and say 'This is mine!'

" There are in Prussia some persons of wealth, very few poor, and not a single beggar; most of the people are in easy circumstances. This is not the case in all the countries of Germany, nor, unhappily, in all the provinces; we must hope, however, that a time will come when every part will resemble, in this respect, the favoured country in which I am now travelling.

" An exception must be made in favour of Prussia, with regard to the unfortunate measures which have led to the excessive division of property in Germany, and the consequent deterioration of estates. This is the only country beyond the Rhine which has endeavoured to prevent these ruinous results by a wise and benevolent system of legislature. In Prussia, every town of any importance has its industrial school, and any lad, above the age of 14, may prepare himself to become a good workman in any branch of art or manual labour. In these schools instruction is given principally in mathematics, mechanics, geometry, chemistry, geography, natural history, modern languages, religion, moral philosophy, drawing, and modelling [2]. "

1. Jacquemin, pp. 3 and 4. — 2. *Idem*, pp. 174 and 322.

It is not alone within her own sphere that the beneficial influence of Prussia is felt; it is extended to the neighbouring nations, and thus tends to make her the head of a great political German body.

"Prussia daily increases the vast importance she has acquired in the midst of the Germanic States. Notwithstanding the antipathies of the inhabitants of the South, much distrust, and continual jealousy and ill-will, Berlin must be considered the true capital of Germany. Every movement in sentiment and opinion confirms the pre-eminence which that city has acquired. This is owing, not to the learning and celebrity of the University alone, nor to the intellectual and brilliant society found in Berlin, nor to the flourishing state of the arts, and the talented and influential aristocracy which Frederick William has gathered around him. The true mark of superiority which distinguishes Northern Germany is the stir, the life, and vigour found there, and the resolute and spirited demands which are sent up thence to the King of Prussia. In proportion as the principles of the French Revolution extend beyond the Rhine, so must all the demands of modern mind and intellect find their way into Prussia; for the very life of intelligence and of philosophic culture has long centered in Northern Germany. To this spot where thought is vitally active, the efforts of all parties must be directed. What, indeed, could be demanded at Munich and at Vienna? It was noble, after Iena, to exert so much mental force for the purpose of raising up the fallen Prussian monarchy; and it was wise and politic also. Never was thought freer and more powerful; and the result of this liberty was the resuscitation of a whole nation which was just about to become extinct. We well know the heroic period of the University of Berlin; the names of Fitche and of Hegel tell the whole. Now this free intellectual development must lead to important consequences. The destiny of Germany depends upon Prussia, and the more the spirit of the times gains strength in that country, the more incumbent will it be upon the Cabinet of Berlin to direct the newly-acquired liberty. There exists in Prussia, at least among a considerable portion of the community, a mass of general ideas, of noble sentiments, of well-grounded expectations, which the events of each day serve to encourage and to strengthen. The present reigning power cannot repress the intellectual vigour of the Northern States; those glorious petitions, those new demands which from day to day, and from hour to hour, are passing to the throne, must be complied with. All the poets have risen at the same time in every part of Germany; but intellectual movements do not proceed so harmoniously as might be wished among the Germanic people. The progress of science and liberty varies in the country with the degrees of latitude, and the man of the south and the man of the north seldom meet in the same road of philosophy and free thought. How great is the distance from Vienna to Berlin! [1]"

Thus we have seen that liberal education, and freedom in every sense of the word, are the two pivots upon which the Prussian Monarchy turns, and that the happy results have been the prosperity of the people and the security of the State. But there is another point still more important for us to consider, viz: that the free and cordial reception of those principles, and also the prosperity which results from them, are the effects not of any particular concurrence of circumstances in Prussia, but of her Protestant Faith. This will appear when we discover, as we are about to do, the same effects in the various German States which profess that faith. Mirabeau shall be our first authority in laying down this universal principle: "Evil," says he, "among Protestant nations, is only slight and transitory. Their religious system is the cause of this; its requirements do not stand in the way of any science; fair play is allowed to all. There is less evil under this religion than under that in which he who teaches that it is the earth which turns round, and not the sun, is in danger of imprisonment; and he who calls in question the historical accuracy of a chart favourable to the Church may possibly lose his life. Moreover, Luther and Calvin had the good sense to deny to their successors (clergy of their own party) the right of opening and shutting the gate of Heaven at their pleasure, and have conceded that right to God alone. And herein lies the grand and important political distinction between Protestantism and Catholicism. The Protestant clergy can never exercise absolute or permanent power over any prince or governor. They could not blind him entirely to his own interest, and that interest is always closely connected with the progress of science, and the prosperity of the State, which are the natural results of toleration [2]."

"Berlin has become a refuge for many suffering from persecution, and may be said to be the centre of much truth. Nowhere can there be found a larger number of educated men in every class of society than in the States of the King of Prussia, and this is owing to the liberty allowed there to thought and opinion. The progress of literature has been highly favourable to industry and commerce. Half the proceeds of the German book-trade flows into the Exche-

1. Taillandier, pp. 134, 172, 212. — 2. Mirabeau, vol. 1. pp. 209, 210.

quer of the Prussian States. Knowledge and intelligence have made rapid progress here in the last twenty years; and the great blessing of toleration has not been confined to the Prussian States, but has spread throughout Protestant Germany. From Berlin, from the States of Frederick II, have emanated those rays which now enlighten the whole intellectual horizon[1]."

M. Cousin, in a work recently published, confirms the testimony of Mirabeau as to those provinces he has himself visited: "I have ascertained," says this able writer, "by unequivocal proof, that general education has attained a high point in this country. Everywhere, even in the smallest villages, I have seen numbers of little children, mostly of the lowest orders, dressed in the blue blouse, with a leathern belt round the waist, and carrying their slates and reading-books under their arms. The general system of instruction is grounded on the Bible, as translated by Luther, the catechism, and Scripture history; and every wise man will rejoice in this, for, with three-fourths of the population, morality can be instilled only through the medium of religion. Luther's forcible and popular translation of the Bible is in circulation from one end of Germany to the other, and has greatly aided in the moral and religious education of the people[2]."

"In Saxe-Weimar, where there are as many schools as villages, and where every master is in easy circumstances, elementary education appears only as an inconsiderable sum in State expenditure. Not only do the schoolmasters receive a handsome stipend, but, when advanced in years, they retire upon a pension equal in amount to half their previous salary[3]."

"Twice in the year the masters of neighbouring villages meet to give an account of the systems they respectively pursue, and to report to one another the progress made. These amicable conferences tend to improve the systems adopted, and to diffuse more widely such methods of instruction as are found most efficient.

"A reading society has been formed, by which every schoolmaster is provided with the best journals, and the best works on the subject of education. These journals and books are circulated among the masters. The necessary funds for the society are supplied by contributions from the members themselves; or, if these are insufficient, assistance may be obtained from the funds of the commune, the church, or the general school treasury. There is a society of a similar kind for the pastors. Thus, it is by no means

1. Mirabeau, vol. I, pp. 231 to 234. — 2. Cousin, pp. 2, 3. — 3. Cousin, pp. 24 to 29.

uncommon to find in the pastors and schoolmasters of the German villages men of extensive and solid acquirements. Education raises their position, and makes them persons of importance in their own spheres.

"Schoolmasters who are found to possess more zeal than learning are allowed to visit the best neighbouring seminaries. Occasionally, they are even invited to pass some time in the great elementary school of Weimar, the best of all institutions of the kind. Here they have an opportunity of improving themselves by the lessons of the Normal School, which has also been established at Weimar, and which may be called the seminary for schoolmasters[1]."

"Not only are all children above the age of seven years sent to school, but special schools are provided in every village for the infants also who are not old enough for the ordinary schools, and must therefore, without such institutions, be neglected, while the parents are engaged in their daily labour. Such poor children, thus left to themselves, early acquire habits of idleness and vagrancy which it is difficult to eradicate in after life. An asylum has therefore been opened for them, to which they are sent by their parents in the morning, and from whence they are taken in the evening. Here they are fed and cared for, and instructed in reading, and in the first principles of religion. There is now not a single village in the Grand Duchy without its infant school, and such institutions are beginning to spread throughout Germany[2]."

"I have myself become acquainted with the secret of the ingenious solicitude of the Grand Duchess for the physical, intellectual, and moral benefit of the people. Public education seems to be the chief object of this truly paternal government. I shall never forget the two days I once spent at Weimar, in contemplating power and influence devoted to the sole object of promoting the improvement and happiness of mankind[3]."

The account of Saxony, taken from other authors, entirely agrees with what we have just quoted from M. Cousin: "Under the last sovereign of Saxony, whose justice and wisdom are universally acknowledged, industry and commerce were stimulated and encouraged; agriculture was improved; the well-being of the middle and lower classes continually progressed; houses of correction and of industry were founded; a refuge for vagrants and beggars was established at Roldetz; hospitals were formed; public

1. Cousin, p. 47. — 2. *Idem*, p. 63. — 3. *Idem*, p. 98.

education was better organised; military schools were instituted; the army itself was placed under regulations more suited to the exigencies of the times; national confidence was secured; and, lastly, the arts and sciences were encouraged and protected by the government[1]. Agriculture is carried in this country to a high degree of perfection, and is particularly favoured there. Neither has the animal kingdom denied its riches to Saxony; a great part of the revenue is derived from the breeding of sheep. The German spoken here is considered to be particularly pure. Nearly the whole of the population is Protestant. Saxony is one of the countries of Germany in which intellectual cultivation is most attended to. Industry may be said to be innate, and it has accomplished great things. Trade, too, has made equal progress[2]. "

" Without possessing either the fertile soil or the genial climate of the Rhine, Saxony has attained to a certain degree of culture, civilisation, and prosperity. The towns are numerous, and most of them contain flourishing manufactories. Dresden, Nambourg, and especially Leipsic, take part in the great commercial enterprises of Germany. In some districts, the villages are as close together as those of Wurtemberg and the Palatinate. Money circulates rapidly, and so much is gained from articles of consumption, that it is evident that the system of internal economy is good, and that there is a wise division of labour. The people are well-housed, well-clothed, and well-fed; and they are characterised by a love of order and a spirit of economy. Every class receives a suitable education, and the dialect spoken in the towns is the purest and most refined of Germany. In Saxony, the press is in active operation; and the book trade is extensive and lucrative. The nature of the productions of the country, and the system of taxation, have given rise to industry in every kind of employment. The cultivation of the fields, the working of mines, the tending of cattle, various manufactures, the exportation of merchandise, which is conveyed both by road and water to different parts of Germany, and commercial speculations, all these matters, in turn, occupy the inhabitants; and the variety of employment serves to sharpen their intellect, and to stimulate and draw out their ideas.

" A concentrated and powerful administration was early formed in Saxony, directing the efforts of the inhabitants to one object, and establishing efficient protection; and arts and commerce, as well

1. *Dictionnaire de la Conversation*, article *Saxe*, p. 310. — 2. *Idem*, p. 313.

as the minds and manners of the people, have experienced the good effects of this administration. The evils of war and disease have been remedied by the wise applications and benevolent measures adopted by the government[1]."

From Saxony let us pass to Wurtemberg: "Manufacturing industry is of some importance in Wurtemberg, although an observer might, at first sight, be inclined to think the contrary. The inhabitants themselves prepare the cloth, wool, leather, and iron utensils which they require. Isolated establishments, in which business is transacted on a more extensive scale, embrace every branch of industry in this country of manufactures.

"The inhabitants are physically strong, and of a vigorous constitution; morally, they are good-tempered, frank, open-hearted, industrious, honest, brave, and religious. As to their peculiar aptitude for the arts and sciences, let us only call to mind that Kepler, Schiller, et Wieland, were born among them. The prevailing religion is Lutheran. General education is the grand object of solicitude with the government[2]."

From Wurtemberg we will pass on to one of the free cities of Germany: "At Hamburg, the victims of misfortune or of ill conduct are never seen in the streets, nor begging from door to door. In addition to the asylums founded many years ago for the relief of the indigent class, a model institution has been more recently established.

"The higher classes have united in the generous design of providing for the poor, in such a manner as to render them useful as long as they are capable of employment. Under the direction of the police, the city has been divided into sections and districts, correct accounts are drawn up of those who need relief, stating their age, occupation, and character. Those who are unable to work obtain relief proportionate to their need; and the rest are provided with occupation, either at their own homes, or in a general workshop. Beggars and vagrants are taken to a house of industry, where they are well treated, but obliged to work. A system of this kind involves a variety of details; such as apportioning relief, appointing work, retaining part of the profits for the augmentation of the general fund, and the care of the children of the poor; to all of which the managers elevate themselves with intelligent and disinterested benevolence.

"The founding of this institution has produced the commence-

1. Catteau, vol. II, pp. 1 to 5. —2. *Dictionnaire de la Conversation*, article *Wurtemberg*, p. 426.

ment of a new era in Germany; and in other countries, inquiries are now anxiously made respecting it, with a view to the formation of similar establishments elsewhere. At Copenhagen, Stockholm, London, and Paris, benevolent and enlightened men are in correspondence with the directors of the Hamburg institution; and the details of its operations, published in the papers, have attracted the attention of the public [1]."

"The environs of Hamburg are almost as thickly populated as the city itself. Here are seen a number of pleasant villas, shaded by avenues of trees; beyond, are flourishing villages, the inhabitants of which are occupied in the cultivation of vegetables and fruit. The riches and activity of the people of Hamburg have extended to the neighbouring districts belonging to Holstein, producing there also an equal abundance of the necessaries and comforts of life. Art has overcome the disadvantages of climate; and sandy soil, and barren and marshy ground, have all yielded to the efforts of man [2]."

To ascertain whether this prosperity results from the soil, or is brought about by men, we must inquire what these reformed Germans are, when removed from their own country.

"The city of Hermanstadt, the capital of Transylvania, is peopled by Saxons. They are distinguished from the aborigines by the superior degree of comfort which they enjoy, the consequence of their industry and sobriety. Their neat, well-built cottages, give an air of cheerfulness to the district they inhabit. Most of them profess the Lutheran religion [3]."

In order that we may better understand what religion can effect, let us take a view of a little society formed under the influence of Christian principles: "What devotion exceeds that rendered to God by men whose sole object is to benefit their fellow creatures, and to spend their lives in doing good! The associations of the Moravian Brethren are perfectly free; they are restrained by no vows; everything done among them is voluntary; and yet they are bound together by one common interest. Their villages are remarkable for cleanliness, and for the good order and harmony of the inhabitants. Their affairs are transacted with so much quietness and silence that, in passing along the road, we might imagine the village to be empty and deserted! The members of the commission who superintended the establishments of the community, perform their duties with that spirit of zeal and patience which a sense of the sacred obligations of religion never fails to produce in the mind.

1. Catteau, vol. I, p. 60. — 2. *Idem*, p. 70. — 3. Marcel de Serres, vol. III, p. 9.

The heads of the community are not distinguished above the rest, even in rank. But what privilege is equal to that of being useful to others? When a brother has been elected head of the community or member of the commission five times in succession, the oldest or most respected person in the district declares his services before the assembled congregation, and each one salutes him with the title of beloved brother. This, with the testimony of his own conscience, is the only recompense he receives for his labours. The more distinguished nations of Europe, amongst whom honour is less prized than pecuniary reward, may learn a useful lesson from such an example. There is one remarkable circumstance which proves that the institutions of the Moravian Brethren are founded upon a knowledge of the human heart, and that they rest upon a solid basis, viz.: that during the whole period of their existence it has never been necessary to banish a member from the society: other slight punishments are inflicted, but for offences so trivial that they would scarcely be noticed in any other community.

"An endeavour has been made to establish perfect equality among the members who live together, and the most complete concord; and indeed a delightful spirit of harmony reigns in this holy brotherhood. In the course of my travels, I have visited several of these communities; and have seen in all of them so much love and union, that I might be tempted to adopt their mode of living myself, were not certain dogmas professed by the Moravians opposed to my own religious tenets. I have also been admitted into the houses of some of the married brethren, who have establishments of their own, and here also I have observed the same calmness, and the same serenity. They all receive the traveller and the stranger with kindness and hospitality, and tell him with honest simplicity how happy they have been since they joined this society of peace and love. In the midst of the desolation which so long spread over Europe, how delightful to find one little spot of earth where wise men, united together by the same sentiment, that of love to their fellow creatures, could pass the brief years of life in harmony and peace!

"Christians, the Moravian Brethren revive in their community the simplicity of the Church in early times, and present an example of true piety to the world. Their whole system may be called a theocracy, for everything is done among them for the honour and sake of religion. This Church seems to be governed by an invisible power. The oldest and most respected member of the community exercises the principal functions of the ministry, and when he feels that another is better qualified than himself to fulfil these sacred duties, he requests him, in the name of his brethren, to speak to them of God. The first time that I went among these good Brethren, I felt myself surrounded by pious recluses, whose only occupations were works of usefulness, and the service of God. True representations of the early Christian Church, their communities show us what sacrifices can be made from the love of truth, and how example may win men over to habits of order and justice. In the present day, these societies are so perfect, that all the members belonging to them seem to possess the same gentleness and goodness; and, wonderful as it may appear, all in nearly the same degree [1]."

We will now take a view of these Reformed Germans in distant colonies:

"The Sclavonians of Hungary are half Germanised. They are superior to other Hungarians in education and civilisation. They have, in conjunction with the Saxons, instructed the Magyars in agriculture. The greater number have embraced the Reformed religion. They are active and enterprising, and well-fitted for any kind of employment [2]."

"The Saxons of the south-east of Hungary are Lutherans; they are well known to be industrious and mercantile citizens, and hard-working and contented labourers. They are all free, and live upon their own lands. They have suffered much from the jealousy of the Magyar nobles, who have endeavoured to enslave them by violence and fraud. They are greatly superior to their neighbours in education and activity; and they enjoy all the comforts of life [3]. "

"Many German colonies now formed in Bohemia were at first attracted thither by the mineral riches of the country, as well as by the invitations of the government, and they have exercised a beneficial influence upon the original inhabitants [4]." Be it remembered that these colonies came from Saxony, and that they are Protestant. "At the commencement of the last century, the country of Saltzbourg lost about 30,000 of its inhabitants. These were Protestants who had long begged for liberty of conscience, but in vain. In consequence of the cruel persecution to which they were subjected, they at last determined to abandon their homes. They were kindly received by several princes, especially by the King of Prussia, who established them in Lithuania. There they have cultivated a large extent of land which had been depopulated

1. Marcel de Serres, pp. 131 to 142. — 2. Rougemont, p. 376. — 3. *Idem*, pp. 378, 379. — 4. *Idem*, p. 364.

by the plague; it now produces, as the result of their labours, abundant harvests, and is again covered with cattle and farms [1]."

"A colony of thirty or fourty thousand persons came into this country, and gradually formed agricultural and mercantile establishments which continue to prosper. Russia is indebted in a great measure to these strangers for the advance she has made in agriculture, in arts, trade, commerce, and science. The indefatigable industry of the United Brethren on the banks of the Volga has led to the establishments of large manufactories among the Kalmoucks and Cossacks, which supply silks, cotton, cloth, woollen goods, and a great quantity of tobacco [2]."

"Most European nations who have gone to the New World have introduced there turmoil and oppression. It should be mentioned, to the praise of the Germans, that they have appeared in America only as benefactors, bringing with them useful arts, honesty, and good principles. A great part of the Northern States of America owes to them the prosperity there enjoyed. We learn from the testimony of travellers that the localities in which they have settled are remarkable for the cleanliness of the habitations, and the cultivated state of the land [3]."

"To avoid the danger of inundations, the inhabitants of Harburg construct their houses upon elevations, and surround their fields with dikes. Notwithstanding this disadvantage, the low lands are exceedingly valuable; they are the most fertile districts of Western Germany. In the nature of the soil, they resemble some provinces of Holland, and they have the same rich cultivation; the produce is even greater, and the general aspect of the country more varied. There are few cities in the country, but a large number of towns, villages, and farms. Most of the villages have ornamented walks of elms and willows; and cleanliness, comfort, and contentment are everywhere visible. Agriculture is in the highest consideration, it being the most profitable pursuit, and one not subjected to the burdens of feudal servitude. The inhabitants have always resisted this yoke, and have made the greatest sacrifices to preserve their personal and territorial liberty. These rich farmers, attached to home, and fond of retirement, have always had a taste for reading: many historical and moral works may be found in their dwellings, but neither poetry nor romances [4]."

Such is Prussia, with her train of Protestant states, and in her colonies. Now let the reader call to mind the picture given by the

1. Catteau, vol. I, p. 104 and following. — 2. *Idem*, pp. 94 to 96. — 3. *Idem*, p. 98. — 4. *Idem*, pp. 104 to 107.

same writers of Austria, Bavaria, and the Southern Popish parts of Germany, and let him declare impartially which side bears away the palm of material, intellectual, and moral superiority? We do not wish ourselves to say a word in reply. In what has already been stated, we have allowed facts to speak for themselves, and we will still listen to others. The contrast between the Catholic South and the Protestant North of Germany is so striking, that most travellers have been, as it were, forced to remark on it. Let us inquire into their verdict, see if they are unanimous, and if the reader will coincide with them after studying the facts we have disclosed.

Let us first notice from statistical figures. We copy from a work by the learned Quetelet, entitled ***Researches on the Propensity to Crime*:**

		Number of inhabitants to one crime against.	
		Person.	Property.
AUSTRIA.	" Dalmatia	535	625
	Gallicia and Bukovina	3,955	1,470
	Tyrol	5,707	1,492
	Moravia and Silesia	12,662	2,689
	Interior Austria (Gratz, Leibach, Trietz)	13,311	2,188
	Lower Austria	17,130	1,382
	Bohemia	18,437	1,881
PRUSSIA.	Prussia	22,741	639
	Saxony	27,588	697
	Posen	31,440	875
	Silesia	33,714	1,086
	Westphalia	38,436	1,045
	Brandeburg	39,486	688
	Pomerania	92,121	1,533"

From this table let us deduce the results affecting our subject.

If we take the average among the States governed respectively by Austria and Prussia, we shall have :

For the Catholic monarchy.

10,248 inhabitants to one crime against persons.
1,675 — — property.

11,923

For the Protestant monarchy.

40,789 inhabitants to one crime against persons.
937 — — property.

41,726

The proportion of 11,923 to 41,726 is nearly as 1 to 4. Thus, with due regard to the numerical difference of population, we have in the countries subjected to Austria nearly four times as many crimes as in those governed by Prussia.

The relative amount of instruction is noted by another statistician: "In Prussia, the number of students is as 1 to 6 ½ inhabitants; in Austria, 1 to 10[1]."

Thus, the condition of Protestant Prussia, compared with Catholic Austria, is, four times less crime, and nearly twice as much instruction. This is proved by incontrovertible statistics; but, for further details, let us examine the reports of the travellers.

We will return to the authors already quoted. Mirabeau shall speak for his time, and Marcel de Serres for ours. This is the opinion of the former as to Austria: "It is a fact, as melancholy as it is singular and remarkable, that precisely in those countries where natural beauties most abound, there the powers of the human mind are most strictly circumscribed, and that this unhappy state is attributable solely to the prevalence of superstition.

"Here is briefly the spectacle presented by Germany. Governed by a variety of rulers, a diversity of mind is necessarily manifest. In the first parts of this extensive portion of the European continent, superstition closes every approach to liberty of thought, and consequently to the knowledge and happiness it procures. Those less favoured by Nature materially are distinguished by moral power, and by the industry and activity which it engenders, and by which they can indemnise themselves for what their climate refuses. Inquire whether there be as many good physicians in a country where ignorance and superstition abound, as in one where knowledge and liberty of thought prevail.

"See in what country beggars are the most numerous; where the natural strength of man is turned to the best account; where fewest crimes are committed. Look at these things, and decide.

"Nature has favoured Bohemia far more than Pomerania; if then we find in the latter more prosperity, if the labouring and still more the middle classes are in easier circumstances, as we have shown to be probable, to what can we attribute this singular difference, if not to the strength of superstition, the absence of knowledge, and the evils of a vicious legislation? The comparison of Pomerania and Bohemia proves even more than we expected; for Protestant labourers do much more work than Romanists, who have at least thirty more holidays in the year.

"Protestantism, being founded on freedom of thought and the right of private judgment in religious matters, which judgment is formed by individual study of the Holy Scriptures, is generally

1. Schnitzler, vol. II, p. 353.

found conducive to liberty. Catholicism entails many political evils, the chief of which is the necessary mental subjection to the pleasure of one who arrogates to himself the right to say : hitherto thou shalt go, and no further, and who can call on the government to enforce his decision.

" The system of monkhood has hitherto been considered one of the greatest evils of Popery, and doubtless it is highly undesirable in the present state of religious communities, for it absorbs a large number of individuals physically well constituted for usefulness, who, though rendering little service to society, still live at its expense, and that alone is a heavy tax. The void in a population caused by war, pestilence, or emigration, is soon refilled by men's tendency to multiply. But the gap of monkhood is of a different kind. There is nothing to replace; the human being is still there; he has simply become useless. He even becomes pernicious, because he submits all his faculties to the domination of a man unconcerned in the political constitution; because he permits this man to mould him to his will; and especially because, as a monk, he increases the mass of superstition by which the people are oppressed.

" Amongst the heaviest exactions of this oppression, are the contributions which the regular clergy receive through the begging friars. To be better off in the next world, or to be able to indulge favourite sins without remorse, people deprive themselves of necessaries, and pay the priest. They neglect the true means of remedying the ills which threaten or befall them, and give themselves up to the influence of devilish illusions, exorcisms, amulets, etc., for which they pay largely. In fact, they are kept in brutish ignorance, in order that they may never escape from slavery, nor attempt its alleviation.

" There is nothing of this kind with Protestants. On the contrary, it is almost impossible that a Protestant villager should fulfil his religious duties without knowing how to read : every candidate for confirmation is required to possess a Bible and catechism, because the pastor is not considered as the only mediator between God and man. In Popish countries, the monk, whether regular or secular, takes entire charge of all matters relating to salvation. Thus, in most of these countries, knowing how to read is the exception, whereas in Protestant lands it is the rule[1]. "

" In Upper Corinthia, in order to deter people from Protestant-

1. Mirabeau vol. VIII, pp. 48 to 57.

ism, the priests barred the entrance of knowledge by closing the schools, under pretence of the inutility of learning to country folks; indeed of its danger, for if they knew how to read they might be found handling heretical books. The consequence is, that not one in a hundred knows his letters, and the most advanced read badly. Being able to read was, at one time, regarded as certain proof of heresy; so much so, that men who had mastered this unusual acquirement positively pretended entire ignorance of it[1]."

"Countrymen, and even countrywomen, who do not know how to read and write, are much more rare in Germany, especially among Protestants, than in France, where, in many respects, greater liberty prevails. Start from Constantinople, cross Hungary, go to Vienna (Popish places) and from thence by Prague to Dresden; on your way buy books and mathematical instruments; seek out the fittest men to instruct you on any subject, or physical or mechanical science, and count up the cities where, during your journey across this vast extent of fully inhabited and much frequented country, you find facilities for satisfying yourself in this respect. Resume your journey. Go from Dresden to Meissen, Leipsic, Weimar, Iena, Erfurt, Gotha-Gœttingen, Brunswick, Luneburg, Hamburg (Protestant places). Try these towns by the same standard, and then pronounce your verdict[2]."

"The professors of literature in Protestant Germany are infinitely better informed than those of Catholic Germany, and have furnished many more distinguished men. The Prussian colleges have benefited by the freedom permitted to thinking and writing. All have taken advantage of the light lately thrown on the subject of education, while in many other countries there is more speculation without result; people, priests, and government striving who shall most effectually exclude knowledge[3]."

"There are two distinct parties in Germany. The endeavour of one is to bring the whole of this vast country under the dominion of one Sovereign. It may be called the Austrian, or Popish party. The other must be truly named the Protestant, or Prussian party; and it embraces all who love civil and political liberty, and freedom of thought, and who desire to bestow these blessings on all men. What the Protestants have to dread, is the constant, secret, and cunning machination of the priests, chiefly the monks, and above all, the Jesuits. When we see the Pope thanking the kings of Spain and Portugal and the Duke of Parma for having preserved the

1. Mirabeau, vol. VIII, p. 100. — 2. *Idem*, vol. VI, p. 386. — 3. *Idem*, pp. 139, 146.

Inquisition, we may be excused for doubting whether tolerance be compatible with Catholicism[1]."

In Mr. Schlœtzer's journal it is stated that a dispute on a new system of education having arisen in the presence of the Empress, the Superior of a religious order in great favour at Court said thus: "If your Majesty allows of this new method of study, which will enlighten and elevate the people, all religion will certainly be destroyed; but if your Majesty wishes to support religion, which is the first consideration, you must leave these things on the old footing, and not corrupt men by inculcating philosophical or licentious ideas, for then they will believe nothing[2]."

"If German literature were more known, it would readily prove the immense difference there is in this matter between Popish and Protestant Germany. It is true that the large town of Vienna has, by means of its wealth, factored some arts and sciences in a higher degree than most of the Romish states of Germany. The large number of strangers who visit it may also contribute to this result. But, generally speaking, instruction is far less widely spread than even in the smaller Protestant towns. M. Nicolaï cites some curious instances of this; we will only give one, which is that the titles of the books approved by the public censor are printed with palpable proofs of the grossest ignorance[3]."

"The clever men occasionally sent forth by the Austrian States are striking chiefly in comparison with the disgraceful ignorance which prevails in the other Popish parts of Germany. In fact, one cannot deny that, whether from timidity or prejudice, they do not rise to the clearness and conciseness manifest in the philosophical ideas of Protestant men of letters. The result is the same when we compare the people of the two countries. In Protestant Germany, they are much more generally instructed[4]."

"In proof of the bad state of the colleges, M. Nicolaï mentions the style of books published for their use. He says, if any one would give himself the trouble of examining these, he would soon see how much their authors had yet to learn. They send forth the most wretched trash, except when they copy, in the most impudent manner, from Protestant writers, as, for instance, Büsching for geography, and Schroeckh for universal history. As to Schroeckh, they have transcribed his work, word for word, both at Vienna and Wurtzburg; in short, wherever it was not judged indispensable that history should have a Popish bias. It is needless to describe more

1. Mirabeau, vol. VIII, pp. 128 to 132. — 2. *Idem*, p. 138. — 3. *Idem*, p. 152. — 4. *Idem*, p. 175.

fully the universities of Vienna. Let facts speak for themselves in this matter. Where are the literary men of Austria? Men known in the world of letters, and held in esteem by foreigners, as are Ernesti, Heyne, Kayt, Feder, etc., in the universities and towns of Protestant Germany? Let the cities of Catholic Germany be examined; take particular note of the universities of Vienna, Prague, Wurtzburg, Cologne, etc.; we do not name that of Mayence, because the small number of distinguished men it contains, such as Muller and Sœmmering, are Protestants, and have been brought from Protestant Germany, where they were educated. Where are the celebrated men, really valuable writers, who have been formed in these universities? Will their number bear the most distant comparison with the same class in Protestant Germany? At the close of the eighteenth century, Mr. de Sonnenfels announced the formation of a literary society. Amongst its members, the good writers who were the objects of emulation were all Protestants; this inscription was placed over their work: Behold those whom you should seek to imitate, if you would be Germans in mind as well as by birth. To prove that the German language is capable of every variety of style, he quotes a large number of authors, exclusively Protestant. If there had been one in Austria, or even in any part of Catholic Germany, M. de Sonnenfels would assuredly have named him. The refined language of these young men was in Vienna ironically called Lutheran German. M. de Sonnenfels himself relates that a person of rank to whom he was introduced for the purpose of requesting some employment, and to whom he wished, in proof of his capacity, to offer some printed compositions of his own, said in an abrupt manner: 'I think you are a Lutheran; at any rate your German is. What, an author! No, sir, you are too learned for my office [1].'"

"Protestant Germany certainly reverences Berlin as the place where true liberty of the press prevails, and as the residence of a number of eminent literary men, but no decided supremacy in literature or science can be allowed her. Men of first-rate talent are scattered over the whole surface of Protestant Germany, and this is no slight advantage of the Germanic Confederation and the Protestant system. In general society in Vienna, one may meet some truly learned men, a few enlightened persons; but in Protestant Germany, all of any position in society, all literary men, all public functionaries, are thoroughly educated and well inform-

1. Mirabeau, vol. VIII, pp. 207 to 211.

ed. The portrait of the University of Vienna, given by Nicolaï, is not flattering, but it is nothing compared with what we read in Schlœtzer, and some authors who have spoken of it :

" The students are idle, in imitation of the professors; a very small number attend any classes not absolutely necessary to teach them a profession, or where the testimony of the professor is not required to enable them to procure employment: 217 students follow the lectures of Mr. Meyer on logic, metaphysics, and moral philosophy, in which the old and inefficient system of Baumeister is adopted, and only 6 attend M. Scharf, who follows Feder's plan, which is a thousand times better. There are only 4 students in the higher class of geometry, and 6 in that of Universal History. Seger has 16 auditors for geography, Mastalier 8 for his course of literature, and Hasslinger 12 for oratory. Further, it is noticed that the number of students in jurisprudence diminishes annually, and that statistics are, at present, entirely deserted. De Sonnenfels has 63 hearers for his lessons on political economy, a number explained by the fact that these lectures, being formerly quite unattended, the learned man obtained an imperial decree, which forbade any one obtaining employment who had not followed his lectures [1]."

" Judging by those who leave the University of Prague, it is the only one which contains truly enlightened men, and who convey verbally important principles; but they dare not write, and some unknown cause acts as a check to their activity. Be this as it may, these universities cannot be compared with those of Protestant Germany which are at all well spoken of [2]. "

" We have not been able to procure the details we desired on the subject of Austrian legislation. Protestant Germany being almost exclusively the seat of learning, no work of general utility ever appears in the Popish States, and the few books which do emanate from them circulate amongst the inquisitive few, as they are very difficult to be obtained [3]. "

Does this contrast between North and South Germany continue to the present day? Marcel de Serres will tell us : " In the North of Germany, titles of nobility are more fairly appreciated than in the South. In the former, a man is valued more for what he is himself than for his titles, which he owes less to merit than to fortune; there it is rarely forgotten that true nobility is in the soul. However, these prerogatives better suit the German

1. Mirabeau, vol. VIII, pp. 215 to 220. — 2. *Idem*, p. 225. — 3. *Idem*, p. 226.

nation than any other, on account of their characteristic gravity. The universities of the North of Germany have enlightened the people concerning the political institutions which most deserve their respect, and have contributed to lessen the severity and harshness of feudal rights. Feudal servitude still exists in some provinces of Austria, where the progress of knowledge is not yet fully influential, but it daily loses its more oppressive features, and will probably, ere long, be entirely abolished. In Southern Germany, before the establishment of academies at Munich and Landshut, there did not exist a single university of the least celebrity; it is well known, on the contrary, what brilliancy the Universities of Gottingen and Halle have cast on the North of Germany, and the influence these great establishments have exercised in the promotion of knowledge. In Austria, where no literary emulation exists, literary merit is little esteemed, because it is feared it might enfeeble military ardour; in truth, it is evident that literary honours cannot be held in much respect where modern European learning has only yet half penetrated. Such titles are even despised, because there are none capable of sustaining them, and that genius is considered of far less value than high birth. The people of Nothern Germany, on the contrary, are passionately fond of reading, and any pamphlet even, which excites attention, is immediately in the hands of every one. In Austria, neither the mechanic nor the labourer care for books or discussions that have no bearing on their own immediate interests [1]."

"We have already noticed that what gives literary men in Northern Germany an influence they would not possess elsewhere, is the demand for political writings by all classes of society [2]."

"A stranger finds more pleasure in the society of Northerm Germany than in that of the South. The aristocracy and great people of the land mix more freely with literary men, and both classes must profit by this intercourse. The nobles of the North are not satisfied with merely seeking the society of literary characters; there are amongst them many who have distinguished themselves in the higher walks of literature, and think themselves honoured thereby. Princes and Sovereigns have rivalled each other in their attempts to give to the study of letters the distinction it claims from a civilised State. Thus, some little town which would otherwise have been unknown to fame, has acquired celebrity by the learned men it has produced. Gotha, Weimar, and Gottingen have alike become

1. Marcel de Serres, vol. III, pp. 193 to 197. — 2. *Idem*, p. 203.

the Athens of the North, and the centre of instruction to a great part of Europe. In a short time, the same will be said of Munich. The illustrious men whom a generous Sovereign has there gathered around him (we have seen they came from Protestant Germany), will soon render the cultivation of literature general in a country where it seemed unknown, and will annihilate for ever the reproaches on this subject, to which the people of Southern Germany are now liable [1]. "

" The nobles of Northern Germany have not forgotten, as many do, their social position. They have not given themselves up to tempting vices, unrestrained pleasures, or the easy duties of a private life, but have always maintained a dignity suitable to their rank. The habits and customs of German families attract the attention of a stranger, and inspire him with respect for a nation which has so successfully rejected innovations.

" When a young man distinguishes himself amid his zealous co-disciples, the nobles and great people eagerly offer facilities for the prosecution of his studies. The Universities of Gottingen and Halle are full of such young men, who, thanks to a generous benevolence, are at liberty to follow the profession of letters, in which they hope one day to distinguish themselves. And, what is not less remarkable in a country where birth is so highly esteemed, they are treated as equals by those lords and princes who throng the Universities, and who, like them, are completing their studies. Thus, in the same enclosure, are trained those who are to govern men, and those who by the strength of reason are to enlighten them. This daily intercourse gives rise to those first friendships, which are the strongest of all, and which have a certain influence on different classes of society.

" Essentially a methodical people, they have always thought that nothing could be efficiently taught, unless in a systematic and orderly manner. It is to this regularity and method that are greatly due the universal information and profound learning which have in every age distinguished the Germans. Who in France does not know that the learned man who astonishes Europe with the variety and extent of his acquirements, obtained them at the Universities, where every branch of human learning is unfolded in the clearest manner? In favour of the German Universities, we might also instance the chief of our French naturalists, who, after having received from them the first stimulus to his fine talents,

1. Marcel de Serres, vol. III, p. 241.

lately proclaimed his admiration of the northern institutions before the official body charged to promote education amongst ourselves[1]."

As yet the authors we have quoted have only mentioned the superiority of Protestant over Catholic Germany in general knowledge and intelligence: let us add a few words on some other points:

Superiority in Industrial Activity. — "The cultivation of flax in the North of Germany is a source of subsistence to a whole nation; it employs all the spare moments which would otherwise be lost, affords a means of usefulness to old people, and preserves a whole country from idleness and its attendant evils[2]."

Malte-Brun generalises this observation: "The people of Northern Germany feed on potatoes, butter, and cheese, with the addition of beer; are healthy, frugal, and enlightened; it is there that Protestantism gains most proselytes. The people of Southern Germany, luxurious in their mode of life, accustomed to wine, even to excess, are more lively, but also more superstitious. In Northern Germany, the multitude of dwellings, the villages ornamented with fountains, the clean and well-kept houses, the good roads bordered with fruit trees, and the well-cultivated fields, all bespeak the intelligence and prosperity of the inhabitants[3]." The industrial superiority brings in its train, as Malte-Brun says, greater material comfort: "There are in Munich 1,275 recognised beggars, who confess to living solely on alms; and above 3,000 persons who receive it. In 1785, there were hardly above 6,400 persons in Berlin who received public aid, and not a single beggar; thus, in proportion to the population, there are double the number of poor at Munich than at Berlin[4]."

Superiority in Morals. — "In Protestant Germany crime is very rare. Everywhere, out of the large towns, you can travel in safety in any costume. The inhabitants on leaving a house do not shut it up, but simply place a stick across the doorway, as a sign that no one is within, and this intimation is sacredly respected, as is often seen in Westphalia. The few thieves and robbers one meets with are either deserters; perhaps some miserable Jews, condemned by long persecution to support themselves by theft; or natives of the Popish provinces, where the people are not nearly so happy, so industrious, or so diligent, and where the number of holydays induces idle habits[5]."

Superiority in National Wealth and Financial Administration. — "The errors of the Sovereigns of Saxony have not thrown the

1. Marcel de Serres, vol. IV, pp. 22 to 28. — 2. Mirabeau, vol. II, p. 202. — 3. Malte-Brun, liv. 86, p. 740. — 4. Mirabeau, vol. VIII, p. 342. — 5. *Idem*, pp. 202 to 206.

country into such an abyss of debt as in Bavaria. The amount of debt was less; the population, and above all the national capital, was much larger in Saxony, even immediately after the war of 1763. A noble result of enlightened knowledge! This is the secret of the immense resources of Saxony, and which has enabled her to repair more recent though almost as great, losses. Bavaria is at present so profoundly plunged in the darkness of superstition and ignorance, that it is difficult to foresee the means by which she can be rescued[1]."

Lastly, *Superiority even in Language.* — "Protestants having been the first to write with intelligence, and consequently with correctness, the language used in the enlightened parts of Germany, this pure style is, in the countries subject to Austria, called ***Lutheran German*** [2]."

It is most remarkable that this superiority should be so conspicuous within the limits of the same nation. We have seen it in Ireland, where the Northern Presbyterians contrast with the Western Romanists; we have seen it in Switzerland, where the district of Morat, in the Canton of Fribourg, is as an oasis in the desert; we shall now see it in Prussia. In Ireland and Switzerland we perceived one brilliant spot in the midst of darkness; here we shall find one dark spot in the midst of light. And this, because in Ireland and Fribourg we were in Popish countries, while in Prussia the prevailing religion is Protestantism. Listen to M. Cousin: "In Prussia there are both Protestant and Romish normal schools. In general, the discipline of the Romish schools, without being precisely relaxed, is less strict than that of the Protestants. The system of these last is almost too severe; if, indeed, discipline can ever be too strict with young men from 16 to 22 years of age. Experience has proved that young men cannot be secluded for two or three years with impunity, unless a strong religious spirit prevails amongst them, and they are kept to their studies by strict rules. Regulations regarding study differ little in the normal schools of the two communities; nevertheless, these are more severe among the Protestants, and it may be said that, in general, their schools are superior to those of the Romanists. It is only natural that the institutions of the less enlightened provinces, such as the Polish, Westphalian, and Rhenish, should manifest the condition of their country, while the superior civilisation of the central provinces bestows on their schools a prosperity which these very results tend yearly to

1. Mirabeau, vol. III, p. 360. — 2. *Idem*, vol. VII, p. 483.

increase. When we enter a normal school in Saxony or Brandenburg, we cannot but be struck with the admirable order and strict discipline which prevail here, as in the Prussian barracks, while freedom and love of study are plainly visible[1]. "

Is it for want of religious guides that Popish Germany is inferior to Protestant Germany? Alas, no: it is not the number which is in fault. It is the only point on which Mirabeau gives it precedence: "Nicolaï remarks that at Berlin, amongst 140,000 souls, there are only 140 clerical personages; consequently, in comparison with Munich, where there are 1,150 ecclesiastics for a population of 33,500, the proportion of this profession is as 1 to 31; besides, in Berlin, the ministers of religion are married, and have children, whom they carefully train up as useful subjects of the State[2]. "

If then there be no lack of spiritual guides in the Romish Church in Germany, what is it that is still wanting? It is the possession of religious truth; for it is this truth which has emancipated Protestant Germany. Yes, the Reformation of the sixteenth century is the cause of the prosperity of Northern Germany, a point we are just about to prove. But, even here, we will allow the witness of the same authors: "It was only after the Reformation that the advantages of the University of Leipsic (Protestant), were developed. A remarkable fact, which proves the efficacy of the Reformation in promoting knowledge, is the excessive difference between the Universities of Leipsic and Prague. The latter has not yet emerged from obscurity; and Bohemia, which continues in a truly singular state of barbarism, has not derived any benefit from it, while the University of Leipsic has not only produced many first-rate literary men, but has elevated Saxony to a degree of civilisation which has had a most marked influence on the character of the people, on industry, and commerce[3]. "

" Protestantism, long since introduced in the Palatinate, has enlightened the people, and dissipated an infinity of prejudices. In this consists the immense advantage of the Reformation; an advantage which renders it of more practical value than all the universities and academies of science. These only enlighten the higher classes; the Reformation has enlightened the people. Based on the perusal of the Bible, all adherents of this sect must necessarily know how to read; schoolmasters have been established everywhere, who teach reading and writing, and this, of itself, is a considerable help to mental development. The Reformation freed the people

1. Cousin, p. 325. — 2. Mirabeau, vol. VIII, p. 432. — 3, *Idem*, vol. VII, p. 6.

from the observance of an immense number of religious holidays, and thus gave fuller scope to activity. This Reformation, having reached the Palatinate, one of the finest countries in the world, where Nature so amply repays the care of the husbandman, doubtless inspired the desire to carry the art of cultivation to perfection[1]."

Here again are more modern authorities :

" Since the Reformation, the princes of the house of Saxony have always awarded independence to the profession of letters. We may boldly assert, that in no country in the world is there so much public instruction as in Saxony and the North of Germany. There Protestantism was born, and the spirit of inquiry has since been manifested with vigour.

" We may judge by the quantity of books sold at Leipsic, how many German readers there are. Workmen of all classes, stonebreakers even rest from their labours with a book in their hands. In France, it is difficult to realise the extent to which knowledge is disseminated in Germany. Even in villages we find professors of Greek and Latin; in every small town there is a good library, and almost everywhere men might be named worthy of notice from natural talent or acquired knowledge. If a comparison in this respect were instituted between France and Germany, the result would make one fancy the two countries were separated by three centuries from one another[2]. "

" Though the government of Saxony was not free by law, that is, not representative, it was so in fact by the customs of the people and the moderation of the Sovereign. The good faith of the people is such, that at Leipsic a husbandman planted an apple-tree by the road-side, and put up a board requesting passers-by not to take the fruit : during ten years it remained untouched. I have looked on this tree with respect. Had it been the tree of the Hesperides, the golden fruit would have been equally respected[3]."

" In the internal government of Prussia, everything was favourable to independence and security. It was one of the countries where knowledge was most honoured, and where liberty actually, if not legally, was most respected. In all Prussia, I did not meet a single individual who complained of arbitrary acts on the part of government. Yet such complaints might have been made without danger[4]. "

" The liberty of the press, the union of talented men, the general knowledge of literature and the German language, so universally

1. Mirabeau, vol. VIII, pp. 432 to 434. — 2. Staël, vol. I, pp. 118, 119. — 3. *Idem*, p. 121. — 4. *Idem*, p. 135.

spread abroad of late, rendered Berlin the true capital of new and enlightened Germany. What must interest all in this country is the intelligence, in conjunction with right ideas of justice and independence, which one meets with among all classes [1]."

"Over the North of Germany are scattered the most learned universities in Europe. In no country, not even in England, are there such facilities for instruction and the cultivation of talent. Intellectual training is perfect in Germany. Sine the Reformation, the Protestant Universities are incontestably superior to the Catholic. All the literary honour belongs to these institutions [2]."

"In Germany, all men above the lowest class are familiar with several languages. On leaving the schools, they usually know Latin very well, and even Greek. Not only are the professors men of extraordinary learning, but they are especially noted for the care and ability with which they impart their knowledge. Thoughtlessness may lead to all the evils which exist in the world; only in a child can it attract, and when time gives a man up to his own guidance, it is only in calm seriousness that ideas, feelings, and virtues will germinate. In Germany, everything is done conscientiously; no one acts without reference to conscience [3]."

"Charitable undertakings ought to prosper in the town of Hamburg. There is such a high moral turn amongst the inhabitants, that, for a long time, the taxes were paid into a sort of poor-box, no one superintending the receipts, and the required sum was always found to be correctly paid. Does it not sound like a legend of the golden age? We cannot sufficiently admire the simple confidence which so facilitates both instruction and government [4]."

"Formerly, the clergy and nobles in Germany possessed many prerogatives extremely irksome to the people. The Reformation first undermined, and then destroyed, the temporal power of the priesthood; every one felt the need of tolerance, the spirit of liberty made some progress, and thus all became changed. The German people could not but rejoice at the new order of things which relieved them from many feudal claims [5]."

"If, with the miracles which Protestantism dispersed, Germany lost something of poetic fervour, she had ample amends. The people became more virtuous and refined. Protestantism had the strongest influence on purity of life and the strict performance of moral duties. Indeed, Protestantism has taken a direction which entirely identifies it with morality. Everywhere a most happy

1. Staël, vol. I, p. 143. — 2. *Idem*, pp. 145, 146. — 3. *Idem*, pp. 154, 155. — 4. *Idem*, p. 170. — 5. Malte-Brun, vol. V, p. 740.

change is seen in the lives of the clergy. With celibacy disappeared the vices and irregularities of the monks, whose place is occupied by virtuous priests, for whom even the ancient stoics would have felt respect. It is necessary to have traversed on foot the whole of Northern Germany before one can understand how much virtue, or, to use a finer phrase, how many evangelical graces, are to be found in the modest habitation of a pastor [1]."

Such is Germany. In the South, Austria and her band of Romish States career in the darkness of material despotism, without consciousness of the noble destiny of man. In the North, Prussia and her company of Protestant nations, blessed with increasing liberty, bask in the bright light of knowledge, in their ceaseless speculations, ever seeking God and immortality. We have now displayed both sides of the argument : the documents are in the hands of the reader, let him consult them and pronounce judgment. And being tolerably satisfied as to the result, we pass on to the consideration of Belgium and Holland, where we shall find a new field for the same demonstration.

1. Henry Heine.

CATHOLIC BELGIUM

AND

PROTESTANT HOLLAND

COMPARED.

Catholic Belgium and Protestant Holland having been alternately united and separated, cannot be so entirely different from one another as the countries we have already compared. During the last half century alone, Belgium has been successively under the rule of Infidel France, of the Protestant Netherlands, and of its own Romanist Government. It is to be expected that these powers will each have left an impression of its own, and thus have modified the contrast which struck us so forcibly elsewhere.

As far back as the seventeenth century, Belgium had Protestant martyrs. It needed the violence of a Duke of Alva, and the machiavelism of a Philippe II, to quench in blood the light of religious truth.

In the following century, the seed of reform produced fruit from which the whole country drew nourishment. It is a Belgian who makes this acknowledgment: " In offering, " says M. Edouard Smits, " a safe asylum to all victims of party violence, whatever may be their creed, we gain not only a material benefit from the stranger who brings us his capital and his trade, but also intellectual advantages far superior to the former. Witness the ever-living fruits of the revocation of the Edict of Nantes! That death-warrant of the noblest part of a nation; that bloody decree yielded by the weakness of an old king to a woman's prayer! Let strangers come; we will profit now, as heretofore, by their superiority in art or knowledge[1]."

Towards the close of the eighteenth century, having passed under the dominion of the French, and mixed with our people then irritated against the priests, Belgians must in some measure have shaken off the same yoke, and lost some of their prejudices; if this was not an advance in good, it was at least a step out of evil.

But it was especially from 1815 to 1830, under a Protestant Government, that Belgium received abundantly the treasures of civilisation.

The first benefit bestowed by Reformed Holland on Catholic Belgium was the creation of numerous schools, under the law of 1806, which, with the Prussian law (also Protestant), M. Cousin calls "the two greatest educational monuments which have yet existed in the world[2]."

"In the space of eleven years, 1,146 schools and 668 teacher's houses were built or repaired; 1,977 masters and 168 mistresses received Government certificates. The published documents stop in 1828, but it is probable the two following years would not present less satisfactory results[3]."

Belgium received these advantages, not only from the State, but from private citizens: "In several of the provinces, societies were formed for the encouragement of elementary instruction; to these are due Sunday-schools and adult evening-schools, in imitation of England and the United States[4]."

Philanthropy followed enlightenment: "Agricultural colonies flourished under the old Government[5];" "institutions for the poor were established; a general increase of population and comfort ensued[6];" as also "that great development of commerce, and that remarkable prosperity which," says Balbi, "have most diminished under the new Constitution[7]." "The manufactures on which Belgium now prides herself made immense progress," says the *Dictionnaire de la Conversation*, "during the union with Holland; instruction spread, art was magnificently rewarded..... But the chief crime of the Protestant Government consisted in not having known how effectually to disarm the Romish clergy."

1. *Statistique nationale*, *Mémoire*, etc., p. 68. — 2. Cousin, p. 156. — 3. Ducpétiaux, vol. I, pp. 60, 61. — 4. Poussin, p. 214. — 5. Ramon de La Sagra, vol. II, p. 163. — 6. *Dictionnaire de la Conversation*, article *Belgique*. — 7. Balbi, p. 363.

It will be admitted that all these Protestant influences (from the trades introduced by the French refugees in the seventeenth century, to the knowledge and commerce imported by the Dutch in the nineteenth) must necessarily have modified Belgium before she was placed, as now, under the guidance of the Romish priesthood, and must therefore lessen the moral distance which separated these neighbouring countries. Still, let us see if this distance is not, even now, great enough to add another chapter to the contrast which, as yet, we have found favourable to the Reformation.

Remark first that here, as in America, as in Great Britain, as in Germany, the disadvantages of soil and climate, on the Protestant side, are considerable: " In Holland," says the *Dictionnaire de la Conversation*, " the soil is entirely artificial; it is the produce of patience, courage, and the love of liberty. Astonishing to relate, the land owes its form and shape to the Dutch themselves, who have also traced the course of the canals, rivers, and lakes, which intersect the country in all directions. Conquered from the Ocean, Holland is covered with rich pasture-lands and smiling plantations, where horticulture is carried to perfection."

Belgium, on the contrary, " has a fertile soil, generously endowed by Nature; a ray of sunshine covers it with abundant crops; it possesses mines of lead, copper, iron, alum, sulphur, and calamine; quarries of marble, free-stone, lime-stone, slate, etc [1]."

In Holland, instead of these natural riches, what do we find? Water! water everywhere. While Brussels, the capital of Belgium, rests upon a rock, Amsterdam, the capital of Holland, is built in the midst of the floods, on thirteen million stakes! Now let us see what Belgian Catholics have done with their fertile land, and compare it with what Dutch Protestants have made of their marshes.

To reclaim, we will not say the soil, for there was none, but the spot where the bright pastures of Holland now gladden the eye, it was needful then, as now, to dry up the sea by dint of machinery and manual labour; in Belgium, they have but to turn up the surface of the soil. What the Dutch have, they made; what the Belgians have, they received, and that chiefly from the Dutch themselves. " It would be a mistake," says one of our writers, " to seek out of Holland for the principle of action; it is within herself that she found strength to struggle with Spain, France, and Eng-

1. *Dictionnaire de la Conversation*, article *Belgique*.

land; it is by her own power that she has become mistress of the seas and of European commerce; by her own innate strength also she has withstood the effects of the violent separation in 1830 from Belgium, to which she had been attached in 1814; there has been no falling-off in this unprecedented situation, where every chance seemed against her [1]. "

Again, dates must be taken in consideration. For centuries Holland has been a commercial nation; it is only of late that Belgium has become industrial. Long ago, the first shook off the yoke of Spain, which the latter continued to wear; and this double difference, so honourable to Holland, explains at once her greatness, and the languid weakness of her neighbour. Let us look back to the time when some few of the United provinces freed themselves from foreign dominion, and formed the Protestant Batavian Republic, while the rest, continuing under that dominion, fell back into Romanism: " When the Catholic religion was established, large numbers emigrated, who were received into the cradle of the Dutch Republic, and associated with that nation, whose commercial power was already dawning. Obtaining soon a complete victory over Spain, Holland consolidated her own independence, and imposed hard conditions on the Spanish provinces. By the treaty of Munster, their territory was diminished, their trade circumscribed; and Antwerp saw with regret her proud rival Amsterdam seize the reins of universal commerce [2]. "

" Art and commerce quitted the land which neglected them; towns became desert, the genius of the people expired; and while Holland rose from her ruins with fresh vigour and wealth, the Belgian provinces, still Spain, fell into degradation [3]."

We will not, however, compare two different things, Dutch and Belgian trade, though the first counts centuries of existence, and spends more than three thousand millions amongst different people; a greater amount, comparatively, than that of all other parts of the world, England alone excepted [4]. We will rather take a comparison where the starting points are the same.

Belgium having a fertile, and Holland an ungrateful, soil, we may suppose that agriculture would be more advanced in the first of these countries than in the second. Let us consult our witnesses. Poussin, after having placed Holland on a level with England as to agricultural development, says of Belgium: " Though the state of agriculture is not, on the whole, unsatisfac-

1. *Dictionnaire de la Conversation.* — 2. John Carr, *Introduction*, p. 44. — 3. *Idem*, p. 45. — 4. Balbi, p. 355.

tory, it is far from being what we have a right to expect in a country so richly endowed by Nature. Belgian agriculture is below that of England [1]," and consequently below that of Holland, with which the writer had ranked it.

"Every traveller, and especially an Englishman," says John Carr, "must be struck with the wisdom with which the Dutch cherish everything which tends to the improvement of agriculture. By this admirable policy, the State maintains a comparatively enormous population, in spite of the disadvantages of her situation. She thus delivers herself from the burden of pauperism, and has an abundant supply of provisions [2]."

The Dutch labourer enjoys an amount of comfort which contrasts strongly with the poverty of Flanders. "One cannot help admiring," says the ***Memoir of the Court of Louis-Napoleon***, "the comfort of the Dutch peasant: neither in himself nor his house is there that lamentable appearance of poverty noticeable in the French labourer. The dwelling of the Dutch cottager is well-kept, his clothes are clean and good; all bespeaks ease and prosperity. Most of these men wear gold buttons at the neck and wrist; others gold or silver buttons to their belt, a silver watch and chain, and gold or silver buckles to both garters and shoes. The women are no less remarkable for their costly attire [3]."

In Holland, agriculture, instead of being given up, as elsewhere, to ignorant routine, is encouraged, as in England, by being made the subject of study amongst all classes. "Purely agricultural school," says the ***British Review***, "have been established. A provincial school of this kind was opened at Groningen, the seat of a University, and the dwelling of some of the most zealous partisans of reform. A similar school exists in the neighbourhood of Utrecht, where scientific instruction occupies a prominent place: the Prince of Hollenzollern has just offered his domains at Heerenberg for an agricultural establishment on a large scale. Humbler schools for rural districts are not forgotten; nurseries, as they may be considered, where the masses grow, and take a good or bad direction. As in Scotland, each parish has its school, where every effort is made to convey to the scholars such an amount of mechanical and agricultural knowledge as will enable them hereafter to obtain their own livelihood. An old and wise regulation obliges theological students to follow a course of agriculture, that they may be able to advise their parishioners. This movement is not likely

1. Poussin, p. 287. — 2. John Carr, p. 309. — 3. *Mémoires sur la Cour de Louis-Napoléon et sur la Hollande*, Paris, 1828, p. 188.

to stop, for the proverbial slowness of the Dutch is still a progressive slowness. With them, prudence is allied to great obstinacy and invincible perseverance[1]. "

The plan of assisting the poor by employing them in agriculture, has answered marvellously in Scotland. Read Ramon de La Sagra on this subject; he cannot find terms strong enough to express his admiration. An establishment of this nature was formed in Belgium by the Dutch, when the two kingdoms were united. What became of it after the separation? De La Sagra says: "I have compared the receipts and expenditure before and after 1830: the result proves that the deterioration of the Belgian colonies dates from the time of the revolution[2]. "

To what is this falling-off to be ascribed? Partly, of course, to the Dutch system of agriculture being superior to the Belgian, but partly, also, because benefactors became discouraged. The amount of subscriptions, which before 1830 "was between 48,000 and 62,000 florins, then fell to 8,476[3]. Six or eight times less! Is it rash to suppose that Dutch patrons had retired, and thence to conclude that before 1830 Protestants alms succoured poor Romanists? This is the more likely, as, while the loss of these institutions is deplored in Belgium, Holland possesses 5,851 public benevolent establishments[4]. "

As the subject of agriculture is here connected with pauperism, let us compare the two countries in this respect: first as to the time when they were united.

Quetelet gives this table:

			Individuals relieved at home.	Population.
District or	jurisdiction of the	Hague.	227,501	2,262,712
—	—	Liége.	128,683	1,132,350
—	—	Brussels.	389,468	2,216,416

The population is not actually given in Quetelet's table, but the materials for the calculation are found in the preceding page of the same work. Nor does this writer speak of the religion of the different districts, but he names the provinces included in each. It happens that the Hague district is entirely Protestant: it is the Holland of the day, the two others forming the present Belgium are wholly Romanist. This circumstance greatly facilitates our comparison. If, then, we consider the individuals relieved out of each population, we shall have in round numbers:

1 pauper for 11 inhabitants in the Protestant district.
1 — 7 — in the two Catholic districts.

1. *Revue Britannique*, 1847, November, December, pp. 139, 140. — 2. Ramon, vol. II, p. 163. — 3. *Idem*, p. 166. — 4. *Idem*, vol. I, p. 115.

In other words, a third more paupers in the Romanists than in the Reformed provinces.

Such was the state of things in 1830. Since Belgium has been under the influence of the priesthood, has this proportion been increased or diminished? In the ***Statistique Générale du Royaume de Belgique,*** for 1841-1850, published by the Minister of the Interior, we find this statement: —

Paupers relieved throughout the kingdom.

Average from 1848 to 1850........................	942,290
Number of inhabitants to one pauper...............	4,65

Or, one pauper to five inhabitants [1].

Thus, under the patronage of the Romish clergy, the number of paupers is two-sevenths more than under Protestant rule; and, in proportion to the population, double that of Holland!

The next consideration is: how may the poor be withdrawn from the moral dangers of their position? By exercising a beneficial restraint on the guilty, or, better still, by the prevention of crime. As to the first point, Ramon de la Sagra, speaking of the classification of prisoners, according to their degree of guilt, says: "In Belgium everything has yet to be done in this respect [2], and I have no hesitation in saying that the Dutch organisation is better than the Belgian [3]." On the second point, the author is equally explicit. He says: "Establishments for the prevention of pauperism in Belgium have not that appearance of wisdom and benevolence which distinguish those of Holland [4]." Let us hear M. Cousin on the same subject: "I was astonished to find that the one central house of detention for young criminals, *for all* ***Holland,*** only contained from 60 to 80 boys, and that, with those expected from Leyden, the number would amount at most to 150, on a population of two millions and a half. The explanation of this phenomenon I found in the excellent schools for the poor, which met me in every direction. At Rotterdam, a commercial town with a population of 100,000, filled with merchandise, and where the multiplicity of canals and ports facilitates theft and even more serious offences, theft is rare; and housebreaking or violence of any kind is so little known, that our guides assured us they would have

1. In this number are included not only those relieved throughout the year, but also those who have received temporary help. We mention this, because the Report especially notes it. But neither are we bound to suppose that those named in the Dutch Report as relieved at home, were so throughout the year. — 2. Ramon, vol. II, p. 241. — 3. *Idem*, p. 242. — 4. *Idem*, p. 179.

difficulty in recalling any instances of it[1]." Malte-Brun adds: "There is much less depravity amongst the lower classes in Holland than in the rest of Europe. One rarely hears of robbery, and still more rarely of other crimes[2]."

Let us now consider the state of education throughout the country, and not only amongst the poor.

We have seen that Belgium owes much to the Dutch government in this respect. "In 1816, elementary instruction, which had been neglected by the preceding (French) government, and left to itself, had entirely decayed; in twelve years, the King of Holland so throroughly revived it that the year 1828 opened with 4,030 masters and mistresses, and 247,496 scholars[3]."

But, putting aside Dutch intervention in this rapid progress, let us consider it as belonging to Belgium, and compare results at this period: on one side in the Protestant, on the other in the Romanist provinces.

Quetelet gives the following figures:

District of the	Hague.	1	pupil for	8	inhabitants.
—	Liége.	1	—	11	—
—	Brussels.	1	—	10,50	—

Taking the medium between these two last numbers, and allowing for the double population of the Brussels district, we shall have

1	pupil for	8 Protestants.
1	—	10 2/3 Catholics.

That is, a fourth more scholars amongst the Protestants, and that at a time when the King of Holland was so actively advancing education in Belgium.

Since then, Belgium has been under the guidance of the Romish clergy: has she retained her system of general instruction? De La Sagra will tell us: "Ducpétiaux, though approving of the agents of the revolution, acknowledges the disorder it created. What have we done, he says, since 1830? We have changed our mode of action, it is true, but have we improved it? We have thrown down edifices, and rebuilt nothing; for several years the ground has been covered with ruins, and no attempt has been made even to clear the space[4]."

But les us quote Ducpétiaux himself: "In various localities

1. Cousin, p. 147. — 2. Malte-Brun, vol. VII, p. 37. — 3. Ducpétiaux, vol. I, pp. 59 to 61. — 4. Ramon, vol. II, pp. 24 and 25.

different plans of usefulness were abandoned after the revolution of 1830. The increase of schools does not necessarily imply real progress; in truth, the greater part of these schools are bad or at least indifferent; numbers of masters are wholly incapable of teaching[1]."

"The old government had commenced the training of useful schoolmistresses; the revolution destroyed these establishments.

"In 1828, out of 4,030 institutions, the number of male and female teachers who received certificates was 2,145. The last report (after the revolution) gives 3,477 teachers, not certificated[2]."

That is to say, after six years' retrograde movement, the number of non-certificated teachers, which had been less than half, rose to nearly two-thirds.

How are we to reconcile the increase of the number of schools with the perversion of the system? Thus: "Under the old regulations, schools existed whose masters were not regularly trained; they were chiefly infant schools, which were tolerated because the usual catechism and prayers were taught, with the rudiments of reading. Since the revolution, several of these teachers have somewhat enlarged their scope of instruction, and all these petty schools figure in the reports on education[3]."

These few lines show that the schools which have swelled the lists are bad, that their masters and mistresses were incompetent, and that the chief instruction was the catechism and the prayers; in one word, the priests' schools. It is worthy of notice that the religious bodies who devote themselves to teaching refused to submit to examination[4].

Clearly, then, it is to Romanism that Belgium owes the weakening of her system of education. What the clergy could not control, they willingly allowed to decay. By claiming unlimited liberty of instruction, that is, by refusing to submit to the inspection of the State, or to receive from it certificates of capacity, the priests freed themselves from all superintendence, and were not sorry that these teachers, who were beyond their influence, should propagate ignorance, true sister of superstition. This is the natural deduction from the following quotations:

"Under the old government, the law adjudged a penalty to those who should be bold enough to teach without a licence; but the Catholic clergy chose to consider themselves exempt from this law. Being however hampered in the exercise of their functions, and indiscriminately mingled with other classes of society, the whole

1. Ducpétiaux, vol. I, pp. 68 and 69. — 2. *Idem*, p. 108. — 3. *Idem*, p. 85. — 4. Ramon, vol. II, p. 21.

body looked at the decree as an infringement of their privileges and an insult to their opinions. From that time they carefully watched for an opportunity of avenging themselves[1]."

"The government having abdicated the influence of authority, fell; and, as Ducpétiaux says, all that had been created by that authority felt the effects of the blow[2]."

"Amidst the general neglect of primary instruction in Belgium, we must remark *the activity of the Catholic clergy in filling the void* left by government. *Moved*, PERHAPS, by laudable zeal, but certainly *inflamed by an ardour of encroachment little compatible* with their separation from secular affairs, the *religious bodies* took the place of ordinary masters[3]."

What was the result of this clerical pretension to freedom from inspection and control? Others took advantage of this false interpretation of liberty; ill-qualified men thrust themselves into the office, and it was not difficult to find a schoolmaster who was an ignorant brute, or worse! "Several barely know," says Ducpétiaux, "what they pretend to teach; some open a school for three or four months in the winter, simply because, at that season, they are unable to pursue their usual employments as carpenters, masons, etc[4]."

The clergy saw no harm in this; first, because, as Poussin says, the whole population (including the ignorant lay teachers) was under their influence; and also because they were not sorry to see darkness spreading over the land. Thus, masons and carpenters metamorphosed into schoolmasters, and teaching nothing, forwarded their work, while, with the old Dutch government which exacted certificates of capacity, inspected schools, and distributed books, there was great risk of light being diffused, the effects of what the priests call a Protestant propaganda.

But, whatever may have been the part taken by the clergy in the Belgian revolution, and whatever their present doings in schools, let us compare the picture just presented of public instruction in this Catholic country with that drawn of Holland by the same authors, with the addition of M. Cousin. Two lines will show the superiority of Holland as to the number of scholars:

In 1836 there was in Belgium 1 scholar for 107 inhabitants.
In 1835 — Holland 1 — 83 inhabitants[5].

Or, proportionately, one-fourth more in Holland than in Bel-

1. Ramon, vol. II, p. 13. — 2. *Idem*, p. 24. — 3. *Idem*, p. 29. — 4. Ducpétiaux, vol. I, p. 91. — 5. Ramon, vol. II, p. 352.

gium. But, though this is an honourable distinction, it is not the most important part of the subject; the capacity of the master and the style of school being the chief points worthy of attention.

"This difference is observable in the scholastic systems of the two countries: in the one the co-operation and influence of the clergy; in the other their exclusion. In Belgium, the priests direct, at least partially, all primary instruction, not only as to religion and morals, but as to every branch of education. In Holland, they take not the slightest part in public instruction; they do not even visit the schools; religious doctrine is not allowed to be discussed, though the master is charged to teach his pupils the rules of the morality and the truths of the Gospel[1]."

"Owing to this happy union of good elements, wonderful effects have resulted in Holland, as far as regards domestic morality, and the acknowledged honesty of all classes[2]."

M. Cousin, who is so well acquainted with educational matters, confirms these assertions. He says: "From all I have seen and heard, I am persuaded that those brought up under the system prescribed by the law of 1806, are honest and pious. In Holland, Christianity pervades the life as well as the minds of the people; yet, in the schools of this religious nation, the only instruction ordered by article 22 is Bible history, with such reflections as are suggested by the narrative[3]."

While M. Ducpétiaux laments the state of education in Belgium, M. Cousin admires that of Holland: "These facts," says he, "are sufficient to show the prosperous state of public (especially elementary) instruction in Holland[4]."

While M. Ducpétiaux acknowledges that in Belgium masons and carpenters undertake to teach that of which they are ignorant, M. Cousin, on the contrary, declares that "the excellence and talent of the Dutch schoolmasters have chiefly contributed to this satisfactory result[5]."

According to M. Ducpétiaux, many schoolmasters in Belgium have become discouraged, and abandoned their profession, while M. Cousin says: "Everywhere in Holland I found the teachers contented and happy. The situation is much sought after; a fact which speaks for itself[6]."

This writer condenses high praises in these words: "I noticed with admiration the Dutch method of general instruction. I had opportunities of convincing myself that to this excellent orga-

1. Ramon, vol. I, p. 64. — 2. *Idem*, p. 106. — 3. Cousin, p. 170. — 4. *Idem*, p. 150. — 5. *Idem*, p. 171. — 6. *Idem*, p. 172.

nisation are due the character of the people, the patriotism of the citizens, and the sentiments of religion and benevolence which animate all classes[1]."

"These happy results have contributed to produce the high esteem which Holland enjoys in Europe[2]."

A passing traveller also notices what close examination revealed to the philosopher: "The Dutch," says John Carr, "have always felt the great importance of education. They are aware that by rousing a spirit of research and industry in youth, they are giving the best hope of success in after life under every government. This system has raised Holland to that high degree of power which is witnessed in the various periods of her history. To this may be attributed the most entire absence of barbarism in her last revolution. Even an English merchant may be surprised in some of the Dutch warehouses by the intricate knowledge of arithmetic displayed by the youngest clerks, by the large amount of business transacted in one day, by the creditable appearance of the ledger, and by the rapid and correct calculations of the different rates of exchange; as, also, by the variety of languages so readily spoken. We are as much astonished at the length and assiduity of their labours, as at their well-regulated habits and life[3]."

It is evident that education in Holland has exactly that tendency which Ducpétiaux regrets it has not in Belgium: it is moral; which brings us to consider the habits of the people.

The vicinity as well as the intercourse of the Dutch and Belgians naturally provokes a comparison between the two nations: it has already been made by Ramon de La Sagra, whom we like to quote, precisely because he professes the Roman Catholic faith.

He says: "There could not be found two people more different from one another than the Belgians and the Dutch. The impetuous and enterprising character of the former contrasts strangely with the caution, patience, and perseverance of the latter, whose qualities, though less brilliant, are not less productive of good results.

"In Belgium, the populace, fond like the French of pleasure, may be seen at theatres, gardens, and all places of public resort. In Holland, the chief pleasure is found at home, and the family circle furnishes the truest happiness. The one need movement, action; the other, freedom from agitation and tumult. Hence the quiet, comfortable existence of the Dutch; hence those pictures of domestic

1. Cousin, vol. I, p. 35. — 2. *Idem*, vol. I, p. 186. — 3. John Carr, p. 48.

felicity, which delight the eye of the traveller. In Holland, life is enjoyed; in Belgium and France, it is recklessly expended. This difference is certainly a characteristic trait in the two people. Now, if any one should ask which of them I think the happiest, I should not hesitate to reply, the one which seems the least so[1]."

M. Cousin will complete the portrait. He says: "In Holland, every one lives at home, and family ties have even greater strength here than in Germany. The Dutchman is a wise and well-reputated being; he does not seek to shine, preferring in all things reality to show. He has more honesty than generosity, more good sense than wit or imagination, more perseverance than enthusiasm. The nation is rather good than great. The general temperament is phlegmatic, which, in favoured individuals, rises to a calm but immoveable firmness, rendering them capable of long and arduous enterprises[2]. The people are amongst the most moral and religious in the world[3]."

But the contrast will be instinctively apprehended by the reader, if we merely place, side by side, two distant pages of the same writer: "A brilliant future," says Malte-Brun, "would be in reserve for the Belgians, if the nation could decide on following the path of real progress; but, blinded by misplaced vanity, it is divided and powerless. The mind of a Belgian does not stretch beyond the limits of his town. Municipal government and religion were of immense service to him, more than two hundred years ago; these ideas of his infancy ought to have expanded since then; they have remained as contracted as ever. The cities are all rivals, but not with that enlightened rivalry which is productive of good; it is petty hatred, rather than noble emulation. The men do not live frugally; taverns and clubs engross a great part of their time; five hours given to business is considered a good day's work for a clerk or a merchant. The young men, particularly in the higher classes, are inexcusably ignorant[4]."

What does the author, who speaks thus of Belgium, think of Holland?

"The parsimony of the Dutch led them to throw off the yoke of the Spaniards, by whom they were so heavily taxed, and to refuse to pay tithes to the clergy and indulgences to the Pontiff. In the great struggle of the sixteenth century, their caution and perseverance triumphed over all obstacles. They felt that religious liberty was the basis of civil freedom, and that only through these could

1. Ramon, vol. I, pp. 30 and 31. — 2. Cousin, pp. 9, 10. — 3. *Idem*, p. 36. — 4. Malte-Brun, vol. VII p. 87.

they insure that of commerce and industry. The number of useful works and establishments in Holland, kept up at great cost, leave a favourable impression on the mind. Those dykes which resist the power of the Ocean, those canals which traverse the country, those hospitals and benevolent institutions, do honour to Holland, no less than the good faith so observable in her mercantile transactions[1]. "

Two short passages from another writer, not meant to be united, offer a still stronger contrast. M. de Rougemont says : " The Dutch are active, laborious, frugal, reflective, prudent, and persevering; their honesty and truthfulness are as proverbial as their cleanliness; elementary instruction is widely spread amongst them[2]. " " The Belgians, " says the same writer, " are known by their excessive intolerance and superstition[3]. " " Flemish towns are celebrated for the rude and dissolute habits of the people[4]. "

Yet the Belgians are often spoken of as essentially religious. What, then, is their religion? M. Poussin will tell us : " In Belgium, society has a great external appearance of devotion, a sort of religious discipline, a tranquil, almost sleepy look : is it really in a better state than ours which is so devoid of religion, so merry, sometimes so turbulent? I cannot think so after all I have heard, seen, and examined. The most shameful vices circulate in low and concealed paths, amidst that half-monastic society[5]." " I am ready to declare that these towns of eighty or a hundred thousand souls foster as much hideous vice as our capital, with her million of inhabitants, is accused of doing[6]. " These lines call to mind, by way of contrast, the following of M. Ramon de La Sagra : " The state of morals in Holland, and the severe organisation of society, check the development of the passions, and preserve the precious candour and innocence of youth[7]. "

Let us close this comparison with the testimony borne to the Dutch by their old king, Louis-Napoléon; a testimony all the more honourable for giver and receiver, in that it was offered after the abdication of the monarch, and when the services of the Prince of Orange had been preferred to his in the then approaching war : " Considering the damp, uncultivated, and desert appearance of the greater part of Holland, the soil constantly inundated, and, so to speak, artificial; on the one side undermined and ravaged by the principal rivers of Europe, which discharge themselves upon it; on the other, continually threatened by the inroads of a stormy sea;

1. Malte-Brun, vol. VII, p. 36. — 2. Rougemont, p. 499. — 3. *Idem*, p. 505. — 4. *Idem*, p. 507. — 5. Poussin, p. 393. — 6. *Idem*, p. 394. — 7. Ramon, vol. I, p. 133.

considering the immense labours necessary to preserve the soil from being swept away, and the incessant activity required to obtain a livelihood where the climate is unfavourable, and the land barren and unsteady, we cannot suppose that this people love their country. We pity them for not being more favoured, and look on them as a band of exiles, forced to live in this unhealthy and ungrateful land. But, when we examine their character and habits more closely, we recognise the virtues of this people; their candour and good sense, their attachment to their duties, their patience, their love of toil, their moderation in their pleasures, their gratitude and love to the Author of all good; when we consider their skill in all they undertake, the great men they have produced in every department without exception, the perfect state of their agriculture and their commerce, their progress in the sciences and arts, the high degree of their knowledge and civilisation, we are induced to change the comparison, and call them a band of philosophers, disgusted with the folly and wickedness of mankind, endeavouring in seclusion to live according to the dictates of reason and conscience, and pitying the noisy pleasures, the show and luxury, of the rest of the world; or rather we look on them as a chosen people, destined by God as an example to others[1]." "Happy nation! amongst you reign justice, reason, humanity. Those who govern you and understand your character will be the happiest of governors, if they follow your good sense, and seek your welfare[2]."

In order to explain the moral distance which separates Holland from Belgium, we must here take into account the religious state of this latter country, so deeply imbued with Romanism; we must speak of those inquisitors of conscience who have no less than sixteen confessionals in one little Jesuit chapel, at Brussels; of those six hundred convents, which, on an average of twenty persons to each, give a total of 12,000 monks or nuns; of that material religion which offers worship to the heart of Jesus, to the wound in his foot, to the nails of his cross; especially must we speak of the Christianised heathen festivals. But we have already so often described Romanism, and we shall have to do it again on so many occasions, that we fear to weary the reader by displaying here the long list of the practices of a church which boasts of being always and everywhere the same. For the sake of brevity, we will merely give one characteristic specimen of Belgian Catho-

1. *Mémoire de la Cour de Louis Bonaparte*, vol. II, pp. 11, 12. — 2. *Idem*, p. 123.

licism, and of those dearly loved *kermesses*, celebrated all over the kingdom. The following details are official, and copied *verbatim* from a programme published by the printer to the archbishopric of Mechlin.

From the preface we learn that this jubilee is kept in recollection of the miracles performed by a miraculous image of Our Lady of Hanswyck. The principal part of the *fête* was a cavalcade which traversed the town of Mechlin four times. It was composed of eight allegorical cars. The 1st was preceded by "Four heralds on horseback, representing the *mirth* of Mechlin, and thirty-six young ladies, also on horseback, representing the *Litanies of the Virgin*, and bearing in their hands emblems of the attributes of the mother of God." The first car contained the "Queen of Angels, surrounded by cherubim and seraphim, etc.;" the 2nd, "the Queen of Patriarchs, surrounded by Patriarchs, and seated under a crown supported by four branches of trees;" the 3rd, "the Queen of Prophets, being represented in the costume of their day, and JESUS CHRIST, the chief object of prophecy, REPRESENTED BY EUGÈNE HAGAERTS;" the 4th, "the Queen of Apostles;" the 5th, "the Queen of Martyrs;" the 6th, "the Queen of Confessors;" the 7th, "the Queen of Virgins;" the 8th, "the Queen of all Saints." Such was the first part of the cavalcade. The second contained "the Philharmonic Society, preceded by its drums and the Virgin of Mechlin, represented by Mimi Vankiel, on horseback, followed by all the Virtues, attributes of the town." The third part represented the royal household, "their Majesties the King and Queen of the Belgians and the young Princes, led by Providence, and followed by Religion, Justice, etc." The last part was: "1st, The three-masted vessel, the *Welfare of our Country*, in which sits Saint Catherine; 2nd, the horse Bayard, ridden by the four brothers Aymon; 3rd, the cavalcade of Giants: the grandfather, grandmother, and three little giants; 4th, the Wheel of Fortune; 5th, two camels, *each bearing a Cupid*; 6th, a detachment of lancers."

"Before proceeding, we feel it necessary to repeat that this was not a masquerade, but a Popish ceremony, winessed by a hundred thousand persons in faithful Belgium, in the month of August, 1838. Let us resume these incredible details.

"The jubilee lasted fifteen days. His Grace the Archbishop himself officiated in the triumphal procession. The Board of Trade, in conjunction with the burgomaster and aldermen, obtained the favour of having 'all the taverns and places of public resort open *all night* during the continuance of the festival,' including two Sundays. During this time there were games with the cross-bow, tilts on horseback, and fireworks, mixed up with sermons and masses, and the whole wound up by a solemn service of thanksgiving. Such is a brief but exact account of the jubilee of Mechlin.

"To crown the work, the Board of Trade, composed of the *curé* and others, by the intervention of the *superior* ecclesiastical authority, had addressed a request to the Holy See to *obtain indulgences* for those who should piously observe the jubilee. The *Holy Father*, by a rescript dated Rome, 11th of May, 1838, granted a favourable reply to the petition.

"The young actors in this religious representation were taken from the best families in the town. A great number of trained horses being necessary for the cavalcade, a demand was made to the Minister of War, M. Wilmar, who hastened to comply with the request.

"It is needless to say that the people thronged to these indecent farces, and that for a fortnight the town presented a continuous scene of drunkenness and debauchery, of quarrelling and foolish pranks, evils that Romish solemnities always tend to promote, but which, on this occasion, were uninterrupted, thanks to the laudable care taken to leave the taverns open all night during this 'pious representation[1].'"

We see that the principal method employed by the clergy to make themselves acceptable to the people is to amuse them, or, at least, to take part in their amusements. It is not the Church that is to convert the world; the world has already converted the Church. To be "all things to all men," in the bad sense of the word, is the great secret of Rome. Clerical influence is immense in Belgium.

"The preponderance of Romish clergy in Belgium," says de La Sagra, "is a bad omen for the future, unless they moderate their pretensions. When we see them not content with the results of a revolution skilfully directed by themselves, invading the province of education, and dexterously profiting by its neglected condition, we tremble for the consequences of such conduct[2]." "The daily encroachments of the clergy," adds M. Poussin, "their spirit of monopoly, their attempt to assume the censorship of the press by interdicting certain journals to the faithful, the unceasing gift of miracles, which they turn to such lucrative account; all these tendencies, so contrary to the genius of the age, make us foresee that

1. *Europe Protestante*, 1839 to 1840. — 2. Ramon, vol II, p. 32.

the numerous exactions of the priest will give great advantage to the liberal party [1]."

"All converges towards a moral and intellectual subjugation, which is what we chiefly dread in the Jesuit system of education; for it aims at nothing less than the extinction of all free will and spontaneous action; that is, of the very life of the soul [2]."

It is in Flanders especially that the influence of the Romish clergy is felt; there Catholicism reigns in all its purity; there, too, ignorance is supreme, and from thence come legions of beggars. "Flanders is the Ireland of Belgium. Some years ago it fell into such extreme misery, that it is now difficult to recover it. It is a constant source of perplexity to the Belgian Government; like Ireland, Flanders is overwhelmed with pauperism [3]."

It is, then, chiefly with Flanders that our comparison must be made; for there is the *maximum* of Catholicism. Its *minimum* is with the Walloons, neighbours of France, who have fallen so thoroughly under our influence that they speak our language, and have largely adopted our customs. Here there is less subserviency to the priests; consequently greater activity, a better state of agriculture, and more relative prosperity. With the Walloons, Romanism is on the surface, infidelity below. "The Belgians," says M. Poussin, "are unanimous in their creed; they are all Catholics, and show great zeal in their worship, of which they observe all the regulations, precepts, and errors, with scrupulous exactness. The people are religious, bigoted, and superstitious. The free exercise of religion has as yet made little progress in Belgium. If here and there is found a follower of Voltaire, you may be sure that his sentiments are confined to himself; in his family, this same man is a stricter Catholic than others [3]."

Is not this a fair picture of the French Catholic? We might say of the Parisian Catholic?

It is a strange or rather a melancholy fact, that the absence of Romanism, even when not replaced by a purer creed, is preferable to its presence. If our comparison had been between not two but three nations, the first Protestant, the second Infidel, the third Catholic, we should have found that the unbelievers held a medium place as to morality. This may be proved by comparing, first, the Dutch, the Walloons, and the Flemish; then the English, French, and Spanish. Whence we deduce, not only Romanism does not improve the character of man, but that it injures it.

1. Poussin, p. 259. — 2. Poussin, p. 240. — 3. *The Times*. — 4. Poussin, p. 29.

We have hitherto compared the effects of Catholicism and the effects of Protestantism on nations more or less civilised. The results which we have verified may be attributed to anterior causes. That no one may fall into this error, let us see what the two religions have done, each in its respective sphere, for the primitive nations on whom they have been the first to operate by their doctrines; in other words, let us compare the Catholic and the Protestant Missions to the Heathen.

ROMAN CATHOLIC MISSIONS

COMPARED WITH

PROTESTANT MISSIONS.

In order to make our comparison complete, it must be directed,

First, to the Missionary Churches;

Secondly, to the Missionaries themselves;

Thirdly, to the people to whom they are sent.

We purpose, then, to contemplate the subject under these several aspects. And, first, let us compare the Churches that send out the Missions. The Romish Church has but one Missionary Society, known under the name of the "Society for the Propagation of the Faith," and having its seat at Lyons, with the whole earth for its sphere, and Christendom for its treasury. Founded in 1822, its character is by this time ascertained, and its mode of gathering funds is admirably arranged. Sanctioned by the Pope, and protected by the bishops, it is also aided by contributions from the laity, which are excited by certain indulgences attached to donations. The organisation of the collectors is also remarkable. They scarcely ask any sacrifice, frequently nothing more than a subscription of a penny a week, for which they remit a copy of the "*Journal de l'OEuvre,*" which is circulated among the subscribers. The rest is made up by the sale of miraculous medals, blessed by the Pope.

The low rate of the subscription to the journal, and the cheapness of the medals, bring both within the reach of the smallest fortunes, and these of course are the most numerous.

The funds are collected throughout the world: we would ask, then, what has been the result? what is the income of this mighty association, organised and in full activity for more than thirty years, and reaching to all the Catholics of the earth. The report of 1850 gives 3,082,729 francs.

Three millions of francs! the annual product of all the zeal, of all the faith, of all the charity of Romanism for its Missionary work. But, as there are 139 millions of Roman Catholics in the world, according to Balbi, if all had contributed each must have given at least two centimes annually! Is this much, or is it little? God alone can determine this positively; we will endeavour to do so relatively. Let us see what is done elsewhere.

Among Protestants, it is not a single society that we meet with; the associations outnumber the nationalities; and we shall not take into the account either the Bible or Tract Societies, with some others, which, although having reference to the Heathen, and being strictly religious works, are yet but what are especially designated as Missionary Societies. It is to these last that we limit our inquiry. The following is a list of them, and of their annual receipts. The elements will be found at the end of the second volume of the "*History of Evangelical Missions.*"

PROTESTANT

DATE of the SOCIETY.	NAMES OF SOCIETIES.	MISSIONARIES and LABOURERS.	STATIONS.
1701	Society for the Propagation of the Gospel in Foreign Parts...	386	341
1701	Scottish Society for the Propagation of Christian Knowledge.		
1705	Society of Missions at Halle for the East Indies...........		
1732	Society of Missions of the United Brethren at Bethelsdorf...	286	61
1786	English Wesleyan Methodist Missionary Society...........	6,860 *	
1792	English Baptist Missionary Society........................	351	102
1816	Universalist d° d° d°........................	6	4
1795	London Missionary Society...............................	250	108
1798	Scottish d° d°................................	18	14
1796	Glasgow d° d°................................	12	
1797	Dutch d° d°................................	24	10
1799	Church of England Missionary Society....................	2,000	93
1800	Jœnike's Institute at Berlin............................		
1810	American General Missionary Society....................	492	97
1814	Society for Baptist Missions...........................	199	48
1816	Bâsle Missionary Society...............................	45	12
1817	Presbyterian d° d° of America.......................	67	14
1819	Episcopal Wesleyan d° Boston U. S.....................	347	67
1820	D° Missionary Society of New York....................	120	29
1823	Berlin Society for the Propagation of Evangelical Missions..	27	6
1824	Paris Society for d° d°.............	40	10
1828	Barmen Missionary Society..............................	36	20
1820	Missions of the Established Church of Scotland..........		
1835	Hamburg Missionary Society............................		
1836	Lutheran Evangelical d° Dresden.......................	9	
1837	Missionary Society of Lausanne.........................		
1838	D° d° for Africa (Glasgow)..................	10	3
1840	D° d° for Foreign Parts.....................		
1840	D° d° of Irish Presbyterian Church (Belfast)....		
1842	Central d° for the Heathen......................	101	22
1842	Norwegian d° d°.................................	2	1
1843	Free Church of Scotland Missions.......................	24	5
1843	Danish Missions (Copenhagen)...........................		
1843	Swedish d° (Stockholm)...............................		
1843	Lutheran America.......................................		

* This number, like many others, very considerable, includes not only the family of the missionary, but those of his assistants, and the native missionaries.

MISSIONS.

INCOME in FRANCS.	SPHERE OF ACTION.
2,000,000 f.	The East Indies, Africa, America, Australia.
	Ireland.
3,000	
337,000	Labrador, N. and S. America, Greenland.
2,570,000	
638,000	
56,000	
1,800,000	
55,000	
130,000	The Malucca Isles, Java, Celebes.
2,570,000	Malta, Greece, E. Indies, Egypt, Abyssinia, E. Africa, North-America, and Australia.
1,280,000	Greece, Turkey, Syria, Persia, Koordistan, China, E. Ind., Afr., Am., Sandwish Isles.
299,000	Greece, China, E. Indies, W. Africa, N. America.
134,000	Greece, Malta, Turkey in Europe, Asia-Minor, E. Indies, E. and W. Africa, America.
300,000	India, China, E. Af.ica, N. America, Texas.
630,000	E. Africa, N. and S. America.
160,000	Greece, Candia, Turkey, Koordistan, E. Africa, N. and Central America.
76,000	S. Africa, E. Indies, N. America.
100,000	S. Africa.
90,000	D° and Borneo.
27,000	E. Indies and New Zealand.
27,000	E. Indies, New Holland, Jews, German colonies in America.
4,500	1. Louisiana, a station in Sioux country, N. America.
	E. Indies, New Holland, New Zealand, N. America.
	S. Africa.
150,000	East Indies, Jews.
	Danish settlements in the E. Indies. The Gold-coast of Af.ica.
	North America.

Thus, against three millions collected by Roman Catholics for the Missionary cause, we have to place fifteen millions collected for the same objects in Protestant countries — a sum five times greater, furnished by a population three times less. Thus, multiplying five by, three we have, with reference to those who support the Missionaries, the expressions of faith, zeal, and devotedness fifteen times less developed among Romanists than among Protestants.

Now let us pass on to the Missionaries themselves. Let us see them at their work. We will not institute any comparison between their respective members, since this is but the necessary consequence of the difference of income between the parties; this applies also to the number of stations. What we have to compare is the nature of the work, the means employed, and the results obtained.

In order to form a correct estimate of the Missionary, let us take him at the moment of departure; let us make an inventory of his suite and of his personal baggage.

A Protestant Missionary is generally accompanied by a schoolmaster, a surgeon, and sometimes by an artisan capable of building a house, or printing a book. This last directs our attention immediately to one of the first objects of the Missionary caravan; a press, or at least books. The schoolmaster, the doctor, the artisans, we foresee, will each and all help to announce the Gospel in their special departments.

Having reached the appointed station, in the midst of a people whose language is neither known beyond their own region, nor written within it, the first employment of the Mission is to learn this, and to commit it to writing. While they are reducing it to the rules of grammar, they are also printing a gospel as well as a dictionary, and thus bringing the nation or tribe within the pale of civilisation. Now, we must bear in mind that this method is not arbitrarily chosen; it is but the necessary development of the Protestant system, which is to teach the Written Word, the Sacred Scriptures. It is by teaching that the Missionary opens up his way.

Look into any report of Evangelical Missions, and at every station you will find a school and a printing-press; and the grammars and dictionaries used by Romish Missionaries in India and in China were all compiled by Protestant labourers, who have thus fixed and stereotyped the materials with which they have to work. In every report you find such details as these: "Doctor Milne (Malacca) sets up a printing-press, opens schools. He has published an interesting journal, the *Chinese Magazine*, as well as several tracts in English, Chinese, and Malay. Two years later, 1818, the famous

Anglo-Chinese College was founded. Doctor Milne died before he had completed his Chinese translation. Doctor Morrison gave a new impulse to the College[1]."

"Schools were established (at Singapore), and the press soon multiplied copies of the books translated into the native language, which penetrated to the heart of Central India. In 1823, Doctor Morrison founded the Malay College[2]. Since 1841, a college for young Chinese has also been founded (at Siam), with a printing press, schools, and religious services. The books and tracts are eagerly sought by the natives. Since 1844, the Missionaries have published a monthly journal."

Nor are these details confined to any particular class of Protestant Missions. The course is the same in all. Schools, printing-presses, instruction; and with this intellectual work philanthropy goes hand in hand, caring for the sick, ministering instruction in the more simple of the useful arts, and thus establishing the empire of the first. In this manner the advantages of science and civilisation are diffused. We might point to an hospital established by a Missionary physician in China, where hundreds of persons afflicted with blindness are received; we might tell of another Christian surgeon who devotes himself to visiting the sick among the heathen. We are not now calling attention either to the self-devotion or to the merits of these men; we speak of them only as pious doctors, gone forth to heal the sick. Farther on, our readers will see the drift of this observation.

Such then are the external modes of action of the Protestant Missionary; and his baggage consists of a book, a printing-press, and a case of surgical instruments. Now, let us inquire into that of the Romish Missionary. The list furnished by himself runs thus: "A breviary for his own private use, a missal for the service of his church, a patine for the communion, chaplets, crucifixes, medals, and images for his converts."

This prepares us for the course of action in which we may expect to find the Romish Missionary engaged among the heathen by whom he is surrounded; his object is not to instruct, but to baptise and to enrol beneath the banner of Rome. He has no need to make a study of a language in order to teach a people who already speak to write it; all he requires is such fluency in the colloquial idiom as may enable him to communicate with the natives. It is to be a means of securing a conquest to himself; not a means of communi-

1. *Histoire des Missionaires Évangéliques*, vol. I, p. 284. — 2. *Idem*, p. 285.

cating knowledge to the aborigines. He avails himself of it not only to teach what he chooses to explain, but to conceal what he desires to hide. With his death, all germ of knowledge dies out; while in the case of the Protestant Missionary, who leaves a written language, he also leaves the means of introducing not only religious knowledge, but the arts and sciences in general, and that in no wise as a contingency of his personal influence, but through all time while the language shall be in use. The germ is deposited in the soil, and that secures the fruits to successive generations. And now let us follow the course of the Romish Missionary in his journeyings among the heathen. He recites a formula, he baptises in haste, he teaches the ***Pater*** and the ***Ave*** by heart, he instructs them to bow, to say the rosary, to carry a cross in procession, and that is all. Doubtless there are exceptions, but this is the general mode of proceeding, at least according to the report of the Missionaries themselves, speaking of their Portuguese brethren. " Certain priests of this nation succeeded, as they relate, in planting Christianity here; but alas! what did we find on our arrival? Scarcely a vestige of it. The faith and piety of the flock had vanished with the pastors; and if from time to time a few zealous servants of the Lord appeared, their ephemeral visits had produced only passing results [1]."

And yet this plan of ephemeral conversion is still persevered in. Here is an instance: " We had been at Fort Albany two mouths; I had baptised more than forty adults, and upwards of sixty children; I had gone through the catechism with more than fifty Indians. ***The Mission was accomplished.*** " We do not mean to say that the Romish Missionaries are never stationary; we only seek to prove that ambulating Missions form part of their plan; for we thus gain a clearer insight into the nature of their operations, and the sort of conversions which they effect. In general, then, their object is neither instruction nor civilisation, but the introduction of a custom, a sacrament, or the giving the sanction of the name of Catholic to some heathen practice previously in use. " If one of them," said a Romish Missionary in speaking to us of a heathen community, " be overtaken by an accident, he goes at once to the magician, makes his confession, and asks for some penance. And what these poor unbelievers do as a mere ceremony, our neophytes are instructed to perform as the most necessary act of the religion they have just embraced [2]. "

We see, indeed, that the transition is by no means difficult.

1. *Annales*, n° 134, p. 6, 1851. — 2. *Idem*, n° 125, p. 137.

Sometimes the mere presence of some object of Roman Catholic devotion is supposed to be sufficient to work conversion : " The sight of the cross that I planted last year," says Father Laverlochère, " make the most salutary impression[1]. " It seems, indeed, that it is not always requisite that the cross should be seen; it is enough that its figure be traced in some secret place. " Before we left Maugarèva, we determined to leave at least the sign of the cross; we therefore cut it on the two little columns of the cabin that had been assigned us, and also on two trunks of trees. M. Laval had even the courage to engrave a cross on one of the pillars of the temple, and to conceal in a corner of the same temple an image of *Our Lady of Peace,* the patroness of the Mission. When our effects were all embarked in the canoe, we addressed the Virgin with confidence in these words, *Iter para tutum,* and departed. In the Island of Akarnaru we found children eaten up with vermin; we cut off the hair of some and washed their heads, in order that we might the more easily baptise the dying without being detected by the natives[2].

It is true that when the age admits of it, the child is previously instructed, but how? Is it a Chinese convert? He is made to recite a Latin prayer: " A little girl, aged only four years and a half, already knows the *Pater noster* and the *Ave*[3]," said one of the Missionaries. The crucifix, the rosary, and penance occupy a prominent place in this propaganda, as we see in such passages as the following, extracted from the *Annales:* " I shall kiss my little wooden corpse and the image of Mary, and I shall plant a cross in my hunting-ground[4]."

Another fasts every Friday, and passes the whole of his life in a state of continual abstinence, eating nothing but rice and a few vegetables, and that to the entire satisfaction of the narrator, who adds: " To the glory of the religion which these two noble Christians know so well how to practice[5]. "

Sometimes the medal is used as a means of conversion: " I asked them if they would not gladly receive baptism? 'Oh! no,' they replied, 'that would make us die.' An answer that shows how much or how little these women understand about the baptism *offered* to them." The Missionary did not however despair: " Seeing all my efforts to win over these prejudiced souls were fruitless, I retired to the recesses of the forest, and there I entreated the Immaculate Mary to interest herself for these unhappy creatures, who

1. *Annales*, n° 125, p. 137. — 2. Otaheiti, pp. 157 to 159. — 3. *Annales*, n° 136, p. 215. — 4. *Idem*, p. 210. — 5. *Idem*, p. 239.

had just refused her medal; and I promised to say a mass in her honour. On the following day the two sick women, still afraid lest they should have died in the night, change their mind, are baptised, kiss the cross and the medal[1]."

In reading such recitals, we were tempted to ask if the senses exercised any influence in these conversions, and three pages further on we think we found the answer to this question: "I saw several of them in tears during the singing of the *Vexilla regis*." Savages moved to tears by a Latin chant! It is possible; but do these emotions flow from a penitent heart or from nervous excitement?

It is plain that the Romish Missionaries aim less at securing a moral reformation than at the accomplishment of certain acts; thus, instead of giving the number of their scholars or of their hearers, they publish lists of their own official services:

"Catalogue of sacraments administered during the year in Corea:

Confessions.............................	6,844
Communions............................	4,929 [2]"

Now, the reverse of all this is the practice of the Protestant Missionaries, who give the numbers of their communicants as bearing on the number of converts, but who would never think of rehearsing each separate season of communication as though there were any merit attached to the act itself.

But there is more, and it is worse. It is not always even a ***short*** residence, a week's catechising, ordinances easy or hard to comply with; sometimes it is a simple rite accomplished without the knowledge of the individual on whom it is practised. It is no isolated fact to which we allude; we have before us accounts of a series of facts, the results of a connected method, and this method the natural consequence of the dogma of the efficacy of baptism for putting away original sin, and taking the baptised person straight to Heaven. Thus, we find Romish Missionaries administering it with peculiar satisfaction to children in dying circumstances; nay, even rejoicing when death comes at once to set the seal to this salvation. Let us not speak a word without book. "It is the gold and silver of Europe," writes one Missionary, "that enables us to administer baptism to so many children in danger of death. The number of little Chinese thus baptised is less this year (1850), than in the year preceding, and this diminution arises from the decrease of your alms; when you are able to send us

1. *Annales*, n° 136, pp. 123, 125. — 2. *Idem*, n° 134, p. 74.

more money, our figures will rise again. Grant us, then, I conjure you, an increasing yearly stipend. For a hundred francs to our baptisers, 300 or 400 children at least can be regenerated, of whom two-thirds go almost immediately to Heaven. Press the rich to open their purses; urge it upon those who would secure the best interest for their capital to send it to Su-Tchuen, where 20 sous, by preserving two souls, produce two fortunes yearly.

The baptism of 94,131 sick children of infidel parents has not been the work of our salaried baptisers alone..... Certain pious neophytes, who profess to cure infantine complaints, have also baptised many for us.

Baptisms of the sick children of heathen parents in sundry of the Asiatic Missions:

At Su Tchuen, 1849	99,807
At Yun Nan, 1848	4,000
At Corea, 1847, 1848	1,225
At Cambodia, 1849	5,000
Among the Bumese, 1849	127
In Eastern Cochin-China, 1849	4,074
— Western d° d° 1849	1,688
— Central d° d° 1849	5,017
At Tonkin (Eastern), 1849	13,506
D° Central, 1849	12,439
D° Western, 1848	9,428
In the same Vicariate, 1849	9,649

With this inventory the Missionaries send the information that three-fourths of the baptised are already dead, and in possession of the heavenly inheritance [1].

It is not a little inconsistent that, in order to accomplish these baptisms, recourse is often had to fraud, and even to falsehood. Thus, in *Les Annales de la Sainte Enfance* for December, 1852, vol. 4, n° 29, page 462, we read: "Our people, so simple in their general habits, are wonderfully adroit where the salvation of a soul is at stake. Those who are somewhat addicted to trickery have singular skill in winning over the children, while they assure the parents that if they are unwilling to consent, they must do as they please, and that family feelings are always respected. One man in particular is spoken of who has some little knowledge of medicine, and who has already baptised hundreds of children without the cognisance of the heathen parents. Some he baptises furtively with a little water from his moistened handkerchief; at other times he asks for water under pretence of washing the child's face, in order the better to ascertain its malady, and then uses it to wash away

1. *Annales*, May 1851, n° 136, pp. 224 to 226.

the stain of original sin from the soul; not unfrequently he makes use of a little instrument by which he administers medicine to children, for the purpose of bringing water in it. He turns again and again as if to bring himself within the child's reach, and when he finds that no one is looking, he discharges the water, and if it be perceived on the bead, it is supposed to be a few drops of the medicine that the patient has not swallowed."

The Protestant method of conversion is very different, and much less expeditious. We have seen something of the preliminary work of these Missionaries, and after all this they often continue their instruction for years, without announcing any conversions. With them it is not enough that a heathen man or woman attend their place of worship and ask for baptism; they require evidence of a change of life, and a process of examination, before any can be admitted as members of the Church. In the Report of the Society of Evangelical Missions, read at Paris in 1853, we find this statement. "Five neophytes, whose religious impressions are of long standing, are receiving instruction preparatory to baptism[1]."

And the following: "The examination of thirty-one neophytes, whose puratory exercises had been long and serious, *lasted three days;* during this time the Church was greatly edified by their frank confession of faith, and by the details they gave of their conversion."

We might cite hundreds of parallel cases from the reports of the same society. Would it be believed that the king of a people among whom the French have had a settlement for the last twenty years, who has favoured their work, attended their schools, joined their assemblies for public worship, and conducted himself in an irreproachable manner, loving the Gospel and admiring its effects, and rejoicing over the conversion of his own children, yet dares not call himself a convert, and is still unbaptised[2]. What a contrast do these scruples, and these catechisms, and these Protestant Missionaries present to the baptisms administered by the Romish Missionary on the very day after his landing on the heathen shore!

But laxity or strictness in the admission of candidates are not the only marks of distinction. The Church of Rome has always taken advantage of State influence. For centuries past she has leaned upon France in Syria, just as more recently she has availed herself of the same alliance in Oceania. We give examples, which, being of recent date, may be easily verified.

1. *Annales*, p. 18. — 1. *Idem*, p. 24.

Otaheiti had been for half a century converted to the Protestant faith. Certain Romish Missionaries, no less zealous against heresy than against paganism, conceived the project of evangelising it afresh. They performed the voyage in vessels belonging the State, and the officer in command published the following declaration: "The chiefs of the island must understand that, to persecute the Catholic religion, to denounce it as idolatrous, and under this absurd pretext to banish Frenchmen from the isle, is an insult to France and to her king." At the same time, the captain asked not only for liberty of worship, which had been given, but also land for the erection of a church, and the deposit of a sum of 20,000 piastres on pain of bombardment. The Queen submitted; and, under protection of the French cannon, the Romish worship was set up [1].

Have Romish agents renounced their civil and military reliance in their subsequent operations? Twelve years after the establishment as we have just read of it, we find the following in the *Journal des Débats* [2]: "We have news from our settlement at Otaheiti down to the 10th of February. France, as the consequence of her Protectorate, has established a station there, filled only by a brigadier and one gendarme. The inhabitants are all either Protestants, or Mormons. Within the last eighteen months certain Catholic Missionaries have established themselves, and have made proselytes; but their zeal having carried them a little too far, a conflict was the result. A Mormon refused baptism, *they would fain compel him, and called in the assistance of the brigadier and the gendarme in order to ascertain the grounds of his resistance.*" The same means were brought to bear in the Sandwich Isles, and with the same success; except, indeed, that here the Romish Missionaries knew better how to take advantage of favouring circumstances. Father Maigret wished to found a high school, and to give the diplomas himself. Captain Mallet, sent from France, came to his aid, required a grant of land for the school, the celebration of marriage without the intervention of the civil power, and the abolition of a law restraining the sale of brandy: all these demands being made in one document, as if to demonstrate more clearly the success of the Church as the result of the power of the secular arm.

Here we see the Romish Missionaries, under favour of a man-of-war, obtaining, first, "liberty of worship; then the right of making converts; then alienation of lands for building a church; subsequently for a school; then the sanction of the government to a por-

1. Otaheiti, p. 260. — 2. Quoted by *La Presse*, May 22, 1853.

tion of the instruction of its youth being committed to the clergy without inspection or control; next, the substitution of religious law for civil authority in the matter of marriage, and thus the giving over of the family in its most important interests to the dominion of the priests [1]."

Our readers may perhaps ask why these Romish Missionaries should select as their field of action islands where the Gospel had been already proclaimed? M. Desgraz, secretary to the commandant Dumont d'Urville, ventures on an explanation: "It will be seen," says that gentleman, "that the object our Missionaries have in view is not the amelioration of the heathen, but the glory resulting from the work; they therefore prefer embracing an opportunity that will bring them before the public by the noise which the edifice they are striving to pull down will make in its fall, to those obscure labours which have for their end and aim the civilisation of some remote corner of the globe, where, should success reward their labours, they would never attract the attention of the public. The spirit of controversy and of fierce dispute has now taken the place of that spirit of peace and toleration which ought to bear rule [2]."

We leave with M. Desgraz the responsibility of his explanation; and, having thus shown the difference of the means employed by Romish and by Protestant Missionaries, we proceed to show the difference of the results obtained.

First, then, what are these results in the case of Romish Missions? Here we are met by a difficulty. We feel that the answer will vary with the witness who may be called before us, and even in some according to the subject on which he is questioned. Still we believe that we have the means of giving an impartial statement. We shall take the evidence of Romanists, and we shall leave them to choose their ground. These Missionaries detail their own progress in a journal published for the last thirty years. From the long annals of the Propagation of the Faith, a friend has selected the most striking parts, and has published these extracts in the form of a pamphlet, entitled, "*Nouveau coup-d'œil sur l'œuvre de la Propagation de la Foi.*"

We take it for granted that a work, the object of which is to obtain subscriptions for Roman Catholic Missions, will set them in the most favourable light. We take our statements from the pages of this work. And lest we should be accused of giving garbled

1. Otaheiti, p. 280. — 2. *Idem*, pp. 195 and 196.

statements, we will give the extracts ENTIRE. We must needs be impartial; let the reader only be patient.

We begin at page 9: "We remember those delightful societies formed during the last century in Paraguay, in which 20,000 savages lived together in a state of peace, prosperity, and innocence such as we cannot recall without emotion. Something of this kind is seen in several of the Missions recently established."

Thus, father Rougeyron, speaking of the Wallis Islanders, observes: "What I have been most struck with is, that form of the Primitive Church which has seemed to revive among these people. The villagers meet every evening in the chapel for united prayer, a catechist presides, and when the congregation disperses they retire some to their cabins, some to the shore, and the rest remain in the valley; and then they recite the rosary, and sing hymns in honour of Jesus and Mary. On Saturday, these hymns are prolonged to 11 o'clock, and even till midnight, so that everywhere their voices are heard, and the whole island joins in praising the God who has saved it. On the following morning these hymns are resumed at sunrise, or even at daybreak. The Missionary rings the mass bell; all hasten to the service. Out of 2,000 communicants, 500 present themselves every Sunday at the holy table. Formerly these people were cheats, thieves, pirates, and cannibals; now, thanks to the power of grace to renew the heart, an excessive mildness is their characteristic feature, an honest frankness seems natural to them, and they hold all theft in horror. Indeed, locks and bolts are no longer necessary; and the Missionary may safely commit to their keeping fruit, wine, money, and effects. Happy people thus to have savoured the gift of God! Even death seems to have lost all terror for them! 'Why should we fear death?' said one day to me a catechumen, 'shall we not be still happier in the next life?' On another occasion I was pitying the sufferings of an invalid: 'Father!' he replied, 'do not pity me; suffering is good for Heaven!'"

The same prodigies appear also among the converted heathen of North America:

"The charity of our Indians is wonderful," writes father Hoecken, a Missionary in those parts, to his Superior; and their union is such that a whole tribe lives as one family. Their submission and love to their chiefs are unlimited, and those chiefs also live in the most perfect harmony one with another. Never, they say, 'do our hearts suggest or our lips demand any but the same things.' The chief regards himself as the father of the tribe; his voice is never raised when he issues his orders; but he never speaks in vain; all hasten to fulfil them. Is an Indian in circumstances of difficulty? he consults his chief, and acts in accordance with his advice. As the father of his people, the chief provides their sustenance. Every animal killed in the chase is taken to his lodge, where it is divided into as many portions as there are families in the tribe; a side of each animal being reserved for those whose business it is to cultivate the ground in spring. The distribution is made with the most perfect justice; the old and the sick, the blind and the orphan, share alike with the hunter. What is this but a return to those happy times when the Apostle tells us that Christians were all of one heart and of one mind? Complainings, murmurings, slanders, are unknown here. Our converts place their glory in the faithfulness with which they serve God, and their ambition is limited to the knowledge of their duty. It is the thought of God that guides the young in the choice of a partner. During the moments of leisure, they flock round the Missionary, besiege him, so to speak, and would even keep him up the whole night, if his strength were proportioned to his zeal. Pride and vain glory are unknown to them. How often do we see grey-haired fathers seated by the side of children of ten and twelve years of age, and listening as pupils to the instruction of these precocious teachers, while they repeat the prayers or explain the figures of the "Catholic Ladder" with all the gravity of a master! And then, in seasons of adversity, when the products of the chase fail them, and they are thus condemned to a rigorous fast, no sign of impatience escapes them. Calm and tranquil, they attribute the failure to their sins; while on the contrary they render thanks and praises to the Lord for every instance of success. But if the first object of the Missionary be to make known to the unbelievers the way of salvation, they nevertheless do not neglect to teach them also those acts which are necessary for this life. It was necessary," writes father Liansu, Superior of the Mission of Gambier, in Oceania, "to provide for our neophytes, to clothe and to lodge them. To this subject we turned our attention, and God has blessed our efforts, so that it is no longer an essay. In the large island alone, we have eight looms, which this year have supplied 4,300 yards of cloth. All the cotton has been prepared in ten weeks, and woven in seven months. Our islanders have determined to build themselves stone houses, finding that their wooden huts perish too quickly, and make great havoc among their finest trees. They have drained all the marshy spots, in order to plant taro; they have rooted up whole forest of useless reeds, and planted the sweet potatoe instead; they have brought the most sterile lands, hitherto covered with fern, under cultivation. We trust that they are thus placed beyond the reach of the scourge of famine."

Now, let us review this long quotation. In the first place, then, what is become of the Jesuit Missions of Paraguay? They are completely annihilated. On the departure of the fathers, the Romanised savages returned to their forests. They had been trained to arms, to labour, all for the benefit of the Society of Jesus... But so little did they appreciate these advantages, that, after having tasted of Romish civilisation, they preferred the life of the savage. They may have been in error, but we must acknowledge that their conversion was not a very deep work, since it left the seeds of such a preference in their hearts.

Father Rougeyron informs us that the Islanders of Wallis recite the rosary and sing hymns on Saturdays up to midnight, resuming them at daybreak. Then, out of 2,000 converts, we have 500 communicants. This is all well; still we have here no indication of anything more than the external work which custom and the love of variety render easy. As to the change said to have taken place in their moral character, the features bear the marks of flattery; but every one must judge for himself.

The pictures of the North American Indians must also be referred to the judgment of the reader. But, when we come to the great Isle Gambier, a farther work has been accomplished; the body has been cared for as well as the soul. Already eight looms are in operation; the natives *resolve* to build stone houses; they have uprooted forests, and planted potatoes, so that in future they *hope* to be beyond the reach of famine.

Such is the result of Romish labour, as set forth by Romanists. And now let us examine the work of the Protestant Missionaries; and instead of consulting their own agents, as we have done in the case of the Catholics, let us take the report of Catholics on this side of the question also. We shall thus place ourselves beyond the possibility of suspicion. As a pendant to the Isle of Wallis, we will take Otaheiti, another Island of Oceania, civilised by Protestants, the island which the Romish Missionaries have endeavoured, though in vain, to detach from the Gospel. What was its state in 1824, that is, just 25 years after the arrival of the first Protestant Missionary? We will give it in the words of the report furnished by Admiral Duperrey to the Minister of Marine: "Otaheiti is very different now from what it was in Cook's time. The

Missionaries have effected a total change in the manners and customs of the inhabitants. Idolatry is no longer practised, and the religion of Christ is generally professed. The women no longer come on board the ships; they are indeed extremely reserved when we meet them on land. Marriage is on the same footing here as in Europe, and even the king has consented to have but one wife. The wives also eat with their husbands. The infamous association of Arreoys (religious assassins) no longer exists. The sanguinary civil wars of former days have disappeared, with human sacrifices, since 1816. All the natives can read and write; they have religious works translated and printed either at Otaheiti, Uljeta, or Eimés. They have handsome churches to which all people repair twice in the week to hear sermons. You may often see individual hearers taking notes of more striking passages of the discourse[1]." And now, having heard the admiral, let us listen to the Minister of Marine, as presiding at the general sitting of the Geographical Society of Paris, on the 11th December, 1829: "It is not the lust of riches that has brought to the light of civilisation that vast portion of our globe, scarcely known prior to the discoveries of the unfortunate but illustrious Captain Cook: I mean Polynesia. What a wonderful event is that moral revolution, brought about as if by enchantment in that Archipelago which within the last twenty years was still groaning under the yoke of the most absurd and at the same time sanguinary idolatry. All at once human sacrifices cease; the priests of falsehood disappear, the altars of them that were no gods fall, and the cruel law of Tabas gives place to the mild and beneficent law of Christ! What glory for Christianity! But her triumph does not stop here. When the idols were broken in pieces, the arts of civilisation were introduced; the natives were inspired with the love of order and the desire of employment. The despotism of arbitrary power has been exchanged for a government which is every day becoming more regular in its action; and beneath the shadow of the Churches where half-cultivated men assemble to worship the living God, are public schools, in which children, formerly abandoned to the grossest ignorance, receive that primary instruction without which the civilisation of any people must be incomplete. O! what cannot love accomplish when enlightened and directed by faith[2]!"

And now, under the sanction of these two authorities, we may surely claim a hearing for our Protestant writers. This is but

1. Otaheiti, p. 112. — 2. *Idem*, pp. 115, 116.

simple justice, when with reference to Romish Missions we have consulted none but Romish authors. We shall select our quotations so that each may bear upon a different object.

We will refer first to the signs of external prosperity, for the conversion of the heart may be denied when it is only manifested in words, but how can we refuse our assent to that which asserts itself in facts? In 1804, then, " Van-der-Kempt was authorised to found a district colony at the Cape of Good Hope. The Boors, who were to choose the locality, fixed on a very undesirable situation, in order, as they said, that the Hottentots, unable to subsist otherwise, might be obliged to come to them for employment. Such was the origin of Bethelsdorp, situated in an arid desert, without vegetation, without timber trees, without water. It now presents the aspect of a well-built village, having a chapel, schools, fine gardens, a printing-press, and all sorts of trades in operation; and the inhabitants, amounting to 600, are decently attired, and distinguished for the purity of their manners. In 1842, they collected among themselves about 3,000 francs for Missions.

Pacaltsdorp is no less remarkable in other respects. When the Missionary Campbell repaired there in 1813, it was but a miserable kraal or village, composed of huts formed of the branches of trees woven together, and having scarcely 60 inhabitants, and these plunged in the very depths of ignorance. When Campbell returnned thither in 1819, he could hardly believe the testimony of his own eyes. It so far exceeded his expectations; it was no longer a wretched hamlet, it was a beautiful village, with elegant houses each in the centre of its garden, fine roads, and a substantial wall all round, to keep out the wild beasts. The Mission on the Kat river affords a striking proof of the manner in which the converted Hottentots reflect the light on those around them. Near to Fish-River, and beyond the district of Albany, there formerly existed a savage tribe, called Gonaquas, who in 1827 had been almost extirpated by order of the government, on account of their depredations. In 1829, the promulgation of the edict of liberty gave freedom to 30,000 Hottentots, who had been held as slaves by the Dutch farmers; of these, 25,000 were provided for by the colony; the rest were invited to settle in a desert region on the Kat river. Eighty little villages rose in succession, the chief of which is Philipton; but the majority of the inhabitants were heathen, brutal, ignorant, and vicious. The government placed 140 Christian families among them, drawn from Bethelsdorp and Theopolis. A touching spectacle was thus afforded by the self-denying charity of these Christians, who thus devoted themselves for the sake of the poor savages. Not only did they attend to their material interests, but they established divine worship, and these wretched Hottentots became attached to them as sheep to their shepherds. Schools where everywhere opened, and Doctor Philips saw men and even half-naked children learning to read, in order that they might teach others. In a short period, the whole mass was leavened, heathenism disappeared, and hundreds were converted to the Lord. Well-built villages were the admiration of the traveller; the population increased to 5,000; there are more than fifteen stations for religious services, and above 700 communicants [1]. "

This Mission is of course English, and as the English have a peculiar reputation as colonists, this success may perhaps be attributed to their skill and genius. We turn, then, to a French Mission, since the French certainly have no prestige in their favour on this head; and it will be seen that the result is the effect of Protestant principles, not of any particular nationality.

There is a French Missionary settlement among the Bassouthos-Betschuanas, in S. America. In 1843, the Missionaries sent home many reports of the manners of this cannibal people, who carried away men, women, and children like animals of the chase. Now, this has ceased, and the whole tribe has come under the influence of the Gospel, and is thirsting for instruction. The French stations are :

I. Bethulia, which is in such a flourishing condition that the number of inhabitants has risen from 600 to 3,000. The effect of preaching has been wonderful. In 1848, the number of communicants, all natives, was 110, and a collection was then made for Missions, which reached the sum of 10,200 francs.

II. Beersheba. In 1842, a printing press was set up here. In 1843, the Missionary Rolland baptised forty-six adults and thirty children.

III. Morija, built in 1833. A town at the base of the high mountains. The Missionary Arbousset baptised here in September, 1844, thirty-five adults, five of whom were chiefs of villages. The work has gone on ever since. Considerable sums have been contributed to build another church.

IIII. Mekutling is a French station of more than 4,000 persons. In 1841, three converts were condemned to death on pretence of magical practices. As they were leading them away to death they were about to bind them, but the victims declared it to be unneces-

1. *History of Evangelical Missions*, vol. 1, p. 57.

sary, as they would not fly; and the executioners, overcome by the calm dignity of their bearing, drew back, and refused to shed the blood of these men. The chief, in a transport of fury, seized a lance and pierced them to the heart. In 1843, the Missionary Daumas baptised seventeen adults; since this time the station has made great progress.

After this proof that the French and English Missions are alike successful, it may be that some persons will be found to attribute their success to the ignorance of the people among whom they labour. "These heathens," they may say, "offer no opposition to a work which costs them nothing." But, besides the sacrifices they have made in furtherance of the cause of Missions, we can now show those who are ready to die rather than give up the faith.

The Missionary Station of Tinouvilli (E. Indies) excited the jealousy of the idolators, who sought to get rid of it by complaining to the government. As they did not succeed, they had recourse to violence[1]. "They organised a society, the members of which swore by the sacred ashes to retain the old religion and the customs of their country, and to oppose Christianity by every means in their power. They sent messengers in every direction with terrible menaces, which they proceeded at once to put in execution. They destroyed chapels, they set fire to houses, they expelled catechists, they committed every possible outrage; but the Christians, instead of being intimidated, found their numbers grow with the danger. From the year 1841 to 1842, the number of converts rose from 13,000 to 19,000, and the excess of baptisms was 500; 234 auxiliary missionaries, natives, proclaimed the Gospel in 360 villages, and the glad tidings are heard throughout six vast districts. In 1844, 1220 converts were baptised."

Such was the result of a popular persecution. We will now turn to one of a still more sanguinary character, originating with the government. The Protestant Missions in Madagascar date from 1818. "In a short time the efforts that King Radama was making for the civilisation of his people was seconded by them with the most extraordinary zeal. Schools were opened, and in 1820 a printing-press was set up. In 1832, 10,000 of the people were able to read. The results of the proclamation of the Gospel were less remarkable; still the idols had fallen into contempt, so that their worshippers took fright and complained. Up to 1826 there were no baptisms. In 1828, the king authorised the administration, and shortly after-

1. *History of Evangelical Missions*, p. 216.

wards died. On this, things assumed a very different aspect. One of his wives strengthened her power by putting to death the members of the royal family. The schools were closed for six months, and the Queen ordered the scholars to be dispersed among the soldiers. All the while the Missionaries continued to print and distribute Bibles, and the preaching of the Gospel was attended with a larger measure of blessing. Complaints were openly made that the Christians despised the idols of the country, were always praying, had ceased to swear, and that the women had become chaste.

At length the storm broke in fearful violence. The Missionaries received orders to give up their work. An assembly of at least 150,000 persons was assembled by the roar of cannon, and all Christians were required to give in their names under pain of death; 400 were turned out of their several employments, others were heavily fined or reduced to slavery. The reading of the Bible and prayer were forbidden; still several of the converts kept their Bibles, but woe to them who were surprised in the act of reading them. One woman was put to a cruel death, another was transfixed with a lance and thrown to the dogs. Horrible sacrifices of children were ordered in honour of the idols. Many Christians fled to the forest, and in the space of eight months, in 1836-7, there were 1016 executions.

After these atrocities, the Missionary John went to Tamalava to visit his afflicted brethren. He found many of them hidden in the woods, where they celebrated divine worship. They were discovered, and the chief, in his refusal to betray his brethren, was put to death. In July, 1840, sixteen converts, seized just as they were about to embark, replied thus to their judge: "We are neither thieves, nor murderers, but men of prayer; if this be a crime in the eyes of the Queen, we are ready to suffer whatever she is pleased to order." Nine were then put to death with spears. Another band of fugitives was overtaken, and of these one hundred were burned at slow fires! This was in 1841. About this time an order was issued that prisoners were no longer to be brought to the capital, but were to be put to death on the spot, by precipitating them headlong into deep trenches, and throwing boiling water over them. Still, rather than renounce the faith, these Christians preferred to live in dens and caves of the forest, and to endure the severest privations. Their number increased, and at last the persecution was at an end[1]."

1. *History of Evangelical Missions*, vol. I, p. 95 and following.

We weary our readers with details; we will proceed to give them a general idea of the Missionary work in a statistical form:

"In 1849, there were 36 Protestant Missionary societies, occupying 1,200 principal stations; 2,500 Missionaries, including their wives; and 3,080 auxiliary Missionaries, all natives. The number of persons then alive, who had been converted by the agency of these Missions, was not less than 800,000[1]."

Some persons may hereupon be disposed to inquire whether the Missionaries have not other means besides those of persuasion at their disposal? Such, for instance, as temporal relief. To remove this suspicion, it suffices to say that often, after years of service, the Missionary bequeaths to his widow and his children no other resource than that supplied by Christian charity. It will be granted at once that if these men had large sums at their disposal, they would not have left their families in want. Nor is this all. We can point to Missionaries who have gone forth at their own expense, and have supported themselves by the labour of their hands, in the midst of the heathen whom they were endeavouring to bring to Christ. Thus, "some Missionaries from Berlin established themselves in Bahar (E. Indies) in 1839. While preaching the Gospel, they were to labour for their daily bread and to found a Christian colony. Their plan was regarded as visionary, but it succeeded even beyond their expectations." "The same plan has been pursued by other Missionaries from Berlin at Tagbor (E. Indies), and Zioushugel, in Oceania. The Moravian brethren had already set the example in 1732. Leonard Dober, potter, and David Nitschman, carpenter, set sail for America with six dollars in their pockets. Mocked and regarded as madmen at Copenhagen, they were received by a planter at St. Thomas, and appointed inspectors of his slaves; but the progress of the work was too slow, and, resigning their charge, they took a house, and opened it for the reception of all the negroes who were desirous of hearing the Gospel. They were frequently reduced to a state of the greatest misery; nothing daunted them. As the night was the season when the negroes were at liberty, these zealous servants of God found little time for sleep[2]."

We close these extracts with the admirable example that these same Moravians have set in Greenland: "When they reached this icy region, they set about providing for their sustenance by hunting and fishing, but in these pursuits they were unskilled, and

1. *Report of Soc. for Missions, in Paris*, 1852, p. 30. — 2. *History of Evangelical*, vol. I, p. 30 and folowing.

violent attacks of illness made them think of departure. In the meanwhile, two more Missionaries, Beck and Banisek, arrive. Having learned to translate the Ten Commandments, the Creed, and the Lord's Prayer, they approached the natives. The study of the language offered great difficulties, and not one of the Greenlanders would come to live with them. The year following brought no supplies from Europe, and the hostility of the people increased. They were extravagant in their demands, and even refused occasionally to sell any provisions to the brethren, so that, in order to stay the cravings of hunger, they had recourse to shell-fish and sea-herbs. If they remained more than one night with them, the savages sought to irritate them by mockeries, imitating their mode of reading, praying, and singing; they even interrupted their exercises by frightful cries, or by beating the drum. Sometimes they even drove away the ambassadors of Christ with stones, spoiled their goods, and sent their canoes adrift. Five years were passed in this manner. In 1738, certain natives arrived from the South and entered the Mission-room while one of the brethren was engaged in a translation of the New Testament. They asked what he was about, and the Missionary joyfully embraced the opportunity of announcing the message of Eternal Life. He read of the Saviour's agony at Gethsemane. One of the savages came up to him and cried, 'What is this you have said? I also desire to be saved.' It was with unutterable emotion that these first words of hope were listened to. Tears of gratitude flowed apace......." But we must abridge: "The first church was built in 1747, at Hernuth, where 230 Greenlanders, 35 of them baptised, were settled. New settlements became from time to time necessary, and thus in 1758 Lichtenfeld was founded; Lichlenau in 1774; and Friedrichsthal in 1824. In spite of famine and contagious diseases, the Mission has continued to prosper. The Greenlanders now have the New Testament, a hymn-book, and some tracts in their mother tongue. The children in the schools show much aptitude. The four stations include a population of 6,000, and of these 800 are communicants [1]."

Missionaries, who have to earn their bread by the labour of their hands, are not the men to *purchase* converts!

Some persons may trace these conversions to the influence of government, but in fact the Missionaries are not only left to themselves; they are often embarrassed and hindered by the temporal power. Thus the East India Company have given their sanction to

1. *History of Evangelical Missions*, vol. II, p. 144 and folowing.

heathen festivals under the fear of exciting popular insurrections, and the Missionaries have in this manner been brought into hostile contact with those who ought to have supported them in their work. It has also been asserted that it is easy to turn the ignorant. Those who say so forget that ignorance and fanaticism united oppose the strongest resistance to change of any kind. Men capable of throwing themselves under the chariot-wheels of an idol are not the subjects ready to worship a God who is spirit and truth. Women prompt to mount the funeral pile of a deceased husband, and there to meet a frightful martyrdom in his honour, do not seem particularly apt recipients of the mild piety of the Gospel. And yet Suttees are abolished, and the car of Juggernaut no longer rolls over prostrate victims... One feature of Protestant Missions, and it is the last, is the preparation of native converts for the Missionary work. Thus " a Chinese association has been formed at Hong-Kong, and the number of preachers already furnished by it is 112[1]. "

We would confess that these scattered traits afford but a faint reflexion of the real character of Protestant Missions. Gladly would we give its portrait as exhibited in all the varying regions of the globe. In the vast Isle of Ceylon, for instance, " where the influence of the heathen priest is fast passing away; where the idol temples are decaying from the failure of their revenues, and where heathen festivals are no longer regarded, schools are scattered all over the island; Christian knowledge is progressing; services for Christian worship are everywhere opened; the natives are employed in building churches for themselves. The Holy Scriptures are in request. The printing-press diffuses millions of tracts in four languages, and the Missionaries do not suffice for the work[2]. "

But our limits do not allow us to enter into the details of a work vast as the earth itself : 15 millions given annually by the Protestant Churches; 2,000 missionaries leaving their homes for distant lands; 800,000 Pagans converted, and whole countries brought under the influence of the Gospel. Such is the state of a work which we admire, but have no longer the courage to compare.

Our parallels terminate with this first volume. In the second, we shall resume the general question under new and not less luminous forms.

1. *History of Evangelical Missions*, vol. I, p. 251. — 2. *Idem*, p. 251 and folowing.

CATHOLIC NATIONS

AND

PROTESTANT NATIONS

COMPARED IN THEIR THREEFOLD RELATION TO

WEALTH, KNOWLEDGE, AND MORALITY.

SPAIN

IN THE 16th AND 19th CENTURIES.

Hitherto we have drawn a parallel between the Catholic and Protestant nations of modern times. It has not been difficult to discern on which side the superiority lies. The proof appears to us at once clear and complete. It is, however, necessary to be doubly armed with reason to bring conviction home to prejudiced minds. Impelled by a desire to gain over the most obstinate, we shall now resume the question with new data, and consider it in a different light. We shall no longer compare one nation with another, but a Catholic or a Protestant nation with itself, and for such comparison to be possible it is necessary to take a view of the nation at different periods. By comparing its former with its present state, we shall discover how much it has gained or lost. This gain or loss will be owing, if not entirely, at least in part, to its religious faith. If it be found that one nation has been constantly improving, while another has been as invariably retrograding, shall we not be led to suppose that its religious persuasion has contributed in a certain degree to these results? And if this rapid or retrograde movement follows the same direction as that which we have already remarked in the nations professing the same religious faith, will not the conclusions already drawn in the reader's mind be considerably strengthened? We think so. We have now only to let the facts speak for themselves.

We shall examine, on the one hand, Spain, a country essentially Catholic; and on the other England, a country essentially Protestant. Our examination will begin from the sixteenth century for each of these nations, whose progress we shall trace down to our own time. Neither of them, assuredly, is now what it then was. Which of the two has gained, which lost, in wealth, in knowledge, in morals? Let us examine this question, beginning by Spain.

Never was a nation so completely under the influence of Catholicism as Spain. Italy herself, subdivided into several nations, each having different tendencies, crossed by hostile armies, visited by foreigners, Italy has not remained so hermetically closed against all external influence as Catholic Spain, founded by Ferdinand, guarded by legions of monks, purged from all heresy by the Inquisition, and finally crystallised in Romanism by policy, by the Church, and even by the popular instincts. Let us now see what Catholicism, with this admirable concourse of wills, of interests, and of power, will make of the Spanish nation in three centuries. In order to measure the distance, let us mark well the starting-point. What was the state of Spain on the eve of the religious Reformation, which she so completely avoided?

Towards the end of the fifteenth century, Spain might, with a view to our subject, be divided into two parts, one subjected to the Moors, the other to the Christians. We are at the eve of the conquest of Grenada, the last bulwark of the Ottoman power; the Church is about to inherit the lands and the intellectual wealth of the Mahometans. Let us now draw up an inventory of what these are about to leave it. We will devote a few words, at first, to an account of the state of the arts and sciences among the Arabs of these regions. We shall present only a simple nomenclature, abridging, much against our inclination, the work of a learned professor of the Sorbonne, M. Roseew Saint-Hilaire: —

"SCIENCES. — Among the different branches of the human faculties, one of those that were most zealously cultivated by the Arabs in Andalusia was history... Their great superiority over the contemporary Spanish chroniclers consists in their giving us a deeper insight into the familiar life of peoples and kings[1].

1. M. Roseew Saint-Hilaire, p. 178.

"We shall not attempt to pass in review the poets; a volume would not suffice[1].

"A branch of literature in which the Arabs have preserved an indisputable superiority, is the tale and the novel[2].

"Statistics, a science so recent in Europe, and geography, were also successfully studied by them[3].

"But the art which the Arabs cultivated with the greatest success was incontestably medicine. Pharmacy made great progress among them. Many terms still in use are purely Arabic, such as syrup, julep, etc[4].

"Physical and mathematical science may be reckoned among the true claims to glory of the Arabs[5]. Our system of numeration, practised by them, was communicated to the west by the learned Gerbert, who had studied at Cordova. Algebra owes its name to one of their mathematicians[6]. Trigonometry, cultivated by the Arabs, is indebted to them for its present form[7]. But astronomy was especially their study; the obliquity of the ecliptic, the annual motion of the equinoxes, and the duration of the tropical year, were all ascertained by them. Although the glory of the discovery of the solar system was to belong to a later century, the motions of the heavenly bodies and the sun's disk were studied with the greatest care, as well as eclipses; and modern science is not wholly unindebted to the labours of these Arabs[8].

"With the progress of civilisation vast colleges were erected, in which youth were instructed in the sciences, etc[9]."

FINE-ARTS. — "The art of music acquired, among the Arabs, a regularity which it never attained among the Greeks; and, as to architecture, the fortress of the Alhambra, a vast enclosure of walls scarcely less than a league in circumference, is the finest specimen of the military architecture of the Arabs; and those red towers, with walls eighteen feet thick, still rise threateningly above the *Vega* of Grenada, which they have ceased to defend[10]."

Nevertheless, as it was perhaps difficult to derive advantage from the knowledge of a nation hated and despised, especially when this knowledge was deposited in a language unknown to the mass, let us not dwell too much on sciences more or less abstract, but take a view of the vulgar knowledge of absolute necessity; that of agriculture, in which all classes are interested, and which the poorest may learn and practise. What was the condition of the soil left by the

1. M. Roseew Saint-Hilaire, p. 181. — 2. *Idem*, p. 185. — 3. *Idem*, p. 186. — 4. *Idem*, p. 194. — 5. *Idem*, p. 194. — 6. *Idem*, p. 195. — 7. *Idem*, p. 196. — 8. *Idem*, p. 197. — 9. *Idem*, p. 199. — 10. *Idem*, p. 218.

Moors to the Christians who expelled them? Let us again hear our author: —"

Agriculture. — "The Arabs made immense progress in agriculture. The art of manuring and watering the soil had been carried to its highest perfection. A narrow runnel of water, by means of trenches skilfully arranged, conveyed fertility over a vast extent of ground. Aqueducts were constructed, artificial ponds (albuheras) were dug to serve as reservoirs for water. All the exotic trees which the climate so varied of the Peninsula permitted them to cultivate, and the balmy flowers of the East, which the Arabs prize as highly as perfumes, were introduced by them. Thus Spain owes to the Arabs her rice, cotton, sugar-cane, saffron, and the date-tree, which ripens on all the coast, and especially at Elche, near Alicant, where an entire forest of them is to be seen. Besides, the number of Arabic works on agriculture would alone prove to what a high degree of perfection the art had been brought in Spain.

"Nothing equals the beauty of the spectacle which must have been presented, in that golden age of Spanish agriculture, by the rich *huerta* of Valencia, one of the most productive and best watered spots on earth; the picturesque *Vega* of Grenada, a garden of olive and orange-trees, thirty leagues in length, watered by five rivers, and sheltered by the *Sierra Novada*, the highest of all Spain; the fertile basin of the Guadalquivir, stretching far out of sight along the verdant swells of the *Sierra Morena*, with thousands of villages grouped round Cordova, the queen of the valley."

As might previously have been supposed, the development of industry kept pace with the progress of this admirable agriculture: "Under the last Ommiades, the empire, on the very eve of its fall, had attained a degree of wealth and prosperity truly fabulous. The population daily increased in this favoured spot of earth, one of the most fertile on the globe. Silk, cotton, and cloth manufactories had been established in all parts of the kingdom, and the Arabs were especially renowned for their skill in dyeing leather and stuffs. To them Spain is indebted for indigo and cochineal, as well as for the beautiful coloured earthenware, so admired at the Alhambra. Lastly, the paper manufactured at Mecca from the year 88 of the Hegira, was introduced into Spain in the twelfth century, and the Spaniards substituted linen for cotton, which the Arabs had used. The soil of the Peninsula abounded in mines of gold, silver, and mercury, and other metals less rare[1]."

1. Roseew Saint-Hilaire, vol. vi, pp. 138 to 141.

We regret that it is not in our power to give more complete statistics of the prosperity of the Moors in Spain at the close of the fifteenth century; but the following lines may to a certain extent supply the place of such: "The pious indifference of governments founded on Islamism never having permitted anything in the shape of a census, it is impossible to estimate, with any degree of certainty, the number of their subjects. We merely know from Conde, that besides the capital and the six provincial chief towns, Toledo, Merida, Saragossa, Valencia, Seville, and Tadmir, they reckoned eighty second-rate and three hundred third-rate towns, without mentioning villages, and towers or strongholds, that were innumerable. Far from being diminished by the fall of the Ommiade empire, this mass of inhabitants was further increased by the invasion of the Berbers, and we shall find the Almoravide Yussouf boasting that in his vast states of the Magreb and Spain the *chotbah* was recited for him from nineteen thousand pulpits [1]."

About the same period, and even still more recently, Catholic Spain presented in this respect no less brilliant a picture. Her power especially extended over the Old and the New World. Let us hear, on this second part, another authority, M. Weiss, professor at the College de France: —

"In the sixteenth century, the Spaniards turned to account every advantage the country possessed: while the nobility gave themselves up to the profession of arms, the other classes enriched their country by assiduous labour. Agriculture was most especially honoured. The kingdom of Grenada, still inhabited by the flower of the descendants of the Arabs, everywhere displayed the produce of the finest agriculture in the world. The Vega of Grenada, watered by the Xenil, was renowned for its fertility, which was prodigious... On all sides irrigation canals and reservoirs distributed water over the remotest and most barren tracts... Industry and commerce added still more to the prosperity of Spain... The most industrious nations of modern Europe had not yet succeeded in imparting to their embroideries and their silk, gold, and silver stuffs the solidity, elegance, and perfection which we admire after the lapse of two centuries, in the products of the ancient manufactories of Spain... Lyons, Nîmes, Paris, have never possessed manufactories comparable to those which formerly existed at Toledo, at Grenada, at Seville, at Segovia, although, undoubtedly, their

1. Roseew Saint-Hilaire, vol. VI, pp. 148 and 149.

manufactories are infinitely superior to those of Spain at the present day. The development of trade was equal to that of industry. A minister of Philip the Second asserted, in an assembly of the Cortès, that at the fair held at Medina del Campo, in 1563, business was transacted to the amount of six hundred and sixty two million five hundred thousand francs... A multitude of trading vessels set sail every year from the ports of Valencia, Carthagena, Malaga, Cadiz, and conveyed to Italy, Asia Minor, Africa, and the East Indies, the products of the national industry. In 1586, the number of trading vessels in the Spanish ports was said to exceed a thousand... More than fifteen hundred vessels, of an inferior class, contributed to give activity to commerce. The smallest towns on the coasts took part in this commercial movement. The mercantile navy of Spain was then superior to that of France, and even to that of England; but nothing equalled the prosperity of Seville: that city, said a writer of the age of Philip the Second, is the capital of all the merchants in the world. Andalusia has become the centre of the earth.

"Spain likewise reigned by her great superiority in the arts, and in literature... Sculpture and architecture reached a high degree of perfection under Juan de Badajoz, Miguel de Ancheta, and their successors. This period was also that of the fine Spanish music; music simple, grand, pathetic. Spain gave birth at that period to composers of the first order, principally in the religious kind. The archives of the chapters of Toledo, Valencia, Seville, Burgos, contained numberless invaluable treasures... In literature there was equal progress, equal lustre. The drama attained a degree of perfection to which it had risen in no other country of Europe. This country produced great men, whose various talents recall Eschylus, Sophocles, and Euripides... Epic and lyrical poetry and history found likewise worthy interpreters... All Europe resounded with the glory of Garcilaso, surnamed the Spanish Petrarch; of Herrera, the Divine; of Montemayor, of Ponce de Leon, and of Quevedo, whom a severe judge did not hesitate to compare to Voltaire... By degrees Spanish literature served as a model to other nations; its influence penetrated as far as England; but France yielded to it more than any other nation. It is perhaps to Spain that we owe the prince of our comic poets... It was long a custom in France, in Italy, in England, and in a part of Germany, to send to Madrid young men, distinguished either by fortune or birth, in order that they might learn Castilian manners and politeness. The palaces of the Spanish ambassadors were in foreign countries the resort of the most elegant society, and Spanish diplomacy everywhere possessed that influence and that moral superiority which France did not acquire until the reign of Louis the Fourteenth[1]."

Such was Spain in the sixteenth century. Let us at once examine her present state: "What I have to exhibit to you," says M. Guéroult, "is the spectacle of an agony which cannot come to an end, an all-pervading confusion to which no term can be assigned, the certain and progressive ruin of a nation that, for a whole century, dictated laws to Europe, that inhabits the richest and most fertile soil perhaps under Heaven, but a nation so disheartened by false experiments, that it feels itself perish, and watches its own decline, as it were, with the resignation of a fatalist, and from this depression vain attempts are made to raise it with the comfort of sonorous words and sounding phrases. Others may employ their efforts to show you order and progress organised on paper, enthusiasm reigning in official proclamations, victory succeeding victory without intermission in bulletins, and lastly the Cortès plying, with gravity befitting the curial chair of the ancient Roman senators, the great work of national regeneration. Our task, more melancholy and stern, will be to bring the broad and sad daylight of facts to dispel all these brilliant phantoms; to show you the evil in its whole extent, and let your ears perceive what a hollow sound is returned by those granite foundations so miraculously raised by the hands of weakness, improvidence, and prodigality. I cannot promise to complete the task I have undertaken; there is a point where the pen drops from the writer's hand: it is not possible to analyse nothingness[2]."

"Here, I confess, I am greatly embarrassed. Is there or is there not a government in Spain? Who commands, who obeys? where is government, where is power? where is strength and authority? and how is it possible to make you, the fortunate inhabitants of a well-organised country, understand the sort of hap-hazard that here regulates all things?... That the country is in a state of revolution is but too evident; that it feels, if not the serious desire, at least an imperative want, of order first, and afterwards of numerous reforms in every branch of public administration; that the re-establishment of the ancient absurd system which has laid asleep for nearly three hundred years, and still lulls the already too apathetic genius of the nation, has become odious to a large portion of

1. Weiss, Introduction, p. 13, etc. — 2. Guéroult, pp. 335 to 337.

the population, and that this re-establishment is well nigh an impossibility, is beyond a doubt[1]."

"There are, on the old trunk of the Spanish monarchy, branches so rotten, that it is difficult to conceive how, when better times render reform possible, the legislator will be able to overcome a contagion which, from the institutions, has passed into the manners of the nation, and which, having been tolerated time out of mind, has obtained a rank among things acknowledged and consecrated. At the head and front of these careless ulcers must be placed the administration of justice. Do not expect, however, from me a minute analysis of this deplorable subject. The story of abuses would never end. As to the history of the institution, a word will suffice: it does not exist. In what concerns justice it is necessary, not to reform, but to create[2].

"If you have a law-suit in Spain, it is to the *escribano* that application must be made in your behalf; if you have had the misfortune, in a moment of necessity or of passion, to take the pocket of a stranger for your own, or to thrust the blade of your *navaja* too deeply between the ribs of a friend, again it is the *escribano* that must be applied to, for he it is that draws up the report of your case, and the judgment likewise, which is signed by the judge in charge. If the judge is hard-hearted, the *escribano* knows what arguments will make him relent; it is he that will inform you exactly how many ounces the death of a man will amount to, and if you give him sufficient encouragement, he will find means, in case of need, to bring you back from the lowest depths of hell. The blackest prison, the deepest dungeon, the closest and thickest bars, nothing can resist the power of the *escribano*[3]."

"Independently of venality (the besetting sin of almost all the magistracy in Spain), there exists, in the legislation itself, various causes of abuse. I shall content myself with pointing out to you a few provisions of criminal jurisprudence, which exercise a more direct and more corrupting influence over morals. It would seem as if the fixed idea of the legislator had been to have his outlays reimbursed at any price, and all his expenses paid; this result has been attained; but you will now see at what cost. A man is assassinated in the street; he cries for help. It is still early; people are passing through the street; house-doors are still open, and lights are seen in the windows. If such a thing happened in one of our

1. Guéroult, pp. 340, 341. — 2. *Idem*, p. 394. — 3. *Idem*, p. 399.

streets, every body would hasten to the assistance of the victim, a crowd would gather round him, the whole neighbourhood would be in an uproar. In Spain, when a murdered man cries for help, what happens? the passers-by flee away with their utmost speed, the doors are closed, the lights are extinguished; the street, a minute ago so full of life and lighted up on all sides, becomes a gloomy desert; in vain the victim's cries redouble, terror has spread silence round him, and the murderers may consummate their crime in perfect security. Whence arises this dreadful selfishness? is it the assassins they fear? No, it is justice; for if, yielding to an instinctive feeling of humanity, you come to the assistance of the sufferer, and fall into the hands of justice, the first act of justice will be to seize you as a witness, and if unfortunately the murdered man or his family are not in a condition to pay the expenses of the law proceedings, it is on you, the witness, that the burden will devolve, and in this manner justice may be lawfully held guilty of the murder committed, and of the cowardly selfishness of all those hidden witnesses who held their breath for fear of betraying their presence.

"One shudders at the dreadful consequences of this fiscal avidity of justice. At Madrid, last year, an old man was assassinated in the street; an application was made on the part of justice to his son, to know if the latter intended to make his complaint. — 'I!' replied the young man, 'you are mistaken, this is no business of mine, I do not know that man!' The unfortunate son was right; if he had made his complaint, the law would have stripped him to the skin, and converted all his property into waste paper. Can we, after this, wonder at the hideous acts which occur too frequently in Spain? should we not rather be surprised to find that some virtue yet subsists in a people who have been for ages wrought upon by so many active principles of demoralisation[1]?"

"The brotherhood of thieves, in Spain, has passed from the militant to the triumphant state; their power is undisputed, and they have for their support prescription and established rights. Justice, divested of its ancient prejudices, negotiates instead of combating, compounds instead of chastising, and evinces towards that respectable corporation the most touching regard, and behaves in the most fraternal manner. A few instances, taken at random, will show you what remarkable progress the spirit of association has made among this body.

"There was, a little time since, on the confines of the kingdom

1. Guéroult, p. 400 to 403.

of Valencia and of Lower Arragon, an alcade, who imagined the following ingenious composition : the fines imposed on robbers are generally divided into three parts : one for the informer, another for the alcade, a third for the judges of the royal court. Now, the above-mentioned alcade, having carefully calculated the average produce of these fines, thought of making a sort of contract with the court : he took the engagement to pay to the court, one year with another, a fixed amount representing its average share of the profits, while he accepted for himself all the chances of the undertaking, of which the profit, as well as the loss, was to be entirely his. The bargain was made, and our alcade, desirous, naturally enough, to regulate his income, imagined the following combination : he raised his police-force to a better footing, gave encouragement to informers, and proceeded to take as many robbers as he could. When once he had them in prison, he began to extort money from them, to bleed them without mercy. When their resources were exhausted, and their wives had brought the last mite, and the family had joined their efforts to pay the prisoner's ransom, you perhaps imagine that he sent the prisoner to the galleys? No, our clever magistrate, true to his word, simply released his thief, who, shrunk and emaciated with the prison fare, and completely ruined, not having a real left in his pocket, fled from his prison to the highway like a raging wolf, scoured the country, and, eager to make up for lost time, accomplished in six months the work of two years. All the environs were filled with alarm. People scarcely ventured abroad. Complaints buzzed about the ears of the alcade, who remained unmoved, and feigned not to hear them; he had formed his plan, and at length, when he deemed that his thief had sufficiently retrieved former losses, the worthy magistrate roused himself from his lethargy and displayed wonderful activity, which, in the space of a few weeks, brought for the second time into his toils the hero of the high school, who was then to undergo a new bleeding not less copious or less often repeated than the former one, and at the end of a few months an inconceivable fatality caused the robber to find for the second time a means of escaping, before even his case could be brought before the judge. By this ingenious system, applied with a truly Arragonese perseverance, the court was regularly paid, the robber who eluded the galleys fled from prison a ruined but a free man, and ready to retrieve his losses : the alcade made his fortune, and every body, except the public, was satisfied[1].

1. Guéroult, pp. 405 to 407.

"Would you believe that to this very day the wretches who assassinated Quesada are proceeding with impunity to search for his son, who has been threatened with the same fate? Would you believe that the assassins are known by their names, and yet remain unpunished? Would you believe that the lewdest rabble have been allowed to go and vociferate impure songs under the windows of the poor widow? And, to crown all, would you believe that the government which tolerates such abominations has the effrontery to affect exhortations and speeches on public order[1]?"

"In Spain, where the police is a nonentity, the robber who takes no pains to conceal himself, but attacks you in broad daylight and by open force, is the king of the highway. He is a sort of independent sovereign, who makes incursions on a hostile territory. For this reason, far from being an object of execration, he is almost always admired by the people, and praised and celebrated in popular strains, which perpetuate the memory of his achievements, so that, by virtue of the immortality conferred by poetry, the name of Jose Maria, the famous Andalusian brigand, has grown, for the people, into something equivalent to that of the Cid, or any other hero of past ages. Add to such moral predispositions the influence of present circumstances, misery, the example of the bands of Cabrera and others, the powerlessness of the government to protect the people since it has hardly strength sufficient to protect itself, and you will easily conceive that highway robbery, favoured by so many united causes, may become one of the most threatening features of the social dissolution towards which this country seems advancing with great strides[2]."

That highway robbery has become a national profession in Spain, that the Spaniard turns highwayman as the Savoyard turns porter, and the Auvergnat water-carrier, seems at first hard to believe; to convince us of such a fact, it is necessary that more voices than one should repeat it. Let us hear it affirmed again, in the ***Revue Britannique*** : —

"...... As to the people, I will ask how the Spaniards have distinguished themselves from the remotest times, unless it be as assassins, or what amounts to the same, as guerilleras? What courage is there in cutting off unfortunate stragglers, in surprising the wounded, in drawing a few isolated detachments into ambuscades, and afterwards massacring them? A blow struck secretly and dishonestly is the blow of a coward, and it is rare that

1. Guéroult, p. 46. — 2. *Idem*, p. 134.

the Spaniard, either in war or in private quarrels, strikes in any other way. Always ready to plunge his knife into the body of his unsuspecting adversary, he has no notion of a fair and open combat with equal arms. .... It is to be inferred from M. Ford's confessions that the Spanish banditti, who make such a noble figure in novels, are the least adventurous, the most cowardly of their species, in any country..... It cannot be denied that Spain is the country of Europe in which the ancient system of robbery by force of arms on the highway has undergone the least change.

"In the first rank, among the robbers, are the *ladrones*, or robbers on a large scale. These are the regularly-organised bands, of from eight to fourteen individuals, well armed and equipped, under the orders of a chief. The robbers of this class are the most dangerous of all; and as they scarcely ever attack travellers without being sure of success, and without having taken all possible precautions, resistance is generally useless, and can only occasion fatal accidents. The wisest course in such cases is to yield, and to obey the summons *boca a bajo, boca a tierra* (not a word! lie down on the ground!) a summons which admits of no refusal.

"The second order of highway robbers is that of the *rat, ratero*. The *rat* is despised, but no less dangerous on that account: he is neither regularly trained to the calling, nor organised; but should an opportunity arise for plunder, he avails himself of it, and then returns to his ordinary occupations. Thus it frequently happens that when strangers pass a night in some town or village, two or three ruffians prepare an ambuscade for the following day, in strict conformity with the proverb : opportunity makes the thief.

"The *ratelliro*, or little *rat*, rarely attacks any but the isolated and defenceless traveller, who, if he is robbed, has only himself to blame, for you must never tempt the Spaniard to do any little piece of business of this nature. The shepherd feeding his flock, the labourer at his plough, the vintner in his vineyard, have each their gun, a weapon ostensibly destined to provide for their personal safety, but which enables them at the same time to attack those who, for their protection, have only their heels and their virtue [1]."

Where such customs prevail, who will be astonished at the following statement of our author? "Laws are enacted, but none obey them; proclamations are issued, which are heeded by none. The people are complimented for their moderation when they have

1. *Revue Britannique*, 1846, May and June, pp. 135 to 145.

just tolerated some infamous atrocity; so that two Spains have been formed; one, a model of a country—a free, powerful, heroic, indomitable people, a people of great men, commanded by chiefs greater still, who succeed in whatever they undertake, the Spain of newspapers and proclamations; but go farther, penetrate more deeply, and you will then come to the true Spain, ruined, torpid, given to fatalism, dislocated, without any administration, or finances with no public spirit, stained with civil war, wearied with diplomacy, protocols, constitutions, asking from Heaven, who refuses the gift, a man, not even a great man, but an intelligent, energetic, and honest man [1]."

"The vice, the scourge of Spain, is a corrupt administration, defective in its mode of action; a torpor and apathy which have given to the most absurd abuses the consecration of ages [2]."

From the summit of the social scale, the magistrates, let us descend to its last degree, the beggars; and let us again hear our author: "As you penetrate farther into Arragon, Spanish misery, that misery to which nothing can be compared, displays itself in all its hideous luxury. At Jaca, a fortified town commanding the mountains, at Guerrea, a wretched halting-place where travellers stop to breakfast, you are assailed by legions of beggars; children are seen in the market-place rolling naked in the dust, and killing each other's vermin. Visit the most impure and wretched quarters of Lyons and Rouen, and even these will not give you an idea of that squalid and disgusting misery. Our beggars seem to suffer from misery and filth; these live on it, dwell in it, are born and die in it; it is to them a second nature. For the rest, setting aside the incidents and the poetry, you find in the filthy inns of that region the physiognomy of the hotels of the time of Don Quixote, vast halls supported by pillars. It is useless to speak of the odious '*ratatouilles*' that are set before you there. You are twenty leagues from France, and you might fancy yourself at a distance of two thousand. The love of gain itself has not had strength to overcome that natural indolence, that carelessness of the morrow, which raises between France and Spain a barrier higher and more difficult to pass over than the Pyrenees.

"Another circumstance that astonishes the traveller, on his entrance into Spain, is the venality, I had almost said the mendicity, of Custom-house officers... A compromise may be made with them

1. Guéroult, pp 48 49. — 2. *Idem*, p. 170.

which will enable you to import the entire kingdom of France into Spain, if you have a mind to do so. You have only to slip a small piece of money into their hands; if you forget to do this, they will remind you of it, and you may, without shocking the sense of propriety of these honest functionaries, give them your alms in public, in the presence of twenty persons; they will not shrink from it."

You will not be surprised to find under the feet of this idle and mendicant population a fertile soil neglected: "The beauty of the Spanish soil is a classical and well-established fact; the romances are full of its praise, the ballads are inexhaustible in their descriptions of the citron groves, and of the fertility of this climate loved by Heaven... That these descriptions were once true, I am willing to believe, but at present we should seek in vain all over France, including the Landes, for regions as naked, barren, and depopulated as the valley of Gallego, leading to Saragossa. This soil, in appearance so sterile, is capable of receiving useful plantations: many trees, such as the fir, the oak, the chesnut, would flourish there admirably, and would besides impregnate the soil with a humidity which it greatly needs; but it happens with this as with many other things in Spain; the Spaniards have the power, but lack the will; they see treasures lying at their feet, but fear the labour of stooping to take them up[1]."

"This soil, at once fertile and uncultivated, this desert, created by listlessness and sloth, on the border of France, those populations so beautiful and yet so wretched, so favoured by nature and so abandoned by human providence, that stubbornness of temper, that attachment to the past in men who themselves appear to be only a generation of the twelfth century lost in our own, that spirit of individuality and isolation, at a period when individuals seem all on the point of being absorbed in the bosom of I know not what gigantic unity, do not all these passing observations, here collected on the highways, lead to the detection of the internal malady which preys upon the vitals of Spain[2]?"

"Spain, reduced to a state of torpor for three centuries past by a system of ignorance, subjected to two foreign dynasties, one of which began by cruelty, to end by weakness, and the other almost always absorbed by court intrigues, Spain is endeavouring, at the present day, with innumerable pangs, to burst this crust of ignorance beneath which she has been groaning too long[3]."

1. Guéroult, pp. 5 to 9. — 2. *Idem*, p. 16. — 3. *Idem*, p. 29.

All this does not prevent the Spaniard from entertaining the highest possible opinion of himself: Hear him speak: "A whim, which, by dint of exaggeration, occasions more harm than a real scourge, is magniloquence in speeches... Here, a general, writing his report of a hostile encounter to a Minister of War, stated that he had ***shed tears of admiration*** at the sight of the exploits of his ***intrepid soldiers***; it was an affair in which two hundred of the enemy had been slain. Gather together all their pompous words, would you not think the nation breathed enthusiasm through every pore; that it was continually inflamed with ardour, that its ordinary feelings were the warmest, the most uncontrollable, the most energetic? After this, interrogate facts, peruse, if you have patience, this history, full of sterile wishes, of abortive attempts, behold the apathy, the profound indifference, the neutrality in which every one enfolds himself, the silence and solitude that surround the government, the incapacity of generals who know neither how to combine a plan of operations, nor how to follow up or turn to account an advantage; compare, I say, words with things, and draw your conclusion[1]."

Our author sums up the Spanish character as follows: "The Spaniards are materialists in their affections, their creeds, their institutions. They have no notion of religion without monks, processions, and ceremonies; they must have relics and miracles, religious orders in picturesque costumes, and convents where not only prayers, but bread and soup, are to be obtained[2]."

And this is not the character of the Spaniard of any particular province; he will be found the same throughout the kingdom; in La Mancha, for instance, M. Guéroult tells us: "The inhabitant of la Mancha, who has little to hope for from his labour, is in consequence idle and vagrant; consumed by misery and filth, the roads are infested with beggars and with ragged children, bearing in their arms other children entirely naked. All, young and old, are beggars, and habits of sloth are almost the only inheritance faithfully transmitted from one to another by these degraded generations. I need not say that the Manchegos enjoy, among their neighbours, a detestable reputation; the inhabitants willingly take to smuggling, to a wandering life, to robbery; they make no scruple of lying in ambush behind a little fir-wood, or in the midst of a ***despoblado***, to wait for and to rob the coach that crosses la Mancha with only two or three ***escopeteros*** on the roof, each armed with a good gun, and a belt filled with cartridges. Thus, it may be said

1. Guéroult, pp. 75, 76. — 2. *Idem*, p. 92.

that one half of la Mancha lives at the expense of the other half. In every inn at which we alighted to take refreshments, we were always informed that outlaws had passed that way two, three, or four times, and that, for fear of a surprise, the kitchen utensils were kept half the time at the bottom of the well[1]."

Of Valencia he has nothing more favourable to say : " As to the corruption of the country round Valencia, it is enormous; this region has the reputation of being the portion of Spain in which most crimes are perpetrated. Murder, robbery, broils, wounds inflicted, amount, in the criminal statistics of Valencia, to a proportion comparatively enormous. Thus, in the year 1832 alone, out of about 700,000 persons comprised within the jurisdiction of the *audiencia* of Valencia, the number of murders and infanticides amounted to 210; that of wounds occasioned by quarrels to 541; that of robberies to 361 ; lastly, of sentences to death there were 34. If to these are added condemnations to the galleys, which are here scarcely ignominious, and crimes unpunished from not finding or not wishing to find the culprit, which last amounted in 1835 to 831, you may form an idea of the species of moral barbarism which desolates these beautiful regions... When a man is assassinated in Valencia, a small black cross is nailed on the nearest wall with this inscription; Here died by misfortune (*aqui murio de desgracia*), such and such a person, such a day of such a year. Now, to give you an idea of the number of these expiatory monuments, it will be sufficient to tell you that in one of the most populous streets of Valencia, that of St. Vincent, which is of nearly the same length as the portion of the rue Vivienne extending from the Palais Royal to the Place de la Bourse, I counted the other day eleven crosses destined to perpetuate the memory of eleven nefarious *accidents.* If then the Valencian passes generally for a traitor and a coward, if the Andalusian himself, who makes so light of his own work, expresses so loudly his contempt for Valencian cowardice, it must be allowed that this bad reputation is not entirely usurped[2]. "

We have sufficiently quoted M. Guéroult. The reader must be desirous of hearing the evidence of more than one person : we will, then, produce a series of testimonies which by their unanimity will obtain credit for all that precedes.

To the evidence of an eye witness let us first add that of an historian, esteemed and greatly admired by the French Catholics : " There is a great country, of which indeed I speak out of regard,

1. Guéroult, pp. 309, 310. — 2. *Idem*, pp. 323 to 327.

out of respect for a noble and unfortunate people, rather than from necessity, I allude to Spain. Human intellect and human society have sometimes appeared there in all their glory, but the instances of such are isolated facts scattered here and there in Spanish history, like palm-trees amid the sands of the desert. The fundamental character of civilisation, general and continuous progress, seems denied in Spain, to the human mind as well as to society. The country presents the spectacle of solemn immovability or fruitless change. Seek for a great idea or a great social amelioration, a philosophical system or an improvement fertile in results, that Europe owes to Spain, and you will find none. This nation has been isolated in Europe; from Europe it has received little, to Europe it has given little. Its civilisation is of slight importance in the history of European civilisation [1]."

To the impartial historian let us add the unimpassioned geographer : "Spain cannot, for its industry, be compared to the principal states of Europe. We must also observe that the manufactories of esparto, formerly so numerous and flourishing, seem to be almost annihilated.

"The want of good roads, the small number of navigable rivers, canals, and hydraulic works destined to remedy that defect of the soil, as well as the unsafe condition of the high roads, almost entirely prevent all internal commerce. Navigation to remote regions has greatly diminished for some years past [2]."

"To Spain has been addressed the severe reproach of having neglected the sciences. Valladolid, formerly a very flourishing city, is now greatly fallen and depopulated : in the time of its splendour it was said to contain more than 100,000 inhabitants; it has now only 21,000 [3]."

After Balbi, let us quote Malte-Brun, better known and no less esteemed : "What evil genius has been able to paralyse or to corrupt so many causes of prosperity, and reduce to a population less than that of France by more than 14,000,000 souls the population of the Peninsula, which in extent exceeds France by more than 2,000 square leagues [4]?"

"The province of Madrid is one of those of New Castille in which the proud indolence of the Castilians is most easily recognised. The inhabitants seem to disdain all kinds of industry; the small number of manufactories, and especially the mediocrity of their products, furnish us with the proof of this. The environs

1. Guizot, pp. 18 and 19. — 2. Balbi, pp. 431 to 433. — 3. *Idem*, pp. 438, 439. — 4. Malte-Brun, vol. VII, p. 486.

of the capital are unlike those of the other great cities of Europe; here you do not witness the life and activity that reign everywhere round Paris and London. You have hardly left Madrid when you suddenly find yourself in a new country: in a few minutes you pass from a world of opulence and luxury into fields abounding with misery and filth. What was formerly said of the German traveller may to this day be applied to the peasant of Castille: the instruments he uses, his occupations, his dress, his food, bear the marks of ignorance and poverty. A sort of blind oredilection for what is old excludes all idea of improvement in matters connected with agriculture and the mechanical arts; and, to complete our disgust at the sight of this miserable population, the high price of linen obliging the poor man to change only once a month, the result is a hideous uncleanliness, producing cutaneous diseases and the excessive increase of that vermin of which they mutually relieve one another in public, in villages, and in the populous quarters of large towns; the population of Madrid is not more delicate in this respect than any other.

"The constancy of women in their engagements almost compensates in the end for the shame of their immorality. Perhaps even to the multiplicity of these ties rather than to the care taken by the police to prohibit places of debauchery, Madrid owes the advantage of being free from the scandalous evil of prostitution [1]."

In contemplating such a society we cannot help desiring that a man of genius would rise from amidst the nation and raise his countrymen by his activity from their sloth, and by his self-denial from their immorality. Such a man there has been. Let us see how he succeeded: "In the reign of Charles III a plan was formed for draining and peopling the richest mountains, so as to render their soils productive. Don Pablo Olavide, one of the statesmen in whom this happy idea originated, was appointed to carry it into effect; this he did with so much zeal and intelligence that he soon succeeded beyond his hopes: 58 villages or boroughs arose on the heights that command La Mancha and Andalusia, and formed under the name of ***Nuevas Poblaciones***, a province whose chief town was called ***La Carolina***, and which soon contained 3,000 inhabitants. But the virtuous Olavide had the misfortune to draw upon himself the hatred of a capucin; he was denounced to the Inquisition for having uttered indiscreet language, and, after having pined in the prisons of the Holy Office, he was con-

1. Malte-Brun, vol. VII, p. 684.

demned to be confined during eight years in a monastery, declared incapable of accepting any office, and despoiled of all his property [1]."

It is evident that the evil is in the nation, or rather in the principles with which it is imbued. Go to the neighbouring people, fostered in the same creed, and you will find the same manners : "In Portugal, everything that recalls the pleasures of the senses has irresistible power. The popular songs would be agreeable and graceful, if the words were not at times too licentious. The national dance, called the *soffa*, is lascivious to such a degree that one cannot help deploring the corruption of the people [2]."

"The fine arts are in a very unsatisfactory state, owing to the want of encouragement from the rich and from the government. Music is, we may say, the only art in which a few Portuguese have attained celebrity. Elementary public instruction is greatly neglected, and, with the exception of Spain, very inferior to Portugal in this respect, there are few countries in which the relative number of scholars is less considerable [3]."

But let us still add to the number of our witnesses ; after the impartial geographer let us consult the precise statistician : "The deserts of Spain," says Moreau de Jonnès, "which extend over half the country, lie under the most beautiful climate most favourable to the human species, and to the cultivation of plants that yield the richest and most abundant crops. These lands, covered with brushwood and withered herbs, were, under the Moorish sway, of prodigious fertility ; if properly watered and cultivated, they might now, as well as then, be made to resemble the flourishing plains of Lombardy [4]."

"There no longer exist, in a civilised country, vasts deserts, like that of the province of Estramadura. In a country gifted by Providence with such ample agricultural resources, it is absurd, impolitic, dangerous, and inhuman, to allow a twelfth part of the population to earn a wretched livelihood by smuggling, robbing, and begging [5]."

Are all the products of this impoverished soil at least equally distributed ? M. Jonnès answers : "Arguelles calculated that the lands possessed by the clergy, added to those of the crown, extended to about a million and a half of *fanègues*, or 12,170,000 *hectares*, making 6,160 square leagues, which is, within a few leagues, one-third of the entire surface of Spain. Thus, in crossing this country,

1. Malte-Brun, vol. VII, p. 631. — 2. *Idem*, p. 535. 3. *Idem*, p. 537. — 4. Moreau de Jonnès, p. 28. — 5. *Idem*, p. 131.

the traveller, every third league, crosses demesne or ecclesiastical property, and this is in general, says Arguelles, the most fertile and best situated [1]."

Does industry produce what agriculture does not yield? Our author solves the question: "The industrial produce," says he, "allows in Spain and Austria 30 francs to each inhabitant, in Prussia 40; in France 58; and in Great Britain 155."

This population, occupied neither with agriculture nor with industry, may be supposed to have at least time to attend to study. To what degree, then, is instruction diffused? "Spain," says our learned authority, "is of all countries in Europe, except Russia, that in which public instruction claims the least attention. The census of 1803 allowed only one student in 346 inhabitants; which is thirty-four times less than in Switzerland, Germany, the Netherlands, England, Scotland, and Prussia, and twenty times less than in France at the present day [2]."

Without agriculture, industry, or instruction, what becomes of this nation? You shall hear: "Moncada estimated at 3,000,000 the number of Spaniards who wore no shirt for want of money to purchase one. Ortess has endeavoured to ascertain how many classes of vagrants exist in the Peninsula. He has found forty, designated by as many specific names forming part of the Spanish language. And indeed the civil history of the country shows that vagrancy is an inveterate disease. We discover by the ordinances from the thirteenth to the seventeenth century, that vagrants stole children and made them lame, in order to excite compassion..... Compamanès calculated that, in 1788, every poor individual cost the state 300 reals yearly [3]."

Sloth and ignorance have made the beggar and the vagrant. What will now become of these vagrants and these beggars? "The judicial statistics of Spain," answers M. Jonnès, "present a series of extraordinary phenomena. We find in them a prodigious increase of open attacks upon individuals, with murder or attempt to murder. These statistics look like the annals of barbarous times, or of those modern nations who, like the Albanese, the Bosniates, the Morlacques, do not enjoy the blessings of social order, education, or the protection of laws [4]."

But our readers would perhaps prefer to the cold analyses of statistics the living pictures of the modern traveller. Let us then follow, in his pilgrimage through Spain, M. de Laborde, an esteem-

1. Moreau de Jonnès, p. 80. — 2. *Idem*, p. 303. — 3. *Idem*, p. 94. — 4. *Idem*, p. 299.

ed writer, attached to the French Court, itself connected with that of Spain, and we shall thus have all desirable guarantees for moderation, knowledge, and sincerity. In order not to alter in the slightest degree the testimony of a man who has seen and felt what he describes, we will not even endeavour to arrange what we borrow from him in the order which the subjects would seem to require, but we will accompany him wherever it pleases him to lead us. If our extracts are of considerable length, the interesting nature of the information they contain will prevent them from tiring the reader. M. de Laborde first explains why Spain has so few visitors: "The principal reasons," says he, "which have hitherto deterred travellers from visiting Spain, are the numberless inconveniences attending excursions through the country[1]. Highway robberies and murders being by no means of rare occurrence, it is necessary for those who travel to be well armed[2]. Spain is not renowned for its inns. A general complaint is made, and with too much reason, against the difficulties you have to contend with in seeking for a lodging. The houses disgust by their uncleanliness, and afford little comfort. The *posadas* are in general disgusting; you find in them at most some wooden bedsteads with old mattresses, the stuffing of which is falling into dust, covered with course sheets, badly washed, rather larger than a large napkin, benches for chairs, greasy dishes, pewter or iron spoons incrusted with the remains of the last repast of the travellers who preceded you. Oily lamps, dirty, inattentive, rude, course, and brutal landlords. The manner of preparing dishes is detestable[3]."

We find, in the *Revue Britannique*, a description of an inn in Portugal, the worthy sister of Spain, which deserves to be quoted in this place:

"The innkeeper of Estrenoz had gone to bed when we arrived. Called in a rude and coarse manner by his wife, he got up and dressed with great celerity, rolled up his mattress and threw it into a corner, drew his bedstead into the middle of the room, and spreading over it, for a table-cloth, the sheet in which he had passed the night, and which had perhaps served this double purpose for several weeks, he invited me to take a seat at this promptly prepared table. I could not believe my own eyes; I thought I must be dreaming; no, I was awake, it was all real; I replied that I preferred breakfasting by the fireside. The cookery of such a host was, as may well be supposed, abominable[4]".

1. Laborde, p. 174. — 2. *Idem*, p. 197. — 3. *Idem*, vol. I, p. 201. — 4. *Revue Britannique*, 1847, May and June, p. 71.

" It is in Estramadura that the traveller must arm himself with courage and patience. The annoyances he has experienced in other parts of Spain are nothing compared to those he has to endure in this province. The posadas in which the traveller seeks repose resemble for the most part bad stables; the rooms and kitchens are dirty, as well as the persons who inhabit them. One has often at one's elbow a pig, an ass, or a mule. The bedsteads are not worth a truss of straw. One finds nothing to eat and often nothing to purchase in the places where these inns are situated [1]. "

"The roads in Murcia are almost all what nature has made them; art has done nothing to relieve the steep ascents of the mountains which must be climbed at every moment; it is often necessary to walk over jagged and almost impracticable rocks, which might afford an easy passage if care had been taken to fill up the inequalities with a little earth. In the environs of Murcia the roads are scarcely traced; they are not kept in repair, and are full of deep ruts [2]. "

Next to the difficulties of the roads and utter want of accommodation in the inns, what first strikes our traveller is the deplorable state of the fields through which he passes: " The difficulty of conveyance is prejudicial to the progress of agriculture; some beautiful roads have been opened within these few years, but they have not rendered the Spaniards more industrious, who still adhere to their old customs, and use at most a few waggons. Catalonia and the kingdom of Valencia are almost the only provinces in which the use of carts has become general. The exportation of commodities is therefore rendered difficult and expensive, diminishing their value for the proprietor, raising their price for the purchaser, and thus discouraging the agriculturist [3]. "

" In Murcia, whatever be the fertility of the soil, it produces very little under the care of the indolent Murcian cultivator, who shrinks from arduous labour. The less fertile portion of the soil is neglected on account of the trouble it would give, and the more fertile lands, producing too easily, banish from the agriculturist's mind the idea of bestowing more care, attention, or reflection on the work [4]. "

" Plantations are extremely neglected in Arragon; one travels over vast tracts of land in that province without finding a single tree. As to irrigation, the neglect is great: they seem desirous to allow nature to do all, without endeavouring to assist or extend

1. Laborde, vol. III, p. 446. — 2. *Idem*, pp. 99, 100. — 3. *Idem*, vol. V, p. 239. — 4. *Idem*, vol. III, p. 78, 79.

her operations. It may be observed in general that agriculture is greatly neglected or imperfectly understood in Arragon[1]."

"An excellent soil extends over the surface of New Castille, but very little advantage is taken of the rivers that cross it. A more enlightened activity might multiply here the experiments which have succeeded elsewhere. One may here cross immense tracts of land without seeing a single tree, and grounds utterly abandoned and uncultivated are common in this province; they however contain germs of vegetation and fertility that require only to be developed[2]."

Not finding any agriculture, M. Laborde seeks for industry and commerce; but, alas! all he can say on the subject is that commerce is passive! Let us hear him: "The present state of manufactures in Spain is, it must be confessed, not very brilliant, if compared with those of France and England. The articles manufactured here have none of the qualities which characterise similar articles in those two countries. The quantity manufactured, far from admitting of exportation to foreign countries, cannot supply the wants of Spain and her colonies; prodigious quantities are imported from France, Germany, Holland, and England[3]."

"The decay of agriculture and manufactures in the sixteenth and seventeenth centuries dealt a mortal blow to trade. It wanted active and intelligent promoters, and suddenly fell away. Spain then scarcely preserved a navy; she no longer had any ships except those purchased in foreign countries; she had no longer any merchants but such as came from other countries; her trade became absolutely passive, and consequently ruinous[4]."

"The rivers Ebro, Guadalquivir, Tagus, Jucar, and several others, formerly navigable, were subsequently neglected, and navigation on them became impossible[5]."

"The commerce of Arragon is almost entirely passive. This province sends its raw materials abroad, and afterwards receives them manufactured. It has neither cloths of any degree of fineness, nor fine linens, nor silks, nor gold lace, nor ribands, etc... [6]"

"The commerce of New Castille is almost entirely passive. This province has none of its products fit for exportation; it imports goods from the neighbouring provinces and from other parts. The manufacture of Toledo is not considerable; it is, as it were, only in its infancy. The other manufactures of New Castille are all of very little importance; they can scarcely supply a portion of the popula-

1. Laborde, vol. I, p. 463. — 2. *Idem*, vol. IV, pp. 300 to 303. — 3. *Idem*, vol. V, p. 370. — 4. *Idem*, p. 377. — 5. *Idem*, pp. 438, 439. — 6. *Idem*, vol. I, p. 481.

tion of the cantons in which they are established. Exportation amounts to a mere nothing in this province, while its importation is very considerable. It however contains all that might conduce to its wealth. The lands require only to be cultivated with care, advantage being taken at the same time of the rivers that flow through them. The Tagus, once navigable, has long ceased to be so. The canal of Manzanarez, undertaken in the reign of Charles III, has not been finished; it is even abandoned [1]. "

" Talavera was a very poor town; the silk manufactories established there by a Frenchman, Jean Bullier, a native of Nîmes, ameliorated its condition. To this Frenchman is due, in some degree, the regeneration of the country, which he would have rendered more agreeable and more flourishing if he had not been arrested in the execution of his useful projects by obstacles which it is not for me to dwell upon here. The manufacture of hats, established also by a Frenchman, began to obtain a certain vogue. The manufactories of earthenware enjoyed much reputation, and gave rise to a branch of commerce of some importance; but they have considerably declined; their work no longer preserves its primitive perfection. Besides the Frenchman who founded the silk manufactories, the manufacturers, designers, and dyers were also Frenchmen. Under the direction of Bullier and the Frenchmen who followed him the establishment rapidly increased: the most beautiful stuffs of France were soon imitated there. When circumstances obliged the French to withdraw, the establishment immediately degenerated, the stuffs were of an inferior quality and of a bad taste, the demand for them slackened. The direction of the establishment has been confided to others; but it is yet far from having regained its primitive lustre [2]. "

" Talavera has absolutely no trade; its situation would, however, be very advantageous if the Tagus were rendered navigable; the town might then have a very brisk trade. The soil need only be assisted by industry: it would be very easy to insure and to increase the crops; but the inhabitants, plunged in an apathetic indifference, do not rise out of the narrow sphere in which they have been educated. Mariana, their fellow-countryman, addressed them this reproach in the beginning of the seventeenth century. The lapse of nearly two centuries has wrought scarcely any change in their condition [3]. "

" Pampeluna has only a secondary and absolutely passive trade;

1. Laborde, vol. IV, pp. 312 to 315. — 2. *Idem*, pp. 225, 226. — 3. *Idem*, p. 228.

it receives almost everything from without, and its manufacturing industry has scarcely anything with which to supply neighbouring towns[1]."

"The productions of Navarre are limited, and insufficient for the wants of its inhabitants. In general, its richest lands are not fully cultivated. Navarre has never had extensive manufactures, nor many manufactories. Its trade is absolutely passive[2]."

"There is in Murcia no establishment on a large scale. The manufacture of silk is confined to a small number of looms; works of this sort are badly dyed and badly glazed. An establishment was organised by the government; a skilful foreigner was called in to improve the manufacture; but the funds were wasted, and the establishment broken up. The other manufactories of the country are unimportant[3]."

"Gold and silver jewelry is neglected in this country where raw materials are so abundant; it is all imported from abroad; hardware and ironmongery are likewise imported. The few articles manufactured in the country are badly executed[4]."

"Indolence and sloth," said Sancho de Moncada, "are the prevailing vices of Spaniards, and foreigners know this so well that they flock from all parts to offer us the products of their industry; they have reduced this poor kingdom of Spain to the condition of the people of Israel, when they were obliged to apply to the Philistines for the simplest instruments of husbandry and of other manual labour[5]."

If at least the people, who will neither plough nor weave, sell nor buy, would allow the foreigner to plough, weave, sell and buy for them! No; jealousy, and hatred of improvement cause them to reject the assistance offered from without. Let us hear M. de Laborde: "Bullier brought from France some improvements in manufactures; Maritz, who came likewise from France, taught better methods for casting cannon; Gauthier, also from France, introduced improvements in shipbuilding; Saint-Laurent, Patras, Scherer, and Vidal rendered similar services; all were persecuted, and some were delivered from confinement only by the intervention of high influence in their behalf[6]."

But what foreigners were not permitted to do among the Spaniards, and for the advantage of the Spaniards, they have done as it were by the side of the Spaniards, and for their own advantage, and this has given rise to comparisons that could not fail to pre-

1. Laborde, vol. IV, p. 292. — 2. *Idem*, vol. I, pp. 298 to 300. — 3. *Idem*, vol. III, p. 93. — 4. *Idem*, p. 372. — 5. *Idem*, vol. VI, p. 430. — 6. *Idem*, pp. 367, 368.

sent themselves to the mind of our traveller : " The Moors," says he, " gave the Spaniards an example of genius, industry, and activity. These two nations had shared between them, as it were, the manufactures of Spain. At the time of the expulsion of the Moors, the manufactures which they directed suddenly declined, The Spaniards, having witnessed the advantages that were derived from them, strove to re-establish them, but never reached the degree to which the Moors had attained [1]. "

" The Moors made a garden of Estramadura. The warmth of the climate and the rivers that watered the country covered it with the most abundant fertility ; but the land is in a measure abandoned to itself. If it yields a few productions, it is not indebted for them to human industry, but to its natural fecundity, which is often rendered abortive by the ignorance of the cultivator killing the seed, which, if left to itself, might have adorned its native soil. It is almost entirely reduced to the state of a forced pasture-land. Zalava contains, in the district of Badagos alone, a tract of uncultivated land, twenty-six leagues in length and twelve in breadth [2]."

" Notwithstanding the advantages which the Andalusias present to those who are desirous of fixing their abode in them, those provinces so rich in varied productions, so full of enchanting sites that claim the cultivator's care, have fallen to decay, and their decay evermore increases. At the time of the Moors, who made it the richest and most enlightened part of Europe, 1,200 villages were seen on the banks of the Guadalquivir; of which not more than 800 exist at the present day. The kingdom of Grenada, which contained 3,000,000 inhabitants, now contains only 692,924. There are, in those fertile Andalusias, districts in such a state of desolation that they resemble tracts of the centre of Africa itself. Thus from Utrera to Xerez, for the space of twelve leagues, not a hamlet is found on those fertile lands that languish uncultivated under a delicious climate. If we may credit the historians, Toledo had a population of 200,000 souls. It is certain that its manufactures alone occupied more than 100,000 persons. You meet everywhere with vestiges of its former greatness and of its decay. You cannot pass through its southern part without a sigh; heaps of earth, bricks, and tiles, are the melancholy remains of houses whose sites they cover. In the other quarters similar ruins are found almost at every step. This town is now reduced to a population of not more than 20,000 souls... It is one of the towns

1. Laborde, vol. v, pp. 321, 322. — 2. *Idem*, vol. III, pp. 440, 441.

most repulsive in their general aspect, and the interior of which is the most disagreeable [1]."

"Toledo has no production to export, and its manufactures are too limited to constitute an important branch of commerce; they were, however, formerly very varied and extensive. Among them were several excellent manufactories of swords. The manufactories of woollen stuffs were very numerous there. The silk manufactories were not less considerable. The decline of these establishments became more and more rapid, and by the middle of the last century not a vestige of them remained [2]."

"Seville was, for a long time, the centre of the commerce and the wealth of Spain. She is now only a body without a soul. At present no activity reigns within her walls. She has, however, great facilities for navigation; ships might easily ascend the Guadalquivir as far as that city. In the time of her prosperity, Seville had numerous and brilliant manufactories, she manufactured silks of all kinds, gold and silver textures, linen and cotton. According to a report presented to the king in 1659, there remained, at that period, only 65 looms: a great number of operatives had left the city for want of occupation; the population had diminished by one-third, and many houses were tenantless [3]."

"Grenada was famous for her manufactures under the Moors. The Spaniards, following their example, established some that flourished until the fifteenth century; but the general causes which occasioned the decline of the arts in Spain produced the same effect at Grenada; agriculture languished, the manufacture of silk was neglected, the manufactories declined, and in the seventeenth century ceased to exist. Efforts have been recently made to revive them, but with very little success; they are, down to the present time, in a state of mediocrity [4]."

"The kingdoms of Jaen and Cordova had a very brilliant trade while their manufactures were in activity: at present they have scarcely any trade left of any sort. The port of Almeria, very famous under the Moors, and carrying on a considerable commerce, has fallen, and has not since been restored [5]."

"The city of Jaen, in Andalusia, was formerly a wealthy commercial city; but its manufactures all went to decay at the close of the sixteenth century, and in the beginning of the seventeenth they were scarcely remembered. An attempt was made to revive them about the middle of the eighteenth century, but the new

1. Laborde, vol. IV, pp. 243, 244. — 2. *Idem*, pp. 275, 277. — 3. *Idem*, vol. III, pp. 258, 259. — 4. *Idem*, p. 331. — 5. *Idem*, pp. 363, 364.

establishments had no vitality. Of old and new no other vestiges now remain than a few wretched looms [1]."

"The Moors, when they had established their dominion in Andalusia, cultivated science and literature with success. It was a brilliant period for that part of Spain. But in their retreat they carried with them their scientific and literary taste, and Andalusia fell back into its former barbarous condition. A disposition has shown itself in this province to countenance study and literature, but the kingdoms of Cordova and Jaen have no establishment capable of lending its aid in such a work; they have, so to speak, no good classes of any kind, but at most a few bad monkish schools, without a sufficient number of masters, without libraries, and sometimes without students; thus, far from being useful, these schools are often prejudicial, from the loss of time they occasion to the pupils who attend them [2]."

"After having compared the Spaniards with the Moors of past times, M. de Laborde compares them with the English of the present day: "It is impossible," says he, "not to do justice to the taste and magnificence of the English, on witnessing the care with which they have embellished the rock of Gibraltar. The have spared no pains to cover it with trees and flowers, to sustain the grounds by walls and other means of support, to open a number of roads on the bare stone, and to render such a soil practicable on horseback or in carriages to the most elevated points. They have even sown some artificial meadows for their flocks; a good example to the Spaniards, who might obtain with much more ease, in their fertile country, similar advantages [3]."

"The English troops attend to cleanliness and military appearance to such a degree, that it seems inconvenient and ridiculous to those who have served in armies less minutely particular in this respect. The same may be observed of the regularity of their buildings, of the valuable and useful execution of all their defensive works; you would think yourself rather in the park and the palace of some monarch than in the fortress of Gibraltar: the cordons of the walls, the embrasures of the cannons, the groins of the vaults, are cut with inconceivable precision in very large blocks of very hard stone, and all the military instruments are constructed, each in its kind, with similar perfection.

"Less neatness and order is observed at Gibraltar in the Catholic tombs than in the others. The Anglican graves have each its slab

1. Laborde, vol. III, p. 344. — 2. *Idem*, pp. 367 to 371. — 3. *Idem*, vol. V, p. 106.

with a laconic and sententious inscription; but the Spaniards do not appear to have venerated these monuments with the same religious respect[1]. "

"The English have neglected nothing at Gibraltar for the security of the place, and they have laboured incessantly to embellish it and render it agreeable... The activity and care of the police preserve the best public order, and effectually provide for the salubrity and cleanliness of the streets. No beggars are to be met with there as in the Spanish towns, nor any of those dealers in second-han d goods, who live at the expense of the poorest classes of the people, nor the quacks who at all hours of the day infest in other places public thoroughfares[2]. "

The *Revue Britannique* seeks for a term of comparison much lower. That journal does not compare the Spaniard with the Englishman, or even venture to place him on an equality with the citizen of any other nation of Christendom, not even with the Turk; it finds his fellow only among the heathens!

"The Spanish peasant is, in our estimation, far below the English, French, German, and Dutch peasant; he will not even bear comparison with the Turk, who has not been spoiled by a residence in Constantinople. It is undeniable that he is perhaps of all men the least scrupulous as to shedding the blood of his fellow-creatures. He is ever ready, in his anger, to strike his adversary with the knife. Like the ancient Carthaginian, he is cruel by instinct, and no less treacherous when his interest is concerned. The *punica fides* is one of the essential characteristics of the Spaniard, taken in the mass or individually. He may be hospitable; but he has nothing to offer worth the trouble of refusing. The Spaniard is a Christian Arab; but, as such, he is far below the Wahabite, who is a little theistical, whereas the religion of the Spaniard, that self-styled Christianity, is nothing but a brutalising superstition, a superstition as contemptible, to speak moderately, as all the forms of paganism that ever prevailed upon earth, with the exception, however, of the Egyptian paganism, to which it is indeed analagous in more than one respect. The Spaniard is patient in poverty and in the midst of privations; he endures his fate, whatever it may be, with the apathetic resignation of the Hindoo. Why so? simply because he finds it easier to suffer than to toil. In this respect, as in many others, the Spaniard is greatly inferior to the Indian of the North American prairies. The Spaniard having within his reach

1. Laborde, vol. v, pp. 108, 109 — 2. *Idem*, p. 115.

all the means of procuring himself the positive enjoyments of life, and of raising his condition in the social scale, prefers living on a little bread and garlic, lying in a wretched hovel, and lounging about in rags peopled with vermin, to working like a man. If by chance he gets a little money into his possession, either from the liberality of a traveller, or from having plundered the said traveller, or from any other source, instead of applying this money to the relief of his own wants or those of his family, or to improving the future prospects of his children, he takes care to make no use of it, to apply it to no purpose whatever, but conceals in some secret place his unproductive treasure [1]. "

But, setting aside all comparison, let us return with our author to a study of the Spaniards themselves. After having taken a survey of the country, M. de Laborde examines the men, and depicts their manners. We will now quote his own words, and first present the least harsh features of the portrait he draws :

" They begin their work late and finish early, and while occupied they are still more slow than thoughtful. They devote scarcely one fourth of the day to toil [2]. The women too are much addicted to idleness; those of the higher classes are scarcely ever occupied, never take a book, never attend to the lighter sort of work so useful in families which falls naturally to the share of the women. Many women of condition leave their residence on the approach of summer, when they can easily procure salad, melons, and other fruit, and above all capsicums; these provisions, purchased at little cost, are sufficient for their sustenance; they say that it is a folly to wear one's self out with labour when it is so easy to obtain food without it..... When persons of both sexes are about to take a walk, they instantly sit down; so great is their fear lest they should be fatigued. Nothing can rouse the Murcians from their apathy [3]. "

" The Murcian passes his days in a state of apathy, in sloth and listlessness. He eats, drinks, counts his beads, and drags his cloak to a place where he sits down to think of nothing. A peasant, a porter who has to carry a light burthen, even if its weight should not exceed twenty-five pounds, puts it on the back of an ass, and refuses to carry it himself. Ignorance and sloth render the manners of the country disagreeable; prejudices are carried to a great extent, and the people are very litigious. A general distrust prevails : they fear and avoid one another, every one lives alone, far from his own kindred, without friends or neighbours; such seclusion

1. *Revue Britannique*, 1846, May and June, pp. 149, 150. — 2. Laborde, vol. III, pp. 110, 111. — 3. *Idem*, p. 113.

leads to sullen, unsociable habits. Discord arises in families, and society takes a tinge of that savageness with which the Murcians reproached the Moors, their predecessors. Cardinal de Belluga said of them : The sky and the soil of the country are good, all between is bad... Some years since, the city was furnished with lamps; this novelty displeased the people to such a degree that on the very first night all the lamps were broken with stones [1]. "

" The Murcian is sad, gloomy, passionate, hypochondriac. His inaction and bad diet may be partly the cause of this. He is persuaded that chronic diseases should be respected, and that it is dangerous to attempt to cure them. Physicians refuse to treat them [2]. "

" In Murcia, every one lives secluded; hence the manners have contracted something wild and awkward. The members of one family scarcely ever unite. The presence of strangers seems to discompose them, and they endeavour to avoid it. The aspect of the people is gloomy; this province is often the theatre of sanguinary contests. To his extreme indolence the Murcian joins the most deplorable superstition. A peasant, suspected of being a spy, and threatened with being shot, replied : 'I defy you to kill me, I have about me an image of Christ that has touched the holy cross of Carovaca.' The poor devil was spared, and doubtless attributed his deliverance to his amulet..... It is scarcely conceivable that manners should have become so rude, so repulsive, under so beautiful a sky and on so happy a soil; they were milder among the Moors whom the Murcians stigmatise with the appellation of barbarians, although, in inheriting their possessions, they have not continued their industry, their activity, or their civilization. The inhabitants of Carthagena are of very different manners; but it is necessary to add that few of them are Murcians, the greater portion being foreigners [3]. "

" Andalusia is the country of those braggarts who differ from other men by their loud and menacing tones, but who threaten only when they are feared, and grow mild as soon as they cease to inspire terror, always to be feared when they can strike without any danger to themselves, known by the name of Majos. There are likewise Majas in the country, women as bewitching as the Majos are repulsive. A free and easy air, a nimble step, are the attributes of these dangerous women; practised in the art of seducing, they know every method of obtaining success. Free in their language,

1. Laborde, vol. III, pp. 46, 47. — 2. *Idem*, p. 49. — 3. *idem*, pp. 113 to 115.

still more so in their attitudes, they provoke, they attack, they invite; it is difficult to resist them. Andalusia was the refuge of the Gitanos, men without house or home, outlaws, the vermin of Spain, the opprobrium of the nation who tolerated them, the terror of the highways and the fields. Protected by the nobility, the Gitanos protected the nobility in their turn. The nobility afforded them places of concealment to screen them and their robberies from justice. They therefore respected the lands, persons, servants, and farmers of the nobility, were acquainted with their feuds, and furnished them with satellites by whose agency they might wreak their revenge[1]."

"The artisan of Valencia is fond of pleasure and good living. The lowest ranks of the people would have the same tastes if they possessed the means of gratifying them. The latter have the appearance of being mild, but they are said to conceal their hatred; they were formerly accused of being familiar with the use of the dagger, and of handling it with skill. Valencia was even reputed to have many hired assassins. It makes one shudder in walking through the streets of this town to find crosses on the walls with inscriptions recalling the names of the persons assassinated below... As soon as the women no longer feel the necessity of working, they give themselves up to idleness until want obliges them to work again. Those of the higher classes do no work of any kind, they do not even read : this indolence is the fault of the parents, who accustom them to inactivity. The women have a singular predilection for the 'place' of Saint Catherine, which is a place of resort for men; the former scarcely ever leave their houses without passing through the place however circuitous the road it may oblige them to take. A man who remained a whole day on that square would see three-fourths of the ladies of Valencia pass before him, generally two or three times. Spain abounds in paupers and vagrants; the former multiply from the facility with which they live on alms; the latter are frequently persons who have escaped from the ***Presides***, and more frequently still unfortunate peasants driven from their homes by misery and the impossibility of finding employment. Both live in destitution and soon perish[2]."

The quarrels of the Valencian are always followed by bloodshed, and very little suffices to provoke them : the pleasure of revenge has for him an irresistible charm; and the gun, the dagger, the knife, and even instruments of husbandry, are the weapons that

1. Laborde, vol. III, pp. 385, 386. — 2. *Idem*, vol. V, p. 139.

he uses to gratify this passion. He fights with the rage of a barbarian. This kingdom has long been known to abound in hired assassins, who, for a moderate sum, undertake to wreak the vengeance of others. Murders are still very frequent there, the prisons therefore are always full, and the twelve existing in Valencia are insufficient.

"The number of idle and dangerous men who fill the convents might be usefully employed on the canals, roads, and in the ports. Without reckoning that a quarter of the population of Spain is composed of men living in absolute sloth, the country contains 100,000 inhabitants who may be divided between smugglers, robbers, mule-shearers, freebooters, and those convicted of murder who have escaped from prison or from the Présides; 40,000 custom-house officers, whose duty it is to arrest them, but who in reality are leagued with them; 60,000 students, the greater number of whom beg alms in the evening on pretence of buying books. Add to all these 100,000 beggars fed by 60,000 monks at the doors of the convents, and you will reckon in Spain nearly 600,000 individuals whose hands are useless either for the cultivation of the ground or for mechanical arts, and whose existence is often dangerous to society[1]."

We shall not be astonished to find profound ignorance prevailing among such a people; but we are determined not to proceed upon supposition, and will again quote the words of our traveller: "The decline of the arts was the same in New Castille as in other parts of Spain. They were destroyed under Philip the Fourth and Charles the Second. Skilful architects, ingenious sculptors, and famous painters had disappeared, and when Philip the Fifth ascended the throne scarcely a faint recollection was preserved of them. This prince founded an Academy at Madrid, which was also patronised by his successors, but it is in vain to seek there any longer for valuable instruction. The Academy has ceased to distribute prizes, and its existence is a mere derision. Except in Madrid, the arts find very few amateurs, and are not cultivated in the least; there is no establishment calculated to inspire a taste for them, or to facilitate their study; few persons even are to be found capable of appreciating them; and in general they are treated very lightly. New Castille has three sham Universities: one at Toledo, another at Alcala, and a third at Siguenza. In these much time is wasted in the pursuit of useless knowledge... The private schools have

1. Laborde, vol. I, Introduction, pp. 18, 19.

the same vices as the Universities, and the same may be affirmed of the colleges... Here an important reflection presents itself, unpleasing, perhaps, but too true. The presence of the Court ought to give life to New Castille, and the benefits of the Sovereign ought to extend over the provinces which surround his residence. By what fatality does the contrary exist in this province [1]?"

"The University of Cervera, in Catalonia, is not equal to the conception which we ought to form of it. It wants many establishments requisite for the formation of good pupils. It possesses neither an amphitheatre for anatomy, nor a botanical garden, nor a laboratory for chemistry and pharmacy, nor apparatus for the study of natural philosophy, nor a course of clinical medicine, and the result is that neither anatomy, nor surgical operations, nor botany, nor chemistry, nor pharmacy, nor demonstrative *materia medica*, are taught there. Professors of medicine still follow the Gelenic system; they have mixed it up with that of Boerhaave, and one disfigures the other. Philosophy is a mixture of the peripatetic school and the precepts of Jacquier, and the result is altogether unintelligible. The professors of theology content themselves with scholastic morality, and do not go so far as the dogmatic [2]."

"The Universities want apparatus, and possess few instruments, no laboratory, no observatory, and their scanty funds leave no hope of their soon obtaining any. The professors are very restricted in the choice of books to be used for their lessons; they are not allowed to adopt those which might contain a clearer and more certain doctrine, or new views and discoveries: for instance, they have obliged the professor of chemistry to follow Baumé for chemistry applied to the arts, and Macquer for chemistry applied to medicine. Science has been greatly enriched with modern discoveries and beautiful experiments, which the Spanish professors are not at liberty to communicate [3]."

"La Mancha is by no means advanced in the cultivation of science and art. Some very indifferent schools of scholastic theology and peripatetic philosophy, and some small grammar-schools, are the only sources whence the people can derive instruction; there is no school for the arts, no establishment calculated to polish and adorn the mind, or to promote industry [4]."

"Estramadura is the most neglected province in all Spain, and the most backward in the sciences and arts. It may, in this respect, be placed on a level with La Mancha; it has no school or

1. Laborde, vol. IV, pp. 317 to 334. — 2. *Idem*, t. II, pp. 99, 100. — 3. *Idem*, pp. 442, 443. — 4. *Idem*, vol. IV, p. 30.

establishment for instruction of any kind. Its inhabitants live in ignorance of what is passing around them in the world of science and art. They have always neglected and contemned study. They know neither how to enjoy the conveniences of life, nor how to procure them. Unaccustomed to society, they fear the approach of strangers, and avoid their company. A certain aversion for employment of all kinds, and the want of instruction, disinclines them to labour, and keeps them in perpetual indolence[1]."

"Old Castille has no establishment favourable to the progress of science. It has, indeed, a few colleges for the education of youth; but nothing is taught in them beyond the elements of the Latin language[2]."

"The sciences and arts do not flourish in Arragon; the inhabitants neglect these two important pursuits; they have not enjoyed that tranquillity so necessary to success in either, nor have they possessed any establishment where the elements of either are taught, or been provided with the means of adding to their knowledge[3]."

And what pupils are formed by these schools? We shall hear. Let us begin by the physicians: "The pupils write their lessons from the master's dictation; their note-books are a shapeless, confused mass of matter, unintelligible even to those who have written it; they omit the words which they do not understand, and many others which they can neither understand, hear, nor write. Yet these note-books are their sole resource; very few of them can procure any books. The pupils may study or not, as they are inclined; their proficiency is not ascertained by means of examinations; they are obliged to provide for their sustenance, and indigence damps their ardour and weakens their courage. Examinations are very trifling in Spain, even those which are instituted for the purpose of filling vacant chairs; the questions for examination are very superficial; the most ignorant students may aspire to the doctorship... If questions are put on anatomy, the candidate answers like a parrot what he has conned by rote from books, though he has a very imperfect knowledge of it, never having seen it on dead bodies...... Many students obtain admission into private families, where they perform the most servile functions, are confounded with the servants, take their meals with them, and do the vilest offices[4]."

"Some surgeons, unknown barbers of old, were appointed professors; to these were added, for form's sake, a few physicians

1. Laborde, vol. III, pp. 450, 451. — 2. *Idem*, vol. I, p. 393. — 3. *Idem*, p. 190. — 4. *Idem*, vol. VI, pp. 195, 223.

without knowledge, skill, or experience, but no students came to attend their lectures; those who remained, finding themselves mixed with a number of barber's assistants, grew ashamed of such company, and withdrew. All the supernumeraries, who had never studied medicine, had their degrees conferred on them in one day, all together, without preparation, without examination, formalities of any kind, or expense. Spain was inundated by this multitude of new quack-doctors, who affected a pride proportionate to their ignorance. The public became their victim, and numbers were mown down by these fatal measures. Notwithstanding their ill-success, the new physicians had the assurance to solicit military grades; they wished to be made captains, colonels, and lieutenant-colonels. This act of madness hastened their ruin [1]. "

Now a word or two on the Spanish historians:

" Most of them have a diffuse, obscure, low or declamatory style, or trivial, always prolix, bombastic, insupportable. Their writings are full of fables, doubtful facts, ridiculous suppositions, inconclusive arguments, digressions, useless matter, allegories, and hyperboles; they will rarely bear reading [2]. "

" The learning of the Spaniards is in general confused, badly digested, mixed with prejudices, propped up with a mass of ideas, passages, reminiscences jumbled together, without any choice or discrimination, order or method; it is a learning which cannot even be complete in its kind, because it is behind all that is written in other countries on the same subjects, owing to the difficulty of communication, and the impossibility of procuring foreign books [3]. "

" The oratorical art is that in which the Spaniards seem to have had the least success. The eloquence of the bar is unknown among them. In the fifteenth century, the pulpit produced only cold declamation, insipid allegories, exaggerated metaphors, trivial jests, misplaced sallies, ridiculous allusions [4]. "

" By what fatality has the Spanish drama, after having been the first in Europe, after having served as a model to all others, fallen so low as to be treated with indifference and contempt by other nations? We find in the Spanish heroic comedies, for the most part, a monstrous assemblage of plots badly accumulated, ill-connected, ill-combined, full of strange and incredible adventures, in which princes and princesses fall as it were from the sky; the plot is often unconnected, the action is interrupted every moment, the audience is suddenly supposed to be transported to a distance of three

1. Laborde, vol. VI, pp. 236, 237. — 2. *Idem*, pp. 247, 248. — 3. *Idem*, p. 193. — 4. *Idem*, vol. VI, p. 252.

hundred leagues. The most critical and interesting situations are often spoiled by dull pleasantries. The dignity of tragedy is degraded by low buffoonery [1]. "

"In the sacred comedies, God, the angels, the saints, the devils, the virtues, and the vices personified are all confounded with each other, to the great scandal of religion and morals. The devil is ordinarily represented in them in a black dress, with stockings, ruffles, a collar, a tail, and ribbands all red... In these comedies are to be seen the wildest freaks of the imagination... Heaven and Hell, the Garden of Eden, souls burning in purgatory, the Conclave, the election of popes, the Holy Sacrament, the devil disguised in the habit of a gray friar..... These plays were pleasing to the multitude; but they offended reason, good sense, morals, and religion [2]. "

"During the past century most nations have laboured successfully to reform their theatre; the Spaniards are almost the only people that have made no progress in this branch of literature; they are in the same state they were in at the beginning and in the middle of the seventeenth century..... The general decline of Spain in almost all possible branches of art and science, under the last kings of the house of Austria, may have contributed to this. By what fatality is the Spanish theatre neglected at the present day in an age when taste is refined, and dramatic art is carried to a degree of perfection which it never before attained? The Spaniards, attached to their ancient customs, disdain to profit by the progress of other nations; they stagnate in a listless and barbarous apathy. The performance of their actors is still more imperfect than their drama; they have no majesty, no softness of expression, either in voice or gesture; all is forced, violent, or lifeless; all is in contradiction to the laws of Nature. Shouts constitute the most important part of their acting; if they threaten, they roar; if they command, they thunder; if they sigh, it is with a painful effort, in which their convulsed respiration is almost exhausted. Their action is mostly monotonous, singular, and ignoble. The women, in their bursts of passion, become furies, warriors become ruffians, generals brigands, and heroes hectors; nothing is pathetic with them [3]. "

When we see such things, we are tempted to ask if there are in such a society any principles, any government, any forms of justice? Yes, all this is to be found in the country; but what justice! "The exceptional tribunals," says M. de Laborde, "are too frequent in

1. Laborde, vol. VI, pp. 321, 322. — 2. *Idem*, pp. 323 to 326. — 3. *Idem*, pp. 336 to 344.

Spain. They withdraw a number of individuals from the surveillance of the local magistrates. The jurisdictions, likewise too numerous, combat and weaken each other. Lawsuits, dragged from court to court, are interminable; often stretching beyond two or three generations. The rich suitor tires out and ruins his poorer antagonist. During the slow progress of criminal trials the proofs die away, the guilty often escape punishment, and the innocent are often punished, by a long confinement, for not being guilty. The prisoners have every facility for communicating with persons outside; they hang baskets without the bars of their prison to solicit alms of passers-by, and afterwards drawing them back with what has been put into them, they thus have an opportunity of receiving letters, and advice or information for their defence or escape [1]. "

What a government! "The labourer, the landlord, the farmer can neither sell nor exchange any of the produce of their lands, their flocks, their farm-yard, or their studs; the sportsman cannot dispose of his game, the manufacturer of his wares, or the tradesman of the goods in his shop, without each time paying a duty. A private man cannot sell his horse, his ass, or his pig, without conforming to the same regulation. No one is permitted to kill a calf, a sheep, or a lamb of his own flock without having declared his intention to do so. Such articles as tallow, grapes, and oil are taxed two or three times as they change their form. These taxes are one of the greatest obstacles to agriculture and industry. They weigh principally on the people, who, being obliged to purchase by retail, thus pay accumulated duty. This leads moreover to inspections and searches, which become vexatious from the faithlessness and avidity of the subalterns, who are with difficulty kept within bounds, since they are certain of impunity [2]. "

"The Cruzada is a tax levied by the popes with a view to a war with the Moors. The bulls which grant indulgences to those who took part in the war are still sold for the advantage of the king, and no one can dispense with buying them every year, without being reputed a bad catholic [3]. ".

"If Spain were to become entirely bankrupt, the expenditure of the State would still exceed its revenues by 400,000,000 reals. I doubt whether it be possible for the finances of any country to be in a more deplorable condition. France is indebted to her institutions, her intelligence, her love of labour and property, for

1. Laborde, vol. VI, pp. 85, 86. — 2. *Idem*, vol. V, pp. 164 to 166. — 3. *Idem*, p. 168.

her financial prosperity. Far from arriving at such brilliant results, unhappy Spain, overwhelmed with the burden of her ancient institutions, drags on a miserable existence under a government destitute of all means of carrying on its administration, without credit abroad or at home, equally incapable of rewarding the devotedness of its servants, and of curbing the audacity of its enemies, and forced at length to implore the assistance of foreign power, in order to obtain from its own people a few compulsory loans, a few wretched taxes, which the hardness of the times renders it impossible for them to pay. Such is now the position of this country, and such it will continue, if the old system, which seems to be revived, be persevered in[1]. "

Finally, what religious principles do we find in Spain! "The Valencian population is one of the most superstitious of the whole country. They mix up religious duties with the most profane customs, and hope, by external practices that have nothing in common with the worship due to the Almighty, to obtain forgiveness for their sins. In the saints especially they place great confidence, attributing to them the power of preserving from accidents and disease : Saint Roch preserves from the plague, Saint Anthony from fire, Saint Barbara from lightning, Saint Casalida cures hemorrhage, Saint Appolina the tooth-ache, Saint Augustin the dropsy, Saint Raymond watches over pregnant women, Saint Lazarus takes care of women during their confinement, and Saint Nicholas of marriageable girls. Every carter carries about him the image of a saint, to whom he testifies his gratitude as long as his journey is prosperous; but, if any accident happens to him on the road, he treads his protector under foot, overwhelms him with abuse, and sends Saint Barbara or Saint Francis to the devil, our Lady of the Carmelites to the infernal regions[2]. "

"*Romerias* are short journeys to chapels, performed on the day preceding that consecrated to the saint. The pilgrims pass the night in the chapel : men and animals are huddled together in tents; the two sexes are mingled; they are riotous with laughter and singing, they lie down to rest, and the darkness of the night is a cloak to licentiousness, and to excesses ill-suited to the sanctity of the day which they have met to solemnise[3]. The mixture of profane things, and accessories that have nothing to do with religious worship, throw more ridicule here than elsewhere on these processions, of which the inhabitants are extremely fond[4]. The processions of

1. Laborde, vol. V, pp. 208, 209. — 2. *Idem*, vol. II, pp. 302, and following. — 3. *Idem*, vol. VI, pp. 448, 449. — 4. *Idem*, vol. II, p. 450, 451.

Passion Week, not more than twenty years ago, were attended by flagellants, by penitents attached to cross bars of iron, by giants covered with cuirasses and helmets, and by other ridiculous personages. Those who formed the processions walked two by two, with a long interval between each pair in order to leave room for the sweep of a train five feet long[1]. On the night of Good Friday a splendid dinner is given to the sick. Individuals of all classes crowd into the hospitals, and jostle one another in their efforts to seize upon dishes in order to present them to the patients. Convinced that they are doing a good action, and desirous to render it still more meritorious, they force the poor patients to gorge themselves with the viands, striving who shall make them devour most, in the name of the Virgin and the saints[2]."

"In the town of Valencia no procession of any importance takes place which is not preceded by eight statues of giants of prodigious bulk. The heads of these giants are of pasteboard, of an enormous size, frizzed and dressed according to the fashion of the day; the bodies are wooden frames, covered with coats or robes, and decked with various ornaments; they are borne by men dressed in flowing garments reaching to the ground, who make them dance, leap, turn, and spin in every possible manner. The attention of the crowd is directed more to the motions of the giants than to the religious ceremony which follows. To perpetuate these giants there exists at Valencia a rather considerable endowment for their support. They have a house belonging to them, in which they are deposited, and two livings have been created in honour of them. The clergymen who hold these livings are bound to take care of the giants and of their dresses[3]. A ridiculous procession takes place on Good Friday: in this procession are penitents wrapped in red cloth sacks, with their heads encased in conical hoods like sugar loaves. The procession is headed by two trumpeters, whose instruments bray with a monotonous and discordant tone; the children who form part of the procession wear wigs that fall over their faces, and crowns of thorns on their heads. Borne on a litter appears the Eternal, arrayed in albe, and stole, and scarf. In one of these processions are to be seen a Christ so naked as to be offensive, lying on a red bed; tambourines covered with black and flageolets adorned with the same colour; idiots or half-idiots dressed in loose

1. Laborde, vol. II, pp. 65, 66. — 2. *Idem*, p. 310. — 3. With reference to endowments, we will here quote an instance of one which appeared to us so extraordinary that we did not venture to insert it in our text. It is the following: "In a cloister adjacent to a church, geese are bred and taken care of! An annuity is provided for their maintenance," Laborde, p. 45.

party-coloured clothes, yellow and blue, with handkerchiefs tied round their necks and staffs in their hands; a garden of Olives surrounded with an osier fence, and other things no less ridiculous. On the day of Corpus-Christi, they imitate the massacre of the Innocents. A man dressed in woman's clothes, mounted on an ass, represents the Virgin Mary. He carries in his arms a child, who personates the infant Jesus; a man leads the ass by a halter, an ox and a horse follow them. Men in a Jewish costume run through the streets as if they were mad, armed with knives, cutlasses, and swords, seemingly bent on murdering all the children; they seize upon all those whom they meet, and apply their knives to the poor creatures' throats. At the feast of Saint Joseph are seen a Bacchus astride upon a tub, a family assembled to kill a pig, a Spaniard and a Spanish woman dancing the bolero, and a giant, in a Dutch garb, making bears dance to the sound of a drum beaten by another figure. At nightfall, the representation is reduced to ashes : this is called the *follas* of Saint Joseph.

"This is the most critical moment: the night favours licentiousness and intrigues; pickpockets now ply their trade in security; lovers come to their appointed meetings, seek and find one another, the night is generally fruitful in events... It is superfluous to draw a picture of the improprieties which are committed in the church of Valencia on the occasion of the representation of the baptism of Saint Vincent Ferrier. To celebrate a miracle of this saint, they bring him into a house where there are two dead children; Saint Vincent, affected by the grief of the parents, approaches the table and blesses the saucepan; at the same instant the two children, restored to life, rise out of it, and gambol, frisk, and dance on the table, and hang about the necks of their father, and mother, of the monks, and of the servant, and overwhelm them with kisses and endearments. The dominican, impatient to receive the pie which the servant is holding, blesses it, and a pigeon which it contained, although thoroughly baked, comes to life at once, spreads its wings, and disappears in the air... In another procession those who carry the banners of the different trades play a thousand antics, and perform feats of strength with them, and poise them with dexterity; but now and then a banner slips from their hands, and in its fall bruises the unwary heads of the gaping crowd; at the same time the noise of the tambourines, mixed with all kinds of shrill and discordant cries, makes a hubbub the confusion of which excites laughter in the beginning, but soon fatigues. Next come the dwarfs that accompany the giants; these have pasteboard heads, which are monstrous from their prodigious size and extraordinary shape; they are dressed after a grotesque fashion; they play castanets and dance as they move along. The regular clergy, the secular clergy, the chapter of the cathedral, and the corporation of the city close the procession... It is difficult to give an account of all that takes place at these feasts; people run from altar to altar to see and to be seen; the streets leading to the altars are filled with persons of either sex; they seek and find one another, and meet; the confusion prevents discovery, and the stupid attention paid to the representation allows many private interviews to pass unperceived amid the innumerable multitude. Night comes on, and the crowd increases. The men's slouched hats and the women's mantillas facilitate numerous intrigues, over which the night draws its curtain. The mother often seeks in vain for her daughter, and the husband for his wife. The darkness of the night hides the sequel to all this disorder. There is little fear of discovery; on all sides are individuals engaged in the same pursuits, and all are reciprocally indulgent [1]. "

" On the morning of Easter Sunday they build up in the public square a gigantic statue representing Judas, and on the passing of the procession this statue is set on fire. The people are more attentive to this spectacle than to the religious ceremony before them; they celebrate it by bursts of laughter, by intemperate shouts, hootings, and exclamations not unfrequently obscene. Another custom, perhaps still more to be condemned, is observed there: during the week preceding Christmas, high mass is solemnised at the Grey Friars'. Children crowd to the place with whistles, and as soon as mass begins the loud and shrill tones of the whistles are echoed back by the vaulted roof of the church, and mingle with the chant of the priests. This scandalous noise is renewed at the elevation of the host, at the communion, and at the termination of mass... The Mondas are a famous feast, in which a number of offerings, varying with the age and devotion of the bearers, are presented to the holy Virgin. Among these offerings are sometimes seen animals adorned in a thousand different ways; lambs, sheep, horses, asses, pigs, etc., are offered to the saint. All these processions enter the chapel, and with them the barrows and carts in which offerings are conveyed; the animals are led to the very foot of the altar. Frequent disputes arise. The meeting of two processions occasions a struggle for precedence, in which angry words are

1. Laborde, vol. II, pp. 316 to 332.

sometimes followed by blows. The processions are often mixed and confounded with one another; battles are fought with the fist, or with clubs, or stones, and bloodshed often ensues[1]."

Such is Modern Spain; such is Spain, once the first, now the last of European nations! Spain, deprived of America, ruined within her own territory, without trade, without industry, without food, and possessing a fertile soil! Let a more skilful pen, that of M. de Lamennais, sum up what is contained in the preceding pages. It is not the socialist of 1848 who speaks, but the *abbé* of 1830, just returned from his pilgrimage to Rome. The following picture is taken from his *Affaires de Rome:*

"After ages bright with every kind of glory, Spain has fallen by degrees into so profound a lethargy that she can be compared in this respect to no other country. Far behind the nations at the head of which she formerly moved, she is now a mere cypher in science, literature, and art; in everything except courage, devotedness, and energy of character. All that has been accomplished for two hundred years in the scientific and intellectual world is as if it had never been for this nation, whose fertile and original genius might have contributed so powerfully to the progress of the human mind and of general civilisation. Instead of this, the apathy, the ignorance of Spain find not their equal in all Europe. Instruction in Spain is now what it was three generations after Charles the Fifth. There has been no change, no advancement; all, on the contrary, has declined from day to day. Intellect, which, to prosper, requires constant activity, has here sunk into a heavy slumber. Both the clergy and the laity are still no farther advanced than the fifteenth century. They remain motionless, with their antiquated methods and ideas, and Aristotle still reigns over the descendants of the Cantabrians and the Visigoths. Besides this, they have no resources for study, no schools to form new artists[2]."

"The history of the decline of Spain would be equally mournful and instructive. It would exhibit to us the grandees, deprived of political influence, shrunk into mere court-puppets, hereditary worshippers of the idol that sits, for the time being, on the throne, degenerating in the midst of sloth and libertinism. We should see the last scions of their race, which has undergone physical as well as moral degradation, left, on the land over which their ancestors shed such renown, mere shapeless phantoms; a ridiculous mockery of mankind. Then we should witness the long series of

1. Laborde, vol. IV, pp. 231 to 233. — 2. Lamennais, pp. 232 to 234.

internal diseases, the grangrene of the social body, which are generated when power, concentrated in the hands of one man, without control or any rule of action but his own caprice, is by turns wielded by a favourite, a mistress, a lackey, a dry-rubber. This Cæsar claims a right to dispose of your property, your persons, your lives, all, without exception. But agriculture languishes, fields lie fallow, industry declines, commerce perishes, the revenue, dilapidated by the courtiers, is encumbered with debts, public bankruptcies succeed each other as regularly as the seasons, the army is disorganised, ships rot in the ports, every department of the public service falls into neglect, and the roads are infested with robbers who negociate with the government as one power negociates with another. The police, unable to protect the citizen, can employ their activity only to disturb the pleasures of the domestic hearth; justice, servile and mercenary, is now the blind instrument of the prince's revenge, and now the privilege of the powerful and the rich, and a warrant of impunity for their crimes. But the country is depopulated, misery increases from year to year, the descendants of the men who fought under the Gonzalvos and the Cortez stretch forth their hands in the streets and public squares to beg a maravedi from the compassion of the stranger; naked men wander on a naked soil. But the very souls of men are here condemned to inhabit a vast desert; only a shadow survives of the old universities, the schools are contemptible; ignorance, proclaimed the prop of the throne, spreads her pall over the national genius. There is gloom everywhere, and thick night; and if in that night a solitary lamp is seen to glimmer in some remote dwelling, that dwelling immediately becomes an object of suspicion, and he whose sight, weary of the darkness, seeks for the sweet light of knowledge, finds, in its stead, only the red and smoky torch of persecution. But all discussion relative to power, its acts, or the public weal, is forbidden, and petition for reform is looked upon as a rebellion. No books, journals, or correspondence, except on private matters, are allowed to cross the frontier. But the whole people are kept in close confinement, thought itself is proscribed; what matters it? this is the sovereign's right, the safeguard of his power[1]."

The contrast that we wish to exhibit between the sixteenth and the nineteenth centuries in Spain is so true, so very striking, that a writer has painted it in such lively colours we might believe that

1. *Affairs of Rome*, Lamennais, pp. 237 to 239.

his picture was intended to serve as a demonstration of our own thesis: "Spain is a dispossessed queen; for two hundred years and more, diamonds have been falling from her glittering crown. The source of her wealth, well or ill-gotten, is exhausted for ever. Her treasures are lost, her colonies are gone, she is deprived of the prestige of that external opulence which veiled, or at least dissembled, her real and utter poverty. The nation is exhausted to such a degree, and has been so long unhappy, that each individual feels but his own misery. His country has ceased to exist for him; even those times are gone when the guerillas called the citizen to arms for the sole and generous purpose of vindicating the national honour. The despondency and apathy of the nation are visible even in the battles fought by the Spaniards among themselves in their civil dissensions. They fight from habit, and discharge their muskets at their countrymen because they can do nothing else, and because every shot from their guns may bring them a piece of bread. A nation reduced to such a state is low indeed: the chill ness of death is very near seizing upon its extremities... What a length of time it will require to heal the wounds of these populations, so brave and so devoted! How much gold, how much blood have been lavished during the past seven years without an object, without any conceived plan. What would Charles the Fifth say, if, rising out of his grave, he saw his great and glorious Spain struggling thus miserably in dread uncertainty of her future destinies? Where are my colonies? where are my Batavian provinces? where is my gigantic power, and the glory of Spain, which resounded from one hemisphere to the other? What have you done with my inheritance, ye cowardly and unskilful men? where are my treasures, where the victorious fleets that crossed the Ocean to bring back in profusion to my empire the gold and gems of the New World[1]!"

But let us pause. Our readers must be fatigued with gazing so long on so sad a spectacle. The question must, we think, at this moment arise in their minds: what can be the cause of so many evils? of such utter misery, such extreme ignorance, such disgusting sloth?

— Tyranny, replies the politician.

— Catholicism, says the Protestant.

— The Inquisition, adds the historian.

But these three replies form but one; they are the three sides of a prism, which, united, give the entire ray of truth. In truth, Ca-

1. Tardif, pp. 105 to 109.

tholicism is the father; the Inquisition and Tyranny the daughters. We are not the first to make this affirmation; we only repeat what we have read in the lines we are now going to submit to the perusal of our readers. It is sufficient for us to have pointed out the connexion of the different causes which will be assigned by our authorities.

That Catholicism produced the Inquisition, a tribunal of priests, judging heretics, it appears to us superfluous to demonstrate : the very nature of the institution renders it evident. It is however expedient to show that one was a necessary consequence of the other; that the ruling idea of Catholicism, the principle of authority, contained the germ of the Inquisition. " It was impossible that the Romish Church should not extend its principle to its penal code; it does not doubt in matters of faith, neither does it doubt in criminal matters. This is the reason why, in the Church, the accused and the guilty have but one and the same appellation. Whoever is arraigned at her tribunal has Heaven and Earth against him; the interrogatory is already a species of torture.

" When the Church accuses, she seems already convinced; all her efforts tend to extort the confession of the crime, which, in virtue of her infallibility, she discovers in darkness; from this anticipated conviction of the guilt of the accused are produced all those ambushes and snares laid for the purpose of obtaining by surprise the confession of the accused. The names of the witnesses are concealed or falsified. Everywhere, in the most trifling details, it is strikingly evident that truth is on one side, and the demon on the other [1]. "

In the second place, that Catholicism has produced the Spanish absolutism of the *Catholic Kings*, is sufficiently shown by the very name given to these kings; but let us rather consult facts: " Another no less deplorable consequence of the position of the clergy in Spain and Portugal is that they have no sooner confounded the cause of religion with that of despotism, than this error, producing its consequences, leads to a monstrous abuse of the word of God. Political fury has invaded the pulpit, and stained it with abject and sacrilegious adulation... The lips whose mission is to preach peace, charity, and mutual love, have spoken the language of hatred and vengeance; horrible vows, abominable threats, have more than once been heard, in the presence of the tabernacles in which abides the Son of Man, who sacrificed his life for the salvation

1. Tardif, pp. 139, 140.

of his brethren[1]." "Spain, since Philip II, has remained closed and uninfluenced by the ordinary progress of the human mind elsewhere. The monkish and despotic spirit has long preserved itself in the midst of ignorance, without, indeed, acquiring strength from abroad, but at the same time without permitting the intelligence of the nation to borrow foreign arms against it[2]."

We shall now see this Spanish Catholicism at work, for three centuries, assisted by its worthy offspring, Absolutism and the Inquisition, and at every ruin, at every crime you meet with, if you ask, who has done this? the reply will assuredly be: the church of the Pope, the tyranny of the Catholic kings, the Inquisition of the priests. To convince yourselves of the fact, you need only put your questions, and listen to the records of history, written, not by us, but by men of talent and skill, who have long enjoyed unquestionable authority.

What was the first fruit of the Catholic Inquisition? — The expulsion of the Jews and the Moors: "Spain," says M. Roseew Saint-Hilaire, "exterminated them for ever, as poisonous plants, from its soil, mortal to heresy. The Jews and the Moors left it in turn, carrying with them, the former trade, the latter agriculture, from this disinherited land, to which the New World, to repair so many losses, vainly bequeathed her sterile treasures. And let it not be said that Spain, in thus depriving herself of her most active citizens, was not aware of the extent of her loss. All her historians concur in the statement that in acting thus she sacrificed her temporal interests to her religious convictions, and all are at a loss for words to extoll such a glorious sacrifice.

"In banishing the Jews from her territory, Spain, then, acted consistently: her conduct was logically just, but according to that pitiless logic which ruins states in order to save a principle. From that period, therefore, a new era begins for Castille. Until then she had been divided from the rest of Europe only by her position; foreign, without being hostile, to the ideas of the continent, she had not begun to wage war with those ideas; but the establishment of the Inquisition is the first step in the career in which she can never stop[3]."

"It required," says M. Sismondi, "about one generation, to accustom the Spaniards to the sanguinary proceedings of the Inquisition, and to fanaticise the people. This work, dictated by an infernal policy, was scarcely accomplished, when Charles the Fifth

1. *Affaires de Rome*, pp. 250 to 254. — 2. *Idem*, p. 53. — 3. Saint-Hilaire, vol. VI, p. 52.

began his reign. It was probably the fatal spectacle of the *auto-da-fé* that imparted to the Spanish soldiers their ferocity, so remarkable during the whole of that period, which before that time was so foreign to the national character [1]. "

Who, employing these instruments, depopulated Spain? — The Inquisition. "To calculate," says Llorente, secretary to the Holy Office, "the number of victims of the Inquisition were to give palpable proof of one of the most powerful and active causes of the depopulation of Spain; for if to several millions of inhabitants of which the inquisitorial system has deprived this kingdom by the total expulsion of the Jews, the conquered Moors, and the baptised Moorish, we add about 500,000 families entirely destroyed by the executions of the Holy Office, it will be proved beyond a doubt that had it not been for this tribunal, and the influence of its maxims, Spain would possess 12,000,000 souls above her present population, supposed to amount to 11,000,000 [2]. "

"The Inquisition ruined and branded with infamy more than 340,000 persons, whose disgrace was reflected on their families, and who bequeathed only opprobrium and misery to their children. Add to these more than 100,000 families who emigrated in order to escape from this bloodthirsty tribunal, and it will be seen that the Inquisition has been the most active instrument of the ruin of Spain. But the most disastrous of all the acts which it occasioned was the expulsion of the Moors. If we add to those who were banished from Spain the countless numbers who perished in the insurrections of the sixteenth century, and the 800,000 Jews who left the kingdom, it will be seen that the country lost, in the course of a hundred and twenty years, about three millions of its most industrious inhabitants [3]. "

"The advisers of Philip III said to him with affright: The houses are falling in ruins, and none rebuild them; the inhabitants flee from the country, villages are abandoned, fields left uncultivated, and churches deserted. The Cortès in their turn said to him: If the evil is not remedied, there will soon be no peasants left to till ground, no pilots to steer the ships, none will marry. The kingdom cannot subsist another century, if a wholesome remedy be not found [4]. "

1. Sismondi, vol. III, p. 265. — 2. Llorente, vol. IV, p. 242. — 3. Weiss, vol. II. pp. 60, 61.
4. Here are, according to M. de Laborde, a few comparisons between the old and the new population.

	Old.	New.
Sarragossa in the 16th century	350,000	10,000
Estramadura under the Moors	40,000	5,000
Carry forward.	390,000	15,000

What ruined agriculture? — The Romish Church and the Catholic kings; first, by " superannuated institutions, that counteract in almost everything the designs of beneficent Nature: no portion of the Old World, with but few exceptions, presents amore naked and wretched aspect than Spain, which ought to be its most beautiful region [1]. "

Next, because " Spain is in want of hands for agriculture, although vagrants and beggars are more numerous there than in any other country in Europe. The clergy, who recruit among those who wish to escape from labour and indigence, deprive agriculture of too many hands [2]. "

Besides, " the excessive frequency of religious feasts tended greatly to increase the indolence of the Spaniards. In Castille the number of holidays a man was obliged to celebrate amounted to one third of his life-time. Thus the labourer is deprived of his occupation, and necessarily contracts habits of indolence. The greatest sufferer is the poor day-labourer, who can maintain his family only by his work [3]."

" Lastly, the ecclesiastical tithe, the royal tithe, and other additional rates, constituted so burdensome a tax, that those who cultivated the ground were discouraged by it [4]."

Who created, supported, and employed the services of those pestilent hordes of beggars and vagrants? — The Catholic convents and monasteries. " The entire Peninsula, at the time of Charles the Fifth, swarmed with vagrants and beggars. The emperor having directed that those who were really in need should be relieved,

	Brought forward.	390,000	15,000
Montijo in the 17th century		10,000	3,600
Kingdom of Seville in the 16th century		200,000	96,000
— of Cordova in the 17th century		60,000	35,000
— of Leon in the 16th century at Rio-Seco		32,000	6,000
— Medina del Campo		60,000	6,000
— Salamanca		50,000	13,000
Old Castille, in the 16th century.	Burgos	40,000	8,000
	Albie	25,000	2,000
	Olviedo	15,000	2,000
Grenada, in the 16th century		80,000	50,000
New Castille, in the 16th century.	La Puebla	10,000	1,200
	Toledo	200,000	25,000
	Casarubiosc	1,000	500
	Santa Olalla	3,000	300
	Valdemoro	6,000	2,800
Ciudadreal		25,000	9,000
Paeza, under the Moors		150,000	15,000
Malaga		80,000	50,000
		1,137,000	103,800

(Pages 127, 128.)

1. Laborde, vol. I, p. 21. — 2. *Idem*, vol. V, p. 234. — 3. Sempéré, p. 205. — 4. *Idem*, vol. II, pp. 111 and 135.

and vagrancy repressed, there was no want of theologians who attacked such measures as contrary to the morality taught by Jesus Christ. The opinion of the defenders of mendicity prevailed. Thus beggars multiplied indefinitely, and in the same proportion there grew up among the people an aversion for labour, and the other vices consequent upon vagrancy and idleness [1]."

Yes, the monks, and the clergy in general, were desirous of preserving the institution of mendicity and vagrancy, and we shall now be made acquainted with their motives : "The honest people of the country they inhabit, who cry death to the constitution! death to the nation! death to commerce! knowing not what they say, but knowing very well that they wish for pillage and murder; those vagabonds, like the locusts of the East, who devour Spain instead of fertilising it, will disappear when those who *use them as their instruments* (the monasteries who feed them) no longer possess *the means of supporting them,* when a vigorous and enlightened administration will know how to keep them within bounds, and find them employment [2]."

The following is still more clearly expressed : "For their mutual interests as castes the clergy distribute provisions among the peasants, and pamper their indolence on condition that the latter will obey, defend, and protect them; and the most palpable result of this alliance is that the clergy, purchasing at a sufficiently moderate price that brutal strength the direction of which they reserved to themselves, became in the end a power out of all proportion with all the others : the principal and predominant power of the State [3]."

"To form an idea of the number of these beggars and vagrants, the monkish militia, it is well to know that there were in Spain, in the seventeenth century, 9,088 monasteries, without mentioning nunneries, which insensibly gained possession of the whole kingdom by donations, brotherhoods, chaplaincies, or by purchases [4]..."

But do not imagine that in this respect the nineteenth century is far in advance of the seventeenth : "The priests, the convents," says M. de Laborde, "the churches, the saints' days, exhaust Spain. The workman's earnings are squandered in providing for the pleasures of the table and in gaming, in presents to monks, to convents, to chapels, in contributions to brotherhoods, in illuminating altars, in alms given to healthy beggars, which last en-

1. Sempéré, vol. II, pp. 202, 203. — 2. Laborde, vol. V, p. 215. — 3. Guéroult, pp. 111, 112. — 4. Sempéré, vol. II, pp. 27 to 29.

courages idleness and vice in a great number of individuals, who often find it more agreeable to degrade themselves by begging than to earn their livelihood by honourable labour: you cannot therefore move a step in the street, especially at night, without being assailed by a multitude of these wretches [1]."

At the present day, as in the seventeenth century, the convents support this militia, which they well know how to make use of: "that horde of vagabonds," says our modern traveller, "from 4 to 500,000 in number, who are supplied with soup at the gates of convents, or beg alms at the churches; *those villains who belong* to the party that pays them, and who compel by terror..."

What has wasted the Treasury? — The Catholic institutions: "The cause of the bad state of the finances in Spain is in the institutions which divert from their proper destination articles made of taxable materials, to sink and waste them in unproductive channels; institutions that destroy in the lower classes the love of industry and property, while they extinguish in the more enlightened classes every feeling, every hope of amelioration. The clergy possess in Spain a revenue which exceeds the whole amount of the taxes. They receive in the tithes what the landed proprietors might devote to the necessities of the State. The government, unable to levy sufficient taxes, is obliged to have recourse to burdensome loans [2]."

"The nobles and the clergy possess almost all the soil; one-third of the Spanish territory belongs to a few families, a few chapters, and a few religious orders. Sufficient establishments are wanting for the improvement of the soil; the farmers have more ground than they can cultivate; the landlords do not watch over their property, their lordly mansions are falling in ruins, their woods disappear beneath the destructive axe of their agents, their grounds are uncultivated [3]."

"The ecclesiastical and civil mortmains impede the progress of agriculture... Almost all Spain is the inalienable property of the nobles, the religious corporations, or the communities, which alliances, successions, and legacies tend continually to increase. The little ground which is, as it were, in circulation is no longer sufficient for the investment of capitals acquired in trade; thus society is solely composed of usufructuaries who are freeholders or farmers, but all equally careless... The farmers, having only leases of three or four years, try to turn the land quickly to

1. Laborde, vol. II, pp. 305, 306. — 2. *Idem*, vol. V, pp. 149, 150. — 3. *Idem*.

account without improving it, and entire fields lie fallow [1]."

"In 1826, there were in Spain 150,000 clergymen, each consuming annually 184 pounds of meat, or eight times and a half the average consumption of a layman, which was from 20 to 22 pounds[2]."

What was the cause of the ignorance so general and so profound in Spain? — The Catholic Inquisition : " At the time of the Reformation, when the minds of all were solely occupied with religious controversies, the Inquisition succeeded in preventing the establishment of any reformed community in Spain by burning all innovators as soon as they appeared. By this terrible example, that body deterred the rest of the nation from all metaphysical speculations and religious meditations; in short, from all occupations of the mind that might lead to such dreadful dangers on earth, and which were represented as exposing the soul to dangers still more dreadful in the life to come.

" The commissaries of the Holy Office received orders to oppose the introduction of books written by the partisans of modern philosophy, as reprobated by Saint Peter and Saint Paul, and ordered information to be given against persons known to be attached to the principles of the insurrection [3]."

" Theological censure attacked even works on politics, and on natural, civil, and international law. The consequence is, that those appointed to examine publications condemn and proscribe all works necessary for the diffusion of knowledge among the Spaniards. The books that have been published on mathematics, astronomy, natural philosophy, and several other branches of science connected with those, are not treated with more favour [4]."

" The Inquisition is perhaps the most active cause of that intellectual death that visited Spain at the close of the seventeenth century. With the illusory object of preserving the purity of the Catholic faith, that tribunal erected an impassable barrier between the Peninsula and the rest of Europe. It encouraged ignorance, and instituted a censorship even for works on jurisprudence, philosophy, and politics, and for novels that reflected on the avarice and rapacity of the priests, their dissolute conduct, and their hypocrisy. It commanded the professors of oriental languages to deliver into the hands of its commissaries the Hebrew and Greek Bibles in their possession..... Certain portions of the Imitation of Jesus Christ were interdicted, as well as the treatises of another

1. Laborde, vol. I, Introduction, pp. 13, 14. — 2. *Idem*, p. 115. — 3. Llorente, vol. IV, p. 99. — 4. *Idem*, p. 420.

author (Luis de Grenada), on prayer, on meditation, and on devotion [1]. "

"Many learned Spaniards, for want of august protection, were arrested (by order of the Holy Inquisition), and underwent much persecution; others were obliged to expatriate themselves. History became clouded with fables; and jurisprudence, far from being unravelled, grew daily more confused and obscure [2]. "

Lastly, if it be asked what has corrupted the morals both of the clergy and the laity of former times and of the present day, the answer is still : Catholic superstition! "There were at no other period, in the Peninsula, so many foundations of convents and chaplancies as during the seventeenth century..... There were in the diocese of Calahorra 18,000 chaplaincies, and in the archbishopric of Seville more than 14,000..... Notwithstanding all this devotion, morals were never so relaxed in Spain as during that period..... 'Lewdness,' said Cespedes, 'has so spread among us that although our morals have been depraved for a very long space of time, they were never corrupted by a greater inundation of vice than at the present time.' Cabrera affirmed that of the 18,000 priests of the bishopric of Calahorra, the greater number were vagabonds. In our own day a great many individuals who abandon themselves to all the excesses of superstition live in the imperturbable belief that they have full permission to continue their criminal practices, without fearing God or the devil, if they always wear on their necks the scapulary of the Virgin of Mount Carmel, and continually repeat a *Salve* to the blessed Mary, because they are persuaded that they shall not die without confession, that they shall go to purgatory, thence to issue on the Saturday following, with the assistance of the Mother of God, in order to ascend with her into Heaven [3]. "

Let us conclude with a few lines from M. de Lamennais: "A testimony too unanimous to leave room for doubt accuses a portion of the Spanish clergy of participating in the relaxation of morals, and thereby giving it a sort of shameful consecration. This practical corruption of Christian morality, fostered by ignorance of the principles of the Gospel, and connected with prejudices oddly superstitious, is the great evil of Catholicism in Spain. Every violation of precepts is tolerated there, and religious practices, badly understood, are made to cover all. The sort of compensation by which some consciences imagine that

1. Weiss, vol. II, pp. 319 to 321. — 2. Sempéré, vol. I, p. 135. — 3. Llorente, vol. II, p. 432.

certain acts of devotion may atone for certain crimes, the little horror they often feel for the greatest atrocities, the simple feeling of security with which they indulge in their vicious habits, or form resolutions of revenge, the strange motives of that security, the undefinable mixture of dissoluteness sometimes carried to the extreme with apparent piety, those souls having all hell within them, calm before the altar, those hands stained with blood joining in prayer without being agitated with the slightest tremor, all this fills one with astonishment and consternation; a false confidence in the protection of a certain saint, or Madonna, has utterly confused the notions of good and evil, and even the notion of repentance. All this most undeniably proves that the internal Christian feeling has been weakened to a deplorable degree. Anything similar is scarcely to be found elsewhere except in Italy, and in particular among the Abruzzi, where robbery excites no indignation, and is even practised devoutly." (*Affaires de Rome.*)

Such details tire in the end. Let us, then, take a general view of those morals which are the growth of Catholicism in Spain: "A remarkable trait," says M. Sismondi, "is the small degree of horror and remorse which the crime of murder occasions in Spain. In no nation are duels and assassinations more frequent. The guilty are exposed, it is true, to the vengeance of the relations, and to the pursuit of justice; but they are under the protection of religion and public opinion, they flee from convent to convent, and from church to church, and all the clergy declare, in their pulpits and confessionals, that it is a duty, abandoning the dead, to shelter the living from the hand of justice. The same religious prejudice exists in Italy: an assassin is always sure to be favoured, in the name of Christian charity, by all connected with the church, and by that portion of the people who are more immediately influenced by the priests; therefore, in no country have assassinations been more frequent than in Italy and in Spain, and when the guilty have performed the expiation imposed by their confessors, they think they have washed away all stain. Such expiations are rendered more easy from their being the source whence the priests derive their wealth. An endowment for masses in behalf of the deceased, an alms given to the church, in short, a pecuniary sacrifice in some measure proportioned to the fortune of the criminal, is always sufficient to wipe out the stain of blood; thus assassinations were more rare in all Pagan Greece than they are in a single village in Spain [1]."

1. Sismondi, vol. IV, pp. 6 to 8.

"Not only those whom passion urges to crime, in Spain, but those who exercise the most shameful and most guilty professions, courtesans, thieves, assassins, are sincere believers; a domestic and daily religious worship is oddly mixed up with their excesses; they continually introduce religion into their conversation, even the refined blasphemies, scarcely ever heard but in the Italian or Spanish language, are an additional evidence of their belief. It is a sort of hostility to supernatural powers, with which they feel themselves in constant relation, and which they delight in braving whenever they think they have cause to be revenged on them[1]."

"The two reigns of Philip III and Philip IV were always more degrading to the Spanish nation. The ministers sold all favours to the highest bidder, the nobility bowed beneath the ignominious yoke of favourites and upstarts, and the people were ruined by cruel extortions. The clergy, joining their despotic influence to that of the ministry, endeavoured, not to reform such odious abuses, but to stifle every voice that rose in complaint. Reflections, thoughts on religion, were punished as crimes; and, while under every other despotic government actions alone, or the outward manifestation of opinion, are amenable to the law, in Spain the monks pursued liberal sentiments even into the sanctuary of a man's conscience, in order to proscribe them[2]."

"We must not attribute to Calderon himself his ignorance of the manners of foreign countries. The circle of uninterdicted attainments was becoming daily more contracted; all books descriptive of foreign manners or foreign culture were prohibited under severe penalties, for there was not one, but in its very silence, was a bitter satire on the government and religion of Spain. How could the government allow the people to acquire a knowledge of the ancients, the very essence of whose existence was political liberty? how suffer them to form an acquaintance with the moderns, the foundation of whose prosperity and glory is religious liberty? Had the Spaniards been enlightened by such studies, would they have tolerated the Inquisition[3]?"

"The Spanish nation seemed endowed with everything: imagination, intelligence, profundity, constancy, elevation, courage; it might have surpassed all others: its religion has almost always rendered these brilliant qualities useless. Let us take care not to allow a mere name to lead us into the error of saying or be-

1. Sismondi, vol. IV, p. 34. — 2. *Idem*, pp. 50 to 53. — 3. *Idem*, pp. 128 to 130.

lieving that the religion of Spain and our own are the same[1]."

"In the former half of the eighteenth century the lives of the saints dramatised were published and represented: these were, for the most part, ridiculous and scandalous, yet they obtained, not only the approbation, but the praise, of the Inquisition[2]."

We will now, before we close the subject, give a summary from the pen of the secretary of the Inquisition himself; let our readers, after the perusal of it, ask themselves, if Catholicism has moralised Spain: "You shall see," says Llorente, "the Inquisitors, abusing the bad policy and the weakness of the Spanish ministry, treat with contempt the viceroys of Arragon, Catalonia, and Valencia, reduce them to the humiliating necessity of craving absolution for having defended ordinary jurisdiction and the royal prerogative, and refuse to absolve these pusillanimous men until they had submitted to the shame of a public penance. I will observe that they contributed to the decline of good taste in literature, from Philip II to Philip V, and almost extinguished the light of knowledge by their ignorance of the canon law, and by their blind deference to the advice of the monks, condemning, as Lutheran, propositions incontestably true.

"It will be acknowledged that the conduct of the Holy Office has been one of the causes that have decreased the population of Spain, by obliging innumerable families to quit the kingdom, by consigning to the flames more than 300,000 persons, and by arresting, out of a blind zeal for religion, the progress of the arts, of industry, and commerce, which would have constituted the glory and happiness of the nation, if free admission into the kingdom had been granted to the English, French, and Dutch[3]."

"The illegal use of the censorship, by means of which this tribunal could strike at will the first magistrates, such as the viceroys, and still more easily subjects of an inferior class, placed in its hands the formidable weapon with which it overthrew all who durst oppose its views; and, if that measure was insufficient, a warrant of arrest was not usually slow in coming to secure the victory in its hands[4]."

"The inquisitors arrogated a right of examining the affairs that concerned the police of the towns, and many others, such as taxes, contraband goods, commerce, the navy, arts and trades, the regulations of the corporations of mechanics, and the preservation of woods and forests. They pretended to a right of judging in all cases

1. Sismondi, p. 179. — 2. *Idem*, p. 221. — 3. Llorente, vol. I, Introduction, pp. 15 and 16. — 4. *Idem*, vol. II, p. 497.

relating to these, especially if among the individuals sued or implicated in such cases there was a single man in any way connected with the Inquisition, were he only a sweeper or some other low functionary, temporarily employed in the service of the tribunal... At the same time they would not allow a criminal, even a robber, to be arrested in an inquisitor's house, either in town or country[1]. "

Before we terminate this account of Spain, taken from documents of several years' standing, we wished to know whether, at the present moment, anything can be said in favour of this poor country. We have procured a work entitled : ***Spain in* 1850 ; *a Survey of her Most Recent Improvements.*** If, then, the above statements can be modified, they will be so by this work, the very title of which shows benevolence towards Spain. We have perused it, and it has only confirmed the opinion we had formed from the documents already quoted. In effect, the author of ***Spain in* 1850**, M. Maurice Block, affirms that the misfortunes of Spain do not proceed from the character of its inhabitants, but rather from the Inquisition. This is precisely what we have ourselves stated. He gives an account of a little progress recently made in agriculture, industry, and commerce. But, besides that it is impossible for a nation not to profit by the progress made in neighbouring countries, it must be remarked that here the progress is especially due to foreigners, to the English; this therefore only corroborates all that we have stated above.

Besides, the improvements described by M. Block belong much more to the future than to the present. At every page he is obliged to say : " There is hope, " " before long, " " probably; " and, as to ameliorations really accomplished, they are so trifling that in reality their insignificance only renders more conspicuous the gratuitous efforts of their apologist to extol them. Every success recorded by M. Block is surrounded by so many restrictions, that, after all deductions are made, what remains is scarcely perceptible. We will quote an example of this from that portion of the work which treats of primary instruction : we shall abridge our extract, not otherwise commenting upon it than by printing in italics the passages to which we are desirous of calling more particularly our reader's attention : " The civil war," says the author, " has greatly retarded the progress of public instruction. The necessity of reform was acknowledged at the very beginning of the century, and numerous attempts have since been made, *but without much suc-*

1. Llorente, vol. II, p. 501.

cess... Until a *rather recent* period, primary instruction in Spain was *in a sad state.* It was at the mercy of the municipalities, who did *little or nothing* for it... In 1825, general regulations were published; these regulations obliged masters to undergo examinations; they were certainly equal to any regulations of the like kind *that existed in the most advanced nations.* Unfortunately they were *scarcely executed at all.*

"In 1835, primary instruction *seemed* to have made some progress. But *what degree of confidence can be placed* in these figures? Without *exaggeration, what was the state* of these schools? This profusion of schools is but a *fallacious* appearance; the existence of a school is *often merely nominal.* Two-thirds of the professors *have not presented themselves for examination.* What can be expected from them but *the propagation of errors,* and so superficial an instruction that it serves only to waste a precious time in sterile occupations? The child who, on leaving school, knows *only how to connect with difficulty* the letters of the alphabet, or *laboriously to trace a few letters on paper,* derives little or no benefit from the instruction received; yet such is *all the knowledge acquired* by the generality of the poorer classes.

"The central school was inaugurated in April, 1838; but great efforts were required to obtain pupils for it.

"We have seen that in 1835 two-thirds of the pupils had no diplomas; at present, in 1848, the proportion is more favourable."

Then follow figures which show that these two-thirds have diminished to one-half. It will be readily admitted that when half the teachers are without diplomas, there is much room for improvement.

Here follows a table showing that there is in Spain only one pupil for twenty inhabitants! whereas, in Prussia, there is one for every six inhabitants, and in England one for every nine.

As to the schools, "there are 10,525 without *buildings appropriated to them.* Some are kept under the church *porch,* or in the *entrance-hall* of the town-house."

It will be admitted that if this state of things is a progress, the previous state must have been very backward indeed.

On beginning this account of Spain, we asked ourselves the following question: Does Catholicism elevate or degrade nations? We described the state of this country at the end of the fifteenth century, civilised by the Moors, enriched by America, luxuriant with prosperity. After this brilliant picture, we presented, without any intervening twilight, the thick gloom of the present:

beggarly, squalid, ignorant, immoral, criminal Spain; and, struck with the contrast, we inquired the cause of it. Many voices have replied: The cause is Catholicism and its offspring, Tyranny and the Inquisition. It is not we that have said it; it is M. Llorente, secretary to the Inquisition; Count de Laborde, aide-de-camp at the French court, attached to the Court of Spain; M. de Sismondi, a learned man, serious, moderate, and universally respected; M. Weiss, professor at the College of France; M. R. Saint-Hilaire, professor of the Sorbonne; lastly, M. de Lamennais, then an *abbé*. All these distinguished men have been unanimous; all have accused Catholicism. Have they all been deceived? We leave our readers to answer the question; for ourselves, to complete our task, after having seen what a nation under the guidance of Catholicism has become in the space of three centuries, we shall proceed to examine what, during the same period, another nation has become under the inspiration of Protestantism. We have taken a survey of Spain; let us now turn to England.

ENGLAND

IN THE 16th AND 19th CENTURIES.

We have seen what Catholic Spain has become, in the course of the last three centuries; let us now examine what transformation Protestant England has undergone in the same lapse of time. If the two nations march at the same pace on the road to progress, notwithstanding the different impulsions which each should receive on account of the dissimilarity in their respective faiths, it will be natural to conclude that this faith plays an inactive part in their civilisation; but if, on the contrary, the two nations take opposite courses; if one advances while the other retrogrades, we shall have double reason for supposing that their religions have severally prepared the elevation of the one, and the decline of the other.

In the first place, let us proceed with England as we did with Spain; and, in order to measure the distance we have to travel over, let us fix the point from which we start. Let us see what the state of England was at the time of the Reformation.

While Spain has seen her population diminish to such a degree, that we have been enabled to furnish a long list of cities that have lost ten-elevenths of their inhabitants, what change has been wrought in the population of Great Britain? During the reign of Elizabeth, "in 1570, it amounted to five millions; in 1830, it rose to 15 millions[1]."

Thus, while Spain has lost 10 men out of 11, in England there

1. De Jonnès, vol. I, pp. 51 and 52.

have been 3 births for 1 death. The relative proportion between the two countries is one to thirty!

If this increase was the result of immigration, it would still be a sign of prosperity, for strangers do not come in search of misery; but we learn from the same author, that since that period mortality in England has diminished by two-fifths, so that the augmentation of the population is evidently the result of an amelioration in their moral and physical condition; and, as M. de Jonnès remarks: "Every individual in England has now twice as much chance of arriving at old age as he had fifty years ago. This is not an increase of population like that which formerly took place in Ireland, where a family saw the number of its members doubled or tripled, without enlarging their habitation; for while under Henry VIII the number of houses in England was estimated at 520,000, at present they amount to 2,463,820." The population is only treble what it was, but the habitations have increased five-fold, which is another indication of prosperity, in the opinion of M. de Jonnès, who considers a small number of persons inhabiting the same dwelling as a proof of a high degree of civilisation; and who adds, "that, in this respect, England is more advanced than the other nations of Europe[1]."

Let us now see what were the elements of this population of England, at that time Roman Catholic.

First, *The Clergy.*—In 1608, there existed in England, 557 large estates in land; 137 of which (*one-fourth*), were religious establishments. Here M. de Jonnès gives an account of the prodigality of the archbishops and bishops of that time, and then adds: "The landed property, the revenues of which defrayed this prodigious luxury, comprised, in 1401, *one-third* of the surface of the kingdom, as we learn from the remonstrances of the Commons, on this subject, addressed to king Henry VIII. Hallam even proves, from other authorities, that this property extended to one-half the kingdom[2]."

If the Catholic clergy had to decide the question, they would probably say, those were the good old times. But we, who form part of the mass of the nation, think it far preferable that the clergy should be less rich, and thereby less exposed to temptation, and that the soil should belong to those who cultivate it, and that wealth should be the reward of labour. We prefer the state of things described by M. de Jonnes: "In 1536, at the time of the

1. De Jonnès vol. I, p. 92. — 2. *idem*, pp. 111 and 112.

Reformation, the regular clergy were composed of 50,000 monks and nuns, who inhabited 508 convents and monasteries, of which the revenues amounted to 752,800 *l.*, making more than 3,760,000 fr. in these days. The number of establishments suppressed, according to Speed, is as follows :

22 Archbishoprics or Bishoprics.	8,803 Benefices.
11 Deaneries.	605 Monasteries.
60 Archeaconries.	2,374 Chapels.
394 Cathedrals.	

" The revenues of these establishments were computed at 1,690,520 *l.*, worth five times as much as now, owing to the difference of prices. These revenues were considerably augmented by alms and gifts. Fish calculated, that, in 1527, England contained 520,000 houses, which gave to each monk one shilling-and-eightpence a year. It appears that there were then above 65,000 ecclesiastics; which gives a priest or monk for every 40 inhabitants, as in Italy in 1788[1]. "

At present there is, " in the Church of England, one minister for 333 persons; amongst the Dissenters 1 for 380. " On an average, 1 minister for 360 Protestants. Nine times fewer ecclesiastics than in the time of the Roman Catholics.

It is usual to reproach the Established Church with the immense revenues of her dignitaries. But, without extenuating the fault, we may retort it with double force on Catholicism. These abuses are an inheritance of the past; and, if they have left traces in England, the reason is that Romish usages had taken such deep root that it has not been possible, even in three centuries, to extirpate them completely. But it must be remarked that now, instead of 1 ecclesiastic for 40 persons, as in papish times, Protestant England has, on an average, including the Dissenters, only 1 minister for 360 laymen, and that the wealth of the clergy of the Established Church, although still too extensive, only amounts to one-sixteenth, not to a half of the landed property. If, now, we reckon all these different data together, the increase of the population, the reduction in the number of ecclesiastics, and the diminution of their wealth, we shall find, on the whole, an immense difference; with regard to the nation on one hand, and on the other to the clergy. The nation, with a population three times more numerous, has to contribute eight times less; this contribution is, in consequence, only the twenty-fourth part of what had been paid before: " As to the

1. De Jonnès, vol. I, pp. 112 and 113.

clergy, the number of ecclesiastics having been diminished by one-ninth, and their wealth by one-eighth, the share of each would be about the same, if the price of things had not increased five-fold [1], which has reduced the average revenue to a fifth of what it was formerly."

In the sixteenth century the nobility rivalled the clergy in riches and powers; for, according to the same author, they possessed the *other half* of the landed property. This is easily understood, at a period when the people were nothing. Villenage had been legally abolished by prescription towards the end of the fifteenth century, but, in fact, some remains of it were still in existence in the following one, since Elizabeth then emancipated the rest of her slaves. The barons, who, under the Norman dynasty, were the sole great landed proprietors, numbered about 700. In order to give us an idea of this powerful aristocracy, M. de Jonnès informs us that: "Count Mortagne had 963 manors; Alain, 422; Robert Mowbray, 280, etc.; and that 557 great proprietors possessed together 515 square leagues.

"In these times of public misery," adds our author, "the riches of these barons were immense. The Earl of Lancaster spent 109,600*l*. annually. The lands of the nobles comprised 3,540 square leagues.

"In 1401, three centuries later, although the nobles were reduced to one-half of their number, they reckoned still 28,575 members [2]."

Now let us transport ourselves at once to the end of the seventeenth century, when the Reformation had already had time to exert its influence, and we shall find that the nobility is no longer diminished only by one-half in three centuries, but by nine-tenths in a single one; and at the beginning of the nineteenth century, of the tenth part that remained, there existed little more than a third. In comparing these two extreme points, we shall find the proportion between the number of the nobles before the Reformation and their number at the present time as thirty to one.

We have not to decide whether the existing aristocracy, and the Established Church of the present day, are a benefit to England; but to compare the present with the past. And it is precisely those who complain of these remains of power being left in the hands of the nobles and the clergy who will be most easily convinced how deplorable was the state of things in former times.

We must anticipate an objection. These changes may be con-

1. De Jonnès, vol. I, p. 113. — 2. *Idem*, p. 114 etc.

sidered as the result of many causes having no connection with the Reformation: but then we may ask why the same results have not been obtained in the Catholic nations of Europe, and especially in Spain, where the nobles, if not rich, are at least numerous, and where they continue to depress the people by their arrogance and indolence as much as in former times?

Now let us examine what was the state of the people next to this clergy and nobility, who divided between them all the wealth of the kingdom? "In 1688, more than a third of the population was reduced to indigence;" and remark, that this state of things was already an amelioration. But even taking this as our point of departure, let any one compare it with the beginning of this century :

"In 1803, this third is reduced to a ninth." Thus, more than a quarter of the nation, in passing from Catholicism to the Reformed faith, passed at the same time from poverty to competence; we may therefore naturally suppose that the comforts of the other three-fourths had increased in a still greater proportion, and precisely at the time when Spain was becoming overrun with mendicants.

The following figures afford another proof of the amelioration of the English people since the Reformation :

"In 1690, the gross product of agriculture amounted to 8,275,000*l.*
In 1832, to . . . . 73,866,000*l.*"

If this increase in the productions of agriculture, at present nine times greater still, was the result of the cultivation of waste land, that of itself would be a great benefit; but it has its source in causes bearing more directly on our subject : "Cultivation," says M. de Jonnès, "has not made much progress in extent; the present superiority is entirely owing to the improvements introduced in the mode of farming, which have obtained an immense increase in crops raised from the same extent of land [1]."

Moreover, the food of the people has not only improved in quantity, but in quality: "In 1760, the quantity of wheat consumed by each person in England was less than half what it is now; or rather the people consumed an inferior sort of bread, and not wheaten bread. At present, the progress of wealth and civilisation has nearly excluded the use of any other grain as food but wheat [2]."

"At the period of the fall of the Stuarts, the consumption of meat was 74 pounds for every person.

1. De Jonnès, vol. 1, pp. 198, 199. — 2. *Idem*, p. 201.

"In 1801, the consumption had risen to 160 pounds and a half. Thirty years later the augmentation was scarcely perceptible in the consumption of each individual, but very considerable in the number of animals killed, since the population had increased by one-half[1]."

Here is another means of judging, at a single glance, of the difference between the past and the present, with regard to the distribution of wealth in England. Formerly the nobility and clergy possessed nearly the whole; now the annual revenue is divided as follows:

"Upper classes...............................	1/5th
Professions....................................	1/5th
Farmers..	1/4th
Tradespeople...................................	1/8th and 1/2
Working classes................................	1/3d and 1/2
Infirm...	1/30th[2]."

That is to say, four-fifths of the annual revenue have passed out of the hands of the upper classes into those of the people, who left Catholicism for the Reformation.

In order to judge of the steps that England has taken in advance, while Spain has been constantly retrograding, we must say a few words of their respective colonies.

Here the advantage is easily ascertained. In the 16th century, England had not a single colony beyond seas: Spain on the contrary was in possession of half the New World. At present we have only to reverse the terms in order to arrive at the truth. Spain in three centuries has lost nearly all; and England, after having planted a colony in America, which now free, enriches and does honour to the mother country, has acquired the richest and most extensive possessions in India. We shall not content ourselves with general assertions, but to obtain more credit we will borrow the words of a learned author disinterested in the question: "The Spanish empire extended itself by degrees in the New World, and comprised during more than three centuries the following countries: Saint-Domingo, Cuba, Porto-Rico, Mexico, Guatemala, Columbia, Venezuela, Rio-de-la-Plata, Peru, Chili, Trinidad, Florida, Louisiana, the Canary Isles, the Philippines, and her penal settlements in Africa; forming together an extent of 471,053 square leagues, with a population of 19,743,000 inhabitants.

"Of this empire, twice as vast as that of Rome, all that remains

1. De Jonnès, vol. I, pp. 217 to 220. — 2. *Idem*, p. 151.

to Spain is Cuba and Porto-Rico, the Canaries and the Philippines; which form an extent of 19,000 square leagues, with 3,858,000 inhabitants."

Spain has thus lost twenty-three parts out of twenty-four of her colonies. Now, let us see what has happened in this respect in the British Empire during the same space of time:

"England directed her ambition towards Hindostan, and laboured unceasingly to establish her rule there. By dint of skill, good fortune, and perseverance, she has succeeded in founding in Asia an empire very differently governed and defended from that of the ancient Spanish colonies.

"This empire, added to the other British possessions in the two worlds, forms an immense empire. We shall estimate its extent, population, and commerce in the following table:

	Number of establishments.	Extent. — Square leagues.	Populations. — Inhabitants.	Total Commerce.
				l.
Europe	14	234	400,000	4,000,000
Africa	9	528	216,000	2,240,000
Asia	9	62,372	90,526,000	9,760,000
America	27	69,700	1,966,000	18,320,000
Australia	5	40	77,000	1,600,000
	64	132,904	93,185,000	35,920,000[1]"

Thus, whilst Spain has lost twenty-three parts out of twenty-four of her colonies, England has conquered a vast territory, well-governed and well-defended, on which she did not possess a foot of land at the period from which our comparison begins; and which at the same time, while Spain has lost 20 millions of subjects, England has conquered 93 millions, and her commerce with her colonies amounts at present to 40,000,000*l*!

We will add a few words on finance, navigation, and education:

Without gold or silver mines, England possessed, in 1836, 80 millions of coined money; five times as much as Spain ever had, even when the mines of the New World were at her disposal. And if we compare the public wealth of Great Britain at the end of the seventeenth century with that of the present time, we shall find that in a century and a half it has more than doubled. Danevant reckons it, in 1698, at 41,360,000*l*., two-fifths of its present amount.

1. De Jonnès, vol. II, pp. 96 to 99.

" As to navigation, its tonnage amounts in these days to twenty-five times as much as under the Stuarts[1]. "

A single fact is sufficient to give an idea of the progress of elementary instruction. There was in England :

In 1734, 1 scholar for every 450 inhabitants.
In 1833, there was 1 in 5 [2].

It is true that the last report comprises the children of Sunday schools, who have in many cases been reckoned already in the day schools. But, even if we suppose this to be the case with all, there would still remain 1 scholar in 10 inhabitants: that is to say, forty-five times more pupils than in the preceding century!

We shall now sum up what precedes, and fix with accuracy the point from which we start. Before the Reformation, the clergy and nobility, with the monarch, were everything in England; and the people, recently emancipated, little or nothing. At that time, agriculture left a third of the population in indigence; no commerce, no manufactures, the finances at a low ebb, and lastly, scarcely two persons out of a hundred knowing how to read. The Reformation of the sixteenth century burst forth; its principles spread abroad, and produced the results that we are now going to examine.

We have seen what was the state of England before the sixteenth century; let us see what it is now. Every one will understand that we cannot undertake to follow her, step by step, during the three hundred years that separate these two periods; for the influence of Catholicism did not cease to be felt from the very moment when communications with the Pope were interrupted, nor could Protestantism produce all its fruits on the day the Reformation was proclaimed. The more distant, then, the two periods are from each other at which we shall examine the state of England, the more certain we shall be to discern in the former period the unmixed fruits of Catholicism, and in the latter the pure effects of the Reformation. However, if we cannot follow the development of the tree in all its stages, let us examine with care what was the seed first deposited in the earth, that we may know to what we should attribute the good or bad fruit that will present itself to our view : " The sixteenth and seventeenth centuries," says M. Guizot, " have produced admirable results; rights have been established, and new manners have been created; and they have not only acted powerfully upon all our social relations, but upon souls... There is no country perhaps in which the principles of religion have possessed,

1. De Jonnès, vol. II, p. 85. — 2. *Idem*, pp. 319 and 324.

and still exercise, greater power than in England; but above all they are practical, and influence powerfully the conduct, happiness, and sentiments of individuals [1]. English civilisation has been particularly directed towards the improvement of society; the amelioration of the external and public relations of men, and not only of his material but his moral existence; to the introduction of more justice into society, as well as more comfort; and to the development of his rights as well as happiness [2].

M. Pichot expresses the same idea: "Of the democratical fermentation of the Reformation, and the guarantees given to the Established Church by the House of Brunswick, the result has been a more abundant circulation of liberal ideas in England than elsewhere, in religion as well as in politics [3]." "There, all the different creeds are full of life [4]."

M. Simon goes still farther: not only he affirms that civilisation in England is the daughter of religion, but he specifies what this religion is, and he contrasts it with that of the fourteenth century in the same nation, and with that of France in our days: "I read," he says, "in an old English chronicle that in the 14th century levity of conduct was one of the great faults of the young girls, who behaved very indecorously at church, where the greatest indecencies were committed. The sanctuary seemed to be transformed into a place for gossiping and amusement: the men came there accompanied with their hounds, and with their falcons on their wrists, to talk of their affairs, make assignations, and display their fine clothes. In the present time, the thousand sects that divide England, from a natural desire of proselytism, have preserved religious fervour by keeping watch over each other. In England, you may be of any religion you please, but you must have a religion, or you would be expelled from society. In France, on the contrary, the Catholic priests would prefer your having no religion, to your being of a different one from theirs. If we have no religion, they hope that we shall come into the bosom of the Church; if, on the contrary, we adopt with fervour some other religious creed, they have less hope (and in my opinion with reason) of converting us [5]."

But this first cause has not ceased to operate. We have seen the source; the stream still continues to flow, and spreads fertility over the field we are about to explore. We shall content ourselves with the testimony of a witness, who cannot be suspected of partiality: "Religion," says M. d'Haussez, "has always a share in the public acts

1. Guizot, vol. I, p. 12. — 2. *Idem*, p. 11. — 3. Pichot, vol. II. p. 38. — 4. *Idem*, p. 42. — 5. Simon, vol. I, pp. 256, 257.

of the English; this necessity is so universally recognised, that if a town or a new quarter is to be built, there is always a place reserved for a church. It is even by this edifice that they begin. It may be objected that the building of the church is a matter of speculation; it may be so, but, if the speculation is productive, we must conclude that the church is frequented by a great number of the faithful: therefore, a religious spirit predominates England. No one on coming out of church complains of the length of the service, and certainly for indifferent people there is no compensation to be found in the trivial eloquence of the orator. Could this be the case if religious sentiments were not firmly rooted in the national mind? A country where religion is never turned into ridicule, where the dogmas of this religion are never discussed but with respect, where it takes part in all the acts of government and administration, as well as in domestic habits: such a country must be religious [1]."

"Now," says M. Léon Faucher, "let any one examine what England has gained in a century and a half in population, wealth, and territory, and declare whether, in the history of the world, without excepting the conquests of Alexander, or those of the Romans, there is an example of such an aggrandisement. England now claims a preponderating influence in Europe, and exclusive possession or dominion in the rest of the world [2]."

But, leaving these general considerations, let us enter into details, which are more easily understood, and traverse the country after the manner of a traveller, visiting towns and fields, houses, manufactories, and marts:

"The first impression produced by England," says M. Custine, "is extremely agreeable. The perfect cleanliness, the attention shown to little things, the elegance of household arrangements, proclaim a prudent and economical people, attached to the spot they inhabit [3]." "The aspect of the interior of the country is cheerful from its perfect cultivation and freshness. The fields carefully tilled, surrounded by hedges and plantations of trees kept in neat order, resemble gardens. It is vain to look for a peasant in the reaper, labourer, or ploughman, or for a peasant girl in the gleaner and haymaker; you would imagine they were all gentlemen and ladies. The villages, built with taste and regularity, are clean, pretty, and kept in good order. The soil being fertile in the greater part of the counties, there is an abundance of all kinds of rural productions, land admirably cultivated, and those magnificent macadamised roads, on

1. D'Haussez, pp. 281, 274. — 2. Léon Faucher, vol. II, p. 394. — 3. Custine, vol. II, pp. 4, 5.

which one travels never less, and often more, than three leagues an hour[1]. Imagine roads, not so broad as our's, not paved, or ornamented with straight rows of trees, but gently winding amidst a succession of wooded hills, cultivated valleys, and green pastures; roads without ruts, and sanded like the alleys of a garden, with a footway running along the side. Add to this perpetual verdure cottages, in which the beautiful is combined with the useful, and all together will give but a faint idea of the mode of travelling in this country, and of the rich aspect that it presents[2]."

"There is a difference (between England and France) in the roads and in the carriages which run on them: there everything is excellent, beautiful, admirably neat, convenient, and finished. One cannot help acknowledging in all an immense superiority over what exists of the kind anywhere else[3]." "At the stages you never hear the swearing of the grooms, and the whip of the coachman is rather a part of his costume than an instrument of correction. In this country, where everything is so perfectly regulated, and every one knows so well how to fulfil the duties of his station, even the horses accomplish their tasks better than those of other countries, and that without the necessity of brutal correction. You may travel from one end of England to the other without ever hearing the sound of the whip or the cries of the coachman, which in France strike so disagreeably the ears of travellers.

"We ought to mention the inns, among the wonders of English civilisation; they are magnificent in many towns, excellent and well supplied in the smallest villages. On arriving, travellers are received by the innkeeper, whose neat dress testifies his respect for strangers. What a traveller prizes most in England is the facility with which he can see everything; thanks to the excellence of the means of communication, he can leave the highway without any fear of being stopped by the bad state of cross-roads[4]."

"The appearance of the country-houses in the counties is as varied as the fortunes of their owners, and the difference in their rank. Here, are seen gardens and fields, running streams and lakes, that present the most delightful aspects; there, canals for agricultural purposes; openings made in avenues to admit the view of a village with its gothic church tower; farm-houses, with their numerous domestic animals; and the humble and picturesque lodge of the gamekeeper lost in the forest, and lending a charm to the landscape. The hand of man, clearing and pruning, is everywhere

1. Solitaire, vol. II, p. 493, 494. — 2. Montuli, pp. 17, 19. — 3. D'Haussez, p. 2. — 4. Solitaire, vol. II, pp. 30 to 32.

visible, but the venerable clumps of trees are generally spared; they stand in the middle of fields, and afford shelter under their immense branches to sheep, deer, fat cattle, young colts, celebrated perhaps for their breed, feeding in picturesque groups in the shade of the foliage. The grass is carefully cultivated by a peculiar process, and one is agreeably surprised at seeing spaces several acres in extent devoted to the cultivation of flowers. On a grass-plot of a rich green, studded with beautiful shrubs, are flower-beds cut into different elegant shapes and full of choice flowers, which vary this delightful picture by their sylvan shapes and the rustic simplicity of their arrangement[1]. "

" You need only enter the cottage of an English peasant, and compare it with the dwellings of the greater number of our small farmers, to see the difference in the general condition of the two populations. Although the French peasant is for the most part a landholder, thus adding a little rent and a certain amount of profit to his wages, he does not in general live so well as the English peasant; he is not so well clothed, lodged, or fed; he eats more bread, but this bread is generally made of rye, buck wheat, or even chesnuts; whereas, the bread of the English peasant is made wholly of wheat. The French peasant never eats meat, and the English peasant does [2]." " In England, more than elsewhere, the country is worthy of God : if it has not everywhere a grand appearance, every field has its peculiar beauty and charm [3]. This small kingdom, traversed by so many roads, canals, and railroads, may be compared to a laurel-leaf, with its innumerable veins. Men, ideas, and newspapers circulate throughout with a rapidity really prodigious. English society is a vast assembly, a great circle, with the consciousness of its existence as a collective body [4]. "

After having taken a view of the country, let us examine several towns, beginning by the metropolis : " On reading the history of London, we see how much has been done for its salubrity. The width of the streets and footways, the drains, the beauty of the parks and squares, the flourishing gardens, the abundance of water, the commodiousness of the dwellings, and the decency and cleanliness of the whole, have rendered London the healthiest city in the world, notwithstanding the humidity of its soil and its inclement sky [5]. In London, the people enjoy liberty as a birthright : there, every one remains in his own sphere, quietly, without compulsion, and with habitual dignity. Much may be learned in that

1. Solitaire, vol. II, p. 500. — 2. *Revue Britannique*, 1853, 1st March, p. 928. — 3. Pichot, vol. I, p. 32. — 4. *Idem*, p. 113. — 5. Bureaud, vol. I, p. 22.

city in industry, commerce, arts, sciences, and even in medicine, for all branches of knowledge have a connection. The English are in advance of all other people, because they are the boldest, the most persevering, and the most enterprising experimenters of the human race [1]."

"On witnessing the grandeur and opulence of London, a foreigner wonders how this metropolis has arrived at such a high degree of splendour. On a survey of its wide streets, its squares, its parks, with the order, cleanliness, and comfort which everywhere reign, we cannot imagine that this city was long the seat of the plague [2]."

"At first sight, a stranger is struck with admiration at the power of man; afterwards, he feels overwhelmed by the grandeur of all around him, and humiliated by a sense of his own littleness. Look at those innumerable vessels, of every size and description, that cover the river for leagues, and reduce it to the size of a canal; the grandeur of the bridges, which appear to have been constructed by giants in order to unite the shores of two worlds. But it is particularly at night that London should be seen. Beheld in the magical light of millions of lamps, fed by gas, London is dazzling! The wide streets, which appear interminable; the shops, where streams of light adorn with a thousand hues master-pieces of human art and industry, produce a bewildering effect: while in the day the beauty of the footways, the number and elegance of the squares, the immense extent of the parks, with their graceful curves, the beauty of the trees, the multitude of splendid carriages drawn by superb horses, which crowd the drives, all these magnificent realities have a magical effect which dazzles one's reason [3]."

"In the wealth, extent, and activity of her commerce, by sea and land, London has not, and never had, a rival in the universe: it is really marvellous that we endeavour to measure its importance, by comparing this city, not only to the greatest commercial marts of the world, but even to the whole of the states most celebrated for their commercial activity [4]."

"The vast basins, known by the name of Docks, where, classed according to their destination, are to be seen the trading vessels of the whole universe, with their cargoes, prove what may be done by the combined efforts of genius and wealth: nothing is more calculated to give a just idea of the height which the commercial

1. Bureaud, vol. I, p. 29. — 2. *Idem*, p. 33. — 3. Tristan, pp. 2 and 3. — 4. Balbi, p. 491.

enterprise of England has attained [1]. The environs of London at every step show marks of incontestable prosperity. The number and style of the country-houses, the splendour and extent of the villages, the activity of the circulation, answer the expectations raised by the grandeur of the capital [2].

" In London, the most scrupulous cleanliness reigns everywhere. The pains bestowed on the salubrity of the town are so much the more worthy of praise, that the sight is not offended, as in our country, by the details of these sanitary operations. One might imagine that the city was superintended by invisible Œdiles [3]. "

" On the whole, London is an immense metropolis, worthy of being seen. It is the capital of a mighty empire; the first commercial city in the universe; the centre of activity, labour, and riches: the Ocean is covered with her ships, and her merchants are the most intelligent in the world. The treasures of the two worlds are poured into her bosom. It is for her that China cultivates her tea; America her cotton-plant and sugar-cane; and Europe the whole of her productions. She spreads over the world these raw materials brought to perfection by her labour. The aspect of London is therefore essentially industrial and commercial; she is the colossus of commerce, and the Queen of the Ocean [4]. "

London has been accused of tolerating evils which are, however, common to all capitals. The multitude of her poor, her thieves, and prostitutes, has been deplored. But, besides that these three classes exist in a fearful proportion in cities where the population is far from amounting to two millions, it must be observed that their presence in London is easily accounted for by the commercial, industrial, and maritime character of this city. We do not attach any weight to the fact that there are numbers of foreigners here, as the same observation might be made with regard to Paris; but we cannot refrain from noticing a class of persons who, although not strangers to the British Isles, are however to England itself, and who in particular do not belong to the religious creed which we have now to consider: we mean those numerous Irish Catholics, who, bringing into London a fearful mass of vice of all descriptions, give a false idea of the state of the English and Protestant majority.

It is a fact, that the Irish Catholic population in London is not equally distributed in all classes of society; since it is nearly exclusively confined to the manufactories, the streets, the brothels, and the prisons.

1. D'Haussez, p. 10. — 2. *Idem*, p. 14. — 3. *Idem*, p. 81. — 4. Dory, pp. 17, 18.

A parliamentary report, quoted by the ***Revue Britannique*** [1], states that ***a third*** of the beggars in London are Irish. Speaking of the infamous haunts, into which the police has not yet dared to penetrate, M. Léon Faucher gives them the name of ***Little Ireland.*** As to the prostitutes, the ***Revue Britannique*** affirms, in the same page, that the fourth part consist of Irishwomen [2]. "

This superabundance of Irish occurs also in the great manufacturing districts of the other counties of England: "Thus, in Lancashire, while the number of Scotch, although they are near neighbours, only amounts to 21,000, there are 105,000 Irish, crowded together, notwithstanding they are forced to cross the sea in order to arrive there. In Manchester and Liverpool, the Irish Catholics are always in a majority in the most immoral and miserable quarters of these cities. Some years ago, the most wretched part of the population of Manchester consisted of Irish. Their dwellings were the dirtiest and most unhealthy, and their children the most neglected. It was in their cellars that spirits of the worst kind were fraudulently distilled; and misery, fever, drunkenness, debauchery, and theft perpetually prevailed there. These cellars were the favourite resort of vagabonds and criminals; and not a day passed but some fray arose, or some crime left its stain of blood in these horrible places [3]."

The same author affords unconsciously, as striking proof of the truth of our assertion, that Catholic Ireland throws a mass of corruption among the Protestants of London, and thus gives a false idea of the entire population, which is considered as Protestant. He is speaking of a quarter called ***Whitechapel***, one of the most miserable in the capital. According to M. Léon Faucher, it is inhabited by three different classes: 1st, the Jews; 2dly, the Irish; and 3dly, by the descendants of the French Protestant refugees. Setting aside the Jews, who are here out of the question, there remain the Irish Catholics and the French Protestants, in presence of each other. M. Léon Faucher has just given the most gloomy description of this quarter. But he makes an exception; in favour of whom? Precisely in favour of these Protestants! He says: "This colony is composed of nearly 150,000 souls, formed by the successive arrivals of French artisans after the revocation of the Edict of Nantes; afterwards by Irish labourers; and, lastly, by the Jews. The descendants of the French

1. *Revue Britannique*, 1845, vol. II, p. 181. — 2. M. Léon Faucher thus speaks of them: "The number of prostitutes is not necessarily a proof of the immorality of a people. The populations of Southern Europe, who have few or no prostitutes, are precisely those who are notorious for the dissoluteness of their manners. The extent of prostitution is in proportion to the greatness of the luxury and the depth of misery. All things considered, prostitution must be more common in London than Paris, because there are fewer means in that city of procuring employment." (Vol. I, p. 78.) — 3. Léon Faucher, vol. I, p. 326.

artisans are a more cultivated race, who show great dislike for the Irish, an ignorant and drunken set, who in their turn regard with profound contempt, from religious motives, the children of Israel. It is these naturalised Frenchmen that have taught the English to weave silk, etc. These weavers may be called the *moral* aristocracy of the place. Their probity has become proverbial, and presents a favourable contrast to the degradation of their neighbours, although the love of spirituous liquors has made some inroads among them. They have the tastes which belong to intelligent beings; they are great readers of newspapers, cultivate flowers, and meet together in the evenings in clubs, where they receive lessons of arithmetic, geography, history, and drawing[1]."

In order to give an exact idea of the share that belongs to the Irish in the corruption of London, we cannot do better than quote an author who has studied them on the spot: "It is not without a sentiment of fear that a visitor penetrates into the narrow and dark lane called Bainbridge (the Irish quarter in London). Before he has advanced ten steps, he is almost suffocated by the mephitic odour, and finds the lane so filled with coal that it is impracticable. Turning to the right, I entered another muddy lane, full of holes filled with soap-suds, dish-water, and worse still. I was obliged to rouse all my courage in order to overcome my disgust and continue my walk through all this filth and mire. In St Giles's, one feels suffocated by the smells; there is neither air to breathe, nor sufficient light to see one's way. This wretched population wash their rags themselves, and hang them upon cords stretched across the lanes, and thus completely intercept all air and sunshine. The filth under one's feet sends forth a poisonous stench, and the rags overhead are dripping with filth. The wildest dreams of imagination cannot equal the horror of this frightful reality. When I had arrived at the end of the street, which was not very long, I found my resolution fail. My physical strength is far inferior to my moral courage; I felt a sickness, and acute pains shot through my temples. I hesitated whether I should pursue my way through the Irish quarter, when I recollected on a sudden that I was in the midst of my fellow creatures, of my brethren, who had been suffering in silence for ages the agony which had nearly overcome my weakness, although I had not borne it more than ten minutes. I conquered my repugnance, and examined minutely this mass of suffering. It was then that an undefinable feeling of compassion

1. Léon Faucher, vol. I, pp. 12 and 13.

filled my heart, and at the same time a gloomy sentiment of terror took possession of my mind.

"Imagine men, women, and children walking barefoot in this horrible filth; some leaning against the walls for want of seats, others crouched on the ground, and children rolling in the mud, like swine. It is impossible, without witnessing it, to imagine such hideous misery, such profound debasement, such complete degradation in human beings? There I beheld children completely naked, young girls, women with children at the breast barefoot, and with nothing on but a chemise in tatters, showing nearly the whole of their naked bodies, old men squatting in a little filthy straw, and young men covered with rags. The interior and exterior of these miserable hovels correspond with the tattered garments of the inhabitants. The greater part of these dwellings have no windows, and the doors no fastenings; they are rarely paved, and all they contain is an old clumsy oaken table, a wooden bench, some pewter ladles; a hole, in which father, mother, sons, daughters, and friends sleep all together : such are the comforts of the Irish quarter. All this is horrible; and yet it is trifling in comparison with the expression of their countenances. All are frightfully thin, wan, unhealthy, and covered with sores on their faces, necks, and hands. Their skins are so dirty, and their hair so matted, that they look like negroes. Their hollow eyes reveal a stupid ferocity; but if you look sternly at these wretched beings, they assume a cringing, supplicating air. I recognised here the same kind of expression that I had remarked in the prisons. It must be a joyful day for them when they enter Cold-Bath Fields. At least, in that prison, they have clean linen, comfortable clothing, clean beds, and pure air! How do this population gain their livelihood? By prostitution and theft. As soon as the boys are nine or ten years old, they are sent to steal; at eleven or twelve years of age, the girls are sold to houses of ill-fame. All, men and women, make a trade of thieving : the old people beg. If I had seen this quarter before I visited Newgate, I should have felt no surprise on being informed that this prison receives fifty or sixty children every month, and as many women of the town [1]."

If we were to sum up all that has been said on the question of the influence of foreigners in London, we might say that the evil, which is an exception, is caused by Catholicism; while the good, which is the rule, proceeds from Protestantism. But we will not form our

1. Tristan, pp. 214 to 217.

opinion of all the towns from a survey of the capital; we are the less inclined to do so that the real people exist mostly out of the metropolis. Let us then take a cursory view of some other cities.

"The persevering industry of the inhabitants of Lancashire has made of this country, the soil of which is sterile, the climate unfavourable, and the winds cold, one of the most prosperous in Great Britain. The land being too spungy, rotted the seed; they dug it up to give it air, and by so doing discovered the rich coal mines which now supply all the neighbouring manufactories. The navigation of the rivers was often impeded by the moving sands, which exist all along their beds; quagmires rendered the roads impracticable during eight months of the year; the inhabitants of Lancashire were the first to substitute canals for these tiresome modes of communication; as later they were the first to adopt the use of railroads. There is not a single useful improvement or discovery that has not been immediately put into pratice, or had its origin, in Lancashire [1]."

"In 1825, commercial enterprise had become so active in England, the manufactories being so numerous, the slow mode of communication by canals ill satisfied the feverish impatience of speculation, and on all sides endeavours were made to find a remedy for this radical defect. Fifteen hours to go from Liverpool to Manchester appeared as monstrous to the merchants of the present day as the eleven days which, in 1720, tried the patience of their forefathers. It was then proposed to apply to outward circulation the system of rails that was used in the mines. In a few months, shares to the amount of 400,000*l.* were taken; the road was opened in 1828, and the distance which divides Liverpool from Manchester was travelled over, by goods, in two hours and a half, and by passengers in one hour and twenty minutes! What rejoicing! what a triumph! what success for this busy population who reckon their existence by seconds, and who are constantly repeating: 'Time is money!' The result of this enterprise produced during the first year 40,000*l.* profit, and on the 31st of December this sum had increased in two years to 85,529*l.* And yet how many difficulties had to be conquered! Valleys to be filled up, hills to be cut through, tunnels to be dug under the towns. All these obstacles were overcome, and in less than four years 800,000*l.* were absorbed in this gigantic enterprise. The number of travellers conveyed daily, by twenty-six carriages, amounted at first to 400; then to 1,200; afterwards to 1,500; and it has now increased fourfold. The fare between Manchester and

1 Saint-Germain Leduc, vol. III, pp. 251, 252.

Liverpool, which was half a guinea on the outside, is now, by railway, only five shillings.

"Manchester, with its environs, for eight or ten leagues round, forms as it were but one vast workshop.

"Liverpool has no manufactories, but sells the productions of the neighbouring towns : it is a mart, nothing but a mart, but the most convenient mart in the universe. All business is transacted in a space smaller than the Place du Carrousel, which contains the Exchange, the Mayoralty, and the Counting Houses. At four or five o'clock, business is at an end for the day : every one shuts his office, and returns to his town or country house. To give an idea of the enormous amount of business transacted in this narrow space, it will suffice to say that lately land was sold there at the rate of 400*l.* for six square feet. I do not believe that land in any quarter of Paris ever fetched half the price.

"Liverpool is the headquarter of the English steamboats; eleven thousand vessels enter her docks yearly. For the last ten years, the exportations of the United Kingdom have amounted regularly to more than 360,000*l.*; two-fifths of these exportations are sent from Liverpool; a fifth of the British customs' dues is levied there, that is to say, the sum of four millions of pounds[1]."

Amidst this whirl of industry of commerce, the inhabitants of Liverpool do not forget that above all things they are religious and moral beings. M. Léon Faucher says : "Religion has always been found to be the only principle that can elevate rude natures. At every step in the streets of Liverpool you meet with some edifice consecrated to public worship (157 churches or chapels). There is even one in the middle of the docks, where an old hulk serves as a floating chapel, for the use of the sailors. The corporation have built five churches, which cost them 3,200*l.* a-year to keep in repair. This has been done, not to ornament the city, as in Paris, but from a principle of devotion[2]."

"At Newcastle, to the beauties of nature have been added the wonders of persevering industry. The country is peopled entirely with artisans, and crossed by railroads in every direction; files of waggons may be seen slowly advancing, drawn by a single horse, or rolling impelled by their own weight from the summits of hills. A prodigious activity reigns everywhere, and yet the most interesting part of the country is concealed beneath the soil. The subterranean works of those coal mines, which furnish the greater part of the

1. Saint-Germain Leduc, vol. III, pp. 267 to 272. — 2. Léon Faucher, vol. I, p. 240.

fuel of Great Britain[1]... The Newcastle mines are very extensive. These subterranean towns and farms deserve a visit from the curious traveller, as much as those on the surface of the earth. At three or four hundred feet under ground, there are streets as regular as those of the best quarters of London. The miners have all a contented look : they enjoy good health, because care is taken to supply them with the proper quantity of air, and frequently renewed[2]. The minds of the citizens of Newcastle are not entirely engrossed by mercantile transactions; they have a great taste for literary pursuits, and have prepossessing manners[3]. "

But why should we confine our examination to the towns and fields? Let us penetrate into the domestic circle, and follow the English into those places where they delight to live alone among themselves. Let us study this family sanctuary, to which they alone have given a name, and for which in France we are obliged to use a periphrase, as if we were strangers to the thing : the *home* of England, and the *chez-soi* of the France. Let our authors speak for themselves : " Home for the English is the centre of their entire existence; it is the stronghold of their fortune, their family, and their liberty[4]. The houses have an air of coquetry : everything is painted, varnished, cleaned, polished, like a mirror. Even on the outside the paint is fresh, and the brass clean. The threshold of the doors, the very pavement, is washed with soap : the floor of the rooms, even in the houses of people of small fortunes, is covered with carpet, as well as the staircase. There are not several families huddled together, as in France, in the same house : each family has its own separate dwelling... The English attach so much importance to cleanliness in person and dress, that it is for them the virtue of the body[5]. " "The family circle is a great source of happiness to the English; it is their *pastime and enjoyment*[6]. "

" Nowhere can be seen such faithful protection on one side, and such tender and pious devotedness on the other, as in married life in England. Nowhere do the wives share with so much courage and simplicity the troubles and dangers of their husbands, wherever the duties of their profession may call them[7]." " All things considered, *ceteris paribus,* thanks to the influence of the manners, the married state in England is happier than in any other country[8]. " " If the attachment of the wife is more durable, the reason

1. Saint-Germain Leduc, vol. III, p. 309. — 2. Pichot, vol. IV, p. 150. — 3. *Idem*, p. 152. — 4. Dory, p. 22. — 5 *Idem*, p. 15. — 6. Solitaire, vol. II, p, 10. — 7. Madame de Staël, p. 108. — 8. D'Haussez, p. 56.

is that the husbands are more faithful; and that the conjugal tie is less an affair of interest than the union of two minds and two hearts, destined for each other. The young girls, before their marriage, are free; they speak and feel freely, and are not concealed by a veil of silence or hypocrisy, as in certain countries [1]." "The Englishwomen are grave and serious; their minds are less occupied with amusements, than with their husbands and their domestic cares. Even women of quality nurse their children. Amidst all the corruption of London, a married woman rarely commits a fault. Her love for her family, her household cares, and her natural reserve, form an insurmountable barrier against the temptations of vice. I will even maintain that there is not a city in the world where the husband's honour is in less danger than in London [2]." "The independence of the Englishwomen before marriage is exchanged afterwards for a submission and a reserve which are most exemplary. These two facts are the rigorous consequences of each other; it is because young persons are allowed to judge and choose for themselves that the marriage tie is strong and durable; for the same reason it is respected, and its rupture is branded with infamy. In France, a separation entails no disgrace. Amongst unions so hastily formed, it is impossible that some should not be found insupportable [3]. On the whole, the Englishwomen ought to be classed among the most remarkable in Europe. To all that constitutes beauty, they add that which gives it its value: devotedness to their duties, varied instruction, and elegant minds; a combination, in short, of all the qualities which constitute the happiness of families and the charm of society [4]."

"It must be allowed that the Reformed faith is particularly favourable to family affection! The Protestant worship is indeed family worship, that of the domestic hearth; inasmuch as the family circle is its best sanctuary. What is the basis of Protestantism? The Bible. Between the Bible and the Protestant there is no medium, no forced interpreter; in consequence, every Protestant Christian, provided he can read, is for himself, as well as for those who listen to him, a priest, a minister of God. To read the Bible is the all-important act of the Protestant religion; on the other hand, this act is in itself perfectly simple, the simplest in private life; and yet there is something solemn about it; but a sweet solemnity, which has nothing fearful or mysterious, like a Catholic mass. I had the pleasure of being present several times

1. Dory, p. 22. — 2. Archenholz, vol. II, p. 156. — 3. Hennequin, p. 138. — 4. D'Haussez, vol. I, p. 103.

at this reading of the Bible, in the house of an honest old farmer in Northamptonshire, who had taken a fancy to me. In the evening, when all the doors were closed, the family took their places round the hearth, where burned an excellent coal fire. The farmer then rose, and with slow steps went to a cupboard, which he opened, and took from it a large quarto volume, which was the family Bible. A family Bible is an object with which so many recollections and ideas are connected, that it might be chosen as the title of a work, which would be a treatise of religion, morality, Christian philosophy, history, etc. The old farmer placed the book on his knees, and immediately every one took up some work already begun; the women their needlework, and the boys their instruments for making nets. It may be remarked, perhaps, that the reading was the signal for work; this habit appeared to me the result of real religious feeling. The worship of the Bible is thus associated with all the occupations of life, even the most humble, which it ennobles and endears. To participate in public worship, in a worship that requires many preparations and ceremonies, it is necessary to bid adieu to our ordinary occupations. Thus, religion awaits us in a higher sphere, whither we must ascend to it, and where we leave it on returning to our ordinary affairs; and it is for this reason we never become better; only more or less devout [1]. "

" As soon as the Lord's Day arrives, all Great Britain becomes silent and serious. Every one goes to church; all bustle ceases, and nothing is heard, except at long intervals the sound of bells, or the chant of a small group of Methodists, repeating in chorus the hymn of some preacher in the open air. A pious or curious crowd surround him; some listen attentively, and sing with heartfelt devotion; others look on in silence; but no one thinks of interrupting or criticising this extemporary service, which is terminated by a short exhortation to the love of God and our neighbour, and also by a collection for poor co-religionists [2]. "

Religion among the English Protestants is not merely, as elsewhere, and among others, a Sunday religion; it is a religion which pervades one's whole existence, regulates morals, and the influence of which is everywhere felt. This is not our own assertion; we quote the Catholic newspaper, *La Voix de la Vérité*, in 1853. These are the very words : " In England, " says M. Etienne, " the respect for religion is so general, that Strauss was translated three times, and neither time could a printer be obtained for the work. A

1. Vieil-Castel, pp. 101 to 106. — 2. Simon, vol. II, pp. 50, 51.

gentleman having broken the windows of a bookseller's shop, in which some blasphemous prints were exposed for sale, the jury acquitted him. A bookseller told me that all the irreligious books he had published had only proved so many losses, and that he continued to publish them merely from a spite against some persons who persecuted him and threatened him with imprisonment. In all private houses, on board steamers, even in hotels, you find the Holy Scriptures; grace is always said at private and public dinners; religion is never mentioned but with respect; and on Sunday every one goes to his own place of worship. The statesmen, with Wilberforce at their head, actuated by religious motives, in spite of long opposition, succeeded in emancipating the American negroes, which emancipation was joyfully hailed by the Church. Men of science endeavour to trace in their discoveries proofs of the greatness and goodness of God; the middle classes, and even the poor, give enormous sums to the Missions and to charitable institutions. If any one wishes to be well received in society, he must beware of wounding the general feeling of respect for religion; or of showing indifference towards things worthy of praise; such as the domestic virtues, the pious observance of Sunday, sincerity, philanthropy, or good faith. "

From domestic manners, let us pass to those of public life, casting a glance at each class of society :

" As every Englishman, " says M. Léon Faucher, " who is not obliged to work in order to gain his livelihood wishes to be thought a gentleman, he is always on his guard either to conquer or conceal his defects; for an impropriety in English society excites more indignation than a crime in Italy or Spain. But what I admire chiefly in these habits is the security which they create in public and private life. A man of any station or birth never tells a falsehood; he would tarnish his reputation by employing artifice or dissimulation. Hence arises the universal confidence which simplifies all social intercourse : in England, everything is transacted verbally as effectually as in France by writing [1]. "

" The French traveller is much surprised, when he visits the manufactories of Great Britain, at seeing the civility of the workmen to whom he happens to speak, and their polite and obliging, but not servile, manners, their respect for their master, and all who appear to belong to a higher class than themselves. They evidently respect the hierarchy of society. Englishmen, in gene-

1. Léon Faucher, vol. II, p. 409.

ral, know how to command and to obey. But, in the latter case, their obedience is rational; they submit to authority, but on condition that the authority is just. They will readily admit that you are a gentleman, and speak to you respectfully in consequence; but your manners must correspond with your pretensions, otherwise they will detect you with exquisite tact, and find means to make you feel that if you have the dress of a gentleman, you have neither the bearing nor the language of one. I was always surprised at the correct and proper manner in which the English workmen express themselves. In the manufactories, every workman speaks without embarrassment, obligingly shows the different operations of his trade, and always makes use of the proper terms, instead of those trivial expressions which disfigure so universally in France the language of the lower classes.

" The English workmen have often been taxed with a sordid spirit: it is a calumny. Not only an English workman never asked me for what is so common among us, something to drink, but on the contrary I have always found much difficulty in persuading men, who had been showing me over the workrooms for hours together, to accept half a crown, or a crown. Several times even I completely failed [1]. "

" To the honour of the English manufacturers I hasten to say that in a great number of the manufactories in Lancashire, Cheshire, Derbyshire, and in Scotland, great pains have been taken to render the workrooms clean, airy, and almost elegant, to the great advantage of masters and men. In the same establishments severe regulations prevent all immorality and profligate language; there are schools for the children, where the young girls learn to sew and knit; libraries for the use of the workmen; rewards given to the children who attend the Sunday schools; and benefit societies have been founded in case of sickness or accident [2]. The word emancipation is written on the standards of France and England; yet in France the middle classes have swallowed up the nobility. In England, the nobility and commoners advance side by side without jostling each other, and this alliance is to us a mystery [3]. "

" In this country of political liberty no one is shocked at the difference of rank. That feeling of jealousy which, before the first Revolution, animated the middle classes and the people against the counts, marquises, and barons, is scarcely known here; a feeling

1. Simon, vol. II, pp. 41 to 43. — 2. Saint-Germain Leduc, vol. III, p. 290. — 3. *Idem*, p. 58.

of pure vanity, which explains one of the highest gratifications enjoyed in our country, that of humbling the nobility... In England, no one dislikes a duke because he is a duke, or a marquis because he is a marquis. Is it because an English nobleman always shows a calm dignity in his pride, while the haughtiness of the French nobleman always more resembles that affected and provoking foppery which Molière was allowed to turn into ridicule for the amusement of the court and city under Louis 14 th ?[1] "

" It is sufficient to examine the list of the House of Lords to be convinced that no class of men can surpass, or even equal, the English aristocracy in learning, talents, or virtues. The reason is, that this aristocracy, instead of being exclusive, as on the continent, is always accessible to all who show themselves worthy of entering its ranks. We must not imagine that privileges, like the satyr in the fable, can blow hot and cold with the same breath; and make simpletons in Austria or Spain, and distinguished men in England [2]."

" Let one of the great lords commit a slight to the man who at first accosted him with the lowliest respect; in an instant you will see a blunt haughtiness replace the respect which is granted to rank, but refused to arrogance. The sentiment of justice is so deeply engrafted in every English heart, that every human consideration disappears as soon as the principles of liberty or social dignity receive the slightest injury. And in this country, so highly monarchical, even the splendour of royalty would not cover the smallest violation of what the citizens regard as their common right [3]. " " The English aristocracy are the instruments of great things; and are constantly occupied in preparing themselves for such. One might almost define them an immense school of government. The heirs of this haughty nobility are to be found in the army and navy, the diplomacy, the colonial governments, and the House of Commons [4]. "

Next to these characteristics, which are peculiar to different classes of society, it is well to place those that distinguish the English in general. You may always recognise the same type, whether he be an accomplished gentleman, an honest workman, a kind master, or a well-informed and unaffected nobleman; he never acts a part, he is always himself. " In England," says Dr. Dory, " the individuality of every man is much more developed than in France. Every one shows himself with his true character, his

1. *Revue Britannique*, 1845, vol. IV, p. 212. — 2. Madame de Staël, pp. 118, 119. — 3. *Idem*., p. 168. — 4. Léon Faucher, vol. II, p. 394.

virtues, or his vices; there is no uniform varnish, as with us, which makes all people resemble each other. The individual stands as it were alone, and thereby acquires greater strength; domestic life is more highly prized, and every one's conscience is the guardian of his faith. It cannot be denied that the individual becomes of more importance from this continual exercise of his strength and faculties[1]." "When a foreigner arrives in England, nothing strikes him so much as the all-pervading spirit of regularity, order, and cleanliness, and the composed and grave aspect that everything wears, betokening precious qualities, which seem to preside over all transactions connected with their gigantic enterprises. This public decorum, this honesty of all the commercial classes, taken collectively, presents an appearance that commands respect. Individual probity is a fundamental quality of the English character. The simple phrase, ***I have given my word,*** contains everything; it is as grave and as full of meaning in the mouth of an Englishwoman about to be married as in that of an Englishman in business : it is the basis of moral security in private life, as well as of confidence in public and commercial life[2]. "

"If we now consider the national qualities of the English, we shall find that they are eminently generous, not only individually, but also as a nation, in the moral signification of the term. They nobly assist the persecuted and destitute, wherever they meet them. This disposition shows itself in the mass of the people, and is their peculiar characteristic : one might almost think that this beneficent disposition has its source in a noble feeling of national pride[3]. "

Study this character, even in its errors under the influence of passion; and if you will in its resistance to authority, when impelled to such resistance by a sense of wrong : "With what profound reflection, " says M. d'Haussez, "the English people act, even while apparently in a whirlwind of passion. How quickly they recover from the emotions which they could not repress! How soon they become calm! How carefully they examine the ground on which they are treading, when they are obliged to advance! The reason is, that good sense forms the basis of their character; and that, for nations as well as individuals, this precious gift is essential to happiness[4]. "

The government, too, in its turn, knows how to yield to good sense, instead of rejecting its claims by violence: "George III,"

1. Dory, p. 54. — 2. Solitaire, vol. II, pp. 12, 13. — 3. *Idem*, p. 44. — 4. D'Haussez, vol. II, p. 232.

says Madame de Staël, " one day gave orders to close a gate and footway in his own park at Richmond, which had been open to the public for many years. A citizen of Richmond, who found this path convenient for himself and the other inhabitants of the town, undertook to defend his own and his neighbours' cause. He maintained that even if the passage had been an abuse at the beginning, it had become, by the lapse of time, part of the public way; that the right was established, and that he would force the king to reopen the gate. Without hesitation, he brought the affair before a court of justice, and gained his suit. If a governor of the Tuileries or the Louvre took a fancy to close any walks or passages which the public had always enjoyed, how many citizens of Paris would lodge a complaint, and how many judges could be found to decide in their favour?

"I saw in London a carriage belonging to a member of the Royal Family seized by his creditors just as he was going to enter it to go to Court. His creditors were very obedient subjects, and men who had as much respect as others for the privileges of rank; but they were also English citizens, who knew their rights, and were determined to enforce them [1]. "

We have taken a survey of town and country, and studied the English character in private and public life; now let us examine the manufactories and marts, and review the industry and commerce of England:

" In Great Britain, " says M. Léon Faucher, "where commerce has in general so much grandeur, tradesmen sell at fixed prices, and the most stupendous affairs are transacted without circumlocution, duplicity, or loss of time, by yes and no [2]. "

" The commerce of England is an immense machine, which is worked by 800,000 merchants or tradesmen, 6,000,000 workmen, 200,000 sailors, and 20,000 vessels, which convey and throw into circulation 12,000 millions of pounds' weight of goods.

" This commerce produces 120,000,000*l.* annually, which serve to pay the workmen and mariners, leaving immense profits, which it is impossible to estimate, and to defray the cost of building 1250 ships yearly, and maintaining a fleet of 560 vessels [3]. The spirit of English trade is, in general, very different from that of the French; and unhappily, in this respect, the advantage is not on our side. There reigns in general among the English, at home and abroad, in wholesale and retail transactions, a good

1. Madame de Staël, pp. 168 to 170. — 2. Léon Faucher, vol. II, p. 54. — 3. Nougarède, vol. I, p. 4.

faith, a punctuality, a frankness, which unfortunately does not exist among us [1]."

"The only expressions that can characterise the commercial transactions of England are 'immense', 'universal.' There does not exist a port or creek in any known sea into which her vessels do not penetrate; not a production but becomes in her hands a means of exchange. From this has resulted an unexampled state of prosperity. With settlements on every coast; sovereigns for clerks; colonies composed of states more populous than the mother country, and for markets states kept by treaties in a state of complete dependence on England; and, lastly, an industry that supplies all these wants, and even exceeds them: such are the general foundations on which rest the commercial operations of England [2]. In its present state, the commerce of England is one of the greatest wonders of a civilisation carried to the highest pitch that it can possibly attain. Its establishments on sea and land, the importance of its transactions, the number of hands it employs, the activity given to capital, the discoveries to which it gives rise in every branch of human knowledge, its results; in short, in whatever point of view we consider them, are above everything that has ever existed of the kind. And even should it be ever reduced to less gigantic proportions, the remembrance of what it was would remain in the memory of nations, and its efforts and success must ever be classed amongt the most powerful levers that ever served to create a revolution in the ideas and material condition of society.

"Industry keeps pace with commerce. In no other country has it been so fully developed, or attained such prosperity. It is nowhere more skilful in its operations, or more successful in its results. There is no want which it cannot readily supply; it can mould itself to any form, and be applied to any use. It is impossible to extol too highly the progress of this industry. The most extraordinary of its creations, however, are not its productions, admirable as they are, but the means it employs, the simplicity, and at the same time the power of its ingenious, we might almost say intelligent, machinery, which possess by their construction all the address with which Providence has gifted human fingers, all the strength that resides in his muscles, without any of the awkwardness, unwillingness, or false judgment, which accompanies the exercise of his faculties, and renders them imperfect. It

1. Nougarède, vol. II, p. 115. — 2. D'Haussez, vol. I, pp. 327, 328.

is this union of capital and of talent that forms a power unknown to the ancients, and which nothing can resist in modern times.

"The spirit of association is stronger in England than anywhere else; nothing escapes its grasp. In Asia, a mercantile company has by conquest formed immense colonies, protected them by armies, and treated the native sovereigns as inferiors. In Europe this spirit has formed extensive establishments, ports, docks, and arsenals, and crushes all individual competition [1]."

"No country," says Balbi, "possesses such numerous and splendid canals. These gigantic works have been undertaken and executed by private individuals, without any help whatever from the government [2]."

"We must not omit another mode of communication in which England surpasses all other nations; we mean the numberless railroads that traverse the country in all directions, and which were the first executed in Europe [3]." "Nearly all the manufactories and their productions have been carried to the highest perfection, and Great Britain may now be regarded as the most industrious country in the world. Nearly all her cities are remarkable for some particular branch of industry. All that history has recorded of the riches and commerce of the nations that have been most celebrated in these respects, during the middle ages and in modern times, dwindles into insignificance when compared with those of Great Britain. While her home trade is probably the richest and the most active in the world, she draws from foreign countries a mass of raw materials to supply her innumerable manufactories, and distributes the excess of her home consumption and the productions of her industry to all the nations of the globe, covering all the seas with her trading vessels, and ruling them all by her invincible fleets and by her colonies, the situation of which has been chosen with admirable skill. Great Britain has raised herself to such a pitch of power and splendour, that her commercial activity extends even farther than her vast political dominion; in fact, her commerce knows no other bounds than those of the habitable globe [4]."

We shall now merely add a few lines more on the extent of the industry and commerce of England: "The number of persons occupied in the cotton manufactories is estimated at 1,200,000. More than 700,000 workmen are employed in the silk manufactures of Great Britain; 500,000 persons find work and subsistence

1. D'Haussez, vol. I, pp. 331 to 335. — 2. Balbi, p. 472. — 3. *Idem*, p. 474. — 4. *Idem*, p. 478, 479.

in the woollen manufactories, and more than 300,000 in the linen manufactories[1]."

"The annual production of the cotton manufactories in England exceeds the prodigious sum of a million; a sum equal to the entire revenue of the extensive Empire of China. Such is the prodigious result of the union of the capital and machinery, the force of which in the United Kingdom equals that of 80 millions of men. The most indifferent observer would feel astonishment at seeing in Glasgow, Manchester, Paisley, etc., the effects of the genius and skill of man. And it is not only in great cities, but in the deepest caverns, on the summit of the loftiest hills, and even in the most remote corners of the country, that may be seen everywhere the admirable results of the use of machinery[2]."

"The silks manufactured in Great Britain and exported yearly, from 1821 to 1831, have amounted : in 1821, to 136,841*l.*; in 1824, to 159,670*l.*; in 1827, to 173,593*l.*; in 1830, to 427,849*l.*; and in 1831, to 500,000*l.*[3]"

We do not pretend to treat the question of the commerce and industry of England as a statistician, but merely to collect some testimonies as to their extent and morality. We could make an almost interminable list of these witnesses, but to avoid repetition we shall close the subject with one more quotation : "Thanks to the wise reserve of government, the efforts of English industry are out of all proportion with what is done elsewhere. For commerce, liberty and encouragement are synonymous. Thus trade and manufactures have attained gigantic proportions in England. One feels as if in a country inhabited by beings greater than men. Intelligent machines grasp weights and enormous masses with a facility, I may say a skill, that is fearful... I have seen galleries half a quarter of a league in length, merely destined to stow away innumerable hogsheads of sugar, until they could be placed in the adjoining warehouses. Under these *depôts* they have dug out subterraneous cities. I wish I could describe the activity of the diminutive beings who bustle about like ants around these instruments created by their genius. I so completely exhausted myself in contemplating this spectacle, that I have not strength to say more upon it. All that is most astonishing in industry in this country can be dated only thirty years back : after stating this fact, judge if it is possible to form an adequate idea of the continually increasing riches of England[4]."

1. Pebrer, vol. II, p. 39. — 2. *Idem*, p. 40. — 3. *Idem*, p. 48. — 4. Custine, vol. III, p. 141.

Now, let us say a few words of the colonies. In 1717, Canada, after having been during two hundred and sixteen years in possession of the French, had a population which only amounted, according to the Memoirs of Chartrain, to 27,000 souls. Twenty years after its conquest by the English, in 1783, it had increased to 113,000. The princes, dukes, and marquises who had succeeded each other, during two centuries and a half, in the government of Canada had done little or nothing for the improvement and prosperity of the colony.

Now, let us see the state of this population under a better government: "In 1790, the Canadians were put in possession, by act of parliament, of the commercial advantages and liberal institutions which are the basis of their present prosperity. Since that time, the colony has progressed rapidly, and increased greatly in importance..... The prosperity of Canada advances at a rate that surpasses all expectations; her population, which now amounts to more than a million, has doubled since 1814, and the quantity of land brought into cultivation is trebled. Her commerce has increased in an equal proportion; the mercantile navy has, on an average, transported more than 400,000 tons during the last three years, and employed 21,000 sailors. The consumption of manufactured products has surpassed 2 millions annually, and the exportation of the productions of the colony has not been less. The public prosperity has greatly increased; all the public works have been executed on a magnificent scale, and at a vast expense. The fortifications of Canada will cost nearly three millions: considerable sums have also been expended on the roads and public buildings [1]."

"Ever since Mauritius passed into the hands of the British government, the colony has constantly improved. The fortifications and public works have been greatly increased. The population has augmented by one-third, and we may say that the wealth and capital have been nearly trebled. The total production of sugar was in 1811 only 20,000,000 pounds; in 1830, the exportation of this article, for England only, amounted to 53,992,800 pounds. The crop of coffee in 1811 was only 600,000 pounds; in 1830, there were 7,066,199 pounds exported to Great Britain. These two articles form the principal productions of this colony; but the fertility of the soil renders all kinds of cultivation productive [2].

"In 1796, Ceylon came into the possession of the British. Since

1. Pebrer, vol. II, pp. 135 to 138. — 2. *Idem*, pp. 174, 175.

the year 1811, great public works have been undertaken or finished; others have been improved, and agriculture has made great progress. The cinnamon gardens are become more numerous and larger; trade has become very extensive; the importations, which in 1813 were only 1,435,262*l.*, and the exportations 545,612*l.*, are considerably increased. The gross value of the cinnamon exported yearly amounts, according to the returns of Colebrooke and Cameron, to 138,000*l.* The cane, which has been introduced into this colony, succeeds admirably. The population of the island has also considerably augmented, and the Cherigulais, or natives, although regarded as the most indolent race in the East, are become industrious under the care of the British government, who have encouraged the natives of the neighouring countries, and especially the Chinese, to come and establish themselves on the most fertile spots in the best parts of the island [1]. "

"All the productions of Europe have already been introduced into the Australian colonies. As to the manufactures, they have attained a considerable degree of prosperity. The population has increased fourfold since 1811; agriculture, commerce, and industry have made great progress; and the navigation is thirty times more considerable than in 1811. All these advantages are enhanced by the numerous literary, scientific, and charitable institutions that have been founded in the country. Indeed, all the improvements adopted by a nation celebrated for its commerce and industry have already been introduced into these distant countries. In order to form a just idea of these important colonies, we must imagine several towns of England transported as if by magic to a distance of 4,000 leagues, with their courts of justice, assizes, municipalities, asylums for widows and orphans, hospitals, charitable institutions, public carriages, markets, newspapers, etc..... Now, if civilisation starts in Australia with all the advantages of the towns of old Europe, what may not be expected in the course of a few centuries? The British people, already profusely scattered in all the quarters of the globe, will finish by covering a great part of it with a race of intelligent, active men; all speaking the same language, and governed by wise and solid institutions [2]. "

" Colquhoun estimated the general population of British India, in 1811, at 40,000,000; Hamilton carried it, in 1822, to 83,000,000; it amounts at present, according to the last official reports, to 89,577,206 souls. Agriculture and all the productions

1. Pebrer, vol. II, pp. 178, 179. — 2. *Idem*, pp. 196 to 197.

of the country have augmented in a relative or even greater proportion. It appears also, from the evidence produced before a committee of the Lords, that land in Berar, which before had been of little value, has now attained a high price. In Bengal, land is sold at 54 years' purchase [1]."

Next to this sketch of the English colonies place that of the Spanish colonies, which have long since disappeared, and the failure of the French colonies, and then say on which side is the superiority?

Such a development given to industry and commerce might lead a reader, who had not visited England, to imagine that agriculture, if not neglected, is only a secondary consideration. But a little reflection will make him understand that intelligence and morality are applicable to all things, to the land as well as to manufactures, and experience will prove the truth of the reflection. Agriculture is not less prosperous in England than industry and commerce. A few short quotations will be sufficient to prove it: "It is often said, and with reason, that if industry in England presents admirable results, there is something still more admirable, which is agriculture. The great landholders watch over their estates themselves, take an interest in all that relates to them, and make all kinds of experiments. Everywhere there are agricultural meetings, where prizes are distributed, and new discoveries or improvements discussed. The Agricultural Society of London has a revenue of several thousand pounds. The intercourse between the English landlord and tenant is much more patriarchal than in France. The losses of the farmer are always met on the part of the landlord by the renunciation of part or the whole of the rent [2]."

"English agriculture obtains with the fewest hands the largest quantity of produce, and feeds the greatest number of cultivators. It follows naturally that the capital must be larger, the methods more rational, knowledge more widely diffused, and the conveyances more easy and numerous than elsewhere; in short, that English agriculture, setting aside some particular cases, has made more progress, and is in a state of greater prosperity and higher perfection, than in any other country in the world. And of this I am firmly convinced, in spite of all the lamentations excited by momentary embarrassments, which party spirit eagerly lays hold of to serve its own purposes [3]."

"We may safely assert that, since 1790, the rents have been at

1. Pebrer, vol. II, p. 222. — 2. Nougarède, vol. III, pp. 907 to 909. — 3. Raumer, vol. I, p. 432.

least doubled in every part of England. This is not an assertion made at random; there are still people living who can prove it; and in Scotland the same fact is publicly recognised. The same farm in Essex, which then paid less than 10 shillings an acre, now fetches from 40 to 50 shillings : and there are farms in Berkshire, which, in the same lapse of time, have risen from 14 shillings to three pounds an acre; that is to say, to five times their original value. One of the causes that has the most contributed to the progress of agriculture is, without doubt, the steam engine. The marshes of Lincolnshire and Cambridgeshire were very imperfectly drained by the windmills. Now that steam has replaced wind, the crops are protected from inundation, and that at a much cheaper rate than by the old method. Several machines have been recently constructed of 60 or 70 horse-power, each being capable of draining 6 or 7,000 acres [1]. "

" The condition of the country people is really comfortable : the dwellings are clean and neat, the food wholesome and abundant; their clothes kept in good order; they turn everything to account. 'Where are the people?' the allied sovereigns exclaimed, on arriving in England in 1815; astonished at not seeing any signs of poverty in the curious crowds who thronged around them [2]."

" Nowhere has the art of improving meadows and pasture grounds, of draining, manuring, turning up the soil, clearing away the stones, embanking, multiplying nutrition plants and weeding out noxious herbs, always so ready to spring up, been carried farther than in England; nowhere is the expense of creating and keeping in repair less considered when applied to a useful purpose; and these enlightened efforts have produced real wonders [3]....." " The superiority of English agriculture is not owing to the nature of the soil or the climate, but to the superiority of the mode of cultivation [4]." " It cannot be concealed that by two or three modes of cultivation, employed on a large scale, the English, by the generality and simplicity of their methods, obtain general results very different to ours. Those of our departments, which most resemble England in the nature and extent of their cultivation have obtained the most satisfactory results [5]. " " The gross produce of the soil exceeds that of France by one-third; this result is enormous, since it is attained notwithstanding the sterility of a part of Ireland, and of all the Highlands of Scotland [6]." " Thus, by a careful comparison of the agricultural pro-

1. Raumer, vol. I, pp. 175 to 177. — 2. Nougarède, vol. III, p. 740. — 3. *Revue des Deux Mondes*, January, 1853, p. 908. — 4. *Idem*, p. 913. — 5. *Idem*, p. 914. — 6. *Idem*, p. 918.

ducts, the number of the population, and the market price of land, it is proved that even in the most moderate estimation the product of British agriculture, taken as a whole, was, five years ago, for an equal extent of ground compared with French agriculture, as 135 to 100; and, comparing England alone to the whole of France, the former produces at least twice as much as the latter. This valuation is sufficient to explain the superiority of the produce of land in England. Notwithstanding the natural inferiority of the soil and climate, the acquired fertility supplies the deficiency [1]. "

"M. Ledru-Rollin, with the intention of depreciating England, describes the soil of this country as being far from equal to that of Arragon and Lombardy. But, in asserting this fact, he bears testimony to the industry and energy of the inhabitants. With a soil certainly much inferior to that of these fertile provinces of Spain and Italy, Great Britain has, by the industry, science, and skill of her people, produced marvels in cultivation and agricultural products [2]."

"The greater part of the land in the country of Suffolk is rented by small farmers, who have only small capitals, and yet the ease and success with which it is cultivated is very remarkable. The fields are kept in admirable order. Everything betokens a population with habits of order, regularity, and neatness; and reminds us of the honest Dutch peasants on the right bank of the Rhine [3]."

We shall more fully comprehend this progress when we learn that agriculture in England is not, as in other countries, a despised profession, but that it is studied and encouraged by the noble, the wealthy, and the learned. "Thus, the Royal Agricultural Society, founded in 1838, has now 7,000 members. The rapid increase of this association, and the interest excited by its meetings, sufficiently attest its importance. The society publishes a journal, in which are reported the results of the experience and practice of the most skilful cultivators, together with an immense mass of facts, gathered from every quarter of the kingdom. It also gives prizes for cattle and agricultural implements, of which there is an exhibition every year in a different town, which excites an ever-increasing interest and growing emulation. Thousands of farmers who go to these meetings imbibe there a spirit of improvement, and acquire a taste for experiments; and on their return home hasten to put in practice

1. *Revue des Deux Mondes*, 1er March, p. 920. — 2. *Revue Britannique*, September, 1851, p. 199. — 3. *Idem*, December, 1852, p. 300.

all those improvements which, without the salutary efforts of the Royal Society, would have taken half a century to reach their localities [1]."

And it must not be supposed that the speculations of these learned bodies remain a sterile theory, or are only put in practice, as elsewhere, by a small number of amateurs, who ruin themselves in experiments. No; this knowledge is attained by the merest peasant: "Nothing shews better the progress that agricultural chemistry has made in England than a quarter of an hour's conversation with the first farmer that you meet. The greater number are already familiar with scientific terms; they speak of ammoniac and phosphate like professional chemists, and they understand perfectly well how greatly such studies tend to increase production. There are a multitude of cheap publications on these subjects; and travelling professors, who are paid by subscription, lecture on them through the country. A special and flourishing school of chemistry and geology, as applicable to agriculture, exists in London, under the direction of Mr. Nisbet [2]."

"Near the historical galleries at Woburn, which are ornamented by a number of portraits by Van Dyck, and where at every step you find traces of the illustrious members of the house of Russell, with princes and great men of their times, you find other galleries, filled with drawings and models of ploughs; sketches of animals of different races; specimens of cultivated plants; in fact, a complete rural museum. The house of Bedford is as proud of these trophies as of the others. The duke has built for his labourers excellent cottages, with small gardens adjoining; schools for their children, churches, etc.... There is no effort that an English farmer is not capable of making when he knows he has a good landlord, who will not impose too hard conditions on him, and who will be ready to assist him in case of need [3]."

"In Lincolnshire may be seen immense estates, and prosperous cultivation on a large scale. The farms present a magnificent spectacle. The agricultural buildings are all in excellent order. The farmers, rich for the greater part, have fine houses, numerous servants, hunting establishments, and fine saddle horses. It is, like Norfolk, the *beau ideal* of large estates and cultivation on a grand scale. I do not specify any particular farm; it would be necessary to mention all [4]."

Such is at present the state of society produced by the Protestant

1. *Revue Britannique*, 2e volume, 1845, p. 254. — 2. *Revue des Deux Mondes*, 1853, October, p. 248. — 3. *idem*, p. 252. — 4. *Idem*, p. 256.

faith; and if any one still asked what is the connection between this material prosperity and that religious faith, we can show him, besides the morality, that we have already pointed out a cause, which every one can appreciate, instruction. We do not even speak of the special instruction drawn from the Bible, but of the general instruction diffused throughout the nation.

"Of all the associations in Great Britain, the Bible Society excepted, none has displayed greater activity, or has obtained more extensive results, than the Society for the Diffusion of Useful Knowledge. It acted upon the perfectly correct notion that it is possible to instruct the people by reading. The greater part of the works published by the society on agriculture, and on the mode of raising cattle, and the almanacks, etc., are very well written : and thus an immense quantity of reflections and useful knowledge are spread abroad in a manner of which, until these times, no one had any idea. This is the best method of destroying bad and immoral writings, always so dangerous for the people [1]."

"It has been observed that the people in England are much more enlightened and judicious than in any other country. One is sometimes perfectly astounded at hearing individuals, belonging to the lowest class of society, reason very seriously on the laws, rights of property, privileges, etc., etc. It is not at all unusual to find this sort of people reading and commenting the public papers [2]."

"The moral strength of nations consists in the average amount of intelligence and in the knowledge of the principles and practical institutions which direct human affairs. It is this ordinary knowledge forms the statesman, the lawyer, the manufacturer, the tradesman; in a word, all the active members of a well-organised community. And in this respect no country can bear a comparison with England. No people has such a homogeneous intellect, and consequently such a strength of cohesion, if I may be allowed to employ this scientific term.

"Our geometricians are more profound, and our engineers more learned; but their mechanicians and manufacturers surpass ours in number and practical skill. In some of our departments, elementary instruction is more widely diffused than in certain countries of Great Britain; but where can be found on the other side of the Channel a whole province where, as in Britany, there is scarcely one child out of five hundred that goes to school? Where

1. Raumer, vol. I, pp. 401, 402. — 2. Archennolz, vol. I, p. 65.

could be found populous towns entirely destitute of all intellectual resources, having neither an institution for education, a reading-room, or a bookseller? [1] "

The most lively faith and the most complete instruction will not make a government unnecessary for a nation; but they may render the task of governing more easy, and authority less burdensome to the people. And there can nowhere be found more respect for those who govern, or more liberty for the governed.

" England is advancing slowly, but firmly, towards the realisation of the desire of the Great Alfred; that it was just that every Englishman should be as free as his thoughts. In England, we rarely see the convulsive efforts which mark the progress of other European nations; but, if we compare past ages with the present, we shall be convinced that no people has advanced so quickly and so wisely towards liberty, and has less frequently, in modern times, imbrued her hands in civil war [2]. "

Equality makes progress in England, as in all the rest of the world. But England has this immense advantage, that it is by the elevation of the inferior classes, and not by the depression of the upper ones, that these inequalities disappear. The people are too proud to claim anything but liberty of action, certain that talent and energy will open to them the road to honours, which are accessible to all. The skill of the legislator, like that of the physician, consists in re-establishing an equilibrium, by fortifying the weaker organs without weakening the stronger, and this, in my opinion, is what we see accomplished in England. The diffusion of knowledge among all classes, the extraordinary progress of industry and talent, tend to augment the democratic principle with much more success than the system of government of any minister, or the intrigues of any party, can strengthen the contrary principle; but this development takes place without any convulsion. From day to day the lower classes draw nearer to the middle classes, and the latter to the highest ranks of society, without the aristocracy having any right to complain that they are deprived of any of the advantages bequeathed to them by the traditions of times gone by [3]. "

" England occupies a distinguished place amidst the happiest and best-governed nations of the present times; and however far back the traditions of history may extend, there are no points of comparison which are not to her advantage [4]. "

1. Madame de Staël, pp. 28, 29. — 2. *Revue Britannique*, April, 1852, p. 283. — 3. Madame de Staël, pp. 173 to 175. — 4. D'Haussez, vol. I, p. 65.

"It is a truth, that does not admit of contradiction, that no civilised people were ever so free as the English are at present; and those who are acquainted with the forms of government in ancient and modern times will undoubtedly be of this opinion. The inhabitants of England enjoy a felicity that is worthy of envy[1]." "Time, in England, has happily consecrated two rights of the people: the liberty of the press, which is never trifled with; and individual liberty[2]."

"An Englishman respects authority, and the agent who represents it, whatever may be his rank, from the Lord Mayor to the lowest policeman; and I hasten to add, that a public functionary very seldom goes beyond the legal limits of his prescribed duties. As he his respected in the exercise of his functions, he encounters no illegal resistance or insult that can excite his anger and prompt him to violence[3]."

"In England, the police is national, and its strength is irresistible. The civilisation of this people is carried so far that we may say with truth that what is wanting at present is ignorance[4]."

This respect of the English for men invested with authority is not so much paid to the man as to the law, of which he is the representative. Thus we see the simple policeman obeyed, and the lord respected: "The House of Lords do not abuse their power," says M. Léon Faucher, "because they feel that it would be weakened by any excess. Besides this natural tendency, public opinion is ever on the watch, and obliges them to conform their decisions to the rules of the most scrupulous equity. Here, again, theory is corrected by practice[5]."

So much for the noble lord, now for the humble police agent: "In France, it excites astonishment that there should be a country on earth where you run no risk of being murdered at the corner of every street, although there is not a gendarme to be seen; where the safety of the government is not in any danger, although it keeps no spies; where there are fine roads, although there are neither special schools for the construction of bridges and roads, nor engineers. Who supply the place, may be asked, of the functionaries that seem indispensable in a well-organised society? Who supply their place? Reasonable beings, who are taught by good sense, custom, instinct, patriotism, and self-love, applied to the interest of the public, to comprehend each other. It is all this which supplies the place of what, in other countries, is established

1. *Tableau de l'Angleterre*, par d'Archennolz, vol. I, pp. 8 et 9. — 2. Pichot, vol. II, p. 81. — 3. Simon, vol. I, pp. 106 to 107. — 4. Custine, vol. II, p. 88. — 5. Léon Faucher, vol. II. p. 425.

by uniform codes, well-administered, but producing a bad result[1]. If a road is to be made? Every one sets to work; the great proprietor indicates the direction; the land surveyor traces it out; the mason constructs the bridges; every one takes a share in the work, according to the nature and extent of his abilities and his rank in society: the road begun by one parish is continued by another, and thus crosses the country and the kingdom. Who conceived the first idea of it? who superintended its execution? No one and every one. It exists, it is used, and society is so much the richer[2]."

"It is by a kind of general co-operation that order reigns everywhere in London. If we were tempted to draw a parallel between the police of England and that of France, we should perceive, not without sorrow, that while ours is mean, meddling, and disagreeably negligent, the English police watches over everything with attention and solicitude, without persecuting any one, and seeming never to interfere[3]."

The best of governments will always be obliged to repress, but its excellence may be shown in the way in which this task is accomplished. We shall therefore say a few words on the prisons, and the more readily that their management is as much the result of the manners of the people as of the laws of the country.

First, a few words on the accused: "An accused person is never put in chains on the free soil of England. The accused are treated there with so much mildness, that they are not even interrogated, during the trial, on the circumstances of the affair, that they may not be forced to criminate themselves[4]."

Now, a picture of the prisons themselves: "By sobriety, cleanliness, regular labour, solitude, religious and intellectual instruction, the maladies of the soul are cured, and by degrees the prisoners acquire habits of order and industry. By depriving them of all communication with others, they are forced to reflect, and are preserved from bad company. In short, it is by this moralising course that they arrive at the complete reform of individuals whom society had rejected, and who seemed to live only to violate all its laws[5]."

"The infirmary of Cold-Bath Prison is an abode of peace and comfort. The care taken of this infirmary shows sufficiently that the governor considers each sick prisoner as an unhappy brother, whom his duty requires him to relieve. There is no

1. D'Haussez, vol. II, p. 130. — 2. *Idem*, pp. 130 to 133. — 3. *Observations recueillies en Angleterre*, by C.-G. Simon, vol. I, p. 106. — 4. Dict. — 5. Simon, vol. I, pp. 227 and 228.

canteen in the prison, and the food is the same for all, without the slightest difference in favour of any one. I saw the prisoners at dinner; each division has its own refectory; the tables, made of excellent wood, are carefully rubbed and washed, and not a spot tarnishes their surface. The small bowl in which the prisoners eat is of pewter, and cleaned and scrubbed till it shines like silver. The food is wholesome and plentiful[1]."

"We passed into the women's prison. There reigns the same cleanliness, order, and silence, and the regulations are enforced with the same severity. The women are more occupied than the men; they make all the linen that is required in the establishment. There is also a superb laundry, drying-place, and ironing-room; a great number of women are constantly employed in washing and scrubbing the floors of the rooms, cells, passages, and staircases; even the pavement of the yards is also washed and scrubbed. It would be possible to go over the whole of these vast buildings in white satin shoes and a muslin dress, without having them stained by a drop of water or a grain of dust. It is really admirable[2]."

"In the Model Prison of Millbank, the floor of the passages, as well as that of the cells, is made of small planks of white wood, like the tables in Cold-Bath Prison; and is so clean and polished that one might draw upon it. The furniture of the cells is not confined to what is indispensably necessary. They have a bed well made, sheets perfectly white, a small press, a table, and a shelf, on which is arranged what is necessary for dressing. All this is fitted to the place, and is as clean and shining as if it were new[3]."

Finally, what neither church, schools, authority, nor prisons can effect, charity will attempt. The number of charitable associations in England is incalculable. Without mentioning the purely religious societies, who for the diffusion of the Gospel at home and abroad spend more than 400,000*l*. annually, we shall quote a few lines on the purely charitable societies, for in this place it is not our intention to exhibit the faith, but the morality, which ought to be a proof of the truth of the religious belief:

"The national character and the legislation," says M. Simon, "co-operate in England in forming associations of every kind, both for the instruction and the relief of the poor. Let an institution of this kind be founded in a town, subscriptions pour in immediately; every citizen thinks it an honour to figure on the

1. Tristan, pp. 193 to 194. — 2. *Idem*, pp. 199, 200. — 3. *Idem*, p. 208.

list of benevolent persons who set on foot a work of charity or education. Legacies are numerous; and, by degrees, an institution, which at first was weak and precarious, becomes settled upon a firm, broad, and lasting basis. I wish I could place one of these subscription lists before the eyes of my fellow-countrymen; how many of them would have reason to blush at their selfish apathy and sordid indifference, at seeing how liberally and generously our neighbours act in circumstances in which, among ourselves, we should scarcely receive a single contribution [1]. "

Let us accompany M. Victor Chevalier in his visits to some of the public institutions for the relief of the poor in England; and first let us listen to what he says of the *Unions* :

" The discipline of these establishments is austere, although parental, and the habits contracted there are satisfactory. They constitute an excellent asylum for aged and infirm persons; but for the lazy and pretended poor they are a hard abode, that drives them back to an honourable life of labour and activity. Thus they form a rampart strong enough to resist the encroachments of false pauperism; for it is sufficient for the relieving officers to oblige those whom they consider as false poor to enter these houses, and in a very short time they abandon the unions, and cease to require assistance. I have been assured that this preventive method had produced such an effect, that there were not in the unions a fifteenth part of the total number of relieved poor, and that the rest received in their own homes assistance very judiciously distributed.

" Such is the assistance granted to the poor who are in their own parish at the time they claim it, or in a parish in which they have resided for a twelvemonth. Those who do not fulfil these conditions go to the nearest parish, where they obtain bread and a hard lodging for one night. The next morning they are sent on in the direction of their own parish; and they receive, if they desire it, bread and lodging in the unions which are on their way, until they arrive at the end of their journey.

" By these severe regulations the love of the poor for their native place is strengthened, and they are in general brought back to the parish where they were born; there they begin life anew, in the midst of their families, and under the purifying influence of recollections of their infant years. They soon resume their old occupations; and those who had abandoned rural life, led away by

1. Simon, vol. I, p. 245, 246.

a false hope of obtaining lucrative employment in cities, return to the more healthful and certain labours of agriculture.

" The rate imposed on each parish, for the support of the unions, varies from one parish to another according to the extent of the parish, or the number of poor requiring assistance. The reduction, then, of their number is a matter of material as well as moral interest. The result is, a complete harmony between the government, the counties, and the parishes in their views and in their efforts for founding institutions destined to render the existence of the labouring classes comfortable, and cause them to acquire habits of industry and good conduct [1]. "

" On the Sabbath, so religiously observed in Great Britain, the children go to school, as on a week day, and are conducted by their masters to divine service; and, besides this, before and after the service, they receive moral and religious instruction; given to the boys by young men, and to the girls by young ladies, belonging to the most distinguished families in the parish. I have been present at these lessons, where the children, ranged in groups of seven or eight round their young and willing teachers, acquired at once sound notions, excellent habits, and true politeness; that is to say, Christian charity applied to our intercourse with each other. By this touching influence of the richer on the poorer classes is established a noble system of patronage, which is perpetuated in one form or another through life, and suggests a word of advice or consolation for every difficulty and misfortune; refines and elevates all the citizens; and forms of this singular society, where the aristocracy enjoys such enormous privileges, a whole harmoniously attached to the institutions of the country.

" When we add that most of the public functions in the parish are gratuitous; that the unions, as well as the schools, are directed by charitable committees, who meet periodically to settle the budget of the past week, and arrange that of the week ensuing; that these committees appoint one of their number to inspect the union daily during the seven days that elapse between two of their sittings; and that it is only the officers in constant employment, residing in the unions, who are remunerated, some idea may be formed of the incessant labours of the rich for the relief of the poor, and the amelioration of the condition of all [2]. "

" In order to diminish the suffering occasioned by the high price of the dwellings of the labouring classes, and also to improve their

1. V. Chevalier, pp. 4 to 8. — 2. *Idem*, pp. 8 to 10.

habitations and render them more healthy, private charity has provided buildings divided into small separate lodgings, which have been constructed of late years in the manufacturing towns. Some of these dwellings are appropriated to single men, others to married persons, and others again to single women; they are kept in good order, and the price of the lodgings is fixed by settlement. Some are sold on condition, that as soon as they are occupied and bring in four or five per cent.; and the capital serves to construct other habitations of the same nature. By these ingenious combinations, the number of workmen's houses will continue to increase until the ordinary prices of healthy and convenient lodgings will have been reduced within proper limits. These are some of the institutions by which a rich and powerful nation gives education to the labouring classes, defends their interests, and assists them in their misfortunes. When they sink into poverty, public charity assists them, and at the same time the government, by its skilful and persevering foreign policy, endeavours to increase the number of markets for trade, in order to procure new work for hands temporarily deprived of employment. Assistance, then, except to the old and infirm, is always considered as an accidental necessity, and private persons unite their efforts to those of the government, in order to render such trials as easy and brief as possible[1]."

"The service of the hospitals is confided to the most eminent practitioners. The excellence of the beds, the cleanliness of the rooms, and the wholesomeness of the food, leave no room for improvement. The different asylums, with a more modest appearance, enjoy the same advantages and in the same degree. As to charity schools, it is not an elementary instruction afforded out of compassion to the children of the poor, but a system of education wisely adapted to their intellectual capacities, and to the professions for which they show any aptitude. A great number of pupils leave these schools sufficiently prepared for the universities. Rich parents could nowhere find, at the greatest expense, a better education for their children in any seminary. It is by hard study that the pupil must obtain, in after life, preferment in the Church, or an honourable situation in law, medicine, or any other profession[2]."

But, as we fear to weary the reader by entering into a detailed examination of such a multitude of charitable institutions, we shall content ourselves with copying a simple list contained in the *Siècle* of the 8th of February, 1854, which begins as follows:

1. V. Chevalier, pp. 11 to 13. — 2. Saint-Germain Leduc, pp. 2, 3.

" London possesses at this time 530 charitable establishments :

	l.
92 Hospitals, with an annual revenue of	266,925
12 Societies, for the preservation of the public health and morality	35,717
17 Societies for the welfare of prisoners and prisons	39,486
13 Societies for the aid of the wounded in the streets	18,316
14 For special accidents	27,387
25 In aid of the Jews, or mixed marriages	10,000
19 For workmen	9,124
12 For pensions	23,677
15 For assistance to the clergy	35,301
32 For different professions and trade	53,467
30 For trade only	25,000
126 Asylums for the aged	87,630
9 For the deaf, dumb, and blind	25,050
13 Orphan asylums	45,465
15 For the children of the parish schools	88,228
21 Societies for the increase of schools	72,247
43 For the home missions	319,705
14 Foreign missions	459,688
5 Societies not classed	3,252
The sale of religious books produces	100,000
To which must be added different revenues	160
The 530 charitable establishments of London distribute annually among the poor and suffering the sum of	1,745,795l."

Let us leave the capital for the country; there we shall find the same charity. For brevity's sake, we will only give a single example :

" Mr. W. T. C. Cooper, the principal landholder in the parish of Toddington, Bedfordshire, determined, in 1829, to try whether, by making small allotments of land to poor families, it would not be possible to lessen the poor-rate. The six families he first selected used every exertion to keep their lots in good condition. Their labour was rewarded by excellent crops, and their ardour for work augmented in consequence. The experiment made by Mr. Cooper having succeeded, all the labourers came and asked for land; he then determined to divide a large field between 41 persons. All these men, who before spent their evenings sauntering about, and often in planning mischief, are now occupied in what they call their field. The stranger who visits this parish cannot behold without pleasure these heads of 41 families, all occupied in digging, hoeing, and weeding the lot that belongs to them, as soon as the day's work for their employer is finished. They remain there until night forces them to cease from their labour, and then return to their families, instead of going prowling about, as before they were in the habit of doing, to see what depredation they could commit. All are now noted for their good conduct.

"Mr. Cooper, in 1831, added 34 more lots to the 47 that he had already granted to his day labourers. They are obliged to pay their rent exactly when due. Whoever should be convicted of an offence, would lose his lot; they are bound to watch over the conduct of their children with the greatest care, and not to allow any of the young ones to be out of doors after nightfall. Up to this time all the tenants have paid their rent with the greatest punctuality. Mr. Cooper, at first, would only grant lots to men noted for their good conduct; he has since granted some to characters relatively bad, and he has had no reason to repent it. One of the latter said to him, on asking for land: 'I know you have not a good opinion of 'me, but give me the means of employing my time honestly, and 'you shall see that my land shall be as well cultivated as that of 'any other, and that my conduct shall be irreproachable.' This man has kept his word, and his lot is one of the best cultivated of all those distributed by Mr. Cooper [1]."

This is England, such as she has been made by the Protestant faith. Now, shall we conclude that she is superior to Catholic Spain?

This would be so poor a pretension, that our readers would accuse us of endeavouring to prove what is evident. We shall take a

1. We will here present our reader, in a note, with a document which reached us too late for insertion in its proper place, in our chapter on the United States. It contains the legacies lately left by Mr. Phelps, an American Protestant.

Mr. Phelps, after having bequeathed to his wife and children what he thought sufficient for them, left the following sums to different religious societies:

	l.
Bible Society	20,000
Missionary Society for the Heathen	20,000
Home Missionary Society	20,000
Society of colonisation for the theological and literary education of the negroes in Liberia	10,000
School of Theology in New-York	1,000
Asylum for the Blind	1,000
Society at New York for sending negroes to Liberia	1,000
School of Theology at Auburn	600
Asylum for half orphans	200
Asylum for orphan negroes	200
To the poor of the Church of Simsbury	200
Total.	74,200l.

A short time before his death, Mr. Phelps had remitted 20,000l. to his son, and desired he would employ the interest for pious purposes.

Finally, after having bequeathed 2,000l. to each of his twenty-two grandsons for their own use, he left each of them an additional thousand pounds, with the following clause:

"I beg my executor to inform my grandchildren that I desire this last legacy should be considered as a sacred trust, which is confided to them in order that it may be placed safely, and that the interest may be consecrated to the propagation of the Gospel and the advancement of the Lord's Kingdom upon earth, I hope, and I feel confident that our Heavenly Father will grant to all of them the wisdom that is from above, and will incline their hearts to be faithful stewards, in order that the same sum may be transmitted entire to their descendants for the same purposes. I know that this legacy is absolute, and that the sum thus given is no longer at my disposal; but I earnestly trust that my desire will be taken for what it is, an obligation which is binding on their integrity and honour." These legacies for pious purposes amount to the enormous sum of 116,200l. (*Archives du Christianisme*, du 11 th February, 1854.)

higher aim. To the glory of the Gospel we will maintain that England is superior to all the other nations of Europe, and, in order to give more weight to our judgment, we shall, according to our rule, leave it to be proved, by French Catholic authorities: "I say it with regret," writes a French traveller, "England is not known. The distance between England and France is immense: on one side, a system skilfully followed up, and so completely inoculated even into the minutest ramification of the social body, that there is not an Englishman to be found, either at home or abroad, in England or at the antipodes, who by his labour does not contribute to the triumphs of the mother country. But, in return, the mother country protects all her children. On surveying what has been accomplished by his country, an Englishman feels himself greater for her conquests, her wealth, her power, her credit, her government: in short, he is proud of being an Englishman, and he is right to be so [1]."

"No nation appears to follow so uniformly a destiny of progress and civilisation: none can advance with a firmer faith than the English nation towards happiness and material prosperity; through all the transformations of ages, it always exhibits its standard qualities [2]."

"On the point of quitting England," says also M. de Custine, "I rejoice at having seen a society whose civilisation has so far surpassed that of all neighbouring States. When we have examined the height she has attained in our times, we may to some extent venture to predict what will be the future destinies of Europe [3]."

"England," adds M. de Montuli, "is advanced so far in civilisation, that, according to the character and opinions of the observer, she must be judged in very different ways. When one has always lived amidst the confusion, negligence, and I might almost say carelessness, of the French, with a natural taste for order and cleanliness, it is impossible not to admire this country, where everything is regulated, and where Nature herself appears to wear her most brilliant colours. As to me, I should be exclusively enchanted with England if I had not already seen Germany, and, above all, the United States [4]. The towns and villages everywhere have an aspect of wealth and cleanliness, and, in justice to England, I must confess that the United States, and some part of Germany, can alone, in this respect, enter into competition with her [5]."

1. Bureau, vol. I, p. 16. — 2. *Idem*, pp. 39, 40. — 3. Custine, vol. II, p. 453. — 4. Montuli, vol. I, pp. 17 to 19. — 5. *Idem*, p. 230.

Let us listen to M. Simon, whom we have already quoted : " My task is nearly ended; I have described successively all the most important branches of the great manufacturing industry, of that industry which has elevated England above all other nations, and made an Island, of moderate extent, the centre of the affairs of the whole world [1]. It is evident that in a great many respects England surpasses France. No national feeling can sufficiently blind our eyes to make us see the contrary : habits of order and calculation long since acquired, methods of operating perfected by long practice, workmen formed at an early age by example and by a serious apprenticeship to industrial manipulations; the genius for mechanism innate in Englishmen, and stimulated by the imperious necessity of producing continually, and at a cheap rate; the abundance of raw materials furnished by the soil; the facilities offered for the arrival of merchandise, and the numberless means of communication; a complete system of banking and credit, and perfect national security; these are the advantages which in a great many points secure an incontestable superiority to Great Britain [2]. "

Finally, we may be allowed to quote a few words from Madame de Staël, after the Catholic writers : " It is impossible to examine England, even with a mind strongly prepossessed against her, without being forced to acknowledge that civilisation has made greater progress there than in any nation on the Continent; that knowledge is more widely diffused; the science of government better understood; and all the movements of the social machine are more rapid and more skilfully combined. To deny this fact, would be in some manner to contest the importance of all the political institutions which have been for centuries the object of the meditation of the wise, and of the efforts of nations [3]."

In concluding our survey of Spain and England, we address to the reader's conscience this twofold question : First, is it not true that Spain, favoured with the finest climate, placed at the head of Europe, enriched with a world, but remaining Catholic, has continued to decline and grow poorer, to sink at last into ignorance, misery, and immorality?

Secondly, is it not true that England, with a sterile soil, a cloudy sky, and starting from the lowest rank among European nations, but having embraced Protestantism, is now prosperous, enlightened, moral, and at the head of the civilised world?

We subscribe beforehand to the answer of our readers, and now

1. Simon, vol. II, p. 247. — 2. *Idem.* p. 249. — 3. Madame de Staël, p. 21.

pass on to our last comparison : Catholicism on the Papal Throne in Italy, and the Reformation crushed beneath the feet of Royalty in France. If, notwithstanding her infallible prop, the former declines; if, in spite of her powerful persecutor, the latter increases in power and influence, we shall be forced to conclude that the fall of the one is owing to the slow but fatal consequences of error; and the triumph of the other to the influence, not less slow but not less certain, of everlasting truth.

CATHOLICISM

ON THE THRONE IN ITALY.

What is the relative value of Catholicism and of Reform? Such, expressed in general terms, is the question we would wish to examine. We have already given to this question two answers, identical in their result: one by comparing two by two those nations following the two Churches; the other, by examining separately each people bending to one or other of these two religious faiths.

We shall again, therefore, take up the problem thus twice solved, and by a third demonstration arrive at the same solution.

This third method of proof will be the study of any one particular nation, being as much as possible the pure produce of Catholicism; of a nation which has sucked no other milk but that which flows from the maternal bosom, reared in the lap of its own family, watched with a tenderness which the fondest parent can but ill bestow on children living apart from the domestic hearth; a nation, in short, which has never been exposed to the venom of heresy, and one we are entitled to regard as the favoured child. We have named Italy. Italy, who enjoins the simple privilege of possessing in her bosom the infallible Head of the Church, the Vicar of God. "The active influence of Papacy," says M. Quinet, "is nowhere more visible than in Italy; it is there it must be studied in order to become possessed of its secret workings, since there the Church reigns sole sovereign mistress. This policy is based upon an unbounded hope, in which the whole nation has a share." Let us see, therefore, what Romanism has done for this magnificent country. The history of Papacy may, for the better management of our subject, be divided into two periods: the one during which the Popes relied upon the people to subjugate Kings, and the one during which they united with Kings in order to subjugate the people. The moment of transition between the two epochs is the sixteenth century. Until that time the authority of the Church had been uncontested. The Sovereign Pontiffs who had preceded that era took small account of the progress of liberty or enlightenment. The *Renaissance*, aided by the discovery of the art of printing, had just begun to disseminate a taste for literature and science. Pope Leo X, himself unconscious of the danger, had proclaimed himself the protector of all liberal arts. But, from the moment when it was discovered that this new light was something more than a mere rocket let off for the amusement of his court, and that the torch was held aloft by the hand of the wise and the learned to enlighten the multitude upon the rights of the people and the errors of the Church, Rome changed her policy on the instant, and deserting the cause of the people, which she had used for her ambition, passed over to the camp of the Sovereigns, whose alliance had now become of the greater value. Henceforward, Popes and Sovereigns made common cause against the people; both having to safeguard the principle of power against the inroads of human liberty. Rome no longer sought to govern the world by her doctrines alone, but to inspire moreover the monarchs of Europe by an identity of interest with her. To extinguish the growing light, to preach the divine right of the Holy See, to persecute learning under the name of heresy, to reward by the bestowal of heaven and earth whoever took service in her behalf, to associate in her glory the populations by which she was surrounded, by proclaiming their soil holy ground, their city an eternal city, their country the centre of Christendom, until it became that of the whole universe; such became from that hour the policy of the Papal Court. Italy accepted this wardship; lured by the hopes of inheritance, she suffered herself to be led, instructed, and became the humble and submissive pupil of Catholicism. It is Catholicism which has formed her people and her princes, inspired her customs and laws, brought about her material position; in short, created and kneaded the whole state to an image of her own likeness. By studying the work we shall therefore become acquainted with the workman; let us examine Italy, and we shall soon learn the worth of Catholicism.

By the foregoing observations, it will be understood that our study of Italy will not go further back than the sixteenth century; before this epoch, Italy had not been so entirely the work of Papacy; in the first place, because her Sovereign Pontiffs had left to the people the enjoyment of a liberty they had not yet dared to dread, and in the second because they had not yet gone over to the camp of the Sovereigns to league against the people. The awakening of altars of arts and science at the beginning of the sixteenth century, even before the Reformation, had been produced by the arrival of the learned men driven out of Constantinople. The Renaissance is Pagan and not Catholic; if proof of this were wanting, it would be enough to remark that is was the Popes who stifled it; the study of Greek and Hebrew, which led to the study of the Book, and consequently to the discovery of the abuses of Rome, was forbidden. And we ask those who dare affirm that the Romish Church was favourable to the Renaissance, because a Pope gave it admission for a moment into his palace, how it happens that from that very time she impeded its progress, and repulsed its advances?

But our documents will throw some little light upon these assertions. Let us examine, first of all, the state of Italy at the time of the Renaissance, just before Papacy had wrought a change in all things:

"From the grandest centuries of antiquity," says Henry Martin, "the world had not presented so magnificent a spectacle as that offered by Italy at the close of the middle ages; she had decked herself with the master-works of the human mind like a queen adorning her brow, for the last time, with the finest jewels of her diadem, when about to descend from her throne to hold out her hands to the shackles of slavery. Her superiority, which had been undisputed in the science of government, was still universally acknowledged in literature, in industry, and commerce, as well as in almost every appliance of human thought to human activity; but above all, and more than ever, in the fine arts.

"The Renaissance continued to march with giant strides, sustained by the printing press.

"The secondary arts, such as the working of gold and silver, the carving of wood and ivory, the graving of metals, joining, engraving, closely allied to the principal branches of high art, aided them by their plastic tendency more defined and vigorous: Polo

Uccello introduced perspective into painting, and Masolino displayed the advantages of chiaroscuro, and the movement of light and shadow; that magical science which till then was unknown by the painters of Bruges, in the sameness of their splendour: painting began then to express, with a newly-awakened truth, nature and reality, without losing the real aim of art, the ideal; and Masaccio united all his progress in a whole so perfect, that it is held up to this day as an example to the painters of modern times.

"The instruments and material resources for the aid of art ceased not from multiplying; the importance given to the quality of precision in form, from the moment when the expression of the countenance alone sufficed no longer to the cravings of the admirers of art, and the human form was disengaged from the floating draperies of the middle ages, brought forward the study of anatomy, and while the art of design was marching towards perfection, colouring was becoming more and more brilliant as it progressed.

"From one extremity of Italy to the other, the fine arts were developing in every direction an ardour, a vigour, and a fecundity almost incredible; illustrious professors and flourishing schools arose in the most unimportant cities; the encyclopedic universality of the men who headed this prodigious march forward, confounds the imagination; the greatest artists cultivating at one and the same time, and with the same degree of glory, every branch of art, placed themselves at the same time at the head of the movement then taking place in the exact sciences, and associated their names with the progress of philosophy and letters."

Such was the end of the fifteenth century; but observe that this prosperity is all material; it is as much as we can do to call it intellectual; most assuredly it was not moral. It was neither the arrival of a few learned hellenists, nor the study of the pagan literature of the ancients, which could purify the moral of the age. These morals were of the lowest tone; there were those of the olden time, anterior to the Renaissance; it had needed the lapse of centuries to establish them; it was these bad morals, and not useful sciences, which Papacy had been employed in forming. Listen to our author: "In the very bosom of Italy the other elements of moral and intellectual life were unable to follow the rapid soaring upwards of the fine arts. Italy was carried away by a sublime fever rather than by activity in the pursuit of her genius; more impassioned for the produce of her arts than penetrated with the principles of their greatness, she was endowed with more feeling than understanding.

"The corrosive principle of materialism found compensation enough for its theoretical inferiority in the ravages which it was allowed to exercise in a society intoxicated with voluptuous luxuries. Italy was in travail, at the same time, with the extremes of *good* and *evil*, and brought them forth together, like those terrible climates of the East whose sun produces at once the most lovely blossoms and the most deadly poisons, the most hideous monster and the graceful bird of paradise. Crime revelled in its peculiar intoxication, as well as genius in its extacies; morality had not sustained itself to the height of the intelligence of the time. Evil had grown and multiplied, political virtue was declining in the citizen, religious conscientiousness was dying in the priest; the Papal dignity, still grand and imposing under Nicolas V and Pius II, with whom political genius, the love of letters, and moral dignity, compensated externally at least for the weakening of faith, Papacy, say we, had plunged itself from precipice to precipice, until the childhood of Alexander VI. Rome, thrown back to the days of Tiberius and Nero, saluted with idolatrous acclamations the monster of impurity, whom a diabolical conclave had just proclaimed vicar of Jesus Christ. Incest, murder, and infidelity had seated themselves on the throne of Saint Peter, side by side with this man who seemed the very incarnation of the spirit of evil. Alexander VI face to face with Perugino! what an ideal and what a reality![1]"

The contrast between the admirable paintings of Perugino, and the abominable deeds of the Pope who reigned at the close of the fifteenth century, is characteristic therefore of the general contrast between the state of art and that of social morality at the same epoch in Italy.

But this "Renaissance," this awakening of the arts and sciences, if not this renovation of manners, to whom did it owe its birth? To the strangers and foreigners from the East, to the literature of the heathens originally from Greece, and not to Papacy. We will prove this from good authority: "The history of the last Crusade, so fertile in events, is merely an episode of the life of Saint Louis. To retrace them here would be to incur the charge of repetition. The saintly king, with one of his sons and a troop of Christians, lost their lives in this Crusade. Many Popes have since attempted to call together the Christians of Europe in that inhospitable land,

1. Martin, vol. VIII, p. 273.

watered with the blood of several generations. The incessant emigrations from West to East have had most important political results. It was the unconscious march of barbarism towards civilisation. These words resume the whole history of the Crusades. The summary result will suffice : the progressive concession of charters, the establishment of districts, the rehabilitation of the royal prerogative, until then a mere nominal dignity without real power, often without honour, but never without danger; total change of morals and customs, brought about by continued migrations from West to East for more than two centuries; the origin and progress of industry, of agriculture, and commerce by this lengthened and uninterrupted communication between nations who hitherto had been unknown to each other even by name. The French went themselves to the East in quest of these rich Indian stuffs and Oriental spices they had hitherto received from the Greeks and Venetians.

"Navigation became a necessity. A merchant navy was formed; the populations of Europe, until then penned in their respective folds, scattered and isolated, were no longer strangers to each other [1]."

"But gradually the arts declined during the reign of the Lower Empire, and sank at length to entire nothingness. The kingdom of Byzantium seemed however to have preserved some importance, when the taking of Constantinople by Mahomet II, in 1453, forced all artists to fly from a city and a country where the sword was the only method of reasoning. The religion of the Turks forbidding the imitation of the human figure, or of any natural object, the artists fled in all haste. Some took refuge in Germany, others in Italy, Venise, or Florence [2]."

The Renaissance, therefore, was an intellectual and not a moral movement. It brought back the taste for literature, the fine arts, and certain sciences; but, circumscribed in its influence, it was not the work of Papacy; it took decidedly its origin in the East.

This Renaissance had needed for its development the blessings of study and liberty. This study and this liberty, first of all applied to profane ends, might have been afterwards adapted to holy purposes. Luther made it understood. The Church of Rome grew alarmed; and, in order to strike at the root of the evil, declared herself inimical not only to the free study of theology, but to every kind of study, to every kind of liberty. We are about to

1. *Dictionnaire de la Conversation*, at the word CROISADES. — 2. *Idem*, at the word RENAISSANCE.

behold her at work to extinguish the light of human reasoning, to compress human thought and impede all progress, both moral and physical, which could tend by elevating the human race to rescue it from her domination. But it is time to let our authors speak for themselves, and prove what we have asserted. We will first of all demonstrate, through them, the inspiring principles of Papacy, and afterwards contemplate the fruits they have borne:

" Up to the date of the Council of Trent," says M. de Sismondi, " the Popes had contracted a species of alliance with the masses against their sovereigns; they were the protectors of philosophy and letters, they acknowledged liberty, and looked favourably on Republics; but when one division of the Church, raising the standard of the Reformation, shook off the yoke, when this rebellious portion of her sons turned against the Popes the light of that very philosophy they had suffered to be kindled, that spirit of liberty they had encouraged, and that public opinion which was slipping from their grasp and becoming in itself a new power, a feeling of profound terror caused them at once to alter their whole line of politics. Instead of remaining at the head of the league against monarchy, they beheld the necessity of making common cause with them, to obtain support against adversaries far more redoubtable. They entered into the strictest alliance with temporal princes, particularly with Philip II, the most despotic of all. Their only occupation became to bend the human conscience to their views, and lead captive the intelligence of man; and soon they imposed upon the human race a heavier yoke than any yet borne by the groaning sons of Adam.

" The Church seized first hold of the domain of moral ethics as being hers of right; she substituted the authority of her decrees in the place of reason and conscience, the study of casuists to that of moral philosophy, and she replaced by a debasing servitude the most noble of all intellectual exercises.

" Moral philosophy thus became completely distorted and disturbed in the hands of the casuists; and became estranged from the heart as well as from the reason; the distinction between mortal and venal offences soon effaced that which the conscience had established between sins of a serious kind, and those easily forgiven. Then were beheld upon the same level, side by side; the crime which inspires the most profound disgust and horror with the simple faults which weakness of human nature will not permit us to avoid.

" The casuists thus delivered up to the most dire execration of mankind in the first scale of malediction all heretics and schismatic reasoners; sometimes they succeeded in fanning a flame of a most bitter hatred against them; the robber, the assassin, the parricide were associated with men to whom involuntary respect was paid by the multitude. The good works of heretics threw doubt and suspicion upon virtue itself; their domination caused reprobation to be regarded as a kind of fatality, and the number of criminals became so multiplied, that innocence appeared impossible.

"The doctrine of penitence occasioned another subversion of morals; there was consolation, no doubt, in the promise of heavenly pardon for repentance; but the casuists deteriorated this doctrine; a single act of faith and fervour was proclaimed sufficient to efface a long list of crimes. Instead of being the constant effort of life, virtue became nothing more than an account with heaven, to be settled at the hour of death; and with this confident assurance the sinner was enabled to give loose to the most disorderly passions.

"I will say nothing of the shameless traffic in indulgences, and of the scandalous price demanded by the priest for the absolution of the penitent; and yet even in our day the priest lives by the sins and errors of the people; the dying man squanders, in the payment of masses for his soul, the money which he has often acquired by iniquitous means, and thus establishes in vulgar eyes a reputation for piety.

"The power attributed to religious ceremonies, the salvation indulgences, all combined to persuade the people that eternal happiness or everlasting torment depended on the absolution accorded by the priest, and this was perhaps the most damning stroke of all to religion and morality. The man the most perverse by nature, the most stained with crimes, might experience one of those momentary returns to virtue to which the most depraved heart is not always a stranger; he might make a worthy confession, a holy communion, an exemplary death, and be secure of Paradise. The flashes of reason and conscience were for ever extinguished by the dictates of theologians. The murderer, all covered with the blood he had just spilt, denies himself meat on fast-days with feelings of devotion, while he meditates the opportunity of committing a fresh murder; the prostitute places near her bed an image of the Virgin, before which she kneels and tells her beads with fervour.

"Charity is the great virtue of the Gospel; but the casuist has taught the philanthropist to give to the poor for the benefit of his own soul, and not to relieve the misery of his fellow creature; he has turned aside, in favour of the begging friar, the funds destined to public charity. Sobriety, chastity, are domestic virtues which preserve the natural faculties of the individual, and ensure the peace of families. The casuist has replaced them by fasting, by flagellations, and by vigils... And, in the midst of all the monkish virtues, gluttony and incontinence may take root unheeded and uncondemned.

"Dog m atical doctors,armed with all the authority of spiritual and temporal power, have forbidden all philosophical research which might establish to rules of probity, founded upon any other basis than those laid down by their own theories, all discussion of principle, all appeal to human reason. Moral doctrines have not only become their exclusive science but their exclusive secret. The scrupulous believer in Italy must abdicate the first of all human faculties, that of studying and learning his duty. He is commanded to forego any thought which can mislead him. It would be impossible to express the degree to which this ill-directed education has been injurious to public morality in Italy. There is not, throughout Europe, any people more constantly occupied in religious practices, or more strictly attached to their observance. There is not one who observes with less regularity the duties and virtues prescribed by that Christianity, to which it outwardly appears so devotedly attached. Each one has learnt, not to obey his conscience, but to tamper with that holy faculty; benefiting by indulgences can give easy play to his passions, and aids them indeed by mental restrictions, and by the prospect of repentance, and the hope of future absolution; and this religious fervour, so far from being a guarantee of virtue and honesty, may be regarded as the cloak of sin and looked upon with distrust.

"When the Popes, led by fanaticism, succeeded those who had been led by ambition, devotion was placed in the weak hands. The Jesuits seized upon all the colleges, and at the same moment everywhere ceased the independent education of thousands of scholars, who were exercising all their powers of intelligence, awakening all their faculties, and appealing without fear to the decision of thought. The monks who succeeded these men of active intelligence were enrolled with the severest care; indifferent to the success of the schools, and solely occupied with the advancement of their order, they denounced all appeal to human reason as a revolt against the doctrines emanating directly from the Divinity. It was no longer permitted to seek the human heart to find those principles on which authority had already pronounced its judgment; all policy was made to conform to the interests of the reigning government, and all noble sentiment was banished from a science which, naturally the most independent of all, soon became the most servile. What could be the value of antique eloquence, when the love of liberty was represented as the spirit of rebellion, the love of country as an idolatrous worship? Of what interest could be the study of law, of moral philosophy, of the customs of antiquity, when they were no longer placed in comparison with the notions of a legislation really free, of a morality purified, of customs born in the perfection of social order[1]?"

This quotation might dispense from citing other authorities; nevertheless, we will add a few lines from two or three authors :

"In this one epoch (sixteenth century) dates the decline of Rome. The Catholic element, passed to the great crucible of the Reformation, lost its power, its prestige, and by degrees became excluded from the political body; it ceased to be the bugbear of princes, who soon began to shake off its influence. By proclaiming the principle of individual independence, Luther was preparing a most glaring triumph to the popular element left without a means of expression[2]."

It is well understood that the Vatican has had no temporal power, since the day when, improvident renegade, it deserted the cause of the people, which was its own. It found itself solitary, without support; and was then compelled, in order not to perish, to seek other sensations. It proclaimed itself a gibelin, and the champion of princes : but, at bottom, it had not renounced its pretension to universal dominion.

"The Holy See has never ceased to increase in power at the expense of the political existence of Italy. By the very logic of circumstances, it has prevented that country from progressing, like every other country in Europe, towards that unity which alone could save it from destruction. It has suspended the very breath of civil life. It has prevented the development and duration of its political state; it has absorbed the vital power of Italy, despoiled and trodden down by the whole world; every one of the great centres of political organisation, the league of Lombardy, Pisa, Florence, Venice disappears in its turn; the temporal world is effaced, it is vanishing before the spiritual.

"When the work of destruction is accomplished, when nought remains of her civil existence; when, in the sixteenth century, Italy, effaced from the political mass of Europe, disappears from the

1. Sismondi, vol. XVI, p. 409 and following. — 2. Didier, p. 326.

region of reality to enter into the life of eternal ruin, at that very moment Popedom exclaims: Thou art dead, but I will make thee still reign; thou hast been sacrificed to me, but I will triumph over the whole world. I have absorbed thy rights, thy entire life, thy whole futurity; in thee nothing shall subsist longer than myself; thou hast consumed thyself wholly for my sake; and now during my reign, it is thee who shall be sovereign; for I will make of the whole earth an Italy like unto thee, without thy joyous sun and wondrous beauty. The thought of death, which arises from thy marshes and thy deserted towns, I will impose likewise upon the whole world, and there shall enter a fatal silence as that which surrounds thee; thou shall recognise it for thine own; thou shall find thyself everywhere, and all shall envy thee the death-crown which adorns thy brow[1]."

Such was the tree planted, in the sixteenth century, by the labours of Papacy in the Roman States, and whose roots extend over the whole Italian soil. Now, let us examine the nature of the fruit which this gigantic tree has brought forth; and when we see secular governments holding up the theory of divine right, of royal authority, of the privileges of race, let us not forget that the pontifical government had begun by proclaiming the infallibility of the Pope, the sovereignty of the Church, and the privileges of the clergy; and that, by the transfer of these pretensions from the spiritual to the temporal reign of power, Papacy itself had prepared every species of abuse, and every description of tyranny.

"Rome," says Sismondi, "who, at the beginning of the century, had beheld in Leo X a great pontiff, a friend of literature, and a generous protector of poetry and art, grown suspicious by the progress of the Reformation, had now no other pre-occupation than that of crushing all spread of thought; and under the reigns of Paul IV, of Pius IV, and Pius V (1555,1572), who had risen to power through the influence of the Inquisition, the persecution of letters and of learned associations was renewed in a regular and systematic manner, to be arrested no more[2]."

"But the calamities which ushered in the beginning of the sixteenth century were less fatal than the death-slumber which ensued. A universal oppression, systematic and regular, succeeded to the violence of war. It would not be an easy task to make known to the reader the government suspicious and apathetic the same time of the three Philips, who possessed the sovereignty over

1. Quinet, p. 58 and 59. — 2. Quinet, vol. II, p. 188.

the duchy of Milan, Naples, Sicily, and Sardinia, and who exercised a rule almost as absolute over the Papal States, and over those of the dukes of Italy, who had implored protection at their hands. Exorbitant tributes, unequally and absurdly levied, had mined all commerce, crushed and depopulated the provinces; internal quarrels, more ruinous by far, had enriched certain governors, while the minds of the people were penetrated with every sentiment of hatred and contempt for a system of government at once so blind and so unjust. All effort of the human mind was considered an attack against the government; all liberty of writing or printing was forbidden to the subject; all public discussion or deliberation was interdicted; every individual possessing books forbidden by these arbitrary regulations exposed himself to the severest penalties, both of a civil and religious nature; for the government, in order to exercise a more vigilant police, and to extend its power over the public mind, had called the Inquisition to its aid, and made it the faithful guardian of every species of despotism [1]. "

" Nothing obtained respect but the vilest abuses; civil liberty was openly violated; men suspected, not of guilty actions but of liberal opinions, were exposed to the most painful death not as punishment but torture, and notwithstanding there was no administration of justice. Convents and churches served as refuge to malefactors; every petty viceroy, every military commander, every agent of the government, maintained an army of banditti under his protection, to whom impunity was secured as reward for those violent and murderous deeds which they committed by his command. The convents themselves had their paid assassins, and, in the conspiracy of father Campanella, the monks of Calabria were found capable of arming several thousand of these bandits. The robbers encamped themselves almost at the gates of cities, and it was impossible to travel without escort from Naples to Caserta or Averso [2]. The state of the Church, during the whole of this century, might be compared to a great desert, which no spark of life was suffered to cheer or animate [3]. "

" The influence of a narrow spirit was found to rule over the administration as well as over the actions of their chiefs; the habits of a minute espionage, of inquiet distrust, of an obstinate aversion for any innovation, was given to every subaltern, and individuals were condemned to vegetate in perpetual constraint. Public morals had yielded to the corruption of the mode, still

1. Sismondi, vol. II, pp. 243, 244, 245. — 2. *Idem*, pp. 246, 247. — 3. *Idem*, p. 250.

more than to that of the passions; a frivolity, become universal, seemed to exclude all thought, all warmth of conversation; the constant habit of idleness relaxed the mind; and rendered it incapable even of the capability of occupation. The adoption of the *sigisbés* (the authorised lover of the married woman), no less debasing to the thought than to the morals, left no time at the disposal even of the professed idler, and furnished hourly duties to those whose lives were ostensibly without aim or end. Men grew accustomed to live without the slightest renewal of ideas, whether for action or conversation; the stoppage of every career, the impossibility of applying any study to any useful end, had destroyed every stimulus to education. The universities, formerly so brilliant, now contained only those whose learning was confined to students of theology, medicine, or jurisprudence, with a view of acquiring a lucrative profession from these studies. The schools, opened in such vast numbers during the fifteenth century, and which had produced so many learned men, were all closed, and there remained only a few colleges and monastic seminaries, wherein the aim of education seemed to be, not to teach, but to repress, and where the scholar was taught to subdue his reason, to curb his will, to be silent, to dissimulate, to fear, and to obey. The nation, in short, was dead in every way[1]."

With his vivid imagination, M. Quinet describes, also, this sixteenth century in Italy: "At the present time the Inquisition has stifled every semblance of life or motion in Italy. The hangman has just torn out the tongue of Vanini; Giordano, Bruno, Dominis have been burnt at the stake. Compelled to abjure all theory or systematic ideas, what remains to Italy? You answer, experience, facts, reality, and, what is invincible with all mankind, mathematical science. Well, then, experience and mathematics are to be condemned, physical science interdicted, geometry excommunicated, that it may be proved to the world that if Italy is arrested in her progress towards perfection, if she ceases to produce, it is because every outlet is closed, and life itself condemned to perish for want of renovating care[2]."

"The ignorance of the ministers of Madrid, who were unacquainted with the very first elements of political economy, was even more fatal to the welfare of Italy than their rapacity and spoliations. They seemed to take to task to invent taxes solely destined to crush all industry, and ruin agriculture. Manufactures

1. Sismondi, *Littérature du Midi de l'Europe*, vol. II, pp. 351, 352. — 2. Quinet, p. 79.

seemed in their decadence; commerce was disappearing altogether; the rural districts of the country becoming deserted; and the inhabitants, reduced to despair, were compelled in short to embrace, as the sole profession open to them, that of highway robbery. Chiefs of high birth or distinguished talents headed the bands of assassins, which became, at the close of the century, organised in the kingdom of Naples and in the Papal States, and this war of banditti often menaced the power of sovereign authority itself. Meanwhile, the provinces remained without defenders, the coast without ships, the forts ungarrisoned [1]. "

" The duchy of Milan found that all recovery from the disasters of the preceding wars would be impossible under the Spanish government. The most absurd imposts were levied, which banished all manufactures and commerce, and if the laws could not accomplish the utter ruin of these fertile plains, at all events they rendered the state of those by whom they were cultivated miserable in the extreme. The government seemed to take delight in augmenting the hateful yoke borne by the Milanese by the establishment of the Spanish Inquisition. The Holy Office of Italy, which had been already for many years in full vigour at Milan, was no longer deemed sufficient to satisfy the savage fanaticism or the policy of Philip II [2]. "

" The Spanish administration drove both Sicily and Sardinia back to barbarism; it had already scared from the cities all enterprise and commerce; it had abandoned the fertile plains of those countries to the devastations of robbers and smugglers, and had left their whole line of coast exposed to the ravages of the pirates of Barbary [3]. "

" For a long time preceding, the Holy See had been filled by men whose sole pursuits were directed towards worldly interests, who had been successively occupied in satisfying their tastes for pleasure, for the arts, or for magnificence and war. Amongst these, some had sought to extend even the sovereignty of the Church; others, on the contrary, had endeavoured to detach from its possession certain fiefs, in order to aggrandise their families; in each and all the statesman had superseded the Churchman, and their conduct was but little guided by religious fanaticism. Such was the characteristic of Papal dignity during the whole space of time between the Council of Constance and the Council of Trent [4]. "

" The government of the Popes who succeeded, from the open-

1. Sismondi, vol. XVI, p. 158. — 2. *Idem*, p. 165. — 3. *Idem*, p. 170. — 4. *Idem*, 181.

ing of the Council of Trent to the end of the century, is found to be polluted by the atrocious persecutions exercised by them against the Protestants of Italy. The abuses of the Court of Rome were more public in that country than in any other; literature had been there cultivated earlier, and with greater care. Philosophy had made likewise more rapid progress in the land; and, towards the beginning of that century, this philosophy had confronted even religious matters with the greatest freedom. The Reformation had acquired amongst men of letters numerous partisans in Italy, but few amongst those poor and labouring classes by which it had been embraced with so much ardour in Germany and France. The Popes succeeded in extinguishing the flame in the blood of its adherents. The Inquisition, during the whole century, became the surest road to the Papal Throne. The Pontiffs ceased not to foment the civil wars then raging in France and Flanders, and the conspiracies against the Queen of England; so that the calamities, which during the latter half of the sixteenth century overwhelmed the whole of Europe, may be entirely regarded as their work.

"The subjects of the Popes, during this second half of the sixteenth century, were scarcely more fortunate than those of the Spanish Crown. By an equally absurd government, they were oppressed to an equal extent, without the experience of the slightest degree of protection; while the most unjust and onerous taxes, monopolies of the most ruinous nature, destroyed all germ of industry amongst them: the administration of subsistence, violent and arbitrary in its nature, by thwarting the commerce of grain, became the source of famine, always followed by pestilence. That of 1590 and 1591 carried off, in Rome alone, 60,000 inhabitants; many of the richest villages in Ombria remaining from that time forwards entirely abandoned. It was thus that desolation and ruin were spread over these extensive plains, formerly so fertile, and that they became the prey of the malaria. The armed force of the State no longer sufficed to protect the citizens against a system of robbery regularly organised. Robbers, grown iusolent by their strength and numbers, and proud of combatting against the shameless government of their country, had ended by considering their lawless trade as the most honourable of all. Even the people, while suffering of their rapine, applauded their valour, and looked upon these bands of outlaws as nurseries for warriors. Numbers of ruined nobles, younger sons of princely families, were sometimes boastful of having served for a while amongst them, and the greatest seigneurs placed themselves at the head of these troops of banditti, to carry on a regular warfare against the Papal army. These brigands, not content with robbing travellers, or hiring bravos to all who consented to pay them for the satisfaction of private vengeance, often surprised villages, and even small towns, for pillage, and compelled the larger burghs to ransom themselves by enormous payments from the burning of their suburbs, and the devastation of their crops. This custom subsists even in our day, and the seigneur is still found sharing secretly in the spoils of the same crime. National honour has remained thus perverted, and still, in that portion of the Roman States where population has not been destroyed (in Sabinia, for instance), the peasant will not scruple to unite the trades of robber and assassin to that of tiller of the soil[1]."

Let us now advance a step with the progress of the world, and we shall see the same state of things renewed: "The seventeenth century in Italy is an era of complete annihilation; its literary history represents it as abandoned to the most corrupt tastes, to puerility, and barrenness, while its political annals hold it up to contemplation as deprived of all activity, and every public virtue, as well as of all elevation of character or important revolution. The further we advance, the greater is our conviction that the history, not merely of the Italian Republics alone, but of the Italian nation itself, was ended with the year 1530. The disasters of the seventeenth century were silent misfortunes; each individual was suffering, but suffering in the bosom of his own family; intercourse of private life was embittered; its hopes destroyed, its fortunes reduced, while its necessities were increasing with each day; the conscience of the citizen, instead of sustaining him under trial and temptation, reproached him with his weakness, and with shame and grief he sought to conceal his misery from the eyes of the world, and to avoid its record from extending to posterity.

"It is this cause which has prevented that, amongst the public misfortunes of Italy, the private sufferings of Italian families have remained unnoticed. The first of these being the attack upon the sacred tie of marriage by the admission of another bond, considered honourable, and foreigners always view with undisguised astonishment, without comprehending it; that is, of the *sigisbés*, or *cavalieri serventi*. This fatal custom, having once been introduced in the seventeenth century by the example of the courts, and placed under the protection of every species of vanity, the peace of fami-

1. Sismondi, vol. XVI, pp. 189 to 193.

lies was banished from Italy; no husband dared to regard his wife as a faithful companion, bound to his existence; none could find in her either a friendly adviser in doubt, a support under adversity, or help in danger, or consolation in despair. No father dared to trust that the children bearing his name were really his own; none felt bound towards them by the tie of Nature; and the pride of conserving a noble name, replacing the most natural and affectionate sentiments, embittered all domestic intercourse. What heavy crimes against humanity have those princes to answer for, who succeeded in depriving their subjects from experiencing the tender feelings of the husband, the father, the brother, or the son[1]!"

"While all these family ties were being destroyed in the seventeenth century by this new state of morals, which, regarded by the Court as the only type of elegance and fashion, was soon of course adopted by the great mass of the people, the commerce of the country received its final blow by the sudden retreat of men of enterprise and capital. Its ruin became complete by the monopolies and by the absurd taxes laid upon the sale of all objects of barter established by the Spaniards in every province dependent on their rule. Nevertheless, ostentation and magnificence seemed to increase in the country, while its resources were diminishing. The Italians acquired, during this century, and it was the Spaniards who taught them the lesson, the art of retrenching from the most pressing necessities of life in order to bestow more expense upon outward show, and it became a high merit in every head of a family to squander large sums upon his vanities or pleasures[2]."

"The laws of the country, its morals, its example, its very religion itself as it was practised, tended to the substitution in every thing of the most hardened selfishness to every more noble incentive. The father of a family, married to the wife he had not chosen, whom he could not love, by whom he was not beloved, surrounded by children of whose paternity he was ever doubtful, whose education he could not follow, whose affection he could not obtain, constrained without ceasing in his own family by the presence of the friend of his wife, separated from those brothers and sisters who where doomed from early childhood to a life of monastic seclusion, wearied with the uselessness of the others, to whom he was compelled to give a seat at his board as their only patrimony, was merely regarded as the steward of the family property, while every member of that family, whether brother,

1. Sismondi, vol. XVI, pp. 220 to 222. — 2. *Idem*, p. 225.

sister, wife, or child, combined together, in secret conspiracy, to turn aside for their sole benefit all that could be secured from the general revenue, in order to enjoy an ease and affluence of their own, without a thought or care for the embarrassment in which its chief was plunged.

"For each unforeseen expense, the head of the family was compelled to draw upon the fund destined to the improvement of the estate, the only resource at his disposal, and the one which ought to have been considered as a sacred deposit. He thus became the despoiler of the family property, because he had not the right to sell it, and numerous families of yeomanry became involved in the fatal effects of his own jurisprudence, or of that of his neighbours, or of the accidental catastrophe which might have befallen his fortunes... If by chance he sought to follow a public career, he could only hope for success by cultivating the arts of intrigue or adulation, and of the most mean subtility; if he engaged in a law-suit, his rights became compromised by the interminable delays of legal chicanery, or sacrificed by the venality of his judges; if he had enemies, his wealth, his liberty, his very life itself were at the mercy of secret perjury, and of the arbitrary administration of the tribunals. Loving nothing but himself, and finding nothing in himself but pains and cares, he was compelled to seek relief from his troubles in the universal rush after sensual delights; and, by abandoning himself to their enjoyment, he prepared for himself new miseries and new remorse[1]."

"No single instance could be found of a father who, by his last will and testament, hesitated to sacrifice all his daughters to his sons, all the younger sons to the eldest, and the widow to the heir. Every domestic tie was distorted by this false distribution of property. Filial respect towards the mother was destroyed, when the mother was thus rendered dependent upon her own son for subsistence. Brotherly affection was equally annulled; for friendship exacts equality, and cannot exist between a despotic master and his hired parasite[2]."

Such, then, were the fruits of the tree planted by Papacy. But would it not be possible to grasp it? To speak without metaphor, would it not be possible to extract from the principle of Catholicism totally different results? Does not evil arise rather from mankind itself than from institutions? No; on the contrary, there have been men good and brave enough to seek to reform this world

1. Sismondi, pp. 227 to 229. — 2. *Idem*, p. 457.

of corruption and iniquity, and they have failed in the attempt. Let us enumerate some of these vain endeavours at reform.

First of all, a vain attempt at Ancona for the preservation of liberty : " The sparks of liberty which still were dispersed about Italy went out by degrees in the Papal States. Ancona alone had preserved a republican and independent government, until the month of August, of the year 1552 ; the little city was in the quiet enjoyment of this liberty, when Pope Clement VII gave warning to its magistrates that the fleet of Sultan Soliman was advancing up the Adriatic, and at the same time offered the aid of a small army, commanded by Louis de Gonzague. The people of Ancona received without distrust the Papal troops; who, having got possession of the outposts, arrested the magistrates, beheaded six of their number, disarmed the citizens, built a strong fortress on Mount San Siriaco, and wrested from the town all its ancient privileges[1]."

Another more recent example : " No Italian State has ever owed so much to any sovereign, as Tuscany to Peter Leopold. He applied himself to reform the abuses which a bad administration of two hundred years had introduced; he simplified the civil laws, and mitigated the severity of the criminal ones; he gave liberty to commerce, and by rousing his subjects to habits of activity and industry which they had long abandoned, he withdrew whole provinces from under water, and doubled agricultural produce. He also endeavoured to check the depravity of the manners, and the excess of superstition; but his ecclesiastical reforms were strongly opposed by the provincial council, convoked by him on the 23rd of April, 1787. The prejudices of the priests, and the vices of the people, were in league against a prince who was perhaps too eager in his desire to do good[2]."

" But neither the wisdom nor the benevolence of Leopold's efforts were acknowledged by a large class of his subjects, a class composed of all that was interested in the maintenance of the abuses he abolished: the priesthood, the noblesse, and the refuse of the people. Convents suppressed, religious orders dissolved, licentiousness reproved, activity called forth, indolence roused from its voluptuous slumbers, and reformation universally suggested or inposed, excited a powerful enmity and resistance against the royal reformer, when, by the death of Joseph the Second, Leopold exchanged his dukedom for the throne of an Empire, and the go-

1. Sismondi, vol. XVI, p. 120. — 2. *Idem.* vol. XVI, p. 326.

vernment of Tuscany lapsed into the hands of his second son. The priests and nobles exhibited their joy at this event, in manifestations by no means equivocal : they well knew that the example of royal fathers holds little influence over their successors, and their opinions were amply justified in the event. The young sovereign, Ferdinand the Third, became the agent of his then major domo *Manfredini:* and, acting under his auspices, he abolished, amidst the plaudits of the rabble, freedom of commerce given by his fathers; he impaired that code, the object of admiration to the philosophical and the benevolent of all countries; he restored capital punishments, and fostered that long-discouraged bigotry, which once more raised its drooping head under royal protection [1]. "

The same has been the case with Joseph II in Lombardy : " By the people he (Joseph II) was not understood; by the noble and the priest he was perfectly comprehended. They saw his aim, and combined to turn it on one side, to save their privileges and preserve their power. Those of his acts which excited the greatest hostility best prove his wisdom and humanity. Such were his decrees of 1781, granting the free exercise of worship to the Greek and Protestant churches. He founded colleges and libraries where his father had raised convents and shrines; he had the Bible translated into the vulgar tongue, hitherto withheld from the knowledge of the people; he took the literary censorship out of the hands of the priesthood. But what was the result? And what was the reward of these voluntary efforts of a prince in favour of his long-oppressed people?... Joseph the Second, the patriot prince, the patron of letters, died of a *broken heart;* unhonoured by one trophy, unlamented by one laureate elegy! The Pope, the priesthood, the princes and nobles of Germany and of Lombardy, united against him; the ignorant and bigoted people believed the avowed enemy of their religion. In Vienna, under the very windows of the Emperor, the more brutal Austrians, in a coarse dialect, exclaimed, 'Let him die!' or, more literally from the German, 'Let him burst!' He expired catching to the last these terrible execrations, and suing to be permitted to die in peace [2]."

In our own day, another attempt made by a powerful hand has met with no better success : " As, by degrees, Napoleon took possession of the provinces of Italy, one after another, the French spirit of reform in the laws and tribunals, the spirit of publicity, of equality, of impatience of tyranny, soon manifested itself, and

1. Lady Morgan, vol. II, pp. 173, 174. — 2. *Idem*, vol. I, pp. 205 to 207.

the Republic of Venice could then judge of the detestation it had inspired in all who possessed any degree of elevation of soul. Inferior minds, it is true, found only in the lowest classes of peasants and workmen governed by priestly influence, and comprehending nothing but what is visible, looked upon every French innovation with horror. The Senate looked to this party for support, and excited its ignorant fanaticism by every means [1]. "

" By the entrance of the French into Italy (1796) arbitrary law was abolished; moral and public instruction replaced, at the tribunals, secret judgments and secret tortures; civil equality had taken the place of the feudal system; education, instead of being conducted on the former retrograde system, had been urged forwards, and the liberty of conscience, both religious and political, had been restituted. The French invasion bore promise to awakening Italy liberty, virtue, and glory. The coalition destroyed this noble work, and replaced Italy entirely under the yoke of Austria, depriving her, with political liberty, of civil and religious freedom likewise, and even that of thought itself, corrupting her morals, and overwhelming her with the lowest degree of humiliation [2]."

" By force of a Papal rescript, dated the 6th of July, 1816, were abolished the magistracy *degli anziani*, that of the tribunes of the people, the tribunal of the *Rota*, the corporation of the arts, the colleges of medicine, philosophy, of civil and canon law, of the advocates, the notaries, and even of theology. The national force was disarmed; all the ancient faculties, and the government of the militia, the administration of tribunals, of studies, of the institute, of the sciences, the right of choosing professors and public officers, and the right of coining money, were cancelled and anulled. By this act of violence, *di Roma che minaccia della s'dgno di Dio senza temerlo*, Bologna is reduced to the same state of servitude as the other provinces; and is subject to the laws of the general sovereignty [3]. "

Thus do we behold that Papacy remains the same throughout all ages. Without possibility of reform, all the change to be expected from this power is that of change in the means of attaining to the same end. Papacy wears the costume of the day; but it is to turn the fashion of the day to its own account. In former times it borrowed the temples, the ceremonies, even the beliefs of Paganism, to gain over the Pagan nations to its cause, without feeling

1. Sismondi, vol. II, p. 262. — 2. *Idem*, p. 266, 267. — 3. Lady Morgan, vol. II, pp. 42, 43.

disquieted with fear lest the disguise might render its own nature Pagan also. In later centuries, Papacy placed itself at the head of the crusades, because, just then, a warlike order stimulated Christianity, and it had become a matter of importance for Rome to appear to direct the movement, in order to preserve and increase her own influence. Later still, this same power has followed in the wake of despotic kings, to profit by this very despotism of which it has ended by adopting the principle. But throughout all these subtle transformations, Papacy has ever remained the same : ambitious, selfish, rendering every human interest subservient to its own advancement; bending to the present without breaking with the past; sharpening for its own usage every arms which seemed the most likely to inflict the most mortal wound; and then, at the hour of triumph, resuming its insolent dominion, in the name of a new principle, distorted to the profit of the ancient cause. Popery can never be modified : Popery will ever absorb into itself whoever seeks to join it. Let us hear our authors on the subject: "It has been the invariable rule of the Church of Rome to observe the tendencies of the age in order to appear to direct them, while in reality she follows and yields to them, so as to secure the great end, ecclesiastical supremacy. Europe, deserted by Papal instigations during the Crusades, was left to the clergy, who did not lose the opportunity to aggrandise themselves. In a more civilised period, at the time of the renewing of Letters, the clergy headed a crusade against ignorance, and when a period of security was succeeded by a moment of danger, when the very existence of Papacy was compromised, the progress of reform was arrested by those faithful champions of error, the Jesuits. More agreeable paths presented themselves to the ambition of the clergy, who found it safer and more convenient to rule cabinets by means of a confessor; mysterious agent, who in turn flattered the vices and awoke the terrors of his superstitious penitents; kings and queens, favourites of both sexes. But when this system was exhausted, and the revolutionary spirit gained the ascendancy, the priest, like another Protius, accommodated himself to the change. In Ireland, the threatening position of the Catholic population has long been openly countenanced by a clergy, who, at any rate, do nothing towards softening the sanguinary barbarity of their manners, and it is at a time when crime had never been so rife in Ireland, that England, with unexampled generosity, lavished her resources to relieve the miseries of this country[1]."

1. *Revue Britannique*, 1848, January, February, pp. 301, 302.

Thus has Italy remained under the inspiration, if not under the empire, of Popery. As in past ages, she has imbibed its very principle: the harvest she is now gathering in with bitterness and tears is therefore the fruit of the seed sown during long centuries by her religious faith. For fifteen centuries ago has Catholicism conceived, nursed, and educated its own beloved people; it has now grown to man's estate at last. Let us see what has become of its faith, its government, its morals, its agriculture, its commerce, and industry:

GOVERNMENT. — "The general policy of the petty despots who rule the subdivided States of this unfortunate country, is no less hostile to its commerce than it is to liberty. But the nullity of Italy is part of the religious and moral system which hypocrisy, joined to the force of arms, has imposed on mankind; and for the present the Italians have nothing to do but to obey[1]."

"The *obscurantism* of the sovereign tyrants of Italy does not tolerate any work that is not dedicated to the propagation of falsehood, and the retrogradation of intellect. The principal movement of mind exists in Lombardy; in Florence it stills struggles to advance; in Rome it sleeps. In this last devoted city, which for more than two thousand years had forged chains for the whole civilised world, there reigns a brutal and entire ignorance of whatever passes without its own walls[2]."

"It is impossible to conceive a greater combination of hostile accidents, operating more successfully against the best interests of civilisation, or more perfectly paralysing all intellectual exertion[3]."

"The ecclesiastical and civil powers of Rome have the same end in view; to proscribe all idea of independence, and all spirit of examination. The Neapolitan clergy have accepted a high office in the police, and they display in this political apostleship an intolerance and fanaticism which exceed even the rigours of temporal power. The evangelical pulpit is converted into a political one; its anathemas are reserved for the oppressed and suffering people; hope is there annihilated, the desire to improve withers, and the powers, constituted and maintained by violence, receive the approval of the Vatican[4]."

We are about to trace this same spirit on every spot throughout Italy. First of all in Piedmont[5]: "The French codes of jurisprudence, celebrated for their lucidity, had been received with joy

1. Lady Morgan, vol. III, p. 113. — 2. *Idem*, p. 148. — 3. *Idem*, p. 150. — 4. Didier p. 233.
5. It is an agreeable task for us, at the moment we pen these lines, to observe that Piedmont has chosen a better path; but it is well known also that the adoption of this new course has drawn down upon her the most violent opposition on the part of Rome and her clergy.

in Piedmont and in Savoy; these provinces might have been enabled to preserve them while ceasing to form part of the French dominions. They have been replaced by the ancient customs, uncertain and contradictory in their nature, which formerly ruled the country. The sons inherit, to the exclusion of the daughters. All attempt to emigration is punished by fines and degrading penalties; confiscation of property reduces to beggary the entire family of any citizen guilty of crime, or even of any misdemeanour; the judges of the tribunals, whose office is revokable at pleasure, determine, according to their own will, the amount of expenses incurred by the adversaries; the royal pardon is even to be bought and paid for under the title of *royal emolument*. In this kingdom the system of centralisation is so admirably organised that, says a traveller, the government can reconsider the verdict of the judges, revoke the free decisions between consenting parties, annul the will of a dead subject, and delegate to its own commissaries the right of decision in causes wherein the interest of the great and powerful are at stake. In criminal trials, neither the accused nor his defender are allowed to be present at the examination of the witnesses; the indictment, the debates, the verdict, are all rendered in secret; and if, in spite of these overwhelming circumstances against the accused, his innocence is recognised, he is only restored to liberty on payment of all the costs of a ruinous and sometimes wholly unjust proceeding.

"The nobles enjoy every favour bestowed by the government; they alone can pretend to any advancement in the army; they alone are exempted from all the forced taxes, with which all other classes are burthened; they are not amenable to the ordinary tribunals. A noble, who refuses to acquit himself of debt, can obtain from the king the permission to abstain for ten or twenty years from payment of the interests of the sums he owes.

"These facts indicate sufficiently the nature of the Sardinian government: it is one of the purest despotism[1]."

The Tuscan government is even worse than that of Piedmont: "The President of Police can arrest citizens in their own houses, and during the night; and upon suspicion, or on secret information, he can commit them to a house of correction, or force them into the military service, as in the case of the *discolato*, that is, of abandoned immoral conduct, or abstinence from religious duties; a practice the more dangerous to personal liberty, from its execu-

1. Didier, vol. VII, p. 290.

tion being committed to the most subaltern agents of the police[1]. The finances of Tuscany far exceed the necessary wants of the State, and are chiefly employed for purposes of corruption.[2]"

But it is at Rome itself that it is of most importance to study the government and administration; for, if the influence of the Pope were ever contested over the rest of Italy, its existence could not be denied in the city over which he reigns, not only as Spiritual Pontiff, but also as temporal and absolute sovereign: "It is not enough for Rome," says M. Briffault, "to preserve in her bosom the barren traditions of her past history; in every intercourse with the governments and peoples of Europe, the Papal Court acts with one sole design, that of driving everything back to immobility; for Roman power a second nature. Under the inspiration of the Sovereign of the Church, the clergy is influenced by one aim alone, that of obtaining admittance into the affairs of the State, in order to bring back to Rome the influence thus acquired over the destinies of the country. Rome no longer thunders forth, from the summit of the Vatican, those anathemas which would now provoke contempt; but she is busily occupied in boring subteraneous passages beneath all those ideas of progress which impede her views; her dark approach is parallel with the march of civilisation visible to the eye of Heaven. Tardy efforts; and which can succeed no better in repairing the ruin of her temporal power than her spiritual influence, which have acted together to their mutual destruction[3]."

"Nothing is so dark and mysterious as the financial administration of Rome; everything is decided by arbitrary rule; everything is obscure and unknown. The public funds are swallowed up and distributed without control. Nobody is ignorant of the fact of the commissions bestowed upon prelates and cardinals, for the exercise of this surveillance, being a mere matter of form. Taxation is unequally distributed. Certain provinces of the Apennines, which for the tast twenty years have been paying 100,000 francs with the Treasury for the construction of roads, are still traversed by the most impracticable footpaths.

"This disorderly management engenders the utmost discontent; this discontent requires renewed efforts at repression, these again demanding increase of outlay, and already the 4,000 Swiss spread throughout the Legations are no longer found sufficient to put down the insurrection, which has peopled the dungeons of Fort Saint Leon and the other State prisons with miserable captives[4]."

1. Lady Morgan, vol. III, p. 102. — 2. *Idem*, pp. 113 and 114. — 3. Briffault, pp. 460, 461. — 4. *Idem*, p. 73.

" As Frenchmen, our existence is not without its charm. We are recherché at Rome, we are welcomed with pleasure, not in the higher regions of society, nor yet amongst the clergy, where our liberalism and philosophy become motives of dislike and dread, but in the middle classes. But, I repeat, Rome is a focus of pestilence, which breathes corruption to the strongest natures, to the most upright hearts[1]."

" The Italian races possess a degree of subtility which leads them involuntarily towards the darkest manœuvres. The perfection to which was carried in Venice the art of espionage and denunciation is well known to all. The annals of the Republic are filled with these mysterious horrors. The other States of Italy adopted, from a natural taste, the morals and the mask of Venetian policy. Rome was the first to follow in this tortuous path, and her domestic annals are filled with these sombre and disloyal traditions. The police of Rome extended far beyond the precincts of the Holy City. By means of the religious orders submitted to its power and discipline, the Holy See was enabled to penetrate into the secrets of the laws, and the feelings of the people. The confessional of every Catholic monarch found its corresponding echo beneath the dome of the Vatican.

" At Rome, almost every member of the government acts with the police, not exactly as a profession, but in order to earn a little in their leisure moments, and add to their means of existence. The whole Church, from the humblest official of the Sacristy up to the members of the Sacred College, is enrolled in this new species of militia. The revelation of secrets and surveillance form part of the oath imposed upon the priests. Flanked by the religious communities, the clerical agencies, and the army of devotees, this vast aggregation becomes complete. The army itself is associated with the system. Another portion of the Roman population takes a share in its operations, that is, the crowd of mendicants, robbers, and courtezans so numerous in Rome; the domestics likewise, the ciceroni, and all that multitude whose existence of chance and adventure is attached to that of the foreign visitors of the city; every element of power and of shame contained in Rome is attached to the police. Fortunately, in that pursuit, as in all others in that country, activity is paralysed by indolence[2]. "

" Upon the Popish territory, " says M. Didier, " things are not examined so closely ; a few galerians obtain by special favour of his

1. Briffault, p. 100. — 2. *Idem*, pp. 105, 106.

Holiness the privilege of not performing any labour, and they pass their time in the delights of an eternal *far niente*. The famous bandit Gasperoni was amongst this number. Tired of the brigand's life, and wishing, as he said, to withdraw from business, he had offered to lay down his arms, upon the sole condition of having his life spared. The Papal government accepted this capitulation. Gasperoni held a species of court, and received innumerable visits in his prison. He loved to recount his exploits, as a general loves to talk of his campaigns; and I have heard him boast of having committed five-and-forty murders. The gaolers professed the highest esteem for him. For them and for the prisoners, he was the greatest hero of the day : such are the morals of this country [1]."

But let us pause no longer to depict the government of such and such Italian country. What we have said successively of Piedmont, of Tuscany, and of the Roman States, M. de Sismondi will confirm with regard to the whole of Italy : " Despotism need seek for no disguise in Italian legislation; a Sovereign power, a power without limit, is the attribute of a Prince. There is no right, however sacred, which is not subject to his supreme will. The laws are simple emanations of the wish of the monarch; the verdicts of the tribunals, whether in civil or criminal cases, may be reversed by his decree. For one, he may suspend the pursuit of creditors; for the other, he can order the restitution *in integrum* of the privileges forfeited by judgment; he can legitimise a third, who may be a bastard, in order to entitle him to a share of his father's inheritance, to the prejudice of his brothers and cousins; he may abrogate, in favor of a fourth, the obligations of primogeniture, that he may dispose of the estates which are entailed upon the children. The privileges of corporate bodies present no greater barrier to his will than those of individuals, and he can change at his own pleasure, and for his own particular purpose, the customs of cities and the prerogatives of their divers orders of citizens. And by the same rule that everything depends upon the sole will of the Prince, everything is accomplished by that will alone, without debate, without public discussion, and without the concurrence of the nation in a matter which may concern its most important interests. To criticise or condemn any system of policy adopted by the government, would be considered a punishable offence. Even the study of modern history is forbidden; it leads to the temptation of pronouncing a

1. Didier, p. 23.

judgment upon matters considered too lofty for the comprehension of the people.

" In countries where the trials of criminals take place in public, each trial becomes a high and solemn lesson for the multitude. The individual learns thence that the crime committed, in secret and solitude, far from human eye, becomes nevertheless matter of inquiry and search. He learns that the public justice watching over him is benevolent, enlightened, and refrains from punishing until the crime is clearly proved. But, where the trial is secret, accompanied by no pleading, no debate which admits the public to a criticism of the verdict, all agree to behold in the administration of justice nothing more than a power of persecution, and odious authority; a league is established to rescue culprits alike from its grasp, and public opinion brands with infamy all those who contribute in any way whatever to its fulfilment. This league against the accomplishment of justice has been found throughout the whole of Italy.

" The profession of an officer of the tribunals, an agent of police, or a sbirri, is pronounced infamous, and it will be readily understood that men who consent to be called by a name which is covered with ignominy have no scruple in committing actions whereby the contempt with which they are visited may not be undeserved. The honest citizen will blush to be suspected of having any intercourse with the bargello, or to have received from that officer any service whatever; although every citizen feels that his reputation, his liberty, his life, are at any hour dependent upon the secret testimony of this officer. Every individual is liable to be arrested at night, torn from his home, bound in chains, transported to a great distance, by the single authority of this man, who is not bound to account for his proceedings to any other than to the Minister of Police, or President of the *buon governo*. Italy is the only country in the world where legal infamy, far from being incompatible with power, has become a requisite condition for the exercise of a certain authority.

" An Italian, of whatever rank he may be, if he has not entirely lost all sense of reputation, will never assist in giving up a malefactor into the hands of justice. An impudent robbery, a frightful murder, may be committed in the public streets; the crowd, instead of arresting the criminal, will make way for him to escape, and close against the sbirri who are in pursuit. The witness, interrogated concerning a crime committed before his eyes, takes offence at being made to answer like a spy. So great is the feeling of compassion towards the criminal, so universal the suspicion concerning the justice of his judges, that the tribunals seldom dare to brave this sentiment by pronouncing a capital condemnation. The criminal gains nothing, however, by this apparent leniency; he either lingers for long years in prison, or he is banished to some unhealthy provinces, where malaria executes slowly, and with pain, the sentence which the judge has not dared to pronounce, while the example of the punishment which follows crime is lost to the people.

"Over almost the whole of Italy, the decision of all cases, whether civil or criminal, is abandoned to the single judge. It is evident that the purity of justice must be compromised by confiding its administration to the hands of a single individual, who must by this universal authority lose all means of distinguishing between his private affections, his passions, his prejudices, and the opinions he may form in his capacity of public officer. The adverse parties brought before him are subjected to the effects of his ill-humour, his impatience, and he is deprived of that salutary restraint imposed elsewhere by the necessity of declaring before his colleagues the motives which have led him to this or that opinion.

"Again, the accused party is taught to regard himself as most fortunate when this unique judge, before whom he is summoned, receives his defence at a regular tribunal; for, whenever the accuser happens to be a person possessing credit or influence with the *buon governo*, the Minister of Police transmits to the vicar or to the bargello the order to plead *per via economica.* In these trials, known as *economici* or *camareli,* the defence of the accused is not admitted. The accusation is not communicated to him; he does not even know the alleged proofs against him, he has but the chance of guessing the nature of the complaint, from the questions of his interrogatory, *in the case where he is interrogated.* The reasons for the sentence pronounced against him are not given.

"Thus, in Italy, the salutary effect which the due administration of justice ought to produce upon the moral feelings of the people has been completely lost, and a contrary effect has arisen in the minds of the greater number. Every subject, trembling before an anthority which is not accountable for its actions, submitted to no law, believes himself to be surrounded for ever with secret spies; he has no faith in the purity of his own conscience, and he is forced to accustom himself to dissimulation and flattery; even by committal of murder he will not forfeit either the esteem of his friends, or the sanctuary afforded by the churches, or the asylum presented by the frontiers of the numerous petty States into which Italy is divided; and certainly no country, with the exception of Spain, has ever been sullied by so many unpunished murders. To all these causes of the general immorality must be added the ferocious habits induced almost down to the present day by the public spectacle of torture [1]. "

M. de Lamennais enters even more freely into the subject, by impressing upon us the necessity of seeking the cause of the corruption of these secular governments in the corruption of ecclesiastical power : " The evil which Catholicism suffers most deeply, and which threatens its daily existence more and more, has its root in the ecclesiastical organisation of the temporal power, and the abolition of the ancient franchises, maintained by Cardinal Gonzalvi, when Pius VII recovered his throne. Hence the impatience with which the people support what is called the priestly administration. The priests, on the other hand, feeling themselves hated by the people, attribute this feeling to the new opinions, the maxims of liberty; and, instead of having recourse to a wise reform in the politics of government, throw themselves headlong into the doctrines of despotism, seeking support in brute force alone, and, worse than all, in the force borrowed from the foreigner. One is very much struck in Italy with the *mollesse,* the apathy, the coldness, the indifference, and in one word with the absence of life, exhibited in the clergy; its members live by their profession, and that is all; they bend to the caprice of the sovereign; they consecrate their pretensions under the name of conscience; they become, in short, the blind instrument of his politics, let them be of what nature they may. Two things contribute to precipitate the clergy of Italy into this dangerous abyss; the first, consisting in the education given to the priesthood, the prejudices imbibed in youth, and the degrading yoke which produces an utter extinction of all intelligence; the second, because the clergy, without examining the real motive of the animosity against the Church, thinking to serve God by serving every species of despotism, alienates the hearts of the people from religion and its ministers. A great number of men have conceived the most unconquerable aversion towards the priesthood, and in order the better to draw away from the priests, they yield to impiety; hating the clergy with all the love they bear to their country [2]. "

" It is painful to avow it, but there is nothing to guarantee good

1. Sismondi, vol. XVI, p. 409. — 2. *Affaires de Rome,* Lamennais, pp. 223 to 226.

administration (in the estates of the Pope), with authorities who are for the most part irresponsible, invested with unlimited privileges, and surrounded by a crowd of greedy underlings who take advantage of the ignorance of their masters. The unfitness of these functionaries is inevitable in an administration where the members are forced upon the Pope, and who are, besides, taken from among the clergy, thus excluding all administrative study, theoretical or practical. A canon becomes treasurer-general, a cardinal directs the war department, a bishop fills the office of the State, and is occupied with Government details. Such are the superior functionaries; and those who direct the secondary branches of the administration are no better, for who are they? monsignori suddenly transformed into jurists, economists, financiers, etc. To these agents of intrigue we must add, alas! recruits from the other sex. The influence of women is not surprising in a State where the celibacy of the priest cannot be scrupulously observed by those who only see in their ordination a door to ecclesiastical honours[1]."

Let us now examine the influence of the Papal government in its very inertness, in the midst of its inaptitude for action, when it would become a duty to exhibit some tokens of life and power:

"Italy," says M. Quinet, "has for the last century and a half followed the counsels of the Church. She is descending to the grave as fast as a nation can sink thither. She suffers herself to be struck deeper down by all who choose to visit her. A *contrat social* is forming between the Romish Church and Italy; the former holding out to the latter the universal supremacy of the mind, to compensate her ruin. If the bargain is accepted, her ruin is complete; the aim is not achieved, and Popery, false to its promise, sits down unrepentant amidst the universal death which extends from Calabria to the Alps.

"It is impossible to witness a spectacle of this nature without extracting from it some useful lesson, at least for ourselves. The whole catastrophe takes its source in one general cause, which is, without a doubt, the secret contempt which the Church of Rome entertains for every species of nationality. For centuries she beheld, without a murmur, the dissolution of Italy; in our day, she has witnessed with the same indifference the fall of Poland. Perhaps a single appeal from the Vatican might have saved that ill-used country, but the idea of that appeal never arose, or it would have shook the whole of Europe. So far from anticipating

1. *Revue Britannique*, 1846, July and August, pp. 135, 136.

the awakening liberties of Greece, M. de Maistre dared to declare that the greatest evil which could happen to that country would be its escape from bondage; such calculation of indifference evidently belongs to a general principle [1]. "

" Does the Church of Rome, in compliance with the duties of her mission, plead for the weak against the strong? Did she remember Ireland, or Greece, or Bohemia, or Hungary, or any of the oppressed, when a word from her lips, falling amid the plenipotentiaries of Vienna, might have wrought a change in the destinies of these neglected countries? Ask her not for attention on such matters; her eyes are fixed on one single spot of earth; she is thinking of Romagna. At least, will you say, she must be pleading for those whom she cannot forget; for the vanquished. On the contrary, she beholds Catholic France overcome, she seizes the opportunity of insisting with the heretic powers for their aid in tearing away a province from France, and to bestow it upon her!

" It is schismatic zeal alone which prevents the outrage! Thus, she beholds the Samaritan Jew lying wounded by the roadside; not only does she refuse all aid and succour, not only does she deny him consolation, but she is influenced by one idea alone, that of despoiling him of his property.

" Has there ever been an instance, amid all the greedy struggles of victorious princes, of the Prince of the Church having sought to overpower the debates of ambition by one of those sublime effusions of universal charity, which would have rendered her in one moment the great moral influence? Has she ever taken advantage of that elevation of soul, of that magnanimity which naturally follows on victory, to remind victorious princes of their oaths towards their people? Such, assuredly, ought to have been her task. The prince of schism, the Emperor Alexander, has sometimes flashed forth with a ray of grandeur of this nature. No such ray has been beheld to emanate from Rome.

" Upon the last agitation of the rights of men, was it Rome who proposed the abolition of slavery, and the penalty of death for political offences? Questions such as this are agitated in the universal conscience, but the Universal Church thinks not of this. At all events the cry of blood restores her to her mission? When the political scaffold is erected in the midst of perishable passion, does Rome send forth her appeal in the name of Eternal mercy? Has she ever stood between the scaffold and impassioned humanity,

1. Quinet, p. 210.

when irritation had produced the blindness of partiality? Ney, Murat, all the brave heroes of that day, pursued by the rage of the victors, did they find refuge in Rome? By extending her hand towards them, did she even spare to their judges the eternal regret of their condemnation? No. In the midst of all, Rome beheld nought but Rome, and France can never forget this [1]. "

"I have already said that Rome denies all nationality; and, moreover, that she holds it in distrust. Observe what is taking place in Catholic Europe; you will soon find out the important fact that everywhere the Church suspects the people, that she aspires but to a separation, and to look for support to Rome alone. There was no need of any public avowal to teach the world that in France the Gallican Church has no existence but in name.

"In Spain, where the clergy had ever been so profoundly incorporated with the nation, every voice re-echoes the one great cry — Rome. The Bishop of Canary, in a work he has just published, places the newly-acquired liberty of the Spanish Church under the absolute dependence and servitude of Rome. This prelate, a man of real merit, incapable of wearing a mask of liberty, betrays the secret of the ecclesiastical coalition when he pronounces a word which none would dare to repeat: 'No man can doubt,' says he, 'that the French Revolution is the work of hell.' In Germany, Gœrres, in the name of the Bavarian clergy, echoes the sentiment expressed by the Bishop of Canary. It may be said that at the present moment every Catholic clergy of the South and of the North of Europe is occupied in divesting with violence the nations of which they have charge of those national characteristics whence they hitherto drew their best defence, and that they are concentrated in Rome to combat together with each of their respective nations against the spiritual unity of the nineteenth century in general [2]. "

"In this duel which has thus been established between the Church and the people, supposing that Rome may have thus lost the nationalities of Europe, has she at all events preserved the support of general humanity? The malcontents will unite, say you: and what security have I? What! Without a single step on your part, the half of Christendom, which has deserted you, will be likely to amend its ways, and without any help from yourself enable you to accomplish in your old age a task to which you were unequal in the hot day of your youth? Besides, where do you perceive the indications of such a movement? Where are the recanting nations

1. Quinet, pp. 220 to 222. — 2. *Idem*, pp. 240, 241.

who are turning back towards you? I behold them, on the contrary, marching forwards with heads bent down towards the future, from which I must conclude them to be seeking elsewhere than in you supreme and universal reconciliation; and all that I can express is a fear that, in your immutability, you will remain isolated from the nationalities of the human race, as well as from human nature itself[1]."

Such is the spirit of Romish legislation. We are ready to anticipate from it what is to be expected from the morals we are about to study:

MORALS. — The better to study the morals of Italy, let us examine one single city at the four extremities of the country, beginning by the metropolis of Catholicism: "In Rome, life seems composed of one long Lenten-time, so punctual is every one in the execution of the outward duties of religion. This great city, which might be made to contain with ease three times the number of inhabitants now gathered there, possesses a sad and deserted aspect, rendered more striking by its spacious squares, width and emptiness of its streets, the numbers of ecclesiastics met with at every turn, and the majestic ruins which greet us at every step. Even in the markets we are struck with the same air of stillness. But this silence is suddenly exchanged at the time of the Carnival for the most boisterous manifestations of delight. Rome seems no longer the same city, so great is her acquired activity; all ranks are confounded, the churches are deserted, and the streets contain with difficulty the population in pursuit of pleasure. During this time of folly we behold young abbés, great magistrates, sometimes even prelates, clothed in masquerade costume, and running after adventures which never fail, for both sexes are in the same pursuit, fully persuaded that a moment of error will be easy of expiation by the penitence and holy self-denial of Lent. The Corso becomes the *rendez-vous* of a tumultuous crowd, the equipages follow each other in endless files, the balconies are covered with rich hangings, a shower of sweetmeats fall amongst the passers-by, and deafening shouts arise from the dense crowd of maskers of every grade. At a given signal, the Corso is cleared in the midst; a troop of horses without riders, urged forward by pieces of metal garnished with spikes, and by a lighted match barbarously introduced beneath the skin, start from the Piazza del Popolo, and rush through the Corso with the speed of lightning, less eager to win the race than to fly

1. Quinet, p. 241, 242.

from the instruments of torture which pursue them. To the follies of the Carnival, which call to mind the *lupercali* of Ancient Rome, succeed, on the night of Shrove Tuesday, the *moccoleldi*, small lighted tapers, of which every one carries a bundle, and attempts to extinguish that of his neighbour. This custom is evidently a remnant of the festival held in honour of the search of Ceres after her daughter Proserpine.

"Clandestine marriages meet with no opposition: a permission to marry, says an author, is delivered by the vice-regent with as much facility as a passport, and with this passport the priest of the parish gives immediately the nuptial benediction. At Rome, the seducer of innocence is condemned to marry the young girl, or to pass five years at the galleys.

"The Church condemns usury; but at Rome she allows the cardinals to practise in secret certain mercantile speculations upon objects of daily necessity. The bakers and grocers are often nothing more than the mere agents of the cardinals. Those agents who would seek to trade on their own account would be exposed to every species of vexation. Elsewhere, the agents of the government tax the price of bread, in order that the people may not pay too high a price: at Rome, the baker is fined who sells it too cheaply. In most of the countries of Europe the immorality of the lottery system has been recognised: at Rome, this fatal tax, levied on ignorance and superstition, is sanctioned by the ministers of religion; and in the presence of the different heads of congregations, and of the cardinals themselves, the prizes are drawn with great solemnity. The child who places his hand in the wheel of fortune only does so after making the solemn sign of the cross; and yet the Church forbids all games of chance.

"At Rome, during the follies of the Carnival, and even before the entrance of the theatres, the public executioner is seen walking up and down near the *cavaletto*, an instrument of punishment destined for to chastise the turbulence of joy which may overstep the license permitted on these days of festival, or the denizens of the parterre of the theatre who may choose to disturb the representations going on within. The culprit is laid upon this little wooden horse, and receives a certain number of blows with a stick. The same chastisement awaits the restaurateur who dares to serve to his guests during Lent any dish forbidden by the Church. For any misdemeanour of a graver kind, the law inflicts the punishment of the estrapade, which consists in raising by a cord the limbs of the culprit, whose hands are tied behind his back, and in causing him suddenly to fall upon his feet; but this punishment, as well as the *cavaletto*, are falling into disuse. The assassin who has struck a priest has his throat cut, and his body is cut into four parts, exposed in four quarters of the town. This mode of execution still prevailed during the reign of Leo XII. It was under this Pope that the first administration of the law began to be carried on in the language of the country instead of Latin, as had been the custom until then. Torture has been abolished for a long time past[1]."

"The Romans, and in general every subject of the Pope, are remarkable for their superstition. They are scrupulous in their fulfilment of the outward forms of religion; but, upon this point, the rule is observed rather than true devotion. Confession is a practice which every one observes more from habit than from Christian humility; rather to shelter conscience, than for the correction of vices. A young beauty will give an assignation to her lover in the church; but, even were she to find herself alone with him in that place, she would neither speak to him, or look at him, before she has finished every bead of her rosary. The people receive the Pope's benediction on bended knee; but it is not at Rome that the head of the Church is looked upon as participating of the Divine attributes; what he gains in temporal power, he loses in spiritual authority. When the week succeeding Easter is past, the priests exact from their parishioners certificates of communion, under penalty of publication of the defaulter's name; no matter in what belief the sick man may die, his body, when carried to the church, will create no scandal; provided he has paid, he will be received with all the honours reserved by religion to all Christians after death.

"It is useless to speak of the *sigisbés*, or *cavaliers servants*; they enjoy as much credit at Rome as in every other great city of Italy. During the occupation by the French, the ridicule thrown upon these gallants had greatly injured their calling; but public morals gained nothing by this measure; amorous intrigue had replaced this species of contract entered into by the husband with the lover he has chosen for his wife. Foreigners who have studied Rome for a little while past agree that upon this point the old fashion is revived: this is a natural consequence in a country where education has done nothing for the regeneration of the people. A government wholly pacific, like that of Rome, might console itself for its political nonentity in the protection given to literature,

1. Malte-Brun, vol. VII, p. 364.

science, and art; but the slumber is universal. Science is less cultivated in Rome than throughout the whole of Italy; notwithstanding this, that city which contains such a fund of archæological treasure has produced antiquaries worthy of comparison with those of France and Germany. If her literary academies enjoy but little fame, and are placed upon a level with the most obscure of our provincial academies, it is the censure by which they are restrained. The Roman school of painting no longer reckons a single name worthy of the bright days of Italy; and, were it not for the *chefs-d'œuvre* with which the city abounds, the Academy of the Fine Arts might have been established elsewhere. The only art in which the Romans excel is in that of mosaic.

"In the higher classes of society, ignorance and idleness are as general as at Venice. The young men who read confine their studies to the lightest poems of Voltaire; the women, who seek compensation for the time passed in convents, give themselves up to the most frivolous and dangerous studies. The people of the city can read and write, but these qualifications are very rare in the country [1]."

After the geographer, let us listen to the traveller: "Here (Rome) everything is formed to charm the antiquary's eye, and feast the poet's fancy; but it is no less calculated to sicken the heart of mere humanity, and to dissipate the philanthropic dream of benevolent philosophy. Here is no resting-place for hope of man's amendment, of the diminution of his sum of suffering, his mass of error; all here is monumental of his folly, or his crime; his credulity, or his imposture. The temples of Romulus and Remus now serve the turn of Saint Cosimo and Théodore; and the games celebrated in the Coliseum in one age, to reduce the people to their original ferocity, are succeeded by rites instituted in another to enfeeble and degrade them [2]."

"The avenues which lead to Saint John de Lateran have no parallel in the history of desolation. A long and spacious street presents itself uninhabited; or if here and there a worn and squalid visage exhibits its sharp and shrivelled features through the shattered framework of a sashless window, it does but add a trait of moral desolation to the material dreariness, and prove that these high and mouldering edifices, once the abode of the powerful and luxurious, now serve as dens to house the lowest and most abject. In this spot the malaria reigns undisputed by human population

1. Malte-Brun, vol. VII, p. 369. — 2. Lady Morgan, vol. III, pp. 244, 245.

(its most efficient opponent), whose ranks, thinned by the institutes of the Church, are daily lessening; and yet, but a very few centuries back, it was chosen for its salubrity as the residence of Popes and cardinals. This desert of walls terminates in a spacious, silent, moss-grown square, in the centre of which towers that mass of sumptuous and ponderous architecture, the Church and Palace of the Lateran[1]."

"It (Church of Saint Peter's) should be approached by pilgrim-steps, slow and difficult; and that great temple:

> "Where majesty,
> Power, glory, strength, and beauty, all are aisled,"

should be reached on foot, and sought through those various details of misery, disorder, and degradation, which distinguish alike all its avenues, and are the elements out of which its grandeur sprang. Around the other great *Basilica* of Rome there reigns a saddening region of desolation; and Saint Paul's and Saint John de Lateran rise on the dreary frontiers of the infected deserts they dominate, like temples dedicated to the genius of the malaria. But the approach to Saint Peter's has another character; every narrow avenue is thickly colonised with a race of beings marked by traits of indigence and demoralisation: and every dark dilapidated den teems with a tenantry which might well belong to other purlieus than those of the Church. It is thus that the altars of Saint Peter's are approached. Here the streets of the filthiest city in Europe are found filthiest! Here forms on which Love has set his seal are equally disfigured by the neglect of cleanliness, or by meretricious ornament; and the young plebeian beauty, lying on the threshold of some ruinous fabric, withdrawing the bodkin from tresses it is dangerous to loosen, and submitting a fine head to the inspection of some ancient crone, smiles on the passing stranger with all the complacency of a *Du Barry*, when she made her toilet for the good of the public, surrounded by the dignitaries of the Church, who emulously canvassed for its services. The streets leading immediately to Saint Peter's occasionally exhibit a spacious but dilapidated palace, mingled with inferior buildings; but many even of these have their façades of marble disfigured by washer-women's lines; and an atmosphere of soap-suds indicates an attention to cleanliness, whose effects are nowhere visible in Rome but

1. Lady Morgan, vol. III, pp. 262, 263.

in the stench which issues from the laundresses' windows in the very finest of its streets[1]."

"The cardinals governed by cabal, and all places were disposed of through their mistresses and their laquais; a class only less powerful than the cardinals themselves. The princes and patricians (and they were of two descriptions) rich, idle, ignorant, and avaricious, were surrounded by dependants and parasites, the indigent followers of rank and opulence, a numerous order in all ill-governed countries. The people, without domestic habits, lived like the commoners of nature, satisfied if bread and church ceremonies sustained life and amused it. Dependence was encouraged by pride, poverty preached as a virtue, and followed as a profession. The parasite came after the prince, and the beggar after the saint. The women of all ranks, divided into vestals and concubines, were either shut up in a convent, or let loose upon society free from the duties of maternity and the ties of marriage, the mistresses of authorised paramours, and the wives of other women's lovers. The passions of all classes were unsubdued by education, unrestrained by law, and all crimes were redeemable by power. Murder had its price, from a basket of figs to a purse of gold; and the murderer his asylum, from the high altar of the church to the cabinet of the palace.

"Assassination was a deed of nightly occurrence; and the careless hand that stabbed for pay not unfrequently mistook its aim, and stopped to excuse its error by assuring the victim '*it was a mistake.*'

"There was no society but such as vice congregated; the interests of the gaming-table, or the intrigues of illicit love. To the former all were devoted, and to forward the latter husbands frequently assisted their wives to get rid of troublesome sigisbés, whose interests interfered with a passion more profitable to the *ménage* than that of the professed ancient cavaliere servente[2]."

"That it (Rome) has fallen is the work of despotism and corruption; and that, like the rest of Italy, it may never rise again from its fearful debasement is the hope and effort of Allied Sovereigns, their cabinets and their dependents[3]."

Let us turn from contemplating the moral miseries of Rome to the less repulsive study of the temporal ones of Genoa; which come next in order: "I never in my life was so dismayed. The wonderful novelty of everything, the unusual smells, the unaccount-

1. Lady Morgan, vol. III, pp. 272, 273, 274. — 2. *Idem*, pp. 403, 404, 405. — 3. *Idem*, p. 390.

able filth (though it is reckoned the cleanest of Italian towns); the passages more squalid and more close than any in Saint Giles's, or old Paris : in and out of which not vagabonds, but well-dressed women, with white veils and great fans, were passing and repassing; the disheartening dirt, discomfort, and decay perfectly confounded me. The court-yards of these houses (great villas), are overgrown with grass and weeds; all sorts of hideous patches cover the bases of the statues, as if they were afflicted with a cutaneous disorder; the outer gates are rusty; and the iron bars outside the lower windows are all tumbling down. Hard by there is a large Palazzo, formerly belonging to some member of the Brignole family. I don't believe there was an uncracked stone in the whole pavement. In the centre was a melancholy statue, so piebald in its decay, that it looked exactly as if it had been covered with sticking-plaster, and afterwards powdered. The stables, coach-houses, offices, were all empty. Doors had lost their hinges, and were holding on by their latches; windows were broken, painted plaster had peeled off, and was lying about in clods. I went down into the garden, intended to be prim and quaint, with avenues, and terraces, and orange-trees, and statues, and water in stone basins; and everything was green, gaunt, weedy, straggling, undergrown or overgrown, mildewy, damp, redolent of all sorts of slabby, clammy, creeping, and uncomfortable life. There was nothing bright in the whole scene but a firefly, showing against the dark bushes the last little speck of the departed glory of the house. Genoa abounds in the strangest contrasts; the rapid passage from a street of stately edifices into a maze of the vilest squalor, steaming with unwholesome stenches, and swarming with half-naked children and whole worlds of dirty people, make up altogether such a scene of wonder, so lively and yet so dead, so noisy and yet so quiet, that it is a sort of intoxication to a stranger to walk on, and on, and look about him. One of the rottenest-looking parts of the town, I think, is down by the landing wharf. Before the basements of the houses is an arcade over the pavement; very massive, dark and low, like an old crypt. The stone or plaster of which it is made has turned quite black; and against every one of these black piles all sorts of filth and garbage seem to accumulate spontaneously. Beneath some of the arches the sellers of maccaroni and polenta establish their stalls, which are by no means inviting[1]."

Lastly, let us cast a glance upon Naples and Venice :

1. Lady Morgan, vol. IV, pp. 234, 235, 236.

"Groups seated at the corners of streets (Naples), at the thresholds of the poorer sort of houses, on the shores of the Scoglio or the Mare-chiano, or the Mola or the Largo,talking, laughing, menacing, or singing, are all domestically (though not often *sentimentally*) employed; wants are supplied or satisfied; trades carried on; Tasso read aloud; and heads cleaned, or heads shaven, all equally *pro bono publico*. A pulchinello and a '*padre predicatore,*' in close contact, call on the sympathies of the dissipated and the devout at the same moment, and share between them the ever-laughing, moving, praying multitude, who seek sensations in proportion as they are denied ideas; and who, consigned unmolested to the influence of their vehement passion by the absence or feeble administration of the laws, are as destitute of moral principles as they are removed from the causes out of which moral principles arise, property and education. Their dishonesty, which rarely rises to acts of violence, except during political commotion, and which is generally accompanied by ingenuity and urged by poverty, is the natural vice of a people left without one conscientious principle, by that government whose laws have always been the slaves of power and privilege, and whose religion has a ready absolution, with its stated price, for every sin [1]."

"They are devoted to a religion which insures them their *feste populari*, they are attached to a government which has licensed their violence and indolence, and not only sanctioned, but allied itself with their predatory bands. The government which most favours disorder, moral and political, will best suit the professional bandit of the Abruzzi, or the brutal lazzarone of Naples [2]."

"What is to be said of a government which reduces the great majority of the people to a slavish insensibility, to national degradation, to a perfect indifference to national honour, a government which renders the subject too ignorant to comprehend the causes of his sufferings, and too listless to seek their removal? Yet to restore such a government was the avowed object of the late crusade ! [3]"

"The *Feste Popolari*, or religious festivals, are so numerous, that scarcely a day passes without some ceremony, which serves as an excuse to idleness and pleasure, and which is frequently sanctioned by the government taking some part in it [4]."

"Ceremonies, appropriated to all the successive holidays, follow to the utter neglect of business and industry. And the most curious part of all this is, that these rites are celebrated with forms

1. Lady Morgan, vol. IV, pp. 238, 239, 240. — 2. *Idem*, pp. 242, 243. — 3. *Idem*, p. 245. 4. *Idem*, p. 250.

so purely those of the ancient idolatries of the Greeks, and the groups are so strictly the same, in costume and countenance, as those preserved in ancient sculpture, that even the ivy wreaths of Bacchus are not forgotten. The sylvan pipe and dance, with movements all grace, and gestures all pantomime, recall at once the groups of Greek Bacchanti, celebrating rites that have no affinity whatever to the sacred epochs of that religion of 'long suffering and sacrifice' whose events they are intended to commemorate. Certain, however, it is, that if other sects have taken surer roads to Heaven, none ever chose pleasanter than those who profess the faith of the Neapolitan Church.

"The religion of the lower classes in Naples is scarcely Catholicism[1]."

"The gross minds and ardent imaginations of the neglected and vivacious people know nothing of the abstract dogmas of religion; they require and possess a tangible creed, a something to see and touch, to complain of, and to adore. The wild Calabrian treats his tutelar Saint according to its merits; he is prodigal of praises to his honour and glory, or he flings him down the mountain, or knocks him off his shrine, as he finds him propitious or otherwise. We were assured that Saint Golagara (the patron of Calabria), had seldom his due complement of limbs and features; but when good harvest brought him into favour, his pardon was asked, his nose glued on, his face fresh painted, and his sanctity replaced in all its honours. The religion of England was not much more spiritual three centuries back; the moment religion takes palpable orms, there is no knowing where folly and fanaticism will stop[2]."

As it is not possible to depict all classes of Neapolitan society, we shall content ourselves with sketching the two extremes, the miseries of the lazzaroni, and the festivals of the court: "Naples contained, previous to the Revolution, ten thousand monks and nuns, and forty thousand lazzaroni, or persons whose sole ranks in the state was their houseless, hopeless, irretrievable poverty. This fact illustrates the whole history of Naples for the last three centuries (for the lazzaroni do not seem to have had an existence as a body previous to the subjection of Italy by Charles the Fifth). Commoners of nature, in the bosom of society, yet denied by their miseries all its advantages, they soon coalesced through the common interests of their forlorn state, and became alike formidable by their numbers and their desperation. By limiting their wants

1. Lady Morgan, pp. 251, 252. — 2. *Idem*, vol. III, pp. 177, 178, 179.

to their means of supplying them, they became cynics without knowing it, and their daily habits of ease, indolence, and frugality illustrated the philosophy of Diogenes, without the ostentatious display of his tub. They who had nothing to give could not be taxed; they who were beyond opinion suffered nothing from its penalty. The two '*grani*' that purchased their daily ration of maccaroni, the two more that went for ice-water and a puppet-show, were surely and easily earned; and a little surplus of ingenuity and industry procured the few yards of canvass which made up their whole wardrobe (a shirt and trowsers), allowing even something for the superfluity of their red worsted sash and cap. These wants supplied, nothing remained but the delicious *far niente,* the lounge in the sun or the shade, the laugh raised indiscriminately at friend and foe, a prayer offered at a shrine, or curses given to the *scrivano,* who mulcts some crime which poverty cannot redeem by a bribe. The miserable offspring of the lazzaroni are the victims of this idleness and these vices; for their wretched mothers, in their sheds or dens, soured by privations and distress, avenge on their children their own hard fate in all the peevishness of perpetual irritation.

" The paternal government of the Bourbons made no effort to redeem this large and fearful class, which festered like a canker in the bosom of the State. It originated no sources of industry; it checked manufacture by exclusion; while it smiled upon the lazzaroni, and spoke their dialect [1]."

We are upon the lowest step of the social ladder, let us mount to the top. There is enjoyment; here is misery. In order to keep more to our subject, let us choose a religious festival:

" The scene of Elijah in the king's court is extremely curious. Acabe accuses him of heresy and sedition; in a word, of being a Radical reformer, disturbing the ancient laws and religion of the state, which, confirmed by ages, had covered the land with unceasing prosperity. To all this Elijah replies, that his mission is from heaven, that he is sent to overturn the reigning religion, and that he will work miracles to prove the truth of his assertions, which shall leave no doubts on the mind of the king. Upon this the high priest of the idolatrous Acabe is called in to back his master, at whose sight Elijah cannot contain his ire, and a dialogue ensues which called forth the rapturous plaudits of the audience. Elijah, in a threatening attitude, calls his antagonist '*un*

1. Lady Morgan, vol. I, pp. 253, 254, 255, 256, 257.

scellerato impio ;' the high priest terms him *' un scellerato ingaunatore ;'* and nothing remains for them but to proceed to blows, when the king, to save the church a scandal, with difficulty parts them, and it is agreed that both are to meet together in a certain cavern, and decide their superiority by miracles. This scene discovers the impositions of the *false prophet,* who is *' tutto confuso,'* when his materials for *miracle-making* are found in the cave, consisting of sticks, matches, pitch, etc., etc.; while a longprayer of the true prophet's not only brings down fire from heaven, which consumes the king, queen, and heir-apparent, but at the same time brings down a fine full-grown angel, vibrating in the air between four pulleys, while the prophet settles himself in an arm-chair for the purposes of translation : first, however, as he was about to ascend, he stepped forward, and gave out the play for the following evening; then, re-seating himself, he threw down an old cloak on his successor's head, who was in look and garb the very image of a Jew clothesman in the streets of London.

" We observed upon this occasion that the theatre was filled with women and their children; and that many of the boxes included the whole family of the lower cittadini class, even to the livery-boy and the baby; for it seems a sort of duty to attend these sacred dramas in Lent; and all that appears so singular and even profane in these exhibitions to the foreign spectator, is by them attended to with reverence and interest. When the false prophet was praying to his false gods, and Elijah kept crying in a taunting tone, *' Più forte! non t'ascoltano!'* (' Cry louder! they don't hear you!') the audience clapped their hands, and exclaimed, ' Bravo Elijah! bravo! [1]' "

Let us now come to Venice, the fourth and last town which we have promised to survey : " But if the foreign traveller once departed from the Lagunes and the revels of Saint Mark's with the same illusions as he first arrived, that moment is now over; and such images of desolation and ruin are encountered, in every detail of the moral and exterior aspect of the city, as dissipates all visionary anticipations, and sadden down the spirit to that pitch which best harmonises with the misery of this once superb mistress of the waves [2]. "

" But this busy spot, once crowded with sixteen thousand workmen, and the occasional resort of thirty-six thousand seamen, its vast sail-room, formerly filled with hundreds of females, whose

1. Lady Morgan, vol. IV, pp. 293 to 295. — 2. Malte-Brun, vol. VII, p. 422.

industry contributed to the Venetian conquests, all now are still, lonely, abandoned; and nothing recalls the great Arsenal of the Republic of Venice, and the naval armament launched from her spacious docks[1]. "

" Five thousand workmen were kept constantly employed in the Arsenal of Venice; while a number considerably under eight hundred are now more than aquedate to its works; scattered over its immensity, they leave it a desert. The state of society, of morals, and manners, in Venice, from the downfall of its greatness, by the failure of its commerce, and the increasing despotim of its government, has been but too frequently and faithfully pourtrayed in the works of successive travellers and historians, from the quaint Amelot to the impartial Daru; and the sum of its corruption has been philosophically illustrated by the latter with an observation that speaks volumes[2]. "

" Convents and casinos, political tyranny and religious bigotry, are dire foes to the virtues which should belong to aspects so bewitching[3]. "

" But, without pausing to weigh those fatal but inevitable circumstances which ever accompany an exhausted nation and a worn-out government, and are at once the causes and consequences of nationale decrepitude, it is sufficient to remark that pusillanimity, corruption, and the absence of a national spirit, are at least as much an inheritance as a consequence of personal vices; and that there is no position more wretched and more worthy of compassion than the having been born under political combination unfavourable to the development of independence and public virtue[4]."

" The Austrian government of Venice, therefore, is not only a pure and unmixed despotism, but a studied and designed aggregation of every abuse that can tend to desolate and oppress, to break the spirit of the species, to damp industry, and to quench hope. The criminal processes are conducted in the strictest secrecy : the accused is allowed no defender; he is left in ignorance of his accuser; he may be detained in prison six months without trial; and, when acquitted, is turned loose on society, with a consciousness of the existence of a secret enemy, whose future machinations he can neither foresee nor parry[5]. The refusal of an advocate to the accused was by no means an oversight. The subject was a matter of formal discussion; and the aulic council of Vienna knowingly and wilfully refused as a favour what the common

1. Lady Morgan, vol. IV, p. 371. — 2. *Idem*, p. 410. — 3. *Idem*, p. 411. — 4. *Idem*, p. 412. — 5. *Idem*, p. 416.

sense and common honesty of mankind instinctively acknowledge as a right[1]. The consequence of this cruel and tyrannical misconduct is, that specie has almost entirely disappeared; a base and valueless coin is nearly all that circulates; and it existed in such small quantities when we visited Venice, that to change a five-franc piece demanded a sacrifice of three *sous*. The agio also on gold was considerably higher that in any other town in Italy. The Venetians, thus plundered of their last sequin, are rendered incapable of conducting the great public works which are absolutely necessary for the preservation of their city. The lagunes are gradually filling up, and the houses falling into the canals, from the impossibility of renewing the piles on which they stand. The population, which was one hundred and forty thousand, is reduced to a hundred thousand. The trade of Venice thus crippled, its resources undermined, and its wealth wantonly exhausted, it is natural to suppose that the bitterest feeling pervades the people with respect to their lawless oppressors; and that mutual jealousy and warranted suspicion multiplies spies, and contributes, with the increasing poverty of the nobility, to break up society and dissolve the links of intercourse and communication[2]."

"The story of Venice has obtained the popularity of a legend. It begins splendidly! — A few free spirits, looking round in vain for some asylum against despotism, find not one spot on earth to shelter them. They congregate on the ocean, and are left the undisturbed masters of mud-banks and sea-weed. They are free and poor; they suffer much, and enjoy nothing, but liberty! They arrive at wealth and national importance under the influence of an energising necessity! Then come power and foreign dominion; and the gangrene of national ruin already poisons the constitutions of the state, and the institutes of society, circulating its infection under the various guises of ambition, luxury, and ostentation, corruption in morals, licentiousness in manners! Power, centered in the few, weighed on the many; a national senate became a state inquisition, suspicion was the leading principle, and spies the efficient agents of government[3]."

From studying thus separately the Italian towns, let us now survey them as a whole. For this purpose we shall follow a celebrated traveller: "One sees everywhere, in Italy," says the abbé de Lamennais, "in these degenerate days, some grievous

1. Lady Morgan, vol. IV, p. 418. — 2. *Idem*, p. 419. — 3. *Idem*, pp. 420, 421.

spectacle, some mark of bondage. The universal misery revealing itself under so many hideous forms contrasts in most places with the native richness of the soil. Idleness, apathy, languor, ignorance, these are the striking characteristics. Even religion, whose past magnificence fills one with astonishment, seems to have done nothing during ten centuries but build itself a vast sepulchre. A dozen or fifteen Franciscans wander in the solitude of the convent of Assise, formerly occupied by 6,000 monks[1]."

"There seems to arise from Rome some indescribable vapour of the tomb which lulls to rest and sleep, soothing the soul to dreams of eternal slumber. We may live there with the hope of death, but never with that of life; for there exists not in the place a shadow of vitality; no movement, save that secret agitation caused by the hidden multitude of small interests which crawl and creep in darkness like the worms amid the gloom of the sepulchre. Power and people, all appear like shadows of the past. The Queen of Cities, throned in the midst of a wilderness, has become the City of Death, who reigns triumphant in all its majesty. Repose, idleness, slumber, interrupted from time to time by spectacles which arouse the senses, such is the happiness offered to men. No public life; nothing, therefore, to provoke activity, nothing social. Over the gate of the palace inhabited by the governor (an office always filled by a prelate), is fixed the famous monogram S. P. Q. R., of which the most exact translation is certainly in this case the French one: *si peu que rien*[2]."

"I need only paint (says the same writer), with local colouring, the effects for ever of illimited despotism; the oppression of spirits thrown back by a brutal power which intimidates all manifestation of thought in its smallest degree; the total absence of all security for persons or property; violence and corruption; the despotism of the government always in suspicion and fear; in the aspect of the people, condemned to vegetate in perpetual dread of the bayonet of the soldier and the eye of the spy; a prodigious amount of misery alike physical, moral, and intellectual; and a debasement so profound that the nation has almost ceased to be aware of its existence. Italy! Italy! The dead heroes of past ages have arisen from their graves; from the slopes of the Apennines the lonely shepherd has beheld them, with sad brow, and their long hair covered with the dust of the sepulchre, gazing around upon this land once so great and glorious; and, as if they could not recognise it for their own,

1. Lady Morgan, vol. IV, pp. 422, 423. — 2. Lamennais, p. 10 to 12.

they shake their heads with a bitter smile, and return to their tombs [1]. "

" With the loss of liberty and civic virtue, Tuscany seems to have lost the genius of science and the genius of art. Some narcotic drug has been mixed with the people's drink, and it has fallena sleep amid the dreams of its ancient glory. In the midst of past greatness the traveller beholds the fellah sleeping on the threshold of the great temples of Thebes and Heliopolis, or the necropolis of the Pharaohs [2]. "

" At every step (in Ferrare) we behold the sad symptoms of incurable decay. We have beheld in a convent, now transformed into a barrack, a Croat nailing the manger of his horse against the wall of a refectory, covered with fresco paintings of remarkable beauty. The stupid barbarian, sent from a far country to maintain what princes have chosen to call their rights, was whistling carelessly, not even aware of the destruction of which he was the instrument. Thus, in a confined space, the traveller beholds at one glance every extremity of human misery, misery of greatness, misery of genius, misery of the people languishing and dying beneath a double oppression. Those who wander among these people can have but one thought, that of the vast cemetery he has before his eyes. Books, papers, even private letters, are all examined at the douane with the most minute care and suspicion; not one of those base and irritating perquisitions invented by political terror, united to fiscal rapacity, is spared to the traveller [3]. "

" I know nothing more sad, and at the same time more instructive, than the spectacle afforded by Venice, fallen as it is under foreign rule. The population, reduced to half its numbers, is compelled to toil painfully to procure a subsistence, which, poor as it is, becomes the object of dispute with the hard taskmaster. That commerce, once the source of its immense riches, has passed to the other side of the Adriatic; a system of police, which fills the mind with terror, can, upon simple suspicion, condemn the citizen to the dungeons multiplied by despotic power, and spreads throughout every relations of life distrust and suspicion, injustice in the laws, and partiality in the tribunals. A few palaces have been confiscated on those slight pretexts which are never wanting with the strong against the weak; almost all of them are falling rapidly to decay [4]. "

" A deep and heavy sadness seizes on the soul when the gaze is directed towards that Rome, once so full of grandeur, and now so

1. Lamennais, p. 103. — 2. *Idem*, p. 112. — 3. *Idem*, pp. 114, 115. — 4. *Idem*, p. 117.

fallen, so feeble. Miserable ruin of ages in the midst of other ruin! silent shadow of the past, mourning by the tomb! What has become of its ancient power? Those who bowed the head in obedience to her commands now give out their dictates with a mocking jeer. She believes in them, and they have no faith in her. What strikes one at first, in the actual state of Rome, is the absolute want of all action, and the humiliating dependence to which she is reduced, on the will of the temporal sovereigns. The immense interests of humanity have stirred the world through whole generations of mankind; they occupy the universal mind; what has she done towards the solving of the one great question? Nothing. A revolution is taking place in the bosom of Christianity; awakened peoples are bursting their antique chains, their ancient laws; they cry alond for a new order of things. What has she done? Nothing[1]."

"What is most to be desired in all classes is the knowledge of the present state of society in Europe, and, out of Europe, of the real causes of events, and of the intimate tendency of all things. In this respect, Rome is behind, and frightfully behind, every nation over whom her influence, for the good of humanity, would be beneficial. She exists in the past alone, in a past which will rcturn no more, and hence the isolation in which she stands[2]."

"Every source of education necessary for the acquirement, in the century in which we live, of moral ascendancy being closed against the priests of Italy, whose studies are forcibly confined to scholastic dryness, it becomes evident that they must be deprived of every influence over certain classes of society, and those the most important. Unfortunately, another evil greater still accrues from this defect. I do not speak of the loose morality or of the habits of pleasure adopted by the greater portion of the clergy[3]."

But let us leave these pestilential cities, and let us see whether we can breathe a less corrupt atmosphere far from the Roman towns. Upon this subject Charles Didier says: "Instead of the green plains which charmed the eyes of Pliny (in the environs of Civita Vecchia), were he to visit them now he would find nought but an unhealthy soil without trees, without cultivation, and almost without vegetable production. Many leagues of this deserted solitude greet the eye. The only habitations of these sad shores are the watch-towers, raised at certain intervals along the coast; the soldiers stationed are scarcely ever free from fever, which undermines their health and strength; the flabbiness of their muscles, their yellow skins, their

1. Lamennais, pp. 210, 212. — 2. *Idem*, pp. 215, 216. — 3. Lamennais, *Affaires de Rome*, p. 223.

languid movements, tell of the venom in their veins; those whom the fever spares are generally dying of starvation, for these sombre deserts are struck by every plague at once. Pursued by hunger, I entered one of these watch towers; but, instead of the rustic frugality I had anticipated, I found nought but sour wine, and bread so hard that it had to be chopped with a hatchet. Even this miserable state of destitution was one of luxury; Santa-Maniella being celebrated for its good cheer! If, however, the provisions might be regarded as scant, the welcome was much more so. The peasant woman scarcely deigned to cast her eyes upon me; she condescended, however, to point to a broken three-legged stool, and to spread out before me, on a pine-wood table, which had never been scoured, the splendid repast I have just described. The manner of this hospitality was that of throwing to an importunate beggar the crust no longer required by the household." But hush! "Nowhere on earth is the knife so ready to avenge offended pride as in the campagna of Rome[1]."

"Aqueducts dried up and destroyed, ancient public ways now untrodden by human foot, temples without gods, cities without men, tombs without corpses, depopulated plains, silent forests, fetid marshes, ports choked up, shores deserted, such is thy glory, O Rome! The sun shines brightly upon it from the heavens; and drags to light thy shame and desolation. Of what use, oh fallen Queen! have been all thy endeavours to hide thy decay, when the sun, pitiless spectator of human vicissitude, comes each day with dazzling pomp to insult thy misery, as if asking thee what thou hast done with all thy glory and thy splendour?[2]"

"I have traversed several villages of the Abruzzi; no language can describe their utter destitution; they might be taken for spots where the plague had passed. If the plague visits them not, famine is their constant guest. A few women and helpless old men, with infants in the cradle, are the only inhabitants of the cottages. Not a single male visage to give them hope and animation; not a single male arm to defend them from danger. Ploughs unused and thrown aside may be seen now and then lying across the streets, where roll *pêle-mêle* the children and the pigs.

"The Italian princes behold these calamities, and their hoggish indolence prevents them from applying any remedy to the evil. The Church is neither more intelligent nor more humane; the only charity she bestows upon the reapers, who come to gather in

1. Didier, pp. 23 to 30. — 2. *Idem*, pp. 137 to 139.

her harvests, is to bury them when they die. It is a terrible thing to declare that death is not only occasioned by malaria in these pestiferous solitudes, but that starvation also does its work, and not only in the campagnas, but even in the capital of the Christian world. I saw myself a man fainting with want and inanition beneath the portico of the magnificent Palazzo Marsini. Another one expired on the marble steps of Saint Peter. The priest was celebrating mass, the hundred and twelve silver lamps were burning round the tomb of the Apostle, and a Christian was dying of hunger at the foot of the altar, all dazzling with gold and precious stones. This is the manner in which at Rome is practised the religion of the crucified Saviour![1]"

"As far as the sight can reach (between Rome and Ostia) not a single habitation or inhabitant can be descried. But, stay; I am in error. I perceive on the edge of the wood a hut of reeds, and two children naked, livid, and swollen by fever, rolling in the dust like savages from Timbuctoo. The wooden crosses, planted by the way-side, indicate the spots where murder has been committed; human life has disappeared from this exhausted plain, and if two men meet therein be sure that one of them has come out to murder the other. The background of this fetid and desolate landscape is occupied by an old crenelated castle, falling to decay, round which are heaped pêle-mêle a few smoky hovels, whose cracked walls, admitting neither light or air, deserted for the most part, are abandoned to reptiles. Some filthy space, designated as a square, and which offers nothing but a collection of dirt and rubbish, forms the approach of a miserable little church, dedicated to the mother of Saint Augustine; all this is encircled and shut in by a wall, entered by a gate which once was the gate of a city, and which was called Ostia!

"The inhabitants are worthy of their habitations. Ostia is a species of Botany-Bay, where out of three men two are generally galley slaves, and the third worthy of becoming so. What kennels, good God! What language must be used to paint these hideous receptacles, infectious, horrible, where the light of the sun has never penetrated, but where, by way of compensation, the smoke of the hearth remains for ever! The four walls cannot be called naked, for they are veiled by a thick coating of dirt and soot; the furniture is composed of a wooden plank upon three feet, which serves as table by day, and as bed by night. The poverty

1. Didier, pp. 158, 161.

of our poorest peasants may be regarded as riches when compared to the Roman wealth [1]."

Charles Didier is not the only author who paints the campagna of Rome in these sombre colours.

Such is the social state of Italy. Where has this people learnt the conduct of its moral condition? In its education. Let us therefore study it:

ÉDUCATION. — The free development of thought experiences every possible obstacle on the part of power. Nothing is left undone to prevent it. If it kills material prosperity, it is by indirect means; but thought, science, become dreaded for themselves; for sooner or later they generate liberty. Thence, the monstrous system of prohibition and of censure to aid in the perpetuation of ignorance amongst the masses, and even amongst the higher classes. The state of morals is in general deplorable in Italy, although less so than in Spain. The absence of all intellectual life, idleness, ennui, drive men to seek, in sensual pleasures, a brutal diversion from this sentiment of existence without aim upon the earth [2]."

M. de Sismondi will enable us to witness, as it were, a course of Italian education: "A young Italian," says he, "never either thinks or feels the want of thought. The profound idleness in which his days are passed would be the greatest misery to a northern temperament. This idleness becomes from habit not only a necessity, but almost a pleasure. The hours of childhood have been employed with a view to guard against the use of his intellectual faculties. The monks, who have had the direction of all his occupations, have retrenched all fervour from his prayers, all invention from his amusements, all attention from his studies, all frankness from his attachments. The pious exercises of the Church occupy the greater portion of the hours of the student; but it is considered sufficient if, by the sound of his voice, his presence can be recognised. While a devotional exercise of short duration might have served as warning to his conscience, the rosary which he repeats as often as three times a day, without comprehension, accustoms him to the entire separation of thought and language; it becomes an exercise of abstraction when it is not one of hypocrisy.

"A certain time, however, is allowed in Italy in the schools and seminaries to recreation and pastime; but monastic discipline follows the student during the very moment which is given to his

1. Didier, pp. 198, 200. — 2. Lamennais, pp. 119, 120.

play. Every day, at the same hour, the long procession of students leaves the seminary; two priests march at its head, others are mingled in its ranks, others again close the train. The step of the promenaders is never hastened, never diminished; they never may pause to gather a flower, or to watch the most curious specimen of insect industry, or to examine the mysterious fabric of a stone; they may never assemble in groups to play, to discuss, to talk in confidence; monastic authority is full of suspicion; it has been taught to mistrust mankind, and to behold nought but corruption in the century. There is nothing which the pedagogue thinks unworthy of his fears, as much for the discipline of his school as for his own authority. The ties of friendship amongst his pupils would be a conspiracy in his eyes; he hastens, therefore, to break them: confidence amongst them would lead to nothing but corruption, and he renders its existence impossible: *esprit de corps* amongst the boys would place a boundary to his power; he attacks it as a revolt; he rewards the secret spy; he accords all his protection to the mean spirit who sacrifices his comrade.

"Unhappy youth, thus educated! What can have been learnt in the schools but the habit of mistrust of his fellow men, of flattery and lies! What remains of all his studies but the disgust of everything he has acquired, and the incapacity of seeking new occupations? His wit has only produced inertness of thought; the distribution of rewards and penalties nothing more than the basest hypocrisy. The monks have taught him distrust of himself and cowardice. The vices with which we reproach the Italian nation belong not to itself, but to its institutions.

"The pupils thus educated by monastic discipline are received on leaving these monastic schools into the legislation of the country, to form them for bearing the yoke, and to fashion into obedient subjects. They have never been taught to examine into the origin of any species of authority, while they have been told that everything in the world must repose upon authority. Their minds have become too indolent ever to mount upwards to the source of what the belief is to which he is compelled to submit. Led blindfold by the priests throughout the whole of their education, they lay the same blindfold obedience at the feet of their princes. It is no longer an heroic devotion to certain families which has entered into the spirit of certain Italian provinces; it is mere indolent obedience, having no further principle of action than the fatigue of struggle, and the constant desire of repose. To obey those in command has become a proverbial maxim, represented as containing at the same time the whole principle of every duty, both private and political. These general principles of Italian education are applied in every part of the country[1]."

"At one period, in the time of the learned Giasone Maino, Pavia contained three thousand students; but it declined in numbers and reputation until towards the end of the eighteenth century; it was so fallen that even its former reputation was almost forgotten; and this splendid establishment, so noted even in the fourteenth century, was without a library, a museum, collections, or any means of affording subsistence to science or public education[2]."

"Formerly the females were taken from the hireling nurse to the cloister of a nunnery; where, to learn their rubrick, and work Adam and Eve in hem stitch, comprised the sum total of their acquirements. The sons were given up in early boyhood by the family chaplain to a monkish college, where their minds were involved in bigotry, as their persons were disfigured by the monastic garb. Of the younger sons, the major part remained to swell the ranks of the Church militant; the rest came forth from the cloister to hang in idle dependence upon the patronage of primogeniture, or to earn a more degraded subsistence as *cavaliere-servente* to some wealthy dame, whose wane of charms threw her on the paid attentions of the noble but destitute *cadet*[3]."

"But impediments are now thrown in the march of mind, with which genius of whatever sex or calling is doomed for the present to struggle. To retrograde, not to advance, is the order of the day in Lombardy; to *dull* and not to *brighten*, their policy[4]."

"At Venice," says Malte-Brun, "the artisans of the city are formed into several corporations, and each of them maintains a school; they are sixteen or eighteen in number, the greater part assembled in sumptuous buildings, ornamented with pictures and statues. Such institutions might create a belief that the Venetian people are more enlightened than any other. Nothing of the kind; the sole honour that could be accorded to this people would be the supposition of its ignorance being less than that evinced by the lower classes elsewhere.

"The public libraries are little frequented; the reading-rooms

1. Sismondi, vol. XVI. — 2. Lady Morgan, vol. II, p. 38. — 3. *Idem*, pp. 349, 350.

are only furnished with the worst kind of romances; and, with the exception of a few choice spirits favoured by Nature, we can only find men of the most ordinary stamp in the city which gave birth to Algarotti, to Gaspar Gazzi, to Goldoni, to Bembo, and to many other distinguished individuals. If the Venetians are illiterate, music has become their favourite art. An author describes thus the manner in which the Venetians of fortune pass their time in Venice: 'They rise at eleven or twelve o' clock, pay a few visits, or walk through the town until three o' clock; they then dine, sleep an hour when the weather is hot, dress themselves, and go to the café until nine, then to the Opera, which is another casino; again to the café for another hour or two, and only retire in summer with the dawn of day. Nobody ever reads. The nobles live in obscurity and poverty in a corner of their palaces; many amongst them dine at the restaurateurs at 2 francs a head, and the more prudent at 16 sous, French money.'

"Notwithstanding the decay in which the commerce of Venice is fallen, it is still one of the most important stores of Italy [1]."

"At Naples, amongst the class of the people, the rising generation can both read and write. True, this degree of education does not extend beyond the walls of the capital. The colleges are frequented by the children of the *bourgeoisie* only [2]. The princes of the house of Savoy seek to spread useful knowledge amongst the higher classes of the population; but they appear to have wholly forgotten the people, who languish in ignorance and superstition. The primary schools are few in number, and little frequented [3]."

"At Parma," says M. Genin, "for a few years past, the government has confided the education of youth to the Jesuits; they direct at Placenza the College of Saint Peter's. In 1846, the municipal body of that town, in speaking of the budget of expenses, expresses itself in these terms: 'The council admits without reservation the 5,200 livres allowed to the reverend Fathers entrusted by government with the direction of the college of Saint Peter's; but, in obedience with the legal necessity registering this expense, the council cannot help thinking that the money thus expended no longer answers the object for which it was voted, nor the hopes which had been conceived. An imperative duty towards the citizens compels them to declare that the state of the college is a source of affliction and complaint to the whole city, and that the

1. Malte-Brun vol. VII, p. 277. — 2. *Idem*, p. 422. — 3. *Idem*, p. 290.

experiments which have been already tried leave but little hope for the future.'

"Parents are in consternation at beholding the entire demoralisation which has invaded these schools; they are indignant at finding the progress of their children to have been made only in wickedness and turbulence [1]."

Such is Italian education; but what has formed it? The Roman Catholic religion. Let this, then, be our study; and the more so that we are now in its sanctuary:

Religion. — "After having admitted the general dogmas of the Church," says M. Sismondi, "the Italian people looked upon them as no longer in need of examination or study; denoting the great respect felt for Christian faith in avoiding the subject altogether. The most dissolute as well as the most reserved in their conduct, the most philosophical as well as the most superstitious in their belief, never breathed a doubt against the doctrines of the Church, as a whole; but, at the same time no single sentiment was ever excited whereby to influence any action of their lives. Religion, separated from reason, from sensibility, from morals, and from conduct, had become a mere habit of the mind, imposing certain practices, and compelling to certain ideas. People had grown accustomed to resistance against the Pope, to making war upon him, and to despising his excommunications. It was known that his court was corrupt, his policy most treacherous, and that the most odious passions were at times concealed beneath the mask of religion [2]."

"Thus, it may be said that in Modern Italy religion, far from serving as support to morality, has perverted its every principle; that education, so far from developing the faculties of the mind, has thrown them into slumber that legislation, instead of attaching the citizens to their country, and drawing them together by the ties of fraternity, has only filled them with fear and with defiance, and given them selfishness for prudence, and baseness for bravery [3]."

"Murder is no longer a duty, but it is not yet a shame. It is an idea with which every one has grown familiar. The Italian regards it as the fatal consequence of an impetuous movment of anger, jealousy, or vengeance; he does not feel in his heart that he will never be driven to plunge his knife in his neighbour's throat, because he has never been accustomed to look upon such an act

1. Genin, p. 73, — 2, Sismondi, vol. XVII, pp. 5, 6. — 3, *Id.*, pp. 442 to 446. — 4, *Id*, p. 370.

with the inexpressible horror inspired by the thought of any odious crime [1]. "

" It is only in Italy and Spain that the vicious habit of blasphemy is met with, entirely unknown amongst the Protestants, and not to be confounded with the gross swearing which the lower classes, in all countries, mingle in their discourse. In every fit of passion of the people of the South, the Saviour himself is attacked, threatened, and loaded with the most foul abuse. Traces of this scandalous habit are to be found in the language and the oaths of other nations; but the will to insult the Divinity by this species of attack could only be preserved in a country where superstition, unceasingly at variance with incredulity, has diminished every object of worship, until it has descended to the level of mankind [2]."

" In the affections of the whole Roman population, the theatre and the Church divide both love and admiration. For the arts, especially for music, the Italian races profess the most ardent worship, and it is to this taste for spectacle that we must attribute the exaltation of a devotion so far from sincere piety.

" The subtlety of the Romish clergy has, in all times, enabled it to take advantage of this disposition, and it is by the double spectacle of the scenery and religious ceremonies that the priests have been enabled to seduce, astonish, and charm those whom they sought to enslave.

" At the bottom of all these acts of the piety of the people, there exists a sensual thought. Sift the motive of the prayer which seemingly mounts to Heaven, and you will find some material interest which draws it back again to earth.

" Formerly, the holiness of the precincts of the Church was so far lost sight of that refreshments were served in the aisle. This usage is being restored, particularly in the chapels of certain convents [3]. "

" As for the Church material, the Saints whom the superstitious crowd invoke with so much fervour are a much better speculation than the Divinity himself, to whom the prayers of low tendency, and the interested demands of the Catholic clergy, must not be addressed. In the legend, each one of these friends of God, as they are denominated by the Church, has some especial attribute, just the same as was the case with the vulgar herd of the Pagan gods, of whom the Romish Church thus continues the traditions with a view to the most shameful traffic.

1. Sismondi, vol. XVI, p. 457. — 2. *Idem*, p. 378. — 4. Briffault, pp. 163, 164.

"Rome places these religious parades amongst the number of its amusements. It is, therefore, to those who treat so lightly all religious things that we must attribute the discredit now thrown upon a worship once so highly venerated [1]."

"In the galleries of the churches, where the women most remarkable for their birth, their beauty, or their gallantry are assembled, frequent disputes arise concerning the places; sonorous and lusty oaths are exchanged in the same manner as in the public markets of the city. The grand dignitaries of the Church, present at these scenes of scandal, may sometimes be heard to join in them by their undisguised laughter, instead of instantly repressing them by their authority. At church or theatre the same necessity for noisy and turbulent demonstrations. In the galleries arise discussions concerning the eloquence of the Christian preacher, just as in the boxes of the theatre the talents of a singer or a prima donna are made subject of debate. The moments which precede the ceremonies are given to noisy salutation, and to loud recognitions between the aisle and the galleries. The audacity of the women in these outbreaks is without bounds; they call aloud to the prelates they wish to attract. The multitude which fills the entire edifice, meanwhile, sways to and fro, chats, moves about, looks right and left, and betrays curiosity and indifference by turns. Its behaviour is free from all restraint, and far from all reserve. It would be easy to imagine oneself in a café on the Corso, or in the foyer of the Opera; for nothing either to be seen or heard can bring to mind the holiness of the place [2]."

"The least inconvenience of the ridiculous superstitions to which are united, as we have just seen, the chief of the Church and the higher clergy, and which keep up in the minds of the people both ignorance and credulity, is to replace in the minds of the population forethought and reflection by the indifference of fatalism, and which seems to rely upon supernatural protection for those prudent cares which ought never to be laid aside. Hence that indolence peculiar to the Roman people, and the persuasion that all the Saints of Paradise are exclusively occupied in watching over the minutest details of existence [3]."

"I have never beheld amongst the Italians of Rome the display of energy save amid the fire of their superstitious demonstrations of devotion. Incapable of rousing their feelings in a noble cause, they have always at command a multitude of emotions for sensual

1. Briffault, p. 167. — 2. *Idem*, pp. 168, 169. — 3. *Idem*, p. 181.

expression. In order to judge these soft and vicious natures, you should follow them in places open to the crowd; there you may see all that is base in the tastes of this people, whose triviality stifles so often the artistic organisation of their Italian nature[1]."

" Sometimes, amid the cloisters, the most lively qualities of spirit and intelligence grow blunted and withered beneath the cowl. Entirely given up to small artifice, to deadened hypocrisy, to all the debasing subterfuge of monastic rivalship, the soul becomes withered and blighted, and beneath this morbid influence the heart dies, and its warm impulses cease. A blind worship, and a complete servility to the interests of an association detached from the general community, bind and compress the ideas and sentiments in a circle of constraint, and nothing more is brought thence into the world than the enfeebled and impotent organisation[2]."

" In Rome, and in many other places, it is common to pray to Mary to favour all the bad desires engendered by the worst of passions. Does not the brigand of Spain and Italy place beneath the invocation of the Virgin his deeds of murder and rapine? Does not the foul courtezan of Rome believe her duty done when she has veiled the image of the Madonna which decks her boudoir? Does not the rosary hang at the assassin's girdle side by side with the dagger and stiletto? Does not the bandit's peaked hat display a goodly show of blessed images? Does not the scapulary cover the breast where crime is engendered? No one would dare to ask of a man what the Roman dares to beg of the Holy Mother of God. What has the Church done to stay these shameless deviations? Has she not, on the contrary, by her complacency, authorised these superstitious beliefs, which submit to her dominion the multitude thus weakened and degraded? Could we not find among certain minute practices the germ of these superstitions? And then, in transporting our examination further into the power and the profits brought to the clergy by these exercises, which have changed both the cause and the aim of religion, are we not led to believe that a vile interest is the mainspring of this favour?[3]"

" The Roman population has remained faithful to its ancient tastes; the ardour for the games of the Circus are still continued in its affection for the magnificence of fêtes, spectacles of all kinds, and for religious solemnities. In the intoxication of pleasure, Rome forgets the rest, and is no longer aware of her sufferings and humiliation. These signs indicate debasement and decay[4]. "

1. Briffault, p. 190. — 2. *Idem*, p. 246. — 3. *Idem*, p. 174 to 176. — 4. *Idem*, p. 49.

" Base, cowardly, insolent, blaspheming, atheistical, superstitious, raising his beaver and crossing himself before every Madonna, while proffering the most blasphemous oaths against his cattle, against the passenger, against even Heaven itself, such is the Italian [1]. "

" Italy, incrusted with Popery, is a country where superstition reigns in all its plenitude, where life is in the stagnation of death, where no new superstition could be established unless engrafted on the old, where they explained the fall of Cagliostro at Rome by these words ; 'He had put no cross upon his pills [2].' "

We have already remarked that in Catholicism the clergy holds an extensive place, and almost constitutes religion itself. By studying the first, we become acquainted with the second. It would be too long a task to go through the various degrees of the Roman hierarchy ; but we will examine the two extremes : the Sovereign Pontiff, absolute monarch ; and the Priest, simple domestic chaplain :

" Owning no ancestry, the Roman Pontiff is alike without posterity ; the present only is his own ; but for him the past has no existence, the future can never be. Hence arise that carelessness of all things, and that eagerness for temporary joys. Hence that wasting of the fortunes of the State, diminished with each reign ; hence the use of pontifical families enriched by the public treasure ; hence, in short, that example of general ruin which each Pope, needy and prodigal, contributes to hasten. There exists in the history of Papacy a fatal sign. The good resolves of the Pontiffs, their efforts for the public welfare, become invariably arrested or distorted by the shortness of their day of power, and the rapidity of their passage to the throne. Doubt and uncertainty allow them not to take a prompt and energetic resolution ; they scarcely dare to commence a work which, after them, will meet with nought but hands ready for its destruction. In the midst of these continued changes the projects which might serve to preserve a century to the gratitude of the world are suffered to perish. Those, on the contrary, who behold in the Papal throne an opportunity of satisfying their passions, hasten to enjoy the pleasures which opulence presents [3]. At Rome, since the attention of Papal authority has all been directed towards things temporal, the spiritual affairs of the Holy See have only become a secondary consideration, and religion, whose dogma should moderate and repress these attacks of

1. Cambry, vol. II, p. 248. — 2. *Idem*, p. 336. — 3. Briffault, p. 239.

worldly vanity, is only put in requisition to keep up the principles the most fatal to the true spirit of Christianity. It would seem almost folly in our day to seek in Rome for the truth of evangelical moral, the sincerity of Christian precept, and the respect of Divine doctrine; all these are things of which no heed is taken [1]."

Now, from this summit of clerical power, let us descend to its last degree: "In many houses of Rome, amongst the most noble, but above all in those of the rich *bourgeoisie*, an individual is met with called *the priest*. This individual is generally the factotum of the house: he overlooks its domestic economy, sees to the service, is the confidant of the wife, the friend of the husband, and the tutor of the children. He meddles likewise with the external interests of the family, and with the care of the fortune. Nothing is done without consulting him, and his opinion, kept in the background, reigns and governs without being manifest. His position is not absolutely a servile one; neither is it reverenced or honoured. He is placed between the master and the servant, by whom he is invariably detested. It is not a rare occurrence to find that the priest is the confidant of the wife's amours, the husband's gallantries, the longings of the maiden, the dissipation of the youth, and the larcenies of the domestics. Then is his power supreme; he holds all the threads by which he can move the puppets it becomes his interest to enslave [2]. "

Between the priest, so called, and the laïc, we find the religious orders. As they also belong to the clergy, we ought to mention them: "The religious orders," says M. Briffault, "are only recruited from the lowest class of society; the one whose total want of education and the rudeness of its habits render the least disposed towards instruction or progress. The individuals of this order, who devote themselves to the cloister, have seldom any other motive then the most narrow-minded selfishness. They are forced to replace by hypocrisy and lies the learning and suavity which are found wanting. Their superiors know well enough how to excite their zeal, and to exalt it to a fanatical devotion, from which they can demand everything. The monk is the instrument which a superior will, isolated like his own from every duty towards the State, can command at pleasure.

"It is from the lowest ranks of this monkish militia that are chosen those furious apostles whose maniacal preachings carry trouble to the bosoms of the lowly, and spread amongst the villages

1. Briffault, p. 435. — 2. *Idem*, p. 443.

that stupid incredulity and perverse intoterance by which they live; from those same lower regions of the cloister do those clouds of locusts arise, who absorb and devour the produce of labour.

" These monks are the most audacious propagators and the most intrepid defenders of all those superstitions which hold the people in ignorance and error, and render it an easy task to plunder them by the most gross manœuvres. Their contact with the inferior classes, from which they emanate, is one of every hour, and always fatal. The monks, in order to keep up in the minds of the people the beliefs necessary to favour their rapines, have penetrated into the habits of indigence, from which they know to extort the very last bajocco. They carry terror and desolation to hearts they ought to comfort and console. They speculate upon the religious hopes and fears which their impostures have sown. In a higher grade of society other monks are found, whose manners are more cultivated. These know how to insinuate themselves into the bosom of families, to seize the gifts of the living, and the inheritance of the dead. They make a study of the confidences of the family to exercise a secret tyranny, and levy a secret tribute.

" Perfidious emissaries, they slide into the houses where a rich heir might benefit the cloister, and satisfy their cupidity. They surprise the confidence of parents, and by the artifices with which they surround them direct their will towards a mystic aim, but always tending towards the aggrandisement of monkish fortune. Sometimes it is by discord that their aim is attained. Masters in the arts of fomenting internal dissension, they seek to irritate the children against their parents, and the parents against the children. They manage to place spies in opulent houses by corrupting the servants, who sell them the secrets of their masters, and favour by this means their avaricious plans[1]. "

Having spoken of the government, of the education of the people, of the religion, and of the clergy, we should now be preparing to speak of the industry and commerce of the country; but, alas! we are reduced to note these down as entirely null and void.

Commerce. — " No kind of industry, " says Sismondi, " can be pursued without a little capital; some small outlay is required even for the slightest apprenticeship; a literary education itself is the result of a long course of expensive study. Agriculture requires land, commerce exacts capital, and the manufacturer cannot pursue his calling without tools and raw material. The greater proportion of

1. Briffault, p. 288 to 290.

younger sons, excluded in Italy from every one of these pursuits on account of their poverty, live in constant dependence and constant idleness. The four-fifths of the nation are condemned to no interest in life, no hope in the future, and to contribute by no exertion to the prosperity of their fellow countrymen [1]. "

" While nothing is done to promote commerce within the Milanese, everything is done to cripple it without. Enormous duties upon foreign manufactures have stimulated ingenuity to evade bad laws, which serve only to multiply sources of licentiousness and corruption [2]. "

In a country where neither commerce nor industry are to be found, where agriculture is neglected, and science unknown, the people must necessarily be supposed to live inactive, and this inactivity leads to mendicity, mendicity to theft, and theft to crime. " The universal taste for the *far niente*," says Malte-Brun, " which distinguishes the Italian is not wholly to be attributed to the influence of climate. It is to a moral rather than a physical cause that we must have recourse to account for the change in the mass of a people who has preserved no vestige of the activity and power of its ancestors. Private charity, so wisely inculcated by the Gospel, but which, in its application, ought to be guided with discernment by the legislators and the expounders of Divine law, has contributed not a little, in countries where industry has received no impulse, to encourage laziness and depravity, and even crimes, to which it may lead the lower classes. Who has not remarked the arrogance with which the beggar demands the price of his importunity? He thinks his destitution gives him a right to the charity he implores. This idea leads to another—that beggary is a trade, a kind of lawful occupation; shame has no longer access to his soul, and if charity procures him a subsistence, he prefers it to work. But, between that first idea of begging without shame, and that of demanding charity with a threat, there is too slight a shade to be observed by the man without conscience and without education. We cannot, therefore, feel astonished if in those countries where mendicity has become a profession, highway robbery has also been followed as a profitable trade. Those great plague-spots of Italy, brigandage and mendicity, are spread over the kingdom of Naples, as well as over the Papal States. Every man carries a carabine, and hangs round his neck the image of the Virgin or of the holy child Jesus! [3] "

1. Sismondi, vol. XVI. p, 457. — 2. Lady Morgan, vol. I, p. 376. — 3. Malte-Brun, vol. VII, p. 415.

What is most singular is, to behold this people refusing to work, yet ending by regarding amid the national indolence this organised brigandage as an acknowledged profession. In order to render it lawful, they have placed it under the protection of Heaven. The Church is commercial; the priest sells salvation under every form; the friar begs in the name of his convent.

"At Genoa," says Lady Morgan, "we met a band of pilgrims, of both sexes, returning from Loretto to their native montains of the Abbruzzi. The staff and scallop-shell hat, the shewy rosary and glittering cross, gave a most fantastic appearance to these devotees, who were trudging on merrily and noisily, absolved from all their sins, and (by the fierce looks of the men, and the looks *not fierce* of the women) disposed to open a new account with the Virgin, at whose shrine they had been so lately purified [1]."

"Loretto, the holiest and poorest of cities, consists almost entirely of little shops and vast ecclesiastical edifices: the former are the bijouteries of the Church, exclusively devoted to the sale of religious trinkets, rosaries of every quality, texture, and value, from the string of wooden or glass beads to rows of amber and other precious materials; crucifixes in tin, copper, or gold, and reliquaries and relics of flowers, feathers, of eyes or noses; in a word, whatever can please or pacify Heaven in a material form, or supply the craving of the devout pilgrim and curious traveller [2]."

If we change the place and the writer, we shall not change the scene: "The inferior classes of the people of Rome," says M. Briffault, "stand in need more than elsewhere of the comforts procured by labour; but the Church, as I have seen, encourages idleness by the number of its fêtes; she nurses, by vain hopes addressed to heaven, disdain and carelessness of more tangible interests, and the greater part of the population is delivered up without defence to the miseries by which it is overcome. The money which could be employed by the poor in procuring comfortable clothing, in wholesome food, and habitation, is absorbed by the contributions, by the offerings, and by the long series of devotional exactions. The rest is expended in the extravagance and dissipation of dissolute pleasures, and also in the certain vanities of dress. And thus it is that in this pious city, so full of the ministers of a religion whose one great precept is that of charity, we find an entire population driven by fever and consumption to the hospitals, whose funds no longer suffice for the maintenance of these vast multitudes of stricken

1. Lady Morgan, vol. IV, p. 300. — 2. *Idem*, pp. 304, 305.

poor[1]. During the daytime, the beggar will devour with hypocritical avidity all that is given to him; but, at night, in his hovel, he will give himself up to all the frenzies of orgie. This abject race mix up with their trade of beggary rapine, espionage, and intrigue. The mendicant friars, who belong to the begging orders, think themselves authorised to penetrate by sheer impudence into every house where they hope to fill their knapsacks; their profession completes that of their accomplices, the street mendicants[2]."

Monks have furnished the beggars; the beggars have furnished the brigands: "At the very gates of Rome the country is infested by the armed attempts of brigands. From within the robbers from without receive those indications which make known to them the departure of the richest forigners; these indications are always of the most scrupulous exactitude; the road they are about to take, the value of they property they bear with them, the designation of their persons, their fortune, their situation, and that of their families, are all carefully set down in the notice transmitted by that part of the Roman population which lives at the expense of the foreigners thus delivered up to the fury and rapacity of the robbers.

"Between the Italians of Rome and their base perfidy, and the audacity of the brigands of the country, there exists the same difference as that between a highway robber and a pickpocket. The result is, to drive this brigandage more slowly away from Italy than from any other Catholic country of Europe; and that, of all the Italian countries, the Papal States remain the most infested by brigands, and where they will be extirpated with the greatest difficulty. A better education, good examples, less encouragement of superstition, and above all an incitement to labour, would spare to the people of Rome all the misery propagated by ignorance and credulity which the Romish clergy cultivate in the hearts and minds of their flocks with a guilty connivance[3]."

If you feel tempted to place this idleness to the score of climate, remember the people of Ancient Rome, and read these lines of Malte-Brun: "Agriculture, enterprise, and labour, if encouraged in Sicily, might be made to nourish, as in the time of the Romans, a population triple its actual numbers; but how many obstacles must be vanquished before they can be carried to the degree of prosperity of which they are susceptible! The nobility must first of all show the example of a great reform; and, what is more difficult, perhaps, they must be made to feel its value. Idleness and

1. Briffault, p. 203. — 2. *Idem*, p. 207. — 3. *Idem*, p. 214, 215.

mendicity would suffer, no doubt; the number of monks would gradually diminish, and we should then be able to judge whether certain factories, in a country where none exist, might not be made to replace with advantage some few of the convents, whose numbers are out of all proportion with the population. The island actually possesses 28,000 monks and 18,000 nuns : in all, 46,000 useless individuals out of a population of 1,650,000 souls; that is to say, one idle monk amongst every 35 inhabitants[1]."

If any doubt could still exist that these evils are the fatal consequence of the Church of Rome, it would be sufficient, in order to convince the reader of the contrary, to find them in every other country submitted to the same religious rule. There are certain expressions which can only apply to Catholic countries, and refuse to connect themselves with a Protestant people. In vain you endeavour to represent to your imagination the idea of the banditti of England, or the swarms of American mendicants; while the mind accepts without difficulty the expression of the swarming beggars of Ireland or Italy, the bands of brigands of Spain, Naples, or the Roman States; and, more conclusive still, we find the same plagues to exist in every essentially Catholic State. The reader will remember, no doubt, that we have seen the same dirt, squalor, and idleness in Ireland, in Brazil, in Spain, that we behold in Italy. We have discovered the same troops of brigands in South America and in Spain that we have found in Italy. One exception exists : no brigandage is admitted in Ireland. This exception, however, rather confirms the rule, for there it is Protestant England whose police keeps the highway. If murder now and then escapes unpunished, it is thanks to the Catholic population, who connive at the murder by hiding the assassin from his judges: a false sentiment of patriotism, inculcated by the priests. Nevertheless, the destitution of a few millions of men, not to be repressed like brigandage, continues naturally to develope itself in Ireland as in Italy.

But let our authorities speak once more. We ought, in order to fill the frame we have set before our readers, present them with a picture of the prosperity of Italy; this picture will bear the tints of ignorance, brigandage, and squalid destitution, and signed by its composer, SUPERSTITION.

Malte-Brun speaks in these terms of Sicily : " The agents of the government are all professed smugglers; the monks direct the

1. Malte-Brun, vol. VII, p. 452.

education of the children, and govern the domestic relations of the families, while their conduct is as disorderly as in the sixteenth century. Bribery had, until very lately, succeeded in protecting robbery in Sicily, as well as in the kingdom of Naples, and some parts of the islands were regular repairs for the concealment of banditti. The government has at length come forward to secure the safety of travellers. In every district they name a *capitano*, chosen from among the richest landowners; they place at his disposal fourteen horsemen, well-mounted, well-paid, and chosen, for greater security, from amongst the most intrepid of the brigands. Under an enlightened government the Two Sicilies would present a very different spectacle to that which they now offer : it would be an easy task to destroy the seeds of idleness which spread such misery among the people, and multiplies the convents of both sexes. In the last few years, the number of men devoted to religious seclusion was estimated at 11,600, of women 9,300, and of priests 26,300 [1]."

Here are a few lines from the pen of M. Cambry, upon this absence of all prosperity :

"Unhappy people of Italy, to what an abject state of slavery has thy superstition led thee! What infection and pestilence at Bergamo! How can men live for a single hour amid the nauseous filth everywhere to be met with in the streets, the palaces, the churches; where the most filthy objects lie beneath your feet, pollute the richest galleries, where the air is never admitted. Debased people of Italy! you have succeeded in dishonouring the richest country in the world; and if population and liberty do not penetrate amongst you, we shall one day behold Tuscany deserted, and Rome without inhabitants! [2] It would seem as if Popery drew from human nature one-third of its strength and virtue [3]. What infection at Padua! Beneath this beautiful sky, amid these fertile plains, everything is destroyed by filth, by stupidity, and ignorance [4]. The Grimani palace at Venice, on the Grand Canal, was one of those by which I was the most struck. These rich fabrics only serve to shew more fully the destitution and degraded state of the surrounding houses. Insolent grandeur, squalid misery, princes and beggars, priests and cripples, are the contrasts often to be met with in Italy. The middle class trembles and crawls, living by lawsuits, by meanness, and by swindling. Filth reigns triumphant in Italy. Happy Benedictins! enjoy in silence the delights that igno-

1. Malte-Brun, vol. VII, pp. 474, 477. — 2. Cambry, vol. II, pp. 111, 112. — 3. *Idem*, p. 121. — 4. *Idem*, p. 160.

rance and superstition have secured to you; go on, with your Senate, your intrigues, and efforts against the bold impertinence of reason which threatens despotism and lies[1]."

One quotation more from Lady Morgan, ere we conclude: "But those deeply touched by the fate of living Italy turn alternately from the Paradise of the natural scenery to the wretched, ragged groups, who, stretching forth their squalid forms from the black dens of Passignano, give the first specimens of the condition of the subjects of the Papal dominions[2]. Yet here we found a friar begging from beggars. Groups of monks and beggars duly notified our entrance into that State, for ages supposed to be under the immediate dominion of the Deity, and governed by the Vice-regent of 'Christ on earth.' Nature was still the same, bountiful and beautiful!... but there was a visible change in the physiognomy of the people. The Tuscan freshness, as well as the Tuscan competency, had wholly disappeared. A few haggard-looking women were performing the field-labours of men: the men (and there were but few visible) were loitering listlessly, muffled to their chins in dark and ragged mantles; and both closely resembled the Irish peasantry in form, expression, and all the exterior of poverty and wretchedness. As we passed along, all held out their hands in silent supplication for charity; a habit universally prevailing in the Roman States[2]. But this tract, where imperial temples and triumphal arches lined the broad *Flaminian* way, is now awfully desolate and dangerously depopulated[3]. The French cleared up these forests, and in many places burnt them up, as the most efficient means of getting rid of the bands they sheltered; and during their government this evil, which, with many others, had so long infested the devoted land, was nearly done away, but it reappeared almost instantaneously on their expulsion[4]."

"When the season of the malaria arrives (Neppi), the innkeeper and his family, and all who can shut up their houses and depart, leave this sad abode to the old and feeble, who stay to die or to survive a little longer the victims of this annual plague. From Neppi, the desert opens in all its heart-chilling sadness; trees dwindle and disappear, shrubs diminish, and the Campagna begins from its extremest verge in striking dreariness, and fades into the remote horizon in unvaried desolation. Here rises no monastic palace; here wanders no mendicant monk. The Church has long withdrawn from the traveller's view. She is found again at Rome,

1. Cambry, vol. II, pp. 189 to 191. — 2. Lady Morgan, vol. III, p. 174. — 3. *Idem*, p. 175. 4. *Idem*, p. 206.

under gilded domes and velvet canopies. But here all that is known of her existence appears in the *waste* she has made[1]. The Pantheon is now the very *comble* of bad taste. The darkest superstition likewise prevails in all its ornaments and decorations, and the temple of all the gods seems, at the first glance, to serve the purposes of an old-clothes shop. The six tawdry chapels, with their colossal virgins and Patagonian saints, which rise between the beautiful pilasters, are covered with offerings that indicate, in very disgusting signs, the moral and physical infirmity of the votarists; and tin noses and wooden legs, old wigs and woollen petticoats, while they disfigure some of the most beautiful proportions of art, indicate a state of society the most degraded by ignorance and bigotry, and illustrate the falsity of the assertion that Modern Rome ever has been the instrument of communicating to Europe those greatest blessings of which human nature is susceptible: civilisation, science, and religion. Let those who have visited her Pantheon on a Christmas Eve, or read her INDEX, judge[2]."

"In the midst of this imposing display of church magnificence sauntered or reposed a population which displayed the most squalid misery. The haggard natives of the mountains, the labourers who had that night deserted their cabins of straw and furze on the Campagna, to avail themselves of the saturnalia and slumber upon precious marbles, were mixed with the whole mendicity of Rome, seeking one night's shelter beneath a roof for heads accustomed to crouch beneath open porticoes and projecting doorways. Some of these terrific groups lay stretched in heaps on the ground, congregating for warmth; and as their dark eyes scowled from beneath the mantle which half hid a sheepskin dress, they had the air of banditti awaiting their prey[3]."

"With no moral law to check, with no religious feeling to restrain, loosened from the potency of opinion, and tempted to the last lure of seduction, that the Italians throughout all Italy should pass their Carnival more in frailty than in crime, more in folly than in licentiousness, is one among many proofs of the inherent tendency towards good, the gentle, genial organisation of that amiable and much traduced people. Love is no sin in Italy. Neither the law, the religion, nor the customs of the land, restrain its impulses, nor limit its ranges: and if love is not the sole business of the Carnival, it at least places a large capital in the venture. The rest is all idle amusement and puerile pleasures[4]." "The shops of

1. Lady Morgan, vol. III, p. 210. — 2. *Idem*, p. 241. — 3. *Idem*, vol. IV, pp. 14 and 15. — 4. *Idem*, pp. 27, 28.

Rome are then gaily lighted; and the *pizzicaroli*, the faithful allies of the Church, now offer 'food for meditation' to the hungry devotees, whose long fasts are about to be recompensed by repletion. In one shop we saw Saint Paul irradiated by a glory of sausages; and in another the ill-boding bird of Saint Peter hung up with the apostle it had warned in vain; Madonnas curiously carved in butter, and Bambinos in lard, warmed the devotion of the inward man; and every eatable of plastic consistence, or of malleable form, was pressed into the service of architectural decoration and symbolic piety [1]."

"Let him (the traveller in Rome), examine the vortex of European wealth, sunk into abject poverty; let him remark the silent desolation of the streets, the poisonous solitude of the environs; let him view the fading splendour of the palaces, the accumulating ruins of the meaner edifices; let him mark the total absence of commerce, the hopeless struggle of lingering industry; let him watch the melancholy dejectedness of the lower classes, the complacent satisfaction of look of the prelates; the hypocritical but cunning obsequiousness of the priest, the more timid and servile humiliation of gesture of the laymen; let him observe the destitution of the multitudinous mendicants, and the freezing discomfort of the nobles beggared by the mismanagement of their overgrown properties: in short, let him extend his glance through every rank of society, from the Pope to the mendicant friar, from the senator of Rome to the lay beggar, and let him ask himself in which of the classes of Roman citizens he would willingly and preferably enrol himself."

"In no part of Europe has tyranny obtained so durable, so perfect, and so unalloyed a possession as in the Eternal City; and the very longevity of which it boasts, while it has accumulated on its head all the physical evils of a too prolonged existence, has concentred in its constitution all the social imperfections, all the abuses, errors, and absurdities of authority and prescription [2]."

These begging habits are such, that the Pope's soldiers are even affected by them:

"The huts of the patrols continue to increase in dreariness, as their inhabitants are deeper steeped in misery. Many of these soldiers of St. Peter were without shoes, and did not scruple to beg a paul from us as we passed. From those to whom we spoke at the post-house we heard a dreadful account of their sufferings, attested by their swollen and jaundiced appearance [3]."

1. Lady Morgan, vol. IV, pp. 64, 65. — 2. *Idem*, p. 79. — 3. *Idem*, p. 100.

About to close this study on the state of Catholic Italy, we beg permission not to pronounce our own judgment, but to provoke that of the reader by a few questions. Would you choose Calabria as a residence? would you accept a Neapolitan woman for your wife, or her *cavaliere servente* for your friend? Have you ever had a thought of pursuing commerce at Venice, or literature at Rome? Would you entrust your honour, your fortune, to those mendicant monks, to those Jesuit priests, nay, even to those Cardinals seated at the theatre with dissolute women? I do not hesitate to declare that your answer would be a sad condemnation of the miserable state of Italy. And who is to be accused of these frightful evils? Is it the country itself, the soil, the climate? No; in that unhappy land, everything from the hand of the Almighty is bright and brilliant; everything beneath the control of man wretched and miserable. Are we bound to accuse the present race of Italians? History protests against the accusation. The name of Roman awakens two distinct ideas, whether we apply it to the days of Ancient or of Modern Rome; that is to say, as one remembers the man of nature still Pagan, or the man of civilisation perverted by Romanism. The Italians of the middle ages struggling against the Papal power, throwing off the yoke, and living under a Republic, bear witness to the worth of this people. *Au reste,* our authors have rendered homage to the Italian character: hear M. de Sismondi: "The Italians are nourished from infancy to old age with the poison of corruption; their energy has been destroyed, their minds condemned to inaction, their pride humiliated, their sincerity destroyed. A profound pity for the fate of this nation, so richly endowed by Nature, so cruelly debased by man, mnst be the result of this examination. In seeking the cause which has inoculated a whole people with vice, we become more convinced that it is not inherent to its nature, and we are more disposed to render homage to the few virtues which remain, to the few qualities still preserved from the pernicious influence of surrounding causes. Not a single vice have we unveiled in the institutions of Modern Italy but should be excused in the Italians[1]."

It is to Popery alone, therefore, that we must attribute the shame of the actual state of Italy; it is the work, the legitimate offspring, the exclusive pupil, of the Papal power. Whatever Popery is able to accomplish, has been accomplished in Italy. No opposition has been offered there. On the contrary, Popery has been enthroned;

1. Sismondi, vol. XVI, p. 408.

princes and people have bowed before it as before an idol; and the head of Catholicism, armed with a triple tiara, held as infallible. This Roman Caiphas, accepted as vice-God, has prepared and consummated that vast ruin we have been contemplating. Popery is there surrounded by the most favourable circumstances; therefore, it has accomplished the utmost of which it was capable. What would have become of it, opposed in its march, or persecuted by monarchs? We know not: but we are about to examine what has become of the Reformation in France, opposed in its development, persecuted by the Great Monarch, and we shall then possess a new and final element of comparison.

PROTESTANTISM

ON THE CROSS IN FRANCE.

The reader will be astonished, perhaps, that, in this series of parallels between nations, we should not have compared France with another country — England, for instance. Before we enter on our subject, we owe an explanation of our conduct in this respect.

First, then, we have intentionally avoided making the comparison. It would have been impossible[1]. But, supposing this were not the case, still we should have felt it our duty to abstain. Our object is not to flatter this or that nationality, but to show forth a broad truth, which shall be profitable for all people.

It is easy to understand, besides, that the question might have become irritating. By reducing it to a personal subject, the author

1. "A parallel has been attempted between France and England; a writer has proved that there are fewer accused persons in the former than in the latter of the two kingdoms; hence, the conclusion that intellectual enlightenment is not productive of good. But it should be borne in mind that the two countries are ruled by totally different laws; and a great number of trespasses, which, in France, would have been considered as bailable offences, are classed, in England, amongst the crimes. In order to draw legitimate inferences, we should compare together crimes of the same nature. Thus, since the beginning of the present century, 25 persons at most are reckoned annually in England as convicted of having shed the blood of their fellow-creatures, whilst, in France, every year, between six and seven hundred wretches, guilty of murder or of assassination, either mount the scaffold or are sent to the hulks. What a melancholy comparison for France! And yet the penalty of death is inflicted there far less often than in England. Thus, in 1825, only 134 individuals were condemned to death by the French laws, whilst in England no less than 1,036 received the same sentence (we should add that 50 alone amongst them were executed)."

Quetelet's *Recherches statistiques sur le royaume des Pays-Bas*, p. 31.

M. Quetelet, whose language we quote, is neither a Protestant, nor an Englishman. He is a Belgian Roman Catholic,

would have composed his work, and the reader perused it, under the impression of a spirit of partiality.

It is not at a moment like the present, when the two nations are united in one common cause, and when their blood is about to flow on the same battle-field — it is not then, especially, that we would raise the slightest irritation between them, merely for the purpose of gratifying the national vanity either of the one or of the other.

We have, in the next place, a still stronger motive for not making a comparison, which has already been drawn by so many writers. In a special point of view, the parallel is not possible. For, if England is essentially Protestant, France cannot be said to be essentially Catholic. The French receive baptism at the hands of the priest, they are married by the ministry of the priest, they bury their dead with the authority of the priest; but, nevertheless, the nation is not inspired by Catholicism; it does not act from it; Catholicism is not the substance of her every-day life.

" France, " says M. Quinet, " has declared upon several occasions that she separates her own destiny from the destiny of her Church. She does not consent to take any substitute for it, but she very cautiously declines beforehand linking her own fortune with that of Catholicism. Whilst refusing to tolerate any other form of worship, she will not pledge herself to accept Catholicism as the ideal of her political faith.

"Strange reserve ! or, rather, precocious distrust of what some people call the liberties of the Gallican Church ! At the very moment that her faith is strongest, France only gives up to Catholicism the one-half of herself, as if she already foresaw that this is not the faith in which she must remain. The Church on one side, France on the other. If the first becomes weak, the second is not bound to it; the nation preserves in its midst the spirit of the past, but resolves not to listen to it. A strange treaty, full of suspicion, and which can alone explain how our country, without receiving Protestantism, has been able to escape from what Saint-Simon calls the *gnawing cancer* of Rome [1]. "

We repeat, then, that France, taken as a whole, is not Catholic; if she is anything in religion, she is deistical; and this is why France cannot be included within the circle of our comparisons between Romanism and the Reformed Religion.

We admit, at the same time, that some of the provinces, Britany, for instance, are really under the influence of the Popish

1. Quinet, p. 312.

clergy. This is a fact which we shall avail ourselves of for the purpose of comparing those parts of France with the districts in which Protestantism has many adherents; thus, instituting a real parallel between French Protestants and French Catholics.

With this view we might have followed for France the course we have already adopted in our account of Switzerland; but here another difficulty meets us. With the exception of the extreme parts in which Catholicism and Protestantism do not intermingle, we must acknowledge that elsewhere, on the contrary, influences exist which, acting either for good or for evil, will not allow us any longer to consider Catholics and Protestants as forming two distinct camps. The comparison between the Frenchmen of both churches must, therefore, in our work, be only a secondary argument. As the title of this chapter sufficiently points out, the history of persecuted Protestantism is the main point to which our attention is invited: we shall examine it at once.

We are not, of course, about to give here the history of the French Protestants, but merely to state the persecutions they have suffered, and the manner in which they endured them. For this purpose, we need only quote from the work of M. Charles Weiss, professor at the Lycée Bonaparte.

With a view to brevity, we shall retrace our steps only as far back as "the Edict of 1620, which re-established the Catholic religion within the dominion of Jeanne d'Albret. In vain did the parliament of Pau protest against this edict. Louis XIII declared that he would go himself and have it registered, and that he would be stopped neither by the advanced season, nor by the poverty of the Landes, nor by the ruggedness of the mountains. He kept his word; and after having completely changed the organisation of that province, so long the hotbed of Protestantism in the south, he returned to Paris, where the people greeted him with cries of joy [1]."

"The defection of Lesdiguières having replaced the Dauphine in the monarch's power, he dismissed all Protestant governors of fortresses, and replaced them by Catholics. In the other provinces the Protestants remained exposed to the hatred of governors, military commandants, priests, and populace. Civil war shortly after covered France with ruins. It was at first concentrated around Castres and Montauban; and such was the exasperation of the royal troops, that soon, in all the environs of those towns, there

1. Weiss's History of the French Protestant Refugees, translated by Frederick Hardman; London and Edinburgh, W. Blackwood, p. 16.

remained neither corn nor fruit-trees, vines nor houses. Everything had been burned. All the Protestants who were within reach in the two towns of Toulouse and Bordeaux were pitilessly massacred [1]. ”

We behold, then, the French Protestants in a position similar to that of the Irish Roman Catholics. Both are persecuted by their respective governments. We know to what depths of misery the Irish Catholics sank; we have witnessed their neglect of agriculture, their idleness, their frightful poverty. Is the same sight offered to us by the equally persecuted Protestants? No: “ Gradually excluded from court employments, and from almost all civil posts, it was fortunately impossible for them to impoverish themselves by luxury and idleness. Compelled to apply themselves to agriculture, trade, and manufactures, they abundantly compensated themselves for their former restraints. The vast plains they possessed in Béarn and the western provinces were covered with rich harvests. In Languedoc, the cantons peopled by them became the best cultivated and the most fertile, often in spite of the badness of the soil. Thanks to their indefatigable labour, this province, so long devastated by civil war, arose from its ruins. On the Esperou, one of the highest ridges in the Cévennes, was remarked a plain enamelled with flowers, and abounding in springs of water, which maintained a fresh vegetation during the summer's most ardent heat. The inhabitants called it the Hort-Diou, that is to say, the Garden of God. In the diocese of Nismes, the valley of Vaunage was celebrated for the richness of its vegetation. The Protestants, who possessed within its limits more than sixty temples, called it Little Canaan. The skilful vine-dressers of Berri restored its former prosperity to that district. Those of the *Pays Messin* became the élite of the population of more than twenty-five villages; the gardeners of the same province brought their art to a degree of perfection previously unknown [2]. ”

“ The Protestants who dwelt in towns devoted themselves to manufactures and trade, aud displayed an activity, an intelligence, and at the same time an integrity, which perhaps have never been surpassed in any country. In Guyenne, they took possession of almost the whole of the wine-trade; in the two governments of Brouage and Oleron, a dozen Protestant families had the monopoly of the trade in salt and wine, which annually amounted to from 1,200,000 to 1,500,000 francs. At Sancerre, by their persevering

1. Weiss, pp. 20, 21. — 2. *Idem*, pp. 23, 25.

industry, and by the spirit of order that animated them, the Protestants became, as was admitted by the intendant, superior to the Catholics in numbers, wealth, and consideration. In the *Généralité* of Alençon, almost all the trade passed through the hands of about four thousand Protestants. Those of Rouen attracted to their town a host of wealthy foreigners, especially Dutch, to the great benefit of the country. Those of Caen resold to English and Dutch merchants the linen and woollen cloths manufactured at Vire, Falaise, and Argentan, thus insuring a rich market to that branch of national manufactures. The important trade that Metz maintained with Germany was almost entirely in the hands of the Huguenots of that department. Accordingly, the governor said to the minister of Louis XIV, 'They hold the trade in their hands, and are the richest of the people.' The merchants of Nismes, renowned throughout the South of France, afforded means of subsistence to an infinity of families. 'If the Nismes merchants,' wrote Bâville (the intendant of the province) in 1699, 'are still bad Catholics, at any rate they have not ceased to be very good traders.'"

"It was also to the Protestants that France owed the rapid development of its maritime trade at Bordeaux, La Rochelle, and the Norman ports. The French Protestants deserved their high reputation for commercial probity.

"Lost, in a manner, amongst a people who regarded them with distrust, unceasingly exposed to calumny, subjected to severe laws, which imperiously compelled them to perpetual self-watchfulness, they commanded public esteem by the austerity of their morals, and by their irreproachable integrity. By the avowal even of their enemies, they combined the qualities of the citizen—that is to say, respect for the law, application to their work, attachment to their duties, and the old parsimony and frugality of the burgher classes—with those of the Christian; namely, a strong love of their religion, a manifest desire to conform their conduct to their conscience, a constant fear of the judgments of God.

"In high repute for their intelligence and commercial activity, they were no less so for their manufactures. More inclined to toil than the Catholics, because they could become their equals only through superiority of workmanship, they were further stimulated and seconded by the principles of their religion. These principles tended incessantly to instruct and enlighten them by leading them to faith only by the path of examination. Thence the superior enlightenment necessarily found in their modes of action, and which rendered their minds more capable of seizing all the ideas whose application might contribute to their wellbeing. The capital possessed by the Protestants enabled them to form and sustain great enterprises. In the provinces of Picardy, Champagne, Normandy, the Isle of France, in Touraine, the Lyonnais, and Languedoc, it was they who created the most important manufactures; and this was made evident by the rapid decline of those manufactures after the revocation of the edict of Henri IV."

"The recent invention of the stocking-loom multiplied the manufactories of woollen, silk thread, and cotton stockings. The Protestants distinguished themselves no less in this new manufacture, which they extended especially in the Sedanais and in Languedoc. A part of this province, the Upper Gévaudan, a mountainous and sterile country, peopled almost entirely by those of the Reformed religion, found an unexpected and precious resource in the manufacture of *cadis*, and serge. Under this name were designated light stuffs, whose extreme cheapness insured them a market. All the peasants had in their houses looms for their manufacture, at which they passed the whole of the time not devoted to the cultivation of their lands. Comfort prevailed in that little country, and extended itself from thence to the adjacent districts."

"The beautiful paper-manufactories in Auvergne and the Angoumois were also in their hands. They had mills at Ambert, at Thiers, and at Chamalières, near Clermont. Those at Ambert produced the best paper in Europe. The best printing of Paris, Amsterdam, and London was done upon the Ambert paper. This manufacture supported a great number of families, and brought in every year more than 80,000 crowns. The manufactures of the Angoumois were not less flourishing and famous. Six hundred mills were at work in that province, and its papers rivalled those of Auvergne."

"It was the Protestants who gave to France the magnificent linen-manufactures that so long enriched her north-western provinces.

"The tanneries of Touraine were renowned throughout the whole of France. The Protestants had established more than four hundred in that industrious province.

The silk manufactures of Tours and Lyons, so flourishing in the middle of the seventeenth century, owed nearly all their splendour to the industry of Protestant workmen[1]."

"The Protestant part of the French middle classes did not devote

1. Weiss, vol. I, pp. 25 to 32.

itself entirely to commerce and manufactures, but entered the liberal professions. A great number of adherents of the Reformed religion distinguished themselves as physicians, lawyers, and writers, and powerfully contributed to the literary glory of Louis XIV's century. A Protestant advocate, Henry Basnage, the learned commentator of the *Coutume de Normandie*, led for fifty years the Rouen bar. His friend and contemporary, Lémery, the father of the illustrious chemist, of whose birth within her walls Rouen is to this day proud, fulfilled, in that same parliament, with rare distinction, the duties of *procureur*. Valentin Courat, at whose house literary men were accustomed to meet, drew out the letters-patent of the French Academy in 1635, at the time of its foundation, compiled its regulations, and was its first secretary. We may also name the celebrated Madame Dacier; Guy Patin, who deserves mention in our annals of learning as a man of letters, a philosopher, and a physician; and Pierre Dumoulin, equal to the best of our classical prose writers. These distinguished persons were all Protestants. The ministry of the Gospel could also bring forward eminent characters: Daillé, concerning whom a Roman Catholic academician, said 'that his sermons were very learned, very eloquent, and very polished;' Drelincourt, renowned for the popular style of his preaching; Allix, whose learning was highly praised; Mestrezat, of whom Cardinal de Retz speaks so flatteringly in his Memoirs; Claude, who, more than all the others, was worthy, by reason of the rare vigour of his mind, by his close logic, and sometimes by his eloquence, of combating at the head of his party; at Montpellier, Michael Lefaucheur; at Caen, Pierre Dubosc; at Metz, David Ancillon; in Normandy, Dufeugueray, Lhérondel, and de Larroque; and at a later period de Langle, Legendre, and especially Jacques Basnage, who published so many learned works which his own century admired, and ours still esteems.

"The synods favoured this literary movement. The four academies of Saumur, Montauban, Nismes, and Sedan, were watched by them with jealous care, and soon the reputation of the schools spread into foreign countries, so that not only many Dutch preachers, but princes of the house of Brandenburg, went to study there. Joachim Sigismond studied at Sedan; John George at Saumur. Montauban, which in France was the stronghold of the doctrine of Calvin, as, in Germany, Wittemberg was of that of Luther, produced Garissolles, Chamier, Bérault; from that of Saumur, founded by Mornay, came forth Cappel, Amyraut, Saint-

Maurice, Desmarets, Tanneguy-Lefèvre; from that of Sedan, Du Rondel, Bayle, Jurieu, Dumoulin.

"In all the principal towns of the kingdom the Protestants supported colleges, of which the most flourishing were those of Nismes, Bergerac, Béziers, Dié, Caen, Orange.

"A portion of the Protestant nobility took part in that literary movement which was the purest and most durable glory of Louis XIV's century. The Duke of Montausier, the Marquis of Dangeau, the Counts of Lude, the Saint-Blancards, the Lords of Cerisy, Count de Gassion, Marshal Guébriand, Marshal Rantzau, Marshal Duke de la Force, the Duke of Rohan, and Marshal Châtillon. All these illustrious generals, and a host of officers who fought under their orders, belonged to the Reformed religion[1]."

"When they saw the prosperity of the Protestants, the enemies of the Reformation thought no doubt that the blows they had dealt to their victim had not been strong enough. They then levelled the club of persecution at that bruised head whose wounds seemed to be healing. Soon an order in council appeared, forbidding Protestants to bury their dead, save at daybreak or nightfall. In 1663, newly-converted Protestants were dispensed from payment of debts to their former co-religionists. Old and barbarous laws against converts who relapsed into the Reformed faith were revived and enforced. Then was once more seen the hideous spectacle of corpses drawn upon hurdles amidst the outrages of the populace. All who had abjured Protestantism, and who, upon their deathbeds, refused the sacraments of Rome, were condemned to this shameful treatment. In 1664, all the letters of freedom granted to Protestants were annulled. A new order prohibited the reception as sempstress of any woman who did not profess the Catholic religion. In 1665, priests were authorised to present themselves, accompanied by the magistrate of the place, at the bedside of dying Protestants, to exhort them to conversion; and if they appeared disposed to it, the work was to be proceeded with, in spite of any opposition offered by the family.

"Already several professions were closed to Protestants. The law often entailed the ruin of their fortunes, and carried disturbance into their families, by pursuing them even on their deathbed with odious controversies. Thenceforward not a month passed without some fresh act of rigour. Protestants were forbidden to abandon the country, and those already settled abroad were recal-

1. Weiss, vol. 1, pp. 33 to 38.

led. The physicians of Rouen were forbidden to receive into their corporation more than two persons of the Reformed religion. Schoolmasters were prohibited from teaching the children of Protestants anything but reading, writing, and ciphering. In 1671, it was ordered that not more than one school and one master should be allowed to exist in the places where the exercise of their religion was still permitted.

"Thus were the Protestants assailed in the daily exercise of their religion, in the education of their children, in the discipline of their families."

After the suppression of the semi-Protestant courts of law, it was nothing uncommon, in purely civil causes, to hear the Catholic invoke this argument: "I plead against a heretic;" and when the Protestant complained of an unjust sentence, "Your remedy is in your own hands," coldly replied the judge; "why do you not become a convert?"

"Now they interdicted Protestant worship in a town in which a bishop was on a visit; then they affirmed that it was impossible to endure the scandal of a Protestant preaching-house in the neighbourhood of a Catholic church. The former was accordingly demolished, and its reconstruction was permitted only in some inconvenient and distant place. To add to all these vexations, ministers were forbidden to hold children's schools elsewhere than in the precincts of their temples, and thus were their young pupils compelled daily to perform long journeys to and from their studies. An edict of the 17th June, 1681, allowed children to return to the bosom of the church as early as at the age of seven years.

"This law had terrible consequences. It undermined paternal authority in Protestant families. It now sufficed that an envious person, an enemy, a debtor, declared before a tribunal that a child wished to become a Catholic, had manifested an intention of entering a church, had joined in a prayer, or made the sign of the cross, or kissed an image of the Virgin, for the child in question to be taken from his parents, who were compelled to make him an allowance proportioned to their supposed ability. But such estimates were necessarily arbitrary, and it often happened that the loss of his child entailed upon the unfortunate father that of all his property.

"The Academy of Saumur, which had existed for eighty years, and was the most celebrated of all, was suppressed in the same year, on the pretext that its foundation had not been authorised by letters-patent. It was sought, by these means, to obliterate that mental distinction and literary cultivation remarkable in the Protestants, and which excited the jealousy of their adversaries.

"Barristers were forbidden to plead, on pretence that they abused their influence to prevent the conversion of their clients. Two months were allowed to all who still held employments at Court, or judicial offices, or who practised as attorneys and notaries, to sell their places or business. Physicians were not allowed to exercise their profession, because, it was said, they did not warn the Catholic patients when the moment came for the administration of the sacraments. This prohibition was extended to surgeons, apothecaries, and even to midwives, accused of sacrificing, in dangerous childbirths, the infant to the mother, at the risk of letting it die without baptism, and of thus exposing it to eternal damnation. Printers and booksellers were ordered to discontinue their trade under penalty of 3000 livres' fine. Domiciliary visits were ordered at the dwellings of the booksellers, ministers, and elders, to seize and destroy all copies of works that attacked the dominant religion.

"To deprive the pastors of the moral influence which long residence and a spotless life might give them over the minds of their congregations, they were forbidden to exercise their holy office for more than three years together in the same place.

"Up to that time the property and the liberty alone of the Protestants had been invaded; now their persons were attacked. The government sent dragoons to those towns in Poitou which contained most Huguenots. They were lodged exclusively in their houses, and even in those of the poorest, and of widows previously exempt from that onerous charge. In many towns and villages the priests followed them in the streets, crying out — 'Courage gentlemen! It is the king's intention that these dogs of Hnguenots should be pillaged and sacked.' The soldiers entered the houses with uplifted swords, sometimes crying. 'Kill! kill!' to frighten the women and children. As long as the inhabitants had wherewithal to satisfy them, they were but pillaged; but when their means were exhausted, when the price of their furniture was spent, and the clothes and ornaments of their women were sold, the dragoons seized them by the hair to drag them to church; or, if they left them in their houses, they employed threats, outrage, and even tortures, to oblige them to become converts. Of some they burned the feet and hands at a slow fire; they broke the ribs and limbs of others with blows of sticks. Several had their lips burned with red-hot irons; and others were thrown into damp dungeons, with threats that they should be left there to rot.

"The soldiers of Béarn, excited by the fanatic Marquis de Boufflers, showed themselves much more cruel than those in Poitou. They were marched from town to town, from village to village; they were ordered to deprive of rest those who would not yield to other torments. The soldiers relieved each other, in order not themselves to sink under the torture they made others suffer. The noise of drums, the blasphemies, the shouts, the crash of the furniture which they threw about, the agitation in which they kept those poor people in order to force them to remain up and with their eyes open, were the means employed to deprive them of repose. To pinch and prick them, to drag them about, suspend them by ropes, blow tobacco smoke into their nostrils, and a hundred other cruelties, were the sports of these executioners. The officers were no better than the soldiers: they spat in the women's faces; they made them lie down in their presence on hot embers; they forced them to put their heads into ovens whose vapour was hot enough to suffocate them.

"In the distribution of quarters, care was taken to separate the officers from the soldiers they commanded, that the latter might be unchecked by any sentiment of decency. The greater share of trade and manufactures was then in the hands of the Protestants; their dwellings were adorned with costly furniture, their warehouses were full of merchandise. All these riches were abandoned to the mercy of the soldiers, and destroyed by them. They were not content with taking what suited them; they tore and burned what they could not carry away. Some gave their horses fine Holland sheeting to lie upon, others converted storehouses full of bales of wool, cotton, and silk, into stables. It was determined to treat with the utmost rigour those who, according to the expression of Louvois, 'aspired to the foolish glory of being the last professors of a religion displeasing to his majesty.'

"The victims were let down by cords into the prisons of the Château-Trompette, at Bordeaux, and daily drawn up to undergo whipping or the strappado. Several prisoners, after some weeks passed in the dungeons of Grenoble, came out without either hair or teeth. At Valence, they were thrown into a sort of well, in which, by a refinement of barbarous cruelty, sheep's entrails were left to putrefy.

"The utmost cruelty was displayed against those amongst the Protestants who had been condemned to the galleys: 'The galley-slaves,' says Admiral Baudin, 'were chained two-and-two upon the benches of the galleys, and employed to row with long heavy oars. . . . . In the axis of each galley, and in the centre of the space occupied by the benches of the rowers, was a sort of gallery, called the *coursive*, on which continually walked guardians, called *comes*, armed with whips of bullock's hide, with which they lashed the shoulders of those unfortunates who did not row with enough vigour to please them. The galley-slaves passed their lives on their benches; they ate and slept there, unable to change their place beyond what the length of their chain permitted, and having no other shelter than a cloth against the rain, or the sun's heat, or the chills of night[1].'"

These dreadful persecutions were not more successful than the first in subduing the energy of the Protestants. Their only result was to remove from the kingdom that prosperity which the Catholics saw with an irritated and jealous eye. The Protestants became refugees. We shall now accompany them to the land of exile, and see the transplated tree bear the same fruits abroad as it had done at home. Truth is not the sap which, productive in one soil, may be powerless in another. Sent from heaven like the dew, it makes every ground teem under its fecundating energy. We may follow from realm to realm the Protestants armed with their Bible; everywhere we see them triumphing over misery, diffusing abroad the light of civilisation, and giving the example of moral conduct.

In the first place, the distinguished military men whom the revocation of the Edict of Nantes deprived France of were extremely numerous: "The Prince of Tarentum took service in the Dutch army, the Duke of La Tremouille in that of Hesse, Count de Roye in that of Denmark. Others went to Brandenburg, whither a concurrence of fortunate circumstances called them. To the Counts of Beauveau and de Briquemault, who set the example, were subsequently added Henry d'Hallard, a distinguished officer, Pierre de la Cave, governor of Pillau and major-general; Du Plessis Gouret, who became colonel and commandant of Magdeburg and Spandau, Count Henry de Montgommery, Colonel Dolé-Belgard, and the Counts de Comminges, de Cadal, de Gressy. The number of officers vho retired into Brandenburg after the revocation may be estimated at more than six hundred: amongst them we may mention the Marquis de Varennes, who had the king for his godfather, and Lieutenant-General Rouvillas de Veyne.

"In 1785, a large number of cadets fled from the frontier towns,

1. Weiss, pp. 51, 77.

and scattered themselves through Holland and Brandenburg. The Prince of Orange and Frederick William formed whole companies of them. The muster-roll of these cadets shows us names that were not undistinguished: Fouquet, Beaufort, Beauchardis, La Salle, Du Périer, de Portal, Montfort, Saint-Maurice, Saint-Blancard. But of all the officers of high rank who quitted France, Marshal Schomberg was the most illustrious.

"The refugees could number, besides, several engineers, the most illustrious of whom, in Brandenburg, were Jean Cayart, a pupil of Vauban, upon whom Louis XIV and Louvois had publicly bestowed the highest praise, and to whom they had intrusted the fortification of Verdun, and Philip de la Chiese, a native of Orange, who made the canal of Muhlrose, to connect the Spree with the Oder, and so to establish a communication between the North Sea and the Baltic. A few gentlemen may likewise be mentioned well known by the functions they discharged either as councillors of embassy, or as intrusted with the direction of ecclesiastical and civil affairs. Olivier de Marconnay, lord of Blanzay, a native of Poitou; Jacques de Maxuel, lord of Deschamps, born at Pont-Audemer; Philip Choudens de Grema; Louis de Montagnac, formerly a king's councillor at the presidial court of Béziers; Henry de Mirmand, the Baron de Faugières, Baron Isaac de Larrey, the Marquis of Chandieu, Francis d'Agoust, Eleazar de la Primaudaye, and Baron Philip de Jaucourt[1]."

To conclude, merchants and workmen belonging to every species of trade scattered themselves throughout the whole world:

"The town of Magdeburg, completely ruined by the Thirty Years' War, but admirably situated upon the bank of the Elbe, which facilitated its trade with Hamburg and the Dutch ports, received a colony of refugees, who contributed to repeople it, and who soon converted it into a rich focus of industry. Three brothers, Andrew, Peter, and Anthony Du Bosc, from Nismes; John Rafinesque, of Uzès; and John Maffre, of Saint-Ambroise, established there a manufactory of cloth, of Rouen serge, and of druggets. Andrew Valentin, of Nismes, and Peter Claparède, of Montpellier, manufactured woollen stuffs. Anthony Pellou and Daniel Pernet, from Burgundy, established a manufactory of woollen and beaver hats. The manufacture of stockings, so far advanced in France, was taken to Magdeburg by six refugees from the Vigan, directed by Pierre Labry.

"The colony of Brandenburg became flourishing after the arri-

1. Weiss, pp. 108, 116.

val of several Norman manufacturers, who made the cloths of Mûniers, Elbeuf, and Spain. This branch of manufacture was especially indebted for its celebrity to Daniel Le Cornu, of Rouen. Frankfort-on-the-Oder, so well situated for the Baltic trade, received several manufacturers from the same town, who founded fine manufactories of cloth, aided by Luke Cossard, their countryman, who had been dyer to the Gobelins[1]. "

"The reputation of the refugees for probity, and that practical piety which distinguished them nearly all, everywhere inspired confidence, and obtained them a degree of credit which insured the success of their enterprises, notwithstanding the slenderness of the funds at their disposal. Little by little they acquired fortunes, which enabled them to extend their transactions, and seek more distant markets. They formed connections with Poland, Russia, Denmark, Sweden, and the agencies they established in Copenhagen, Hamburg, and Dantzig, opened to Brandenburg an inexhaustible source of wealth.

"After the manufacture of woollens, that of hats was one of the most productive that the refugees introduced into Brandenburg. The Elector was naturally glad to make those industrious strangers welcome, who brought him a manufacture which would prevent considerable sums from leaving the country, and soon would bring in money from foreign lands.

"The tanner's art was rendered perfect in Brandenburg by the refugees. They established tanyards at Berlin, Magdeburg, Stettin, Potsdam; and soon they so fully supplied the country that the importation of leather from Silesia and the Northern States entirely ceased.

"The arts of the shamoy-dresser and of the tawer, and that of the glover especially, were introduced into Brandenburg by the refugees, who likewise founded manufactures of silk, velvet, gold and silver brocade. They made ribbons, gold lace, and other fashionable articles, which before had been brought from Paris. Carpets and tapestry became, owing to the interest the Court took in them, important articles of a trade which engaged the industry of the exiled Protestants.

"They contributed to bring to perfection the glass-worker's art, and they added a manufactory of mirrors, the first seen in the country. The Neustadt mirrors were equal to those of France and Venice, and had a considerable sale in Germany.

1. Weiss, pp. 123, 124.

"Persecution also drove into Brandenburg a host of artisans skilled in every kind of craft; miners from the comté of Foix, and from Dauphiné, who took up the working of the iron and copper mines, with which the government had as yet but little busied itself; men experienced in the fashioning of metals, armourers, polishers, locksmiths, and cutlers. In the very first years that followed the revocation, Berlin beheld the arrival within her walls of Frenchmen practising those two arts, who formed considerable establishments, and originated a traffic which never ceased to increase during the whole of the eighteenth century. The art of engraving, the lapidary's art, both imported by workmen from Languedoc, sprang from the same source. The use of clocks and watches did not extend through the Elector's dominions, and thence into neighbouring countries, until after the arrival of the working watchmakers from France.

"Embroidery, in which France excelled, was taken to Berlin by four brothers from Paris. The first manufactures of printed calicoes had the same origin; gauze-makers came from Picardy, Normandy, and Champagne.

" At first the refugees sold retail, seeking an honest living rather than aspiring to wealth. Then they had neither cashier, book-keeper, nor clerk. It was the dealer himself, his wife, and his children, who filled all these departments. These simple customs, this severe economy, were the foundation of more than one large fortune. As their means increased, they sought to extend their connections. Soon they ceased to confine themselves to the home-trade, and frequented foreign markets. The trade in hardware, which has become so important since, owed its origin to the refugees."

In proportion as the national industry revived under the powerful impetus they gave to it, trade found new resources[1]:

" Agriculture was not less indebted to the refugees than were trade and manufactures. Before their arrival, in all parts of Brandenburg, the traveller's gaze rested upon vast monotonous plains, and upon land uncleared for lack of inhabitants. The colony of Bergholz owed to them the high degree of prosperity it ultimately attained. The villages of Gross-Ziethen and Klein-Ziethen, burned in the Thirty Years' War, were rebuilt by them, and the surrounding country was cleared and cultivated for the first time since that calamitous period. The county of Ruppin, which had hard-

1. Weiss, pp. 126, 133.

ly any inhabitants left, was cultivated by French labourers. The most important of the new branches of cultivation, by which the refugees enriched Brandenburg, was that of tobacco. A special service which these industrious men rendered to Brandenburg was the improvement — we may almost say the creation — of the art of gardening. They converted into gardens those vast suburbs of Berlin which as yet were but uncultivated fields. Such prodigies had never before been witnessed by the Berliners [1]."

"The principal colony of the refugees was that of Cassel. That town, then of 18,000 inhabitants, living in rudely-constructed wooden houses, was indebted to its new guests for the flourishing state in which it soon found itself. They created numerous manufactures previously unknown in that part of Germany. A profusion of goods, quite novel to the natives, were soon exposed for sale in handsome shops; and so great was the advantage to Cassel, that, in the year 1688, the old town no longer sufficed for the increasing population [2]."

"The Brandenburg refugees are still renowned for their temperance and sobriety. They are all in confortable circumstances—a result due to labour. Hospitable to strangers, they afforded an asylum to unfortunate stragglers from the rout at Leipzig [3]."

"It appears certain that the revocation of the Edict of Nantes sent into the three kingdoms about 70,000 manufacturers and workmen, most of whom proceeded from Normandy, Picardy, the maritime provinces of the west, the Lyonnais, and Touraine.

"The English were indebted to them for the introduction of several new manufactures, which soon contributed to the public wealth, and for the improvement of others still in their infancy. The refugees taught the English to manufacture superior qualities of paper for themselves, and, moreover, showed them how to produce silks, brocades, satins, velvets, light tissues of linen and wool, clocks and watches, glass-ware, cutlery, hardware, French locks, and surgical instruments.

"Of all the manufactures with which the refugees endowed England, not one acquired a more magnificent development than that of silks. England and Ireland then presented the memorable sight of a manufacture borrowed from the foreigner, consuming foreign materials, and which nevertheless succeeded in equalling, and even in surpassing, the products of those countries where it had long been cultivated.

1. Weiss, pp. 126, 137. — 2. *Idem*, pp. 188, 189. — 3. *Idem*, p. 192.

"The manufactures taken to England by the refugees, and the great development they attained, deprived France of an annual return of 1,880,000*l*. sterling.

"Thus, English commerce profited by the impulse given by the refugees to the national manufactures, and the export trade of France received a fatal blow, from which it has not yet recovered[1]."

"The American colonies were largely remunerated for their wise and generous hospitality by the services the refugees rendered them. The uncultivated banks of the river St. James were by them transformed into fields covered with rich harvests. All Virginia admired the flourishing state of their model farms in the environs of Mannikin. In the State of New York, the founders of New La Rochelle recoiled from no fatigue that might render productive the virgin land on the banks of East River. Men, women, and children unceasingly laboured until they converted a wilderness into a smiling landscape, and in South Carolina they reared magnificent plantations on the banks of the Cooper..... The agricultural colony on the banks of the Santee surpassed all those formed in the same province by the English, although these brought with them considerable fortunes, and all that was necessary for the success of their plantations. The fugitive French hardly possessed the things indispensable to life; most of them were not even accustomed to the kind of work; and they had, moreover, to contend with a proverbially unhealthy climate. But, stimulated by want, sober, industrious, ready to help one another, they succeeded more rapidly and completely. The English traveller Lawson, who visited their establishments in 1701, admired the cleanliness and decency of their dress, the convenient arrangement of their solidly-constructed houses, and all the external signs of a prosperity much superior to that of the other colonists. He beheld with astonishment a country, recently covered with swamps, formed by the overflowing of the river, rapidly assuming the appearance of the best-cultivated parts of France and England. 'The French colonists,' he said, 'live like a tribe, like a family. Every one makes it a rule to assist his countryman, and to watch over his fortune and reputation as if they were his own. The misfortunes which assail one of them are shared by all the others, and every one rejoices in the progress and prosperity of his brethren.'

"The arrival of these honest and laborious men was a fortunate acquisition for the newly-founded colony of Charlestown. As in

1. Weiss, pp. 251, 261.

England, the traditions of elegance and good taste, brought over by the artisan emigrants of 1685, were incessantly revived by the arrival of fresh fugitives[1]. "

Let us hear on this subject, not an historian, but an eye-witness, the American Mr. Baird : "The French Protestants formed a considerable element in the population of the American colonies; hence their precious blood flows in the veins of many citizens of North America at the present day. One feels, besides, what a boon must have been conferred to the colonies through the arrival of those men, distinguished, generally, by their simple honest piety, and whose strong and lively faith was attested by their presence in America. To their posterity belong some of the best families in New York, Maryland, Virginia, Carolina, and other states besides.

"Out of the seven presidents which Congress had during the war of the Revolution, no less than three descended from the Huguenots, and all three were celebrated men : Jay, Laurens, and Boudinot. Never did any individuals better acknowledge the hospitality granted to them. The names of French refugees appear with distinction amongst the great bodies of the state in our halls of judicature, in the ministry of the Gospel. No one need blush in America of having amongst his ancestors one of those respectable Huguenots, for it has been more than once observed, and the remark is, I believe, correct, that nothing was ever more uncommon than to see them appear as an accused party before a court of justice[2]. "

"In Holland, as well as in England and Germany, the refugees exercised a powerful influence upon politics and war, literature and religion, industry and commerce[3]. "

"Natural history, medicine, physics, and especially the methodical sciences, so generally cultivated in France since the time of Pascal and Descartes, owed to them the strong impulse they received in Holland[4]. The commerce and manufactures of the Low Countries were indebted to the refugees for an immense increase. The manufacturers who settled in the United Provinces endowed their adopted country with several new manufactures, assisted in the re-establishment of those that were in a declining state, and communicated a vigorous impulse to the national trade[5]."

"The city of Amsterdam, previously entirely occupied by maritime commerce, received a fresh population, composed of manufacturers and skilful artisans. A host of embroiderers in silk and thread, designers of flowered stuffs and laces, makers of

1. Weiss, pp. 306, 309. — 2 Baird, vol. I, *De la Religion aux Etats-Unis*, pp. 178, 179. — 3. Wess, vol. II, p. 130. — 4. *Idem*, p. 101. — 5. *Idem*, 130.

serge and drugget, spinners of gold and silver thread from Lyons, and linen-cloth-makers from Aix, in Provence, whom the Dutch magistrates had induced to emigrate by promising them large profits, flocked to Amsterdam. A great number of articles that had previously been purchased in France were now made in Holland by the refugees; serges of various kinds, single and double taffeties of all colours, crapes of wool and silk, fans, caudebecs, embroideries in gold and silver, in thread and in silk, point-lace *à la reine*, of which a manufactory was founded in the Orphan-house, brocades, ribbons, plain and flowered gauzes, beaver hats. When the town received its last addition by the construction of the streets comprised between the Jews' quarter and the rampart, from the Amstel to the Rapenburg quay, the new houses were occupied in great part by French artisans, and especially by hatters. 'All these manufactures', wrote Scion to the magistrate of Amsterdam, 'have been established in two years' time, and without expense; whereas, with all their endeavours, your predecessors were never able to obtain them, and the greatest ministers of the Most Christian King spent several millions upon them. They fill the city more and more with inhabitants, increase its public revenues, strengthen its walls and its boulevards, multiply arts and manufactures, establish new fashions, circulate money, erect new edifices, make trade flourish, fortify the Protestant religion, bring an abundance of all things, and will soon attract buyers from every country — from Germany, the kingdoms of the North, Spain, the Baltic Sea, the West Indies and American islands, and even from England. They contribute, in short, to render Amsterdam one of the most famous towns in the world.'

"The manufactories established by the refugees increased the prosperity of Amsterdam with a rapidity that astonished Europe. This may be judged of by the report addressed in 1686 to the Elector of Brandenburg, by his ambassador in Holland. The prodigious success of the French manufactures, that of lustrings — so long deemed impossible to be made elsewhere than at Tours and Lyons — the fall in the price of silken stuffs, which had formerly fetched fifty sous, and had fallen to thirty-six; that of beaver hats, which had cost ten crowns, and now cost but six, — such were the benefits this city owed to its generous hospitality, and which Frederick William's envoy reported to his master.

"But nowhere did French industry flourish more than at Leyden and Haarlem. The manufactures established there did not attain their highest point of perfection until after the arrival of the Protestants of France. From that date forward, they produced the finest cloth, the best camlets, and the most esteemed serges in Holland. They acquired a European reputation, and the high wages tempted even the Catholic soldiers of Louis XIV.'s armies, who deserted and went to Leyden in the capacity of workmen.

"Haarlem, which had likewise received amongst its citizens a large number of artisans from Flanders, also owed the increase and improvement of its manufactures to the French refugees, to whom the beauty of its situation and the salubrity of its climate proved particularly attractive. They introduced the manufacture of plush, particularly of flowered plush, known in the trade by the name of *caffas.* The prodigious extent of Dutch trade in all parts of the world nevertheless gave a reputation to its plushes, flowered silk-stuffs, and stuffs of mingled silk and wool, which insured them everywhere a sale. These products of refugee industry acquired so great a reputation, that instances were known of particular sorts of velvets being manufactured at Milan, sent to Holland, then sent back to Milan, and sold there as Dutch velvet.

"Five hundred workmen, chiefly French, had helped a Dutchman, James Van Mollen, to create in Utrecht a magnificent establishment of watered silks. This town soon had also important manufactories of velvet. Founded, or early taken in hand, by refugees, their products had a solidity and lustre which those of Amsterdam did not attain to. The French manufacturers, and especially those of Amiens, who endeavoured to imitate them, were soon unable to dispose of theirs, excepting under the name of Utrecht velvets. In fine, the ancient cloth-manufactories of that town, chiefly those of black cloth, were brought to great perfection by the refugees. Most of them passed into their hands, and were indebted to them for a long period of prosperity.

"Thus did almost all the Dutch towns receive from the refugees an increase of wealth, owing to the manufactures these either brought into them or improved. Not only did they create new manufactures, and elevate those they found already established; they did still more. By their intelligent toil they greatly improved the mechanical arts, the humblest trades. They taught the Dutch better processes than they had previously employed for refining sugar, salt, sulphur, rosin, for bleaching wax, making soap, etc., etc. Thus, by the high finish of their work, the refugee manufacturers and artisans acquired a reputation that kept in the country considerable sums by which France, and especially Paris, had formerly profited; they won public esteem for manual aptitudes previously despised, and thus raised the condition of the middle classes, which gained both in prosperity and in respect[1]."

"The activity of the refugees, who had to begin the world again, excited the liveliest emulation on the part of the Swiss, and led to the most surprising and happiest results. Agriculture, in the first place, was indebted for great progress to the intelligence of those peasants of Languedoc and Dauphiné who had quitted their cottages to seek religious liberty on a foreign soil. The daily food of the inhabitants was coarse and monotonous. The refugees completely transformed the fields allotted to them. They formed model-gardens, which the Vaudois soon imitated. The guardians of the charity schools took advantage of the opportunity, and apprenticed several lads to these skilful agriculturists.

"In the course of a few years the refugees assisted greatly in the development of manufactures and trade in almost all the towns where they settled. Not only did the refugees introduce new manufactures, which enhanced the prosperity of Lausanne, but they were the first to open shops, and so to substitute regular trade for the occasional traffic to which that province had previously been restricted[2]."

"If French Switzerland was indebted to the refugees for superior polish, more elegant manners, and the inestimable benefit of a first assertion of the principle of religious liberty, it had no less to congratulate itself on their happy influence upon arts, sciences, and literature[3]."

"Thus, as regarded religion, literature, and politics, as well as agriculture, commerce, and manufactures, the refugees exercised a favourable influence on the destinies of Protestant Switzerland, and even reacted, to a certain extent, on those of their former country, The salutary action of those distinguished men and their descendants continued during the whole of the eighteenth century, and has not ceased even in our own day. The progress of agriculture in the Pays de Vaud is in great part their work. The flourishing state of the country around Lausanne sufficiently proves the superiority of the modes of cultivation they introduced into that country, already so favoured by nature. The manufactures they took with them became for French Switzerland, and for the canton of Berne, a source of wealth which has never since run dry. The fine silk-manufactures with which they endowed their new country have never ceased to improve in their hands, and to afford

1. Weiss, p. 439, 448. — 2. *Idem*, pp. 503, 504. — 3. *Idem*, p. 524.

employment to a vast multitude of native as well as French workmen."

"The refugees powerfully contributed to the progress of agriculture in the Danish monarchy. Some settled in Iceland, and there introduced the cultivation of hemp and flax. The others, fixed in the Danish peninsula, in the islands of the Baltic, and in Holstein, introduced the superior processes of French agriculture, and originated several new objects of cultivation. King Frederic IV succeeded, by great promises, in establishing a colony of those skilful cultivators at Fredericia. This little colony did not disappoint the expectations of its royal founder. In spite of obstacles, it never ceased to prosper and multiply, so much so, that at the end of the eighteenth century it formed a society of more than a hundred families, composed of five hundred or six hundred persons, who commanded public esteem by their industry and activity. To them the town of Fredericia owed the flourishing condition it soon attained. As early as the middle of the eighteenth century, its prosperity was unmistakable. It sufficed to compare the magnificent spectacle presented by its highly cultivated plains with the fields surrounding other Danish towns, which also owed their subsistence to agriculture. The difference was striking. To the refugees belonged the glory of having brought about this happy change; for, before their arrival, no part of the kingdom presented so unprosperous an appearance[1]."

"The French refugees in Denmark set an example, during the whole of the eighteenth century, and up to our own times, of the most rigid propriety of manners, of the most irreproachable morality, of the most touching charity. All the emigrants were remarkable for their love of labour and their frugal manner of life. Nothing less than these habits of order and this rigorous economy would have enabled them to live at first, and afterwards gradually to rise to that degree of ease and comfort which rewarded their exertions. We must add that the colony of Fredericia has ever done its utmost to keep its young men at home. They lived under the eye of their families, remote from all example of corruption; and their simple and austere habits assured the fecundity of marriages, in contracting which inclination was far more considered than interest. The young girls, on their part, were stimulated to strict virtue by the hope of speedy establishment, and rarely departed from the right path, knowing that by misconduct they would forfeit all chance of marriage in the colony. Exempt from that licentiousness

1. Weiss, pp. 544, 567.

which vitiates both mind and body — exempt from the luxury which creates new wants, and often prevents a man from thinking of choosing a wife — the colonists married young, and thus insured themselves a healthy and numerous posterity. Their undeviating confidence in Divine Providence made them consider large families a source of riches. Sure of their subsistence, free from all uneasiness about the future, the more arms they had to help them the more works they undertook — works which contributed to their wellbeing, and enabled them to support in society a rank proportionate to their modest desires [1]. "

" In conclusion, let us follow the Protestant refugees as far as the very extremity of Africa; there, again, we shall see them prosper, as far as external circumstances allow them to do. Towards the end of the seventeenth century, there were about three thousand French refugees established at twelve leagues to the north of the Cape, in a fertile valley, which bears, to the present day, the name of ***French Valley.*** The members of the French tribe of Charron have always had as chief an old man chosen amongst the elders of the community, and without consulting whom no important enterprise is undertaken. This patriarchal government, so conformable to the democratic ideas of the first Calvinists, has been favourable to industry. It has not been less useful to the maintenance of pure morality, simple habits, faith, and piety, which have remained uncontaminated amongst the descendants of those expatriated families. There is a fourth village, the most considerable of all, that of ***La Perle,*** whose inhabitants, exclusively devoted to agriculture, are the richest in that old Dutch colony, now belonging to the English.

" This population has not forgotten the rigid principles and fervid piety of their ancestors. The traveller who crosses their hospitable threshold invariably finds upon the table one of those great folio Bibles which the French Protestants were wont to hand down from father to son, as a sacred patrimony and inestimable treasure. The date of birth and the names of all the members of the family are invariably inscribed in it. Sometimes, too, one finds pious books in their houses, such as the Psalms put into verse by Clement Marot. An affecting custom has been preserved amongst these simple and austere men. Night and morning the members of each family assemble for prayer. There are no formalities or pompous ceremonies; they content themselves with praying with all their hearts, and with reading the Bible. Every Sunday, at sunrise, the farmers set out

1. Weiss, pp. 576, 577.

in their rustic vehicles, covered with hides or with coarse cloth, to attend divine service, and at night they return peaceably to their homes. Gambling is unknown amongst them, and the refined corruption of European civilisation has not reached them. The useful arts and practical instruction are all they care for and cultivate. They seek to diffuse them amongst their former slaves, whom they have always treated with kindness, and they willingly devote much time and pains to the propagation of the gospel amongst the idolatrous races that surround them [1]. "

We may sum up in the following words the various particulars introduced above: "The fugitives, dispersed over the whole world, unconsciously became the agents of God's mysterious will. They were destined, especially in America, to temper Puritan fanaticism, to foster the germ and to favour the triumph of that spirit of independence, regulated by law, of which the United States to-day present to us the magnificent example; in Europe, to develope for Prussia, to increase for Holland and England, the elements of power and prosperity contained in those three countries, whose present greatness is, in some respects, and to a certain extent, their work. Have they not contributed, in the most critical circumstances, to defend them by arms, and to help them to repel foreign invasion? Have they not aided, in some degree, to maintain them in the political path that has so long preserved them from despotism, that preserves them from the dangers of anarchy, and that, by preventing them from being disturbed by revolutions, which succeed each other at regular intervals, assures them the inestimable benefit of institutions at once stable and liberal? Have they not enriched them by improving their manufactures, by the introduction of new ones, by stimulating their commercial activity, by teaching them the superior processes of French agriculture? Have they not, by propagating the language and literature of France, raised the standard of intellectual cultivation, and consequently, of public morality? Have they not, by their own writings, spread the love of literature, of science, and of art? Finally, have they not set the example of urbanity in social relations, of politeness in language, of austerity in morals, of the most inexhaustible charity towards the suffering and the indigent? [2] "

"It was admirable to observe that this people, excluded for more than a century from all employments, impeded in all professions, hunted like wolves in the forests and mountains, without schools,

1. Weiss, pp. 458, 460. — 2. *Idem*, p. 586.

without any family recognised by law, without any certain inheritance, had lost nothing of its ancient energy. By its enlightenment, its morality, its civic virtues, it was worthy of the great reparation reserved for it by the Revolution [1]."

We now state our question once more: Persecution, it is said, has scattered away the Irish Catholics as beggars and sufferers; how is it that the identical cause has, on the contrary, sent the Protestant refugees to prosper in the same regions side by side with the outcast Irish? If we may quote an example we have already adduced, why do the descendants of the Huguenots constitute the aristocracy of Whitechapel, whilst their Celtic neighbours are its disgrace? Why are the children of the French reformers landlords, merchants, and bankers in Dublin, whilst the Irish are workmen and beggars in London? The only cause for this difference is that the truth was on one side, and error on the other. Here, God; there, the Pope: unless some persons would venture to say that there is no God, and that it does not signify whether we follow truth, or are led astray by error.

But only half of our argument is as yet proved. Suppose such an objection as this: if the refugees prospered out of France, it is because they were beyond the reach of persecution. Let us see, then, what became of the Huguenots who remained exposed to its fury. What is now the condition of the French Protestants in France? The answer to this question shall bear upon the three points which constitute all our comparisons: material prosperity, intellectual culture, morality.

Material Prosperity. — Persecuted during centuries, deprived of their property, the French Protestants might be expected to be, as far as wealth goes, not on a level with the rest of the nation, but far below, at the present day. Is this the case? If we wished to appeal merely to public opinion, we are certainly entitled to say that the reader's conscience has already answered, and thus we should have done with this part of our subject; but our desire is to affirm nothing, not even what is self-evident, without supporting our assertions by documents. Those we have procured for this special purpose are authentic, and of the highest value. As the source from which they are drawn is not accessible to the public, we must beg to explain how we came to discover it. The fortune of the citizens in France can be estimated neither according to their landed property, nor the profit they derive from trade; for

1. Weiss, p. 592.

it often consists of the interests of a funded capital, which it is impossible to state. Amongst tradesmen themselves, we could not adopt as a sure basis the account of licences granted, for they do not all take one. The safest criterion is the personal tax, as being alone in the same ratio as the individual's fortune; for generally speaking, each one has a style of living corresponding to his means; and, even if this fact were not always correct, we might here suppose it to be so because we adopt as a uniform weight both for the Catholics and the Protestants.

In order to make our comparison, it would, therefore, be necessary to know the personal tax of all the Protestants in France; but this is a fact which the government itself could not ascertain; for, up to the present time, religion has never been taken notice of in the census-tables, and the particulars of the taxation, besides, will never be published. Then, how voluminous the undertaking, supposing it was accomplished! But, if impossible for the whole of France, a research such as this is practicable within the limits of one department. We have done it ourselves for the department of the Seine from documents which were procured in the following manner. In 1852, the Reformed Church of Paris, having to reappoint its consistory, had a list drawn out of all its parishioners who were voters. This list, lithographed, is in our possession, for, athough not extensively circulated, several copies of it were struck off. We forwarded it to the Prefecture of the Seine, and obtained the statement of the personal tax paid by each person whose name and direction appear thereon. We then ascertained from the same authority the average of personal tax paid by all the inhabitants of Paris; supplied with these documents, we added up together the different items paid by the Protestants enumerated on the parish list; we divided the total by the number of tax-payers, and we thus finally obtained a Protestant average, which we here place opposite the general one:

Account of personal tax for the city of Paris:

Average paid by all the inhabitants........	33 fr. 14 cent.
Average paid by the Protestants...........	87 fr. 01 cent.

According to this basis, therefore, the fortune of the French Protestants is, at the present time, very nearly treble that of the Roman Catholics belonging to the same country! And, if the fact is taken into consideration that the general average is increased by the triple taxes which the Protestants forming one twentieth of the nation, have to pay, it will be seen that the result we have just offered, as an approximating number, is really very correct. We repeat it, if we take for our standard the amount of personal tax paid by the department of the Seine, the French Protestants are three times as rich as their Catholic countrymen. But the above calculation being our own, authentic, irrefutable as it is, we wish to compare it with the results arrived at by other persons on so novel a subject. We can have, of course, no direct document to bring forward; but on the other hand our readers will understand that any piece of information supporting our discovery only in an indirect manner will be so much the more valuable as it has evidently not been put together for the purpose of making good our argument.

This is the reason which induces us to publish the following facts: It is well known that the departments of the Gard and the Upper Rhine contain the greatest number of Protestants. Every body is aware, too, that the departments of Finistère and Morbihan not only are exclusively Roman Catholic, but that they are more completely than any other under the influence of the priests. Now, what place do those departments occupy on the list of patentees or license-holders?

In the Upper Rhine there are. .	38	patentees for every	1,000 inhabitants.
In the Gard.	38	—	—
In the Finistère	17	—	—
In the Morbihan.	18[1]	—	—

In the two essentially Protestant departments, the number of patentees is consequently *more than double* what it is in the two exclusively Catholic ones, and our preceding calculation is thus confirmed, which stated the fortune of the Paris Protestants to be *nearly three times* that of their fellow-citizens. We shall now see the same fact proved by a third demonstration. The following facts are given to us by a late mayor of Nismes: — "At the time of the census of 1846, the whole population of Nismes amounted to 50,000; viz., 35,000 Roman Catholics, and 15,000 Protestants: 816 voters paid more than 200 francs of taxes, and 389 amongst them were Protestants." This is nearly one-half instead of one-third, which would be the proportional numbers. "Out of the 300 most heavily taxed patentees, 202 were Protestants;" that is to say, double the proportional number.

1. Schnitzler, vol. III, pp. 171, 172.

This fact is acknowledged, too, by one of the writers whose views are most hostile to Protestantism. M. Rubichon confesses "that a great number of French Protestants are at the head of our manufactures and of our commerce; they are, therefore, richer than the same number of French Roman Catholics[1]."

No one who has perused the articles published by the *Revue des Deux Mondes* on the subject of Protestant Missions will accuse that periodical of partiality for the Protestants; well, in its number for October 15, 1853, we find the following paragraph relating to the point under discussion: —

"The development of education varies a little at Mazamet, according to the different religions. Out of 10,000 inhabitants, about 4,000 belong to the Reformed creed. All the master manufacturers, except one, are Protestants, whilst the majority of the workmen are Catholics. There is less instruction amongst these than in the industrious Protestant families. The latter, being in better circumstances than the former, have been enabled to devote more care to education[2]."

The same might be said of Nismes, Marseilles, Lyons, and Bordeaux; but as we cannot enter into details such as the above for all the cities in France, we shall limit ourselves to the significant documents we have given respecting Paris: documents open to inspection to any one who may feel inclined to verify our statements.

Our last quotation connects the subject of intellectual culture with that of material prosperity; let us, then, go on to the second point we have to examine:

Intellectual Culture. — Here our sources of information are not less precise; they will have, moreover, the advantage of rendering the truth in some manner visible and tangible.

Although scattered over the length and breadth of France, the Protestants may be subdivided into two distinct and pretty considerable groups. Those belonging to the Lutheran Church, in Alsace; those professing the Reformed faith, in the Gard, and the neighbouring departments, the Drôme, the Ardèche, and the Hérault. Alsace is not altogether Protestant, no doubt, but there the Protestants are most numerous, and are thus more likely to modify educational statistics. We say the same of Languedoc. Impos-

1. *L'action du Clergé dans les Sociétés Modernes*, by Rubichon. — 2. It would be erroneous to reckon up for France the children attending Protestant schools, because we must take into consideration the pupils of mixed schools. This is, however, what the Protestant Almanack has done, so that the editor's result, in 1844, for the whole kingdom is quite contrary to the one he obtained in 1842 for the department of the Gard. Such statements may serve as a text for declamatory exhortations, but they can give no support to the cause of truth.

sible, as we find it, to make a correct division in both these provinces, if we consider them as Protestants, it will be noticed that the error is quite to the advantage of Catholicism. For, if the exclusively Catholic departments were more enlightened than the mixed ones, we might presume that the superiority proceeds from the Popish faith; but, should the reverse be the case, the superiority of the mixed departments must come from the Protestant element they contain; so that, in considering them as exclusively Protestants, our want of correctness is a real profit for the Catholic cause.

According to Mr. Schnitzler, the six departments which supply the primary schools[1] with the greatest number of pupils are the Meurthe, Upper Rhine, Lower Rhine, Haute-Saône, Vosges, and the Moselle. The very six departments which comprise the majority of the Alsace Lutheran!

The same author gives as the six departments numbering the smallest amount of pupils: the Allier, Indre-et-Loire, Upper Vienne[2], Morbihan, Corrèze, and the Côtes-du-Nord. That is to say, those containing the most exclusively Catholic populations, and the most zealous Catholics!

But at what distance are both extremes from each other?

On the Protestant side we find 1 pupil for every 6 inhabitants.
On the Catholic side we find 1 — 25[3] —

The contrast can be rendered visible to the reader by a reference to Baron Charles Dupin's figurative map of primary instruction in France. On this map each department is shaded with darker and lighter tints, according to the greater or smaller degree of ignorance; a number shews, besides, how many persons must be reckoned for one who knows how to read; so that the higher the number, the deeper the ignorance. What we purpose doing now will be to copy exactly from Baron Dupin's chart the departments we have just been alluding to. The reader must compare for himself. Our reproductions are *fac-similes*. We have even left the verso of each page quite clear, in order to avoid increasing the darkness of the shading.

1. Écoles primaires, corresponding to our national schools in England. — 2. The Protestant churches and schools opened in this department are of more recent date than Schnitzler's statistics. — 3. Schnitzler, vol. II, pp. 345, 346. The above numbers differ from those of M. Dupin, inasmuch as the latter concern only male pupils; besides, the dates do not correspond.

FAC-SIMILE TAKEN FROM M. DUPIN'S MAP.

(Departments essentially Roman Catholic.)

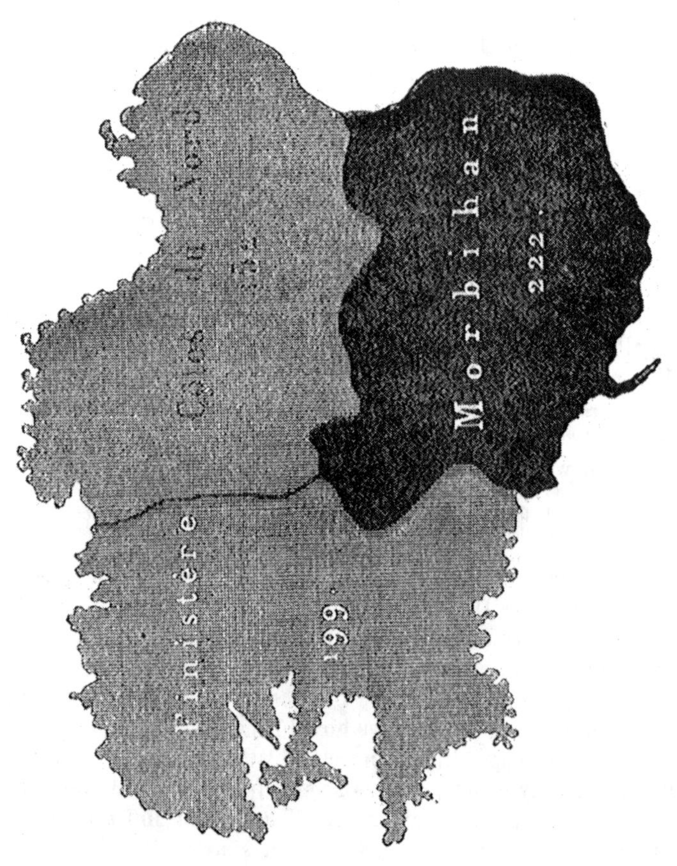

FAC-SIMILE TAKEN FROM M. DUPIN'S MAP.

(Departments including the great agglomeration of the Protestant Lutheran Churches.)

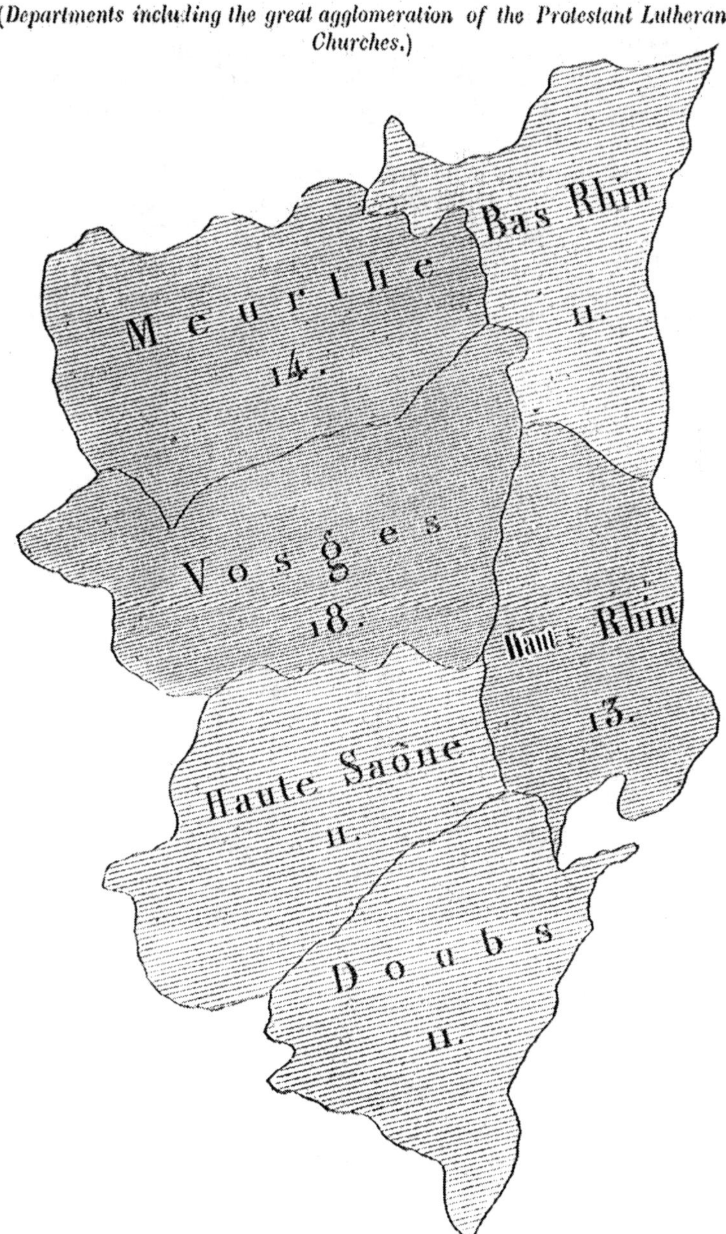

After having thus considered the Lutheran Church, let us now examine the state of the case in the Reformed community. By a reference to M. Dupin's map, we shall find, towards the centre, a frightfully dark spot. This includes the departments of the Cantal, Puy-de-Dôme, Corrèze, and the Haute-Loire. Now, with the exception of three little village congregations, these departments are entirely Roman Catholic.

But, on the other hand, if we look round that gloomy centre, we observe that it is girt as with a zone of light, comprising the departments in which is gathered the densest cluster of Reformed churches. Now, therefore, we meet again the contrast we have already found betwen the east and the west, between Alsace and Britanny.

FAC-SIMILE TAKEN FROM M. DUPIN'S MAP.

(Departments essentially Roman Catholic.)

FAC-SIMILE TAKEN FROM M. DUPIN'S MAP.

(Departments including the great agglomeration of the Protestant Churches.)

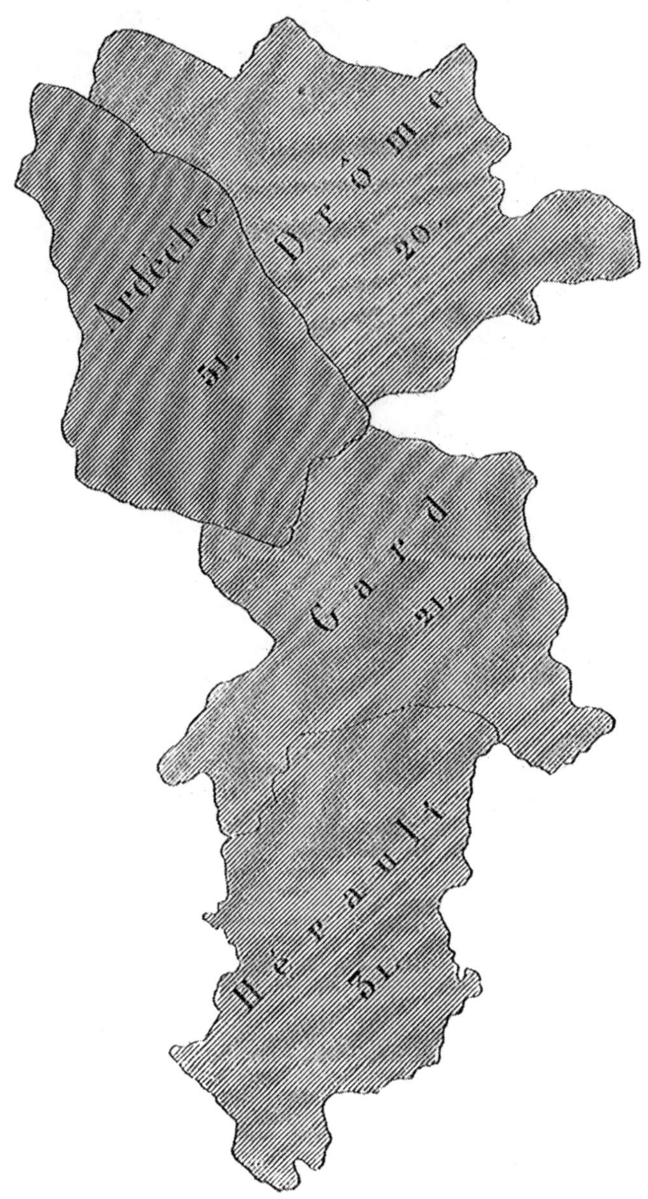

Lastly, M. Dupin's map exhibits a third contrast in the results given by two departments almost adjoining each other, the Deux-Sèvres and the Indre-et-Loire: the former has 1 pupil in 28 inhabitants; the latter, 1 in 229. Now, the Deux-Sèvres contain 21 large Protestant churches, and the Indre-et-Loire not one.

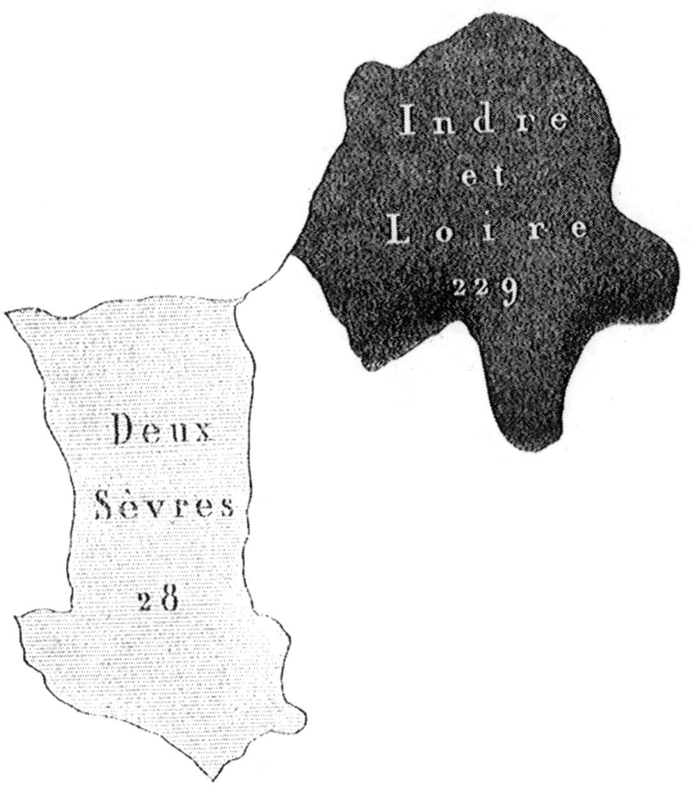

Thus, a uniform conclusion is arrived at, after a threefold experiment made, both upon groups of departments and upon departments taken singly.

The result supplied through our own observations is corroborated in the following statement, the full value of which will now be better understood by the reader :

" *Departments presenting the maximum of ignorance.*

Finistère (Rom. Cath.), 709 in 1,000; Côtes-du-Nord (Cath.) 702.

Departments presenting the minimum of ignorance.

Lower-Rhine (Prot.), 64 in 1,000; Doubs (Prot.), 109; Upper Rhine (Prot.), 139 [1].

This affirmation, besides, is not made by ourselves, but by a Roman Catholic professor. M. Lorain, a man whose experience no one will question, speaks as follows in his ***Sketch of the State of Primary Instruction in France drawn up from Authentic Documents*** [2].

" A fact which should stimulate the zeal of the other Christian denominations is, that those who profess the Reformed religion are infinitely beyond us in point of primary instruction. And I am not alluding here to the towns where it might be supposed that the presence of influential Protestants tells powerfully upon the happiness of the children, and the management of the schools; no, even in the most distant, the most obscure, the loneliest villages, the influence of the austere forms of Protestantism is felt in the religious care with which children are sent to the school; and more than once, when, in glancing over the map of a department, I saw all those school-less districts composing the great desert of primary instruction, the depths of some unknown valley exhibited to me a real oasis [3]. "

" The Catholics and Protestants (of the Charente) have forgotten the dissensions of their forefathers. The Protestants have more piety than the Roman Catholics.

" All things, besides, being equal, I have ascertained that in the department of the Drôme civilisation and instruction are less advanced amongst the Roman Catholic than amongst the Protestant populations.

" The Protestant religion prevails in the arrondissement of Florac (Lozère). There the civilisation is greater than at Mende (Roman Catholic); all or nearly all the districts (*communes*) are provided with teachers.

" The best schools (in the Lower-Rhine) belong to the Protest-

1. Schnitzler, vol. II, p. 368. — 2. *Tableau de l'Instruction primaire, en France, d'après les documents authentiques*. — 3. Lorain, pp. 54, 55.

ants. At Strasburg, in the canton of Oberhausenbergen, which I have visited, almost all the best schools are Protestants. This superiority of the Protestant over the Roman Catholic schools arises chiefly, as I have already stated in another report, from the fact that Protestant children frequent the school up to the age of fourteen, when they are admitted for the first time to the Lord's table; whilst the Roman Catholics discontinue their attendance as early as the age of twelve, when they generally make their first communion."

"In conclusion, in the arrondissement of Niort (Deux-Sèvres), canton of Saint-Maixent, the fifteen districts (communes) supply a sum total of 28 schools, mostly Protestant. This flourishing state of things is owing to the influence of the views of progress generally adopted by Protestant Christians, and warmly encouraged by their pastors[1]."

"The superiority of the Protestant schools may be traced to several causes: 1. Protestant children, for the most part, frequent the school all the year round, whilst during the summer months the Roman Catholic schools are nearly deserted; 2. Protestant children discontinue their attendance only when they are fourteen years old, whilst the Roman Catholics cease coming as soon as they have made their first communion; that is to say, at the age of twelve or thirteen; 3. Protestant ministers are generally more zealous than the Catholic *curés* in helping, encouraging, and superintending the teachers[2]."

The same author explains to us, not only why Protestant schools are so superior, but also why the level of the Roman Catholic schools is so very low. The motive of this last fact he finds in the conduct of the Roman clergy, which is precisely the reverse of that he has had to notice in the Protestant pastors. The priests are opposed to instruction, at least when instruction is not under their own management.

The same opposition will, of course, be found amongst their inferior agents *the Brethren of the Christian Doctrine*. M. Lorain does his best to deal gently with the *Brethren* and the clergy, whom he would fain bring over to the cause of liberal education; and yet, in spite of his gentleness, he cannot help speaking out his inmost conviction. A few extracts will reveal it to the reader: "We are not sufficiently acquainted," says he, "with the fundamental constitution of that society (the Brethren of the Christian Doctrine) with the power which governs them, with the en-

1. Lorain, pp. 264, 265. — 2. *Idem*, p. 264.

gagements which bind them to the ecclesiastical, nay, perhaps, to the papal, authority, to supply in this respect the particulars our readers might naturally expect; we think, moreover, that the secret of this connexion has been kept well enough to allow us nothing but conjectures. In the eye of many people, the principles and the direction which regulate this society will for a long time bear the reproach of being surrounded by mystery [1]. "

" Despite the conservative spirit which actuates them, the *Brethren* have made up their mind to introduce into their method important modifications; competition has warmed them, and they have understood their own interest [2]. "

" In the *arrondissement* of Angers (Maine-et-Loire) the *Brethren* have declined the books sent by the University, and they have persisted, up to the present day, in not making known to the *Academie* [3] the numerous mutations occurring amongst them; hence the material impossibility of ascertaining what is the staff of teachers belonging to those schools [4]. "

As might have been expected, the female teachers under the authority of the priests are still more below the intellectual level of their profession. We give respecting them the opinion of several inspectors, quoted by M. Lorain: " Each village (in the Upper Loire) has its '*béate;*' the priests, those enemies of intellectual freedom, exercise there a most fatal influence. The state of education is deplorable. Almost everywhere I have found elementary teaching intrusted to a girl professing strict views of devotion (*une fille dévote*), and who goes in each village by the name of '*béate.*' Those girls impart such erroneous principles of reading (the only thing they teach), that, for the pupils coming afterwards to the town schools, their lessons are rather a hindrance than a help.

" In each small village or hamlet are to be found female teachers, called '*béates,*' or '*Roubiaques.*' These pious but ignorant girls teach embroidery, reading, and sometimes writing. They live upon little, cost nothing, and impart to both boys and girls the first elements of religion. This is sufficient for the priests, and, consequently, for the parents; who, as far as education goes, are entirely ruled by clerical influence [5]. "

We must remark, too, that neither the ignorance of the teachers nor that of their pupils should be ascribed to their own idleness; the whole blame rests with the fixed determination of the clergy. The facts we have given arise, not from neglect, but from syste-

1. Lorain, pp. 77 and 85. — 2. *Idem*, p. 82. — 3. The local board of education. — 4. Lorain, p. 322. — 5. *Idem*, pp. 326, 327.

matic opposition. "The government," says M. Lorain, "should carefully watch the dark and continual intrigues which the majority of the *curés* are opposing to all improvement in education, the monopoly of which it is their constant object to secure."

"Instead of furthering the views of government (in the Mayenne), for the amelioration and diffusion of elementary instruction, the *curés* do all they can, and avail themselves of all their influence, for the purpose of preventing the municipal councils from voting the necessary funds towards the establishment of a district school (*école communale*). They have exclusively the upper hand in rural parts[1]." "To sum up our statements, the Roman Catholic schools are inferior to the Protestant ones, both as to number and to quality; a double difference, arising," says M. Lorain, "from the fact that the Protestant pastors are more zealous than the Roman Catholic *curés* in encouraging the teachers."

But the inferiority we have described does not stop with the pupils of elementary schools; it reaches those belonging to training establishments (*écoles normales*), and even the students of the theological seminaries. Our readers may judge. As it is the Roman Catholic influence we wish to ascertain in the education question, we must distinguish between the lay training-schools which exist in various parts of France, and the clerical training-schools which do not exist. For the new law, answering admirably to all the expectations of the clergy, exempts from all attendance at a training-school, nay, from all examination, such pupils as have merely resided for five years with a teacher as probationers.

Now, see how exactly this law meets the wants of the Brethren of the Christian Doctrine. According to their statutes, they are obliged to go two together, so that the bishops can, without the least expense, place with every real teacher a mere probationer knowing always sufficiently to keep the class in order, and who in course of time is always sure of getting a teacher's diploma. The law fits itself so well to the views of the priests, that it seems as if it had been drawn up on purpose to please them. Under its sanction, therefore, we must expect to see the lay training-schools vanish away for ever; the best pupils of these last-named establishments cannot stand against so powerful a competition; then, when the last has disappeared, we shall see exclusively throughout the whole extent of France Roman Catholic schools under the direct

1. Lorain, p. 402.

influence of the clergy, and ruled by masters who have not studied, but *resided* with the "*Brethren.*"

But let us pass on to the lay teachers. Every examination at the Sorbonne is attended by Catholic and Protestant candidates; at every examination, the result is the same as the one we have just stated. In November, 1853, for instance, there were 49 Roman Catholic and 6 Protestant candidates; two only out of the former obtained a diploma, whilst, out of the latter, four received theirs — the superiority being as 1 to 2.

Teachers, we see, are what we might have expected from their position as students. We must now ascertain whether the spiritual guides of the community are at all better. And, first, what is the condition of theological *facultés?* "Six Roman Catholic divinity *facultés,*" says M. Schnitzler, "are open at Paris, Bordeaux, Aix, Lyons, Toulouse, and Rouen; two belonging to the Protestants exist at Strasbourg and at Montauban." The Roman Catholic *facultés* stand merely *pro formâ;* they are not useful realities, nor are they valued as they should be. In an excellent report on the state of public instruction, presented in 1836 to the Chamber of Deputies, one of the University councillors alludes to "the deplorable condition of these *facultés,* and the complete solitude to which they are reduced." "Science," says M. Dubois [1], "in all its power, its strength, its fulness, is the only thing that has in it the elements of life; religion, as well as all other human institutions, is subject to this law. Now, really, when we see to what a low ebb theological teaching has fallen in France during the last eighty years, on the subject of doctrines, discipline, or ecclesiastical history, we are struck at once both with terror and with shame; limiting ourselves merely to secular considerations, the comparison of our schools with those abroad is for us a matter of confusion. The ideas, the systems, the institutions, which since the last century form the basis of every history, of every civilisation, are taught nowhere amongst us according to their importance, and to the part they are playing in the history of this world [2]." "We need hardly hesitate to affirm that, in the theological *facultés,* the only auditors are those who attend the lectures of Protestant professors. And yet, in the higher *séminaires,* there are generally more than 7,000 pupils. In 1837, the number was as much as 7,888 [3]."

The word *séminaire* is applied exclusively in France to Roman

1. Dubois, p. 70. — 2. Schnitzler, vol. II, p. 318. — 3. *Idem,* p. 319.

Catholic theological schools. It may be objected that *séminaire* answers the purpose of theological *facultés*. No doubt; but this does not clear the difficulty. Why should the future conductors of the Church be trained in schools where no one, not even the State, can control the teaching imparted to them? We are now touching upon a delicate question; one which we can answer only in Latin. This answer is before us, notwithstanding the following caution with which the volume opens:

"IMPORTANT CAUTION.

"Every application for this work must be accompanied by an authorisation from either the superior of the high *séminaire*, belonging to the diocese, or a vicar-general. Without this indispensable formality, no copy can be sold."

Modesty forbids us quoting from the volume in question, even in Latin; so we shall just extract a few headings to be found in the table of contents:

"De fornicatione.
"De meretricio.
"De incestu.
"De clericis ad turpia sollicitantibus.
"De pollutione.
"An liceat gaudere de pollutione inculpabiliter contingenti.
"De sodomiâ.
"De bestialitate[1]."

The whole book treats of the like topics. Our readers will thank us for not analysing it, even though it would supply us with a thousand strong arguments against our opponents!

The end of the work, however, throws an indirect light upon a system of teaching which we shall reveal in order that every one may know why some persons had rather *whisper* their doctrines behind the walls of a *séminaire*, than explain them publicly in the Sorbonne. For instance, after having said that it is not allowable to open the corpse of a dead woman for the purpose of baptising the fœtus, *against the parent's wish*, how could a lecturer dare, in the presence of medical students, to add: "If, however, the persons who are appointed to watch over the dead woman, or to bury her, could be persuaded to open the body secretly, and attempt to save the child, these means might be tried, but it would require the

1. *Dissertatio in sextum Decalogi præceptum*, etc.; *auctore*, J.-B. Bouvier. Paris, 1849.

greatest precaution[1]." In the presence of law-students, how could any one dare to say that "government has persecuted and condemned to a fine individuals who had performed that operation (the cesarian) with the greatest precaution, ***under the pretence*** that they had practised surgery illegally!" And, will it be credited, that, after having allowed the illegality of an operation which a surgeon has not performed, the author proceeds to teach persons not belonging to the medical profession how they should perform it themselves! "Surgeons have instruments," says he, "and other persons who have none must employ the means they may find within their reach![2]" How could any one dare to say, before the old pupils of MM. Michelet and Quinet (authors of ***The Jesuits,*** and of ***Priests, Women, and Families***) that when a girl big with child is in danger, the only authorisation needed for the autopsy of her body, immediately after death, is a letter neither written, nor even signed, but merely given by her![3]"

Ah! we can well understand why such teaching is buried in the depths of the *séminaires!* We can well understand that such impurity, that illegality so criminal, should produce amongst those who sanction it a feeling of shame!

But we are now led to the moral question; the third and last point we have to examine:

Morality. — In our review of countries, whether Roman Catholic or Protestant, our object is neither to exalt the one, or abuse the other; our sole intention is to show what doctrines are worth, by describing the men who have been trained under their influence. This was an easy task when we had to deal with material prosperity, which can be handled, or with intellectual culture, which is easily perceptible, as the motives of action are the only tests of morality: our work now is more difficult. The dread of opinion may, as well as the voice of conscience, suggest outward propriety of behaviour. To this difference we shall first direct our attention.

Catholicism is not in France now-a-days what it was in times gone by; what it is still in countries where it enjoys unlimited sway. The Reformation has reformed, amongst us, even the Roman Catholic church; as far, we mean, as externals are concerned. The morals of the clergy have benefited especially from this improvement; and we quote the fact to show the respective merits of both doctrines... The one unwittingly gives a lesson; the other, unwittingly likewise, is obliged to receive it.

1. *Dissertatio in sextum Decalogi præceptum*, etc., *auctore*, J.-B. Bouvier. Paris, 1849, p. 208. — 2. *Idem*, p. 209. — 3. *Idem*, p. 211.

Perhaps, however, the moral amelioration of the Roman Catholics through Protestant influence is a mere hypothesis on our part? We might be satisfied with appealing to public opinion. We prefer in this case, too, supporting our assertion by written documents.

Our first quotation is a letter from one of the ministers of Louis XIV, exhorting the Catholic clergy not to estrange the Protestants from the Holy Church by the sight of their customary worldliness and avarice: —

(To My Lord the Archbishop of Paris.) Fontainebleau, Nov. 6, 1685.

"SIR, —

"A complaint has been made to the King that the theatines, under the plea of devotion to the souls in purgatory, have a real opera performed in their church. Every one goes for the purpose of hearing the music; the gate is guarded by two *Suisses*; sittings are let at ten sous each; all the changes introduced, all the means employed to increase devotion are made public by bills, as if it were the first performance of a new play. Whereupon his Majesty commands me to write to you, in order to ascertain whether there be any ground for this complaint, and to inform you that, considering the present state of the Protestants with regard to their conversion, it would perhaps be better to avoid public exhibitions which are painful, as you yourself know, and which would only increase the dislike Protestants have for our religion."

We now give another epistle, in which the coadjutor of Rouen complains of the scandal given to the Protestants by the debaucheries of persons belonging to religious associations: —

(To M. de Chateauneuf.) " Dec. 11, 1685.

"SIR,—

"The coadjutor of Rouen informs me that one of the greatest obstacles he has met with in his attempt to convert the Protestants has been the scandal created by the religious associations belonging to that city; for those who become presidents of such associations are obliged every year to spend large sums of money in festivities, which are only incentives to drunkenness, and which, nevertheless, they cannot dispense with if their object is to fill some municipal office. The King commands me to lay this fact before you, in order that you may write to the *intendant* for his advice, and endeavour to find some means of suppressing the aforesaid religious associations. R. S. [1]."

The very influence of the Protestants, then, has improved the morality of the Roman Catholics, and especially amongst the priests. Let us now see, at least comparatively, what that morality is at the present day.

Our readers will easily understand that we can only supply on this point incomplete statements. Roman Catholics and Protestants are so mixed up together in the population of France, that it is impossible to ascertain their respective influence. An inquiry can be made only in the cases where both denominations are placed one near another; for instance, in statistical accounts, in hospitals, and prisons. A word on each of these points.

M. de Guerry, well known by his works on the moral statistics of France, has pointed out in a few paragraphs two results which deserve notice. He shows that the departments where the Roman clergy is most influential are also those : 1, "where crimes against persons are most common;" 2, "where (with the exception of Britanny, Alsace, Lorraine, and La Vendée), illegitimate children are most numerous;" 3, "where donations made to the poor by testators occur most frequently." Now, M. de Guerry tells us that "he has considered as indirectly bestowed upon schools and upon the poor gifts which are made to the Brothers of the Christian Doctrine, and to Sisters of Charity!" And that we may know the share which falls to the lot of ecclesiastical establishments out of these legacies, said to be bestowed upon the poor, M. de Guerry adds that "these dispositions constitute nearly half the total number of donations and legacies." In conclusion, M. de Guerry proves by the calculations contained in official reports, that during the years posterior to 1820, "the number of legacies and gifts to the clergy has increased to nearly double; whilst, in the same space of time, donations to the poor have only increased in the proportion of 45 per. cent., that is to say, one-half less." And yet M. de Guerry considers as given to the poor the bequests made to Sisters of Charity!

How instructive the few facts we have just adduced! We shall leave the reader to draw his own conclusions, and examine the details which the same author gives respecting the Protestants.

M. de Guerry points out a circumstance which we must first notice, because it evidences an enlightened liberality: "it is amongst the Protestants that schools find most benefactors." But M. de

1. *Bulletin of the Historical Society of French Protestantism*, July and August, 1853.

Guerry obtains another result, which he will explain himself. He states that Protestants give less to the poor than Roman Catholics. This must be, of course, in a statistical document, which describes as given to the poor the donations made to the Brethren of the Christian Doctrine, and to Sisters of Charity. Protestants never give to either pastors or teachers; they think it more prudent to bestow their alms upon churches and schools, and it is the consistory — a lay body — which receives and dispenses these charities. The result would have been quite different if the legacies made to the Brethren and to the Sisters of Charity had not been put down as belonging to the poor, since "these bequests amount to nearly half the total number of donations and legacies."

But M. de Guerry himself explains this anomaly. He adds: "It is only fair to remark that if the Protestants give less to the poor than the Roman Catholics, it often happens that by giving to their fellow-believers, they do not forget our charitable establishments." Thus, where M. de Guerry alludes to the gifts made by Protestants to the poor, he only means those they bestow on their fellow-believers; and if we were to add, besides, donations made to Catholic charitable institutions (an item which M. de Guerry takes no notice of in his parallel), the proportion would still be reversed.

Let us mention a last fact. From our foregoing remarks, it follows that Protestants give more to schools, whilst Roman Catholic liberality is more centered upon the clergy. Now, does the reader wish to know whose donations are dispensed with the least ostentation? M. de Guerry makes the following remark: "Donors, whose names remain unknown, are *five times* more numerous amongst those who give to the schools, than amongst those who dispose in behalf of the clergy."

The reader may judge for himself. We shall now make hospitals the subject of our inquiry: —

Let us consider the city of Nismes, where three-tenths of the population are Protestants, and where the two parties are, by exception, so deeply separated that no confusion need be feared.

We have before us statements, derived from official sources, both ecclesiastic and municipal, which we could produce, if needed. These documents supply us with the following tabular view of natural children, born in both communions during the space of five years: —

Years.	Natural children.		Catholic.		Protestant.
In 1849	 146	of which	134	and	12
1850	 155	—	148	—	7
1851	 148	—	138	—	10
1852	 119	—	107	—	12
1853	 136	—	131	—	5
	704		658		46

That is to say, one-fourteenth instead of one-third; — or, four times more immorality on the side of Rome.

In this account we have taken no notice of exposed children, whose origin is unknown. But here the disproportion must be greater still, because these children being brought up in the hospital as Roman Catholics, Protestant mothers must feel more reluctant than others to send their children there. We shall now test the results we have just obtained. Misery must exist in the same proportion as vice. In the *Hôtel Dieu* of the same city, there are, not including military beds, 176 beds, viz., —

152 occupied by Roman Catholics.
23 — Protestants.

Likewise the *Hospice de l'Humanité*, destined to old people, gives us 230 beds, being

195 occupied by Roman Catholics.
35 — Protestants.

Thence, we find as a total,

347 Roman Catholic poor.
60 Protestant ditto.

If the first number were in the same proportion as the population, it would be only double the second; whereas it is nearly six times greater!

Nismes, it is true, contains a Protestant asylum where poor people are received gratuitously. But the number of sick persons there is comparatively small; the existence of such an establishment, besides, only proves more forcibly the wealth and liberality of those who support it, in order to prevent sending to mixed hospitals invalids belonging to their communion; the beds destined to such persons being often unoccupied.

If we go on from a town to a department where Protestants are most numerous, we shall find, according to the *General Statistics of France, published with the authorisation of the Minister of the Interior, by Alex. Ferrière*, that "the Protestants of the Deux-Sèvres are distinguished by great union, by a pure morality, and by more active industry[1]." In the Moselle, "some anabaptist fa-

1. Alexander Ferrière's *Statistique Générale de la France*, p. 45.

milies are remarkable by the simplicity of their manners. Patient, submissive, docile, they avoid law suits and contestations. The Republic has no subjects more peaceful [1]. "

But from a department let us rise to the whole State, and quote facts of a more general nature.

For the purpose of obtaining documents beyond all discussion, we sought them from official sources. We had already consulted the archives of the Department of the Seine; in the same manner our researches have been directed amongst those of the Public Instruction Office, the Home Office, and the Admiralty (*Ministères de l'Instruction Publique et des Cultes; de l'Intérieur; de la Marine et des Colonies*). In order that our data might be more recent, we have obtained them not in the dust of public libraries, but in the Government-bureaux. Some have been given to us in print, others in MSS., some *vivâ voce.* We are willing to supply any one with the proof of our various assertions. So much by way of preface; now let us come to the point.

Our first research bears upon the numerical proportion between the Roman Catholic and Protestant populations in France. On this subject two opinions prevail; some give 2,000,000 as the amount of French Protestants; others lower the amount to 1,500,000. No official report has ever been published to elucidate this point. The Census made in 1851, both by the government authorities and by the consistories, has allowed a state of uncertainty to subsist which, no doubt, will prevent the publication of the results [2]. We give, nevertheless, the number we have derived from authentic sources: —

Roman Catholic population.	34,741,658
Protestant ditto..........	1,538,181

According to these items, the Protestants are to the Catholics about as 1 to 22; but, that our conclusions may be beyond all dispute, we shall take as the basis of our calculation sometimes the proportion of 1 to 20, sometimes that of 1 to 25, uniformly selecting the one which the nature of the comparison instituted makes more favourable to Roman Catholicism. We now examine our

1. Alexander Ferrière's *Statistique Générale de la France*, p. 24. — 2. We must explain here how the last Census has been made, that the reader may understand how unfair it is to the Reformed populations. Every person who did not acknowledge himself as either Jew, Protestant, or Mahometan, was put down as Roman Catholic! If an opposite system were adopted, we should probably find in France not only one million, but several millions of Protestants! Another proof of the erroneous results given by the Census: How many individuals, do our readers think, are there in the department of the Seine, whose religion is stated as unknown? One! Yes, one! Thousands, evidently, never gave a personal answer.

remaining question, that of morality. Morality, we have already stated, can be only negatively appreciated. Let us, then, consider the prisons, and, first, the *maisons centrales.* According to the information, for which we are indebted to the Home Office, there were, at the date of March 1st, 1854, —

Protestants...............	503
Roman Catholics..........	19,943 [1]

In round numbers, the proportion is as 1 to 40; hence it follows that, taking the whole population as a term of comparison, the Roman Catholic prisoners are almost twice as numerous as the Protestants. From the *maisons centrales*, we proceed to the hulks.

Here our printed documents have been supplied by the Admiralty. The exact title is as follows :—

Admiralty Office. Statistics of the hulks, for the year 1852. *Paris Imperial Printing Press.* 1854 [2].

In the tabular view, No. 16, we read the following :—

Population of the hulks, subdivided according to their religion—

Roman Catholics...		6,415
Lutherans....	35	180
Calvinists	143	
Anglicans....	2	

Dividing 6,415 by 180, we have for quotient nearly 36 and not 25, a number which expresses in an exaggerated manner the proportion between the Catholics and the Protestants. If we apply the term morality to mere absence of crime, the Protestants, then, have a moral superiority measured by the numerical difference between 36 and 25. This is nearly what we had found for the *maisons centrales*; here as 36 is to 25; there, as 40 is to 25.

Let us examine the problem under another point of view. We have seen that the three departments of Gard, Hérault, and Drôme comprise the greatest agglomeration of Reformed Churches; the three neighbouring departments, on the contrary, namely, Puy de Dôme, Cantal, and Upper Loire, are exclusively Catholic. We shall compare these two groups with respect to the quota they contribute to the inmates of the hulks, taking due account of the respective populations. The amount of these not being stated in the statisti-

1. It might be objected that some Protestants declare themselves Roman Catholics on entering into prison, in order to avoid the ill will which they imagine is entertained against the minority. But as, on the other hand, many Roman Catholics call themselves Protestants that they may escape from the control of a chaplain priest, the compensation is more than established. We might quote facts which fully justify our last assertion. — 2. *Ministère de la Marine et des Colonies. Statistique des Bagnes*, année 1852. Paris, imprimerie impériale, 1854.

cal work we are now examining, we shall borrow the particulars from Balbi's geography :

Puy-de-Dôme	573,000	inhabitants	94	convicts.
Cantal.......	259,000	—	72	—
Upper Loire.	292,000	—	79	—
	1,124,000		245	or, 1 for every 4,546 inhabitants.
Gard........	357,000	inhabitants	65	convicts.
Drôme	300,000	—	44	—
Hérault......	346,000	—	58	—
	1,003,000		167	or, 1 for every 6,005 inhabitants.

If we neglect the fractions in both calculations, we shall therefore find on the Protestant side a superiority equal to that of 60 over 45; or, in other words, the relative amount of the population being taken into account, the Roman Catholics are more numerous at the hulks by one-fourth than the Protestants.

This result is not so favourable to the Protestants as the former; but then, in our second calculation, it should be borne in mind that we took three departments together as if they were completely Protestant, which is not the case; the first tabular view, on the contrary, reckons only those individuals whose religious belief is well identified. The first statement, consequently, is the true one; but we can ascertain what the error in the second amounts to. Supposing the population of the three departments to be exclusively Protestant, instead of being mixed, the moral advantage then would be doubled, and the comparison with the three other Catholic departments would supply the result already furnished in the calculations of individual cases; viz, a Protestant superiority of one-half instead of one-fourth. So, the reader will perceive that we have verified mathematically, within one unit, the numbers 36 and 25 previously found.

If we have dwelt upon this point, it was only to prove how easily truth can be found, provided we are on our way towards it.

In the table No. 13, where convicts are classed according to their profession, we discover nine clergymen; their religion, it is true, is not stated, but we have a clue to it, for out of these nine we find five condemned for immoral practices! What an argument against compulsory celibacy! And yet there is nothing in that statement to astonish us; ecclesiastical discipline cannot reform human nature.

M. Kératry, on reading the above facts, would be astonished, not that criminals of the last-named description exist at all, but that their proportion is so small : " the Roman Catholic clergy," says he, " scandalously countenances those amongst its own members who have disgraced the sacred ministry; hence it is that government appears sometimes to connive at guilt in consequence of judicial sentences not receiving their application; hence it is that sentences of acquittal are recorded, the clauses of which are so many imputations against the purity of those who serve at the altar, whilst at the same time we blush at having to enter them in the records of justice. If the disciplinary rules were revised, we should be spared the scandalous scenes which are not to be met with in other religious communities, besides having a pledge of safety as to the purposes of a system unfortunately too contrary to our social order. Gregory VII knew well what he was doing when he imposed celibacy upon the priests; he gave them the clergy as their family, a priest for their sovereign, and Rome for their country. He thus deprived at one blow the nations of their moral and civil securities; what the result has been amongst the Roman Catholic populations, is very well known[1]."

But the most valuable piece of information we have found in this statistic of the hulks, bears upon the question in its widest extent, and although it relates, not to France exclusively, but to Europe, we shall state it here, because it belongs decidedly to our subject. We allude to foreign convicts. Our comparison, now, will have to be instituted between the number of criminals suplied by the various nations, relatively to the number of the entire population and their distance from us. For it is clear that, in proportion as a state is removed from France, the probability will decrease for its inhabitants coming amongst us to undergo sentences of condemnation. Let us then select, to compare them by twos, nations equally removed from us, and whose population is nearly the same, in order to get nearer the truth; we shall afterwards take the average on both sides.

Austria and Great Britain, two empires of first-rate importance, may be brought into parallel together; the one is separated from us by a narrow channel, and the other by a small state. Now, the following is the number of convicts they both supply to the population of the French hulks: —

Austria (Roman Catholic)	11	convicts.
Great Britain (Protestant)	2	—

That is to say, five times more criminals in Austria than in Great Britain.

Spain and Prussia are our next door neighbours; the population

1. *Du Culte*, by Kératry, p. 70.

is nearly the same in both countries; they may, therefore, be appropriately compared together, and we find as the result —

Spain (Roman Catholic).	96 convicts.
Prussia (Protestant)....	15 —

six times more criminals for the Catholic nation.

The distance and population of Bavaria and Holland suggest another parallel :

Bavaria (Roman Catholic).	14 convicts.
Holland (Protestant).....	3 —

Nearly five times more criminals in Bavaria than in Holland.

Denmark is farther than Belgium, whilst its population is less numerous. In order to render the comparison true, let us double the number of convicts for the former country, and we shall have : —

Belgium (Roman Catholic)................	36 convicts.
Denmark (Protestant) (double number).....	20 —

Nearly double the number of criminals on the Catholic side, as before.

Switzerland contains a strong Roman Catholic minority; we shall, however, consider it as entirely Protestant, and, if our principle is true, we may reckon upon finding a smaller advantage for the nation which we have erroneously set down as exclusively Protestant.

Sardinian States (Roman Catholic).	58 convicts.
Switzerland (Protestant)...........	39 —

A result which corresponds with our anticipations.

We come, finally, to the last and most singular part of this parallel.

The Roman States are at a much greater distance from France than Wurtemberg; but the population is double that of the last named little kingdom. These two circumstances being in inverse ratio, balance one another, and our comparison remains quite fair.

Roman States.....................	80 convicts.
Wurtemberg.....................	7 —

His Holiness, consequently, supplies France with from eleven to twelve times the number of criminals which come from the dominions of a Protestant Prince! He that hath ears to hear, let him hear!

In order to be more exact still, let us keep a strict account of the population, and take the average number of convicts : —

ROMAN CATHOLIC COUNTRIES.	POPULATION.	CONVICTS.	PROTESTANT COUNTRIES.	POPULATION.	CONVICTS.
Austria............	32,000,000	11	Great Britain.......	23,400,000	2
Spain..............	13,900,000	96	Prussia............	12,164,000	15
Bavaria............	4,070,000	14	Holland............	2,558,000	3
Belgium............	3,560,000	36	Denmark............	1,950,000	10
Sardinian States....	4,300,000	58	Switzerland........	1,980,000	39
Roman States.......	2,590,000	80	Wurtemberg.......	1,520,000	7
			United States [1].....	23,000,000	3
	60,420,000	295		66,572,000	79

Our readers will see that although the Protestant population is the greatest, the number of convicts it supplies is from three to four times less. This general result proves the correctness of the partial facts we have already obtained, and the whole sum of our illustrations, taken together, confirm our previous statements respecting the various nations.

We have examined prisons and the hulks; but there remains a class of criminals who escape beyond the reach of hulks and prisons; we allude to suicides. If, however, we endeavour to ascertain the religious belief of those unfortunate individuals, we find in M. de Guerry's work a test with which he unwittingly supplies us—a test the more valuable, because it carries along with itself the condemnation of the religious doctrine which encourages crime.

We have already noticed that when crimes can be compounded for, a criminal is seldom deterred from committing them. The Italian robber, the Spanish prostitute, satisfy the claims of conscience by dividing their profits with the Virgin Mary. We find in history that more than one murderer has taken the holy communion as a preparation for the crime he was about to perpetrate. Something similar occurs in the case of suicides. M. de Guerry gives us a long list of instances in which that crime has been committed under the safeguard of the Roman Catholic religion. Sometimes it is a man who hangs himself in asking God's pardon; or a woman, on the point of taking poison, begs that masses may be said for the good of her soul. On other occasions, the self-murderer has provided himself with amulets and small prints which reveal the state of his thoughts. The greater number ground their hopes of heaven on the fact that they have suffered here below;

1. We place here the United States, which we could not compare with any country in our series of parallels, because their natural point of contrast is to be found in the colonies which belong to Spain. By adding the United States to this tabular view, the Protestant total exceeds by more than six millions the Roman Catholic one.

they present as an expiatory offering the apparent sacrifice of their life, in conformity with the Roman Catholic doctrine that he who suffers may offer his troubles as a pleasing oblation to God. But the learned statistician must speak for himself : — " Many persons will no doubt be astonished at this manifestation of religious feelings, at the very moment when the individual who expresses them is on the point of committing a deed which religion condemns as a crime. A fact such as this will appear to them unaccountable. Similar discrepancies, yet, are more common than one might suppose. Several suicides cross themselves before hurrying into eternity; others kneel down and say their prayers; on a few are to be found rosaries and devotional books [1]. "

Can *one* case be quoted in which a Protestant has justified from the Bible an attempt on his own life?

The following question meets us at the close of every one of the parallels we have drawn : " Are we right in ascribing to religious faith, correct here, erroneous there, the differences which strike us between the state of civilisation in various countries? " It would seem that an affirmative answer to this question is pre-eminently correct here, when both terms of the comparison are taken on the same soil, in the same nation, under the influence of the same laws. We wish, however, to render this truth still more evident by a quotation which shall bring before our eyes French Catholicism — not the Catholicism of unbelieving Paris, but that to be met with in Britanny, where the priests are absolute masters. We borrow the following paragraph from a Roman Catholic writer, who has seen what he relates : —

" Will you have an idea of the eagerness and success with which our clergy enlighten the people and help on the progress of civilisation? I shall not describe the degradation of Spain and Italy under clerical domination; nor shall I turn your attention to the *prosperity* of Catholic Ireland; — Ireland who has suffered at the hands of her priests quite as much as at those of the English. No; I only say, look a few yards off, look at Britanny. There the clergy enjoy full swing; no one thwarts their actions; they bask in all the liberty they have sued for; their rule is despotic; what a state of destitution, consequently, both for the body and the soul!

" I have visited the celebrated *pardon* [2] of Saint Anne d'Auray, in Britanny. Pilgrims flock there from a distance of fifteen or twenty leagues in every direction. Dirty, wearied by a long jour-

1. De Guerry, p. 68. — 2. The name *pardon* is given to religious pilgrimages in Britanny.

ney through detestable roads, those wretches lie down promiscuously for rest under hoops fixed in the ground and covered with sheets..... There are plenty of shops for the sale of rosaries and sacred prints; but no books, not even prayer-books; this would suppose that the purchasers know how to read. Now what is the use of that? The rosary is enough for people to pray by. You may see a goodly number of men and women going round the church on their knees; give them a trifle, and they will offer to do the same on your account; they will save you the trouble, and for the sum of five or six sous you purchase merits in heaven.

"The ear is struck at once by a metallic sound, which is kept up without any interruption; it proceeds from a cascade of sous falling as heavily as a storm-shower into a couple of casks, placed on each side of the choir. Behind these casks stands a priest, who brings the patena to the lips of each pilgrim as he approaches, a wax candle in the one hand, and his offering in the other. At the moment he is about to kiss the patena, a sacristan lights the wax candle; this ceremony is hardly gone through when a second sacristan blows the candle out again, and sets it aside, for the church..... Those peasants would never dream of reflecting, of reasoning on such facts. The priest has spoken, therefore it is all right, all true.

"Each Breton church has its relic or its wonder-working saint. The last-named worthies, in their turn, have each a special province, from which they are requested not to depart. One is a chiropodist; another cures head-aches; gout, cholics, ophthalmias, nervous diseases are presided over by distinct saints, and no one is allowed to encroach upon his neighbour's grounds. The chapel at Loc Ronau in the Finistère, exceptionally, is a sort of neutral district, where every neighbouring *curé* has a right to send his saint; it is a real miracle fair. The priest does not attend himself, custom forbids it; but he opens in his parish a species of auction for the letting of the miraculous image; the highest bidder gets it. The *curé* once paid, the other trader proceeds to drive at his own risks whatever bargains he can. This is an ingenious manner of bringing the theory of stock-exchange speculations within the ideas and resources of the country.

"One of the *curé's* tenants had made a first-rate collection, but his drinking propensities happened to be quite as great as the faith of his customers; after numerous visits paid to the public house, he felt his head rather heavy, his sight had become confused; in short, he found it impossible to go on with the sale. Two hours still remained, however, before the close of the day; determined to make the best of them, he cried out, 'Who will buy the remainder of my saint's privileges? I take thirty sous for them!' 'Thirty sous? here you are.' Our drunkard pockets the money, goes to sleep, and his successor sits down at the table; but he had only collected twenty-five sous when the first purchaser returned. This one insisted upon the other shutting the shop; the sub-tenant was determined to continue the sale by candle-light. A fight ensued in the presence of the plaster-saint, who kept looking on with the greatest gravity, whilst the crowd, quite as impassible, formed a ring around the two champions.

"As an insurmountable bulwark against the invasion of philosophical ideas, the clergy is most careful to keep up the use of the bas-breton dialect. The Jesuits have at Pontcroix a school, where they teach both Latin and Greek to 300 pupils; but as for French, not one word. In country districts it would be impossible for any one to make himself understood, and the only interpreter is the *curé*. Whatever information you wish to impart to the people must be conveyed trough the medium of the priest. Suppose the case of a political crisis, and of the clergy declaring against the Government, what will you do? Will you go and speechify before breton peasants? Will you prove to them who is right and who is wrong? It would be throwing away your eloquence. On the other hand, by pronouncing one word which you cannot understand, the priest is able to raise a mob against you, and to have you torn in pieces.

"Britanny is still the land of the Druids; the only difference is that the Druids now-a-days are called *curés* or *rectors*. For example, the forest of Brocéliaude is celebrated in the romances of the *Round Table*. There might be seen the vale from which no one ever returned, the enchanter Merlin's tomb, the platform, and the fountain of Baranton. By pouring some water from the fountain on the platform, one could raise a cloud in the sky. A Christian clergy has retained this celtic superstition.

"People go to pray at the chapel of our Lady of Hatred in the neighbourhood of Tréguier, to obtain the death of an enemy; there the rosary is the murderer's weapon, and the virgin is his accomplice.

"Britanny abounds in fountains possessed of marvellous qualities. Men and women, young and old, healthy and diseased, all bathe there indiscriminately. If you are in good health, a dip will preserve you from the attacks of illness; if you are sick, this is the best cure for the ague. Rheumatism is cured by pouring water inside the patient's coat sleeves; everywhere the priests are proprietors of the *good fountain*, and applicants must pay to make use of them.

"In another locality, near Landernau, horses are brought to church at least once a-year; they attend mass; it is true that they go to the offertory only by proxy.

"I have seen in a village church a distaff covered with flax, stuck up at the entrance of the choir. This distaff is offered to the Virgin by one of the female parishioners. On Sunday the *curé* will appoint another woman to spin out this offering — an honour which is most earnestly solicited. The ceremony is renewed every week, that is to say, fifty-two times a-year. The produce, of course, goes to the *curé*.

"The Breton *curé* has quietly managed to re-establish tithes or their equivalent in kind. He then sells these offerings publicly at the very foot of the cross, where they have been brought. This is called *a sale under the cross*. Such a sale is always highly productive; in the first place, because the various articles being selected for God are all of a superior quality; secondly, because the ceremony of consecrating has increased their value.

"Generally speaking, every species of offering is accepted; at some *pardons*, however, the nature of the oblation is distinctly specified. At Our Lady of Ralecq, for instance, white hens only used to be presented; but, as such fowls are scarce, the *curé*, out of pity for the perplexity of his parishioners, has decided at length that two black hens are as acceptable to God as one white one. What a relief for those poor people!

"Those who derive from such means their power and their income, are they likely to desire earnestly and with all their heart the progress of enlightenment? If they say so, they are only telling another untruth. No; it is impossible for me to admit that the interest of the clergy is to give information to the people. I therefore cannot believe such to be their earnest wish. An absolute sway over them is the only thing they desire[1]."

But Roman Catholicism and Roman Catholic clergy are perhaps different in the remainder of France from what they are in Britanny! No; we may be deceived by the difference between the various populations; but this affects neither the clergy nor their doctrine. If Roman Catholicism is not exactly the same every-

1. Kératry, pp. 49 to 61.

where, it is certainly aiming at uniformity: now it selects its patron not in London or in Paris, but at Rome and at Madrid. It is the same with epochs as with places. The mediæval clergy entertained the pretensions afterwards harboured by those of modern society; the priests of the new empire are exactly the counterpart of those who lived under the Restoration. Whilst we read M. Kératry's book, published in 1827, we might believe that its date is 1854. By quoting from it, we exhibit the character of the Catholic clergy during the whole of this century. Let the reader peruse the following extract, and he will no longer be astonished at the contrast we have just now been considering: "It is well known," says M. Kératry, "that Roman Catholicism, by encouraging within its pale the multiplication of emblems, rash practices, religious associations, mysticism, useless, local, and material ceremonies, which have overgrown it, has favoured throughout France a low tone of public morality. In many a district village of the kingdom to which we belong, in many a *commune* of Lower Britanny, for instance, Christian worship has been so completely turned aside from its noble origin, that were it not for that inner voice which is never entirely quenched, even by the most deplorable aberrations of our reason, we might say that in such localities our Heavenly Father is neither known nor worshipped.

"Ultramontane nations have moulded the Creator too much according to the pattern left by Epicurus. They have transformed Heaven into a large machine, where everything is active, is busy, is at work — except God himself. This is the degradation of Christianity, nor are we to feel astonished that human degradation follows wherever such ideas penetrate [1]."

"In the prostration of human reason, Rome had admitted a mass of superfetations which ought to have vanished away before the light of the Gospel. She has ever been consistent with her own views. Look at part of the South and North-west of France; consider, likewise, the various denominations of Protestantism; compare and judge! [2]"

"The pretensions of Ultramontanists, favoured by the revival of religious feeling which followed our civil disturbances, have everywhere intruded upon public worship, thus destroying the generous hopes of many. The numerous subdivisions of Roman Catholicism at present into brotherhoods and associations, all derived from absolute power, are in accordance with that power

1. Kératry, pp. 41 to 63. — 2. *Idem*, p. 45.

alone. They are destined either to destroy representative government, or to be swallowed up by it themselves. Between such a disposition and the feeling of hatred, there is only one step, for there can be no concord between servility and liberty. It would be easy to prove that Ultramontane authority has become more temporal than ever. It has its arms, it raises it subsidies, it organises its tribunals, it enrols its men; without taking the slightest notice of the ideas of justice, which they have oftentimes perverted, since they have assumed the right of deciding upon them, the Ultramontanists are unceasingly interposing themselves between the subjects and the laws of the State, between the citizens in their civil relations to one another, between contracting parties, between servants and masters, whose secrets they have thus taught their inferiors to reveal. There is no place where Ultramontane authority will not penetrate for the purpose of laying down the law according to views merely human. Question the maiden, the young wife, or the mother; see those anxious forebodings respecting the rights which our French Charter has vainly insured to us, respecting our modern institutions, respecting the children whose legitimate birth is acknowledged by the country, and the settlement we intend making for them, respecting the vote which the father gives when he is called to take a part in any electoral transactions, respecting even the use he makes of the money he has derived from labour and industry; consult the grave itself, and it will tell you that the kingdom of our new Catholicism does belong to this world! Forms have become everything; they carry along with them the substance which is now reduced to an accessory of very little importance. Countenancing above all, as they do, superstitious opinions, they go so far as to prescribe the education of youth; what they aim at is man's self-abdication; they impose it upon us, they lead us on by a straight line to bigotry: we call to witness the teachers who have the charge of the rising generation. When we see walking about our streets those beardless pedagogues destined to train up citizens and to educate men; those new-fangled professors, just fresh from the plough, where, even, they had no abilities to spare; that herd of youths withdrawn from manual labour for the purpose of adding a whole kingdom to the realms of ignorance, we cannot imagine that we have before our eyes the successors of the celebrated *École Normale*[1], the suppression of which has distressed all the true friends of the country. No; we cannot believe that

1. The *École Normale*, or superior training school for professors and lectures, was temporarily suppressed in 1822. It is now re-established.

by such means the prosperity of French industry is to be fostered; and if we did not generally see by the side of these vegetative beings a *gendarme* ready to lend them his assistance, we might fancy that we are witnessing some grotesque ceremony soon to be concluded by the presence of the magistrate.

"The duty of religion should be not merely to drive away the accredited agents of error and superstition who have crept out of the ground at the voice of Ultramontanism; the Reformation must bear upon the power which has called them forth; religion itself must be freed from the circumstances which degrade it, and which bring it continually in a state of hostility against the country. It is not astonishing that Rome should trifle with the scanty remains of religion she has left in Europe [1]."

"The old faith exists no longer either within the Church, who endeavours to restore it once more, or amongst the councils of princes bound together under a mystic title [2]."

"Supposing a complete restoration of faith were possible, would it not bring back along with it all the bloody incidents of Saint Bartholomew's Day! We will venture to affirm that there are points in the tenets of Roman Catholicism which no one can be thoroughly convinced of without hating to the death him who does not pay to such tenets every honour and respect believed to be due to them [3]."

"Roman Catholicism, organised according to a plan in harmony with the wants of barbarous ages, has either been unable or unwilling to help on the social progress. It has vented all its hatred upon public prosperity; it has remained aloof from modern society; and modern society in its turn, not anxious for self destruction, has likewise kept at a distance. The immense majority of the nation, thinking, acting, strict in its morals, commendable by its domestic habits, avoids the influence of Catholicism.

"Nobles and government servants, it is true, are regular at their attendance at public worship, but as far as the forms are concerned we feel inclined to think that, after having suffered from the spirit of irreligion which they had contributed to spread in former days amongst the lower classes, they have now settled themselves in the nave of the Church actuated by the dispositions of a man who wishes to be about his business. As for the government agents, prayer is for them a duty of the same nature as the election of deputies. Thus surrounded, the priest, standing before the sacred

1. Kératry, pp. 46, 53. — 2. Allusion to the Holy Alliance between Russia, Prussia, and Austria. — 3. Kératry, p. 55, 57.

and mysterious symbols of the faith, seems to be there only for the purpose of concluding a compact. We feel pained as we write it; but, from the present direction given to worship, and from the thoughts which it suggests, the very altar has been transformed into a board upon which two contracting parties have signed a treaty of mutual insurance against the nation.

"We have no right to be astonished at seeing a citizen belonging to a religion which he abstains from professing; he constantly finds it armed against his liberty, his civic rights, against all the things which he holds most dear. He claims from the Church prayers which are without importance in his own eyes, because they have no influence on the character of those who pronounce them; and he sends his daughter to a place of worship the road to which he has forgotten himself. It is a just subject of amazement that faith, whose duty it is to lead men to happiness, begins by pulling down everywhere the monuments of genius, destroying industry, impoverishing the citizens, and reducing the number of the population; yet this is nevertheless the sight offered to us at the present time by the three countries the most Catholic, but in fact the most irreligious and the most wretched in the whole civilised world [1]."

Such was the French Roman Catholic society in 1827. Such it is in 1854: Rome cannot change, but it can perish. God grant that her last fate may not meet her on the ruins of another nation, fallen a prey to her cruelty. God grant that "*the Protestant Church, remarkable by its high degree of intellectual culture, by the fervour of its religious sentiments, and by the great purity of its morals* [2]," may not one day be compelled to follow the example of its forefathers in carrying abroad the benefits it would have bestowed upon its native country.

After having brought to an end this comparative study of the various nations, both Protestant and Roman Catholic, we were so struck by the superiority of the one over the other, that we were on the point of drawing our own conclusions. But a scruple occurred: what might be said in favour of opposite assertions? Hence we have resolved upon examining likewise the statements brought forward by objectors.

1. Kératry, p. 445. — 2, Schnitzler, vol. II, p. 135.

THE OBJECTIONS EXAMINED.

Our subject has recently been discussed in two Roman Catholic theological works. The first is entitled: ***Protestantism and Catholicism Compared in their Connexion with the Civilisation of Europe***, by Jacques Balmès; and the second, ***on Protestantism and all other Heresies in their Connexion with Socialism***, by Auguste Nicolas. M. Balmès begins with the question of principles; he goes so high and so far in the region of metaphysics that we lose sight of him. But it is no concern of ours. Our question is, above all, a question of facts. The world is tired of ranting; it knows long since that the tongue of man can utter both sweet and bitter words, can plead both for and against with equal facility. It will no longer put up with high-sounding sentences; nothing short of well-proved facts will do. Consequently we are not going here to refute such and such a chapter of M. Balmès' work, in which the author endeavours to prove that man must of necessity be intolerant, that the Church had the right of establishing the inquisitions, etc., etc. This may be the opinion of M. Balmès; it is not a fact, and so we leave it.

In the second place, M. Balmès dates Catholicism as far back as Jesus Christ, and asserts that all the good that has been done in the world for the last eighteen hundred years is the work of Catholicism; but the writer forgets one very simple distinction: viz., that Catholicism and Christianity are far from being synonymous; to confound the one with the other is to lay down as a fact precisely what is a matter of discussion. It is to assert that the Faith of Rome is the same as that of Jerusalem, that the doctrine of the Popes is the same as that of the Apostles; and that the Italians and Spaniards of the present day lead the same life as the Christians of the Primitive Church. Now all this we deny. The Roman Catholic Church sprang up about the fourth century; she has gained ground and grown older; she is no longer what she was in her infancy; neither, above all, does she resemble the Church of Christ, such as this church appeared eighteen centuries ago. The works, therefore, of the Protestantism of our own day cannot be compared with those of the Primitive Church; for the children of the Reformation might say, as well as the disciples of Rome, and with better reason still : the Primitive Church is my mother, for I am like her, and you are not!

As M. Balmès delights to throw around Catholicism the garb of antiquity in order to render it respectable, so he likes to keep Protestantism in the cradle, that he may taunt it with the faults of its infancy. But the child has grown and come to maturity; a man for the last three hundred years, it travels the world everywhere, showing itself and acting. What matters! our author is determined to know it and to study it, as it appeared during the sixteenth century. From this point of view the comparison of course must become favourable to the Romish Church; she wraps herself up in the ancient mantle of the apostles, and tearing from the Reformation the cloak of modern civilisation, she says to the world : judge between us! Our readers will perceive here a double act of of injustice. It is not at the day of his birth that one can appreciate a man, but when he has attained the age of maturity. According to the same rule, you should take both the Protestantism and Catholicism of our own times, and institute a comparison between *them.* When a new faith spreads itself throughout an old society, two distinct effects are produced. An extraordinary fervour is developed in some, whilst the prejudices of the past impair the faith of others. Thus, at Jerusalem, even in the days of the apostles, the power of the Christian life manifested itself admirably amongst the true disciples, whilst at the same time judaising Christians, nay, St. Peter even, to the great indignation of St. Paul, preserved many practices belonging to the Mosaic dispensation. In the same way the reforms of the sixteenth century had remained so long in the Church of Rome, that they had retained many of its characteristics. An unfrocked priest loses neither at once nor ever completely those mechanical habits under which his body has become bent, his eye quailing, his step embarrassed. So that at the present time it is as easy to point out an ex-priest as a quondam Israelite. Luther, Calvin, and many others, then, have, to some extent, persevered in the ways which the Pope first taught them; they confounded, for instance, temporal and spiritual things, and from this confusion many evils have issued. But, since then, this wound, the sad legacy of Roman Catholicism, has healed under the salutary influence of the principles of the Reformation; if not entirely closed everywhere, in some places it is cured, and in others it is gradually disappearing; the vital strength of Protestantism supplies the remedy, and if people will not judge of the Reformation by what it must naturally become, let them judge of it at least by what it is already. America has entirely rejected State religion; the Dissenters form half the population of England; elsewhere, the Reformed Church, if assuming the character of a national establishment, is tolerant: the priests celebrate mass in London, in Berlin, in Amsterdam, whereas no Protestant minister is allowed to preach publicly at Rome, Madrid, or Lisbon. Do not judge of a religion either from first enthusiasm of her converts, or from the old prejudice of her neophytes; let us wait till the tree has produced its fruits, and then we can judge. In a word, let us compare the Protestantism and the Catholicism of our own day — not the Reformation of the sixteenth century, then new-born, with the Catholicism of the time of Jesus Christ — a Catholicism which did not exist.

These general considerations simplify, as we see, many subjects. We are now limited to the discussion of facts, and almost exclusively of contemporary facts. The question, thus examined, becomes easy, interesting, and of present importance. We have circumscribed it within limits from which we will not depart. So, in the work of M. Balmès, we take no notice of his long disquisitions on the doctrines of Thomas Aquinas, on virginity, on the influence of chivalry and the manners of the barbarians, on the march of intellect since the eleventh century, etc., etc.

Our field of inquiry is already singularly circumscribed. The work of M. Nicolas will not enlarge it; for not only does this author reproduce the ideas, but the very words of the former writer. It is then, finally, to the examination of M. Nicolas's volume that we must limit ourselves.

This work may be divided into two parts: in the first, M. Nicolas seeks to prove that Protestantism and Socialism are one; in the second, that Protestantism is contrary to toleration, intellectual development, and morality. Our business is not with the first part and by far the longest part of the book; we need only confine ourselves to an examination of the second, which is comprised in 150 pages. Let not our readers, therefore, be frightened. This critique cannot be long, especially as our task will be chiefly limited to the mere quoting from a work which carries along with it its own refutation.

Nothing helps so much to judge a composition as an acquaintance with the author. This must be our preliminary step, and we shall endeavour to derive this knowledge from the book itself. We should like to insert here in its integrity an article published by the ***Revue de Strasbourg*** (for January, 1853): the author of this paper proves that M. Nicolas sometimes plagiarises, and sometimes misquotes; on one occasion he mistakes men for cities; on another, cities for men; but, as our readers can peruse in the Revue the excellent article we are now alluding to, we prefer illustrating the elasticity of M. Nicolas's conscience by a specimen which we have studied for ourselves.

The assertion of M. Nicolas is as follows: Protestantism tolerates unbelief and immorality (that's all); now for his arguments: "Protestantism is for immorality what it is for unbelief: toleration itself. Do you require a singularly conclusive instance of this fact? Here you have it. One of the most upright, pious, pure-minded doctors of Protestantism, the *lamented* M. Vinet, writing a treatise on the qualifications necessary for the sacred ministry, says: 'Can doubts render the vocation null? We answer: 1. There would be few legitimate calls, if a man was disqualified by his doubts. 2. Study, experience, the exercise of the ministry itself will raise new surmises; but it will be objected: a man sent to solve mental difficulties of others, can he be a doubter himself? No, not absolutely; for we are not speaking of a minister who is a sceptic or an infidel, but of a man who is not quite clear upon all subjects, and who sometimes will have to acknowledge it.' So much for faith; now we come to morality: 'Can *certain* feelings annul the call? The feelings we have in view are scruples of conscience, and the difficulty is answered by the principles already stated [1].'

"These words need no comment," adds M. Nicolas; "we may judge of the flocks by the pastors [2]."

M. Nicolas, we see, asserts that: "the lamented" Protestant M. Vinet tolerates unbelief and immorality amongst ministers. Such is the conclusion to be drawn from the foregoing passage; and, to

1. Treatise on Pastoral Theology, pp. 107 and 108. — 2. Nicolas, p. 573.

speak the truth, the words here quoted as those of M. Vinet authorise such an inference. Now, what would you say, reader, if you were told that the words of M. Vinet are so mutilated that, were they restored to their original, they would have a directly opposite meaning? Be convinced of this by reading what M. Nicolas has taken good care not to quote: " Speaking of evil inclinations: but if they are evil," says M. Vinet, " they are alike incompatible with the professions of Christianity, and with the ministry. At the same time, as the scandal would be greater in a minister than in a private Christian, the following question may be put: Will it not be necessary for him to begin by conquering these inclinations as a private Christian? He answers, perhaps, I can do so still more easily as a minister. This is venturing much: double or quits. If the church is a hospital, the ministers are not the patients, but the physicians. They must enter it in a good state of health. No doubt they may benefit themselves, but there is something very repugnant in such a calculation. They run the risk of injuring the work of the ministry instead of being benefited by it [1]."

In one word, evil inclinations are incompatible with a profession of Christianity, but still more so with the pastoral office. Such is M. Vinet's affirmation, and yet you are bold enough to say that he tolerates... But wait: this is not all.

Not only does M. Vinet not tolerate evil inclinations, either in the minister or in the private Christian, he goes so far as to forbid the former " to indulge certain tastes, which, although innocent in themselves, are not convenient for the minister. They annul the vocation," says he, " if the vocation does not either annul or overcome them. " And this is said, not in another work, not even in another chapter, but in the very same page quoted by M. Nicolas, and you are bold enough to say... But wait a little: we have not yet done with this falsification.

So much for morality: let us see the part which concerns faith. M. Nicolas quotes M. Vinet in the following manner: " Should doubts disqualify a pastor for his vocation? We reply, 1st, that there would be few legitimate vocations if this were the case; 2[dly], That study, experience, the exercise of the ministry itself, will often raise fresh doubts." This " 2[dly] " belongs to M. Nicolas. M. Vinet had put " 3[dly];" why, then, alter the numbers? Simply for the purpose of concealing the suppression of the real " 2dly," which stands thus: " According to this hypothesis, the number

1. Vinet pp. 108 and 109.

of private Christians, even, would be few. For, although a man may attain to a state of mind in which all is light, (*des êtres disgraciés*) incomplete beings alone have never doubled. "

Thus the doubts of which M. Vinet speaks may exist in a man who will afterwards have a clear apprehension of all things, and, some few lines lower down, the author adds : "It is not, of course, of a sceptic or infidel minister that I am writing, but of a man who does not see clearly through every question."

And such is the writer *a propos* of whom it is affirmed that "Protestantism is for unbelief toleration itself!" He has just been saying that he does not allude to a "sceptic" minister, and, on the strength of this plain assertion, M. Nicolas boldly declares that he does apologise for unbelief! Well, we are not afraid of making another statement, and it will be this : M. Alexandre Vinet has been basely calumniated and hypocritically *lamented!*

Our readers know now the character of the individual who is about to prove that Protestantism is intolerance, darkness, and immorality; whilst Catholicism is identical with liberty, intellectual culture, and morality!

M. Nicolas starts thus : "For the last hundred years men have agreed to say that in the great struggle between barbarism and civilisation, the Church has shown itself intolerant, opposed to intellectual progress, nay, even favouring corruption; whilst it is to Protestantism and to philosophy that we owe liberty of conscience, mental development, and a high standard of morality[1]."

Certainly, as M. Nicolas asserts more than once, *it is* generally acknowledged by public opinion, and even by those writers who do not set up for the apologists *quand même* of Catholicism, that to Protestantism we owe liberty of conscience, mental development, and a higher standard of morality. Moreover, in a time like the present, when every one examines for himself, it strikes us that an opinion which becomes so general must have some foundation, and that we may place some trust in a cause supported by so many champions, against M. Nicolas who stands almost alone. But, after all, we do not think a majority of votes sufficient here; let us examine the words of our author himself. His arguments may perhaps outweigh what "men have agreed to say."

"Catholicism," says he, "in this impleading, has besides been condemned unheard. It has not had a judge, but only accusers; interested and unjust accusers."

1. Nicolas, p. 439. — 2. *Idem*, p. 440.

It is very easy to brand as an accuser any person who judges us. At this rate, no one could hold an opinion of his own; for, as soon as he gave an unfavourable judgment, he would be called not a judge but an accuser. *We* appeal to our readers: have we not selected our authorities against Catholicism almost uniformly amongst Roman Catholics, even amongst their clergy? Is it our fault if Romanists by birth, the moment they begin to reflect, are not Romanists by conviction? It would be rather too odd if we were called upon to produce a condemnation of Roman Catholicism from the lips of its apologists: M. Nicolas himself, for instance.

Never mind, let us try. As he has undertaken to prove to us the erroneous nature of the general opinion, it is worth while listening to him. First, then, M. Nicolas appeals from our Protestant prejudices to the *honesty of our sentiments*.

Is this a little flattery in order to seduce us? We do not like to think so, and if it is seriously that we are reminded of the honesty of our sentiments, we are at a loss to understand how the same man can ascribe to all Protestants *Satan* as their common father; how he can tell them that the end of their doctrines is the "suppression of all morality, and the destruction of society."

After these preambles, M. Nicolas comes to the point. His first argument is the identification of Catholicism with toleration, and of Protestantism with intolerance. But this trick of legerdemain can be accomplished only by altering the proper meaning of words. So, M. Nicolas begins by telling us that for those who find fault with Roman Catholicism "liberty of religion has become liberty of irreligion; nay, the liberty of attacking religion [1]."

To be sure; and we belong to that number. There is no liberty, as we believe, in a person's walking towards a goal marked out to him beforehand. Whilst we claim the freedom of saying *yes*, we are quite as anxious that M. Nicolas should enjoy that of saying *no;* the unbeliever even has the right of contradicting us both. If it were not that critics are at liberty to assail religion, what would be the worth of apologetic writings! The very interests of the truth, which for us is the Gospel, make us wish that persons may be free to attack it; it is in defending itself that truth will identify itself as such. With God on our side, we dread not the struggle, and M. Nicolas supplies us with a good opportunity of proving so to him.

In order to make out that Protestantism has been in France the persecuting party, M. Nicolas — clever man! — begins by grant-

1. Nicolas, p. 448.

ing a concession. "Protestantism," says he, "has been first attacked, repulsed, persecuted, in this country (France) and, carried away by the deplorable excess of legitimate defence, the Catholic society was so exasperated against it, as to become its executioner, in order to avoid being its victim[1]."

We must bear in mind this concession: "Protestantism has been persecuted; and, carried away by a deplorable excess, Catholic society became its executioner."

We could not have said more, but our inference would have been different; for it seems to us that the intolerant party is the one which persecutes even to the death!

But the point we would especially insist upon in this astonishing defence, is the motive alleged to justify the crime: viz., the fear of becoming a victim... What! is this your justice? You might happen to be killed, *ergo* you begin by murdering? At that rate, what crime could not be justifiable? Suppose a thief saying of the travellers whom he has assassinated: "I only wanted his purse; but, lest he should send me to prison, I blew his brains out!" Of course, it would be waste of time to dispute about such principles; but we wish to show by what successive degrees M. Nicolas justifies the executioner and curses the victim.

Here our author turns round, and by means of a quibble he endeavours to put in his first accusation. The object is to establish that Protestantism has brought about in society the confusion of things temporal and things spiritual: "Protestantism, by destroying the authority of the Church, has destroyed spiritual authority in contradistinction to temporal power; *that is to say*, it has immolated the rights of thought and of conscience to human strength and human might[2]."

This "that is to say" is rather extraordinary; *white*, that is to say, *black*; *yes*, that is to say, *no*; the authority of the Church, i. e., the rights of thought; the authority of the Pope, i. e., the liberty of conscience. But, M. Nicolas, the Church, represented in your community by the clergy, is not identical with the thoughts of all human beings! The Pope's authority is not identical with their conscience! When the authority of a special body no longer exists, it is precisely then that the thoughts of all are free. I should have been ashamed to expose this blundering of yours in the very a, b, c, of a system, but I thought it right to prove how you consciously confound the authority of the Church, that is to say of *one* man —

1. Nicolas, p. 449. — 2. *Idem*, p. 450.

the Pope — with the rights of thought and of conscience: the rights of the whole human race.

And, on the other hand, to whom can we trace this confusion of the temporal and the spiritual power? Is it to Luther or to Hildebrand? To him who only followed the errors of your church, or to those pontiff kings who wear a triple tiara, and distribute crowns, placing them on with the hand, and overturning them with the foot? Who was it released a whole kingdom from its oath of fealty to the monarch? Who was it sent a pretender to possess himself of the crown of the dethroned king? Who was it changed a dynasty, and transformed a mayor of the palace into an usurping ruler, in order to make of the legitimate prince a cloistered monk? Was it Luther? was it Calvin? or is this enough in your eyes to make a wise and profound distinction between things temporal and things spiritual?

We allow that during the sixteenth century our reformers, still imbued with your Roman ecclesiasticism, did not sufficiently resist those tendencies which induced princes to maintain state religions; but, since the Reformation has followed its natural course, it is on its side, not on yours, that the powers are divided.

Look at the United States, where the reciprocal independence of both powers is so complete, that no one single form of worship, not one single ecclesiastic, is supported by government; look at England, where half the Protestants are Dissenters, and actually struggle on behalf of the Catholics; look at France, where Protestant chapels are increasing every day, and may be found wherever the national church exists; look at Belgium, where the evangelical communities had an opportunity of joining the State Church, but declined the faith. Of course, you can hold up to our view the national churches of England, Prussia, and Sweden; but you must acknowledge at the same time that these are only remains of Romanism, diminishing every day. Show us, if you can, a Roman Catholic church which would refuse an income from the government, as we have pointed out to you Protestant congregations declining every yoke and every pay granted by the political Budget. Why, your own Irish fellow religionists have gladly received an endowment for Maynooth, for the National Board, and for some of their priests. Whenever she can, your Church unites herself with the secular power; she offers to political rulers her services, in return for their protection; she even makes her own conditions as she formerly did in France. As soon as you can adduce a Roman Catholic congregation proclaiming itself a free church like that of Scotland, or of the Canton de Vaud, then we shall begin to think that you desire a separation of the two powers, and that you have confidence in your cause. Until such an event comes to pass, allow us to say that Protestantism alone favours and realises liberty of conscience.

But to proceed. After having accused Protestantism of bringing about the union between the temporal and the spiritual powers, M. Nicolas goes still farther, and says: " Protestantism began not by being persecuted, but by persecuting. I do not speak of what Protestantism has done since, but of what it did before its progress was stopped in France [1]. "

In accordance with this affirmation, you will doubtless imagine that M. Nicolas is going to tell you of some grand massacre done by the Reformers, or of some Bartholomew's Day contrived by the Protestant party! No such thing. After having made a statement concerning the French Huguenots, he passes on, without transition, to Denmark, Norway, and Ireland. Further on, he quotes an author who declares that the French Protestants were desirous of becoming stronger, in order to enjoy religious liberty in all its fullness; and that they assemble together for the purpose both of defending themselves and of assaulting others [2]. "

Such, then, is the crime of the Protestants of France: They wished for "full religious liberty; they wished to defend themselves, and even to assault others!" But where do you see persecution in this? Would you have been more pleased at seing them refuse religious freedom, and oppose no resistance to the attacks directed against them?

Doubtless, we disapprove as much as you do the political position assumed by the French Protestants of that age, the fortified towns they insisted upon holding as a pledge for the execution of treaties, etc., etc. But you must allow that before coming to such a state of things they " had been *first* attacked, persecuted," by executioners "who dreaded to be their victims." According to your own avowal in p. 449, this is the best answer we can oppose to your accusation in p. 459. This answer is yours; this *first* was penned by yourself, M. Nicolas; and we would ask you how you reconcile these words, "The Protestants were first persecuted," with these: " Protestantism in the *first place* was not persecuted?" Then, if as you say " you do not speak of what Protestantism has done since," you thereby agree that the Protestants were persecuted neither first

1. Nicolas, p. 359. — 2. *Idem*, pp. 460 and 461.

nor last. During the course of your persecutions they defended themselves. That is their crime. What the French Protestants required, previously to your attacks, previously to the resistance they were obliged to offer, was the liberty of worshipping God according to their conscience; and as, instead of allowing them to do so quietly, you deprived them of their goods, you threw them into prison, you banished them, you burned them at the stake, then, and not till then, their children had the boldness to escape from your bad treatment. Such is the extent of the persecution they contrived! And this is so true that you cannot quote a single instance where the French Protestants have persecuted the Catholics!

Now comes the question of the religious wars of the sixteenth century, the establishment of Protestantism in Germany, England, and elsewhere. Here the Catholics accuse the Protestants, and *vice versâ*. We will not enter upon this interminable dispute, because we are speaking not of *then*, but of *now;* in the sixteenth century the Reformation had not yet produced all its fruits; the Protestant populations were still half Roman Catholic. In order to understand what Protestantism is now doing, we must study how it has acted upon the communities which it has been leavening for the last three hundred years; we must study the states, the institutions, the men who are under our own eyes. This will be an easier task than the survey of the men, the institutions, and the states that have vanished three centuries ago! We will not return to this subject, but leave unnoticed the insults to which our reformers have been falsely exposed, though it would be a very easy matter for us to retort upon our adversaries!

As to the present time, besides, the only epoch of which we desire to speak, M. Nicolas admits that we are right. "I do not examine," says he, "what Protestantism has done *since.*" Of course not; because you would be compelled to bear a favourable testimony.

After having asserted, without either fact or proof, that Protestantism is intolerant, M. Nicolas is about to prove Catholic toleration, but his case appears so bad that he feels obliged, first of all, to apologise for certain peccadilloes, such for instance as Saint Bartholomew's Day: "It would be almost useless," he says, "to assert that neither religion, nor the church have ever dictated or approved the crime of Saint Bartholomew's Day. And yet an insinuation such as this has been grounded upon the satisfaction with which the news was received at Rome, and upon the fact of the *Te Deum* which Pope Gregory XIII ordered to be sung on the occasion. . . . . The suppression of an impending conspiracy, the deliverance of the king and kingdom from the massacre to which this conspiracy would have led : such was the circumstance the Court of Rome intended to celebrate, and did celebrate. This sentiment was surely, I will not say excusable but lawful; and yet, in the midst of the thanks it inspired, the features of one man appeared sorrowful, tears suffused his eyes; his lips, under the influence of tenderness and pity, ceased not to repeat these words, which the injustice of our adversaries has left us the honour of preserving and quoting : '*Who shall assure me that a great number of innocent people may not have perished?*' These paternal words, these paternal tears, were the words and the tears of Gregory XIII [1]."

To the Pope's words, to his tears, we will only oppose one fact—a medal struck by the same Pope. Gregory XIII, who wept for the innocent Huguenots, caused the words "The Massacre of the Huguenots," to be engraved on brass; and, as if to rectify this event, he had his own effigy placed at the back of the inscription. Do you doubt the existence of this medal? Here is a copy; the original is in our possession; it will moreover be found reproduced in the work of the Jesuit Bonanni, printed at Rome at 1699, and deposited in the Imperial Library at Paris.

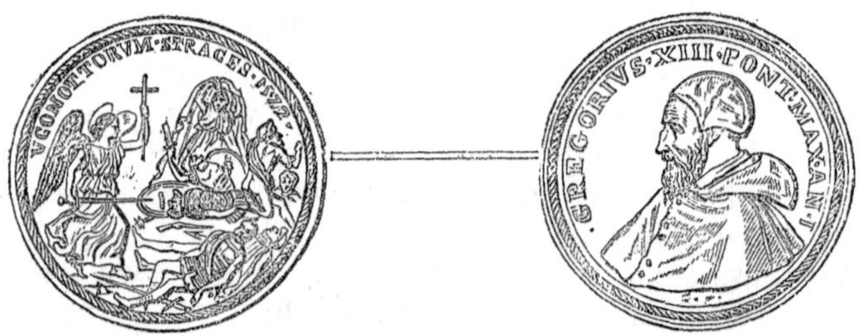

But an idea strikes us, which may perhaps explain both the Pope's tears and his medal. The innocents whom Gregory XIII mourned for, were they not, perchance, some of the Roman Catholic executioners? Joy was for the slaughtered Huguenots, and the tears for their unfortunate executioners. The medal is there, at any rate; and it proves that the Pope did not mourn over those whom his elder son had slain.

Now, as the Pope stands cleared of the crime perpetrated on St. Bartholomew's Day, the next thing was to acquit Bossuet, and even Louis XIV, of the *Dragonnades* and the persecutions. M. Nicolas, therefore, makes us notice that, "thanks to the influence of

1. Nicolas, pp. 465 and 466.

the Bishop of Meaux, the king's message to the *intendants* and his letter to the bishops allowed the Protestants a free return in France, with restitution of their property to them, provided only they *would consent to receive instruction.* No compulsory period was assigned to them to state the result of *the catechising* they had received[1]."

Is it seriously that a man can write such things? . . . . But let us examine the arguments he gives, and judge for ourselves.

In the first place, if his Majesty condescended to recall the Protestants, it must have been because he had begun by expelling them. This does not prove the toleration of the Romish Church. We note, in the second place, that the Protestants are likewise led to hope for the restitution of their property; this property must, consequently, have been taken away from them, and unjustly so; for we have never heard of persons restoring back what they had a right to take. Never mind, however; such deeds are of no consequence when Protestants must be persecuted! What we wish to insist upon here, in order to show the strength of M. Nicolas's arguments, is, the meekness displayed both by the king and by the bishop. They consent to allow a man's return, and to restore him to his property, provided he will consent to receive instruction for the purpose of becoming a Catholic. The time of his conversion is not fixed, certainly; but it must be some time or other; for you would not imply, would you, that the catechumen might remain such till the day of his death! As well receive him unconditionally. We see, then, the extreme gentleness of Roman Catholicism: we forgive you, provided you become one of our party; you are at liberty to be instructed, provided your instruction infallibly ends in your acknowledging our infallibility. But this is downright mockery; and we have not the courage to proceed.

M. Nicolas at length designs to examine modern times, in order that he may make manifest the intolerance of Protestant countries: "In most nations belonging to the Reformed faith, the Roman Catholics at the present day are still reduced to hope for an Edict of Nantes[2]."

A phrase like this will produce a certain effect upon a person who has not a clear idea of the edict in question, and who is perhaps in the dark as to the legislation of Protestant States now-a-days; but this effect speedily vanishes away when an attempt is made to dispel the obscurity which surrounds the whole point.

1. Nicolas, p. 475. — 2. *Idem*, p. 480.

The Edict of Nantes may be summed up in a few words: liberty of religious worship, and restricted admission of the Protestants to the dispensing of civil and criminal justice, both rights being secured by *guarantees*. Are these important privileges refused, in our own days, to the Catholics of England, the United States, Prussia, Holland, Sweden, and Denmark? No; in all Protestant countries the Roman Catholics enjoy the liberty of worship. Everywhere they may fill not only magisterial but even political offices. To recall merely well-known facts, who does not know that O'Connell was a member of the British Parliament? Who has forgotten that a Roman Catholic archbishop for a long time annoyed the Prussian Government on the subject of mixed marriages? Who has not lately read in the newspapers that a *concordat* now exists between the Pope and Holland? Let our opponents name one Protestant country, a single one, in which the religious worship of the Roman Catholics is impeded as that of the Protestant is at Rome, Naples, Florence, Milan, Madrid, Lisbon — where the law forbids their discharging any civic functions; then we shall acknowledge ourselves to be defeated. But, as long as we are taunted merely with statements unsupported by either proofs or facts, we must beg leave to adhere to our own opinion.

Since M. Nicolas here enters upon the question of religious liberty, which did not properly belong to the design of this work, we shall answer him by giving a statistical account of this liberty throughout all the nations of Europe, both Protestant and Roman Catholic: the sketch we are about to quote, recently drawn up and admirably executed, will show at last on what side religious liberty is to be found.

The author of this paper — our extract must be an abridged one — attempts to compare from the stand-point of toleration the Roman Catholic and the Protestant countries. He begins by a review of the former, as follows:

"Since, then, the convulsions of Europe belong to the history of politics, the struggle of the spirit of tolerance has become one of opinion and moral force. The idea re-discovered in the Reformation — the right to think and to differ — gradually spreads, and penetrates through the bigotry of the most despotic states, despite the vain efforts of tyrants to prevent the free development of thought. The great landmarks have remained; changes have been wrought, but imperceptibly, not by striking epochs. Protestantism no longer struggles for life, and therefore more calmly diffuses its principles, and improves its example. In nearly every country we may trace some progress towards liberality, yet we cannot but be surprised how so much stagnation should have been preserved in so many states, amid the downfall of ancient theories, the change, the tumult, and collision of modern ideas.

"It is a hopeful prospect for the rest of Europe to look on BELGIUM, with its richly cultured plains, its populous cities, and thriving manufactures, and see that the elements of progress and liberality are attainable in a Roman Catholic country. It is, however, an instance that their rulers are not likely to originate these new modes of thought, and that such must be in a manner forced upon their acceptance. We should not forget that Belgium was for ages under the rule of a Protestant government, and of one which employed its ascendant power but to confer a perfect religious equality on the less powerful sect. The Belgians were Roman Catholics, but the Netherlands were Protestant; and perhaps no more striking proof of the leniency of their rule can be adduced, than that the Pope condescended to make a *concordat* with the Protestant William I in 1827, and that the latter made such concessions as satisfied his Holiness. The constitution was thus established, the laws framed — nay, even the *concordat* with the Pope ready made — and when the Revolution of 1830 tore the kingdom into two separate states, Belgium had not the credit of devising a new system; it but continued in a separate form that which it had enjoyed while united with Holland. Perhaps, therefore, we should rather set down its liberality to the credit of Protestantism, which was undoubtedly its creating cause, or at least to the popular generosity, which accepted and prolonged its results. Indeed, the only efforts of their clergy since then have uniformly been to restore the reign of intolerance; and here, as in every other part of the world, they have put forward the most arrogant claims to the exclusive control of the public education[1]. With all its backsliding, would that the rest of Europe could learn the same lessons as Belgium, and in a similar school!

"Of FRANCE we need not say much; it is ever in a transition state, never permanent; our criticism may be that of a by-gone era ere it meet the public eye. Under the semblance of universal toleration, in the frenzy of democratic equality, its first revolution annihilated all religion, and refused to tolerate any. The restoration of any one could hardly, after this, be exclusive, though we fear indiffer-

1. See the public letter of the Archbishop of Malines to his clergy, in November 1851, desiring them not to celebrate masses for any colleges or schools "not under the authority or control of the local priest!"

ence or atheism had more to do with such liberality than enlarged views or nobler sentiments of charity. France has now, however, on more rational grounds, confirmed that tolerance, and is therefore entitled still to rank as a tolerant nation; though its descent to a very opposite system seems likely to be as rapid as has been its progress to despotism. The political influence of the clergy was bargained for; the clergy bought the imperial recognition of their religion. They have kept their part of the contract, and have helped to establish imperial authority. Who can limit the return they may now exact? It will require great concessions to atone for the flattery they did their conscience the violence of listening to without rebuke, for the profane addresses they did not oppose, for the episcopal benedictions bestowed upon this great 'man of God[1].' Accordingly, without any repeal of fundamental laws, we already find Protestantism effectually discouraged, its publications prohibited, and its schools, under various pretexts, successively suppressed — results that flow from the ascendancy of the ultramontane clergy, but that are combated by those Roman Catholics, who remember that their forefathers manfully shook off the papal yoke, without abandoning their creed, in the famous declaration of the 'Gallican liberties.' Never, perhaps, was the struggle more fiercely carried on in the bosom of the church than at this very moment.

"Not dissimilar is the story of AUSTRIA. For ages the centre of despotism and persecution, the whole fabric of its ancient policy was torn down by the sudden violence of a popular outburst, and the imperial dynasty was only saved, amid the convulsions of 1848, by a timely abdication, with the pledge of a free constitution at the hands of their young monarch. The constitution of 1849, accordingly, promised much, and has accomplished nothing. It stifled the popular movement for redress of grievances, and gave the Emperor power to gradually nullify its provisions, and finally, despite his solemn pledge to uphold it, to formally repeal it by his *ipse dixit*[2]. One of its advances in liberality had been to permit the public profession of the Protestant, as well as of the established faith, though the same liberty was not conceded to any other forms

1. See, amongst others, the Bishop of Chalons' address to his clergy, in September last. "May he be blessed, this man of God, this great man, for it is God who has raised him up for the happiness of our country, to cure all the wounds which sixty years of revolutions had inflicted! Once more may he be blessed." This may be simple hyperbole, but the address presented in the department of the Hérault was an outrage on religious feeling that should have been sternly rebuked by any who professed to be the ministers of religion. — 2. The constitution of March, 1849, was formally annulled by a series of Imperial decrees published on the 1st of January, 1852.

of belief. These concessions are supposed still to remain, but they may be swept away any hour by the same breath that annihilated the hopes of political freedom. Meanwhile, toleration exists nominally, but little more than nominally. All religious meetings require the sanction of the police, and those who know how effectually, by petty delays and difficulties, they can prevent anything they do not wish, without appearing to prohibit it, will see that laws are of very little consequence. The executive is everything; it makes the laws, and enforces them as it pleases. In inquiring into the condition of such a state, therefore, we should ask, not what is the constitutional statute, but what is the private feeling of him who makes and unmakes statutes and constitutions. That this is rapidly reactionary is plain enough. The formal restraints on the publication of papal bulls, adhered to with strict firmness, as a necessary safeguard to themselves by other Roman Catholic States, have been abandoned; those who presumed to publish or propagate the Bible have been banished at the instigation of the clergy; the haughty demands of the episcopal assembly have been acquiesced in. 'The Catholic Church can never, and *nowhere*, renounce her claim upon the exercise of a decisive influence on religious instruction;' and again, in reference to the popular schools[1], 'the Catholic Church does not claim the right to the religious instruction of the Catholic youth alone, she is appointed by God to educate *mankind* for eternal life.' True, there is still the possibility of other schools, but their certificates of education are valueless in a country where, without such certificates, no promotion or occupation is permitted. Though, therefore, we now charitably class the Austrian Government among those that profess to be tolerant — even the affectation of virtue is a homage to its merit — but a little further progress in its present direction will suffice to change the verdict.

"A moment we may pause in BAVARIA, ere we bid adieu to the fairer specimens of Roman Catholic liberality. Here we find the same extent of religious freedom that pervades the rest of Germany. Surrounded by free Protestant states, and, like many of these minor principalities, very roughly treated in the convulsions of Europe — their kings bundled in and out, and their territories sliced, to suit the public convenience — it would be strange, indeed, if it alone had opposed the current of feeling in the grand confederation of which it is a part. Still it has a right to its distinct laws, and to

1. See the report drawn up by Count Thun, the Minister of Public Worship and Education, April 13th, 1850, and approved by the Emperor.

its own expression of opinion, and must receive its due merit for having adopted the religious freedom of its neighbours[1].

"The scene now changes, and we commence the dreary catalogue of intolerance. Nor yet shall we plunge at once into its thickest darkness, but accustom our eyes to the gathering gloom by the least startling transition we can find. In PORTUGAL, men can now *think* as they please, provided they do not dare to speak lightly of Roman Catholic dogmas, or to impugn their truth, and, at least, they are no longer dragged before the terrible inquisition; nay, they may worship God as they think right, if they take care to do so at home, and not to offend the public eye by allowing it to observe their rebellious deviations from established orthodoxy. This, too, is something by comparison, as we shall see anon, though, despite of this concession, we must set down Portugal in the list of intolerants; it cannot stand the simple test—public worship is prohibited, the public expression of opinion is criminal.

"About SPAIN there is no doubt. But one religion is professed, and none other is permitted in any shape. To be a Spaniard, implies necessarily to be a Roman Catholic. He who dares to forsake that faith is banished by law, lest the poison of his heresy should spread contagion; while those who may have tempted him from his faith are liable to the mild punishment of five or seven years' imprisonment. Hitherto, the mere traveller or foreigner was looked on as a necessary exception, as a passing evil that could not be avoided; now, by the decree of November 17, 1852, he must bury his thoughts within his bosom, and give no evidence of his dissent; he is no longer permitted to '*profess* any but the Catholic religion.' It is true that diplomacy, with its dexterous mystery, has stated that this will not affect English travellers, but it is a plain outrage on all notions of national honour or generosity, and, even if not enforced, it will be but a symptom of our strength and of Spain's weakness. Thus, he who has most freedom there, the English stranger, must, while living, hide his creed, and when dead he must be satisfied to have his corpse hurried obscurely to the cemetery which treaty alone has secured for him; but if he would have the prayer or forms of his religion to hallow his tomb, his friends must choose some secret hour or opportunity, when the crime of performing such a service will be connived at, because of its secrecy! We shall see much more savage intolerance

1. Bohemia is not entitled to be considered as a separate kingdom, at least for the purposes of our present argument. It is so completely incorporated with Austria, as to be incapable of forming a separate or independent opinion. Its decision on the subject of tolerance is not its own, and only follows the dictates of its imperial master at Vienna.

elsewhere, but very little so despicable and so ungenerous as this.

"And now we have reached the mighty ALPS—the barrier that has so often turned back the tide of papal usurpation, and separated ultramontane arrogance from the struggle long waged by Roman Catholics themselves against complete mental slavery; and now we look down on the rich plains of Italy — beautiful, unfortunate, and degraded! Let us descend into SARDINIA, where the new-born aspirations for freedom threaten to shake the peninsula by the presence of an idea so novel and so formidable. But the movement towards freedom must not be mistaken for its accomplishment. Public feeling is here allowed to find expression in the press, and thus controls the operation of unjust laws; the executive abhors the principles of enactments, which yet it has not had the courage to repeal; it is a mistake to suppose that toleration is yet the rule — it is the exception to the constitution; they chafe under the yoke, but have not yet flung it off. 'Sono schiavi, ma schiavi ognor frementi!'

"The despatch from the Chevalier Azeglio to Sir R. Abercrombie, of Sept. 30, 1851, perhaps fairly states the present transition state of the laws. The Vaudois Protestants have been allowed to build a church in Turin, but the intolerant laws with reference to these subjects of the state 'have not been expressly abolished.' He intimates an opinion that other Protestants would be allowed to perform their worship, 'if it did not take place with such external circumstances as should offend the Catholic faith,' in other words, if it were private and unobserved. In exact accordance with this view is the conduct of the government. In the recent prosecutions for heresy, the victims[1] were saved, not by the laws of the country, or its judicial decision, but by the Minister of Justice extending to them the royal pardon, for what he admitted to be still a legal crime. The general opinion of the liberality of Sardinia is drawn from the expression of public feeling that wrung this and similar concessions from the laws, and that replaced the Professor Nuytz in his professor's chair, when condemned by a papal bull,[2] for questioning the most objectionable dogmas of the pontifical canons; but the laws still provide that, 'in accordance with the sacred canons,' the secular aid should be ever extended to execute the ecclesiastical sentence; that in cases of 'suspicion of heresy and blasphemy' — and we know that reading the Word of God some-

1. One of these, however, Mazzinghi, was first pardoned, and then banished. — 2. This was in December, 1851. The Sardinian minister protested against the reception of this bull.

times falls under this definition — the civil power should give exclusive jurisdiction to the ecclesiastical; that this latter should, indeed, have its own ministers for enforcing its proceedings, but that, the sentence once pronounced, the culprit should be handed to the State, to inflict the sentence their Christian mercy has awarded. Such, it should be noted, has ever been the system, except in the case of the Inquisition, which scoffed at pity or decency, and outraged every feeling of humanity; bigotry has always had the tact to make the state its executioner. Of old, it organised a war of extermination, or sent forth a holy military order; in later days, it never wields the sword or the axe, but it often brings those who incur its anger to suffer under the arm of the civil law the chastisement it cannot itself administer. The same effect is produced, and the odium falls on the despotism, rather than on its cause. Yet, with all its failings, its yet undeveloped hopes, would that we had more countries as promising as Sardinia.

" TUSCANY and NAPLES have been so oft discussed and exposed of late, that we need not expose them again. The one is notorious, and the other despicable in its intolerance. Tuscany we may shortly describe, in the words of a despatch of its minister[1] — ' the canon law forms a part of its legislative code! ' What more can we add? It is true the Leopoldine law of 1782 abolished the Inquisition, as they would an acknowledged bore or a public nuisance, but they did little more. Nor let it be imagined, as has been ignorantly put forward in the House of Commons [2], that these laws were framed in a spirit of hostility to the Roman Catholic Church; they cannot possibly be so considered, unless the speakers, who made this crude assertion, choose to identify their Church with the maintenance of the Inquisition. It was against this latter alone that they were aimed, and they certainly left ample powers of persecution to satisfy the most intolerant[3]. "

1. Despatch from the Duke of Carigliano to the Hon. P. C. Scarlett, September 25, 1851. In this he takes care to point out that the privileges granted " to enrich the commerce of the town of Leghorn," as well as the narrow connivance at the service of their rich English visitors, should be considered as distinct " exceptional cases, " and not as any deviation in principle from the established rule. — 2. See debate of February 17. — 3. The last rule is worth recording. " That the usurped right of taking cognisance in causes of religious faith be henceforward *restored* to the various bishops; and that the proceedings in such causes shall in no way differ from those of right, observed in every other *ecclesiastical criminal cause.*

" We will, and do trust, that the bishops will voluntarily make it a law, to have present in their minds, that the publicity of a trial and condemnation often produces greater scandal than even the transitory error it is intended to correct; that the admonitions, exhortations, and every thing which charity, such as it is incumbent on them to profess for an example to others can suggest, tend far more effectually to correct the guilty, and edify the rest; but that whenever the circumstances of the case shall be such as to demand *rigour and the assistance of the secular arm* — provided always it be proved to us that the adoption of the abovementioned means have not succeeded — *we shall think it our duty to grant it.*"

Despite this little lecture on " charity, " there seems here very slight appearance of the abolition of coercion.

"The mild spirit of Leopold for some time animated the administration, but that, too, has perished, and his laws have been abolished. The last two years attest the change and prove its severity. The journals have furnished a catalogue of martyrs of oppression; need we recal the names of the Count Guicciardini and his six companions, or of Savi, Byche, Madiai and his wife; Manelli, Fantoni, Pasquale, Casacci, and more recently Guarducci? Some have been fortunate enough to escape with banishment; others have been consigned to the living tomb of an Italian dungeon. Those who have seen their horrors could well imagine a brave man being less daunted by the quick and sharp penalty of death, than by so lingering and revolting a doom.

"It is in vain to palliate these cases by seeking to give them a political aspect, or by calling them civil offences! They are only one or the other, in so far as ecclesiastical censures consign them to the 'rigour of the secular arm.' We have only to read the officially published acts of accusation and conviction to see that it is for religious belief, exercised and discussed only within their own houses, that they now suffer. It is for this reason that the British public selected the Madiai case for the expression of their indignant sympathy. Many others occur from time to time, but they are usually complicated with circumstances that create a difficulty in separating political punishment from religious persecution. It would be unbecoming in us to interfere if the government of a foreign state were to tell us that the accused was arraigned for an offence nowise connected with his religious belief. Here, fortunately, the Tuscan executive has removed all such scruples of delicacy, by placing us in possession of its official details. It was a plain, avowed case of religious persecution, and none seek to fritter away this obvious conclusion, who do not make us at heart suspect their sympathy with such intolerance when exerted against their opponents. Indeed the termination proves the conscious guilt of their persecutors. Had there been any defensible grounds for vindicating the punishment, they would never have released them; but they tardily yielded to the overwhelming cry of shame, smuggled forth their victims from the dungeon, and hurried them from their dominions, reft of all but life.

"And Naples, too, with its glorious forms of nature's beauty, and its ever-smoking volcano — symbol of the earthquake that lurks beneath the now still peninsula — Naples has, in days of yore, coped with the haughty pontiffs of Rome, rejected the greater portion of the decrees of the famed Council of Trent, and proudly trampled upon papal bulls. Those days are gone; and now its government, at once imbecile and violent, bigoted and profligate, lends the swords of its venal army to wreak on its own citizens the bidding of Rome. Its people violate every precept of morality, and observe every ceremonial of religion. Ignorant of the meaning of freedom, they possess it not themselves—they seek not to accord it to others. They are, indeed, steeped in the servitude of intolerance, without alleviation and without hope.

"Thus have we at length penetrated to the great centre of Roman Catholic teaching, and next find ourselves in ROME; before us the majestic temple of the tutelary Apostle; on the right the pomp of the Vatican; on the left the palace of the Inquisition. The emblem of heaven's religion, the pride of earthly power, and the monument of man's unhallowed passions, are thus strangely grouped together. If others have admitted unjustifiable papal claims — if other countries have harboured the Inquisition, or sanctioned the canon law, it was from here that the haughty thunders were launched — here was the organisation framed, and here grew that unscrupulous code. Others may faintly deny the imputation — may admit part, and explain away more; here there is no evasion; the canon law is proclaimed an inwrought portion of the constitution.

Intolerance reigns supreme. Here it had its birth, and here it has made its throne.

"Rome, unfortunately, prides itself on its immutability in doctrine, and is prone to apply it to what it was never meant to refer; and thus, in its temporal claims and temporal rules, it only means obstinate adherence to error, and an incapacity to adopt improvement. The Vatican fulminates at once against the unfortunate professor at Turin. Does Spain relapse into the intolerance of by-gone centuries? The Pope, in a studied allocution, congratulates Christendom on so glorious an advance in its Christianity. Across the Atlantic, the state of New Granada sets a noble example in conceding what, for the ideas of these regions, was an unwonted freedom in education, in the press, and in the exercise of religion. Another allocution, not yet six months' old, condemns such fearful approaches to hated liberty, and it is denounced as 'a horrible and sacrilegious war against the Catholic Church.' But the remedy is at hand. No subjects should obey the state when it displeases the Church, and therefore they are stimulated to a holy rebellion against their rulers. 'We, raising with apostolic liberty our pastoral voice, do censure, condemn, and *declare utterly null and void* all the aforesaid decrees, which have been there enacted by the civil power.'

"But we must not forget that civilisation claims another quarter of the globe. The story of American tolerance is briefly told. NEW GRANADA we have just mentioned as having excited the papal indignation, and, therefore, we may safely class it as tolerant, or meaning to be so, though its efforts are, perhaps, very much below what would entitle it to the name in Europe. The same glory we willingly give to the unostentatious republic of VENEZUELA. The remaining Roman Catholic states we may group together into those that are intolerant, and those that are so exclusively intolerant as not only to prohibit the public worship, but even the *private* profession of any but the one religion. In the former we may place BUENOS AYRES, and the federal republic of CENTRAL AMERICA, since 1832[1]; and in the latter we may class BOLIVIA, CHILI, EQUADOR, MEXICO, PERU, and URUQUAY. All these vast tracts were once the seats of European greatness across the Atlantic; now they have sunk into stagnant decrepitude, beside the wondrous growth of the mighty nations that have been raised by the Saxon and the Celt; the spirit of freedom has prospered, while bigotry and servitude have wrought decay.

"Call this, then, tolerance, and what is the general result? Out of *twenty-two* Roman Catholic states, there are just *seven* tolerant, or less than *one-third*. But what is still more striking is, that out of the fifteen intolerant, there are no less than *ten* that are *absolutely and exclusively so*. This is the most remarkable feature, as we shall see when we institute a like examination into the Protestant states of the world.

"Our induction, however, would be but half complete were we to pause here; we must finish our panoramic view by glancing also at the position of intolerance in Protestant countries.

"We shall commence with SWEDEN and NORWAY, which have of late been much cited as a triumphant answer to the claims Protestantism puts forward of being the ally of toleration. How far its exceptional case alters the general argument, we shall not see till we come to cast up results; meanwhile we shall not spare its violations of Protestant principles, though we shall also do what has not yet been fairly done—place the actual facts, the real extent of its delinquency, before the public. Of Norway we may very briefly dispose,

1. Until 1832 it was exclusively intolerant. It now consists of five states, united under one federal government, but differing somewhat in laws as well as in their degrees of intolerance. Our judgment may be taken as a fair average.

as it is now under precisely the same laws, in this respect, as Sweden. Formally united to it in 1814, it for long retained its own constitution, and the complete absence of any dissentient religious sect left legislation on the subject a matter of unimportance. Even now there are scarcely 500 who are not members of the Established Church. When attention was at length called to the subject, a resolution of March 6, 1843, gave liberty to Roman Catholics to establish a church, and perform public worship; and this edict was confirmed, and made general for the benefit of all dissenters, on the 16th of July, 1845.

"Now, we have no wish to palliate such narrow bigotry as still lingers in these Scandinavian regions; but it is fair to know precisely what should be the extent of our condemnation. It has been asserted, that this is a parallel case for Spain, Tuscany, or Rome. A moment's examination will show that it does not, in the slightest degree, approach their exclusive intolerance, nor even that of other countries, such as Portugal, which have made comparative advances in liberality. The laws still in operation were promulgated on the 24th of January, 1781, by Gustavus III, and profess to establish 'a free and unconstrained exercise of religion, and a perfect liberty of conscience.' Even this declaration, however imperfectly carried out in practice, is a tribute to the truth of the general principle, and at once distinguishes the state that professes it from those that explicitly repudiate it. The acknowledgment of what is right is the first step, and a necessary condition to its practice.

"We find that there is perfect freedom to each one to *continue* in his own religious opinions; full liberty to construct as many churches as may be required, to appoint and maintain proper ecclesiastics, to perform every act of public worship within the appropriated precincts, but avoiding public processions in the streets (ceremonies that cannot be said to be a necessary part of their ritual, and that might naturally lead to angry collisions with the majority) the right of endowing schools for the instruction of their members in their own religion, and of sending teachers for the same purpose where no schools exist. No one of the dominant religion is permitted to ridicule the Roman Catholic doctrines, under a penalty of from ten to fifty dollars, and any one who interrupts their service is liable to a fine of twenty-five dollars. No Lutheran clergyman is allowed, under severe penalties, to intrude on any but his own flock, or to force his services where not required.

"The plain, insurmountable charge against Sweden is, that it will allow no man to *change* his religion, except for Sthat of the ate.

To no other will it permit any efforts to spread its tenets. No Lutheran can attend any service but his own, without being subject to a fine of ten dollars; those who attempt his conversion are fineable to the extent of 100 dollars, and should their efforts be successful, he is subject to banishment, or confiscation of his property.

"Having said thus much, we have said all, and unhesitatingly denounce so timid, narrow, and un-Protestant a policy. It will, however, at once be plain, that this forms no set-off to the darkness of Italy; in contrast with it, it is actually light. Can Italian Protestants establish public churches, endow schools or clergy for teaching their children the Bible? or are their opinions protected from insult or oppression? This one question shatters at once the fancied parallel.

"And now our task is nearly done. We have visited Protestant Sweden with a severity that Roman Catholic Austria could not have stood, had we applied as severe a test; henceforth we shall have little more than to complete our catalogue, marking, perhaps, any striking differences in the degree of toleration afforded, but finding none that do not more than satisfy our definition.

"As the most antiquated and the least progressive, we may commence with DENMARK. Here it is only of late years that the universal exercise of religion has been made a fundamental law; previously the Roman Catholics (who, however, number but 2,500) had been restricted in their places of worship; at present, they possess all they are able to maintain in Copenhagen, Fredericia, Frederichstadt, Altona, and Kiel.

"The NETHERLANDS may be briefly and satisfactorily dismissed. Leo XII condescended to the very unusual course of making a *concordat* with the Protestant King, William I[1], for the government of the Roman Catholic Church. This is a very unusual proceeding with a heretic prince, and argues the belief of the Vatican, that it had to deal with a government of no ordinary liberality. The internuncio at the Hague is also head of the Papal Church in Holland, and as such receives a pension from the state. It has even been formally announced, that it is the intention of the Vatican to establish an organised Roman Catholic hierarchy there; perhaps to prove to the world that Holland is on the point of being converted, but with about as much truth as if a sudden importation of coffins were to be made, to persuade the sturdy inhabitants that they were all inevitably dead men.

1. See the correspondence in *Tablet*, of June 18, 1827, with the Protestant Alliance.

"We may take our testimony in favour of PRUSSIA from the papal bull of August, 1822, known as *De Salute*, which regulates the Roman Catholic Church. We shall only add, that the correspondence of religious communities with Rome had been then subjected to the state regulations that are ordinarily imposed in Roman Catholic countries, and to no other, and that even these have been removed by an article in the constitution of January, 1850. The followers of the Pope can hardly complain, when he is compelled formally to announce, as the result of his 'efforts to preserve the Catholic faith' — 'Our wishes in this respect have been greatly seconded by the aforesaid King of Prussia, whom we have found, and gratefully acknowledge, to be animated by the most benevolent wishes towards his very numerous Catholic subjects; so that at length we are able to bring everything to a happy and prosperous conclusion, and we can constitute the churches anew, and divide the dioceses, and provide all places that require it with their own fit and worthy pastors.'

"HANOVER we cannot pass without noticing a curious incident in its dealing with the papal hierarchy within its realm. These are regulated by a bull, issued March 26, 1824, which divided this country, where they could have but one-ninth of the population under their spiritual direction, into episcopal dioceses, with much the same *sang-froid* with which England was recently similarly parcelled out. To this bull our own sovereign, then also King of Hanover, gave his royal sanction; but we should add, that his sanction was sued for *before* the bull was published.

"The kingdoms of WURTEMBERG and SAXONY are the only other states of the German Confederation that we mention apart from the whole of Germany. In both nearly equally complete toleration exists. In the former, where education is very much advanced and very generally diffused, the striking feature is the number of Roman Catholic schools. In the latter the reigning family is Roman Catholic, although there are not 30,000 of that persuasion out of a population of more than 1,600,000. Both, however, are on an equal footing, not only as to religious but as to civil rights, both have members in the Diet. It is true there are limitations as to conversions from one religion to another, but these are perfectly mutual, and are adopted by both — whether wisely or not — as safeguards against fraud, not as restraints upon convictions [1]. Thus,

1. These are prescribed by a mandate of Frederick Augustus, dated January 20, 1827.

after the age of twenty-one, no one can be prevented from changing his religion; he must, however, give notice to the clergyman of the persuasion to which he has hitherto belonged, and must continue four weeks before taking the final formal step. All improper inducements to proselytism, whether by bribes or intimidation, are severely punishable.

"Of what remains of GERMANY — that great centre of the intellectual activity of Europe — after deducting those greater kingdoms which are entitled to the dignity of a separate consideration, we still find no less than twenty-four independent states, each preserving its own internal laws, though portions of the one great federal alliance. In each of these it is competent to differ from its neighbours by enacting intolerant laws, and, therefore, the decision of each is a distinct expression of opinion.

"It is not our object to swell the number of Protestant tolerant states, by counting these *per capita*, as no less than twenty-two are Protestant, and but two are Roman Catholic; but it would be equally unreasonable to omit the aggregate as a unit, when it represents more than six millions of men, and conveys their decision all the more forcibly that it has been taken in detail. The degree of toleration differs in particulars, especially in the amount of civil privileges accorded to the minority; but in none is there any impediment to the free exercise of any form of the Christian religion. In Baden, where, strange to say, there is a much larger proportion of Roman Catholics than in any other state, there are some singular regulations as to convents. None are allowed to take the monastic vows for more than seven years; and a government inspector, at the appointed time, presents himself to each immate, and proffers the means of escape, should any be so inclined. Doubtless, the *power* of obtaining freedom often checks the longing that would spring up within the bosom, were it hopelessly lost for ever; and, at the same time, it must insure a management in harmony with the wishes of the immates. In some other states no new convents are allowed to be established; but it does not appear that there is any occasion for more than those that exist at present. Their ideas have not, in many respects, expanded to our latitudinarianism; but they seem to distinguish, not unreasonably, between allowing the essentials of a religion, and encouraging its ornaments or luxuries. There is also a general notion, that, as man is not to be suffered to voluntarily take away his own life, so he is not to be permitted to vow away his liberty; or, at least, the step should not be irrevocable — there should be left some *locus penitentiæ*.

"SWITZERLAND — the cradle of the Reformation, and the champion of freedom — is not without peculiarities. The general federal government has formed no regulations as to religion; each canton acts independently. Out of its twenty-two cantons, there are but seven Roman Catholic, and about four-fifths of the population are of the Reformed faith. All, however, adopted the same principles, and did not suffer religious opinions to be made any ground of disqualification. Thus they lived in harmony till about 1830, when a series of political revolutions commenced, that led to a permanent conflict of religious interests. To the intrigues of the Jesuits, who sought to abuse the liberty accorded them, by obtaining an exclusive and ascendant power, these internal dissensions were attributed. We cannot pause to discuss how far they were its sole cause; but, unquestionably, they exasperated differences, and flung themselves into the turmoil of political agitation. This led to a retaliation by the Protestant cantons, carried to an undue excess — as all popular retaliations are — and the Jesuits were expelled by force, as the *causa teterrima belli*. It should, however, be observed, that these acts had their origin in political causes, and not in any intolerant laws; and it should be remembered, that there is no Roman Catholic country that has not, at some time, been compelled to adopt the same course towards these too-active politico-ecclesiastics. Even conceding the injustice of individual acts, it is impossible to deny the perfect freedom that is allowed to the ordinary exercise of every Christian religion in Switzerland. An establishment of Jesuits can hardly be called an essential to any, after the solemn declaration of a Pope to the contrary [1].

"For a moment we must cross the Atlantic, to dismiss almost in

1. It is so common to confound the Jesuits with Roman Catholicism itself, that it is well to advert to an often-quoted document that proves the contrary—we mean the Brief of Clement XIV., July 21, 1783. Speaking of his predecessors' efforts to control the turbulence of the Jesuits, he says: — "In vain did they endeavour to restore peace to the Church, as well with regard to *secular affairs*, with which the company ought not to have interfered, as with regard to the missions which gave rise to great disputes on the part of the company with the ordinaries, with other religious orders, about holy places and communities of all sorts in Europe, Africa, and America, to the great loss of souls, and scandal of the people; as likewise concerning the practice of certain idolatrous ceremonies adopted in certain places, in contempt of those approved by the Catholic Church; and further, concerning the use of certain maxims, which the Holy See has, with reason, *proscribed as scandalous*, and manifestly contrary to good morals. . . Complaints and quarrels were multiplied on every side; in some places dangerous seditions arose, tumults, discords, scandals, which, entirely breaking the bonds of Christian charity, excited the faithful to all the rage of party hatreds and enmities. Desolation and danger grew to such a height, that the very sovereigns, whose piety and liberality towards the company were so well known as to be looked upon as hereditary—we mean our dearly beloved sons in Christ, the Kings of France, Spain, Portugal, and Sicily—found themselves reduced to the *necessity of expelling from their states* these very companions of Jesus, persuaded that this step was necessary to prevent Christians from rising against one another, and from massacring each other in the very bosom of our common mother, the Holy Church." As he appropriately concludes by abolishing and suppressing the order, we may infer that a state may amply tolerate Roman Catholics, and yet expel the Jesuits.

a sentence the mighty nation that overspreads the western world, the UNITED STATES. Neither the federal government, nor any of the individual states, permit any laws either for the encouragement or the suppression of any particular form of religion. They have cut the gordian knot of legislative difficulty, rather than arrived at its philosophical solution. It is not for us here to discuss how far a nation can abjure all national character or responsibility, and become purely a political association; it is enough to notice the fact that such is there the case. We need here only remark that the states must, undoubtedly, be classed amongst the Protestant countries. It derived the foundation of its laws from England; from thence it drew its spirit of freedom, and its religion it still retains. In a country whose growth is so rapid, it is not easy to be precise; its population changes day by day; but we may safely assume the Roman Catholics as not more than one-eighth of the entire[1].

"Were we anxious to swell an already overwhelming majority, we might fairly add Canada to the list of Protestant countries. Though but a colony, it has been entrusted with large powers of self-government; and recent legislation has placed in the power of the Assembly to deal with, as it pleases, the property held for years by the Established Church, under the name of the clergy reserves. As, however, we are determined to deal more severely with our own than with our opponents' side, we shall not press it into our ranks.

"Thus have we made the grand continental tour of Europe, and traversed the entire globe, in the effort to condense from each, into our panorama, the striking features that bear on this great question, that each day more and more agitates the heart of Europe. We have at length returned home, and find ourselves, not displeased if somewhat fatigued, in GREAT BRITAIN again. It is but a unit in the account, but one that surpasses in magnitude the aggregate of nearly all the rest. Circling the wide globe with its dependencies, embracing under its sway some portion of every quarter of the earth, its 160 millions would outnumber the inhabitants of all the states that own Roman Catholic rule[2]. Its free institutions are therefore of incalculable value to the progress of

1. This is the report of the Rev. Mr. Mullen, who was sent over last year to make a collection for the projected Newman University. He conceives that, out of more than fifteen millions, there are less than two millions of Roman Catholics. He would be more correct in making the numbers twenty-three and three millions. See *Freeman's Journal*, April 24, 1852. — 2. These do not exceed at most 150 millions. Those under Protestant laws are about 220 millions.

the human race, and its scattered possessions are centres whence a kindred spirit may diffuse itself amid surrounding oppression. It, therefore, fitly closes our list of tolerant states, and enables us to pause and view the general result.

"Out of eleven Protestant countries, we have found but *one* intolerant, and *not one* such as we have called above 'exclusively intolerant,' or wholly forbidding the profession of any but the Established religion.

"Out of twenty-two Roman Catholic, we could detect but *seven* tolerant, and there were *ten* 'exclusively intolerant.'

"Thus the in-tolerance of Protestantism is *one*-eleventh, and the toleration of Roman Catholicism is but one-third of their respective numbers; or, to reduce them to a common standard of comparison, Roman Catholic intolerance is just *thirty-three* times more general than Protestant!"

Although M. Nicolas denies the Protestants the merit of toleration, he goes so far as to allow that they profess the principle. There is, then, a chance that this principle may come into practice; whereas it is impossible that those who deny the theory should ever admit the application. Men pass away, principles remain, and that is enough for the cause we are defending. But it is curious to see how M. Nicolas turns against us the arms directed at his own church. "The intolerance of Protestantism is so much the more crying," he says, "because, different from that with which Catholicism is reproached, it is without excuse; it is quite arbitrary, and sins not only from excess, but from principle..... the intolerance of *authority* is legitimate; for whilst it does not allow of licentiousness, it secures liberty..... such intolerance has a necessary foundation, and is perfectly justifiable: such has been the intolerance of Catholicism[1]."

All this may be reduced to the following few words: "We, who have been arrogating to ourselves so much authority, cannot be intolerant, to whatever lengths we may go; but you, who depart from the principle of liberty, however slight your deviations may be in practice, they are criminal. For us, Catholics, that which we do not tolerate must necessarily be licentiousness; "our intolerance is necessary, and by our principle it is perfectly justifiable." Why, no doubt it is, since it is you who have framed both the principle and the application! That is just what we blame you for; you set up for masters, you arrogate to yourselves the right of saying: this

1. Nicolas, p. 481.

is lawful, but not that; you bestow upon yourselves an inquisitor's patent, and then naively exclaim, may we not burn you if we please? — No, you may not, and your first fault was to use that right, by claiming absolute authority.

But the conscience of M. Nicolas rises against the consequences of his theory; she obliges him to stoop from the accuser's part to that of the accused. Let us hear how he tries to prove that the Inquisition is not the work of the Roman Catholic church: "Catholicism," he says, "is not called to bear the responsibility of the Inquisition; it is not her work, it is that of Philip II, and especially of Ferdinand and Isabella. True, clerical divines took a part in this institution, and composed the tribunal, but it was for the purpose of deciding cases of heresy; somewhat after the manner of a jury, pronouncing upon the fact of culpability, without inflicting the penalty[1]."

Thus, ecclesiastics take part in the Inquisition, and make up the board; but merely to decide on cases of heresy, and not to apply the penalty. They know perfectly well that if the crime of heresy be found, an *auto-da-fé* must follow; but that goes for nothing; so much the worse for the heretic, if the law condemns sins; his reverence has merely said "you are guilty of heresy." Now we ask, which of the two is most guilty, Caiaphas or Pilate? Caiaphas saying of our Lord, He hath blasphemed, or Pilate answering, Well, crucify him yourselves? The Caiaphases of the Inquisition in fact so palpably did the duty of crucifyers that the heretic was arrested at their request, questioned by them, by them put on the rack, condemned, and finally led to torture. The character of an executioner would be honourable, we admit, in comparison with this; for an executioner is compelled to obey the orders he has received.

We shall, however, follow M. Nicolas as he passes on from tolerance to intellectual culture, and see how this new subject supplies him with an opportunity of endeavouring to prove the superiority of the Catholics over the Protestant nations.

The first, the great, we had almost said the only, fact M. Nicolas adduces to make his proposition good is the building of cathedrals! There he finds everything, the whole of the arts and sciences, from Alpha down to Omega. We do not refute his arguments, we merely note them as they occur.

The second proof M. Nicolas gives of the partiality of the Roman Catholics to the diffusion of knowledge, is the favourable manner

1. Nicolas, p. 485.

in which the Pope regarded the invention of printing. We have but one word here in answer. Since the favourable reception just now alluded to, the results of printing, as far as the pontifical states go, are only known to us by their list of forbidden books.

Here M. Nicolas turns round upon the Reformation, and affirms "that, after having sacrificed everything to the rights of private reason, Protestantism has sacrificed reason to the Scriptures, and the Scriptures to reason[1]."

What a deal of meaning in this concise sentence! In the first place, everything is annihilated by Scripture; then Scripture is annihilated by reason; finally, reason is annihilated by Scripture. In short, amongst the Protestants we find nothing but complete annihilation, darkness, and chaos!

Words! Words! Words! we refer, for facts, to the two volumes our readers have just perused.

After having made it quite clear that the breath of Protestantism extinguishes every torch, both human and divine, M. Nicolas attacks Luther, and quotes passages where the Reformer reviles, in succession, nearly every book in the Bible, beginning with the Pentateuch, going on with the Gospels, and concluding with the Revelations. We have already shown to what degree of confidence the quotations of M. Nicolas are entitled; we, then, confine ourselves to notice here a curious fact. The *Revue de Strasbourg* (January, 1853), proves that the alleged passage has been altered, and signifies nearly the contrary of what M. Nicolas undertakes to make it say. To cut the matter short, we would ask : is it likely that Luther destroyed, leaf after leaf, a book he spent years in translating; a book which was the sole foundation of his work as a reformer; a book the perusal of which he had a hundred times recommended; a book..... but we must bear in mind that we are not refuting; we are only exposing the arguments of M. Nicolas; for, in this case, to expose, is to have refuted[2].

As, when he examined the principle of toleration, so now that he is treating of intellectual culture, M. Nicolas is driven, by the very nature of things, to forsake the attack and put himself upon the defensive. Forgetting his task, viz., the demonstration that Protestantism and *obscurantism* are identical, he sets about clearing his

1. Nicolas, p. 503. — 2. If the reader will refer, not even to Luther's works, but to M. Alzog's second-hand quotations from which M. Nicolas has taken, selected, and arranged his own, he will see that the German reformer rejects only the apocrypha; if he prefers one Gospel or one Epistle to another, he really condemns neither any of the Epistles, nor any of the Gospels.

church of the crime of having condemned Galileo. Let us follow him on this ground.

" Galileo, " says he, " was not condemned as a good astronomer, but as a bad divine[1]. "

Do you not admire the power of this distinction? Why, Monsieur Nicolas, if the earth turns round the sun, it is true in theology as it is in astronomy. With respect to such a question as this, the qualities which make a good astronomer cannot produce a bad theologian. Neither Galileo nor the Bible were in error. Who, then? Merely the divines who condemned Galileo, and put upon the Word of God a wrong interpretation. Thus we see that on this point, the sole object of condemnation, Galileo was the good divine, whilst the unsound men were the inquisitors, and their president the Pope!

M. Nicolas is desirous of proving, not only that the comdemnation was just, but also that Galileo was pleased with it; and he quotes a letter of the persecuted sage, where, in the midst of equivocal phrases, torn from his as him retraction itself was by the torture, we find the following sentence, which plainly reveals the nature of his thoughts: " I have been *obliged* to retract my opinion [1]. "

What! you have the courage to quote, in defence of the judge, these words of the accused: " I have been obliged, forced, constrained, to retract my opinion? " It is a courage well worthy of the inquisitors, imposing the torture, compelling a man to say things he does not believe, and then sending him either to the dungeon or to the stake.

M. Nicolas does not seem very satisfied with his own defence of the Inquisition, for he denies the Holy Office: " The tribunal of the Holy Office," he says, " does not absolutely represent Catholicism itself. " The Inquisition, no doubt, did not constitute the whole of Catholicism; but it was its work, and that is sufficient for us to judge the workman.

After having justified Catholicism of the accusation of not favouring intellectual culture, M. Nicolas proceeds to condemn our reformers: he alludes to Luther's interview with the devil, to the ghost which appeared before Zwingle. We must be allowed to repeat what we said at the beginning: we are not sitting in judgment upon the reformers of the sixteenth century, but upon those of the nineteenth. At the same time, we shall mark here the futility of such arguments, in order to show better the weakness of the cause.

1. Nicolas, p. 508. — 2. *Idem*, p. 510.

Zwingle had, the preceding evening, a warm public discussion on the actual presence of the body and blood of Jesus Christ in the consecrated bread of the sacrament administered every day for fifteen centuries in thousands of places. He was full of his subject; he thought of it after the closing of the discussion; he thought of it in the evening, in the night, nay, in the midst of his dreams. Correct ideas mingled with strange images presented themselves to his mind. His imagination awoke in spite of the fatigue which overwhelmed his body, and supplied him with a good argument. Is there any thing astonishing in this? Has M. Nicolas never had any rational dreams even in the midst of fantastic images? And would any one think of calling him, for that reason, either a superstitious or an ignorant man? Certainly not. Well, then, apply to Zwingle the rule by which you would like to be measured yourself?

Such was Zwingle's dream, related by himself as such: "*Somnium enim narro,*" says he. Now, would you believe, M. Nicolas gives as a fact what Zwingle declares to have been a dream. "Zwingle, the father of Protestantism in Switzerland, was assisted likewise by a certain devil or spirit, either white or black, etc[1]."

I ask the reader: is it fair to present as a fact what was actually nothing but a dream? Can any one be made responsible for his dreams?

But there is something still worse in the conduct of M. Nicolas. Not only did Zwingle speak of this event as of a dream, but he never even said that a devil took part in it. This devil is the invention of M. Nicolas or his friends. Let us state the plain fact: Zwingle, on awakening, not being able to recollect the appearance of the person he had dreamt about, and wishing to express his own uncertainty on the subject, said he could not remember even if it were black or white: "*Ater fuerit an albus nihil memini;*" and M. Nicolas, who has already changed the dream into a fact, slips in slyly the word *devil;* thus, in the twinkling of an eye, he transforms an intelligent thinker, who reasons well even whilst dreaming, into a superstitious man who talks nonsense even whilst wide awake.

Our intention was also to have spoken of Luther's devil; but the example we have quoted shows the worth of a critic who can judge so lightly. Luther believed in the devil; but M. Nicolas, who believes that Satan was the first Protestant, does not he also believe in him? Luther thought the devil was hostile to his translation of the Bible, destined to enlighten the people on the errors of Papacy, and

1. Nicolas, p. 516.

that, on this account, the evil spirit came and disturbed him in his labours whilst confined within the fortress of Wartburg. Does M. Nicolas, then, believe, as a good Catholic, that the devil only torments people who take his own side of the question; St. Anthony, for instance? M. Nicolas, in this case, is schismatic in the church to which he belongs; for in every age the priests have exorcised and cast out devils; nay, if we believe his bishops, legions of evil spirits at the present time are making tables both talk and turn. We admit that Luther was wrong in supposing that the devil visited him in prison. But what does this prove? First, that the source from which he drew so erroneous a fancy was Catholicism; and, secondly, that God did not allow the devil to assault Luther, as has been the case for so many Catholic saints. We cannot see, however, a proof of the ignorance of Protestants. M. Nicolas, at last, grapples with his subject; he is going to show us Catholicism working for the good of mankind, endeavouring to spread light all over the world. By what means? Through the agency of the religious orders; the Jesuits, amongst others. Here again we decline entering upon a controversial discussion, and opposing to the learned labours of a few orders the ignorance and scandalous deportment exhibited by the rest. Our only object is to place before our readers some arguments which they might have thought strong, had they not known them. Let us then fully understand that the light of which Catholicism boasts is that spread abroad by the various religious orders, benedictines, oratorians, capucins, and Jesuits. These last, especially, excite our author's admiration; he enumerates fondly the universities which they have established and governed; that of Vienna, for example, of which M. Saint-Marc-Girardin says: " It has no renown, no celebrated professor, no clever work has ever gone forth from the midst of it;" although, or, rather, because, " the influence of the Jesuits and their method prevail in the frequent examinations of the *Faculté*[1]:" that of Freyburg, " a town whose population," says M. de Rougemont, " are ignorant and superstitious," although, or, rather, because, at Freyburg " there is one priest for every 18 inhabitants! the canton, besides, has produced very few celebrated men[2]." M. Nicolas tells us of the wonderful visions of the Jesuits in Paraguay — a country where the savages learnt to handle the pick-axe and the gun for the benefit of the reverend fathers, and at the king of Portugal's expense;—where the converts returned to the bush as soon as their masters were

1. Girardin, p. 182, 183. — 2. Rougemont, p. 317.

gone; — where there is no trace, at present, of the Jesuit mission, except the tyranny of Dr. Francia! After having done with his eulogy of the Jesuits, M. Nicolas returns to his accusations against Protestantism, and thus enters fully upon the subject which we have discussed. He will show us precisely the reverse of what we thought we had understood in the course of our two volumes; he will prove that England, and especially Scotland, have degenerated from their ancient splendour; he will cause the light of antiquity to shine in the midst of modern darkness. Edinburgh, the Northern Athens; Glasgow and its industry; Sir Walter Scott, the poet; Dugald Stewart, the philosopher; Adam Smith, the economist; James Watt, the inventor of the steam engine; must they all hide their diminished heads... before what? Before one of the Hebrides which once contained some convents. Excuse me, courteous reader; but were you aware that there existed in a corner of the world an ilot called Iona? I doubt it, for this place is not even marked on the generality of maps. Well, it was there that more light was to be found in days of yore than can be discovered at present throughout the whole of the Scotch Church; and, as a proof that the country had degenerated, M. Nicolas "*does not know* whether the present inhabitants" of an ilot which formerly could boast of so many monks, "have now even a minister to instruct them[1]."

We beg the reader's pardon, but we cannot coolly discuss such arrant nonsense. Because an island, selected long ago by certain monks as a place of shelter from a barbarous country, is now abandoned by *savants* who can live quietly in any part of civilised Scotland, is that a reason why Protestantism should have extinguished the torch of intellectual progress? Why speak of Iona, the residence of a few fishermen, and leave unmentioned Edinburgh, Glasgow, Aberdeen, the most learned cities in the world? Why not have compared the Catholic London of the fifteenth century with the Protestant London of the nineteenth? There was the point... and your condemnation!

Now, shall we enter into the same particulars respecting three Scotch and three Irish cities, whom M. Nicolas casually names? No; but in the meanwhile, as we do not wish to seem as if we avoided the objection, we shall say that the cities described are more flourishing now than they formerly were, and that the only way of reconciling with truth M. Nicolas's vague assertion is to take into serious account the designation he makes of *episcopal* and

1. Nicolas, p. 530.

abbatial cities. As such, these localities have been deteriorated, no doubt; nor is this fact astonishing, for the Scotch towns are now Protestant, and the Irish ones have gained in industry what they lost in priests. On the other hand, if the last-named cities, which are still Roman Catholic, are shorn of their intellectual glory, it is no fault of the Protestants; the Catholics even are not to blame; for in one of them, at Thurles, are still to be found a Catholic church, a Catholic college, Catholic convents, and a Catholic monastery. The fault, then, is not with man, but with the principles of the Catholic religion, which has allowed the torch of human intellect to become extinct, or at least has preserved only the faint glimmer of the middle ages, whilst the broad light of truth was flashing elsewhere. To quote Catholic cities which have fallen from their bygone intellectual eminence, is to condemn Catholicism, which has allowed or caused their decay.

M. Nicolas at length draws up a list of illustrious men who have belonged to Catholicism and to Protestantism, respectively, in order to exalt the former and to depreciate the latter. He says, indeed, he will not discuss individual cases; we think that it was impossible to treat even the general question; but since M. Nicolas attempts to do so, we ought at least to show his way of thickening the ranks of the men of genius who have belonged to his church, diminishing, as a matter of consequence, the number of those whose names are found in the annals of the rival community. It is thus that he presents to us, as the offsprings of Catholicism, Molière, the author of *Tartuffe,* and Pascal, the Jansenist, the author of the *Provincial Letters,* whom he elsewhere calls "a calumniator full of genius!" Thus again, on the other hand, M. Nicolas, obliged to acknowledge that Newton and Kepler were Protestants, says that this proves nothing in favour of Protestantism; for, "if they were learned men and great discoverers, it was at their own expense, so to say....." At their own expense? We do not understand; let us proceed; the idea will become clearer. "Bacon and Leibnitz reflect the greatest credit upon humanity; but the former belonged to that class of solitary minds, unconnected, as far as genius goes, with the society of which they are members[1]. The general idea of M. Nicolas may, then, be expressed as follows: a man of genius, born in a Catholic community, be he a stage-player or a Jansenist, is the boast of Catholicism. Another man of genius, Newton, for instance, publishing works on divinity, nay,

1, Nicolas, p. 532.

commentaries on the Book of Revelations, and calling the Pope antichrist, goes for nothing. Intellects like his have nothing to do with Protestantism! Let us proceed. We are now on the true ground of discussion; we are approaching our own times. But for what glorious names has M. Nicolas prepared the crown of Catholicism? Three in all : M. de Bonald, the adversary of the French Revolution; M. de Maistre, the author of a book on *The Pope,* in which the common hangman plays so conspicuous a part; and M. de Châteaubriand, of whom it is acknowledged, in the same page, that he " romanced the Gospel! [2] "

M. Nicolas gets gradually nearer the difficulty; at last he touches it, and tries to explain how it is that the Protestant nations are not plunged now-a-days into complete obscurity. It is because the light of Catholicism has penetrated them. There is only one little objection to make to M. Nicolas. If the Protestant nations are now compelled to borrow their light from the Catholics, can you account for the fact that the Catholic torch is extinguished in Spain, in Portugal, in Italy, in Ireland? Will you explain why the borrower is richer than the lender? the disciple better instructed than the teacher? If Prussia, for instance, has been indebted for so much to Austria and Bavaria, whence is it that these two last-named countries are reduced at present to seek in Protestant nations their literature and their professors? If England and Scotland are penetrated by the beams of the Catholic sun, how is it that Ireland cannot boast of one intellectual meteor? Here again we pass on.

It now only remains for M. Nicolas to prove — a difficult task — that the morality of Catholic countries is greater than that of Protestant ones. Before coming to facts, he examines the principles. In all our doctors, from Luther downwards to Vinet, he finds revolting tenets, and a very low code of morality. We have already shown how upon this subject M. Nicolas alters texts just to suit his own purposes; we have made it quite clear that he goes so far as to say that such and such a writer tolerates amongst clergymen certain bad inclinations, whilst, on the contrary, the incriminated author not only reproves these inclinations both in the clergy and the laity, but is scrupulous enough to condemn in the former "many tastes which in themselves are quite innocent." We will not return to this subject, nor will we lose further time in refuting the objection a hundred times refuted, that the Protestant doctrines sanction

1. *Revue de Strasbourg*, January, 1853.

looseness of morals. To show the absurdity of this objection, it would be sufficient to state it in M. Nicolas's own words. How can we reply to the following assertion? "Seeing that it was unable to reform society, Protestantism has adduced this incapacity itself as a reform, and instead of regulating the morals of men according to the standard of doctrines, it has shaped its doctrine according to the general tone of public morals[1]."

This is still the old calumny refuted by Saint Paul: "Let us sin that grace may abound." It is the common burden of all the detractors of Protestantism, who accuse our religion of saving man gratuitously, in order that he may be authorised to commit sin. We maintain, that any one who can believe such a doctrine to be preached by a church which has existed for three centuries, must either be a liar or a fool! The Protestants have proclaimed the doctrines of grace, like the Jansenists, Saint Augustin, and Saint Paul; a doctrine which, instead of sanctioning vice, insists upon sanctification, without making a merit of it. But all this has been said so often, and so well, that we have not the courage to repeat it.

It now remains to be proved whether the lives of the Protestants correspond with the abominable doctrines ascribed to them. It may be easily perceived that here M. Nicolas is rather puzzled by facts; he is obliged to confess that Protestants are better than Protestantism[2]; and he tries to get out of the difficulty by a distinction. If there is any virtue amongst Protestants, it is not because they are Protestants, but because they have preserved some traces of Catholicism! A very happy subterfuge! When, elsewhere, M. Nicolas feels obliged to confess to evil among the Catholic nations, he will turn his arguments and say that it is not because they are Catholics, but because they have been tainted by Protestant venom. With the help of such arguments any cause might be defended; but, as some persons would hardly credit that they have been broached by a writer of our own times, we shall quote one sentence of M. Nicolas's: "It is to Catholicism," he says, "that we must trace whatever slight remains of religious principles are to be found in the Protestant nations; and to Protestantism what is impious in Catholic countries[3]."

After that, you will not be surprised if M. Nicolas sometimes humbles France, calling her "actually Protestant;" and presently exalts her "on account of those centres of action, full of charity,

1. Nicolas, p. 552. — 2. *Idem*, p. 55. — 3. *Idem*, p. 572.

self-denial, devotedness, and holiness..... keeping up in the heart of the nation a sense of moral and religious worth far superior, after all, to that of all the other countries[1]."

Is that all? No; England, too, must be humbled, and national jealousies aroused by a comparison with France. This is what we have avoided; but, since M. Nicolas attacks Great Britain, we are constrained to answer his accusations.

He reproaches England for her many poor, being doubtless ignorant of the fact, that, under the influence of Romanism, one-third of the people were in a state of indigence[2], from the very plain reason that the clergy, at that time, preserved half the landed property[3]. If there is poverty in the British Isles, Ireland is especially its hot-bed; at all events, Protestant England relieves her poor bountifully, and in Scotland their number is comparatively few.

M. Nicolas quotes M. Léon Faucher on the subject of *Whitechapel*, but he is not aware, as we have elsewhere remarked, that in that spot it is the Irish Catholics who are sunk in misery and vice; whilst the descendants of the French Protestant refugees are remarkable by their moral and intellectual superiority[4].

M. Nicolas quotes moreover a report of M. Eugène Rendu, writen *a propos* of the Crystal Palace, and in which it is said that "the city of London alone..." But why speak of the city of London *alone?* Is London identical to England? London, whose very prosperity attracts so many strangers, can it be fairly considered alone when speaking of the crimes of a nation? Can London, in this respect, be compared with Paris — Paris, which has no sea-port, no manufactories — comparatively speaking — and, above all, no Irish?

This anti-English effusion brings to our mind the one directed against the United States of America. M. Nicolas wishes to prove that New York cannot appreciate the fine arts, and as an evidence of this he tells us of the "enthusiastic applause lavished by this merchant people upon..... Lola-Montes![5]"

Do you feel all the force of the argument? The merchants of the United States have applauded Lola-Montès; therefore it is impossible that from amongst them should ever spring a Saint Theresa, a Saint François de Sales, a Corneille, or a Raphael!

We have only three answers to give. In the first place, the fine arts of which M. Nicolas here makes special mention have not much to do with religion. One must understand the Scriptures after the Roman Catholic fashion to give so much importance to

1. Nicolas, p. 576. — 2. De Jonnès, vol. I, p. 147. — 3. *Idem*, p. 112. — 4. Léon Faucher, vol. I, pp. 12, 13. — 5. Nicolas, p. 539.

painting and music. Secondly, if the United States have produced neither a Saint Theresa, nor a Saint François de Sales, nor a Corneille, nor a Raphael, they have given birth to Washington, Franklin, Cooper, Irving, General Jackson, John Clay, Webster, and many others, in the course of a few years, not of a few centuries.

A last word, besides, to overturn your argument at once. Your famous Lola-Montès, a Spaniard and a Catholic — Lola-Montès, made Countess of Mansfeld by a Catholic King as a reward for her adulterous *faiblesses,* and driven out of the country by an indignant people; — Lola-Montès *never* received in the United States the applause of admiring crowds! You mean, perhaps, Jenny Lind, the singer, who has neither been the wife of two or three husbands at the same time, nor the mistress of many lovers, nor even an opera dancer; Jenny Lind, singing only in concert-rooms, and giving most of her large income to the poor and to religious institutions; Jenny Lind, the Swedish lady, who received a bible from the hands of the Bishop of Norwich, must be a Protestant. Now, Monsieur Nicolas, what remains of your famous argument about Lola-Montès?

We should reproach ourselves were we to prolong this discussion; there is, no doubt, plenty more to say, but we wish to remember that the force of our arguments consists in simply exposing the objections, and allowing the mere statement to carry the refutation along with it. We, however, thought it right the reader should know them, that he might perceive our adversaries have nothing serious to say.

Thus far we have directed our attention only to the objections made by the Roman Catholic party. There are others which, although not brought forward with the same noise, exist nevertheless silently amongst infidel minds. Some persons believe they are raising themselves to a great height when they deny the importance of religious faith, either as a source of civilisation or a corrupting principle; at the same time laying great stress on the influence of races and climate towards the formation of manners. Let us examine this new pretension.

Climate, certainly, does act upon the development of civilisation; but has this element the importance generally ascribed to it? Does it not allow plenty of room for the action of religious faith? Such is the first question.

Let us remark, to begin with, that climate acts in various ways. A high temperature enervates the mind, whilst it renders the earth fruitful; so man gains on one hand what he loses on the other. A cold temperature stimulates the intellect by the wants it produces; but it makes the ground sterile, and deprives it of part of its produce. In this manner, although they are giving to climate an influence which it does not possess, some persons might at the same time maintain that it acts in opposite ways; and, as our comparison bears on all points, we may believe that whilst it is favourable on the one hand, it acts prejudicially on the other. There is, then, a compensation.

But climate has not the importance ascribed to it. If it were the chief cause of civilisation, man would become little else than a vegetable, ripened or retarded in its growth by the changes of wet and heat! If climate is the most powerful cause, they should tell us in what manner it acts. Is it the heat or the cold that developes intellect? Suppose this question is answered, we shall require to be shown that the influence of climate has always followed the same law. Now this is contradicted by facts; civilisation flourished at one time under the blue sky of Greece, when foggy England was still in a state of barbarity. The climate of both these countries has remained much the same, but barbarism and civilisation have completely changed places [1]. The Moors formerly prospered on the same soil where the Spaniards are now sunk in wretchedness. To cut the matter short, let us fix our attention on three countries: The United States in the middle, Canada on one side, Brazil on the other. Now let us hear which point of the compass helps on civilisation. Is it the north or the south? If the north, why is Catholic Canada inferior in intellect and in wealth to the United States? If the south, why are the United States superior in all respects to Brazil? Remark, too, that climate, taken as a cause, only applies to certain nations; whereas the religious test bears upon all; it is a key which has opened every door, solved every difficulty. An hypothesis which explains all the cases of a problem must be a true one.

Do the human races account for the progress of intellect better than climate? We do not pretend to be more absolute on this point than on the other. To deny the influence of races would be to deny the bond which unites the physical with the moral world. Influence does not imply domination; we grant something to this agent, but at the same time we would have our adversaries grant us that it is not everything. If they decline doing so, as in the case of climate, we need only oppose both objections against each other; they would mutually destroy themselves.

1. The civilisation of England has done more to alter its climate, than the climate to form the civilisation.

In fact, the argument usually brought forward is a strange one. It is found that the Saxon race has chiefly embraced Protestantism, and is making rapid strides in the arena of civilisation; whereas the Latin family has remained Catholic, and moves very slowly in every sort of progress, when it does not become stationary. Then, without taking any notice of the religious convictions which animate the heart and quicken the mind, some say : These progress, because they are Saxons; those are stationary, because they are of Latin origin. Why should they not say : These advance, because they are Protestants; those hold back, because they are Catholics? Is the former assertion better proved than the latter? In assigning race as the cause of civilisation, do they show the necessary relation it bears to the effect produced? In nowise : it is an affirmation, nothing more. In pointing out faith as a cause of moral life, we state an opinion which is supported by plain common sense; we do not feel compelled to prove how this is brought about. Whoever takes the trouble to listen to his own thoughts, or observe his own actions, must be conscious of the influence which his inward principles exercise upon his outward conduct. I do not know whether my understanding has anything to do with my white skin; but I know that I flee from evil, because I fear God. Take away my faith, and the colour of my skin will not prevent me from giving myself up to injustice and selfishness.

Besides, here again we can answer by facts. The Irish celts belong to the same race as those which inhabit the Scotch highlands; and yet, why are the two tribes so different from each other! Because the former are idle Catholics, and the latter industrious Protestants. The Italians and the French of our southern provinces belong to the Iberian race; how can we account for the difference which exists between our Huguenot refugees and the Neapolitan lazzaroni? The former, under the liberal principles of the Reformation, have developed their minds by examining for themselves; whilst the others have stupidly submitted to the authority of a clergy which has always discountenanced instruction. The same Saxons have spread over Germany and England: if religion does not make the difference, why the striking contrast between the Englishman and the Austrian? To conclude, why should Switzerland, setting aside origin, be divided throughout into two distinct parties; the one, well-informed, rich, and Protestant; the other generally poor, ignorant, and Catholic?

Strange to say we see every day extreme differences between the children of the same parents; we explain these differences by the circumstances in which they have been brought up: education, society, fortune, etc.; but, as soon as religious faith is the point moved, some persons dismiss from their considerations the various causes just now stated, and will not acknowledge that faith or unbelief, which lies hid in every soul, can have any influence; they introduce afresh the question of race, in order to ascribe to it all the discrepancies which strike us among individuals! But, then, be consistent: draw a logical inference. Man, turned out of a brass mould, is irresponsible; he has neither vices nor virtues, but simply physical predispositions, erroneously called moral tendencies, and which he can neither strive against, nor strengthen! Thus, to argue is, we see, to deny the influence of education and the use of laws; it is to overthrow the whole fabric of society.

In reality, the question of race and of climate are identical: yes, climate does influence mankind; yes, races do diversify men in general; but these differences of races have been created partly by the difference of climate, here by the latitude, there by the elevation of the soil, elsewhere by a thousand accidental causes too long to enumerate. It is the persistency, the perpetuity of such climacteric causes, which in the long run increases the variety of races, and the sum of our argument may be stated thus: physical man is liable to be modified by the physical element in which he moves; these modifications, in their turn, go so far as to influence his moral being; but, finally, the whole is restrained within limits which allow to religious faith a vast field of action. Man is neither a plant, nor a beaver; he is free, intelligent, moral, and responsible.

In order to say all we think upon this subject, we must add that whatever, in the races of mankind, cannot be accounted for by climate, finds its explanation in the moral man: he, on the other hand, modifies the climate, so that the two causes assigned to civilisation are themselves modified by a primary and more general cause: the moral man himself. Physical influences may act upon the man; but it is in retarding, not in developing, his intellectual progress: the source of development dwells in him. Let him be enslaved, as he is by Catholicism, and he will lose all his powers; let him be unrestrained, as under the direction of Protestantism, and his faculties will become more and more expanded. Liberty alone will make him richer and more intelligent; then, the Word of God coming in, will render him happier and better.

To conclude, Protestantism has been reproached for exciting in the sphere of politics a revolutionary spirit by proclaiming in religion the principle of free inquiry.

We might merely ask here whether no revolutions are to be read of in history anterior to the sixteenth century; nay, whether the Popes themselves did not excite disturbances abroad by starting up the animosity of subjects against their sovereigns; and at home by exasperating so much their own people that more than one pontiff is known to have fallen a victim to their indignation. On one hand we see the Crusades begun by a monk, preached by the bishops of Rome, executed by the most Catholic princes and nations; on the other, we see the Popes encouraging the son of Henry IV in his revolt against his father; sanctioning in France the usurpation of the mayor Pépin in dethroning his lawful prince; fighting in Italy to secure a crown for their own relations; all these facts would supply us with a formidable array of recriminations and defence. But let us come to a closer view of the question, and see what has been the state of Christendom in this respect since the dawn of Protestantism.

In the first place, in order to ascertain whether it is the nature of Protestantism to create internal revolutions, we must not look at the origin of this religious franchise; for the nations which adopted the reformed principles were then, as we have already said, quite impregnated, so to say, with Roman Catholicism; and these struggles, besides, resulted from the efforts of the Romish party to oppose the progress of the Reformation. Religious war originated precisely from a wrong application of the principle of authority to spiritual things. What we have to examine is, whether by its doctrines Protestantism fosters rebellion; whether, in fact, it has done so since it has begun to rule over nations.

We admit that Protestantism, taking as its starting point free inquiry in matters of religion, has applied this principle to all things, politics included: we admit even that the public mind has become deeply imbued with it: what follows? precisely the reverse of the opinion we are now refuting. The Protestant, brought up in the spirit of inquiry and of liberty, applies its rule to every circumstance in his life, throughout all the classes of society. As a clergyman, a magistrate, a legislator, a monarch, whatever be the sphere in which he moves, he acts upon these principles to which he was trained since his youth. This spirit, leavening the whole lump, prepares both rulers and ruled to political changes which the march of intellect points out as necessary. It is not when everybody is walking forwards that collisions take place;

it is, on the contrary, when those who take the lead offer resistance.

Experience has proved what theory leads us to expect. Study the history of nations exclusively Protestant, and you will not find there the revolutions they are so rashly accused of. Civil war has disturbed neither England, nor Holland, nor the United States since they have become independent States. Progress of every description has been obtained in those three states without turmoil, quietly, by the mere development of the national institutions. Petitions, speeches, books; such are the barricades thrown up by Protestant revolutionists. And it is rather remarkable that these weapons have been especially made use of in England towards the emancipation of the Roman Catholics!

Let us now glance over the second term of the comparison, viz., Spain, Portugal, Italy, Brazil, Peru, the whole of Southern America, France itself. What do we see there? an uninterrupted series of riots, revolts, bloody revolutions. To consult only contemporary reminiscences, who is not frightened at the mere thought of the political disturbances which have taken place in those essentially Catholic countries? Mexico changes so often its president, and the Brazils are so constantly in a state of war, that it will be no offence to our readers if we remind them how ignorant they are as to the power which, for the present, rules in those countries. Is it Rosas? or Ribeiras? or General Santa-Anna? or any other *quidnunc* whose existence is revealed to-day by the newspapers, but who is doomed to fall on the morrow. In Spain, we have seen Don Carlos, Espartero, Queen Christina, and her daughter contending for power. Although civil war has only ceased for the last few years, we already see fresh riots bursting forth in several localities. In Portugal, Don Pedro and Don Miguel were contending for the throne. Quite recently, a political party rose in arms against the government, and if there was no bloodshed it was only due to the cowardice of both factions. For twenty times within a very short space of time Italy has seen conspiracies originated and stifled. *Carbonari* is an Italian name: we know of Milanese exiles: amongst its conspirators, Piedmont reckons a hero lately dead, Charles Albert. The Pope himself, after having been driven back out of his dominions and brought back again, can only be maintained in his infallibility by foreign bayonets. Shall we mention Naples, where Swiss troops must always be keeping the population in check? And Florence, whose sovereign withdrew in 1850 the liberties he had sworn to defend in 1848? Not one Italian city but has contributed its quota to the number of refugees we are now harbouring. It is the same with Spain. And our poor native country! how many revolutions has she not seen for the last sixty years? Louis XVI, Robespierre, Bonaparte the Consul, Napoleon the Emperor. By an exception, Louis XVIII dies on the throne, but only after having lived through the *Hundred Days,* and in spite of several conspiracies. Then the series of revolutions begins again: Charles X dies in exile in Germany; Louis-Philippe, an exile in England; the Republic was still-born; and Louis Bonaparte has been successively member of the Legislative Assembly, President of the Republic, and Emperor of the French. How can any persons be found bold enough, with all these facts before their eyes, to raise their voice and accuse the Protestants of stirring up revolutions.

Let us leave those nations which are essentially Protestant or Catholic, and turn our attention to those where the two elements are mixed; and, strange to say, we shall find that, when revolt lifts up its head, it is always in the name of the Catholics. Thus, in the British Isles, it is Catholic Ireland which is riotous, rebellious, and keeps hard at work the greatest part of the army. In the Netherlands, Catholic Belgium revolts, and separates herself from the mother country. At Geneva, the radical party triumphs by the force of arms, with the help of Roman Catholic bands come expressly from Savoy for that purpose. When the whole of Switzerland took the field, it was in order to suppress the Sunderbund: a Catholic conspiracy. To conclude: the electric spark which spread throughout Europe in 1848, and shook semi-Catholic Prussia, as well as all other countries, was kindled in Catholic France! Thus, we may seek in vain during the last century for a revolution amongst a Protestant people; whereas we shall find ten for every Catholic community, where the spirit of liberty is constantly struggling against the spirit of despotism more or less avowed.

Thus, the objections drawn from politics and from science, as well as those founded on religion, fall before the facts of history, and such being the conclusion, we remain perfectly justified in the following opinion we have maintained throughout this work: — If we compare the United States with the Brazils, Ireland with Scotland, the Swiss cantons together, Austria with Prussia, Spain with England, Catholic Italy with Reformed France, we shall find that from the threefold standpoint of physical comfort, intellectual progress, and morality, the superiority is always and everywhere on the Protestant side. But does this legitimate conclusion, drawn from a survey of the countries above-named, apply equally to those beyond the circle of our observation? In other words, is the superiority of the Protestant over the Catholic nations so general that the cause may be ascribed to the very principles of the Reformation? Such is the last point we have to examine.

GENERAL SUMMARY.

We have gone through the circle of the Protestant and Catholi nations: on each point of the circumference we have been enabled to make the same remarks. We might, therefore, legitimate generalise for ourselves, and say of Christianity as a whole what we have proved respecting each particular section of it.

We shall, nevertheless, commit this task to fresh authorities; and our quotations, instead of being confined to such and such a country, either Protestant or Catholic, shall bear upon the whole of the Catholic and Protestant world at large.

And first, let us note this fact: Catholicism is disappearing; it is abandoned with disgust by every thinking, disinterested man, though he may not have embraced the doctrine of the Reformation: "The fact cannot be concealed," says M. de Lamennais, "that, at the present day, Catholicism is in a stage of weakness and suffering. The Church is sick, she languishes, and has ceased to extend her conquests. Scarcely able to preserve the acquisitions she made in past ages, she is like the sea abandoning the shores it used to wash [1]. Where is the influence which Rome was wont formerly to exercise on every mind? What has become of it, especially for the last four years, in France, in Germany, even in Poland? Has she, in those countries, modified to the slightest extent public opinion, and public conscience? Except a few followers, men belonging to another age, who cares even to inquire about what she says? Forget coteries and their wretched agitation, look at the masses;

1. Lamennais, *Affaires de Rome*, p. 207.

where are those which Popedom controls and directs? Everything has its reason; what, then, is the reason of this decay of the Papal power? Rome knows full well that her authority has long been less efficacious in Italy than anywhere else. The Italians hate Rome with an implacable hatred, for they consider her as the chief cause of their country's misfortunes[1]. "

"Assemble," says M. Quinet, "the bishops and archbishops of the whole earth; if this council assumes the right of deciding absolutely on questions connected with the spiritual world, its tyranny will be as insufferable to me as that of the Bishop of Rome. Who would, in the present day, repudiate his thought, his moral right, the strength of internal evidence, before a convocation of the clergy, however numerous? If the priests were to summon at the bar of a council the Husses, the Jérômes of Prague, the Luthers of our days, they would run the risk of summoning the whole world. They have lost the majority; and if their fate is to be settled by a vote of nations, how will they stand it [2]."

Whilst this decomposition of Catholic societies is going on, what has become of the Protestant nationalities? We shall begin by taking a general view : "Wherever the religious revolution of the sixteenth century prevailed, if it did not effect the entire enfranchisement of the human mind, it procured for it a new and very great increase of liberty. It resuscitated and maintained in Germany a liberty of thought greater perhaps than anywhere else..... In Denmark, also, by the influence of the Reformation, thought was enfranchised and freely exercised in all directions. In Holland, in the midst of a republic, and in England, under constitutional monarchy, the emancipation of the human mind was likewise accomplished. Lastly, in France, in a country where the Reformation had been conquered, there even it was a principle of intellectual independence and liberty; a liberty which tended to the profit of science, to the honour of the French clergy, as well as to the profit of thought in general. Religious thought was then far more bold, and treated questions with more freedom, than the political spirit of Fénelon himself in Telemachus. This state of things did not cease until the revocation of the Edict of Nantes.

"Wherever the Reformation penetrated, wherever it played an important part, victorious or vanquished, it had, as a general, dominant, and constant result, an immense progress in the activity and liberty of thought, and towards the emancipation of the human

1. Lamennais, p. 283. — 2. Quinet, p. 315.

mind. . . . . Let us now take the counterproof of this inquiry; let us see what happened in countries into which the religious revolution had not penetrated, where it had never been developed. History shows that there the human mind has not been enfranchised; two great countries, Spain and Italy, will prove this. Whilst in those European countries where the Reformation had taken an important place, the human mind, during the last three centuries, has gained an activity and a freedom before unknown, in those where it has not penetrated it has fallen, during the same period, into effeminacy and indolence. . . . . Impulse of thought, therefore, is the essential character of the Reformation, the most general result of its influence, and the dominant fact of its destiny [1]."

"Throw a glance upon the history of the Jesuits; they have everywhere failed. Wherever they have interfered to any extent, they have carried misfortune into the cause into which they mixed. In England they ruined kings; in Spain, the people. The development of modern civilisation, the liberty of the human mind, all these powers against which the Jesuits were called upon to contest, fought and conquered them. And not only have they failed, but call to mind the means they have been obliged to employ. . . . They have acted only by underhand, obscure, and subordinate means. . . . The party against which they struggled, on the contrary, not only conquered, but conquered with splendour; it did great things, and by great means; it aroused the people, it gave to Europe great men, and changed, in the face of day, the fashion and form of state [2]."

"I might exhibit the Reformation in the diversity of its relations with the social order, bringing on in all directions results of mighty importance! For instance, it awoke religion amidst the laity in the world of the faithful. It caused a general circulation of religious creeds; it opened to believers the field of faith, which, hitherto, they had no right to enter. It restored the independence of the temporal power [3]."

Leaving this general view, let us descend to a few particulars. The Roman Catholic nations themselves were the first to reap the earliest fruits of the Reformation. The spirit of rivalry compelled the Popes to make concessions: what a downfall, from Hildebrand to Pius IX! Villers says: "The Reformation alone could oppose a mound to this torrent. It struck by one blow both the rivals who were aspiring to impose chains upon Europe. Haughty Austria

1. Guizot, *History of Civilisation in Europe*, *Hazlitt's translation*, lect. IV, vol. I, pp. 122, 123. — 2. *Idem*, p. 227. — 3. *Idem*, p. 233.

humbled and brought under restriction for ever. The Roman Pontiff lost a part of his dominions, and retained only a precarious power in those which he preserved. Powerful governments, too, have arisen, which, rivalling one another in whatever contributes to the glory and happiness of nations, commonly second the operation of that new spirit which animates the people, and hasten to remove every trace of the barbarism of the middle ages.

"The gradual progress of knowledge," we may be told, "would insensibly have produced the same consequences, and have saved all the evils which sprang from such terrible commotions and lengthened wars. But those who object so do not reflect that, in the system of an Infallible Church, all the decisions of which are dictated by the Holy Spirit, such a Reformation as is requisite becomes impossible, and that it is contrary to the very spirit of Roman Catholicism. It is at least reasonable to doubt whether the desired change would have happened so soon, and have been so complete. It is certain that, at the period of the Reformation, the heads of the Catholic religion, who at first had discovered nothing in the revival of letters but glory and pleasure, or some tendency towards the refinement of manners, and who encouraged them under that idea, began to perceive their own danger in too much knowledge, and manifested a very distinct resistance. That opposition has not speedily ceased in Austria, in Spain, in Italy, in the Netherlands, where all the means of inquisition and censure were employed to restrain the operations of mind, and turn improvement backwards. Let any one compare the political, literary, and religious condition of the greater part of those countries during the succeeding ages with the condition of Saxon Germany, of Holland, and England in the same respects; and let him judge, without prejudice, what could have been expected from the same policy, extended in all its rigour over Europe.

"As to what might have been expected in course of time from Popes and the clergy, if they had been allowed to proceed as they chose in the full career of their power and credit, we may form a judgment from the physical and moral condition of the kingdoms immediately subject to ecclesiastical princes. The spirit of Popery, it is impossible to deny, is exclusive and intolerant: now the spirit of an intolerant institution cannot cease without putting an end to the institution itself. A testimony sufficiently decisive is, that the humane and virtuous Innocent XI was scarcely able to execute any of his laudable designs during a pontificate of twelve years. The Popes, since the Reformation, more cautious, reduced, indeed, to the last stage of debility, have yielded by necessity in several encounters; but what they wanted was strength, not inclination[1]."

If the beneficial influence of the Reformation was felt even by those people who had not embraced it, what must have been the blessings it imparted to the nations by which it was freely accepted? The freedom of thought is the one we shall mention first, because even our adversaries admit it as incontestable :

"Let us reflect" continues M. Villers, "upon the immense apparatus of censures, of prohibitions, and of inquisitors which the Romish Church employed to keep all eyes shut at a time when every new opinion was a heresy, that is, a crime worthy of the direst punishment, and against which the rigour of the secular arm was required, and we shall shudder at the danger to which the human species was exposed before the sixteenth century. Had not the mind, by the happiest and most extraordinary concurrence of favourable circumstances, obtained, in rapid succession, new aids and fresh fuel to its activity, what would have become of that feeble spark of light which began to shine under the system of extinguishment and *obscuration* adopted by the Court of Rome? Had not the art of printing and the reformation of religion proceeded from the bosom of laborious Germany; had not the colossal power which bound the consciences and oppressed the minds of men received so many shocks in rapid succession, for how many ages might not the culture of the human mind, and the improvement of the political condition of man, have been retarded! Let us put the question to the southern parts of Germany, to the people of the Two Sicilies, of Spain, and of Ireland. Let any impartial observer, after having fairly ascertained the state of knowledge in those countries, make himself acquainted with the degree in which it exists in Switzerland, in the two Saxonies, in Holland, and England; the contrast cannot escape him. It is not asserted that in the Catholic countries above-named superior men, persons on a level with the most elevated of their age, are not to be found; but they are rare; and only the masses of the people in different countries ought to be compared. True it is that in the close connection in which the different nations of our little Europe live together, it is impossible that the knowledge existing in one country should not in some degree penetrate into the others. The wall of separation cannot be so raised, cannot be so vigilantly guarded, as to prevent individuals in all from

1. Villers, Mill's translation, pp. 128, 131.

communicating with one another. But undoubtedly on the part of the Catholics no precautions have hitherto been neglected to ward off, as a dangerous disease, the liberal ideas of Protestantism from their boundaries. It was at Rome that the censorship of books was first invented, and the example was religiously followed by the governments devoted to Rome. Leo X, that vaunted protector of the arts, issued, in 1515, severe restrictions against printing and publishing any books translated from the Greek, Hebrew, or Arabic. At the same period that, five years afterwards, he fulminated against the Reformation that famous bull which begun: "*Exsurge, Deus, judica causam tuam,*" (Arise, O God! judge thy own cause), in which Luther and his adherents were attacked with the most terrible anathemas, and in which all men were prohibited indiscriminately from reading any of their books whatsoever, and on what subject soever they might treat; at that very moment, I say, this pontiff did not blush to publish, in the name of JESUS CHRIST, a bull in favour of the profane poems of Ariosto, threatening with excommunication those who should find fault with them, or obstruct their sale. What was to be expected from such a spirit as this, from such an abuse of things, violently converted into things sacred, nay thrust into the place of the very oracles of Heaven itself? France, the most enlightened of all the Catholic countries, more enlightened than several Protestant countries, and in which Popery never reigned with unlimited sway, in spite of all its efforts to confirm its hold and to introduce the inquisition — France itself, in which even a species of half reform existed, under the title of Gallican liberties, was not entirely exempted from that system of extinguishment. In Spain, in Italy, and Austria the prohibitions and censures went much farther, and in those countries still impose many shackles on the liberty of writing and thinking. These facts, and an immense number of others, which are repeated every day, characterise the spirit of Catholicism in regard to the propagation of knowledge, and the liberality of instruction. The maxim of the middle ages is yet preserved in those countries in all the vigour in which it is possible to preserve it in the present times; 'to retain the minds of men on certain subjects in complete stupidity; to keep them as much as possible empty, that they may be afterwards filled with anything which is found agreeable, and that superstition may find a convenient reception.' Besides this, the Romish inquisitors prohibited in the mass all books printed by sixty-two printers which they denounced without any regard to their contents; adding further, a general prohibition to read any book issuing from the press of a printer who but once in his life had printed anything produced by an heretic. By this means, says an historian, nothing was left to read. Never was a better secret found to benumb and corrupt men by religion.

The Reformation broke all those shackles imposed upon the human mind, and overthrew all the barriers erected against the free communication of thought. Within its boundaries nothing remained forbidden except productions offensive to modesty and public morals. By recalling the memory of those shackles and barriers, by considering the long continuance of barbarity which they might still have maintained upon the earth, have we not sufficiently proved how much the Reformation has contributed to the progress and to the diffusion of knowledge? As soon, indeed, as by its means the path was opened, men proceeded boldly and publicly to discuss the best interests of human kind, and to speak like men of things pertaining unto men.

The principle of examination calls forth light, of which it is the friend, as that of blind submission is the promoter of darkness. And who can calculate the immense extent of the influence of a fundamental principle, admitted as the basis of religious, and by consequence of moral, instruction in a nation? The man who is free in the inmost sanctuary of his soul looks freely and boldly around him. He becomes enterprising, active, and disposed for everything that is great and useful. He who is a slave in his conscience, in the very centre of his being, is, without knowing that he is so, a slave in his whole conduct. He is by birth a slave, from the stupefaction and apathy which unnerve his faculties[1]."

The liberty of thought, applied at first to religious topics, was soon, by a natural consequence, extended to moral philosophy, sciences, the fine arts, and even the soil itself, which man, having become more intelligent, could better cultivate: "Agriculture and industry, in Protestant countries, grew rich from the suppression of numerous feast-days, pilgrimages, nocturnal processions; these festivals, lost for activity amidst Catholic communities, are pernicious inducements to idleness and disorder; they are really negative quantities, diminishing by so much the sum of national labour and riches.

"How long might the true spirit of commerce, might navigation and discovery, have yet languished, if two states, rendered active

1. Villers, pp. 287, 296.

by the Reformation (states in which the whole nation unfolded its powers, employed all its resources, and seconded the operations of government) had not found themselves drawn, and as it were constrained to seize upon the trident? Without the religious impulse produced by Luther, such would not have been the order of events. Holland, a poor portion of the Austrian dominions, would have remained without a navy and without commerce; England would not have had that volcanic power she exerted against Spain, nor would it have been turned in that direction. In place of this, the maritime and commercial system in Europe has, by means of those two nations, acquired a magnitude and power proportioned to the vigour which inspired them. Their fleets and skilful sailors have traversed every sea, and surrounded the globe itself with their track. Their example has been followed by France. Thus has the fermentation produced in Europe by religious opinions raised up a new order of things more beneficial to human nature [1]."

Material prosperity, however, is only one of the results of that freedom of thought; a more immediate consequence was the diffusion of knowledge. The first spark came from theology — theology, so disdained at the present time, precisely because all that is known of it is a Romish shred or two. Let us listen to M. Villers: "The whole system of studies relating to Protestant theology differs from that of Catholic theology. They are two worlds in opposite hemispheres, which have nothing common except the name. But that unhappily is sufficient to deceive all those who never go farther than the name. The Catholic theology rests on the inflexible authority of the decisions of the Church, and therefore debars the man who studies it from all free exercise of his reason. It has preserved the jargon, and all the barbarous appendages of the scholastic philosophy. We perceive in it the work of darkness of the monks of the tenth century. In short, the happiest thing which can befall him who has unfortunately learnt it, is speedily to forget it. Whoever wishes to be instructed in history, in classical literature, and philosophy, can choose nothing better than a course of Protestant theology. Clergymen reared in this manner, proceeding from the universities, go to fill the place of pastors and teachers in little villages, and in the country. It very often happens that there they establish excellent schools, and spread around them the light which they have received from their

1. Villers, pp. 281, 282.

masters. The class of our village curates and vicars has in general been always very respectable and exemplary; yet, it must be acknowledged, and all those who have been enabled to observe it will acknowledge without difficulty, that this class is not less exemplary among the Protestants, and among them it is much more, and much *better* instructed.

"In the mean time, it ought to be observed that this movement could have free and unlimited course only in Protestant countries. It was alien and contradictory to the system established in the Catholic states. Among these, philosophy is to be regarded as a disturber of the public peace, or, if you will, of the public apathy; which in the opinion of many people comes nearly to the same thing. In Austria, in Italy, and Spain, this philosophical impulse was soon spent; and the usual lethargy quickly recovered the ascendant. Even in France, a country which ought by no means, as we have already demonstrated, to be ranked in the same class with the other Catholic countries, the philosophical spirit was soon extinguished after the death of Descartes, who indeed, as is well known, found the greatest number of his partisans in Holland. The interest excited by philosophical truths and systems among the English, the Swedes, and the northern Germans, on the other hand, far from losing any of its force, appeared to go on invariably increasing. London, Halle, Geneva, became the schools from which Frenchmen drew their information. Locke and Hume, Wolf and Bonnet, became our masters.

"For the influence of the Reformation on the study of morality has not been less decisive than on the other branches of philosophy. That science, which is the same thing with regard to the conduct of man that metaphysics are with regard to his knowledge, had fallen from the time of the last Roman moralists into almost total oblivion. It is well known that the fathers of the Church, who exhausted all the resources of their minds in doctrinal controversies, did little, or indeed nothing, toward the moral sciences; the schoolmen less; and under their long reign true morality disappeared altogether, giving place to casuistry; a degenerate species of morality, in which the duties of man towards God, and even towards his fellow-creatures, were reduced almost entirely to his duties toward the Church; in which a multitude of superstitions and practical subtleties corresponded but too well with the superstitions and subtleties of the theology of that dark period. When the Gospel recovered its station, and resumed the place of casuistry, the pure and divine morality which it teaches recovered its station likewise in the pulpits and the writings of the spiritual pastors.

"Those religious disputes, relating only to different opinions in matters of theology and faith, have contributed to preserve alive in Protestant countries that spirit of religion, and that attachment to Christianity, which is found much more conspicuous than in Catholic countries. Far better is it, after all, to dispute about religion, than peaceably to consent to have none. Much rather dispute about the manner of worshipping God, than disbelieve in him altogether, and lie down in neglect and indifference about everything which concerns our relation to the Divine Being. Still better is it, undoubtedly, sincerely to worship God, and leave every man at liberty to perform this great act in his own way. This is precisely what the different Protestant people, some sooner, some later, came at last to do. They began with argumentation and controversy; they have ended with philosophy and toleration; and the religious spirit remains[1]."

In conclusion, M. Villers himself compares the results produced by the Reformation with those of Papacy: "The members of that clerical body were besides the pastors, the instructors, the depositaries of all knowledge, the masters of all minds. Occupied with the external practices of devotion, with the maintenance of the rights of the Church, these were almost the only subjects, too, on which they addressed the people. Hence resulted a profound ignorance and indifference with regard to the most precious interests of man in society. Agriculture and all kinds of industry were in a state of the most deplorable degradation. Such is nearly, at this day, their condition in the fine provinces of Naples and Rome, in Spain and Portugal. Misery, laziness, immorality, and every species of vice, arise among a people from such dispositions; and the state remains weak and ill-governed. What activity, on the other hand, what perfection in agriculture, in rural economy, in the general administration of affairs, strikes the eye of the observer amid the cold and barren fields of Scotland, in Great Britain, and in Holland! There the hand of man creates everything, because there it labours for itself; it is there all-powerful, because there it is free, and because corresponding information directs it. The contrast of these indubitable effects of the two religions is more especially perceptible in Germany and in Switzerland, where

1. Villers, pp. 307, 310, 316, 320, 361.

the different territories intersecting one another make the traveller every moment pass from a Protestant country to a Catholic one.

"If you enter a wretched hovel built of mud with a thatched roof; if you pass through neglected fields, where you are met by low, common-looking peasants, and innumerable beggars, you may guess pretty safely that the country is a Roman Catholic one. On the other hand, are the dwellings clean, pretty-looking[1], offering the aspect of ease and industry; are the fields well enclosed and widely cultivated, you are most probably amongst Protestants, Anabaptists, or Mennonites. Thus, the aspect of nature seems to change in proportion as he whose right it is to give laws to her enjoys his freedom more or less; whilst, however, she seems to delight in lavishing her gifts upon the Catholic population inhabiting the finest countries of Europe. The limited Helvetian territory illustrates this singularity in a striking manner. Compare the fertile plains of Soleure with the much less favoured soil of Aargau; the stony, barren canton de Vaud, exposed to northern influences, with the magnificent Italian Switzerland, or the sheltered Valais; the Neufchâtel district with the fruitful locality only lately under the rule of the abbot of Saint-Gall; finally, within the states of that prince-monk, compare together the part which followed the Romish religion, and the much smaller one which, under the protection of Zurich and Berne, had been enabled to preserve its adherence to the Reformed faith; you will see in all cases man's activity and enlightenment superior even to the bounties of lavish nature, whilst those lost benefits are, so to say, wasted upon idleness and indolence. Agriculture is brought to such a high state of perfection in the country of Berne, that several methods introduced by Bernese cultivators have been adopted in England; and it is to the agronomical society they have established that we owe the true theory of irrigation, the importance of which is sufficiently known to farmers[2].

1. What traveller has not been struck by the contrast between the filthiness which prevails in Roman Catholic countries, and the extreme cleanliness of the northern Protestant people, the Dutch and the English? Whence the apathy of the one, and the activity to be found amongst the other? Whence is it that, here, we find the spirit of order and of labour; there, indolence and idleness? The reason is plain enough. As for mendicancy, everybody knows to what an odious and revolting excess it is carried amongst the most Catholic countries; so that we see it increase sensibly as we get nearer the centre of Catholicity, throughout the whole of Italy, till we get to Rome, where it reaches its highest point. Whoever, besides, has seen only a few Protestant towns and Catholic cities, must have remarked, at one glance, the difference which exists between them on the important question of mendicancy.

2. "If we proceed from the cultivation of the earth to intellectual culture, Switzerland offers the same contrast. How many celebrated literary men have sprung from Geneva, men whoms science and the belles-lettres claim with pride amongst us! Berne, Lausanne, Bâle, Zurich, Schaffausen, can boast of their annals, crowded with illustrious names. The antiquarian *Morel*; *Haller*, the creator of philosophy, and equally distinguished as a poet; the two *Turretini*;

What the reformers could not effect themselves, the good spirit which they had introduced accomplished naturally and by degrees in the end. It is remarkable that during the last three centuries, beside a great number of inferior establishments, Germany has been enriched with more than twenty universities, of which three-fourths are Protestant. England founded three and Holland five. On the part of the Catholics, six were founded in Italy, eight in Spain, and three in France. Not only have the Protestants the advantage, which might be equivocal, in point of number, but no reasonable person will entertain a doubt that they have it also in respect to the instruction which is given in those universities. It would not, I apprehend, be considered a very extravagant paradox if I were to assert that there is more real knowledge in a single university, such as that of Gottingen, or Halle, or Jena, than in the eight Spanish universities of San-Yago de Compostella, of Alcala, Orihuela, etc. In these is taught what must be believed whether agreeable to reason or not; in the other is taught how a person may arrive at a reasonable belief in whatever is presented to his mind. In the one place the Decretals are given as infallible oracles; in the other no oracle is acknowledged but reason and well-established facts. On this account it is natural that pedantry, the child of the scholastic discipline, should be infinitely more rare in the Protestant schools than in the others [1]."

"Finally, the morals of Protestant nations are incontestably more strict and purer than those of Catholic people. Is this fact the consequence of the nations being Protestant? or is it vice versâ? I leave others to decide the question [2]."

We see plainly, therefore, that the weightiest authorities affirm, respecting the generality of Protestant nations, what we have ourselves recognised as true of the most considerable amongst them. We are, then, perfectly justified in applying our conclusions to the whole of Christendom, and in ascribing to the principles of the Reformation itself the great superiority of Protestant communities.

The liberalism which is its essence has brought about the progress of human intellect; it began by breaking the fetters under which the mind of man was groaning; then, confident of the merits

the father and the son; *Crousaz*, the *Buxtorfs*, the *Werenfels*, *Bernoulli*, *Euler* (*Christopher* and *Isaac*), *Iselin*, the first who conceived the idea of writing a philosophical history of mankind; the Wettsteins of Basle; Gessner, the naturalist; Gessner the poet; Bodmer, etc., etc., who have contributed so much towards the revival of polite literature in Germany; and a host of other great men, in fine, whom it is superfluous to enumerate. Catholic Switzerland, on the contrary, has not one illustrious name to mention in any branch of human learning." (Villers.)

1. Villers, pp. 328, 330. — 2. *Idem*, p. 303.

of its cause, it did not dread to court inquiry, whilst Popery, from a totally opposite motive, prudently proscribed free examination.

To the ethical doctrines enforced by the Reformation are due the comparatively pure morals of its adherents. Liberty may instruct, but it does not moralise; hence, a second proof that the Reformation is really built upon the truth.

To conclude, the material prosperity of the same communities, the natural result of labour, intelligence, and good order, must be ascribed to the union of the liberalism and the moral tenets advocated by the Reformation. Without morality, what would be temporal happiness but an incentive to the passions, a blossom destined to perish in the course of one day? But, as we see prosperity developing itself in a contrary direction, we may consider it as an offshoot of the tree of life.

Such is the present condition of Protestant nations: from the facts already stated we shall now deduce what their future is likely to be.

FUTURE DESTINIES

OF PROTESTANT NATIONS.

If we acknowledge that intellect, prosperity, and morality are the fruits of Protestantism, it is as much as to say that the future is its own; and, in fact, when we study the actual position of the Protestant nations, and their rapid progress in the path of civilisation, we cannot help being struck with their immense resources, and the giant strides they are making towards the conquest of the world. Let us first remark that the two most prosperous countries, England and the United States, are Protestant. England, who owns one hundred and sixty millions of men, has been compelled, by sheer necessity, to turn her thoughts to navigation; the very thing which will carry her influence and ideas to the remotest points of the globe. Doubtless, her hundred and sixty millions of men are not all Protestant; but they are all likely to become so. Ireland, for instance, now no longer under the Great Agitator's influence, and sufficiently calm to listen to Protestant preaching, Ireland is entering the true road of reform. The Romish clergy, who accuse the Protestants of buying these conversions, acknowledge, by this charge, the fact of which they complain. Others emigrate to the United States, and there, free from the fear of their priests, they quietly adopt the belief of the country they inhabit. In consequence both of these conversions at home, and emigrations abroad, the change has been such, that Ireland, which was lately three-fourths Catholic, is now nearly half Protestant. Twenty-five Protestant societies continue the work of proselytism, and carry it on by every available means. Churches are erected, schools, hospitals, and workshops established in order to instruct and relieve the poor suffering Irish Catholics. In India, the progress is not less remarkable; there, the heathen temples are falling to ruins, the priests are discouraged, the native youth congregate in the institutions of the English, and the people, formerly idolatrous, flock round the preachers of the Gospel. We will not argue on the intrinsic merits of Christian doctrines, in order to predict the conversion of India to Protestantism; but the unbeliever himself must admit that the wealth, the power, and the intellectual superiority of the English, compared to the Hindoos, will, as a matter of consequence, finally procure a complete triumph for the faith of the former over that of a people already quite reduced to their political rule. Old prejudices are shaken, a general movement will soon follow; the least that we can say of it is, that it is a mere question of time.

And the United States of America, do they not admirably second the work of their mother country? Does it not seem as if the whole of Europe was acting under the direction of a providential impulse, when it throws out its population towards Protestant North America, who, in her turn, transforms them, and scatters them abroad throughout the Catholic regions of the South? At the very time that the revolutions of the Old World are frightening its inhabitants, the gold mines of California attract to the New World Irish, Germans, French — all Catholic; and, though we will not venture to say that they uniformly become Protestants as soon as they arrive there, yet they, at least, willingly allow their children to be instructed in the great truths of the Gospel. The Irish, supposed to be so fondly attached to their religion, but who are often only intimidated by their priests in their own country; the Irish, who, in the course of a few years, have given to the United States millions of emigrants; the Irish, we say, have become there, five-sixths of them, Protestants. In those countries religious, or, if you prefer, clerical activity follow the movement imparted to agriculture, industry, and commerce. It is the same activity, the same life. Catholics arrive from all parts; the Protestant populations open to them churches, schools, workshops, colonies, and the two races are so completely assimilated that in the second generation they form one homogeneous whole. The proof of this is the fact that the United States, composed in great part of emigrants; the United States, which have seen, in the course of twenty years, their population increase from 12 to 23 millions, are now Protestant for 39 out of every 40, although the emigrants, on their arrival, were chiefly Catholics! At the same time that the Protestant United States absorb the population which they attract from without, they likewise invade and assimilate to themselves the neighbouring countries; California, Texas, Mexico, have each come to join the Union, as if constrained by the force of an irresistible attraction. In order to ground our assertions upon a true basis, we have consulted the last census published by order of Congress, and the following are the results;

	FORMERLY.		AT THE PRESENT DAY.	
	Catholic churches.	Protest. Do.	Cath. churches.	Protest. Do.
Maryland.	all.	0	68	800
Florida	all.	0	5	147
Louisiana	all.	0	55	223

The first of these three states was colonised by the English; the second, by the Spaniards; the third, by the French.

Nationality, therefore, has had no influence; everywhere Catholicism has equally disappeared. Texas, originally Spanish, and recently annexed to the United States, has now only 13 Catholic churches, and already 161 Protestant. Protestantism is now also the religion of the majority of Californians. In a word, the whole of the United States contain only 1,112 Roman Catholic places of worship, capable of accomodating 621,000 persons; this is about one-fourth of the entire population; yet how many went out as Catholics from Ireland, France, Bavaria, and Austria. If we look at the social position of this half-million of Catholics in the United States, we find that they are as wretched as their number is small. Very few of them are to be met with in the catalogue of statesmen, orators, magistrates; but they form the majority of the inmates of unions and prisons. In a judicial inquiry recently made at Boston, a Protestant city, it was proved that out of 40 children imprisoned for crimes and misdemeanour, 38 were the children of Catholics. At nearly all the public executions it is a priest who accompanies the criminal, thus showing plainly what his religion is. We repeat that these facts are uniformly drawn from official documents lately published by Congress.

The day is not far distant when Cuba, either purchased or conquered, shall pass from the drowsy dominion of the Spaniards to the vivifying influence of the Anglo-Saxons. Whilst the populations of Europe and of America are becoming one in the Reformed religion, the Congress at Washington meditates the commercial conquest of Japan, just as England lately secured that of China. That these two nations should succeed in the first instance is out of the question; but they have made the undertaking: this is the important point, and we know their perseverance.

The foregoing considerations lead us to touch upon a fact most extraordinary, if we think of the natural course of events. A rebel, as obscure a few years ago as he is now illustrious and powerful, a rebel, who has already conquered the greater part of the Celestial Empire, and is at present besieging the capital — this rebel, in his victorious march, destroys the idols, calls himself a Christian, and circulates the Scriptures. We do not pretend to approve either of revolt or massacre; but, looking at results which alone can here engage our attention, is it not admirable to see a nation, forming one-third of the human race, — a nation until lately walled-in against European influence, — to see them, we say, sweeping away the rubbish of their heathen temples, in order to facilitate the entrance of the English and American missionaries, who are already preaching in their sea-ports, nay, even further inland! Here, again, can we not foresee at some future time, more or less remote, the final success of the two great Protestant nations, when we think that commercial treaties bind them with China, that they have already gained possession of her towns, and that their believing populations are ready to spend not only money but life in the propagation of true religion. Have we not a right to expect much from two countries, one of whom has so liberally answered to the call of the Bible Society, and supplied the necessary funds towards sending to China one million Bibles, whilst the other has already opened Chinese Christian churches in San Francisco, the very seat of the gold fever.

The influence of England is felt not only far off, but nearer home; in Portugal, where commerce seems exlusively in the hands of the British; in Spain, where navigation and trade are conducted by subjects of the United Kingdom; Piedmont, where, according to the Romish clergy themselves, a continual flow of travellers leave behind them thousands of Bibles, and where Protestant churches are daily erected in every city; the Legislative Chambers, in the meanwhile, depriving the Popish priests of their means of influence over the people.

In France, for the last fifty years, the work of Protestantism has been carried on by the organised remains of a church which, before the season of persecution counted thousands of members, whilst it is now recovering its strength through its victories over the Catholic population. M. Nicolas says : "France is Protestant." This assertion is only half true. She is Protestant inasmuch as she has rejected ultramontanism; the people are Protestant in name, but not in faith; that is all. Although they have never taken the sacrament twice, they send their children to make their first communion; they marry their young people at a church where they are never to be seen either on Sundays or fête-days; respect for public opinion alone makes them call in a priest to bury their dead. No: France is not sincerely, thoroughly a Catholic country; and as soon as she can be openly told and made to understand that the religion of Christ is not the religion of the Pope, then France will listen to the Gospel as she did in the sixteenth century, and has done even in our own time.

Shall we not speak of the progress Protestantism has made in the Polynesian Islands, those islands formerly peopled by savages, and now declared so well instructed that the American missionaries feel warranted in withdrawing to other spheres of action. Shall we allude to the coasts of Africa, where colonies of liberated negro slaves prosper without the interference of their white rescuers! Shall we enumerate the missions spread over the habitable globe! No; let us be silent ourselves, but invoke, by way of conclusion, the testimony of the *Journal des Débats* in favour of the subject which is now engaging our attention: —

"If we consider," says M. Michel Chevalier, "the progress made since 1814 by nations which are not Catholic, and compare it with the increase of power obtained during the same time by Catholic countries, we shall be astonished at the disproportion. England and the United States, both Protestant, have acquired, to an extent hitherto unknown, the dominion over immense regions destined to be one day widely populated, and over numerous tribes of people already existing. England has sought to conquer those mighty and densely inhabited regions known under the general name of India. In America she has spread civilisation throughout the northern continent, in the deserts of Upper Canada. The industry of her children has procured for her the whole of Australia — an island which is as large as a continent, and she has thrown off branches in the principal groups with which that vast ocean is studded. The United States have mightily increased in population and riches throughout the superficies of their ancient territory. They have removed the boundaries which confined them, formerly drawn to a very narrow limit, on the borders of the Atlantic: they are now seated upon both oceans. San Francisco is another New York, and seems likely to become soon equal to it at least. They have proved their superiority over the Catholic communities of America, and assumed, in that respect, a power which is not even disputed. To England and the United States, after the attempt made by the former in China, is apparently reserved the glory of overcoming the two greatest empires in the whole East, viz., China and Japan; two empires which comprise, numerically, the half of the human race. In the meanwhile, what has been the progress of the Catholic countries? The first of all, the most united, the most glorious — France, which, fifty years ago, seemed to give laws to the civilised world, has seen her sceptre broken, and her power overthrown by unheard-of disasters. It is true that she has roused herself with the noblest courage, with indomitable energy; but whenever the observer may have thought she was about to make a sudden effort, some revolution, sent as a scourge by the ALMIGHTY, has paralysed her energy, and brought her to the ground. The balance of power between Catholic and non-Catholic civilisation has evidently been broken ever since 1789[1]. "

Let us confirm the authority of M. Michel Chevalier by that of M. John Lemoinne: —

" The spirit of Him who walked upon the waters, " says this writer, " pursues across the seas the work of expansion and of propagation which will only finish with time itself. ' You go to the right; ' I go to the left; ' says the proverb: ' thus, walking round the world, we shall at length meet again.' Well, these words will be accomplished, and by the sons of that adventurous race scattered in every locality of whom it has been said *toto divisos orbe Britannos*. The English and the Americans have started, the former towards the East, the latter towards the West; and they will meet again after having journeyed round the globe. The great wall of China is the only obstacle theyhave to overthrow, and within a little while English and Americans will have taken between two fires that last entrenchment.

" We are writing no fable. Sooner or later the English will take possession of China; further extension is a necessary condition of their conquests.

" Whilst the English march forwards to the attack of Ancient Asia, on the other hand the Americans are putting themselves in

1. *Journal des Débats*, Sept. 1853.

motion in order to reach the same terminus by way of the Pacific Ocean. The United States government have sent a squadron to Japan; they have issued a kind of polifical manifesto, from which we shall quote the principal passage:

" 'We do not allow any nation, occupying any part of the habitable world, the right to refuse all commercial intercourse with other nations. Civilised and Christian governments may force barbarians to submit to the general law [1].' "

If we have quoted these words, it is because they place together the two antagonistic principles which, at this present time, are continuing in the far East the struggle begun for the last eighteen centuries: the principle of expansion, and the principle of exclusion. The English and Americans are not merely conquerors; they are the missionaries of civilisation, of humanity, of the rights of nations, of social life; in a word, of Christianity.

" Governments no longer carry on religious wars; the work of proselytism is one with which they have nothing to do. We even see the governments of England and the United States disclaiming most expressly all intention of religious proselytism. They may say what they please, but they are missionaries in spite of themselves. Proselytism is not conducted by an official society; the missionary army consists of volunteers; it generally recruits its adherents amongst the dissenters. It is all very well for the governments of England and the United States to tell the Chinese and Japanese that they do not wish to convert them; they can no more hinder the work of religious propagandism than prevent the earth from turning on its axis."

However rational these surmises may be, we acknowledge that they lead us beyond our subject, which is the present state of nations; to our subject, therefore, we return, for the purpose of drawing our inferences.

1. John Lemoinne, *Journal des Débats*, May 3 and 10, 1852.

INFERENCES.

Our first inference has surely been already drawn by the reader's mind; we shall therefore just state it: taken either separately or together, the Protestant nations are superior to the Catholic, under the threefold point of view of Wealth, Knowledge, and Morality.

This preliminary conclusion implies a second, which it is right we should insist upon. A man who knows anything of the modern history of the world must acknowledge, not only that Christianity is superior to every other religion, but that its superiority is immense. The civilisation of the Romans was warlike, that of the Greeks, artistic. The Chinese are distinguished by industry: Christian civilisation alone is moral, and that single feature must place it infinitely above every other form of social development. It is Christianity which has liberated the slave, raised woman to her proper station, given an impulse to charity, by opening hospitals at home, and sending missionaries abroad; thus realising the Scripture precept, "Ye are all brethren;" and introducing into the world the new doctrine of self-denial practised with humility — self-denial towards all; even our enemies! We might also notice that Christianity is superior to every other religion with respect to the arts and sciences. Elsewhere, discoveries have been made; *we* have mastered principles. We proceed from consequence to consequence; allow us time, and we may depend upon reaching the promised end. Christian knowledge, therefore, must necessarily be progressive; intellectual vigour, on the contrary, of a merely human character, has decayed in Greece, and it is now languishing in China. But we desire to keep to the one point of morality, and to show, in doing so, the immense superiority of Christianity.

This fact, besides, is so evident that we do not think any of our readers will question it; we only recall it in order to arrive at the following conclusions :

If Christianity is superior to every other religion, and if at the same time the Reformation is better than Popery, it follows that Protestantism comes nearer true Christianity than Romanism does. We do not pretend to affirm that Protestantism has already borne all the fruits which it is capable of producing ; all we maintain is this : the Roman tree never yielded a crop so nourishing, so pleasant to the taste. Perhaps we shall be more accurate in representing Romanism as the wild tree; whilst the Reformation is a young plant bearing the graft of the Gospel. In a word, Protestantism is much more like Christianity.

We hardly think that any attentive reader of the foregoing work will dispute the truth of this second conclusion, but it is only for us a link which brings us to the third inference, the most important of all.

We do not flatter ourselves. Many of our readers, we know, will stop at the point we have now reached; many will say : Protestantism is more in accordance with the Gospel; it is more favourable to civilisation; we sympathise with it, and, if needs be, we will lend it our support. But, reader, there is one more reflection you should make : if Protestantism, or rather its parent, Christianity, is by far the religion most calculated to do good, this religion is then the true one. We stated it at our very outset :

" Good deeds are the result of truth; evil is the result of falsehood; two modes of expressing the same idea : the true and the good are intimately connected, or, to speak more correctly, they are but one. "

Our legitimate conclusion, then, is : Christianity is Truth ; it comes from God; for it professes to be a revelation, and cannot lie.

No doubt this last inference reaches far beyond the former ones; we even acknowledge that it is only indirectly the result of our previous statements; but, mark, such an indirect proof is only the more powerful and the more simple; it comes to this argument of the divine founder of the Gospel, " By their fruits ye shall know them. A good tree cannot bear evil fruit, neither can an evil tree bring forth good fruit. Do men gather grapes from thistles, or figs from thorns? " No. Therefore Christianity, which alone has brought down charity upon earth, and produced good will amongst men; Christianity, which regenerates a fallen creature, Christianity is the truth!

LIST OF AUTHORS QUOTED IN THE WORK.

(Our quotations are often abridged, but we have always preserved their textuality.)

ANNALES de la Propagation de la foi.
ARRAGON (Madame, membre de l'Athénée de Paris). Souvenirs d'un voyage en Suisse.
ARCHENOLZ (d'). Tableau de l'Angleterre.
AUBIGNÉ (Merle d'). Trois siècles de luttes en Écosse.
BALBI (Adrien). Abrégé de géographie.
BEAUMONT (Gustave de). L'Irlande sociale, politique et religieuse.
BERNARD. Histoire de l'Autriche.
BONAPARTE (Louis). Documents historiques sur la Hollande.
BOUVIER. Dissertatio in sextum Decalogum præceptum. Paris 1849.
BRIFFAULT (E.). Le secret de Rome.
DUBLIN UNIVERSITY MAGAZINE, 1853.
BUCHON. Quelques souvenirs de courses en Suisse, et dans le pays de Bade.
BULLETIN de la Société du Protestantisme français, 1853.
BUREAUD (docteur de la Faculté de médecine de Paris). Londres et les Anglais des temps modernes.
CAMBRY. Voyage pittoresque en Suisse.
CATTEAU. Voyage en Allemagne et en Suède.
CHEVALIER (Victor). Étude sur l'assistance publique en Angleterre.
CHEVALIER (Michel). Lettres sur l'Amérique du Nord.
COXE. Voyage en Suisse.
COUSIN. Mémoire sur l'instruction secondaire dans le royaume de Prusse.
— Rapport sur l'état de l'instruction publique dans quelques pays de l'Allemagne.

COUSIN. De l'instruction publique en Hollande.
CUSTINE. Mémoires et voyages.
DEPPING. La Suisse, ou tableau historique, pittoresque et moral des cantons helvétiques.
DESCOMBAZ. Histoire des Missions évangéliques.
DESPREZ. Les Peuples d'Autriche.
DIDIER (Charles). Campagne de Rome.
DICTIONNAIRE de la Conversation.
DILL (E.-M.). Ireland's miseries : their cause and cure.
DORY (Alphonse). Souvenirs d'Angleterre.
DUCPÉTIAUX (Ed.). De l'État de l'instruction primaire et populaire en Belgique, par Ducpétiaux, inspecteur des prisons et des établissements de bienfaisance.
DUBOIS (député de la Seine-Inférieure). Rapport sur l'instruction fait à la Chambre des Députés en 1836.
DURAND. Statistique de la Suisse.
EUROPE PROTESTANTE, 1839 et 1840.
FAUCHER (Léon). Études sur l'Angleterre.
FERRIÈRE (Alexandre). Analyse de la statistique générale de la France, publiée sous l'autorisation du ministre de l'intérieur.
FRANSCINI (S.). Nova statistica della Svizzera, 1847.
GENIN. L'Église ou l'État.
GIRARDIN (Saint-Marc). De l'instruction intermédiaire et de son état dans le midi de l'Allemagne.
GOODRICH (S.-G.). Les États-Unis de l'Amérique, par Goodrich, consul des États-Unis à Paris.
GUERRY (de). Statistique morale.
GUÉROULT. Lettres sur l'Espagne.
GUIZOT. Histoire de la civilisation en France.
HAUSSEZ (baron d'). La Grande-Bretagne en 1833.
— Alpes et Danube.
HEINE (Henry). De l'Allemagne.
HENNEQUIN. Voyage philosophique en Angleterre et en Écosse.
JACQUEMIN. L'Allemagne agricole, industrielle et politique.
JOHN CARR. Voyage en Hollande.
JONNÈS (Moreau de). La Prusse, son progrès politique et social.
— Statistique de la Grande-Bretagne et de l'Irlande, 2 vols.
KÉRATRY (ancien député). Du Culte en général.
LABORDE. Itinéraire descriptif de l'Espagne.
LAMENNAIS. Affaires de Rome.
LAUTIER. Les Voyageurs en Suisse.
LEDUC (Germain). L'Angleterre, l'Écosse et l'Irlande.

LLORENTE. Histoire critique de l'inquisition d'Espagne.

LORAIN. Tableau de l'instruction primaire en France, d'après des documents authentiques.

LUTHEROTH (H.). O-Taïti, histoire et enquête.

MALTE-BRUN. Géographie, 16 vol. in-8°.

MARTIN (Henri). Histoire de France.

MINISTRE (de l'intérieur, Belgique). Statistique générale du royaume de Belgique, publiée par le ministre (période de 1841 à 1850.)

MIRABEAU. Monarchie prussienne.

MONTULI. Voyage en Angleterre.

MORÉ. Le Brésil en 1852 et sa colonisation future, notice écrite sur des documents communiqués par le consulat suisse à Rio-de-Janeiro.

MULLER. Histoire de la Confédération suisse.

NICOLAS (Auguste). Du Protestantisme et de toutes les Hérésies dans leurs rapports avec le Socialisme.

NOUGARÈDE. Lettres sur l'Angleterre.

OMALIUS. Notions élémentaires de statistique.

ORBIGNY (d'). Voyage dans l'Amérique méridionale, exécuté en 1826 et 1833, par Alcide d'Orbigny, publié sous les auspices de M. le ministre de l'instruction publique.

PEBRER. Histoire financière et statistique générale de l'empire Britannique.

PICHOT. L'Irlande et le pays de Galles.

PICOT. Statistique de la Suisse.

PORTER. Progrès de la Grande-Bretagne sous le rapport de la population.

POUSSIN. La Belgique et les Belges depuis 1830, Paris, 1845.

PRÉVOST. Voyage en Irlande.

QUÉTELET. Recherches statistiques sur le royaume des Pays-Bas. Bruxelles, 1829.

QUINET (Edgar). De l'Ultramontanisme.

— Le christianisme et la révolution française.

RAOUL-ROCHETTE. Lettres sur la Suisse.

RAUMER (professeur d'histoire à l'université de Berlin). L'Angleterre en 1835.

REVUE BRITANNIQUE.

REVUE DES DEUX-MONDES.

REY. L'Autriche, la Hongrie et la Turquie.

ROUGEMONT. Précis d'éthnographie, de statistique et de géographie historique.

RUBICHON. De l'Action du clergé dans les sociétés modernes.

SAINT-HILAIRE (Rossew). Histoire d'Espagne.
SCHNITZLER (J.-H.). Statistique générale, méthodique et complète de la France, comparée aux autres grandes puissances de l'Europe, 4 vol. in-8°.
SEMPÉRÉ. Histoire d'Espagne.
SERRES (Marcel de). L'Autriche.
SIÈCLE (Journal le).
SIMON. Observations recueillies en Angleterre.
SISMONDI. Histoire de la liberté en Italie.
— Républiques italiennes.
— Littérature du midi de l'Europe.
SOLITAIRE (le). Souvenirs d'un voyageur, ou Méditations sur le caractère national des Anglais.
SOMMERLATT. Géographie de la Suisse.
STAEL (Madame de). Lettres sur l'Angleterre.
— de l'Allemagne.
STATISTIQUE NATIONALE de la France.
STATISTIQUE des bagnes en 1852. Paris imprimerie impériale, 1854, publié par le ministère de la Marine et des Colonies.
TAILLANDIER. Histoire de la jeune Allemagne.
TARDIF. Des Peuples européens.
TOCQUEVILLE. De la démocratie aux États-Unis.
TRABAUD. Notes et sentiments sur les îles Britanniques.
TRISTAN (Madame Flora). Promenades dans Londres.
TROLLOPE (Mistress). Vienne et les Autrichiens.
UNIVERS PITTORESQUE.
WALSH. Voyage en Suisse.
WARDEN. Chronologie historique de l'Amérique.
WEISS. L'Espagne depuis le règne de Philippe II.
— Histoire des réfugiés protestants de France, 1853.
VINET (Alexandre.) Théologie Pastorale.
VIEL-CASTEL (comte de). De l'Angleterre et de la France.
VILLERS. Essai sur l'esprit et l'influence de la réformation de Luther.
WILNES (Journal le).
ZSCHOKKE. Histoire de la Suisse.
ZURLAUBEN (le baron de). Tableaux de la Suisse.
ANONYMES. De l'Autriche et de son avenir.
— Mémoire sur la cour de Louis-Napoléon et sur la Hollande.

www.ingramcontent.com/pod-product-compliance
Lightning Source LLC
LaVergne TN
LVHW021056110826
845150LV00001B/90

9781425566784